THE STAIR SOCIETY

MISCELLANY TWO

BY

VARIOUS AUTHORS

EDITED BY

DAVID SELLAR, B.A., LL.B.

WITH A PREFACE BY

The Right Hon. LORD AVONSIDE

EDINBURGH

THE STAIR SOCIETY

1984

ISBN: 0 90229210 2

Printed by Clark Constable, Edinburgh, London, Melbourne

CONTENTS

iv CONTENTS

PREFACE

A PREFACE is, almost by definition, at risk of being tedious. At best it should present the least of barriers between the reader and what he wishes to read. Its proper function is to offer thanks.

Miscellany One was published in 1971, the preface written by Lord President Clyde. It is a lively volume, a pleasant mixture of learning and light. To the present writer there is exceptional interest in the personality of the Chairman of Council, himself a contributor, then a Queen's Counsel and now, this year, the first United Kingdom President of the European Court of Justice.

This is the Jubilee Year of the Society and it is very pleasant and proper that it should be the year of the publication of Miscellany Two. Such a volume demonstrates abundantly the varied learnings and skills of the contributors and, most importantly of all, their willingness to put their gifts at the disposal of the Society. Without such generosity the Society could not exist and this Miscellany must be the envy of many.

We do not have a Bank raid, as had the last volume, but it is almost frightening to read of the indents for weapons lodged by those who took part in Trial by Battle; we go into Ettrick Forest; we read some of the material prepared for the advisers to Mary, Queen of Scots, as she was later to become, on aspects of Scotland as it then was; uniquely and importantly, we have a fragment of a rare document written in our Gaelic of the 17th century, and there is a striking contribution from the Historiographer Royal. One could go on and on — but that is for the reader.

I have been asked to thank on behalf of the Society — and do so with great pleasure — Winifred MacQueen who gallantly undertook the great work of compiling the Index and Hector MacQueen who assisted in proof reading. The Society also acknowledge with thanks the contributions from the University of Glasgow and from Balliol College towards the publication costs of Professor Stones' article on John Snell.

Miscellany One, so far as I can find, paid no acknowledgement to any editor. This Miscellany is fortunate in having David Sellar, not only as a contributor, but as Editor. He is the only person to whom he has not asked me to express thanks, but I am sure that the Society will join me in feeling deep gratitude for his diligence and skill in completing a demanding task.

IAN H. SHEARER.

ILLUSTRATION

LIST OF ABBREVIATIONS

These abbreviations are supplementary to the references and abbreviations which appear in the various contributions. *The List of Abbreviated Titles of the Printed Sources of Scottish History to 1560* (Supplement to Scottish Historical Review, October 1963) has generally been followed.

Acta Sessionis (Stair)	*Selected Cases from Acta Dominorum Concilii et Sessionis* 1532-3, ed. I. H. Shearer (Stair Society, 1951).
ADA	*The Acts of the Lords Auditors of Causes and Complaints*, ed. T. Thomson (Edinburgh, 1839).
ADC	*Acta Dominorum Concilii — The Acts of the Lords of Council in Civil Causes*, edd. T. Thomson and others (Edinburgh, 1839 and 1918-).
ADC (*Public*)	*Acts of the Lords of Council in Public Affairs 1501-1554: Selections from Acta Dominorum Concilii*, ed. R. K. Hannay (Edinburgh, 1932).
Adv. or *Adv. MSS.*	Advocates' Manuscripts, National Library of Scotland, Edinburgh.
APS	*The Acts of the Parliaments of Scotland*, edd. T. Thomson and C. Innes (Edinburgh, 1814-1875).
Balfour	Sir James Balfour of Pittendreich, *Practicks* (1754), reprinted and edited for the Stair Society by P. G. B. McNeill (Stair Society, 2 vols. 1962, 1963).
Bracton	*Bracton on the Laws and Customs of England*, trans. S. E. Thorne (Cambridge, Mass., 1968-).
Carnwath or *Carnwath Court Book*	*The Court Book of the Barony of Carnwath* 1923-42, ed. W. C. Dickinson (Scottish History Society, 1937).
CDS	*Calendar of Documents relating to Scotland*, ed. J. Bain (Edinburgh, 1881-8).
Complete Peerage	*The Complete Peerage of England Scotland Ireland Great Britain and the United Kingdom by G.E.C.*, edd. Vicary Gibbs and others (London, 1910-40, reprinted Alan Sutton, 1982).
Craig, *Jus Feudale*	Sir Thomas Craig, *Jus Feudale* (1655; 1716; 1732; translated by Lord President Clyde, 2 vols. Edinburgh and London, 1934).
De Verborum	See Skene.

DNB	Dictionary of National Biography.
Dunfermline or *Dunfermline Court Book*	*Regality of Dunfermline Court Book* 1531-8, edd. J. M. Webster and A. A. M. Duncan (Dunfermline, 1953).
ER	*The Exchequer Rolls of Scotland*, edd. J. Stuart and others (Edinburgh, 1878-1908).
Erskine	John Erskine of Carnock, *An Institute of the Law of Scotland* (2 vols., 1773; 8 eds. to 1871).
Fife or *Fife Court Book*	*The Sheriff Court Book of Fife 1515-22*, ed. W. C. Dickinson (Scottish History Society, 1928).
Foedera	*Foedera*, ed. T. Rymer, Record Commission edition (London, 1816-69).
Glanvill	*The Treatise on the laws and customs of the realm of England commonly called Glanvill*, ed. G. D. G. Hall (1965).
HMC	*Reports of the Royal Commission on Historical Manuscripts*, (London, 1870-).
Hope, *Major Practicks*	Sir Thomas Hope, *Major Practicks*, 1608-33, 2 vols. (Stair Society, 1937, 1938).
Hume, *Commentaries*	Baron David Hume, *Commentaries on the Law of Scotland respecting Crimes* (2 vols., 1797; 4 eds. to 1844).
Hume, *Lectures*	Baron David Hume, *Lectures on the Law of Scotland*, 6 vols., ed. G. C. H. Paton (Stair Society, 1939-58).
JR	*The Juridical Review*, Edinburgh.
Jus Feudale	See Craig.
Mackenzie, *Institutions*	Sir George Mackenzie, *The Institutions of the Law of Scotland* (1684; 8 eds. to 1758).
Mackenzie, *Matters Criminal*	Sir George Mackenzie, *The Laws and Customs of Scotland in Matters Criminal* (1678, 1699).
Mackinnon, *Catalogue*	D. Mackinnon, *Descriptive Catalogue of Gaelic Manuscripts in the Advocates' Library, Edinburgh, and elsewhere in Scotland* (Edinburgh, 1912).
Maclaurin	Maclaurin, *Arguments and Decisions in Remarkable Cases, before the High Court of Justiciary* (Edinburgh, 1774).
PRO	Public Record Office, London.
Quoniam Attachiamenta	*Regiam Majestatem and Quoniam Attachiamenta*, ed. Lord Cooper following Sir John Skene (Stair Society, 1947). Also edited in *APS*. vol. i.
Regiam Majestatem	*Regiam Majestatem and Quoniam Attachiamenta*, ed. Lord Cooper following Sir John Skene (Stair Society, 1947). Also edited in *APS*, vol. i.

REO	*Records of the Earldom of Orkney*, ed. J. S. Clouston (Scottish History Society, 1914).
RMS	*Registrum Magni Sigilli Regum Scotorum*, edd. J. M. Thomson and others (Edinburgh, 1882-1914).
RPC	*The Register of the Privy Council of Scotland*, edd. J. H. Burton and others (Edinburgh, 1877-).
RRS	*Regesta Regum Scottorum*, edd. G. W. S. Barrow and others (Edinburgh, 1960-).
RSS	*Registrum Secreti Sigilli Regum Scotorum*, edd. M. Livingstone and others (Edinburgh, 1908-).
Scots Peerage	*The Scots Peerage*, ed. Sir J. Balfour Paul (Edinburgh, 1904-14).
SHR	*The Scottish Historical Review*.
Skene, *De Verborum*	Sir John Skene, *De Verborum Significatione* (1597 and 1599).
SRO	Scottish Record Office, Edinburgh.
Stair	Sir James Dalrymple (Viscount of Stair), *Institutions of the Law of Scotland* (1681, 1693, 1759, 1826, 1832; edited D. M. Walker, Edinburgh and Glasgow, 1981).
TRHS	*Transactions of the Royal Historical Society*.
Willock, *Jury*	I. D. Willock, *The Origins and Development of the Jury in Scotland* (Stair Society, 1966).

COURTESY, BATTLE AND THE BRIEVE OF RIGHT, 1368 — A STORY CONTINUED

By DAVID SELLAR, B.A., LL.B.,

Department of Scots Law, University of Edinburgh

Chapter 63 of George Neilson's *Trial by Combat* is headed 'Three Half-told Stories, 1362-85'. In it Neilson notes that English records give details of preparations being made in 1367 and 1368 for a judicial duel to be fought in Scotland 'according to the law of Scotland, for certain causes' — *juxta legem Scotiae ex certis causis* — between James Douglas and Thomas Erskine. Both Douglas and Erskine petitioned Edward III for permission to buy the necessary arms and armour in London. These included a pair of plates, a haubergeon, gauntlets, a helmet, bracers and leg armour, long arms and coverings for two horses, two daggers and the head of a lance for Douglas, and plates, bascinet, bracers, cuisses, greaves, a chaffrein for a horse, a dagger, a long sword, a short sword and a pair of iron gauntlets for Erskine. But there, for Neilson, the story ended: 'As is too often the case in the history of Scotland the intimations of the English records serve only to tantalise. One hears of duels which are to be, but lacks the satisfaction of knowing the event. The story ends with the beginning.'[1]

For once Neilson was mistaken. Tucked obscurely away in a Latin footnote to W. F. Skene's edition of John of Fordun and largely unnoticed save by peerage writers and family historians, there is a near contemporary account of the duel between Erskine and Douglas, fought before King David II himself.[2] We know both the event and the 'certain causes' from which the duel arose. As the story is a dramatic one and the causes of considerable interest, we may regret the lack of an account from Neilson's sparkling pen.

In 1353 Sir William Douglas of Liddesdale, a man who had notoriously lived by the sword, was assassinated in Ettrick Forest by his namesake William, lord (and later first earl) of Douglas. He left considerable estates, mainly in the south of Scotland. Some of these were inherited by his only child and heir, Mary; while others went to his nephew and heir-male, James Douglas (later Sir James Douglas of Dalkeith), one of the protagonists in the duel in 1368. James Douglas had already been granted the barony of Aberdour (Fife) by his uncle and on his death he also acquired the baronies of Dalkeith (Midlothian) and Kilbucho and Newlands (Peeblesshire) by virtue of a tailzie executed by Sir William in 1351.

---

[1] George Neilson, *Trial by Combat* (Glasgow, 1890), 216-17; *Rotuli Scotiae*, edd. D. Macpherson and others (1814-19), i, 915b-917b.

[2] *Johannis de Fordun Chronica Gentis Scotorum* [*Fordun*], ed. W. F. Skene (Historians of Scotland, Edinburgh, 1871), i, 370n. I am most grateful to Dr. A. Grant for first bringing this note to my attention. It is noticed in *Scots Peerage*, v, 597, vi, 345 and W. Fraser, *Douglas Book* (Edinburgh, 1885), i, 253.

Mary Douglas succeeded to the unentailed lands, which included the baronies
of Calderclere (Midlothian), Linton-Rothrik (West Linton, Peeblesshire),
Roberton (Lanarkshire), Buittle (Galloway), and half of Preston (Galloway).[3]
Mary was married first to Reginald Mure (or More), son of William Mure
of Abercorn, but this marriage was annulled, and she then married Thomas
Erskine, the other protagonist in the duel. In or about 1367 she died in childbirth
and her child died with her, leaving James Douglas as her nearest heir (Table 1).
James Douglas claimed the inheritance — he was served heir to Mary in the
baronies of Buittle, Preston and other lands, by brieve of succession (otherwise
inquest) at Dumfries on 30 June 1367[4] — but Thomas Erskine claimed that he
was entitled to a liferent of his wife's not inconsiderable heritage by right of
courtesy.

Fordun narrates the death of Sir William Douglas of Liddesdale and then
provides this vivid account of the duel:[5]

> Hic reliquit post se unicam filiam nomine Mariam heredem, quae nupsit
> Reginaldo Mure filio et heredi domini Willelmi Mure, sed postea per
> quasdem causas exquisitas divortiata fuit ab eodem et postea nupsit Thomae
> de Irskyn filio et heredi domini Roberti de Irskyn quae, impregnata per
> eundem, in partu periclitata mortua est. Terras vero domini Willelmi de
> Dowglas idem dixit sibi deberi pro tempore vitae suae ex curialitate Scociae,
> eo quod, ut dixit, de dicta maritagia genuit prolem vivam, sed Jacobus de
> Dowglas filius domini Johannis de Dowglas fratris praefati domini Willelmi,
> se opposuit dixens dictas terras sibi debere, jure hereditario, eo quod, ut dixit,
> dicta proles non fuit viva nata. Super quo debato acceperunt duellum apud
> Edinburgh coram rege David, et in introitu parcae idem Thomas est effectus
> miles per patrem suum, et Jacobus per dominum Archibaldum Dowglas est
> miles effectus; qui simul pugnantes autoritate regia sunt divisi et extra parcam
> ducti. Sed quia post longos tractatus hinc inde habitos concordare non
> potuerunt, iterum dominus rex adjudicavit eosdem infra parcam convenire
> complecturi finaliter. Sed, ipsis ibidem introductis, rex cum magna diligentia
> tractavit inter eos, et data quadam summa pecuniae dicto Thomae per dictum
> Jacobum quam ante in prioribus tractatibus optulerat, et alia summa per
> ipsum regem ex sua magnificentia propter concordiam et dilectionem
> utriusque personae, idem Thomas cessit esse et, ipsis simul eductis de parca,
> terrae universae ipsius domini Willelmi penes dictum Jacobum jure
> hereditario remanserunt.

'He left behind him a single daughter called Mary who married Reginald
Mure, the son and heir of William Mure. But afterwards she was divorced from
him on certain intricate grounds and she married Thomas Erskine, the son and
heir of the lord Robert Erskine. She conceived a child by him but died in

---

[3] *Scots Peerage*, 'Morton', and *Registrum Honoris de Morton* [*Morton Registrum*] (Bannatyne Club,
1853). The career and landed interests of Sir James Douglas are considered in A. Grant, 'The
Higher Nobility in Scotland and their Estates, c. 1371-1424' (Oxford Univ. D. Phil. Thesis, 1975),
240ff. — copy in the Scottish Record Office. Dr. Grant points out that Mary Douglas was a more
substantial heiress than *Scots Peerage* suggests.

[4] *Morton Registrum*, ii, no. 83.

[5] *Fordun*, i, 370n.

childbirth. Now he [Thomas Erskine] said that the lands of the lord William Douglas ought to be his for his lifetime by the courtesy of Scotland, because, he said, he had fathered a live child by the said marriage, but James Douglas, the son of the lord John Douglas, brother of the aforesaid William, opposed him saying that the said lands ought to be his by hereditary right, because, he said, the said child was not born alive. They agreed to a duel at Edinburgh on this debate in the presence of King David to settle the question, and at the entrance to the park the said Thomas was made a knight by his father, and James was made a knight by the lord Archibald Douglas; they then fought but were separated by royal command and led outside the park. But after long further negotiations they were unable to agree and again the lord king adjudged that they should meet in the park to settle the matter finally. But, after they had been led in there, the king mediated very carefully between them, and after the said Thomas had been given a certain sum of money which had already been offered by the said James in

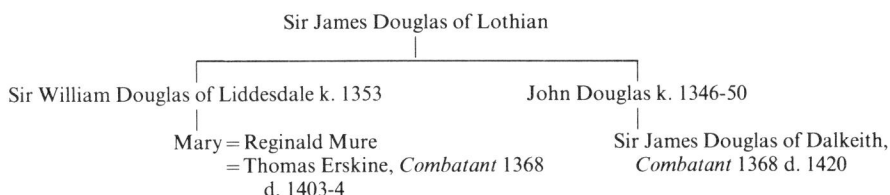

Sir James Douglas of Lothian

Sir William Douglas of Liddesdale k. 1353   John Douglas k. 1346-50

Mary = Reginald Mure   Sir James Douglas of Dalkeith,
     = Thomas Erskine, *Combatant* 1368   *Combatant* 1368 d. 1420
       d. 1403-4

Table 1 — COURTESY 1368

previous negotiations, and a further sum by the king himself out of his own magnificence for the sake of concord and because of his affection for both parties, Thomas yielded his claim. Both parties were led simultaneously from the park and the whole lands of that lord William remained with the said James by hereditary right.'[6]

The detail and precision of the account is remarkable and must surely be taken from a legal document drawn up to record the event: the knighting of the participants by Sir Robert Erskine, Thomas's father, and by Sir Archibald Douglas; the two stages of the combat; the intervention and anxiety of the king; the final settlement by which neither party lost face; and the simultaneous departure from the lists — *simul eductis de parca* — all are carefully narrated. The relationship of the parties and the nature of their claim is clearly set out. Erskine claimed by the courtesy of Scotland — *ex curialitate Scociae* — while Douglas claimed by hereditary right —*jure hereditario*. The point at issue between them was not one of law — for the law seems to have been clear enough — but one of fact: had the child born to Mary Douglas been born live or stillborn? If live, then Erskine was entitled to his courtesy. If stillborn, then Douglas took his heritage untrammeled by a liferent. To determine this fact they were prepared to duel, if need be to the death. We are also told that it was Erskine who relinquished his claim — *idem Thomas cessit esse* — which suggests that the issue on which battle was joined had been raised by him. We may be sure, incidentally, that the date of

---

[6] The translation is my own.

the duel was 1368: at the beginning of that year Erskine was still buying arms and armour, as has been seen, while by December 1368 James Douglas is being styled '*miles*'.[7]

The king's anxiety to achieve a settlement is understandable. Both combatants were closely connected to leading members of the royal circle. To judge from the frequency of their appearance as witnesses to David II's acts, Sir Robert Erskine and Sir Archibald Douglas, who knighted the combatants, were second to none in importance in the counsels of the king.[8] Sir Robert was Chamberlain of Scotland and had been Justiciar both North of Forth and of Lothian. At the time of David II's death in 1371 Sir Robert controlled Stirling Castle, while his son Sir Thomas, the combatant, controlled Edinburgh.[9] Sir Robert was a trusted servant of Robert II, both when Steward and when king, as well as of David II. Sir Archibald Douglas, nicknamed 'the Grim', was the illegitimate son of the celebrated Sir James. He controlled the rich inheritance of Bothwell and Petty, by virtue of his marriage in 1362 to Joanna Moray. In 1369 David II granted him all royal lands in Galloway between the Cree and the Nith in free barony. Later he became lord of Galloway and earl of Douglas. His daughter Marjorie married Robert III's eldest son, David, duke of Rothesay, and his son Archibald, earl of Douglas, married King Robert's eldest daughter.[10] David II had everything to gain from a reconciliation of the parties.

The dispute between Erskine and Douglas is one of the earliest recorded Scottish cases on the right of courtesy (*Anglice* curtesy), and the point at issue illustrates one of the peculiarities of that law. A widower could not enjoy the courtesy of a liferent of his wife's heritage unless a child had been born of the marriage and that child had been heard to cry. This requirement is as old as the law of courtesy itself.[11] It is to be found in *Glanvill*, it is found in the *Leges Quatuor Burgorum*, it is found in *Regiam Majestatem*.[12] Sir John Skene, in his *De Verborum Significatione*, waxes positively lyrical about it:[13]

> Curialitas, curialitie, curtesie, from the French *Curtoise* civilitie, gentelnesse, humanitie, for the law of curtesie, is an gentill and favorable ordinance or constitution, granted and observed in this Realme, and nocht universallie

---

[7] *Regesta Regum Scotorum* [*RRS*], vi, Acts of David II, ed. Bruce Webster (Edinburgh, 1982), nos. 413 and 417.

[8] *RRS*, vi, *passim*; Bruce Webster, 'David II and the Government of Fourteenth Century Scotland', 1966 *TRHS* 127.

[9] Ranald Nicholson, *Scotland — The Later Middle Ages* (Edinburgh, 1974), 150, 169-70, 185; *ER*, ii. Nicholson's account of Erskine's part in the accession of Robert II is doubted by Dr. A. Grant. Sir Robert first appears as Justiciar north of Forth in 1358/9 (*RMS*, ii, no. 3717).

[10] *Supra* n. 8; *RRS*, vi, no. 451, and see Nicholson, *Scotland — The Later Middle Ages* and *Scots Peerage*.

[11] The further requirement in the later Scottish law of courtesy that the child, had he or she survived, should have been the mother's heir, in the sense of heir-at-law, may not have been part of the medieval law.

[12] *Glanvill*, vii, 18; *Leges Quatuor Burgorum* c. 41 (*APS*, i, 340); *Regiam Majestatem*, ii, 53 (*APS*) or ii, 58 (Skene/Cooper). Pollock and Maitland, *History of English Law* (2nd ed. re-issued with introduction by S. F. C. Milsom, Cambridge, 1968) discuss curtesy at ii, 414-20. There is no adequate treatment of the history of courtesy in Scotland, but see P. Fraser, *Husband and Wife* (2nd ed., Edinburgh, 1878), 1118 and J. C. Gardner, *The Origin and Nature of the Legal Rights of Spouses and Children* (Edinburgh, 1928).

[13] *De Verborum Significatione* (1597), 'Curialitas'.

keiped, or used in uther cuntries, And therefore it is called *Curialitas Scotiae*, the curtesie of *Scotland*. And in the laws of *England lex Anglie*, or the curtesie of *England*, within the quhilk twa realmes and none uther this law is in use. That is quhen onie man maries lauchfullie ane wife, and receivis lande and heritage with her: And it happen that he beget with her ane bairne, quha being borne, is heard cryand betwixt foure walles of ane house: and thereafter his wife deceasis before him, he sall bruik and possesse, all the landes quhilks perteined to her, in-during his lifetime, albeit the bairne live or decease . . . The curtesie hes nocht place quhen na bairne is borne in lauchfull mariage, for it is necessar that ane bairne be borne maill or femaill, quick and liveand: And for probation theirof, he mon be heard cryand, for the curtesie hes place *in puero clamante*, (or as it is written in sum buikes) *brayand*, squeiland, or loudlie cryand. For in French *brayer*, in the latin *vagire*, is to crie or greite with ane loud voice. Quhilk word in our language is alswa attributed to Horse, Hartes, and uther beastes.

Already in the thirteenth century, as Maitland pointed out, English lawyers were at a loss to account for some of the peculiarities of the law of curtesy, including the requirement that the child be heard to cry. Yet these peculiarities remained part of the Scottish law of courtesy until the end, and in the fourteenth century men were prepared to resort to battle to satisfy them.

The judicial duel in England could be either civil or criminal, and in *Trial by Combat* Neilson demonstrated that this was true of Scotland as well.[14] 'The proof for the judicial duel in a plea of land in Scotland', he writes, 'is very indefinite, yet there is such a body of floating provisions on the subject that in spite of the poverty of testimony it is reasonable to believe that it had at least some short existence there.'[15] The criminal duel was appropriate in the appeal of felony where the appealer appealed the accused of felonious crime and offered proof by his body. The classic situation where the civil duel was competent in England was in procedure on the writ of right, the writ which raised the question of the best and most ancient right to land, rather than more recent possession or seisin. In the writ of right, but not in the 'possessory' writs of novel disseisin and mort d'ancestor, the 'tenant' (defendant) could choose whether to let the question be decided by an inquest or assize, or whether to defend and prove his right by battle. In the civil duel, but not in the criminal, the parties would be represented by champions (*campiones*), the 'demandant' (plaintiff) necessarily so, the tenant at his option. Recent research has done much to elucidate the history of the brieves (or writs) of right, of novel dissasine and of mortancestry in medieval Scotland.[16] As their name indicates these brieves were modelled on the English writs, although they were by no means exact copies, and once established had a

---

[14] Neilson's *Trial by Combat* remains a classic for both Scotland and England. For England, see now also M. J. Russell, 'Trial by Battle and the Writ of Right', and 'Trial by Battle and the Appeals of Felony', 1980 *Journal of Legal History*, 111-64; and M. T. Clanchy, 'Highway robbery and trial by battle in the Hampshire eyre of 1249' in *Medieval Legal Records*, edd. Hunnisett and Post (HMSO, 1978), 26.

[15] *Trial by Combat*, 87.

[16] Hector L. MacQueen, 'The Brieve of Right in Scots Law', 1982 *Journal of Legal History*, 52-70 and 'Dissasine and Mortancestor in Scots Law', 1983 *Journal of Legal History*, 21-49; see also MacQueen, 'Jurisdiction in Heritage and the Lords of Council and Session after 1532', below, p. 61.

different history. As in England, the brieve of right appears to have raised deeper
and more ancient questions of right than mere recent possession, and as in
England, battle was at one time presumably competent on this brieve. The brieve
of right was the ultimate touchstone of right to heritage and recognised as such
by the fifteenth-century poet Dunbar in his description of hell in *The Dance of the
Sevin Deidly Synnis*:

> Nae menstrallis playit to them but dout,
> For gleemen there were haldin out,
> By day and eik by nicht;
> Except a menstrall that slew a man,
> Sae til his heretage he wan
> and entert by brief of richt.[17]

As more rational methods of proof were adopted the original duel of law went
out of favour, especially in civil matters. After 1300 there appears to be no record
of a duel of law actually fought over heritage in either Scotland or England.
However, as the duel of law declined it was to some extent replaced, at least in
courtly society, by the duel of chivalry. In some respects the duel of chivalry was a
continuation of the duel of law, but there were important differences. The duel of
chivalry was confined to the knightly classes. The parties fought in person and
not through champions. They fought on horseback, fully armoured and bearing
weapons of their choice, unlike the combatants in the original duel of law whose
dress and whose weapons, prescribed by law, were archaic and repulsive: the
combatants in the duel of law fought on foot, shavenheaded and barelegged in
sheepskin coats, and attacked each other with batons tipped with horn which
resembled small pick-axes. The duel of chivalry took place before the Constable
or the Marshal and not in the ordinary courts. Typically the duel of chivalry
arose from an accusation of treason or other serious crime — indeed Neilson
habitually refers to it as 'the treason–duel of chivalry'. But is was also
appropriate, to judge from English evidence, to decide the right to armorial
bearings, which are a type of heritage, and we need not doubt that it would have
seemed appropriate, at least in the fourteenth century, to deal with questions of
disputed right such as might arise on the brieve of right.

Neilson argues for, and indeed proved, the existence of a court of chivalry in
later medieval Scotland. He pointed to two fifteenth-century manuscripts which
regulated procedure in that court: 'The Manner of Batale' and 'the Order of
Combats'. He also noted, as a further distinguishing mark between the original
duel of law and the law of chivalry, that the duel of law could not be stopped by
the judge, 'for, so to speak, the battle itself was the real judge';[18] whereas the duel
of chivalry could be stopped, and frequently was. 'As in England', he says, 'the
duels were rarely fought except in the royal presence, and as in England, they
were often stopped in mid-fight by the king. He did this in virtue of a royal *nobile*

---

[17] Stanza 18.
[18] *Trial by Combat*, 189; chapter 66 is headed 'The Maner of Batale' and chapter 74 'The Order of Combats'. See also R. K. Hannay, 'Observations on the Officers of the Scots Parliament', (1932) 44 Juridical Review, 125.

officium peculiar to chivalry. In both countries he was the head of this battle court …'[19] The Scottish court of chivalry may not have been fully choate in 1368, but we may recognise in the combat between Erskine and Douglas a classic example of the duel of chivalry, fought between knights on horseback and in armour, and determining a question of heritage.

It seems more than likely that the duel of chivalry between Erskine and Douglas arose out of some process at common law. The English records speak of a judicial duel to be fought 'according to the laws of Scotland, for certain causes'; and Fordun's account mentions several legal words and phrases — '*ex curialitate Scociae*', '*jure hereditario*', '*Super quo debato acceperunt duellum*', and '*rex adjudicavit*'.[20] However, we can only speculate as to the exact nature of that process. In England, there was a writ of right of dower (terce) and on this battle was competent.[21] But the widow's right of dower differed in many important respects from the widower's right of curtesy and it appears that there was never a separate writ of curtesy in England.[22] In his great treatise, however, Bracton does indicate several methods by which the issue in curtesy of whether a child had been born live and heard to cry — or worse, whether a monster and not a child had been born (an eventuality which seems to have caused Bracton particular concern) — could be raised.[23] The widower would normally be in possession of the lands on his wife's death. He might then be dispossessed by the heir. In that case the widower would take out a writ of novel disseisin, to which the heir, after the necessary general denial, would admit the disseisin but put forward the 'exception' that the widower was not entitled to curtesy because no child had been born live of the marriage. In later English parlance he would 'confess and avoid'.[24] Thus the birth of a live child would be put in issue. Alternatively the heir might take out a writ of mort d'ancestor (or of cosinage) alleging that the widower stood between him and the land to which he was entitled by ancestral descent. In this case it would be the widower who would 'except' and place the birth of the child in issue. Neither of these possibilities would involve battle at common law. But there was a third possibility: instead of a writ of mort d'ancestor the heir might have to proceed, or choose to proceed, by writ of right, claiming that the widower stood between him and the land to which he was entitled by hereditary right. Again the widower would 'except' and place the birth of the child in issue. In this third scenario battle would be competent.

The evidence for medieval Scottish pleading is distinctly scrappy and has

[19] *Trial by Combat*, 273; the best known instance of royal intervention is the treason–duel between Hereford and Norfolk in 1398 stopped by Richard II; Kenneth Nicholls 'Anglo-French Ireland and after', *Peritia*, i (1982), 377, suggests that the judicial duel was often used as a device to enforce arbitration rather than as an end in itself.

[20] Above, p. 2.

[21] *Glanvill*, vi, 11; cf. *Regiam Majestatem*, ii, 13 (*APS*), ii, 16 (Skene/Cooper).

[22] S. F. C. Milsom, 'Inheritance by Women in the Twelfth and Early Thirteenth Centuries' in *On the Laws and Customs of England*, edd. M. S. Arnold and others (Univ. North Carolina, 1981), especially 83ff.: 'There was no action by which the husband could claim curtesy, and he never had to sue for it. He had had the land ever since the marriage.'

[23] *Bracton*, fols. 168 (3: 34), 169b-170 (3: 38), 216 (3: 151), 271 (3: 293), 278 (3: 311), 438-438b (4: 362-3); Milsom, 'Inheritance by Women', 83-5.

[24] On exceptions in England, see *Pollock and Maitland*, ii, 611-20; S. F. C. Milsom, *The Legal Framework of English Feudalism* (Cambridge, 1976), 13-17.

seldom been studied, but it is clear from legislation, surviving treatises and the early records of Council and Session that the system of pleading by exception existed in Scotland also.[25] It seems probable that in Scotland too the issue of childbirth in courtesy could have been raised in any of the three ways described by Bracton — by brieve of novel dissasine by the widower, or by brieve of mortancestry or brieve of right by the heir, followed by the necessary exception. In Scotland, however, the scope of the brieve of mortancestry, albeit extended by Robert Bruce's legislation of 1318 to include grandparents as well as parents, brothers and sisters, uncles and aunts,[26] does not appear to have been extended further, as in England, by writs of cosinage, and so it is the more likely that the heir in Scotland would have to rely on the brieve of right. Thus James Douglas would not have been able to use mortancestry to succeed to lands of which his cousin Mary had been in sasine: he would have had to resort to the brieve of right.[27] If then a process at common law lies behind the duel of chivalry between Douglas and Erskine, we may speculate that Douglas, having been served heir by inquest to some of Mary's lands in June 1367,[28] found Erskine unwilling to relinquish possession, and was forced to proceed by brieve of right in the sheriff court. Erskine made the general denial and then pleaded by way of exception that he was entitled to a liferent by the courtesy of Scotland because a child had been born live of the marriage. On this exception issue was joined, and the duel of law competent at common law on the brieve of right was transmuted into a duel of chivalry before the king. The issue was Erskine's: 'He who excepts must, like a plaintiff, offer to prove his case',[29] says Maitland: and thus it was Erskine who eventually yielded his claim, as Fordun informs us. This explanation, however, it should be stressed again, is speculative and likely to remain so.[30]

Sir Thomas Erskine and Sir James Douglas both enjoyed long and distinguished careers after 1368. Both were to demonstrate again their appreciation of the finer points of law. After Mary Douglas's death Sir Thomas married as his second wife Janet Keith, great grand-daughter of Gratney, earl of Mar, and, in the eyes of Sir Thomas, the heiress-presumptive to that earldom. In order to safeguard the rights of his wife and of their heirs, Sir Thomas appeared in full Parliament in March 1390/1 before King Robert III and made a protest in

---

[25] On exceptions in Scotland, see *inter alia* P. J. Hamilton-Grierson in his edition of Habakkuk Bisset's *Rolment of Courtis* (Scottish Text Society, 1920-6), iii, 69; Bisset himself 'Anent the ordoure of proponyng of exceptionis,' *Rolment of Courtis*, i, 172; Balfour's Practicks, ii, 343 'Anent exceptiounis and essonzies'; *Regiam Majestatem*, i, 10, 11 (*APS*) or i, 11, 12 (Skene/Cooper); *Quoniam Attachiamenta* c. 20, 35 (*APS*) or c. 34, 52 (Skene/Cooper); *Fragmenta Collecta* c. 7 (*APS*, i, 742); *APS*, ii, 10 c. 10 (1425/6), 14 c. 5, 7 (1427), 17 c. 3 (1429/30), 101 (1471), 253 c. 40 (1504), 502 c. 5 (1557); *John son of Walter* v. *Thomas Scot* 1368 (*APS*, i, 505); *ADA*, index 'Exceptions', *ADC*, index 'Dilatory Exceptions'. For a discussion of procedure in the church courts see S. Ollivant, *Court of the Official in pre-Reformation Scotland* (Stair Society, 1982) 108. I owe several of these references to Mr. Hector MacQueen.

[26] *APS*, i, 472. c. 23.

[27] The reference in *Morton Registrum*, ii, no. 107 to a brieve of mortancestry in connection with a dispute between Sir James Douglas and William Cresswell over the barony of Roberton (which was part of Mary Douglas's inheritance) presumably relates to Cresswell's ancestral claim.

[28] Above, p. 2.

[29] *Pollock and Maitland*, ii, 616; Maitland cites *Bracton* and the *Digest*.

[30] I am indebted to my colleague Mr. Hector MacQueen for much of the argument in the last two paragraphs and for making available to me the results of his research on medieval Scots pleading.

the vernacular, using these or similar words — 'dixit in vulgari prout sequitur vel saltem in verbis consimilibus':[31]

> My lorde the kyng it is done me til understand that thare is a certane contract made bytwene schir Malcolme of dromonde and schir John of Swynton apon the landis of the Erledome of Marr and the Lordship of Garvyauch of the qwhilkes Erldome and Lordship Issabell the said schir Malcolms wyf is verray and lauchfull ayre And failliand of the ayrez of hir body the half of the forneymt erldome and lordship perteignys to my wyfe of Richt of heretage Therefore I require you for goddis sake as my lorde and my kyng as lauchful actornay to my said wyfe that in case gif ony sic contract be made in preiudice of my saide wyfe of that at aucht of Richt and of lauch perteigne til hir in fee and heritage failliand of the saide Issabell as is before saide that yhe grant na confirmacion thare apon in hurtyng of the commone lauch of the kynryk and of my wyvis Richt swa that sic contract gif ony be make na preiudice no hurtyng to my fornemyt wife of that at scho aucht to succede to as lauchful ayre To the qwhilk our lorde the kyng answerit saiand that he had weel herd and undirstand his request and said that hym thocht his request was resonable And said als that it suld nocht be his wil in that case no in nane othir oucht to do or to conferme that suld ryn ony man in preiudice of thair heritage attour the commone lauch and namely in oucht at rynyt the said schir Thomas or his wyfe in sic manner Apon the qwilk our lorde the kynges grant the said schir Thomas and als apone his said Request Requerit me notare before said to make hym ane Instrument.[32]

Interestingly, this notarial instrument appears to be our first record of the vernacular in use in the Scots Parliament. The parliamentary record itself does not change from Latin to Scots until 1399. Erskine was right to suspect double dealing regarding the earldom of Mar, for it is notorious that his descendants were excluded from that earldom, despite frequent protests, for over one hundred years until they were finally granted the title (which still remains in the family) in the sixteenth century. Sir Thomas Erskine died in 1403 or 1404.[33]

Sir James Douglas of Dalkeith enjoyed the favour of successive kings and became one of the most powerful magnates in Scotland.[34] Many surviving documents attest to his close attention to legal matters. There is, for example, in the recently published *Regesta* of David II a brieve of mortancestry taken out by Douglas in 1368, not long after the duel of chivalry, to gain sasine of the lands of the barony of Kilbucho and Newlands, entailed on him by his uncle in 1351.[35] But the best evidence for his legal activity lies in the chartulary of the Douglases of Dalkeith, a treasure of evidence for the medievalist and legal historian, and one of the very few lay chartularies to have survived from medieval Scotland. The bulk of this was published last century as *Registrum Honoris de Morton*. Perhaps

---

[31] *APS*, i, 578.

[32] For details of the Erskine claim see *Complete Peerage*, 'Mar', especially VIII, 409-10.

[33] *Complete Peerage*, VIII, 414.

[34] Both Cosmo Innes, in the preface to *Morton Registrum*, and A. Grant, 'Higher Nobility, c. 1371-1424', 240ff. discuss the career of Sir James Douglas.

[35] *RRS*, vi, no. 417; MacQueen, 'Dissasine and Mortancestor', discusses this and others of Douglas' legal actions. Above, p. 2 for the entail of Kilbucho.

the most interesting documents in the chartulary are two wills drawn up for
Sir James in 1390 and 1392, the earliest known Scottish wills extant. In them Sir
James makes special mention of his books: books of romances, books of
grammar and dialectic, but also books of law, both civil law and Scottish statutes
— *libros meos . . . civiles et statuta Regni Scocie*.[36] A direction later in the will to
return books which had been borrowed to their owners confirms the impression
of a literate, articulate layman. There may have been several such in late
fourteenth century Scotland, but Sir James is one of the few for whom we have
clear evidence. Also specified in the will are various items of armour, some of
which, one imagines, may date from the combat in 1368! Sir James married first
the sister of the earl of March, Agnes Dunbar, whom David II may have wished
to make his queen.[37] He married secondly Giles (Egidia), half-sister of Robert II.
His eldest son married Elizabeth, daughter of Robert III. Sir James died in 1420,
more than fifty years after the combat with Erskine, 'a man of enormous
territories and great real wealth'.[38]

Before concluding, it is worth noting another tantalising reference, in no way
less dramatic, to the law of courtesy in medieval Scotland. As the aged Walter
Stewart, earl of Atholl, lay in prison on the afternoon of 26 May 1437, awaiting
execution later that day for his part in the murder of his nephew King James I,
he was visited by Sir Thomas Maule of Panmure, accompanied by various
gentlemen and a notary. There, after making his last confession, Walter Stewart
swore a solemn declaration that after his wife's death he had possessed the lands
of Brechin Barclay by the courtesy of Scotland — *possidebit simpliciter ex
curialitate regni Scotie*. Some of these lands he had resigned into the king's hands,
but others in Fife he had not. This declaration was recorded for Sir Thomas
Maule in a notarial instrument.[39] Atholl's wife had been Margaret Barclay, lady
of Brechin, and heir to her father, Sir David Barclay. Maule's interest in the
matter is not stated in the instrument, but it appears from a document drawn up
in Scots eleven days later on 6 June 1437 — 'the soothfast witnesing' of Thomas
Bisset of Balwillo.[40] In it Bisset carefully traces the relationship between the
countess of Atholl and Sir Thomas Maule:

> suth fastli I make knawin that dam Jehan Barclay the wif umquhil of scher
> David Flemying was ful systir til the last scher David Barclay umquhile lord
> of brechyn and at the Said scher David [Barclay] had na brothir that mycht
> succed til his heritage bot alanerlie a douchtir the quhilk was merit witht
> Walter Stewart Knicht erl of Athol sumtym. Heir atour, suthfastli I mak
> knawin that the said dam Jehan Barclay the wyf umquhil of the said scher
> David Flemyng had twa douchters an callit Jonet an uthir Marioun and Jonet
> bair Alexander of Seytoun, and Marioun Thomas de Maule the quhilk decisit
> at the Harlaw. Alsua suthfastli I make knawyn that in my yuthed I was

[36] *Morton Registrum*, ii, nos. 193 and 196.
[37] Nicholson, *Scotland — The Later Middle Ages*, 182-3: in 1371, before she married Sir James
Douglas, Agnes Dunbar was granted 1000 merks a year from the customs of Aberdeen and
Haddington by David II.
[38] Cosmo Innes, *Morton Registrum*, xv.
[39] *Registrum de Panmure*, ed. J. Stuart (Edinburgh, 1874), ii, 228.
[40] *Panmure Registrum*, ii, 230.

Sir Archibald Douglas = Beatrice Lindsay
k. 1333

Sir Robert Erskine = Christian Menteith[1] = Sir Edward Keith
d. 1385   d. 1387/8   of Sinton

Sir David Barclay = Margaret Brechin
k. 1350   Lady of Brechin

Reginald Mure = Mary Douglas
d. c. 1367

Sir Thomas Erskine = Janet Keith = Sir David Barclay
d. 1403-4   d. 1412-13   Lord of Brechin
                                      d. 1366-9

Jean Barclay = Sir David Fleming = Isabel of
                 of Cumbernauld   Monycabock
                 k. 1406

Walter Stewart = Margaret Barclay
Earl-Palatine of Strathearn, Earl   Lady of Brechin
of Atholl and Caithness ex. 1437   d. pre. Aug. 1404

Alan Stewart
Earl of Caithness
k. 1431

Janet Fleming
= Sir William Seton

Marion Fleming
= William Maule

Sir David Stewart
Master of Atholl d. 1433/4

Sir Alexander Seton[2]
d. 1440/1
= Elizabeth Gordon

Thomas Maule
k. 1411

Sir Robert Stewart
Master of Atholl ex. 1437

Alexander, Earl of
Huntly

Sir Thomas Maule
1437

Table 2 — COURTESY 1437

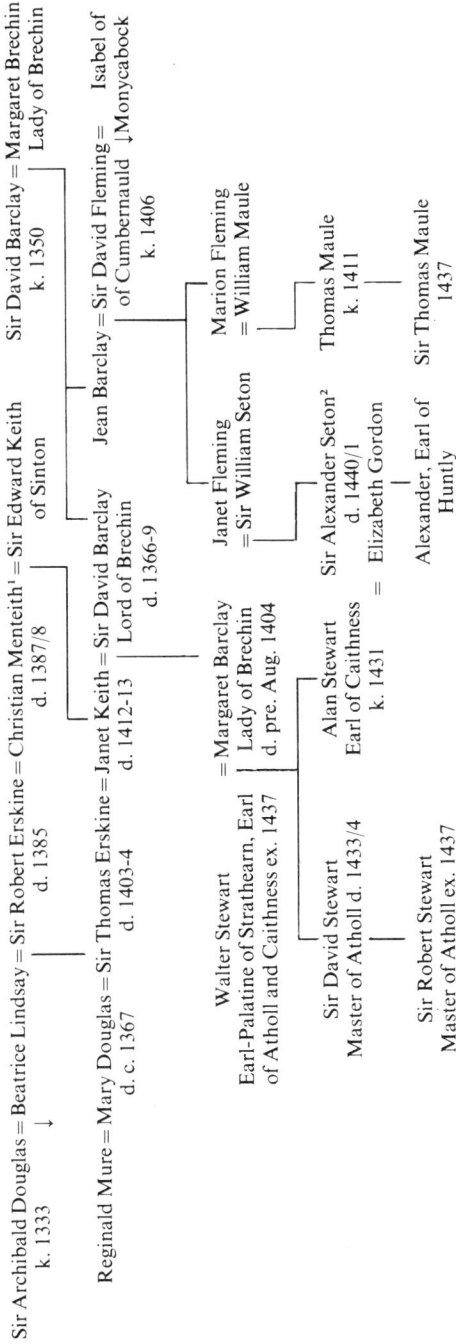

[1] Christian Menteith was both stepmother and mother-in-law to Sir Thomas Erskine. It was through her that the Erskines claimed the Earldom of Mar.
[2] Sir Alexander Seton's elder brother Sir John Seton was probably the son of an earlier marriage.

servant on to my lord scher Thomas of Erskyn [the duellist of 1368] and of continual houshald and oftymes I herd my lord beforsaid and my lade Dam Jehan his wif that was modir to David Steuart's modir, suthfastli say that failyeand of David Steuart and of his modir that Seytonis and Maulis war verra ayris to the Barclayis landis . . .'[41]

Table 2 sets out some of the complicated relationships involved. The point is, however, that failing issue of Margaret Barclay and Walter Stewart — and Walter died predeceased by all his descendants, his grandson Sir Robert Stewart having been executed some days before him — Sir Alexander Seton and Sir Thomas Maule were the nearest heirs to the Barclay inheritance, through heirs portioners.[42] It would be pleasant to record that Sir Thomas Maule did actually succeed to some of the Barclay lands, but the evidence is otherwise.

The duel between Erskine and Douglas in 1368 and the last declaration of Walter, earl of Atholl, provide two of the best and most dramatic instances of the operation of the law of courtesy in medieval Scotland before the records of the central judicial bodies and of the Court of Session provide a clearer picture. The duel in 1368 may strike us as an extraordinary combination of a bizarre rule of evidence and an archaic method of proof, but before we rush to condemn our fourteenth-century ancestors we would do well to reflect that the requirement that a child be born of the marriage live and heard to cry remained part of the law until the abolition of courtesy in 1964, and that it is at least arguable, following dicta in *McKendrick* v. *Sinclair*,[43] that trial by battle is still competent in Scotland.

DAVID SELLAR

I am indebted to Dr. A. Grant and Mr. Hector MacQueen for reading and commenting on a first draft of this paper.

[41] I have followed the text in *Panmure Registrum* but, with the aid of the facsimile included there, corrected some small mistakes.

[42] Thus both Seton, who appears to have been the father of the first earl of Huntly, and Maule were heirs to the Barclay inheritance, and not Maule alone, as is often stated.

[43] 1972 S.L.T. 110; S.C. (H.L.) 25 and especially per Lord Reid at 54: the argument would assume that the 1819 Appeal of Murder Act which abolished trial by battle in England after the celebrated case of *Ashford* v. *Thornton* does not apply in Scotland, and follows Lord Reid's view that 'Loss of a common law remedy by desuetude would, I think, be a novelty in our law, and I see no advantage in introducing such a principle. No one knows what may happen in the future.'

PROBLEMS OF SOVEREIGNTY AND LAW IN ORKNEY AND SHETLAND

By Gordon Donaldson, d.litt., f.b.a.,

Historiographer Royal for Scotland;
Professor Emeritus, University of Edinburgh

It is among the most picturesque and therefore best remembered episodes in Scottish history that King Christian I of Denmark and Norway, unable to raise the 60,000 florins of the Rhine which he had promised as the dowry of his daughter, Margaret, on her marriage to James III, King of Scots, pledged his lands and rights in Orkney for 50,000 florins in 1468 and his lands and rights in Shetland for a further 8,000 florins in the following year.[1] But those transactions were no more than incidents in a long process whereby the islands were gradually transferred from Norwegian control and were stage by stage incorporated into the Scottish kingdom. They did not in themselves mean an abrupt substitution of Scottish rule and Scots law for Norwegian rule and Norse law.

Much had already happened before 1468-9 — in the first place in the international scene. In 1266, by the Treaty of Perth, Norway ceded to Scotland the Isle of Man, the Hebrides and all other islands on the west and south of the great 'Haff' or sea, in return for 4,000 merks in four annual instalments and 100 merks yearly in perpetuity[2] — the 'Annual of Norway' which remained a Scottish liability for two hundred years but which was seldom paid. Orkney and Shetland were at that time expressly reserved to Norway, but, only fifteen years later, a treaty arranging the marriage of Alexander III's daughter to King Erik of Norway provided that, should the Norwegians not fulfil the terms, then Orkney was to be ceded to Scotland:[3] the possibility of a cession of Orkney had thus been envisaged two hundred years before 1468. Soon after the treaties of 1266 and 1281 Scotland was preoccupied with her relations with England, and — although the Treaty of Perth was confirmed by the Treaty of Inverness in 1312[4] — relations with Norway did not figure much in Scottish history again until Scotland recovered stability after prolonged wars and periods of weak administration. But in 1426 the obligation to pay the Annual of Norway was reaffirmed.[5] Then in 1460, when the possibility of a marriage of Princess Margaret of Denmark to James III was first discussed, the Scots proposed that to make up her dowry the

---

[1] The best text of the Orkney treaty, with translation, is in John Mooney, *Charters and other Records of the City and Royal Burgh of Kirkwall*, 96-109. The text of the Shetland treaty is in *Norges Gamle Love*, Anden Raekke (ed. O. A. Johnsen et al., Oslo, ii, no. 116, 1934), and Barbara E. Crawford, 'The Pawning of Orkney and Shetland', *SHR*, xlviii, 52-3.
[2] *APS*, i, 420.
[3] *ibid.*, 423.
[4] *ibid.*, 461-2.
[5] *Diplomatarium Norvegicum*, xx, 764-6.

Annual of Norway should be extinguished and Orkney and Shetland should be ceded to Scotland.[6] These events should be seen in the general setting of Scoto-Norwegian relations over two centuries. With the death of Haakon the Old in 1263 it may be said that the imperialist phase of Norwegian history came to an end, even while Norway was still an independent state. Then, in the fourteenth century, when Norway passed under the Danish crown, responsibility for Norwegian dependencies passed to Denmark, which was interested not in possessions overseas to the west but in its relations with the Hanseatic League and the Baltic lands, so that Norwegian interests were neglected.

Thus, even in the international scene, the transfer of Orkney and Shetland in 1468-9 did not represent anything startlingly novel. But much had also been happening before 1468-9 within the islands, where Scottish influence had long been infiltrating. One need look only at the succession of the earls to see this. It is usually said that the Norse line of jarls ended with John in 1231, but the fact is that both John and his brother and predecessor, David, were at least three-quarters Scots, and their father, Harald Maddadson, had been Scots on the male side. Indeed, intermarriage between Orkney earls and Scottish families had started at least as far back as the end of the tenth century, when Sigurd II married a daughter of Malcolm II, and the male line of the Norse earls had not continued beyond Earl Rognvald, who died in 1158. At any rate, after 1231 the earldom passed to a series of Scottish families — the Angus line (1231-c. 1320), the Strathearn line (1321-57) and finally, in 1379, the St. Clair line. All these earls were mainly Scots or Scoto-Norman in race, their interests were primarily Scottish and some of them may never have set foot in Orkney. They had a dual allegiance, for, while they held Orkney from the kings of Norway, they also held Caithness or other property from the kings of Scots, and as Scottish magnates they played their parts in Scottish affairs: Magnus, earl of Caithness and Orkney, was one of the barons in whose names the Declaration of Arbroath was sent to the pope in 1320. Precisely what influence these earls had in Orkney may be debatable, but they assuredly can have done nothing to strengthen or even to maintain the connection with Norway. Shetland, however, did not wholly share Orkney's fortunes. In 1195 it had been detached from the earldom, and was ruled, like the Faroes, by a governor appointed in Norway. This arrangement lasted until at least 1379, when the St. Clair earls came in, but, although they certainly had interests in Shetland, whether they were actually invested in Shetland as well as Orkney remains debatable.[7]

It is true that the formal superiority of the king of Norway over the earls of Orkney, Scots though they were, was maintained. Indeed, between the last of the Strathearn earls and the first of the St. Clair line the Norwegian king took the earldom into his own hands for twenty-two years, and after the death of the second St. Clair earl, in 1420, the Norwegian king again took the earldom into his own hands, this time for fourteen years. Certainly the St. Clair earls, and presumably their predecessors also, were invested on terms designed to safeguard

[6] *Diplomatarium Christierni Primi* (ed. Hans Knudsen, Copenhagen, 1856), 128. I am indebted to Dr. Barbara Crawford for giving me a photocopy of this item.
[7] Barbara E. Crawford, 'The earldom of Orkney and lordship of Shetland', *Saga Book* (Viking Society for Northern Research), xvii, 157, 165.

the rights of the Norwegian king: they were to govern only during his pleasure, they were to be answerable to him for their administration, they were not to build castles in the islands without his consent and they were to provide men for his service.[8] If these provisions suggest that the king was apprehensive lest Orkney, under its Scottish earls, might slip from his grasp altogether, his fears seem to have been justified. The first of the St. Clair earls did build a castle in Kirkwall; the last of them, when summoned in 1460 and 1461 to give his personal allegiance to Christian I of Denmark and Norway, excused himself and there seems to be no evidence that he ever did homage to the king.[9] Besides, the earls were clearly withdrawing from active participation in Norwegian affairs. In 1389, when twenty Norwegian councillors declared that King Erik was the rightful heir to the Norwegian crown, the second name in the list was that of Henry Sinclair, Earl of Orkney.[10] By contrast, after Christian I came to the throne in 1448, there was no representative present from Orkney either when he was elected as Norwegian king, when he was proved to be the true heir, or when he was crowned at Trondheim.[11]

Just how strong Scottish influence in Orkney had become is shown by the fact that even when the Norwegian king took the earldom into his own hands Scots continued to play important parts in Orkney. Already in 1357, when the king resumed the earldom after the death of the last Strathearn earl, the people of Orkney petitioned him for protection against the activities of a Scot, Duncan Anderson, who claimed to be acting for the rightful heir of the earldom.[12] After 1420, when the king again resumed the earldom after the death of the second St. Clair earl, the administration was nonetheless carried on (though in his name) by Scots — Bishop Thomas Tulloch from 1420 to 1423 and 1426 to 1434 and David Menzies of Weem from 1423 to 1426. There is also evidence that before 1468 the king of Norway was finding it impossible to collect the revenues due to him from the islands.[13] It looks as if it was impracticable for the Norwegian king, whatever his intentions, to make his power effective in this distant dependency.

In view of the long succession of Scottish earls, a certain amount of penetration of Scottish influence in the secular field is not surprising. But it extended also to the church, and only four years after Henry Sinclair became earl of Orkney Robert Sinclair was nominated as bishop of Orkney. This is perhaps rather more surprising, because the bishopric of Orkney did not form part of the Scottish province but was subject to the Norwegian archbishop of Trondheim. That Scottish influence was paramount in the church in Orkney became evident during the time of the Great Schism (1378-1417), when rival popes competed for the allegiance of western Christendom. Norway, like England, supported the pope at Rome, and Scotland, like France, the pope at Avignon. Clearly, the will of the Roman pope should have prevailed in Orkney, and yet it seems that in practice the voice of Avignon, which meant Scotland, was not ineffective, with

[8] *REO*, 21-2, 48-9.

[9] Crawford, 'Pawning', 41-2.

[10] *Diplomatarium Norvegicum*, v, no. 484.

[11] Lecture by Mrs. Thelma Jexlev, Assistant Keeper of the Danish Archives, at Kirkwall, reported in *The Orcadian* 29 August 1968.

[12] Joseph Anderson, in Introduction to *Orkneyinga Saga* (1873), lix-lx.

[13] Crawford, 'Earldom', 162.

the appointments of Robert Sinclair, dean of Moray and later Bishop of Dunkeld, and Alexander Vaus, later Bishop of Caithness. Nominations were of course made on the Roman side as well. One of them was the realistic one of John, parson of Fetlar, presumably a native candidate, but after him came the nomination of an Englishman, a papal chaplain, who was recognised in Norway but apparently never set foot in Orkney. It seems that the Norwegian candidates, the Roman candidates, were repulsed by the Scots, with the support of the earls. The important fact is that from 1383 onwards there was a succession of Scottish bishops of Orkney, including latterly two Tullochs — the Thomas Tulloch already mentioned and then William Tulloch, who was keeper of the privy seal of Scotland and an active figure at the Scottish court.

It was perhaps even more remarkable that Scots were finding their way into the church in Shetland (which, even when detached from the earldom of Orkney, was always part of the bishopric). In the archdeaconry of Shetland there were a couple of Buchans, obviously Scots, in the 1380s, and during the Schism it seems that it was Scots, nominated by Avignon, rather than natives or Norwegians, who obtained possession. After the Schism, the archdeaconry of Shetland, like the bishopric of Orkney, fell into the hands of Tullochs — three of them in succession, Malise, David and Thomas. Thus even Shetland, though to some extent screened from Scotticisation in secular affairs, was exposed to Scottish influence through the church.

The Scots who filled the leading positions in church and state brought their kinsmen and clients in their train: one of the Orcadians' complaints against Menzies of Weem in the 1420s was that he introduced 'foreigners' (i.e. Scots) who oppressed the people,[14] and it is evident that there must have been a substantial Scottish immigration before 1468, to produce a fair number of officials and landowners.[15] There is a telling illustration in the linguistic field. The latest extant Orkney document in Norse is dated so early as 1426, and even it was composed in the official Norwegian of the day and not in the local Orcadian Norn. Ten years after that, namely in 1436, the lawman of Orkney was writing in Lowland Scots — a generation before the transaction of 1468. As we should expect, it was different in Shetland. As to Scottish immigration, it seems unlikely that more than a small number of Scots can have settled in Shetland before 1469, and even thereafter, until the second half of the sixteenth century, the process was slow. It is not surprising that the latest Norse document extant in Shetland belongs to so late as 1607, nearly two hundred years after the latest Orkney one. Clearly, Scotticisation was much slower in Shetland than in Orkney.

Looking over the whole field, can one doubt that much had happened before 1468 and that the Scots had come to Orkney and had come to stay? It is hard to believe that by 1468 the king of Denmark and Norway can have considered that the effective reintegration of the islands into his dominions could be practicable. The transaction of 1468 may not have been a mere recognition of a *fait accompli*, but it did not amount to the transfer to Scotland of something that was an integral part of the Norwegian kingdom. This may have been less true of

[14] *REO*, 37.
[15] Storer Clouston, *History of Orkney* (Kirkwall, 1932), 271, 281.

Shetland than of Orkney, and 1469 was perhaps a more significant date for Shetland than 1468 was for Orkney.

But what did in fact happen in 1468-9? What was the scope of the transactions and what exactly was pledged? A substantial transfer of some kind must have been made, for the king of Scots was not going to waive the bulk of the dowry in return for a mere paper concession. What was pledged must have been considered to represent a value of 58,000 florins. The treaties specified 'our lands of the islands of Orkney' and 'our lands of the islands of Shetland', with 'all and sundry rights, services and rightful pertinents belonging to us by royal right'. Whatever else may have been comprehended, crown lands clearly had first place. There were assuredly lands in Orkney which had belonged to the Norwegian crown, and when Henry St. Clair was installed as earl in 1379 there is a reference to 'the lands of our said lord the king', as well as to the king's rights, on which the new earl was not to encroach.[16] We know less about crown lands in Shetland, and if royal estates were less extensive there that would help to explain the discrepancy between the sum of 50,000 florins for Orkney and only 8000 for Shetland — bearing in mind that Shetland, though far less fertile than Orkney, has an area about 50% greater.[17] On the other hand, it may be doubted if the negotiators were thinking of a precise valuation, and perhaps King Christian could hardly have pledged a quarter or a third of Shetland.

Besides lands which may have been considered royal demesne, there were lands of which the crown was superior or landlord. It is true that udal tenure, which obtained in Norwegian territories, involved allodial holding, with no superior in the feudal sense, but clearly the king was in some way the superior of the earldom of Orkney and, besides, there must have been land which was let and from which the crown derived rents. Among crown renenues there were not only rents but profits of justice, especially fines. We know that in 1195 half the fines from Orkney were assigned to the crown, and in the 1420s David Menzies of Weem was accused of wrongfully uplifting them.[18] There were also taxes, and in 1469 King Christian commanded the people of the islands to pay their taxes to the Scottish king and obey him.[19]

A comprehensive transfer of crown rights should have included a voice in the selection of bishops, the patronage of other benefices and the enjoyment of the temporalities of bishoprics during vacancies. In 1266, when the Hebrides were ceded, the crown patronage in the bishopric of the Isles had been expressly mentioned, but there was no such clause in 1468 and some uncertainty seems to have persisted. In 1502 a nominee of the king of Denmark contested the archdeaconry of Shetland with a nominee of the king of Scots,[20] and so late as 1662 a conveyance of land in Shetland which had once belonged to the cathedral of Bergen and had fallen to the Norwegian crown was confirmed by King Frederick III.[21] On the other hand, there is ample evidence that from the very

[16] *REO*, 26; Crawford, 'Pawning', 44.
[17] Crawford, 'Earldom', 164-5: Mr. Brian Smith, Shetland Archivist, deduces from a reference c. 1500 to 'the kingis landmaill' that the crown lands in Shetland were 'very meagre indeed'.
[18] *REO*, 38.
[19] Crawford, 'Earldom', 163-4, 168.
[20] *RSS*, i, 755.
[21] Gilbert Goudie, *Celtic and Scandinavian Antiquities of Shetland* (Blackwood, 1904), 97-9.

beginning of the sixteenth century the Scottish kings regularly exercised their regalian rights in the bishopric of Orkney and also made presentations to benefices in the islands without further challenge.[22]

Crown lands, revenues and rights had the pecuniary value with which the negotiators of 1468-9 may be presumed to have been primarily concerned. It may be doubted if they thought of the more abstract concept of sovereignty, but there are positive indications that sovereignty was deliberately excluded from the impignoration. A comparison with the Treaty of Perth is again instructive. The western isles were ceded in comprehensive terms, with express exclusion of 'the islands of Orkney and Shetland, which the said king of Norway reserved to his *dominium*, with all their lordships, homages and revenues, services and all their rights and pertinents'. The marriage treaty of 1281 envisaged the possible cession of 'the whole land of Orkney'. The draft treaty of 1460, in its turn, proposed to transfer 'all right and *dominium*' which the king of Denmark and Norway had in the islands of Orkney and Shetland (*omne jus et dominium quod habet et habere pretendit in insulis Orchadie et Chasteland*).

In the terminology of 1468-9 there is no mention either of *dominium* or of the whole land of Orkney and Shetland. King Christian pledged only 'our lands of the islands of the Orkneys' and 'our lands of the islands of Shetland'. That may or may not have in itself meant less than 'the Orkney islands' or 'the islands of Shetland' would have done, but it has been argued on the strength of this phrase that the impignoration extended only to the royal estates.[23] It is more revealing that the treaty of 1468 contains a contrast between 'the islands of the Sudreys and Man' and 'our lands of the Orkney islands'. Why this qualifying phrase, '*our lands of* the Orkney islands'? It does look as if Norway was ceding less in Orkney in 1468 than she had ceded in the Sudreys in 1266 and less in Orkney in 1468 than she had reserved there in 1266. The 'something less', whatever else it may have been, surely included sovereignty. It may be objected that the Treaty of Perth was two hundred years old when the impignoration of 1468-9 took place. But, though old, it was not forgotten. It had been reissued in 1426, it had been referred to in the negotiations of 1460, when a draft treaty contained an abridgment of its terms,[24] and it was referred to in the treaty of 1468 itself, one clause of which finally extinguished (as the treaty of 1460 had proposed to do) the Annual of Norway payable in terms of the treaty of 1266. It can hardly be doubted that those who drew up the treaty of 1468, if they did not actually have the treaty of 1266 before them, were fully conversant with its terminology.

In later attempts by the Danish kings to redeem what they had pledged, it was more than once claimed that sovereignty had not been renounced, and this claim was not, apparently, disputed by the Scots. When Frederick II raised the question of the redemption of the islands in 1560 he said that the Scots must be aware that the *dominium* of the islands pertained to him. Again that word *dominium*, which in the context must mean sovereignty. His words were: 'of the Orkney islands, which your people have kept for some time, the *dominium* pertains to us and to our kingdom of Norway' (*insularum Orcadum, quas aliquo*

[22] *RSS*, i, 1031 and *passim*.
[23] *The Viking Congress* (ed. W. Douglas Simpson, Aberdeen, 1954), 81-2.
[24] *Diplomatarium Christierni Primi*, 125-6.

jam tempore gens vestra detinet, dominium ad nos nostrumque regnum Norwagie pertinet).[25] In 1585 Frederick again asserted that the islands 'are acknowledged indisputably to form part of our kingdom'.[26] And in 1667 the Danish case was that the islands 'belonged to the kingdom of Norway as an inseparable and inalienable dependency, and still belong to it'.[27]

It is therefore reasonable to maintain that sovereignty was never formally transferred, even in pledge, let alone by complete cession. On the other hand, in practice, Scotland, and subsequently the United Kingdom, have long and continuously exercised sovereign rights, to the exclusion of any Scandinavian authority, and it has therefore been concluded that sovereignty has in the course of time been transferred by use and wont, by tacit agreement or acquiescence and, for many generations now, without challenge. An expert in international law has written recently: 'At the present time, and indeed for some considerable time past, the United Kingdom has exercised full sovereign powers over Shetland: the islands are under the British crown, governed by the government of the U.K., bound by the statutes made at Westminster, subject to the Scottish legal system of local government and the U.K. administrative network.... The Scottish, and later U.K., title to Shetland derives from the exercise of a full range of governmental functions over a large number of years without interruption.' It is argued further that, despite the 'whensoever' (*quandocunque*) of the document pledging Shetland, which gave the Norwegian crown the right to redeem at any point in the future, yet by this time acquiescence and delay have now barred Norway from invoking the rights of redemption.[28] It has been from time to time suggested that all possible ambiguity should be removed by a brief treaty between Britain and Norway, perhaps along with Denmark for any interest that country might be thought to have, just to make it clear once and for all that sovereignty over the islands belongs to Britain,[29] but in view of the opinion just quoted this would appear to be quite superfluous. The link of Orkney and Shetland with Britain may resemble a marriage by habit and repute, but it is nonetheless a legal marriage. There remains, however, one point of ambiguity. Granted that British sovereignty now exists by prescription, no one has ventured to pronounce on the date at which such sovereignty became effective *de jure*, and it may be considered to remain uncertain whether Scotland had acquired sovereignty before 1707 or if it was acquired by the U.K. after that date: it might therefore be asked whether Orkney and Shetland, while legally parts of the U.K., are legally parts of Scotland. At the moment this question is purely academic, but in the event of Scotland becoming independent it might conceivably have to be discussed.

Examination of the question of sovereignty, and in particular of what precisely was pledged in 1468-9, must take the documents of those years as meaning what they say and as being legally impignorations. It has, however, been contended that Christian I had no intention of redeeming what he had pledged.

[25] *National MSS of Scotland*, III, xliv; translated by Goudie, *op. cit.*, 217-18 (where 'dominium' is wrongly rendered 'lordship').
[26] Goudie, *op. cit.*, 219
[27] See note 115 below.
[28] John P. Grant in *The Shetland Report* (Nevis Institute, 1978), i, 139.
[29] *Shetland Times*, 9 July 1965.

The argument is based partly on the diplomatic of the documents. In the private law of Scotland the pledging of land by a wadset, as it was called, was commonplace, and specimens of reversions, whereby the grantee undertook to return the land on payment of redemption money, are frequently found in private muniments, containing words and phrases with which the student of Scottish documents is thoroughly familiar. While it would not be true to say that there is an absolutely rigid style, or that all reversions contain precisely the same clauses, certain provisions were nonetheless normal: the place where payment was to be made was specified, payment had to be made on one day between sunrise and sunset, there had to be warning in advance (usually, though not always, forty days) of the intention to pay, the coin in which payment was to be made was stipulated, and arrangements were sometimes made for handing over the money to a third party should the person entitled to receive it not appear.

Of all those characteristic phrases, which would seem to have been of the essence of a true reversion, not one appears in the documents of 1468-9, with the single exception that the Shetland treaty specified the place for repayment — the cathedral of St. Magnus in Kirkwall. It is not impossible that this is an indication — taken along with the *quandocunque* already mentioned — that the pledging of Shetland was a shade more realistic than that of Orkney: Christian may have reflected that, while he had little hope of raising 50,000 florins to redeem Orkney, he might raise 8000 to redeem the much less Scotticised Shetland. It is true that it would have been in order for those characteristic phrases to appear not in the grant by King Christian to King James but in a separate document in which James undertook to restore what had been pledged when the money was paid over. But, while the treaty of 1468 itself has survived in both the Danish and the Scottish archives, there is no trace in either of such a reciprocal undertaking;[30] the treaty of 1468 is itself so full, reciting for instance the procuratories of the Scottish ambassadors, that it would have been expected to recite such a document had one existed; and, as the treaty of 1469 mentions the place for repayment, other provisions would surely have been inserted there as well had they been in mind.

Comparison may also be made between the Orkney and Shetland impignorations and several other documents issued by Chirstian I, who pledged many parts of his dominions, ranging from the duchies of Holstein and Slesvig to a castle or a few parishes. The other impignorations are in German or Danish and not in Latin, and they have no standard phraseology, so an argument from simple diplomatic is not possible. Yet the differences are significant. An examination of over half a dozen of Christian's impignorations, haphazardly selected, shows that although the clauses usual in Scottish reversions are not to be found regularly in them, yet similar phraseology does sometimes occur. 'In general it is stated how long notice must be given when redemption was wanted, and very often it was also mentioned that notice could be given only at certain times of the year. Furthermore there was often a clause indicating in which sort of currency the payment was to be made, and there was almost always an indication

---

[30] Storer Clouston, *op. cit.*, 258, states that James III formally promised to give back the islands to the king of Norway on redemption of the wadset, but the source he cites turns out to be nothing other than the document pledging Shetland.

of the place in which it was to be handed over.'[31] The inclusion of such provisions in Christian's other impignorations makes their omission from the 1468-9 documents the more striking. It is true that most, probably all, of the other areas pledged by Christian were sooner or later redeemed. None of them, however, were either outlying and detached territories already deeply infiltrated by a foreign power, or territories the outright cession of which had already been discussed, and to that extent they were in a different case from Orkney and Shetland. It would therefore be unsound to argue that Christian meant to redeem Orkney and Shetland also.

It is not a novel suggestion that Christian had no intention of redeeming Orkney and Shetland, for half a century ago a Norwegian historian wrote: 'It is not probable that the Danish king Christian I ever seriously contemplated the redemption of the islands'.[32] The question is, did Christian use an ostensible reversion to cover up his real intention of complete alienation? The negotiations of 1460 had been for a straightforward surrender of all Christian's rights and *dominium* in Orkney and Shetland: the treaties of 1468 and 1469 were impignorations of 'our lands of the islands of' Orkney and Shetland. Are we to believe that the Scottish government had climbed down and decided to settle for so much less than it had wanted eight years before? The explanation is surely to be found on the Danish side. Christian was obliged, by conditions laid down at his accession, not to decide any matter touching the Norwegian crown without the consent of his council, and he was not to alienate or even pledge any honours, fiefs or revenues of the realm. Whether Christian obtained Norwegian consent to the transactions of 1468-9 remains debatable: it has been pointed out that he did visit Norway in 1468 and it has been suggested that he obtained consent to the Orkney transaction of 1468 but not to the Shetland transaction of 1469.[33] If consent was given it was much more likely to be given to an impignoration than to a cession; and if it was not given, then Christian may have thought that a pledge was a more venial breach of his obligations than outright cession would have been and also that by giving up lands and rights, but not sovereignty, he was surrendering the substance but retaining the formal title. However regarded, the impignoration was an exercise in face-saving. It does not affect this argument that the 1468 document provided that, should James die before Margaret, and she chose to leave Scotland, she was to have 120,000 florins for her terce from Scotland, less the 50,000 florins unpaid of the dowry, and the lands of the islands of the Orkneys were to revert to Norway. At the time, in 1468, Christian's habit of pledging territory was the setting for his ingenious device which avoided

---

[31] Information from Th. Lyby Christensen of the University of Aarhus, in a letter of 10 February 1976. He prefaced the sentence quoted with the following: 'It is quite true that Christiern I made some sort of sport out of pledging parts of his dominions, and quite a lot of mortgage deeds are still extant. I looked through the two classical collections of documents from his times, viz. the *Diplomatarium Christierni Primi*, ed. Hans Knudsen (Copenhagen, 1856) and the 'Registrum König Christian des Ersten', ed. Georg Hille (Kiel, 1875), which is vol. iv of the *Urkundensammlung der Gesellschaft für Schleswig-Holstein-Lauenburgische Geschichte* and contains material pertaining to the Duchies. Both of them abound with impignorations, but although I went over them both, I have not been able to find any other examples of impignorations in Latin than those already known to you'.

[32] A. W. Brøgger, *Ancient Emigrants* (Oxford, 1929), 196-7.

[33] Scheel (see note prefixed to Appendix), 385.

difficulties with his Norwegian subjects and saved his pocket to the tune of 50,000 florins by parting with islands in which he had ceased to have much more than a nominal interest.

Events which happened within a very few years of 1468-9 seem to confirm the view that redemption of the islands was not regarded as likely. The 'lands of the islands of Orkney' and of Shetland pledged in 1468-9 had not, of course, included the lands of the earldom. They were not the king's to dispose of, but belonged to William St. Clair. In 1470, however, Earl William resigned to the king of Scots his rights in the earldom of Orkney and lordship of Shetland.[34] That transaction, whereby the Scottish king acquired permanent ownership of the earldom, was actually more important than the transactions of 1468-9 — if, that is, those were, as they purported to be, only redeemable pledges and constituted only a temporary title. This meant that had the pledge been redeemed after 1470 the king of Scots would have continued to hold the earldom and lordship and would have held them as a vassal of the king of Denmark and Norway. This would not have been an impossible or unparalleled situation, but it tends to increase doubts about the genuineness of the supposed pledge in 1468-9. It may be that from the outset the Scottish king had his eyes on the earldom property, and the 1468-9 treaties were steps towards his acquisition of it. In February 1471/2 the Scottish parliament 'annext and uniit the erledome of Orkney and lordschip of Scheteland to the croune, nocht to be gevin away in tyme to cum ... except alanerly til ane of the kingis sonnis gott of lachfull bed'.[35] This is of course related to the earl's private property and had no direct bearing on either sovereignty or the international status of the islands. In the very next year, 1472, when the archbishopric of St. Andrews was created, the bishopric of Orkney was included in the Scottish province — which would have been a strange proceeding if the islands had been regarded as genuinely in pledge and likely at any time to be redeemed. There is an air of inevitability about the sequence of events year by year: 1468 — impignoration of Orkney; 1469 — impignoration of Shetland; 1470 — resignation of earldom; 1471/2 — annexation of earldom to Scottish crown; 1472 — incorporation of Orkney into Scottish province. Already in 1469 the bishop of Orkney had attended the Scottish parliament and had been appointed to a committee,[36] but the determining factor in a bishop's eligibility for parliament was the territorial and not the ecclesiastical affiliation of his see. Thus two bishops had long appeared in Scottish parliaments because their dioceses were politically parts of Scotland although not parts of the Scottish ecclesiastical province — Galloway, which had been in the province of York, and The Isles, which, though politically part of the Scottish kingdom from 1266, had remained ecclesiastically subject, like Orkney, to Trondheim. The presence of the bishop of Orkney in the Scottish parliament in 1469 might therefore be taken to suggest that the 1468 treaty was understood to imply something more than the transfer, in pledge, of the lands and rights of the Norwegian crown in the islands. All in all,

---

[34] *RMS*, ii, 997-1002. It should be kept in mind that the entries in the Register are meagre abridgements of documents not themselves extant, and too much should not be read into their apparent brevity.
[35] *APS*, ii, 102.
[36] *ibid.*, ii, 93.

it hardly looks as if contemporaries thought that the arrangements regarding the islands were makeshift or temporary.

Curious language was used by the Scottish council in 1540 when it ordered the restitution of ships which had been seized 'out of the sey besyde the north ilis callit the Fyre Ile' in Shetland and 'out of the se beside our soverane lordis north ile callit the Fire Ile', one of those vessels being 'at the fischeing in our said soverane lordis north seis'.[37] The terminology may not have been calculated, but it does seem to imply not only the Scottish crown's property in Fair Isle but also its sovereignty over the surrounding waters (though to what limit is not defined).

Yet, whatever the meaning of the contracting parties in 1468-9, or the meaning of the language of 1540, the position about sovereignty remained ambiguous. In so far as the integration of the islands into the Scottish administrative system was significant as some kind of token of the extension of Scottish sovereignty, the process can be followed in the records of parliament and privy council. The first act which seems to put it beyond any doubt that the islands were regarded as fully within the Scottish administrative system is in September 1566, when the council, concerned over the inefficiency of the system of 'sercheouris' whose responsibility it was to look for goods which had avoided the payment of customs dues, discharged 'all generall lettres of sercheorie owir all the haill realme, and in particular within the boundis of Orknay, Zeitland and Caithnes'.[38] Eight years later, when parliament passed an act for the reorganisation of 'wapin-schawingis' or musters for military training throughout the realm, it made provision for Orkney and Shetland exactly as for other sheriffdoms.[39] In the later 1580s we come on a series of acts which point to the further integration of the islands into Scottish administration. In July 1587 parliament, in an act for the reorganisation of criminal justice which foreshadowed the system of justices of the peace, ordained that in Orkney and Shetland fourteen landed men were to act in this novel capacity. One wonders where men 'experimentit in the lovable lawes and custumes of the realme, actuall indwelleris in the same schires' would have been found in the islands, but — and it is no surprise — no names are given and we do not even know if this proposal ever got beyond paper.[40] In October of the same year, the council, making a fresh attempt to organise or reorganise a High Court of Justiciary for the trial of crime throughout the realm, made provision for Orkney and Shetland as for other shires.[41] In July of the following year, 1588, when the council drew up a list of commissioners who were to take action against various delinquents, it proceeded to name individuals, sheriffdom by sheriffdom, until it reached Orkney and Shetland, where alone no names are given.[42] Only in March 1590, when similar commissioners were appointed, was a commissioner named for Orkney and Shetland, and the name was that of Robert Stewart, the Earl, which hardly suggests a strengthening of central control.[43] Presumably the remoteness of the

---

[37] *Acts of the Lords of Council in Public Affairs*, 496-7.
[38] *RPC*, i, 481.
[39] *APS*, iii, 91.
[40] *ibid.*, 459.
[41] *RPC*, iii, 217-18.
[42] *ibid.*, 301.
[43] *ibid.*, 463-5.

islands, as well perhaps as hesitation about the propriety of extending Scottish administration to them, explains the apparent difficulty about applying all the intentions of the central government in the north, but the council itself, in 1598, offered a different explanation, in the shape of a flattering testimonial: because 'the boundis of the cuntrayis of Orkney and Zetland is ane civile cuntrey, and the ... inhabitantis thairof ar and evir hes bene maist obedient to his hienes and lawis of this realme', the islands were exempted from provisions intended for the Highlands and Borders, where people were 'daylie subject to commoun reiffis, spuilyeis, heirschippis, slauchteris and depredationis'.[44] However, twelve years later, when there came a full nomination of justices of the peace for all the sheriffdoms of Scotland, named justices were, for the first time, appointed for Orkney and Shetland.[45] Meantime, in 1599, when machinery was set up to operate a register of sasines, it was provided that a register for Orkney and Shetland should be kept at Kirkwall, and the same arrangement was repeated when the register was re-established in 1617.[46] The first act of council designed to deal specifically with a problem peculiar to the islands was the well-known one in 1619 forbidding the 'rooing' of sheep,[47] but the application of that whole series of acts to the islands is conclusive about their incorporation into the Scottish administrative system, at least in intention.

If the proceedings of parliament and council illustrate the tendency to integrate Orkney and Shetland into administration under the Scottish crown, the Register of the Privy Seal illustrates the extension of the crown's authority in other ways. The crown, for instance, had power to legitimate bastards, and as early as 1497 there is an example in the case of a cousin of the bishop of Orkney.[48] In the event of a bastard dying intestate and without heirs of his body his movable goods went to the crown, and this practice likewise was soon applied to Orkney, with an example in 1529.[49] Under the privy seal the crown could issue various privileges and licences: in 1530 there was a protection to the vicar of Northmavine,[50] but it was perhaps more remarkable that as early as 1509 the crown licensed the bishop of Orkney to 'win and fyne' (that is, quarry and refine) lead in the islands for the re-roofing of the cathedral.[51] Such gifts by the crown indicate a considerable measure of Scottish sovereignty.

The question of sovereignty has to be related not only to administrative integration and the powers of the crown, but also to the law which obtained in the islands. It is wrong to believe that sovereignty has a necessary connection with law to the extent that sovereignty involves uniformity of law. There are plenty of examples to the contrary. The United Kingdom as at present constituted is one example of a political unit without uniformity of law and even without right of appeal in criminal cases from one judicial system (the Scottish) to any British court. Equally, Britain took over French Canada without abrogating French

---

[44] *ibid.*, v, 436.
[45] *ibid.*, ix, 79-80.
[46] *APS*, iv, 184, 237, 546.
[47] *RPC*, xi, 510, xii, 111-12.
[48] *RSS*, i, 135.
[49] *ibid.*, ii, 216.
[50] *ibid.*, ii, 554.
[51] *ibid.*, i, 1856.

law, and took over the Cape of Good Hope with abrogating Dutch law. On the other hand, appeals can lie to a court in a land which does not possess sovereignty over the territory where the appeal originated: the judicial Committee of the Privy Council is an example of this. Yet a connection between sovereignty and law has been assumed. When the Inner House of the Court of Session gave judgment in the Case of the St. Ninian's Isle Treasure, both Lord Patrick and Lord Mackintosh based their opinions in favour of the crown partly on their belief that 'since 1468 the right of sovereignty over the islands has belonged to the kings of Scotland and afterwards of Great Britain'.[52] Professor T. B. (now Sir Thomas) Smith, who presented an argument in the case, accepted that Christian I impignorated the sovereignty of the islands.[53] Although none of those lawyers explained their grounds for believing that sovereignty had been transferred, yet the fact that their arguments were based partly on the issue of sovereignty demonstrates that discussion of the question is not merely an academic one.

The development in both law and government since 1468-9 must be viewed in a wider context. For centuries before that point there had been something like a northern commonwealth of nations or a North Atlantic community, stretching from the Baltic to the Greenland settlements, through Sweden, Norway, Denmark, Shetland, Orkney, the Faroes and Iceland, and from the Isle of Man to the North Cape. Essentially one race, one language, one culture, one set of political and legal institutions extended over that wide area, and Orkney and Shetland were not on its periphery, but at its centre. In the course of the centuries that unity has been disrupted. The political link was the first to go. There are now six or seven distinct political units, and Orkney and Shetland, almost alone of the parts of the old community, have for five hundred years been attached politically to a state itself outside that northern commonwealth. Other aspects of the old unity vanished less perceptibly. The Norse tongue ceased to be spoken in Orkney and Shetland in the eighteenth century. Unity of race was disrupted by the immigration of a considerable number of Scots into the islands: even in Shetland by the late sixteenth century such immigration had become something of a flood, and by 1600 something like a quarter of the inhabitants had names pointing to a partially Scottish ancestry.

It is against this background that the erosion of Scandinavian legal institutions must be viewed. In Orkney Norse law had been under threat even before 1468. When Bishop Thomas Tulloch was put in charge of the islands by King Erik in 1420 he promised to 'keep law and justice according as the Norse lawbook mentions',[54] and perhaps it is significant that such a promise had to be exacted. Whether the bishop kept his word does not appear, but David Menzies of Weem, who succeeded him as administrator, was accused by the people of Orkney in 1424 of imprisoning the lawman and depriving him of his seal and of the lawbook, and they petitioned that their judges and governors should be bound to observe the ancient laws approved by King Olaf.[55] It would appear, however, that there must have been at least a partial restoration of Norse law and

[52] Court of Session Cases, 2 August 1963, pp. 556, 561.
[53] A. Small, C. Thomas and D. M. Wilson, *St Ninian's Isle and its Treasure* (London, 1973), i, 151.
[54] *REO*, 31-2.
[55] *ibid.*, 36-48.

practice after that, even in Orkney, and it is unlikely that in Shetland Norse law was under any threat until some time after 1469. It has often been said that the treaties of 1468 and 1469 expressly preserved Norse law in the islands. But there was no such provision. However, the very silence of the treaties on the subject may be revealing. Once again there is a contrast with the treaty of 1266 which ceded the Hebrides and which states that 'the men of the said islands, as well lesser as greater, shall be subject to the laws and customs of the realm of Scotland'. The absence of any such clause in 1468-9 suggests that the men of Orkney and Shetland were not intended to be subject to the laws of Scotland.

An admission by the Scottish government that Scots law did not apply, or might not apply, in the islands is clear from the records of parliament in 1503/4. An act was originally drafted to read: 'That all our soverane lordis liegis, bath within Orknay, Scheteland and the Ilis, be reulit be our soverane lordis aune lawis and the commoun lawis of the realme and be nain other lawis'. This draft was next strengthened by the insertion of 'and other placis' after 'Orknay, Scheteland and the Ilis'. Then there were second thoughts, and the objection perhaps raised that the law of Scotland could not be applied to Orkney and Shetland, at least specifically. The mention of those islands by name was therefore cut out, and the act amended to read: 'All our soverane lordis liegis beand under his obesance and in speciale all the Ilis'. Finally 'all' was deleted before 'the Ilis'.[56] These changes may have been intended to leave it open to doubt whether the people of Orkney and Shetland were indeed under the obedience of the king of Scots, in other words whether the sovereignty of the islands pertained to him. The phrase 'the Ilis', especially with the omission of 'all', may have been designed to introduce a certain ambiguity, and at a later date it was argued that the act did apply to Orkney and Shetland.[57] However, the deletion of the names of those islands, the fact that in normal usage 'the Isles' meant the Western Isles, and the fact that in the first draft Orkney and Shetland had been distinguished from 'the Ilis' all make it more likely that the act indicated that Scots law was not intended to apply in the northern isles. The batch of acts which includes this item contains another, relating to a proposal for additional justices and sheriffs, in which 'The Ilis' clearly meant the Western Isles and no more.

Some sixty years later, in 1567, the question was once again discussed in the Scottish parliament. It was asked 'Quhidder Orknay and Yetland sal be subject to the commone law of this realme or if thai sall bruke [i.e., enjoy] thair aune lawis', and the answer was: 'Findis thai aucht to be subject to thair aune lawis'. This, however, was only an 'article', with a comment, and there is no conclusive evidence that it was the foundation for an act or had any statutory authority.[58]

[56] APS, ii, 244, 252 and facsimile facing p. 241.
[57] Shetland Islands Authority Archives, SC 12/65/3: Information for James Sinclair of Scalloway. (I am indebted to Mr. Brian Smith for giving me a photocopy of a transcript of this document.) The statement also contended, with less credibility, that the matter had been settled by an act of James I (d. 1437) 'that all the kingis liegis live and be governit under the kingis lawis and statutis of the realme allenarly'. Mr. Smith has also drawn my attention to the remarks in the Report of the Napier Commission on the question of a separate law.
[58] APS, iii, 41. The MS. is contained in a portfolio titled 'Acta Parliamentorum 20 December 1567–28 August 1571', but the title is relatively modern, probably early nineteenth century, and does not in itself mean more than that the contents of the portfolio are parliamentary papers. The item relating to Orkney and Shetland is an integral part of a long series of articles, numbered consecutively,

Apart from parliamentary record, there is other evidence of the recognition of a distinct legal system. In 1525/6, when Margaret, Lady Sinclair, agreed to appoint her son, William, Lord Sinclair, as justice-depute of Orkney, he received authority to administer 'according to the commoune law and apprevit consuetude of Orknay'.[59] But when Oliver Sinclair was appointed sheriff in 1541, his commission was in standard Scottish form, with no allusion to special laws or procedure, and from that point the lawman of Orkney disappears from the scene while the sheriff is found acting on every occasion when the lawman had formerly acted.[60] In Shetland, however, the change came later. When Lord Robert Stewart received his feu charter of the islands in 1565, the Scottish crown granted him the 'foudrie' or office of foud of Shetland,[61] and much of the old system survived for another generation or more.

A few instances of continued reference from Shetland to Norway have often been cited. In 1485 the lawman of Bergen and the lawman of Shetland, along with the councillors of Bergen and the lawrightman of Shetland, gave a decision relating to land in Shetland. In 1538 a decree of the king's court at Bergen confirmed a decree of a court held in Yell, Shetland. And a deed of sale of land in Shetland, executed at Bergen in 1536, was ratified by the lawman of Bergen in 1544.[62] Other documents of sixteenth-century date illustrate the survival in Shetland of Norse land tenure and methods of conveyancing.[63] Several of them are in Norse, but even when they are in Scots they contain phraseology and clauses foreign to the practice of Scotland. Property extended from the highest stone in the hill to the lowest stone in the ebb, contrary to the Scottish understanding that private property stopped at high-water mark and that the shore belonged to the crown; property was divided among heirs (a daughter's share being half a son's), instead of passing to the first-born (who had, however, the right to the 'heid buile' or chief place); the consent of the family had to be obtained before land was sold. Besides, Norse terms, sometimes in corrupt form, are preserved: for example, the apparently enigmatic phrase 'all aing owthill ryt roith samaing and reversion' incorporated the words *eign*, meaning possession; the recognisable *odal* or *udal*; *roith* or *raedi*, meaning rule or control; and *sameign*, joint possession. There is an even more cryptic amalgam of Norse and Scottish jargon in 'all eing and outhwell, ryt and roith, eis and intres, hous and harbry, toftis, thowns, moillis, inpastor and outpastor'. Some of those

---

presented to the parliament of December 1567. These articles had been prepared by a gathering of commissioners of barons and burgesses, with some ministers, which first met on 15 December, the day of the opening of the parliament. Each article bears a marginal annotation, often merely 'Apprevit', and the annotations which are dated bear dates from 22 to 28 December. As the last recorded act of this parliament was dated 29 December, it is hard to avoid the conclusion that the annotations represent decisions of the parliament, yet these decisions were not, so far as we know, embodied in formal acts. The possibility that they were so embodied cannot be excluded, for in the parliament of 1560 (admittedly an unusual parliament) at least one act was passed which does not appear in the parliamentary record.

[59] *Acts of the Lords of Council in Public Affairs*, 240.
[60] *REO*, 61-3.
[61] *RSS*, v, 2078.
[62] *REO*, 72-3, 96-9; cf. Goudie, *op. cit.*, 87-91.
[63] Many are reproduced or summarised in Goudie, *op. cit.*, and there are more examples among the Symbister Papers, now in the Shetland Archives (GD 144, especially 21/10 and 262/8).

documents show that inheritance of property was still arranged by Norse procedure (rendered 'sheunds', 'schuynds' or 'schounds' and 'airffis'), which enabled an udaller to assign his land as well as his movables by testament and which provided machinery for division of heritage among children.

But alongside these survivals of Norse usages there is plenty of evidence of the infiltration of Scottish practice. A very important agency in this process, and one which was effective at least in Orkney long before 1468, was the presence in the islands of many clergy of Scottish origin. These men were the most literate in the community and to them the natives perforce had to go when they wanted transactions committed to writing, which the clerics were likely to do in the Scots tongue and in phraseology which would at least be influenced by Scottish legal terminology. Not only so, but among those many clergy were a number of notaries, trained in Scottish legal styles and obviously more apt to draft deeds in the terminology of Scotland than in that of Norway. Notarial instruments by Scottish notaries are to be found in Orkney from the 1530s, as examples printed in *Records of the Earldom of Orkney* show. The survival of such material is fortuitous, and there is more consistent proof of the extension of Scottish practice in the records kept by the central government. Orkney and Shetland naturally figure in the records of crown grants of land from an early date, because, whatever else the Scottish kings may have had in the islands, they did possess certain properties, even if held only in pledge, and they could clearly make grants of these properties.[64] There is at first nothing to show that such grants were necessarily at variance with traditional tenures, but in 1535 the crown granted a feu charter to James Sinclair of Sanday and his wife of the islands of Sanday and Stronsay, to be held without division among heirs — a clear innovation.[65] Ten years later there appears a confirmation of a conveyance of lands in the islands, which seems to represent a crucial stage in the introduction of a feudal system: it was one thing for the crown, in its capacity as a proprietor, to make grants of lands which were its property; it was quite another for the crown, in its capacity as a superior, to confirm charters by private proprietors, who were thus put into the position of feudal vassals, and the concept of the crown as the ultimate owner of all land was acknowledged or implied. The first of many such confirmations, dated 30 April 1545, is of a charter dated the previous 23 January by the sons of Andrew Halcro of that ilk to their cousin Hugh, of the lands of Halcro, Holland and others, entailing the subjects on Hugh and his heirs. It is in the normal feudal form, and while it does not expressly forbid partition among heirs such a prohibition is certainly implied.[66] Such confirmations, because of their acceptance of the crown's superiority and because of their prohibition of partition among heirs, represented in simple terms the introduction of feudal law. It would appear that some years passed before confirmations were extended to property in Shetland. In March 1575/6, in a somewhat unusual style, the crown confirmed two dispositions of land in Shetland, pronouncing that the lands were to be held by the disponee 'nochwithstanding ony ... constitutionis of the said cuntre of Yetland ... that may be objectit or allegit, ... dispensand thairwith be

---

[64] e.g., *RMS*, ii, 1974, 2232, 2414.
[65] *ibid.*, iii, 1479.
[66] *ibid.*, 3101.

thir presentis'.[67] This may indicate that the crown was still feeling its way in Shetland, but within the next two or three years a decisive tone crept into the confirmations there too. Early in 1577 the crown confirmed a charter by Andrew Mowat of Hugoland to John, his son, of lands in Shetland, to be held without division.[68] Two years later there was a particularly interesting example. In this case the proprietor, Oliver Sinclair of Brow, had divided his heritable estate among his three sons, according to 'the custom of the country of Yetland', but a charter was then granted by the crown to one of them, conferring on him his third and specifying that it was in future to be held by him and his heirs according to the usual procedure of succession in Scotland.[69]

Possibly even more than land tenure, civil justice raised the question of the way in which the northern isles were brought within the Scottish judicial system, and it would be desirable to define the date at which cases arising in the islands were heard by the Lords of Council and their successors, the Court of Session, and the stages by which Scottish law was applied in Orkney and Shetland. This is a subject difficult to handle, because although for the sixteenth century there are in all some 220 volumes of Acta Dominorum and Acts and Decreets, there is a dearth of guides, no indexes and little in print. A case was indeed heard by the Lords of Council as early as 1485, concerning 150 merks due to Thomas Simson, sheriff of Fife, when he was comptroller of the king's rents from the lands of Orkney, money which Henry Sinclair had appropriated.[70] That can hardly be regarded as meaningful, since it was a dispute about crown property, and that the Scottish crown had had property in the islands since 1468 is not open to debate. That is the only case relating in any way to the islands in the first printed volume of the *Acta Dominorum*, covering 1478-96, and the second volume, for 1496-1501, has no Orkney or Shetland entries at all. Thereafter we are on largely uncharted seas so far as the judicial proceedings of the central civil court are concerned. There are Stair Society volumes, one for 1501-3 and one for 1532-3, in which we again draw a blank. The only thing resembling a guide to the voluminous proceedings of those days is Sir James Balfour's *Practicks*, compiled in the 1570s. That work contains no reference to cases concerning Orkney and Shetland or their inhabitants. This absence may not mean very much, partly because Balfour's work is such a small selection from a vast archive and partly because Orkney and Shetland could not have yielded him much material unless he had wanted to enter on a discussion of their peculiar usages. This he had no intention of doing, and indeed he gives no indication of being aware of, for example, the existence of any rule of succession other than by primogeniture among male heirs, a preference for males over females, and partition only among heiresses, or of the existence of any tenure other than feudal tenure with its accompaniments of the casualties of ward, marriage, relief and nonentry. Balfour does have a section on the laws of the Borders, but none on the laws of

---

[67] *RSS*, vii, 502. Only ten years earlier, a precept had ordered an enquiry into the ownership of land in Shetland 'according to the auld ordour observit in thai partis' (SRO, GD 164/50/404/7).

[68] *RMS*, iv, 2672.

[69] *ibid.*, 2850. A disposition of Shetland lands in 1589 stated expressly that the subjects were to be held 'but [i.e., without] divisione, efter the forme in successione usit to landis in Scotland' (Shetland Archives, GD 144/27/1).

[70] *ADC*, i, *112.

the northern isles. There is another invaluable and wide-ranging guide to the Acts and Decreets in general in Morison's *Dictionary of Decisions*, a digest of significant cases from the early sixteenth century onwards. But it is a dictionary of subjects, designed for the use of practising lawyers, with an alphabetical index of the names of parties. A search for material relating to Orkney and Shetland could be complete only if one read through all Morison's twenty volumes, but a certain amount of sampling under headings which seemed especially promising yielded no result.

Since there is no continuous and consistent guide to the judicial proceedings of the central civil court, we are thrown back on stray items gleaned from various sources. There is, for instance, a complaint to the king and council by William, Lord Sinclair, as justice of Orkney, against James and Edward Sinclair for assaulting his servants and compelling him to surrender the 'Kingis hous' at Kirkwall, and it relates that in May 1529 Lord Sinclair had obtained the king's letters against them in the first, second, third and fourth forms — the familiar procedure of 'letters in the four forms'.[71] In the hope of finding this case in the court records I searched the *Acta Dominorum* from the beginning of May 1529 to 25 March of the following year, without finding any reference to the action, though I noticed that on 31 May 1529 Lord Sinclair's procurator entered a protest before the Lords in a case between him and the Bishop of Orkney.[72] A few years later a letter dated 12 May 1535 was sent by the Scottish crown to English authorities in connection with a case before the council in which Thomas Millar, an English merchant, pursued James Sinclair of Kirkwall for the spoliation of goods in North Ronaldsay from a ship called the *Andrew*.[73] Next comes a testimonial, dated 18 September 1566, by the bailies of Kirkwall to the 'cunsall of the realme of Scotland' relating to the theft of a ship.[74] This case I thought would probably have constituted Privy Council, rather than Court of Session, business, but when I found that the printed *Register of the Privy Council* had no mention of the affair I went through the three volumes of Acts and Decreets covering the period from September 1566 to the end of the year, again with no success. There is yet another instance of casual evidence about the Court of Session: William Bruce of Simbister obtained a decreet from the Court of Session in an action of spuilzie relating to lands in Shetland in 1609.[75] What can reasonably be deduced from these stray pieces of information is that the central civil court was acting from time to time in Orkney or Shetland business from a fairly early date. But it is to be observed that none of the proceedings thus traced related to any peculiar northern law or indicated Scottish intervention in such law.

However, apart from the records of the Court of Session, in their uncharted state, we have the *Register of the Privy Council* and, as the council continued to act judicially despite the differentiation between it and the Court of Session, this record helps us to determine at what point the central civil judicature of Scotland began to operate regularly in the islands. It is not easy to know what precise

[71] *REO*, 57-60.
[72] *ADC*, xl, 48v.
[73] *RSS*, ii, 1665.
[74] *REO*, 375-7.
[75] *Archeologia Scotica*, iv (1857), 385. I am indebted to Mr. Brian Smith for this reference.

significance to attach to the well-known 'Complaints' of the people of Orkney and Shetland against the oppressions of Lord Robert Stewart and Laurence Bruce of Cultmalindie which came before the council in 1575,[76] except in so far as they seem to demonstrate an acceptance of the sovereignty of the Scottish government; it does not seem to have occurred to anyone that complaints against oppression should now, as in the case of Menzies of Weem in 1425, go to the Norwegian government. The first clear indication of the strictly judicial functions of the council in relation to the islands seems to occur in February 1575/6. A complaint was made by Nicol Oliverson, son and heir of the deceased Oliver Randveill, heritor of udal land in Gairsay in Orkney. The complainer had been in Norway for forty years and had returned three or four years ago because, as he explained in a pretty compliment to the Regent Morton, he had heard that justice was 'ministrat the better within Orknay sen my lord Regentis grace regiment than afoir'. He had obtained a decreet in his favour from Lord Robert, as sheriff, but Lord Robert subsequently intruded one Isobel Brown into his heritage. For Lord Robert it was alleged that the lands pertained to him 'be the law and practik' observed in Orkney. The pursuer's procurator was ordered to produce 'the bukis of the said law'. He duly did so and on 4 April the council ordered Lord Robert to enter the complainer in his heritage and keep him there.[77] Thus the council was giving judgment in a dispute over udal property and taking Orcadian law into account — showing that uniformity of law and unity of jurisdiction did not necessarily go together. Thirteen years passed before another case from the islands came before the privy council, and this time it was a less significant one. On 2 July 1589 James Pitcairn, minister of Northmavine, appeared before the council. He had been summoned by letters dated 22 January 1589 at the instance of his parishioners to compear to answer their complaints. However, although Pitcairn turned up the pursuers did not.[78]

There is yet another key, besides the *Acta Dominorum*, the Acts and Decreets and the Privy Council Register, to the relationship of the islands with the Court of Session, and that is the Register of Deeds or Books of Council and Session, of which there is a brief Calendar, with an index, from its beginning in 1554 down to 1595. This shows that the Register does contain deeds to which people in the islands were parties and which were drawn up in the islands and duly recorded in the Books of Council and Session. There is one example in 1563 of a contract between a party in Shetland and a party in Orkney.[79] The mere fact of registration, taking into account the formula used, implied recognition of the jurisdiction of the Court of Session, so that this Register is further proof that long before the end of the sixteenth century the court was the acceptable judicatory in the islands for civil justice at the highest level. There is a large number of entries in the Acts and Decreets and the Register of Deeds which *relate* in one way or another to the islands; many are cited in Peter D. Anderson, *Robert Stewart, Earl of Orkney* (1982), and in my article on 'Bishop Adam Bothwell and the

[76] David Balfour (ed.), *Oppressions of the sixteenth century in Orkney and Zetland* (Abbotsford and Maitland Clubs).
[77] *RPC*, ii, 488-9, 517-18.
[78] *ibid.*, iii, 400-1.
[79] Register of Deeds, vi, 338b.

Reformation in Orkney' in *Records of the Scottish Church History Society*, xiii. But the more significant items are surely transactions to which at least one of the parties was a native of the islands.

Criminal law deserves as much study as civil law. Here our main source is the records of the High Court of Justiciary, material from which was printed by Pitcairn in his *Criminal Trials*, but supplementary information comes from the *Register of the Privy Seal*, which records respites and remissions for offences and also escheats of the goods of persons convicted of crimes. It is evident that from an early date Scottish rights were held to include responsibility for the maintenance of order in the islands, so that in 1539, for example, we find the respite to Edward Sinclair and thirty others in Orkney for their conflict with the Earl of Caithness at Summerdale ten years earlier.[80] In 1544 Oliver Sinclair of Havera, foud of Shetland, had a respite for the slaughter of certain Lewismen who had invaded the islands in the previous year; he had another respite later and finally a remission in 1564.[81] Persons guilty of an affray in Kirkwall were tried in the High Court of Justiciary in 1562 and the case then remitted to the justice ayre of Orkney.[82] A particularly explicit Shetland case arose in 1581: Thomas Boyn was summoned to the High Court in Edinburgh for the murder of Patrick Winram and, on his failure to compear, was put to the horn.[83] In 1596, when Henry Colville, parson of Orphir in Orkney, was murdered at Nesting in Shetland, the persons accused were all tried in the High Court of Justiciary.[84] It would seem, therefore, that in criminal as in civil cases the central court in Edinburgh was accepted as the appropriate judicature for Orkney and Shetland some time before the act of 1611 abolishing Norse law in the islands.

Yet, although courts in Edinburgh might from time to time exercise jurisdiction in the islands, local justice, at least in Shetland, still reflected the survival of Norse law and practice, as the *Court Book of Shetland, 1602-4*, amply shows. It is at once evident that it represents much of the old Norwegian laws as they were printed by Laurence Larson,[85] and Professor Robberstad identified the law operating in Shetland specifically as the law found in the lawbook of Magnus the Lawmender (1263-80).[86] The language of the Court Book is Scots, but there are many survivals of Norse terminology and procedure. A man accused of a crime could clear or 'quit' himself with the aid of compurgators or oath-helpers, two, six or twelve in number, the number apparently depending partly on the nature of the crime and partly on the accused's past record. As in the Norwegian code of law, various degrees of assault and injuries were defined: penalties were more severe when wounds were 'beneath the end', as the Court Book has it, that is, beneath the breath. It made a difference, too, as in the Norwegian laws, where the assault was committed: attacks in a trading or market-place — 'ane frie coupsta' — or in a boat, for instance, were more severely punished. The Court Book also shows that the Lawbook of Shetland was still consulted and it

[80] *RSS*, ii, 3151.
[81] *ibid.*, iii, 980, 1542, v, 1794.
[82] Pitcairn, *Criminal Trials* (Bannatyne and Maitland Clubs), I, i, *413.
[83] *RSS*, viii, 37, 40.
[84] Pitcairn, *op. cit.*, I, iii, 386-97.
[85] Laurence M. Larson, *The Earliest Norwegian Laws* (New York, 1935).
[86] *Historisk Tidsskrift*, xli (1961-2), 65-9.

confirms that udal practice was still at least partly observed. Anyone looking in the Court Book for Norse survivals will find them there in plenty. But what it reveals is an amalgam of Scottish and Norse terminology and procedure and it represents much the same kind of duality as we have already seen in isolated documents. Two systems had clearly been to some extent merged, presumably over a considerable period. The very structure of the judicature, or at any rate its designations, reveals the duality. The local headman in a district was still called the foud; but the judge in whose name the central court was held was styled justice general and sheriff principal. By a curious reversal of usage, the local courts were called courts, not *things*, but the central court was officially styled 'the Lating'. Similarly, in the local or parochial organisations, the lawrightman and the ranselman had Norse titles, but there was also an 'officer'. And for the jury in each court, whether central or local, there seems to have been no other term than 'assize', a word the Scots had taken over as part of their borrowing from English or Anglo-Norman procedure. Some of the terminology which looks Norse is also, however, Scottish, and does not necessarily represent Norse survivals. Thus 'bluidwyt' is identifiable with the Norwegian *blodvite*; but it was also regularly used in Scottish charters and had been adopted at an early date from England. Equally, 'skayth', meaning damage or harm, can be equated with the Norse *skade*; but it was a term in constant use in Scots law and indeed is still standard English, if a shade archaic, in the form 'scathe'. And there is the term 'fang', in the phrase 'taken with the fang' used of a thief apprehended with stolen goods in his possession; again the term is both Norse and English, and 'infangthief' and 'outfangthief' were standard terms in Scottish charters from the earliest times. Neither Norwegians on one side nor Scots on the other need jump hastily to the conclusion that many terms used in the Court Book are definitely or exclusively Norse or Scottish. It is also noticeable that the Court Book contains several allusions to the Court of Session: persons in Shetland were at one stage forbidden to raise actions there except in default of justice within the islands, but at least one action had been raised in Edinburgh before that act was made; several deeds are recorded in the Court Book which contain the usual clause giving consent to registration in the Books of Council and Session; and the volume contains a copy of letters under the signet which demonstrate the normal operation, within Shetland, of the proceedings of the Court of Session.[87]

When one reviews the duality or coexistence which the evidence discloses, it becomes plain that it would be totally wrong to believe that the Norse system survived until it was abolished at a stroke in 1611. There was clearly some truth in the Privy Council act which did in that year finally abolish the Norse law when it stated that the rulers of Orkney and Shetland had for some years past 'taken upon them ... to judge the inhabitants of the said countries by foreign laws, making choice sometimes of foreign laws and sometimes of the proper laws of this kingdom'.[88] But it was wrong to allege that the rulers — the Stewart earls — had necessarily made an arbitrary choice between the two systems. One reason, probably the main reason, for the act of 1611 was the policy of James VI,

[87] *Court Book of Shetland, 1602-4*, ed. G. Donaldson (Scottish Record Soc.), 48, 40, 137-8, 138-9, 142-3, 148, 152.
[88] *RPC*, ix, 181-2.

determined as he was to make the whole of Scotland a unified country, obedient
to him and to a uniform law. But Professor Robberstad did point out that in 1604
there had appeared in Norway a revised code of law, the revision of Christian IV,
and it would have been difficult for Orkney and Shetland either to adhere to the
now superseded older code or to accept a new code at the hands of someone now
regarded as a foreign king.[89]

It has sometimes been suggested that the act of 1611 was beyond the
competence of the Privy Council,[90] especially if the Norse law in the islands had
previously been safeguarded by acts of the Scottish parliament. But, even if they
had been so safeguarded, the competence of the privy council in legislation was in
practice so extensive that it would be hard to challenge any of its acts as *ultra
vires*, and the fact remains that this act seems never to have been so challenged in
a court of law.

The act of 1611, perhaps in conjunction with other events, had an immediate
effect in ending the duality or coexistence of two judicial systems. When next we
have a Shetland Court Book, in 1615, its procedure approximates much more
closely to that of a Scottish sheriff court and it bears little resemblance to the
book of 1602-4. Certain unusual administrative and judicial practices long
survived at parish level — the appointment of ranselmen, for example, until the
nineteenth century[91] — and there were 'Country Acts' with something of the
character of bye-laws, but any distinction in substantive law had disappeared.

The act of 1611 had said nothing specifically about land law, and there is no
evidence that it was thought of as necessarily bringing udal tenure to an end. But
only six years later, in 1617, there was finally established the Register of Sasines,
in which all transactions relating to heritable property had to be recorded, and
this may have had a strong influence in bringing about uniformity in the
procedure for the conveyance of land. The Register certainly enables us to
examine land tenure in Shetland in the seventeenth century in a systematic
manner not possible for earlier periods. The first volume of the Register of
Sasines for Shetland is not extant, and the second begins in 1623. Abstracts of a
series of sasines from this volume were printed by the Viking Society for
Northern Research, and they reveal a somewhat confused situation. There is
land called 'udal land', land called 'feudal land' and land not designated as either.
One sasine expressly limited property to the flood mark, so that it did not include
the foreshore in the udal manner. There is an instance of the inheritance of udal
land by two brothers, but on the other hand 'udal land' was disponed by the
'eldest son and heir' as if he had inherited by primogeniture. A charter was
granted by a man designed as 'udaller and heritable proprietor'; 'udal land' was
held of the crown and even held by a feu charter; and a crown precept could be
obtained for infeftment in 'udal land'.[92] On the whole, therefore, it appears that
already some 'udal land' was udal only in name and that the substance of the
feudal system of conveyancing and tenure was prevailing. It fits in with this
erosion of true udal tenure that in 1624 the Court of Session decided that udal

[89] *The Orcadian*, 22 August 1968.
[90] A. Small et al., *op. cit.*, 155.
[91] Goudie, *op. cit.*, 241-6.
[92] *Orkney and Shetland Records* (Viking Club), ii, nos. 1, 10, 11, 12, 42, 83, 121, 167, 174.

lands 'behoved to be bruiked by some lawful title and that naked kindness and possession were not sufficient to possess them'.[93] The situation was complicated, and confusion increased, by the fact that there was evidently a good deal of opportunism: some contended that udal land had been wholly abolished, while others — including some quite recent comers to the islands — claimed to be udallers when they saw any advantage in doing so.[94]

The Register of Sasines was examined in detail, for three sample periods in the seventeenth century, by Dr. Frances Shaw in her Ph.D. thesis.[95] She observed, as others had done, the absence of large compact estates in Shetland in the early seventeenth century and the vast numbers of small proprietors; this was almost certainly the consequence of the udal system of division among heirs, and a sharp reduction in the number of small proprietors was likewise the result of its supersession by feudalism. At the beginning of the century there are allusions to the sharing of property among heirs, to an udaller obtaining the consent of his kinsmen to the sale of land and to the transmission of land without charters.[96] However, changes came rapidly. In 1633 there was a petition to parliament by the 'udallers' craving that none be interposed between them and the crown, but that they should be vassals of the crown until the king should adjust their rights in conformity with the law of Scotland:[97] this amounted to an acceptance by the udallers of the feudal principle of the crown's ultimate superiority over all lands. In 1664, on the ground that 'udal right' was 'merely a possession and no kind of fundamental right or title by charter or sasine', the Earl of Morton, who then held the crown lands, was authorised to grant feu charters to the 'udallers', many of whom took feu charters at that time.[98] It is true that in 1690 an act of parliament gave a limited measure of protection to a certain class of udal lands, and then only where the value did not exceed £20 Scots,[99] but — apart from the fact that this was a very limited measure — the damage had by that time been done. Dr. Shaw's analysis shows that by the end of the century conveyances by udallers made up only 4% of Shetland sasines.[100] So late as 1716 it was said that three quarters of the land in Shetland was 'udal',[101] but most land in Shetland had long ceased to be udal in the full sense, for it was held by feudal and not by allodial tenure; most 'udallers' were so in name only, and Shetland was nearly as completely feudalised as the rest of Scotland. The practice of partition among heirs ceased in general to apply — though it was upheld by law as late as 1893[102] — and the only significant vestiges of udal law which remained effective related not to the terms on which the proprietors held their lands but merely to certain rights which the holders of 'udal land' continued to claim within their own properties.

[93] *Sinclair* v. *Hawick* (1624), Mor. 16393.
[94] Shetland Islands Authority Archives, *loc. cit.*; cf. Goudie, *op. cit.*, 135.
[95] Her findings have now been published in Frances J. Shaw, *The Northern and Western Islands of Scotland: Their Economy and Society in the Seventeenth Century* (Edinburgh, 1980).
[96] *ibid.*, 36-7.
[97] *ibid.*, 39.
[98] *ibid.*
[99] *APS*, ix, 200.
[100] Frances Shaw, *op. cit.*, 41.
[101] A. Small et al., *op. cit.*, 158.
[102] *The Viking Congress*, 159 — the Sheriff Court case of *Hawick* v. *Hawick*.

The Scottish machinery for succession to heritable property held of the crown — and, with modifications, to other heritable property as well — was by way of a precept which instructed a jury to ascertain the rights of the heir and report their findings in a document called a 'retour' — strictly an *inquisitio retornata* — which constituted the 'service' of the heir. Our earliest records of retours have not survived, but we do have information from the middle of the sixteenth century and that is early enough for our purposes in relation to Orkney and Shetland. Actually the confirmation under the great seal in 1579 of a third of the estate of Sinclair of Brow, referred to earlier, states explicitly that the heirs were in future to enter 'by brieves of inquest of the royal chancery and according to the rule of succession of the realm of Scotland'.[103] The extant records of retours show that the system was in operation in the islands by 1605 and that it continued thereafter.[104] Moreover, the Sheriff Court Book of Shetland for 1615-28 contains some thirty services in favour of sole heirs, though in a few cases protests were entered on behalf of those who claimed that they should be acknowledged as heirs portioners according to Norse practice.[105]

So far as the moveables of persons deceased were concerned, in 1549 the general council of the Scottish Church laid down that the law and practice of Scotland should be extended to the diocese of Orkney.[106] It is quite clear, however, that there was no immediate and sweeping change, for the machinery for the division of property according to Norse practice proved tenacious and seems to have been in regular use for another two generations. A commissary (who would normally have dealt with such matters in other parts of Scotland) was operating in Shetland by 1590,[107] but his scope must have been limited by the persistence of 'sheunds and airffs'. It was remarked in 1611 that the office of commissary in Orkney and Shetland had been 'thir mony yeiris bigane verie far obscuirit, pairtlie be the iniquitie of the tyme and be the usurpatioun whilk utheris judgeis and magistratis within the saidis boundis took upoun thame of a grite many of the actionis and causis proper and competent to the commissariat jurisdictioun'.[108] The alleged 'usurpation' may in truth have been the survival of Norse practice. It was not until 1611, when Norse laws were in general abrogated, that a Record of Testaments, barely distinguishable in character from those elsewhere in Scotland, existed for Orkney and Shetland.[109] That it was a real innovation is indicated by its inclusion of testaments of persons who had died many years before — one as far back as 1573. From that point the practice was to apply the rules for the division of moveables operating in Scotland: if the deceased was survived by a widow and children then the relict and the offspring (collectively) were each entitled to one third, leaving a third for disposition by will, and if only a widow or children survived then a half was available for bequest.

[103] *RMS*, iv, 2850.
[104] *Inquisitionum Retornatarum Abbreviatio*, ed. T. Thomson (1811-16), i, Orkney and Shetland section.
[105] A calendar of those services is inserted in the copy of the 'Retours' in the Historical Search Room, H.M. General Register House.
[106] Patrick, *Statutes of the Scottish Church* (Scot. Hist. Soc.), 115-16, 137-8.
[107] *RPC*, iv, 546-7; cf. *Court Book*, vi.
[108] *RPC*, ix, 182.
[109] Robert S. Barclay, *Orkney Testaments and Inventories* (Scottish Record Soc.).

It remains true, as was remarked earlier, that there is no necessary connection between sovereignty and uniformity of law, in the sense that sovereignty does not necessarily imply uniformity of law and uniformity of law does not necessarily imply sovereignty. Yet, in the circumstances of Orkney and Shetland in the sixteenth and seventeenth century, it is hard to see how the consistent acceptance of Scottish law, and more particularly the acceptance of the jurisdiction of Scottish courts, can have meant anything else than the existence of Scottish sovereignty, certainly *de facto* and probably even *de jure*. It is impossible to be conclusive, but there is certainly a strong case for believing that Scottish sovereignty by prescription was effective before 1707.

The one thing that remains to be looked at, among the developments since 1468-9, is the series of attempts by Denmark to redeem the islands. Much has been written about them in detail, and it is unnecessary to do more here than offer some general comments. About the attempts there was sometimes, perhaps always, an air of unreality. On the Danish side, the fact that so many attempts were made does not necessarily meant that there was ever any serious hope of getting the islands back. The fact is that each Danish king from Hans in 1483 to Frederick III in 1648 was obliged by the equivalent of a coronation oath to make an attempt to reunite Orkney and Shetland to his crown. No such obligation was imposed on later monarchs, simply because the Danish monarchy became absolute in 1665. Now, Scots believed, or professed to believe, that in making attempts at redemption the Danish kings were just going through the motions in order to comply with their accession undertakings.[110] Perhaps they were right, but they may have put this view forward in order to ease their own consciences. This they had much need to do, for their attitude throughout was something less than honest. It is true that a number of Scottish writers related that the right of redemption had been surrendered by Denmark when the future James IV, son of James III and Margaret of Denmark, was born in 1473;[111] but this tale was for home consumption only and they never dared to bring such an untruth forward in answering Danish representations. When Denmark opened negotiations, or tried to, the Scots never denied that the right of redemption existed. They contented themselves with trying to shuffle out of their responsibility, they found some pretext for evading the issue, and indeed their attitude was little better than the simple one that possession was nine tenths of the law.

On more than a dozen occasions Denmark raised the question of redeeming the islands from Scotland.[112] It is perhaps less well known that in 1535, when Denmark was anxious that England should cease aiding Lübeck against her, an offer was made to Henry VIII: if he paid a sum equal to the 58,000 florins, he could have the Danish rights in Orkney and Shetland.[113] The question was raised

---

[110] Sir James Melville, *Memoirs* (Bannatyne Club), 343.
[111] Hector Boece, *Scotorum Historiae* (edn. 1574), fo. 389. Ferrerius, Boece's continuator, said that he heard (*audio*) that the renunciation, in writing, was preserved among the Scottish royal archives. Sir Thomas Craig, in his *Jus Feudale* (ed. J. A. Clyde, 1934), written about 1600, stated that the Danes 'gave up their reversionary rights by the treaty between ... James IV and Christian II of Denmark. This treaty was confirmed by the authority of Pope Alexander VI and recorded in the registers of the papal court.' It may be pointed out that Alexander VI died in 1503 and that Christian II did not become king until 1513, seven months before the death of James IV. Cf. Goudie, *op. cit.*, 215.
[112] See Appendix.
[113] *Letters and Papers of Henry VIII*, viii, 1160.

in some sense so late as 1749, to the extent at least that the Danes then claimed the exclusive rights of fishing in Orkney and Shetland waters and asserted that they still had the right of redemption.[114] However, the last serious attempt at redemption seems to have been at the making of the treaty of Breda in 1667. The Danish representatives wanted to insert in their agreement with Charles II the following article: 'It has been sufficiently proved by documents that for many centuries the Orkney isles belonged to the kingdom of Norway as an inseparable and inalienable dependency, and still belong to it, and that they have been pledged and pawned to the king of Scotland for a certain sum of money on condition that they should be restored and returned on reimbursement and payment of the same sum, and that they would be given back and reunited to the kingdom of Norway; yet, although reimbursement of the same sum has been many times offered on the part of Denmark, nevertheless the restitution of the islands has not been made: it has therefore been agreed and accorded . . . that the abovenamed islands . . . be restored and returned to the king of Denmark or to any other to whom he shall give power to receive them, in the condition in which they are at present, without any retention and without delay'. The English reply was predictable: they protested that they had no instructions on this matter. The Danes therefore agreed, though under protest, that the article should be erased from the draft treaty.[115]

Since then the issue has been an academic one. The question has sometimes been raised whether the right of redemption, if it still exists, would now pertain to Denmark or to Norway. The Treaty of Kiel, in 1814, seems to be conclusive on this point. There it was laid down that the territories surrendered by Denmark comprehended not only the Norwegian mainland and the islands along the coast, but also the Norwegian dependencies, except Greenland, the Faroes and Iceland. The specific exception of those three named territories from the lands ceded by Denmark clearly implies that all other overseas dependencies of Norway were surrendered. If, therefore, it was still true in 1814 that sovereignty of Orkney and Shetland pertained to the Dano-Norwegian crown, then it can be accepted that that sovereignty was transferred or reserved to Norway by the Treaty of Kiel. It has, however, been argued, perhaps over-ingeniously, that as the islands were not mentioned when Norway gained its independence from Sweden in 1905, the sovereignty and the rights of redemption really pertain now to Sweden.

The matter therefore remains where it was left at Breda in 1667. The Danes then agreed to give up their claim for the surrender of the islands, but only 'on condition that the suspension and withdrawal of the demand for the restitution of the islands should be understood not to prejudice the rights of their lord the most serene king [of Denmark] and should not derogate in any way his claims, which remain whole and entire until a more favourable occasion, whether it presents itself sooner or later, for demanding the restitution, according to such claims'.[115]

[114] *Gentleman's Magazine*, 1749, p. 428.
[115] J. Dumont, *Corps Universel Diplomatique du Droit des Gens* (Amsterdam, 1731), VII, pt. i, 56.

APPENDIX

References to attempts to redeem Orkney and Shetland

[The most comprehensive accounts are given by Thormodus Torfaeus, *Orcades seu Rerum Orcadensium Historia* (Havniae, 1715), and Fredrik Scheel, 'Orknøerne og Hjaltland i Pantsaettelsestiden, 1468-1667', *Historisk Tidsskrift udgivet af Den norske historiske Forening*, series 5, i (Kristiania, 1912), 380-420. Gilbert Goudie, *Antiquities of Shetland* (Edinburgh, 1904), 216-29, reproduces information from those authorities and adds quotations from Scottish sources. The following list provides some supplementary references.]

1485   A Scottish embassy to the Pope was to seek 'a confirmacioun of the convencions, confederacions and bandis maid betuix our soveran lord and the king of Denmark that last deceissit of the donacioun and impignoracioun of the landis of Orkney and Scheteland and of perpetuale exoneracioun, reversacioun and discharge of the contribucioun of the Ilis efter the forme of the said convencions' (*APS*, ii, 171). The 'exoneracioun' is of course of the Annual of Norway, as provided in the Treaty of 1468, but is a careless reading of this phrase the origin of the tale that the right of redemption of Orkney and Shetland had been surrendered?

1549   A letter of 1585 (see below) states that Christian III (1535-59) attempted to recover the islands, and this is presumably to be identified with an initiative taken in 1549, when it appears that a special tax was levied to procure money for redemption (Scheel, 410, citing *Danske Magazin*, series 4, iv [1878], 363).

1560   In a letter to the Governors of Scotland, 23 October 1560, Frederick II claimed that the *dominium* of the islands pertained to him and went on: 'It is of the greatest importance that these islands be at length, after so many years, restored and added to our kingdom; and we to this end do not decline [to make] payment of the money due; and . . . we request Your Highnesses that together you . . . cause these said islands to be delivered up and restored to us, in return for the payment of the money due, which we offer' (*Nat. MSS. Scot*, III, xliv; cf. *Cal. State Papers Scotland*, i, 493, 516).

1564   When William Douglas of Whittinghame went on an embassy to Denmark his instructions included this: 'In cais ony thing be proponit to yow tuicheing Orkney and Zetland, twiche nawise that string, bot, as fer as ye may, flee the clos, allegeing that ye ar nawyse instructit ony thing in that heid' (*Warrender Papers* [Scot. Hist. Soc.], i, 40). The Danish council did in fact raise the question (*RPC*, xiv, 196-201, 203-5).

1568   James Hepburn, Earl of Bothwell, who had been created Duke of Orkney when he married Mary, Queen of Scots, in 1567, declared that he had intended to obtain Danish help by surrendering Orkney and Shetland (Scheel, 416, citing Frederik Schiern, *Life of Bothwell*).

1570   Scheel (p. 416) quotes a letter of 10 June 1570 from the French ambas-
         sador to Denmark, Charles de Dancays, to Catherine de Medici, from
which it appears that the Danish Council will try to get the islands back as soon as
possible.

1572   Accusations of Lord Robert Stewart, feuar of Orkney and Shetland,
         included the allegation that in 1572 he offered the 'supremacy and
dominion' of the islands to the king of Denmark, and it was reported that that
king gave him a confirmation and gift of them and sent Laurence Carnes as
lawman (*Cal. S.P. Scot.*, v, p. 205; Peter Anderson, *Robert Stewart*, 87).

1585   A Danish embassy for the redemption of the islands is referred to in
         Warrender Papers, ii, 36, 46n, and its purpose is described in a letter from
Frederick II to Queen Elizabeth of England, 4 May 1585: 'Although an attempt
was made to recover the islands by Christian III and even by ourselves some years
ago, nevertheless the governor and councillors of the kingdom [of Scotland]
urged in excuse partly their own occupation in operations of war and partly the
minority of the queen as the cause of the restitution being hitherto always
deferred. Now, therefore, we, offering anew the required sum, demand, as in duty
bound, that these islands, which are acknowledged indisputably to form part of
our kingdom, should be restored to us. For which cause we have despatched to
the kingdom of Scotland ... ambassadors ...'. (Goudie, 219-26, gives a full
account of this episode, with several quotations.)

1587-9   Negotiations in connection with the marriage of James VI and Anne of
           Denmark. The Danes pressed hard for redemption, and 'the matter of
Orkney' was prominent in the negotiations in 1587 (*Warrender Papers*, ii, 37-42).
In 1589 the question was explicitly left open: 'All further claim or repetition of the
foresaid isles upon whatsoever pretended right or interest alleged thereto by that
crown [Denmark] shall be superseded and continued for their parts [i.e. on the
parts of the two kings] unto the said elected prince's [Christian IV's] perfect age'
(*APS*, iii, 566; *RPC*, iv, 824; cf. Goudie, 228).

1621   In a treaty between James VI and Christian IV it was agreed that the
         question should rest during their lifetimes (Scheel, 418, citing Rymer,
Foedera, vii, pt. 2, 216).

1640   Christian IV raised the question after Charles I had capitulated to the
         Covenanters (Scheel, 418, citing Torfaeus, 227).

1651   From the diaries of the Danish politician Christen Skeel it appears that
         the question was mentioned in the Danish Council on 6 December 1651
(Scheel, 418, citing *Nye Danske Magazin*, series 3, iv, 134).

1660   Some documents concerning Orkney were sent to the Danish ambassador
         in London (Scheel, 419, citing evidence of a private letter of 18 August
1660, in *Danske Magazin*, series 5, iv, 180).

1667   The negotiations for the treaty of Breda, referred to above (Scheel, 419-
         420, cites *Historia of Verhael van Saken van Staet en Oorlogh* [The Hague,
1669], pt. 10, 409 sqq).

1749   An attempt by Frederick V (Scheel, citing *Genealogisch-Historische
         Nachrichten von den allerneuesten Begebenheiten* [Leipzig, 1749], cxl, 695).

THE STATUTES OF ETTRICK FOREST, 1499

By JOHN M. GILBERT, M.A., PH.D.

Introduction

The Statutes of Ettrick Forest were issued on Tuesday, 30 April 1499 in the tolbooth of Edinburgh in full court of the forest.[1] They were promulgated at that court by the commissioners of crown lands who had been appointed a fortnight previously.[2] These twelve statutes brought the old forest law up to date and adapted it to the particular circumstances of Ettrick Forest. They represent, therefore, an adaptation of national law.

To understand the unique nature of Ettrick Forest and to explain why new laws were required in 1499 it is necessary to know something of the history of that forest. Before presenting the text of these laws their compilation and promulgation will also be considered. After the text a detailed commentary will explain the content of the laws while a more general commentary will endeavour to elucidate their significance.

Brief History of Ettrick Forest

Ettrick Forest, or Selkirk Forest as it was called in the twelfth and thirteenth centuries, is first recorded in that part of David I's foundation charter of Melrose Abbey which can be ascribed to 1136.[3] Previously, David, as earl of Huntingdon, had some sort of hunting establishment in southern Scotland perhaps based on Selkirk Castle but he does not appear to have made that area a forest till the 1130s.[4] The forest of Ettrick was adjoined by the forests of Traquair and Tima, first mentioned in 1136 and 1165 × 1169 respectively.[5] Ettrick Forest itself was split into several administrative divisions. The division of the forest north and south of the Tweed appears in 1264.[6] Since, in the twelfth and thirteenth centuries, royal forests were usually administered by sheriffs it seems likely that the sheriff of Selkirk was the chief administrator of this forest. If the sheriffdom of Selkirk did not exist in the reign of David I then it would no doubt have been the sheriff of Roxburgh who then controlled the forest. By the later thirteenth century the area north of the Tweed was certainly administered by the sheriff of Roxburgh, while Traquair Forest was perhaps supervised initially by the sheriff of Edinburgh and then by the newly created sheriff of Traquair/Peebles. The forest of Tima was alienated to Melrose Abbey in 1235/6.[7]

---

[1] *Exchequer Rolls* [*ER*], xi, 394.
[2] *ER*, xi, 396.
[3] *Early Scottish Charters* [*ESC*], ed. A. Lawrie (Glasgow, 1905), no. cxli.
[4] *ESC*, no. xxxv.
[5] *ESC*, no. cxli, *Melrose Liber* [*Melr. Lib.*], no. 39.
[6] *ER*, i, 29, 30, 35.
[7] *Melr. Lib.*, no. 264.

41

This careful division of administrative responsibility was all the more necessary because this area in the twelfth century was not uninhabited. The population no doubt centred on the *veterem villam* of Selkirk and on the new town round the royal castle, but there must also have been other settlements along the valleys of the rivers Ettrick, Yarrow and Tweed which lay within the forest.[8] The existence of these settlements increased the difficulties of the sheriffs who were trying to enforce the forest law.

Few details of the work of this administration in the twelfth and thirteenth centuries survive. The sheriffs had to maintain the area as a hunting reserve and ensure that the local population did not hunt there without permission. They were no doubt also expected to supervise the grazing of cattle and sheep and wood-cutting by the inhabitants of the forest as well as by outsiders such as Melrose Abbey[9] and the men of Ashkirk[10] to whom these rights had been granted. Ploughing must also have concerned them. They would have had to ensure that the men of Ashkirk did not plough beyond the fence erected for them on 21 October 1179. Other matters relating to boundaries such as the dispute between the men of Wedale and the monks of Melrose settled in 1184 over pasture rights would also have been part of their remit.[11] These forester-sheriffs had also to provide a revenue for the king from pannage, the toll levied for permission to graze pigs, and from herbage, the toll to graze animals, probably on the summer grass. Herbage was collected from 'Fulhope', the modern Philiphaugh, which at one time had supported royal stock, and which in 1288 × 1290 was let by Alexander Balliol, the chamberlain.[12] The sheriffs must also have seen to the distribution of the animals and money collected as rents or tolls, sending some to royal castles and others to local abbeys or officials as directed. They no doubt had to supply venison when required and to prepare provisions and equipment for royal hunting trips, although evidence of these duties has not survived.

Thus, by the end of the thirteenth century Ettrick Forest was characterised by various features which other forests did not possess to the same extent, if at all. Firstly, the forest was divided into several administrative areas. Secondly, most if not all the land in the forest was rented out and so the forest was exploited not only by outsiders to whom special grants had been made but also by its inhabitants. Thirdly, the king saw the forest as a source not only of sport and game but of revenue, both by grazing his own herds or flocks there and by collecting rents for lands and tolls for certain economic activities.

Throughout the fourteenth and fifteenth centuries these features were more fully developed. In 1291 and 1292 and from 1296 to 1306 Edward I appointed foresters to administer Ettrick. He preserved a tripartite division: the area north of the Tweed, Traquair, and the rest of the area south of the Tweed. He thus continued Scottish practice.[13] When, however, the lands of Ettrick were granted

[8] *An Inventory of the Ancient and Historical Monuments of Selkirkshire [RCAM]*, 21, 22.
[9] *ESC*, no. cxli.
[10] *Regesta Regum Scottorum, [RRS]*, ii, p. 263.
[11] *The Chronicle of Melrose* (Facsimile Edition), edd. A. O. Anderson and others (London 1936), 44.
[12] *ER*, i, 29, 30, 35.
[13] *Calendar of Documents Relating to Scotland [CDS]*, ii, no. 1646.

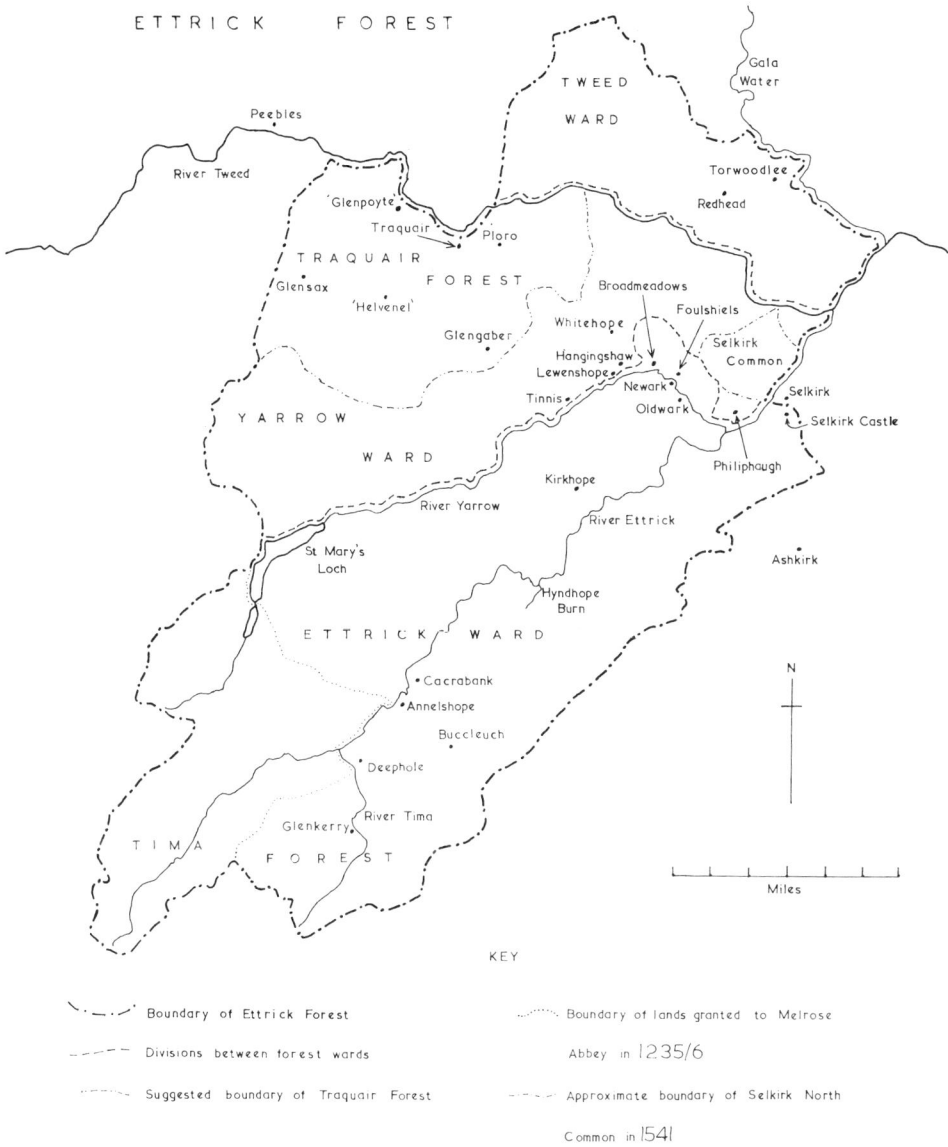

ETTRICK   FOREST

TWEED WARD

Gala Water

Peebles

River Tweed

Torwoodlee

Redhead

'Glenpoyte

Traquair   Plora

TRAQUAIR   FOREST

Glensax

'Helvenel'

Glengaber

Broadmeadows

Whitehope

Foulshiels

Selkirk Common

Hangingshaw

Lewenshope

Newark

Tinnis

Oldwark

Selkirk

Selkirk Castle

YARROW

WARD

Kirkhope

River Yarrow

River Ettrick

Philiphaugh

St Mary's Loch

Ashkirk

Hyndhope Burn

ETTRICK   WARD

N

Cacrabank

Annelshope

Buccleuch

Deephole

River Tima

Glenkerry

TIMA   FOREST

Miles

KEY

Boundary of Ettrick Forest

Boundary of lands granted to Melrose

Divisions between forest wards

Abbey in 1235/6

Suggested boundary of Traquair Forest

Approximate boundary of Selkirk North

Common in 1541

Tima Forest—In 1165 × 1169 this forest appears to have lain across the headwaters of the Ettrick and the valley of the River Tima. (*Melr. Lib.*, no. 39.) In 1235/6 Nigel de Heriz held lands in the Tima valley. (*Melr. Lib.*, no. 264.) In 1415 Robert Scott of Rankilburn granted lands to the west of the River Tima, at Glenkerry, to Melrose Abbey. (*Melr. Lib.*, no. 548.) The Rankle Burn flows past Buccleuch to join the Ettrick at Cacrabank. In the second half of the fifteenth century the exchequer rolls record no stead of Ettrick Forest farther south than Deephole. The valley of the Tima, therefore, must have been deforested during the thirteenth and fourteenth centuries.

Traquair Forest—Between c. 1320 and 1334 it was probably incorporated into what was later called Yarrow Ward.

Settlement sites—These are marked only approximately and are not based on fieldwork. They are taken from Craig-Brown, T., *The History of Selkirkshire or Chronicles of Ettrick Forest* (Edinburgh, 1886), *An Inventory of the Ancient and Historical Monuments of Selkirkshire* (Edinburgh, 1957), 6 and *Ordnance Survey, 1: 50,000 Second Series, Galashiels and Ettrick Forest* (Sheet 73) and *Hawick and Eskdale* (Sheet 79).

to James Douglas c. 1320[14] the divisions of the forest appear to have been Ettrick, Selkirk and Traquair. The introduction of 'Ettrick' suggests that the ward south of the Tweed had been found too large and that the forest had been split into two more equal portions: north of the River Yarrow including the areas later called Yarrow Ward and Tweed Ward but excluding Traquair; and south of the River Yarrow comprising the area of the later Ettrick Ward. The description of the larger portion as Ettrick might explain why the forest in the fourteenth and fifteenth centuries was no longer called Selkirk Forest but Ettrick Forest. This change of name suggests that the *caput* of the Forest was moved from the royal castle of Selkirk to the baronial castle of Oldwark in Ettrick Ward, itself replaced by Newark Tower *ante* 1423.[15] In the short time before the English re-occupation in 1332 the Douglases may have incorporated into Ettrick Forest some lands which appear to have been part of Traquair Forest, namely Ploro, Glengaber, 'Helvenel', 'Glenpoyte' and Glensax. If these holdings, which are grouped together in the royal rental books after 1455, were not once part of Traquair Forest then that forest must have been a relatively minor reserve. Whatever the fate or the original size of Traquair Forest, in 1334 and 1343 the English record refers only to the forests of Selkirk and Ettrick.[16] The Selkirk division presumably contained the whole of the forest between the Rivers Yarrow and Tweed, including Traquair as well as the area north of the Tweed. By 1354 when the forests of Ettrick, Selkirk, Yarrow and Tweed were granted in free regality and free warren to William, Lord of Douglas, the Douglases had probably created the wards through which the forest was to be administered till 1499, namely the wards of Yarrow, Ettrick and Tweed,[17] marked on the accompanying map.

To clarify the rather complicated development of the forest administration in the fourteenth century the names given to the various geographical areas of the forest at different dates are listed below. The geographical areas of the forest are listed along the top.

Date	Area north of Tweed	Traquair Forest	Area between R. Yarrow and Tweed	Area S. of River Yarrow
1291-1306	North of Tweed	Traquair	South of Tweed	
c. 1320		Traquair	Selkirk	Ettrick
1334 & 1346			Selkirk	Ettrick
1354	Tweed		Yarrow	Ettrick

Table 1   *The Development of the Forest Administration*

When the forest was annexed to the crown in 1455 the wards of Ettrick, Yarrow and Tweed were retained. While some other Scottish royal forests such as Alyth

[14] *Registrum Magni Sigilii* [*RMS*], i, app. 2, 232.
[15] *RCAM, Selkirkshire*, 23, 61.
[16] *CDS*, iii, nos. 1127, 1425.
[17] *RMS*, i, app. 1, no. 123.

and Mamlorne had internal divisions and while some were broken up into smaller forests, for example, the large reserve round Elgin, Forres and Inverness, only in Ettrick, so far as the evidence tells, were the wards so fully developed, and only in Ettrick did the wards form such an integral part of the administration.

At what point in its history Ettrick was completely rented out to tenants can not now be determined. It would seem likely that those people resident on this area of royal demesne before it was afforested by David I continued to pay their customary dues in kind or services, or they may have received short-term leases for a fixed rent or ferme. This process would have continued after afforestation. The whole forest, however, cannot have been set at ferme at this date since it was still possible for William I to refer to his waste of Selkirk in 1193[18] and for Alexander II to describe Tima as waste in 1236.[19] To judge from the distribution of bronze-age and iron-age sites[20] and from the location of Selkirk and Oldwark in the eastern part of the forest the population of the twelfth and thirteenth centuries probably concentrated in the river valleys in the eastern part of the forest. During the thirteenth century settlement may have moved up the valleys of the three main rivers and then along their tributaries but this is only surmise. Hyndhope Burn Mouth is recorded in a forged charter of c. 1290[21] supposedly relating to events in 1171. William I had hunted at St. Mary's Loch in 1166 × 1171[22] and if he ever was at Hyndhope Burn Mouth he may have been hunting there. There may have been small settlements at both places. In 1288-90 the chamberlain fermed out Philiphaugh, and in 1306 Aymer de Valence was permitted to lease lands in the forest.[23] Even by 1304 × 1305 there may still have been areas of unlet land in the forest since English receipts in that year amounted to £17 13s 4d from Traquair and only £20 from the far larger area to the south of the Tweed.[24] The comparative paucity of the rent from Ettrick at this time could, however, be equally well explained by the war in which the control of Ettrick was claimed by both Scots and English. From the numerous references to the foresters and tenants of Selkirk it is clear that a considerable part if not all of the forest was let by the early fourteenth century.[25]

When light is next shed on the leasing of Ettrick in 1423/4 it is obvious that the whole system of wards, officials and tenants had crystallised into its more fully documented fifteenth-century form. At Oldwark on 2 March 1423/4 Archibald Douglas let to William Middlemast the two forester steads of Lewenshope and Hangingshaw between the stead of the master of Yarrow, Whitehope, and that of the curour of Yarrow, Tinnis.[26] During the fourteenth and early fifteenth centuries, therefore, the Douglases as head foresters of Ettrick had divided the forest into three wards, had let holdings called forester steads within these wards to tenants or foresters, and had placed in charge of each ward a curour and a master who were paid by the tenure of a stead in the forest. In 1455 when the

[18] *RRS*, ii, no. 367.
[19] *Melr. Lib.*, no. 264.
[20] *RCAM, Selkirkshire*, 17, 19.
[21] *RRS*, ii, no. 119.
[22] *RRS*, ii, no. 75.
[23] *CDS*, ii, no. 1839.
[24] *CDS*, ii, no. 1646.
[25] *CDS*, ii, nos. 1226, 1227, 1307, 1782, 1978.
[26] *RMS*, ii, no. 59.

exchequer rolls for Ettrick take up the story this system operated unaltered. The master by then was the master currour, and the head forester, the bailie. The forest was thus entirely set at ferme to about 100 tenants and so the problems which these royal officials had to face when enforcing the forest law were considerably greater than in any other royal forest.

The third distinguishing feature of Ettrick Forest, closely related to the leasing of the forest, was the amount of revenue which it contributed to the crown. Royal exploitation of the forest took various forms. Firstly, Ettrick was visited by most Scots kings and must have been used for royal hunts although they are seldom specifically mentioned in the sources.[27] In this context there are references to deer being transported from the forest to Edinburgh and Stirling.[28] These deer may well have been transported live as was common in the sixteenth century. They could then have been hunted on arrival, slaughtered as fresh meat, or used to restock a royal park. Secondly, royal livestock was kept in Ettrick Forest. The earliest reference to this practice in Philiphaugh has already been mentioned. In the early fifteenth century James I kept sheep on one of the steads of William Middlemast in the forest even although the lands of the forest were in the hands of the Douglases.[29] This, of course, was the custom known as steelbow where the king's animals were kept not by his own *nativi*, as may have been the case on Philiphaugh before 1288, but by tenants on land which was rented to them. In addition to a royal stud James IV kept 6,000 to 8,000 sheep in Ettrick, more than in any other royal forest.[30] By far the largest contribution to royal revenue from this forest came from the rents of the tenants after 1455 in money and in kind. In the later fifteenth century the returns from Ettrick Forest were one of the largest sources of royal revenue. That the land was rented and not alienated points to a desire for revenue from royal lands which was not to be disappointed. The rent expected in 1461, but not fully collected, was £519 13s 4d. In the years before 1499 the actual revenue from rents, proceeds of courts and arrears could on occasion exceed £1,000. The desire for revenue was, therefore, a much greater obstacle to the maintenance of a hunting reserve in Ettrick than it was in those forests such as Darnaway or Clunie let only to a few tenants, or such as Glenfinglas of which only small areas on the periphery were let.[31]

It is against this background that the Statutes of Ettrick Forest must be seen.

The Need for the Statutes

When Ettrick Forest returned to royal hands in 1455 James II continued to operate the administrative system of the Douglases. Table 2 illustrates the administrative hierarchy of the forest. The officials of the forest were all paid by the remission of the fermes of a forest stead, the name of which is given in brackets.

The duties of the currour in each ward were to collect rents, grassums and entries, make allowances for other officials, dispose of the revenue to the royal

---

[27] *RMS*, ii, no. 664; *ER*, x, 505.
[28] *ER*, vi, 371, 372; vii, 25.
[29] *ER*, iv, 576.
[30] J. M. Gilbert, *Hunting and Hunting Reserves in Medieval Scotland* (Edinburgh, 1979), 250.
[31] Gilbert, *Hunting*, 123, 174, 331.

chamberlain or otherwise as ordered, collect fines levied in the forest court and present accounts to the exchequer. The accounts were usually presented in June or July. The year was divided into two terms named after days at the start of the term, All Saints or Allhallows on 1 November, and Lammas or St. Peter *ad Vincula* on 1 August. The currours were in effect the executive of the forest. The master currour, who presumably supervised the currour in his ward, seems to have been responsible for bringing to the forest courts cases concerning

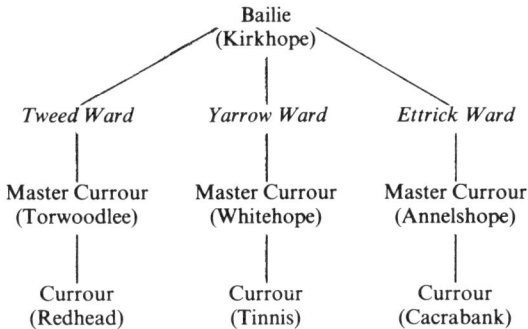

```
                              Bailie
                            (Kirkhope)
              ┌────────────────┼────────────────┐
         Tweed Ward        Yarrow Ward        Ettrick Ward
              │                │                  │
       Master Currour    Master Currour     Master Currour
        (Torwoodlee)      (Whitehope)        (Annelshope)
              │                │                  │
          Currour           Currour            Currour
         (Redhead)          (Tinnis)          (Cacrabank)
```

Table 2   *The Officials of Ettrick Forest*

poaching, wood-cutting and other forest matters.[32] The tenants of the forest had to assist the master currour in these duties since a condition of their lease was that they were responsible for the vert and venison, that is the vegetation and the game.[33] If they did not fulfil their duties they were liable to lose their lease. In practice it must have been very difficult to make this system work since there was nothing to stop the tenant committing an offence and not reporting it. The ability of the master currour and currours to supervise the tenants must have been extremely limited. The bailie, the overall head of the forest, could help to lease the steads and hold special forest courts when necessary.[34]

The bailie, however, was not the only person to have judicial competence within this forest.[35] The main forest courts were the All Saints and Beltane courts held by the commissioners of crown lands appointed by the king. In the absence of the commissioners the courts were presumably held by the bailie. These courts were latterly seldom held on the days after which they were named and on occasion were both held at the same time. Although after 1461 separate courts should have been held for each ward, there was usually one Beltane and one All Saints court for the whole forest either at Newark or at Peebles. There is some evidence that the All Saints court may have been mainly concerned with collecting unpaid rents while the Beltane court dealt with all forest matters. The leasing of the forest, the *assedacio*, was usually conducted at the Beltane court. In order to try to punish offenders who came from outwith the bounds of the forest bound courts were held once per year by the commissioners of crown lands or the

---

[32] *ibid.*, 142.
[33] *ER*, ix, 30, 606.
[34] *ER*, vii, 527; *RMS*, ii, no. 1921.
[35] Gilbert, *Hunting*, 148-50.

bailie. The bound courts may have been held separately for each ward but there is little direct evidence relating to them.

The non-forest law was also enforced in Ettrick:[36] the courts held by the bailie and commissioners of crown lands could deal with lesser civil offences; the sheriff of Selkirk tried civil and some criminal offences from the forest; and the justice ayres tried the pleas of the crown and matters delegated to them by parliament. In 1424/5 illegal wood-cutting was made a point of dittay[37] as was the theft of hawks in 1474.[38] There was, consequently, some overlap between the justice ayres and the forest courts and so it is not surprising to find that the currour of Tweed in 1495 was also the coroner of the ward.[39]

With what would appear to be such an all-embracing administrative and judicial establishment it might be thought surprising that new laws and arrangements had to be issued in 1499. There could, however, have been several cogent reasons why it was felt necessary to issue a series of statutes for Ettrick Forest.

The crown quite simply was having difficulty enforcing the forest law in Ettrick. It has to be remembered that Ettrick in the early sixteenth century was part of the area associated with the Border reivers. In 1495 the justice ayre at Selkirk heard over 100 cases of theft of stock and numerous cases of murder, burning, pillage and receipt of stolen goods.[40] These problems were compounded by the fact that the judicial system itself did not function efficiently.

Before the early 1480s the Beltane and All Saints courts met fairly frequently but thereafter problems ensued. From 1484 to 1488 the returns of courts were not made on time and so fines were not collected until the following year if at all.[41] From 1489 to 1499 these courts were held extremely erratically. In Ettrick ward for instance, out of twenty-two possible courts only eight were held, and the courts of 1496 to 1498 were all held on 20 July 1498. The accession of James IV saw a virtual breakdown in the holding of the forest courts in Ettrick for a variety of reasons. On seizing the throne in 1488 James may have felt that the late or non-collection of court fines during his father's reign had done so much damage to the wood and game that it could not be repaired. There had also been a considerable change-over in the tenants of the forest between 1485 and 1490, perhaps because they had supported James III.[42] Consequently, the forester-tenants, the lowest echelon in the administration, would be unsettled and perhaps less willing and able to fulfil their duties. Bearing in mind that James IV's favoured hunting areas lay in the Menteith-Balquhidder area James may not have been too concerned with the decline of Ettrick as a hunting reserve. Moreover, the recent memory of what had befallen his father as a result partly of financial mismanagement, and the threat of insolvency may well have encouraged him to concentrate on revenue collection rather than on the maintenance of a hunting reserve.

During the 1480s the arrears of Ettrick ward rose to over £2,000. While the

[36] ibid., 246-7.
[37] The Acts of the Parliament of Scotland [APS], ii, 7, c 10.
[38] APS, ii, 107, c 15.
[39] Scottish Record Office, Justice Ayre Journal Books, RH 2/1/5, 124.
[40] ibid., 109, 116.
[41] Gilbert, Hunting, 162-3, 174.
[42] ibid., 333.

arrears of other wards varied less dramatically, they both took a marked turn for the worse in 1489. In other words in the last years of James III's reign the currours were not collecting the rents and court fines which the exchequer expected them to collect.[43] This may well have worried James IV for he carried out a minor re-organisation of the adminstration by replacing John Cranston as bailie of the forest with Alexander, second Lord Home[44] whom he also made master currour and currour of Yarrow,[45] a ward in which revenue collection had proved particularly troublesome in the 1480s.[46] Under his guidance and with the help of allowances from the exchequer the arrears of Ettrick were greatly reduced and the accounts of Yarrow actually balanced in 1494 and 1495. In 1494 out of a real revenue of £862 10s the comptroller received £477 13s.[47] In 1499 after concentrating on revenue collection for nine years James appears to have decided to redress the balance. Enough time had elapsed since the upheavals of 1488, and enough of the tenants removed in 1488 had returned for an attempt to be made to improve the administration and to persuade the tenants to carry out their forest duties effectively.

Given medieval standards of communication and transport the administration was being asked to do too much. To preserve the vert and venison while the whole forest was inhabited was impossible. The administration lacked the coercive power to ensure that all the tenants performed their duties. In short, the leasing of the forest severely hampered the reservation of the vert and the venison, but the financial gains to be obtained from leasing the forest ensured that leasing would never be discontinued. After the minor administrative reorganisation of 1488 more fundamental measures were required in 1499.

The administration of Ettrick was hampered not only by its own short-comings and by the behaviour of the tenants of the forest but also by the nature of the law which it had to enforce. The traditional forest laws of Scotland belonged to the twelfth, thirteenth and early fourteenth centuries. By the late fifteenth century this forest law was still relevant in principle, but in practice it was out of date and in many ways was unsuitable and inadequate for Ettrick Forest.[48] Firstly, prevention of unlicensed hunting, grazing and wood-cutting within the forest were still the main aims of the Scottish forest officials as in the twelfth century, but in Ettrick there were many exceptions to be made for which the law made no allowance: tenants were allowed to keep animals, to cut wood and to travel through the forest. Secondly, while the officials referred to in the traditional forest law were foresters, there were no officials with that name in Ettrick. Thirdly, many of the penalties stipulated in the traditional forest law were altered in Ettrick. Instead of confiscating sheep found grazing illegally according to the traditional law, in Ettrick the owner of the sheep was fined. Instead of imposing a £10 fine for cutting all trees lesser fines were imposed for trees other than oak. Instead of imposing a £10 fine for killing deer lesser fines were imposed for deer other than stags.[49] Control of wood-cutting in Ettrick was

[43] ibid., 173.
[44] RMS, ii, no. 1921.
[45] ER, x, 650, under Whitehope; x, 97.
[46] ER, viii, 420, 473.
[47] Gilbert, Hunting, 331.
[48] ibid., 291-7.
[49] ibid., 165-8.

no longer the sole responsibility of the forest courts as in the traditional forest law, but was now also within the competence of the justice ayres. In Ettrick the fines imposed on outsiders committing offences in the forest did not correspond with the various penalties, such as confiscation or imprisonment, given in the traditional forest law.[50]

More generally the laws were out of date not only for Ettrick but for other forests in Scotland. Bondmen and *nativi* frequently mentioned in the laws were no longer to be found in the late fifteenth century. The custom of collecting pannage to permit pigs to graze, mentioned in clauses 7 and 8 of the forest laws, had died out in the fourteenth century. More seriously, the traditional law did not mention numerous activities which would have to be regulated where a hunting reserve was completely let out. Cultivation, drainage, enclosures, building, sub-letting, absentee-landlordism and wood-based industries were not controlled by the traditional law.

These shortcomings of the traditional law had been felt before 1499. The commissioners of crown lands who held the All Saints and Beltane courts did, of course, have the power to make laws for the forest as for other royal lands. When James III appointed commissioners for Ettrick he instructed them to enforce 'actis and statutis of our said forest maid of befor for the reuyle of the samyn' and 'utheris thocht expedient of new to mak and sett to be kepit in tyme cumming'.[51] The process, therefore, of revising and augmenting the law was well under way. No copy of these earlier statutes has as yet come to light. One of them, mentioned in 1471, stated that the fine for an illegal yard or enclosure was 6s 8d.[52] Another, mentioned in clause 8 of the statutes of 1499, required that a tenant of the forest had to keep his stead 'nychtbourlike accordin to the auld statutis'. How comprehensive these local statutes were is a matter of debate. One can perhaps conclude that since none of them were copied into the royal rental books as were those of 1499 they were not so comprehensive as the 1499 statutes. By 1499 it was realised that the time had come to consolidate these earlier statutes and to prepare a group of laws which were up to date, adapted to Ettrick's administrative system and would render that administration more effective.

Composition and Promulgation

The royal rental book for 1499-1507 opens with twenty points of inquest to be held on royal lands, twelve statutes for Ettrick Forest, a copy of a privy seal letter appointing the commissioners for crown lands, and the rental of Ettrick Forest for 1499.[53] The rental book does not record who compiled the Statutes of Ettrick Forest, but it must have been the commissioners of crown lands. Firstly they were empowered to make local laws. Secondly, the laws were issued, and the *assedacio* or rental made, in the one forest court in the tolbooth of Edinburgh on 30 April. Thirdly the commissioners of crown lands held the *assedacio* which was 'maid . . . efter the forme of the said statutis'.[54]

[50] *ibid.*, 150.
[51] *ER*, ix, 605.
[52] *ER*, viii, 44.
[53] Scottish Record Office, *Rentale Domini Regis*, E 40/4, 1-9.
[54] *ER*, xi, 395.

The commissioners, appointed on Thursday 18 April, were William Elphinstone, Bishop of Aberdeen, George, Abbot of Dunfermline, James, Abbot of Scone, Sir Patrick Hume of Polwarth, comptroller, Sir Robert Lundy of Balgownie, treasurer and Sir Henry Alan, archdeacon of Dunblane and clerk of the royal household. They were joined at the *assedacio* by Archibald Campbell, second earl of Argyll, master of the household.[55] In their letter of commission James stated that they were appointed after his general revocation to lease all royal lands. This revocation, made on 16 March 1498,[56] annulled all tacks and leases on royal lands which had, consequently, to be renewed, hence the commissioners' appointment. Before a tenant could renew his tack he would, of course, have to pay an additional sum of money called an 'entry', to the crown. The revocation was, consequently, a way of raising money from these 'entries'. The commissioners' letter of appointment also records that this revocation was made when James had reached his 'compleit, perfit and lauchtfull' age, i.e., twenty-five. He had made a similar revocation when he was 21.[57] The Statutes of Ettrick Forest may, therefore, be seen as part of a general initiative on royal lands taken in 1498 and 1499.

The letter of commission also authorised the commissioners to hold courts within the royal lands, to raise amercements, to punish trespassers and to do whatever was necessary in law in all these matters. As with other commissioners of royal lands they were entitled to hold forest courts and make local laws as they saw fit.

The commissioners had thirteen days to assemble, call the court of Ettrick and prepare the statutes, a tight schedule. Which of the commissioners drafted the statutes cannot now be determined, but Sir Patrick Hume the comptroller, and Sir Henry Alan were the two people with most direct contact with Ettrick. The comptroller received money from the currours of the forest and Sir Henry Alan had been his assistant since 1491 and a commissioner of crown lands from 1492-5.[58] In view of the detailed administrative arrangements in the statutes and the obvious influence of the comptroller in clause 1 it seems likely that they provided the driving force. One may guess that prior discussion had taken place with Alexander, second Lord Home, the bailie of the forest and great chamberlain. The influence of William Elphinstone must also have been strong. He was interested in the efficient holding of leases on royal lands and in improving the laws. It is known that he spent as much as ninety-three days a year in Edinburgh hearing cases which had originated in local courts.[59] Elphinstone, the two abbots and Sir Henry Alan were all lords of council in 1499,[60] and so the commissioners as a group had more than enough experience and vision to compile a set of statutes. They may also have compiled the points of inquest which they had to hold on royal lands. The time available to compile the laws, from 18 to 31 April, was not unduly short when one remembers that the lords of

[55] *ER*, xi, 396.
[56] R. Nicholson, *Scotland: The Later Middle Ages* (Edinburgh, 1974), 544.
[57] *ibid.*, 541.
[58] J. H. Cockburn, *The Medieval Bishops of Dunblane and their Church*, (Edinburgh, 1959), 179, 263.
[59] L. J. McFarlane, 'William Elphinstone, Founder of the University of Aberdeen', *Aberdeen University Review*, 39 (1961), 1-18, at 9, 10.
[60] Gilbert, *Hunting*, 160; Cockburn, *Bishops of Dunblane*, 263.

the articles could prepare legislation for a Scots parliament in six days in 1469 and in sixteen days in 1485.[61]

The Statutes of Ettrick were 'publist to the forrestaris in the plane court in the tolbouth of Edinburgh'. The tolbooth stood to the west of St. Giles church on the High Street. The use of the phrase 'plane court' implies a more authoritative and more legally powerful court than a normal court because the requisite number of suitors and officials had to be present. It also implied that the proceedings were open and public.[62] The 1499 court was, consequently, well suited to the promulgation of the statutes. The location of the court in Edinburgh and not as usual at Newark is puzzling. The commissioners held the Ettrick court on Tuesday 30 April but their next *assedacio*, held in Edinburgh, that of the royal lands of Ballincrief in Lothian, did not follow till Saturday 4 May. The commissioners then moved to Stirling to carry out further rentals of other royal lands on the following Monday, Tuesday and Wednesday and finished up at Cupar on Monday 13 May.[63] There had been plenty of time for the commissioners to have held the Ettrick court in Newark and then moved to Edinburgh for the Saturday. One can only assume that they leased Ettrick in Edinburgh in order to cut down on their own travelling, to give themselves extra time for the leasing and for dealing with other business in Edinburgh and to stress the importance of the court. The next forest court to be held in Edinburgh was another *plena curia* to commence the feuing of the forest in 1506, an equally important matter.[64]

The 1499 Statutes of Ettrick Forest

The only copy of these statutes is in the royal rental book for 1499.[65] This copy is, therefore, contemporary. One or two errors show that it is not the original version of these laws but the possibility of major errors and omissions may be discounted. The text has already been printed accurately in volume XI of the *Exchequer Rolls* at page 394.

In this edition *thorn* is given as *th* and *yogh* as *y*. Abbreviations have been expanded and italicised. Modern capitalisation and punctuation have been used.

Ultimo Aprilis anno domini etc nonagesimo nono publicatum in pretorio de Edinburgh.

Primo. It is thoucht expedient that the vj steidis of office be takin in the kingis handis and the comptrollar mak officiaris to gadder in the malis and extretis of the courtis and pay thaim thair feis tharfor, and ordane men to gev in the entres of the wardis in ilk court for the kepin of the forrest forrestlike as he will ansuer tharfor, the quhilkis officiaris ordanit be him sall considir the destruccion of wod and der.

Secundo. Item it is thocht expedient for the kepin of the said forrest forrestlike

[61] Nicholson, *The Later Middle Ages*, 426; *A Source Book of Scottish History*, edd. W. C. Dickinson, and others (London, 1963), ii, 39.
[62] *Sheriff Court Book of Fife*, ed. W. C. Dickinson (Scottish History Society, 1928), 402-5.
[63] *ER*, xi, 396-419.
[64] *ER*, xii, 658.
[65] SRO, *Rentale*, E 40/4, 3-5.

and for hanging of wod and der that thar be na fyris upon ane steid bot thre allanerlie, the quhilkis salbe twa bowis and j sper to the kingis ost eftir the auld consuetude.

Tertio. Item it is thocht expedient that ilk forrester keip and have the der *and* wod within his steid as he will ansuer to the king undir the pane of tynsale of his steid *and* eschaetin of his gudis being tharupon.

Quarto. Item that na forestar hald undir him in his steid haggar, flegeour, turnour, barcar, colebyrnar, pelar of bark, scab, pikar, wrychtis, swyne, nor gait, undir the pane of tynsale of his sted, eschaetin of the gudis apon the said steid nor yit he sall nothir geve nor sell ony maner of wod till ony personis, nor yit cut nor distroy himself undir the sammyn panis bot till his awne neidis within the said forrest.

Quinto. Item[a] for schutaris, slaaris of calfis, foneis or rakiddis, or slaaris, of deir be hunting or ony uthir maner of way within the bondis of the forrest [the forrester][b] of the said steid quhar the der or best is slane sall othir find ane slaare for the sammyn or ellis be punist tharfor himself *and* pay the auld unlaw but favour.

Sexto. Item anent the kepin of the said forrest it is thocht expedient that thar be na telin, sawin, delfyne or ony maner of corne with[in][c] the forsaid forrest undir the pane of tynsale of[d] the steid *and* eschaeting of the said corne *and* gudis being tharupon.

Septimo. Item it is thocht expedient that thar be na mureburne nor na maner of yardis nor dikyne of na maner of wod fra thinfurtht except it be of thorne, saucht or erde undir the pane of tynsale of his takkis[e] quhar it beis fund.

Octavo. It is thocht expedient that thar be na steid of the forrest set to ony maner of persone bot gif he remane tharupon himself or ellis ordane ane sufficient tenant *and* nychtbour tharto that beis abill to keip the said steid nychtbourlike accordin to the auld statutis and undirly the ordinance abon writtin.

Nono. Item it is thocht expedient that the balye hald foure balye courtis in the yer at the lest for the seing of the said thingis and reforming of plantis of nychtbourhed *and* uthiris *and* ma gif it neidis, *and* see gif ilk steid beis boding with twa bowis *and* a sper with hors *and* ger as accordis tharto as said is, and als mony as beis findin falyeing in the said ordinance he sall put thaim in the rolment of his court and deliver the sammyn to the commissionaris of the Beltan *and* Alhallow courtis quhen thai ar haldin undir the pane of tynsale of his office *and* all his stedis gif he has ony.

Decimo. Item it is thocht expedient that becaus it is plenyeit that the marchis *and* the induellaris within the bondis about the said forrest distroyis the wod *and* der grettumlie for the quhilkis thar has ben na remeid this langtyme to gret prejudice[f] *and* hurt of the king *and* his forrest *and* landis, that thar be yerelie ane bond court haldin be the kingis comptrollar *and* commissaris for the reforming *and* remeid of the said hurtis *and* skaith.

---

[a] 'It' written by mistake by the scribe after 'Item' and then scored out.

[b] The scribe has written 'the forrest', scored it out, and then written 'the forrest' again with the result that 'the forrester' was omitted.

[c] Abbreviation for 'in' omitted.   [e] The *ER* edition gives 'stakkis' incorrectly.

[d] 'his' written and scored out.   [f] The scribe has, of course, written i not j.

Undecimo.[g] Item it is thocht expedient that fense eftir the auld consuetude be
kepit undir the pane of tynsale of the steid *and* [h]eschaeting of the[h] gudis being
tharupoun.

Duodecimo. Item it is thocht expedient that gif it happinnis ony forrester within
the said forrest to tak remission or respitt fra thin furth for common theif,
pikry or reset tharof or happinnis to be convict tharwith that thane his stedis
salbe forfalt, and his gudis being tharupoun salbe eschaetit without ony uthir
*pro*cese of law *and* the stedis wacand.

[Conclusion.] And all thir statutis abone writtin togidder with the auld statutis
of the forrest be observit *and* kepit undir the panis contenit in the sammyne
and this assedacioun undirwrittin maid be the commissaris eftir the forme of
the said statutis *and* publist to the forrestaris in the plane court in the
tolbouth of Edinburgh the day *and* yer abone exprimit.

Notes on Text

Clause 1.

The *steidis of office* were those steads which were given to the officials of the
forest rent free as part of their remuneration. *Malis* are rents and *extretis* are the
fines imposed by the court. They were so named because they were listed on an
extract of the court's proceedings.[66] *Entres* in this context means the list of
offences committed. The official would make entry of offences in the court.[67]
Forrestlike was a frequently used word to summarise the preservation of the
venison from poaching and of the vert from wood-cutting, agriculture and
grazing.

Clause 2.

Haning in this case means protecting rather than enclosing. *Fyris* means
weapons. The provision of two bows and a spear for the king's host was not new.
In 1490 the tenant of Mid-Fauside had to have one lance and two archers for the
king in war time.[68] It would seem likely that it was not simply the weapons but
also the soldiers which had to be provided as part of the military service of
Ettrick. Since the fifteenth century or earlier inhabitants of a forest had been
expected to provide a bow and a spear not a bow and arrows since a bow and
arrows could easily be used for poaching. Such arrangements may have been
current in Robert I's reign when poorer men were expected to provide a bow with
either arrows or a spear.[69] It is ironic that Ettrick was renowned for its archers.

Clause 3.

Tynsale means forfeiture, in this case loss of lease in Ettrick. *Escheat* meant
the same in effect. The tenants' goods would be taken over by the king. The

---

[g] The scribe wrote 'Ultimo' then scored it out and wrote 'Undecimo'.
[h-h] Inserted by the scribe above the line.

[66] *ER*, ix, 317, 414, 467.
[67] *ER*, xii, 658; Gilbert, *Hunting*, 149.
[68] *ER*, x, 675.
[69] *APS*, i, 752; 473, c 24.

technical meaning of escheat was that a person's goods would be returned to the king because he had no heirs.

Clause 4.

This clause bans from the forest anyone involved in an industry or trade which used wood or would disturb the vegetation. The following words are used:– *haggar* hewer, *flegeour* arrow-maker, *turnour* turner (on a lathe), *barcar* tanner, *colebyrnar* charcoal-burner, *pelar of bark* bark-stripper — oak bark for tanning — *scab* a thief. In the Oxford English Dictionary under the fifth meaning of *scab*, *scab* and *pikar* are placed together as *scab picker* and are said to mean one who treats sheep for the scab, a sheep disease. This would obviously not be someone to be excluded from this forest and so cannot apply here. *Pikar* robber, *wrychtis* tradesmen or wrights as in wheelwrights. This clause also banned pigs and goats since they could have an extremely harmful effect on woodland vegetation. Sheep were, in fact, permitted in many parts of the forest.[70]

Clause 5.

While hand guns were introduced to Scotland in James IV's reign they were rare, and *schutaris* here refers to the use of bows and arrows and crossbows. Calves, fawns and roekids are specified as the young of red, fallow and roe deer. If the young survived then the deer population would thrive. The ways of killing deer other than hunting would be by nets and traps.[71] The old unlaw was £10. This statute is reminiscent of the traditional forest law which stated that if someone saw a poacher at work in the forest and did not raise the hue and cry in the nearest settlement or inform the forester then he would be at the king's mercy.[72]

Clause 6.

In this clause *telin* means ploughing, *sawin* means sowing and *delfyne* means digging or ditching. All would disturb the vegetation. *Corne* means corn, grain.

Clause 7.

Moors might be burnt to clear them or to encourage the growth of new grass and so improve the grazing. In 1401 parliament forbade muirburn except in March.[73] The best time to renew the pasture was in March when the vegetation had not completely dried out and so the fires could be more easily controlled. Burning in summer or autumn could get out of control and could kill off the heath rather than regenerate it. Whenever it was done an area of land would for a while be bare of vegetation and nearby trees might catch fire. For these reasons it was banned in Ettrick. This does tell us that there were areas of heath and moorland in Ettrick in 1499. The fine for muirburn outside the permitted time in 1401 was 40s. Good timber was not to be used for dykes and fences. Thorn and willow (*saucht*) could be trained into a living or quickset hedge. Banks of earth (*erde*) were also permitted.

[70] Gilbert, *Hunting*, 267.
[71] *ibid.*, 57.
[72] *ibid.*, 297.
[73] *APS*, i, 576.

Clause 8.

This law applies to civil rather than to forest law. Good neighbourhood in medieval society covered a variety of matters such as proper maintenance of hedges and ditches to ensure that stock did not stray, assessing damages caused by straying cattle, disputes relating to pasture boundaries and to joint tenancies, not overgrazing common land and the duties of maintaining the local mill.[74] *Nychtbourlike* meant in accord with the requirements of good neighbourhood. The *auld statutis* were no doubt previous rules and laws passed by the commissioners or the bailie in previous Beltane and Allhallows courts.

Clause 9.

Complaints about matters concerning good neighbourhood, therefore, lay within the competence of the bailie. Horse and gear is added to the provisions given in clause 2. Gear could mean arms and armour or personal equipment. In this clause it probably meant food, clothing and weapons as well as the horse's harness. The rolment of the court would be the official record of the court. This clause shows one reason why the clerk of the court had an important task.[75]

Clause 10.

This law begins with a preamble describing the faults it is trying to rectify. *Marchis* must refer to people living on or beyond the marches or boundaries of the forest. The last recorded bound court before 1499 was held in 1477 × 1478.[76]

Clause 11.

Fence was the time when the deer were fawning. In the traditional forest laws permission was required to graze beasts in the forest from 9 June to 9 July. This is the first known use of the word *fense* in Scots with this meaning.

Clause 12.

This clause concerns corrupt and offending foresters. It states quite clearly that if a forester was convicted of theft or reset of stolen goods then his stead would be forfeit. The first part of the clause, however, is not quite so clear. It could mean that if a forester granted a remission to an offender or let him off and did not report the offence to the forest court then his stead would be forfeit. Alternatively it could mean that if the forester himself received a remission or a respite for an alleged offence then he lost his stead.

The former meaning raises problems since there is no evidence that foresters could hold court themselves and so they should not have been granting remissions. This, of course, could have been the point of the law: to stop foresters taking the law into their own hands and letting offenders off lightly. The latter meaning also raises problems since it seems to imply that the forester could receive a remission without being convicted. There is no recorded example of a remission in Ettrick preceding trial but there are several examples of remissions

[74] *The Barony Court Book of Carnwath*, ed. W. C. Dickinson (Scottish History Society, 1937), pp. cix, cxv.
[75] *ibid.*, p. lxxxii; *Fife*, ed. Dickinson, p. lxi.
[76] *ER*, viii, 477, 478, 482.

following trial. Nonetheless the possibility that this statute is envisaging a remission before trial seems more likely than the possibility that it relates to foresters granting remissions. Remissions before trial had occurred in Scotland in James III's reign and were common again in the seventeenth century. If the forester was found guilty of theft or reset and the penalty set, whether or not he obtained respite or remission of the penalty or paid the full penalty, his stead would be forfeited and his goods escheated. Given the turbulent nature of Border society and the amount of thieving and reiving which occurred, as evidenced in the justice ayre journal books, this clause was an attempt to ensure and enforce a law-abiding character amongst the foresters.

Respitt means prorogation or respite of punishment. 'Without any other process of law' presumably meant that forfeiture of the stead and escheat of goods followed directly without any further legal procedure.

Conclusion.

The old statutes would include statutes previously made for Ettrick and possibly the traditional forest law. The *assedacio* or leasing of the forest followed the publication of these statues. *Plane* court is used here in the sense of legal, public and open.

General Commentary

These statutes were passed, it has been argued, to remedy the weaknesses of the administration in Ettrick and to provide an up to date set of laws adapted to the circumstances of Ettrick Forest for that administration to enforce.

The administration of the forest was re-organised. The old system of currours and master currours was abolished and two sets of officials, appointed by the comptroller, replaced them (Clause 1). One group of officials, obviously replacing the currours, had to collect rents and court fines. The comptroller could now hope to have more control over the officials who collected the revenue and so to receive more revenue. The other group of officials, perhaps replacing the master currours, had to bring breaches of the forest regulations to the courts. The central government could thus exercise much greater influence on the officials, hopefully resulting in more arrests and convictions for destruction of wood and deer.

To assist this second group of officials the forester-tenants were clearly informed of their duties. Each forester-tenant had to protect the wood and deer on his stead (Clause 3) and if he did not he would lose his lease and his property. He had also to prevent the pursuit of any wood-using industries or trades. (Clause 4). He could not keep goats or pigs (Clause 4) and if any deer were killed on his stead he had to find the poacher or else pay the penalty himself (Clause 5). The forester-tenants would no doubt report cases to one of the comptroller's officials. To ensure that the forester-tenants were there to perform their duties Clause 8 forbade absenteeism amongst tenants. These statutes, therefore, tried to make the forester-tenants more efficient by reminding them of their duties and by threatening loss of lease and goods. If the forester-tenants did not function efficiently then offenders would slip by unnoticed or unreported.

The system of courts was also covered. The bailie had to hold at least four courts in the year which could try all forest cases and matters of good neighbourhood and supervise military provision in the forest (Clause 9). The commissioners were still to hold the Beltane and All Saints courts. In view of the irregularity of these courts before 1499 the revised bailie courts were no doubt to become the main court of the forest. In this way the compilers of the statutes must have hoped to ensure that the courts met more regularly than in the past. Similarly bound courts were to be held once per year.

The statutes of 1499 give a very clear example of the revision and augmentation of the traditional law by local statute. Clauses 1, 3 and 5 adapted the control of vert and venison to the conditions of Ettrick. The principle behind these statutes was not new but the regulations for the comptroller's officials, the forester-tenants, the bailie courts and the bound courts were. The law was adapted to the way in which Ettrick was administered and to the existence of a large number of tenants within its bounds. The regulations about animals were modified. Only goats and pigs were forbidden. Sheep and cattle which were common in this forest were not banned as they had been in the traditional law.

The new matters covered by the Statutes of Ettrick Forest were the limitation of weapons on a stead, the control of wood-using industries, the forbidding of agriculture and the forbidding of absenteeism. These statutes, therefore, filled gaps in the traditional law.

One regulation of the traditional law, fence, was continued but the penalty was revised to loss of stead instead of eight cows. How exactly this law was to operate in Ettrick after 1499 is not clear. The traditional law stated that beasts were not to be allowed to enter the forest in time of fence, that is when the deer were fawning between 9 June and 9 July, according to the traditional law. To enforce this was obviously impossible in Ettrick. Perhaps in fence time in Ettrick the tenants were to keep their stock in enclosures or to herd them out of certain areas.

To what extent these statutes improved the administration is not recorded. The currours were abolished but the comptroller's officials are never mentioned as such in the exchequer rolls. The money discharged to the comptroller after 1499 was regularly paid by the same people who may, consequently, have been the comptroller's financial officials.[77] From the financial point of view they were fairly successful since the amount of money returned to the comptroller rose from £427 4s in 1498[78] to about £850 in 1499.[79] Lord Home and his son made the accounts of the forest balance in 1503 and from 1507 to 1510. On the judicial side the comptroller's officials may not have been so successful since the tenants in 1506 were asked to make entry of offences against the vert not to these officials but to the commissioners' court in Edinburgh. This might argue that they were not functioning satisfactorily.[80]

The bailie courts which must have become the everyday court of the forest were similarly never recorded by name and one can only assume that the

[77] *ER*, xii, 35, 36.
[78] *ER*, xi, 99-102.
[79] *ER*, xi, 243, 245.
[80] *ER*, xii, 658.

amercements and the forfeitures recorded in the exchequer rolls in 1502 and 1503 were imposed in the bailie court.[81] After 1499 while the names Beltane and Allhallows court disappear from the record the commissioners did continue to hold courts in 1500, 1501, 1506 and 1510.[82] It would, therefore, seem likely that courts were held more frequently after 1499 than before. Whether or not they were held as often as the statutes required, *assedaciones* for the forest were held every year and they were usually held in association with a court.[83]

The statutes themselves provide the best basis on which to assess the performance of the forester-tenants. They were allowed to take wood in the forest for their own needs (Clause 4). At the same time they had to preserve the vert and the venison on their steads. Forfeiture for failure to do so may sound severe but one wonders how many tenants simply cut what wood they wished, poached game or hid carcasses and never reported the offences. After failing to find a poacher one suspects that few tenants would report their failure and pay the £10 fine unless one of the comptroller's officials happened to witness the event. In 1510 many of the inhabitants of the forest were fined by a justice ayre for Ettrick and among the offenders were at least five of the forester-tenants and the sheriff of Selkirk.[84] Nonetheless, offences were reported and tried in the forest courts.

The one occasion when forester-tenants could be held to account was when they came to renew their leases. It was no coincidence that these statutes were published in conjunction with the *assedacio*. In this it is possible to see the influence of Bishop Elphinstone for it is known that he wished royal leases to be held efficiently on all royal lands under pain of loss of lease.[85] The deterrent effect, however, of even that penalty was greatly minimised because in many cases it was composited to a fine of sheep or money. The court's most effective weapon was thus seldom used.[86]

To a large extent the work of the legislators and administrators was doomed to failure. The revenue to be obtained from rents, remissions and compositions was too valuable to lose. In 1501 the length of the leases was extended to nine years in return for an increased rent with the result that in 1502 the revenue from the forest rose to £1779 while the comptroller received £718 14s 10d. At the same time many privy seal letters of tack, while they still required the tenants to keep the forest forestlike, permitted the tenants to sublet, to plough and to sow.[87] Some even exempted the tenants from the forest courts.[88] Obviously the 1499 statutes were laid aside for financial advantage. This is clearly seen when James IV started to set the forest in feu ferme between 1506 and 1510.[89] In return for a further increase in rent, not so large as the 1501 increase, the tenants received tenure for life and were encouraged to develop their holdings, to construct

[81] *ER*, xii, 31, 110.
[82] *ER*, xi, 403, 319; xii, 658, 659; xiii, 649.
[83] Gilbert, *Hunting*, 149, 164.
[84] SRO, *Journal Books*, RH 2/1/6, 283ff.
[85] McFarlane, 'William Elphinstone', 9.
[86] *ER*, xi, 396ff.
[87] *Registrum Secreti Sigilii* [*RSS*], i. nos. 1858, 1859, 1867, 1872.
[88] *RSS*, i, nos. 2037, 1858, 435.
[89] *ER*, xii, 658-9; Gilbert, *Hunting*, 330.

orchards and gardens, plant oak trees, make fishponds and to build and maintain farmhouses with outbuildings. Consequently, the desire to improve the administration of Ettrick as a hunting reserve, which gave rise to the statutes of 1499, was soon overridden by the ever-present need for money.

The impact of the statutes on the life of the inhabitants of Ettrick was, as a result, greatly reduced. If they had been strictly enforced the prohibition of ploughing and subletting would have caused considerable upheaval. As it was, several people were fined in 1499 for ditching, ploughing and sowing but thereafter no fines or forfeitures for these offences were recorded in the rentals.[90] Although steads in the forest changed hands after 1499 as they had done ever since 1455 it is not known whether this happened because steads were forfeited in accordance with the penalties in the statutes or for other reasons.[91] That tenants continued to rent lands in the forest argues that the forest statutes were not strictly enforced partly for financial reasons but also because even the revised administration could not cope with the somewhat turbulent nature of Ettrick society.

The Statutes of Ettrick Forest were the result of a conscious rationalisation of the laws which applied to the forest, the traditional forest laws and earlier *ad hoc* local statutes. As such they were included in the royal rental book. They were tied to the practical everyday concerns of life. They were not theoretical or philosophical in any way but they were idealistic in that they represented the aims of the commissioners of crown lands rather than what could actually be achieved. The statutes were also of local application only. They were published in a court of Ettrick for Ettrick. Although they were revising the national forest law they did not apply to the whole of Scotland. It is a feature of the history of royal forests in Scotland that after their inception the law enforced in them was variable. No parliament legislated on forest law. It was presumably held to be a matter for the king alone. While the commissioners of crown land may have created a certain amount of uniformity there must still have been variation in offences, penalties and arrangements throughout Scotland. Alternatively, parliament may simply not have been interested and may have been quite content to leave to local courts the adaptation and development of laws which in practice were causing no great hardship.

[90] *ibid.*, 166-8.
[91] *ibid.*, 332-3.

JURISDICTION IN HERITAGE AND THE LORDS OF
COUNCIL AND SESSION AFTER 1532

By HECTOR L. MACQUEEN, LL.B.,

Department of Scots Law, University of Edinburgh

In May 1532 the Scottish parliament passed an act instituting 'ane college . . . for the doing and administracioune of justice in all civile actiounis'.[1] Legal tradition has for long seen this act as founding the Court of Session. But Professor R. K. Hannay in a number of writings demonstrated that it was in fact only 'a plausible pretext for obtaining money of which the Crown stood desperately in need'.[2] There was no real change in judicial arrangements as a result of the act of 1532 or, indeed, as a result of its subsequent confirmations by parliament in 1541 and 1543.[3] Over the previous forty to fifty years there had been gradually emerging from the king's council a group of councillors whose particular function it was to sit in judicial sessions and to determine litigations.[4] It was this group, the 'lords of council and session', who were now to form the new college. The purpose of the Scottish king James V was very simple. He wished to strengthen the financial position of his crown, and one of the principal methods used by him to this end was to exploit the wealth of the church. This was facilitated by the desire of the papacy, in the face of the forces of reformation then sweeping much of Europe, to retain the allegiance of the Scots.[5] This became particularly important following the start of the Henrician reformation in England in 1531. The idea of establishing a College of Justice was put forward in that year by the Scots, and accepted by Pope Clement VII, as a justification for imposing an annual tax of approximately £10,000 Scots on the Scottish church.[6]

Historians have accordingly attached little importance to the act of 1532 in the development of the Court of Session. Thus, for example, Professor Gordon Donaldson:[7]

> All that had happened was the inadequate endowment of the 'session' of semi-professional and specialist judges which had already been taking shape:

---

[1] *Acts Parl. Scot.* [*APS*], ii, 335, c. 2.
[2] R. K. Hannay, *The College of Justice* (Edinburgh and Glasgow, 1933), 37.
[3] *APS*, ii, 371, c. 10; *APS*, ii, 443, c. 7.
[4] See A. A. M. Duncan, 'The central courts before 1532', *Introduction to Scottish Legal History* (Stair Society, 1958), 321-40, and T. M. Chalmers, 'The king's council, patronage and the governance of Scotland 1460-1513' (Aberdeen Ph.D. 1982) chs. 3 and 4.
[5] See G. Donaldson, *The Scottish Reformation* (Cambridge 1960), 37-41.
[6] The most detailed study of these events is still Hannay, *College of Justice*, chs. III-V; for a summary, see G. Donaldson, *Scotland: James V-James VII* (Edinburgh 1965), 46-8.
[7] Donaldson, *James V*, 48. See also the terse comment of Duncan, 'Central courts', at 336: 'It is clear that the creation of the College of Justice was no more than an excuse to mulct the Church'.

of the fifteen judges named in 1532, all but one had been on the session in 1531. Nothing at this stage did much to accelerate or complete the separation of 'session' from 'council': only after 1540 did separate registers appear for the proceedings of the privy council on one hand and the acts and decreets of the court of session on the other; and not until 1554 did a separate register of deeds emerge for the court of session.

It is interesting therefore to note the recent comment of Dr. A. L. Murray that 'though historians have tended to play down the significance of the events of 1532, contemporaries saw them as marking a definite change in the nature of the court'.[8] This remark occurs in his article on the *Practicks* of John Sinclair, a collection of the decisions of the court from 1540 to 1549 made by one of its judges. His analysis of the cases reported by Sinclair shows that in the period covered by his *Practicks* the court was expanding its jurisdiction and indeed claiming exclusive jurisdiction in certain types of case; justification for this could be found, on occasion at least, in the act of 1532 which explicitly gave the court jurisdiction 'in all civile actiounis'.

As Dr. Murray notes, an important field into which the court extended its jurisdiction was that of heritage, the ownership of land. The conciliar courts of the fifteenth century had no jurisdiction in cases which involved disputes over such questions, and it would seem that this continued to be the position as the institution of the session developed, for in 1532 the court still could not deal directly with matters touching heritage.[9] However by 1587 it was accepted that the lords of council and session were the most appropriate judges for disputes over heritage, as an act of parliament in that year makes clear.[10] It seems therefore that this change followed the institution of the College of Justice.

We can perhaps pinpoint the period of the change to the 1540s, the decade covered by Sinclair's *Practicks*. Both Sir James Balfour of Pittendreich and Sir John Skene refer to the jurisdiction of the session in heritage, respectively in the *Practicks* written between 1574 and 1583,[11] and in the *De Verborum Significatione* published in 1597. Both cite cases of the 1540s as authority for the proposition that heritage pertains exclusively to the lords of council and session. Thus Balfour:[12]

> Item, The Lordis of sessioun alanerlie, and na uther Judge, ar Jugeis competent to actiounis of reductioun of infeftmentis, evidentis, or sasines, and of all actiounis of heritage betwix all the liegis of this realme, spiritual or temporal, and to all obligatiounis and contractis followand as accessory thairupon, 20 Mart. 1545, Sir James Caldwell contra Sir James Maison.

Skene points out that, in earlier times, questions of 'the ground richt and propertie of lands' had been determined before the justice general by the brieve of

[8] A. L. Murray, 'Sinclair's *Practicks*', *Law-making and Law-makers in British History*, ed. A. Harding (Royal Historical Society, 1980), 90-104, at 98.
[9] See H. L. MacQueen, 'The brieve of right in Scots law', *Journal of Legal History* 3 (1982) 52-70, especially at 66-7.
[10] *APS*, iii, 445, c. 23.
[11] Balfour, *Practicks*, ed. P. G. B. McNeill (Stair Society, 1962), i, xxxiii.
[12] Balfour, *Practicks*, i, 269.

right; but, he adds, the lords of council and session had determined this process 'nocht to have bene nor yit to be thir mony yeires in use and theirfore they find themselfe, conform to the institution of the Colledge of Justice, and jurisdiction granted to them, to be judges competent in all causes of heretage, ult. Februar 1542, Patrick Weems contrair Forbes of Reres'.[13]

Sinclair's *Practicks* contain no reports of cases decided between March 1544 and July 1546, so that there is no reference by him to *Caldwell* v. *Maison*.[14] But he does report the case of *Weems* v. *Forbes* in terms showing that his *Practicks* were the source for Skene's gloss of the case. The report is headed, 'That reductioun of auld infeftmentis pertenis to the lordis of sessioun', and continues:[15]

> The last of Februar anno eodem in causa Patricii Weymes contra dominum de Rires, the said lairdis procuratour allegit that the lordis of counsall wer na judges competent to the reductioun of his infeftment *vi* yeiris auld, becaus thairthrow vald cum in disputatioun of the rycht of his landis, quhilk ground rycht of *landis* aucht be act of parliament to be decydit be ane *breif* of rycht befoir the justice and nocht befoir the lordis of sessioun. The lordis of counsall nochtwithstanding decernit thame competent judges in this mater, sic as thai wer thir divers yeiris in use of calling sic materis befoir thame, and divers *sic interlocutoris* gevin, ut in causa domini de Sanquhair et in causa cuiusdam Pringill de Torsounis et aliis diversis, and als becaus the breif of rycht is nor hes nocht yit bene mony yeiris usit in this realme.

It seems clear that Skene used Sinclair's report, not merely borrowing the words, but also the historical error that the brieve of right pertained to the court of the justice or justiciar when in fact it was competent only in the burgh and sheriff courts.[16] This may well support the lords' statement that the brieve had long been in desuetude in 1543. The act of parliament referred to was probably that of 1458 in which the lords of session were empowered to 'know apone ... civile acciounis the quhilkis concernys nocht fee nor heretage'.[17] This suggests at least some awareness of the institutional antecedents of the lords of council and session and their willingness in the 1540s to cut loose from these historical restrictions.

It seems then to be worthwhile to set out the official record of these two cases, to test the accuracy and reliability of these notes by Sinclair, Balfour and Skene, and to see if any further information can be obtained. The cases will be dealt with individually, in chronological order; after which some more general conclusions will be advanced.

[13] Sir John Skene, *De Verborum Significatione* (Edinburgh 1597) s.v. '*Breve de Recto*'.

[14] Murray, 'Sinclair's *Practicks*', 95-6.

[15] The text from Sinclair's *Practicks* is based on Edinburgh University Library Laing MS. III 388a, with amendments suggested by a collation of that MS. with Edinburgh University Library Laing MS. III 429 and with National Library of Scotland Advocates' MSS. 22.3.4 and 24.1.11. The amendments are indicated in the text by italics: for 'vi' read 'vi^{xx}'; for 'landis', 'auld'; for 'brief', 'schiref'; for 'sic interlocutoris', 'sicitouris'. The consulted MSS. differ only on whether the infeftment was six or six score years old: I have taken six, as the infeftment of Arthur Forbes was in fact only of six years' standing, while one hundred and twenty years would go too far into the past. See below, pp. 65, 78. For the MSS. of Sinclair's *Practicks*, see Murray, 'Sinclair's *Practicks*', 91-2.

[16] See MacQueen, 'Brieve of right', 53-7.

[17] *APS*, ii, 47, c. 2.

Wemyss v. *Forbes*[18]
Ff. 249v.-250r. (28 February 1542/3)
    Ultimo Februarii licet hic subscribitur

Maister Thomas Marioribanks, prolocutour for the lard of Reres in the actioun and caus persewit be Patrik Wemis of Pettincreif aganis him, protestit for all his defens in the mater swa that be the proponing of ane he intendis not to pas fra utheris.

It was allegit be Maister Thomas Marioribanks, prolocutour for Arthour Forbcs of Reres in the actioun and caus movit be Patrik Wemis aganis him tuiching the reductioun of the said Arthour's infeftmentis, allegit the said mater was auld and that the lordis war na competent jugis thareto, becaus thare was divers sesingis, retouris and infeftmentis past thareupoun and as yit standing unredusit. The lordis be sentence interlocutour decernis that thai ar jugis competent in the said mater as it cumis befor thaim. Maister Hew Rig, prolocutour for the said Patrik Wemis, askit instrumentis of the said interlocutour. Maister Thomas Marioribanks protestit for remeid.

Maister Thomas Marioribanks, prolocutour forsaid, askit documentis of the productioune of ane decrete, berand that Arthour Forbes suld be put in possessioun of the landis of Reres and utheris that war recognist, and remane with the said possessioun as he was of befor, without preiudice of the ground rycht clamit be the said Jhone Wemis ay and quhill thai be recoverit be him fra the said Arthour; quhilk decrete was of the dait, at Edinburgh the xxi day of October the yere of God i^m iiii^c Lxxxvii yeris. [1487]

Maister Hew Rig, prolocutour for Patrik Wemis, askit instrumentis of the dait of the charter producit be the lard of Reres, maid to Elizabeth Wemis, lauchfull apperand air of Thomas Wemis of Reres, knycht, and doychter of umquhile Michell Wemis, his eldest sone, and of all the landis and barony of Lucheris Wemis, with tenentis and tenendriis, viz, Westhouss and the thrid part of the landis of Balbuthy, the kirktoun of Lucheris, the Myltoun, Pursk, and Baltongue, lie Brigend, le Auld Muris, lie Nethir Muris, with pendiklis and pertinentis, Stratheboyis, Nethir Pirnie; quhilkis landis of Lucheris Wemis with pendiklis etc was the said Thomas and Margaret his spous in coniunctfeftment and resignit, reservand the frank to the said Thomas and Margaret of Lucheris Wemis, and reservand the frank of the landis of Strathboyis and Nethir Pirny to the said Thomas and reservand the terce to the said Margret; quhilk was of the dait, apud Edinburgh secundo Septembris, anno etc iiii^c Lxxvii^o [1477: see *Reg. Mag. Sig.* [*RMS*], ii, no. 1304]; and of the uther charter maid be [read 'to'] Arthour Forbes of the landis of Reres cum tenentibus tenendriis etc, Fawfelds, Frostleys, Bowhill, Cabriswallis, cum molendino et jus patronatus capelle de Rires que fuerunt Thome de Wemis de Reras militis hereditarie et resignata, reservato

---

[18] Scottish Record Office, CS. 7/1/1, ff. 248v.-250r. In editing this record, I have rationalised punctuation and capitalisation in accordance with modern conventions. The term 'frank' which appears in the text is shorthand for 'frank tenement', to be equated with the Latin *liberum tenementum* and our modern liferent. On this terminology see T. M. Cooper, 'Freehold in Scots law', *Jur. Rev.* [*JR*] 57 (1945), 1-5 and W. C. Dickinson, 'Freehold in Scots law', *JR* 57 (1945), 135-51, especially 142 ff.

tenemento dicto Thome et reservata tercia Margrete Malvile, sponse sue, apud Edinburgh secundo Septembris anno etc Lxxvii° [1477: see *RMS*, ii, no. 1305]; and of the instrument of sesing of Arthour Forbes of all and hale the landis of Reres except the annuale rent of viii markis thareof and jus patronatus pertening to the airis of umquhile Thomas Wemis of Bowhill [read 'Pettincreif'? — see *RMS*, ii, no. 3052] with the myln of Reres cum presentatione juris patronatus capelle de Reres cum pendiculis quhilk was the xiii° Aprilis anno etc xxxvii° [1537]; and of the uther instrument of sesing of Elizabeth Wemis, narrest and lauchfull air of Thomas Wemis of Reres, knycht, and sone [read 'doychter'] of umquhile Thomas [read 'Michell'] Wemis, his eldest sone, of all and hale the landis and barony of Lucheris Wemis cum tenentiis et tenendriis, viz, the Westhouss, tercia de Balbuthy, lie kirktoun de Lucheris, lie Mylnetoun, Pursk, Baltounye, lie Brigend, lie Auld Muris, Nethir Muris cum pendiculis et pertinentiis, quhilk was at manis of the landis forsaidis the x day of September anno etc iiiiᶜ Lxxvii yeris. [1477]

Maister Thomas Marioribanks askit instrumentis that he producit ane contrair and desirat per modum dilatorie contrar Patricium Wemis ane terme to call his warand conform to the tenour of the samin becaus it is maid titulo oneroso. Maister Hew Rig askit instrumentis and protestit that the lard of Reres suld haif na terme assignit to him to call Patrik Wemis quha persewis him for his warand.

Ff. 248v.-249r. (5 March 1542/3)

In the actioun and cause persewit be Patrik Wemys of Pettincreif, air male and of talze to umquhile David Wemys of Pettincreif, and als air and successour male and of talze of umquhile Thomas Wemys of Pettincreif, his fader, fiar of the landis and baronyis of Reras, Lucheors Wemys and utheris underwrittin, aganis Arthur Forbes, now pretendit lard of Reras, air to umquhile William Forbes of Reras, knycht, his gudschir, the sone and air of umquhile Arthur Forbes of Reras and Elizabeth Wemys his spouse, and als the said Arthur as air and successour to the said umquhile William his gudschir, Arthur his grandschir and Elizabeth Wemys his grantdame, to bring with him and produce before the lordis of counsale the tua pretendit charteris and infeftmentis with the sesingis thareof, gif ony past thareupoun; that is to say, ane of the saidis pretendit charteris and infeftmentis thirof maid and gevin be umquhile King James the thrid of gud mynde, quhom God assolze, to umquhile Elizabeth Wemys, allegit lauchfull air to umquhile Schir Thomas Wemys of Reras, knycht, and to hir airis heretably of all and hale the landis and baronyis of Luchris Wemys, with tenentis and tenendryis thareof, viz, the Westhouss, and thrid part of the landis of Balbuthy and kirktoun of Lucheris, Mylntoun, Pursk, Baltunny and Briglandis, the Auld Muris and Nether Muris, with the pendiklis and pertinentis thareof, liand within the schirefdome of Fiffe, the landis of Strathyboyis and Nether Perny with the pertinentis liand within the erldome of Strathearn and schirefdome of Perth [*RMS*, ii, no. 1304]; and that uther pretendit charter and infeftment maid be the said umquhile King James the thrid of gud mynde forsaid, to the said umquhile Arthur Forbes, spouse to the said Elizabeth, to his airis heretablie of the landis and lardship of Reras, with the tenentis and tenendryis thareof, that is to say, the manys of Reras and Fawfeldis, the Frostleyis, Bowhill, Cabiriswallis, with the mylnis of the samin, and with the presentatioun of the chaplanrie of Reras, maid and gevin be resignatioun [*RMS*, ii, no. 1305]; to be sene and considerit, and to heir and see baith the saidis tua pretendit charteris and infeftmentis be retretit, rescindit, cassit and adnullit for divers resounis and causis, likas at mair lenth is contenit in the summondis, actis and lettres maid thiruppoun of before. Baith the saidis partyis being personaly present, the said Arthur producit ane indenture maid at Edinburgh the x day of July the yere of God i^{m}v^{c}vi yeris [1506: see *RMS*, ii, no. 3052] betuix umquhile William Forbes of Reras, knycht, on thar ane part, and Thomas Wemys of Pettincreif on thar uther part, quhilk is maid titulo oneroso, and tharefor desires ane terme to call the said umquhile Thomas Wemys airis quhatsumever for his warand. Therfor the lordis of counsale assignis to the said Arthur Forbes the xxv day of Aprile next tocum with continuation of dayis, to call the airis of the said umquhile Thomas Wemys quhatsumever for his warand, as he may of law, and to have summondis to that effect as he pless to libell; and in the meantyme continewis the said mater in the sammin forme, forss and effect as it is now but preiudice of party. And the partyis prolocutouris and thare procuratouris ar warnit heirof apud acta.

The record of the case from which this transcript is drawn is to be found in the first volume of the acts and decreets, the series of council and session records which begins in 1542. The case is not recorded in the series known as the *Acta Dominorum Concilii et Sessionis*, where there is a gap between May 1542 and March 1546.[19] The relevant entries in the first volume of the acts and decreets are to be found at folios 248v. to 249r. and at 249v. to 250r. From this, it would seem that protests and pleadings in the case were heard on 28 February 1543, during which the lords decerned that they were competent judges in the case. It is clearly this sitting to which Sinclair's report refers. The final decree, of which Sinclair makes no mention, was given on 5 March. However, in the acts and decreets, the final decree appears first (at ff. 248v.-249r.) and is immediately followed by the earlier pleadings and interlocutors (at ff. 249v.-250r.). This is not uncharacteristic of the first volume of the acts and decreets, it would seem, where many entries are similarly inserted out of their chronological place. Such insertions are known as 'licets', because the date of the entry is followed by the words, '*licet hic subscribitur*' (although written here).[20] As will be seen, this practice was followed by the clerk who wrote the record of this case.

No sederunt is given for 28 February. However the sederunt for 5 March includes John Sinclair as dean of Restalrig.[21] Sinclair was also sitting on 20 and 26 February,[22] so that it seems likely that he was on the bench which heard the pleadings on the 28th. This lends credence to his statements about the argument advanced on behalf of Forbes of Reres at this sitting concerning the jurisdiction

[19] The present classification of the council and session records in the Scottish Record Office, created by Thomas Thomson, masks their essential unity. It is hoped that the tangle will be unravelled in the near future by Dr. A. L. Murray.
[20] I am indebted to Dr. Murray for this information.
[21] Scottish Record Office, CS. 7/1/1, fo. 240v.; also RH. 2/1/9, p. 76.
[22] Scottish Record Office, RH. 2/1/9, p. 75.

of the lords to reduce old infeftments. There seems to be no further record of the case: the court did not sit on 'the xxv day of Aprile next'. It would appear that Patrick Wemyss, confronted with the somewhat paradoxical position whereby he had to warrant Arthur Forbes against his own action, conceded defeat. Certainly in subsequent charters in the great seal register we find the Forbeses continuing to hold the barony of Reres as well as the barony thereafter known as Leuchars Forbes.[23] The family is known as Forbes of Reres while their erstwhile opponents continue as Wemyss of Pittencrieff.[24]

Yet the baronies of Reres and Leuchars had both belonged to the Wemyss family at one time, as can be seen from the record of the case. It was an action of reduction of two 'pretendit charteris and infeftmentis with the sesingis thirof', granted by James III (king from 1460 to 1488) to Arthur Forbes and to his wife, Elizabeth Wemyss. The charters in question were, as indicated in the transcript above, recorded in the register of the great seal and are printed in the second volume of the *Registrum Magni Sigilli* series. Examination of these and other records reveals that the 1543 action was the culmination of a dispute which had been going on since the late 1470s and which had its origins in the apparent attempts of the Wemyss family to prevent the diminution of their heritage.

The situation in which the family of Sir Thomas Wemyss of Reres found itself in the 1460s was seemingly accurately summarised in the nineteenth century by the family historian, Sir William Fraser.[25] Sir Thomas, who was married to Margaret Melville, had five sons. The eldest was Michael, who predeceased his father, leaving a daughter, Elizabeth. The next three were John, Thomas and Alexander, and the youngest was Andrew. Finally, there was a daughter, Margaret. Sir Thomas held the lands of Reres and Leuchars in Fife, as well as a number of other properties, in chief of the crown. Leuchars had been granted to his great-great-grandfather, John Wemyss (a cadet of the family of Wemyss of Wemyss) by Robert I.[26] Reres had been acquired by Sir Thomas' grandfather from another branch of the Wemyss family by resignation in the 1370s. It was held of the earls of Fife, but in 1425 the earldom had been forfeited on the execution of Murdoch Stewart by James I and, in accordance with an act of 1401, all its constituent baronies would thereafter have been held of the crown.[27] There was, then, no doubt about Sir Thomas' title to the lands in the 1460s.

---

[23] *RMS*, iv, nos. 584, 585 and 3033.

[24] *RMS*, iv, nos. 650, 1311, 1529, 2339 and 2687.

[25] W. Fraser, *Memorials of the Family of Wemyss of Wemyss* (Edinburgh, 1888), i, 60-1; but see below p. 71, where it is suggested that Michael, the eldest son, was not the son of Margaret Melville.

[26] *RMS*, i, app. 2, no. 488; also nos. 1734 and 1742. The lands which formed the barony of Leuchars Wemyss can only be partly identified today. Milton, Pursk and Balmullo are all just to the south west of the modern town of Leuchars, Fife. The 'auld' and 'nether' muirs are now covered by the Tentsmuir forest, to the north east. Whitecroft may have been between the muirs and Leuchars, near Cast and Wards. Westhouse was on what is now Leuchars airfield. Brigende is also no longer in existence; it may have been at Morton Lochs in the north, or between Guardbridge and Inner Bridge to the south.

[27] Fraser, *Wemyss* ii 15-17; ibid., 29; *RMS*, i, nos. 870, 871; *Scots Peerage* iv 15; *APS*, i, 576. Reres is modern Rires farm in Kilconquhar parish, Fife. There is also a Reres wood to the east of Leuchars today. In the 18th century the farm belonged to Alexander Bayne, first professor of Scots Law at Edinburgh University: *JR* 36 (1924) at 62. The 'Faufeldis' are represented today by Northtown of Falfield, Falfield, Falfield Bank and South Falfield, to the north west of Rires farm. Nearby, to the east, are North Bowhill and South Bowhill Farm. The other parts of the lands of Reres have not been identified.

The immediate problem for Sir Thomas at that time was most likely caused by the death of his eldest son Michael, which left his grand-daughter, Elizabeth, as heir to his lands. This opened up the possibility of the lands being carried out of Wemyss hands should Elizabeth marry; moreover his four surviving sons were as yet unprovided for. It seems probable that Sir Thomas' actions were guided chiefly by anxiety to preserve the heritage of his line, to defeat the possibility of Elizabeth inheriting on his death, and to confer landed status upon his sons.

His first step was to make provision for his eldest surviving son. In July 1466 he resigned his lands of Pittencrieff to the king, who regranted them to John Wemyss and his wife, Elizabeth Dishington, in conjunct fee. Significantly, John is here described as the 'son and apparent heir' of Sir Thomas, suggesting that some attempt was being made to obscure the claims of Elizabeth Wemyss.[28] The next entry in the register of the great seal is the king's confirmation of an entail by Sir Thomas in favour of his sons, over the third part of the lands of 'Luchris Wemis . . . Logymuirtho, Westir Cruvy, Reras and le twa Faufeildis' in the sheriffdom of Fife, and the lands of 'Strathboys and Nethirpurny in the earldom of Strathearn in the sheriffdom of Perth'. Sir Thomas would hold the lands for life, and on his death they would pass to John (again described as his son and apparent heir) and the 'heirs male of his body lawfully begotten'. If John's line failed, then the lands would pass to his brother Thomas and his heirs male, whom failing, to the next son Alexander and his heirs male. If all these failed, the lands were to pass to their father's lawfully begotten heirs male — that is, to any other sons; and if they failed, then the lands should pass to the 'lawful and nearest heirs male' of Sir Thomas whomsoever.[29]

Sir Thomas was clearly anxious to ensure the passage of these lands to male heirs, but he did not forget the needs of his wife, Margaret Melville. In the entail he was careful to reserve a terce for her which, given that he had deprived himself of the fee, she would otherwise have been unable to claim. Moreover in the following year the king confirmed that Sir Thomas and Margaret were jointly to hold a third part of the lands of 'Luchristoune, Westhouse, Brodeland, Mylnetoun, Pursk, Balcougye, Brigend, Toftis and Muris, also the lands of Logymurtho and Westercruvy'. Presumably this third part was quite separate from the third entailed in 1466. The grant was expressed in the classic terms of a conjunct infeftment, that is, to man and wife and the longer liver of them and, after their decease, by the lawful and nearest heirs of Thomas whomsoever — which would therefore enable Elizabeth to take the lands in due course.[30] It was presumably to defeat this possibility that in September 1473 the provisions relating to the succession to these lands were adjusted; they were to be held after the decease of the conjunct fiars by the true and lawful heirs of Sir Thomas 'as contained in the old entail'[31] — that is, the entail of 1466 in favour of Sir Thomas' surviving sons and the male line.

[28] *RMS* ii no. 881. Pittencrieff was to the west of medieval Dunfermline. For its history as a Wemyss possession, see *Regality of Dunfermline Court Book 1531-1538*, edd. J. M. Webster and A. A. M. Duncan (Dunfermline, 1953), 156-7. It is to be distinguished from the Pittencrieff just north of Cupar, Fife, which was owned by the Spens family. See *Dunfermline Court Bk*, 184 and *Sheriff Court Book of Fife 1515-22*, ed. W. C. Dickinson (SHS, 1928), 250-1.

[29] *RMS*, ii, no. 882. The Strathearn lands are Strathy and Pairney, by Aberuthven, Perthshire.

[30] *RMS*, ii, no. 900.

[31] *RMS*, ii, no. 1139.

In July 1476 the king again confirmed the entail of 1466, as well as what appear to be two further gifts of lands to his heirs of entail by Sir Thomas, by which he divested himself of half parts of both the lands of Leuchars, and the lands of Reres, reserving to himself only a life interest.[32] In effect Sir Thomas was rearranging the settlements of 1466 and 1467 so far as the first gift was concerned. The lands of Leuchars, in one third of which Sir Thomas had retained a life interest, and another third of which pertained to his wife and himself in conjunct fee, were now given over to the extent of one half to the heirs of entail. Not all of this could have come from the remaining third which was presumably still Sir Thomas' heritage. It is difficult therefore to see how this gift was worked out on the ground. The second donation adds half of the lands of Reres to the one third entailed in 1466. Presumably this left one sixth to Sir Thomas, and, in due course, to Elizabeth, in heritage.

It is apparent throughout these transactions that Sir Thomas was acting in favour of his surviving sons, seeking to control the inheritance of his lands, and thereby depriving Elizabeth of lands which at common law would have come to her on the death of her grandfather. We do not know to what extent Sir Thomas was acting as a free agent in these transactions. It is possible that he may have been coerced by his sons; it is perhaps more likely that he acted out of paternal concern for them and to prevent the lands passing out of the Wemyss family, as they would should Elizabeth marry. Whatever the motivating force which lay behind them, the arrangements made by Sir Thomas were struck down in a series of charters granted by James III on 1 and 2 September 1477. The first of these suggests that the actions of Sir Thomas had all been of his own accord. It narrates that 'the king, through the lamentable story told him by Thomas Wemyss of Reras, knight, understands that the same Thomas, through evil zeal and against good conscience, had a certain entail made for his second-born son John of Wemyss, in disinheritance of Elizabeth of Wemyss, lawful and nearest apparent heir of the same Thomas and daughter of the late Michael of Wemyss his first-born son'. After listing all the lands which had been involved from 1466 to 1476, the charter continues:[33]

> Therefore, considering the foregoing and because having constituted several other gifts in less age etc, the king grants, by authority of parliament and on the deliberation of the three estates of the realm, and being in his perfect age of twenty five years, and revokes the said grants and infeftments, and especially he revokes and annuls the said entail and infeftment of the foresaid lands to the said John of Wemyss and all charters, sasines, etc. given to the said John of the said lands or any part thereof.

There are a number of points to be made about this royal act. It appears to be an exercise of the privilege in law whereby the transactions of one's minority (or less age) may be revoked — a privilege of which the fifteenth-century Stewart kings made extensive use. But such revocations could only be made during the *quadriennium utile* — that is, during the four years following a man's twenty-first birthday. The twenty-fifth birthday therefore marked the end of the privilege and

[32] *RMS*, ii, no. 1245.
[33] *RMS*, ii, no. 1302.

the attainment of a man's 'perfect age'. It is important to observe that this landmark had been reached by James III in May 1477, three months *before* this particular revocation.[34] There must accordingly be some doubt as to its legality, at least on that ground. The reference to the 'authority of parliament' must mean the act of revocation passed in July 1476, which revoked all previous grants (including entails) prejudicial to the crown.[35] But this act, which was clearly an exercise of the king's rights within the *quadriennium utile*, was passed on the very day — 10 July — on which the king had confirmed the arrangements made by Sir Thomas in favour of his sons. Presumably therefore the confirmation represented an exemption of those arrangements from the provisions of the act. Moreover that confirmation could be seen as an act of majority by the king ratifying the acts of his minority; in which case it could be argued that he was barred from any subsequent revocation. To this the answer might be that the king's confirmation was given in ignorance of the position of Elizabeth Wemyss and of Sir Thomas' 'evil zeal' to disinherit her. Certainly it was relevant that nowhere had there been any indication of consent to the arrangements by Elizabeth as heir, which might have been thought necessary to their validity.[36]

It is also worth noting that the revocation appears to apply only to grants made in the king's minority and in particular to those in favour of John Wemyss. What then of the confirmation of September 1473 (after the king's twenty-first birthday which would be in May of that year) by which Sir Thomas and Margaret Melville were to hold lands in Leuchars in conjunct fee? It was true that this provided for the succession of the heirs of Sir Thomas as contained in the entail of 1466, which was certainly struck down by the revocation if valid; but in its other aspects the grant could still be regarded as unaffected by what the king had done. Succession to that might be covered by the common law if the words of the confirmation on the point could not be applied.

This seems to be borne out by the subsequent action of the king in relation to Leuchars. The lands were granted to Elizabeth, following a resignation by Thomas *and* Margaret. Moreover a liferent was reserved to them jointly and to the longer liver. This suggests that the confirmation of 1473 was still seen as essentially valid despite the revocation. Such a conclusion is further supported by the fact that Elizabeth was also given Sir Thomas' lands in Strathearn but this time under reservation of a liferent to her grandfather only and of a mere terce to Margaret.[37] She had never had any right to them, and accordingly the resignation of them to the king was carried out by Sir Thomas alone.

The king made two further grants of Sir Thomas' lands. In one he gave the demesne lands (*terras dominii*) of Reres to a certain Arthur Forbes, following the resignation of Sir Thomas. Again a liferent was reserved for him and a reasonable terce to Margaret.[38] It is clear that it was reduction of this charter and of the one

[34] A. I. Dunlop, 'The date of the birth of James III', *SHR* 30 (1951), 201-4; N. A. T. Macdougall, *James III: A Political Study* (Edinburgh 1982), 7 and 125.
[35] *APS*, ii, 113.
[36] See *Regiam Majestatem*, bk. II, cc. 15 and 16 for the requirement of the heir's consent to the alienation of heritage. Here the *Regiam* follows Glanvill, but the rule disappeared in England subsequently: see A. W. B. Simpson, *Introduction to the History of the Land Law* (Oxford 1961) 48-9. It is unclear what happened in Scotland but see e.g. *RMS*, i, no. 882, a grant of 1407.
[37] *RMS*, ii, no. 1304.
[38] *RMS*, ii, no. 1305.

in favour of Elizabeth Wemyss which was sought in the litigation of 1543. Finally, there was a charter in favour of Andrew Wemyss, the youngest son of Thomas and Margaret. He was given the lands of 'Myrecarny, Westircruvy, Logymurthto and Brighous'. Some at least of these lands were part of the barony of Leuchars; they were accordingly given to Andrew after a resignation by both Sir Thomas and Margaret and with the reservation of a joint liferent to them and to the survivor.[39] This again bears out the view that as a result of the confirmation of 1473 Sir Thomas and Margaret had a conjunct fee in Leuchars and that this was unaffected by the revocation of 1477.

If this be accepted, then the destination in Andrew's charter regarding the succession to his lands becomes even more interesting than it already is by virtue of the fact that it gives us additional information about the family of Wemyss — information not noted by Sir William Fraser. The lands are to be held by Andrew and his heirs, whom failing the heirs lawfully begotten by Thomas and Margaret whomsoever, whom failing to Elizabeth and her lawful heirs whomsoever. This seems to suggest that Elizabeth could not have taken as heir to an heir lawfully begotten by Thomas and Margaret, but had to have a special provision in her favour. In other words her father Michael was not a son of Thomas and Margaret, but rather of a previous marriage of the former. The significance of this for subsequent developments should not be underestimated. If the king's revocation was ineffective, then so were the grants which had followed it. The entail of 1466 might be invalid also, whether or not the revocation stood, since the common law heir, Elizabeth, had not given her consent. But the confirmation of Leuchars in conjunct fee would stand even if entail, royal revocation and post-revocation grants all fell. Who then would be entitled to succeed to Leuchars on the death of the conjunct fiars?

The answer to this would not have been clear-cut in later law, and was said by Craig to depend upon the intention of the parties. He stated that there was a strong presumption that the heirs of the husband, as opposed to the heirs of the wife, should take on the deaths of the conjunct fiars.[40] But this arose from Craig's own favouring of the view that the feudal fee could only vest in one person at a time and that male should be preferred to female. It is far from clear that medieval conveyancers setting up a conjunct fee would have subscribed to the former of these points. They would be more likely to have seen the conjunct fee as a means of providing something beyond terce for the widow and lands for the children of the marriage.[41] Thus, while Elizabeth was undoubtedly heir to Sir Thomas, this did not necessarily mean that she could take Leuchars on the death of her grandparents. The children of Margaret Melville by Sir Thomas might have a preferable claim.

However so long as the revocation and subsequent grants stood these questions could not arise. The pleadings of 1543 tell us that Elizabeth was infeft in Leuchars on 10 September 1477. They also tell us that she was married to

---

[39] *RMS*, ii, no. 1303. Myrecairnie is some two miles north of Cupar, Fife, while Logie, Brighouse and Cruivie are all within a couple of miles of each other to the north east.

[40] Craig, *Jus Feudale*, II, 22, 6. Craig's view seems to have settled the law: Stair, *Institutions*, II, 3, 41; Erskine, *Institutes*, III, 8, 36.

[41] Compare the English jointure. See K. B. McFarlane, *The Nobility of Later Medieval England* (Oxford, 1973), 64-8.

Arthur Forbes, who had received Reres. This is borne out by an entry in the register of the privy seal in 1502, which speaks of Forbes enjoying the lands of 'Strathiboyis and Nethirpirny' in Strathearn by the courtesy of Scotland through the decease of his spouse Elizabeth Wemyss, 'heretar' of the said lands.[42] Elizabeth, it will be recalled, received these lands in 1477. It is possible that Forbes received Reres because he was already Elizabeth's husband, but this seems to be contradicted by a case in June 1478 before the auditors of causes and complaints.[43] Here Sir Thomas Wemyss, Margaret Melville and Elizabeth were pursuing an assize for error in the service of a brieve of inquest. The assize had apparently declared that Arthur Forbes was 'ourelord' of certain lands in Leuchars. The auditors decreed:

> The said persons of inquest has errit in the serving of the said breve because it was declarit be our souverain lordis charter schewin and producit befor thaim that the said Arthur was never in the barony of Luchris Wemis quhar throw he mycht be ourelord of the said landis.

This was a manifestly correct decision, but the appearance of Elizabeth as one of the pursuers is not inconsistent with the view that she was already married to Forbes. It was her grandparents as liferenters who would act as overlords in Leuchars and the action was probably brought at their instigation. But since Elizabeth held the fee, her name would be brought into the action for her interest. The confusion of the assize could hardly have arisen unless she were married to Forbes, since the marriage would have given him managerial powers over her heritage even while she was alive.

The next significant event in the history of this dispute was the death of Sir Thomas Wemyss sometime before March 1479. In that month Arthur Forbes raised an action of spuilzie against John and Thomas Wemyss, 'sons to umquhile Schir Thomas of Wemis of Reras'. The brothers were accused of taking thirty oxen and large quantities of crops 'out of the maynis of Reras'. Now by the charter of 1477 the death of Sir Thomas should have given Forbes a title to Reres burdened only by the terce of Margaret Melville. Nevertheless the case was 'Referrit and Remittit be the lordis of counsale to be determit before the Juge ordinare because the landis that the said gudis was takin of Is clamyt fee and heretage be baith the said parties and the questioun of the Richt dependis apoun heretage'.[44] Clearly therefore John and Thomas were putting in some sort of claim to Reres. We do not know the result of any litigation before the judge ordinary; but in October 1479 John of Wemyss had again been summoned by Arthur Forbes 'anent the taking and intrometting with the house and place of Reras and braking and casting doune of the office house of the samyn'.[45]

The picture was further complicated by the rapid remarriage of Sir Thomas' widow, Margaret Melville, with Baldred Blackadder. Having survived Sir Thomas, Margaret was entitled to liferents of the barony of Leuchars-Wemyss and of the lands of Myrecairnie, Wester Cruivie, Logiemurtho and the

---

[42] *Reg. Sec. Sig.* [*RSS*], i, no. 868.
[43] *Acts of Lords Auditors* [*ADA*], 65.
[44] *Acts of Council* [*ADC*], i, 22.
[45] *ADA*, 93.

Brighouse, as well as to terce in the lands of Reres, Strathibois and Nether Pirny. She was in short a well-endowed lady, which doubtless accounts for the speed with which she remarried. A husband would be able to assist in protecting her rights, and these would also make her an attractive proposition for any suitor. Certainly Margaret's new husband appears to have been solicitous of her rights, for in October 1479 he too was suing John Wemyss 'for spuilzie of certain vitalis pertaining to him be Resoun of his wif and hir malis of the barony of the Luchris'.[46] At the same time Baldred also sued John's son, David, for taking three oxen from the lands of Myrecairnie.[47] In the following year, John was found liable to pay Baldred forty marks,[48] but himself sued John and Adam Anderson for the spuilzie and wrongful withholding of an annual due to him from the lands of 'Perthyok' (presumably Pursk in the barony of Leuchars). The case was remitted to the judge ordinary by council, 'becaus it is fe and heretage and kan nocht be decidit but one of the partiis be hurt in the richt of thir heretage'.[49] It is not clear if this case was connected with any dispute over the lands of Sir Thomas, but it does illustrate how an action of spuilzie might be an incident of a contest of right.

It seems clear from all this that each of the parties was seeking to exercise rights in the various lands in order to maintain his or her claim. Equally this had to be challenged by the other claimants; normally, it would seem, by an action of spuilzie. The most significant contest was that between Arthur Forbes and his wife on the one hand and John Wemyss on the other, since the interest of Margaret Melville and Baldred Blackadder would only endure for the former's lifetime. It is interesting to note that John put forward a claim to both Reres and Leuchars immediately upon the death of Sir Thomas, suggesting that he sought to rely upon the entail of 1466 and its subsequent additions. There could be no other basis for a claim to Reres by him. The claim to Leuchars was complicated by the holding of the still-surviving Margaret Melville, but it could nevertheless be argued that his father's death had given John a right of fee, albeit one burdened by the widow's liferent. All this would of course depend on whether or not the entail had been validly struck down in 1477.

It may be noted that Arthur Forbes seems to have adopted a policy to take account of the contingency that the revocation and subsequent grants of 1477 might be held to have no legal foundation. Thus in 1480 Baldred Blackadder sued a certain James Bonar for spuilzie of the lands of Wester Cruivie.[50] Now, as we have seen, by the royal grant of 1477 Andrew Wemyss held the fee of Wester Cruivie subject to Margaret Melville's liferent; this would be the basis of Blackadder's action. Nevertheless council remitted the case against Bonar to the judge ordinary because the question touched his entry and the problem of identifying his overlord; a matter depending, as was pointed out, on the heritage. Bonar then produced 'a letter of testimoniale schewand that he was enterit as are to his fader ... be Arthur of Forbace as his oure lord'.[51] Now under the

---

[46] *ADA*, 93; *ADC*, i, 37.
[47] *ADA*, 93; *ADC*, i, 39, 80.
[48] *ADC*, i, 66, 48. See also ibid., 108*.
[49] *ADC*, i, 63.
[50] *ADC*, i, 65.
[51] *ADC*, i, 66.

arrangements of 1477 Forbes' wife had only a future interest in Wester Cruivie as a possible heir of entail, and this would provide no justification for his action. If however these arrangements were set aside, then new issues would arise. Were the entail arrangements valid, given that the consent of the heir-at-law Elizabeth had not been obtained? If they were not, then Elizabeth would have a *prima facie* claim to the fee of Wester Cruivie and to the superiority of its tenants. But even then the issue was far from clear, since Wester Cruivie was part of Leuchars in which, apparently regardless of what had happened in 1477, Margaret Melville was a conjunct fiar. The question of whether Elizabeth could succeed to the fee on Margaret's death was, as we have seen, debatable. Little wonder then that council declined to entertain Blackadder's action of spuilzie which clearly turned on much deeper questions of title.

Probably by this time the whole complex issue had become focussed by the commencement of procedures to determine the various claims, for in April 1481 the dispute over Reres reached parliament. From a procedural point of view, however, it was still at a very early stage. The record of the parliamentary proceedings makes it clear that the debate was still only about who should have possession of the lands until the question of right was settled. When the ownership of lands was in dispute, it was the law that the superior should recognosce them into his own hands and 'let them to borgh' to the last lawful possessor: that is to say, the last lawful possessor would be given possession once he had found caution that the lands would ultimately be handed over to the person who had established his right of ownership. The question of who had been the last lawful possessor could of course be the subject of litigation just as much as the question of right,[52] and it was this which was at issue in 1481. John and Arthur were unable to agree on who the judge should be and upon which of them should be the pursuer or the defender on this point. Parliament continued the case, but decided that the lands of Reres should be recognosced by the king, 'for staynchin of debate betuix the saide partiis but nocht lattin thaim to borgh to nowther of thame'.[53]

The question was still at issue in 1485 when Arthur sued John before council 'anent the asking of the landis of Reris to borgh quhilkis ar Recognist in our soverane lordis handis for the debatis betuix the said partiis'. It would seem that John was now in possession for it was 'complenit be the said Arthur that the hous of Reras Is takin fra him be uncoursable lettrez purchest be the said Johne of Wemis'.[54] The outcome of this seems to have been the recovery of possession by Forbes. According to the pleadings of 1543, there was a decreet on 21 October 1487 that he should be put in possession of Reres. This is borne out by the records of the parliamentary auditors which in 1491 state 'that our soverane lordis faider quham god assolze let the said landis of Reres to borgh to the said Arthure Forbes efter Congnitioun of the cause him self sittand in Jugement'.[55]

This decision of the king was of course far from settling the question of right

[52] On recognition see *APS*, i, 492; *APS*, i, 575; *APS*, ii, 37, c. 18; *APS*, ii, 47, c. 2.
[53] *APS*, ii, 134.
[54] *ADC*, i, *107.
[55] *ADA*, 159. No conciliar records are extant from April 1485 to July 1488 inclusive to give us any information on the decreet by which Arthur Forbes gained possession of Reres.

between John and Arthur. Its effect was to put Arthur in possession and to compel John to establish his claim. By October 1488 John was suing Arthur before council although the cause of action is not specified in the record and indeed the pursuer failed to compear.[56] However it is unlikely that this represents a stage in any claim of right by John, since, as we have seen in the history of this case, it was firmly established that council had no jurisdiction to determine such questions of fee and heritage. Instead John would be obliged to raise an action by some pleadable brieve.[57] He could not have used the brieve of dissasine since, even if he had had possession of Reres, he had been put out by a judgment in favour of Forbes. By a statute of 1430[58] he could not use the brieve of mortancestor, which was available only to lineal heirs and not to heirs of entail. In any case the ancestor from whom his claim was derived had not died vest and saised of Reres as of fee. This would leave only the brieve of right. We do not know whether an heir of entail could gain entry to his lands by this brieve, although we may speculate that if he could, he would also have been able to challenge the title of the defender. The nature of the heir of entail's right may well have been a subject of debate in fifteenth-century Scotland. The act of 1430 suggests that it had been previously regarded as a fee, comparable to that of the heir of line and therefore recoverable by the latter's remedies, but is completely silent as to how it should be treated thereafter. In the sixteenth century, the heir of entail entered formally by a brieve of tailzie, the equivalent for him of the lineal heir's brieve of succession, so that plainly lawyers had come to see some differences between the two claims.[59] But in the present state of knowledge about later medieval Scots law, we cannot say much more about how John Wemyss might have proceeded to vindicate his claim. Perhaps he and his advisers were unsure in any case, for there is no evidence to show that any action of right was ever raised by him against Arthur Forbes.

We may note that, at this stage, John was only laying claim to Reres. He seems to have taken no action with regard to Leuchars, presumably because his right under the entail would only vest on the death of Margaret Melville. Perhaps he also hoped to have a claim at common law to those lands, as eldest son and heir of the marriage of Margaret and Sir Thomas Wemyss. We have nothing to show that he was their eldest however, and since John predeceased Margaret when he died sometime before May 1491, he was never able himself to make any further claim to either Leuchars or Reres.

The death of John did not however mean the end of the dispute. His widow took out a brieve of terce for the lands of Reres. The assize ruled that John died 'last vested and sesit as of fee' in these lands and found accordingly that his

---

[56] *ADC*, i, 97.
[57] On the basis of the rule that no man needed to answer for his freeholding except by the king's pleadable brieve: see MacQueen, 'Brieve of right', 64.
[58] Not in *APS*, but printed in W. C. Dickinson, 'The acts of the parliament at Perth 6 March 1429/30', *SHR* 29 (1950), 1-12 at 5.
[59] The nature of the difference is however obscure. See Dickinson, *art. cit.*, 8 and references there given. The subject clearly needs more detailed discussion and research than is possible here. See also H. L. MacQueen, 'Dissasine and mortancestor in Scots law', *Journal of Legal History* 4 (1983) 21*-49* at 36*-8*, also printed in *New Perspectives in Scottish Legal History*, edd. A. Kiralfy and H. L. MacQueen (London, 1984).

widow was entitled to a terce. Arthur Forbes sued the assize for error, arguing that the lands pertained to him heritably. The verdict of the assize was overturned, although it was noted that Arthur only held the lands in borgh.[60]

The continuing possibility of a challenge to his right to Reres may have guided other actions by Arthur Forbes at this time. In October 1491 he made an agreement with Baldred Blackadder and Thomas Wemyss regarding corns on the third of Reres. Thomas was the heir of John,[61] and his involvement in this agreement suggests some anxiety on the part of Arthur to reach a settlement. However it is indicative of his tense relations with the Wemyss family that he and Thomas each gave lawburrows as part of the agreement that the one would be 'scaithless' of the other.[62] Similarly in March 1491, Andrew Wemyss of Myrecairnie, John's youngest brother, had found lawburrows that Arthur would be 'harmeles and scaithles of him and all that he may let but fraude or gile, baith in his persone and his servitoris personis gudis and landis of Reres bot as the course of commoun law will, under the pain of ane thousand pundis'.[63] The large amount of the penalty suggests some fairly serious transgressions or threats in the past.

The appearance of Baldred Blackadder in the agreement of October 1491 is a reminder that Margaret Melville was still to the fore with her terce of Reres and her liferent of Leuchars. Undoubtedly this was also an irritation calculated to disturb Arthur Forbes' peaceful possession of his rights. This must have been particularly true after the death of his wife, which left him with only the courtesy of Leuchars. There is some indication that he sought to eliminate Margaret's interest in Reres by taking a tack or assedation of her terce.[64] Leuchars, in which each of the parties had a life interest, was more contentious. The issue seems to have been focussed by the Ramsays of Brackmont, owners of lands just over a mile to the west of Leuchars. In October 1493, Arthur and Margaret were both sued by Ramsay 'to schew quhat richtis ilkeane of thaim has of the superiorite of the landis of Brakmont', but the case was continued and remained at issue in November 1495.[65] Thereafter nothing more is heard of it until April 1498. By this time, it seems, Arthur too had died, for the action was continued so that James Stewart, the Duke of Ross and Archbishop of St. Andrews, 'quhilkis has the ward of the landis and mariage of Arthur of Forbes ayeris be gift of our soverane lord', could be called for his interest.[66] A couple of days later, Margaret and Baldred appointed their procurators for the action. At the same time John lord

[60] *ADA*, 159.
[61] See *RSS*, i, no. 220.
[62] *ADC*, i, 205.
[63] *ADC*, i, 182.
[64] W. Robertson, *Parliamentary Records of Scotland* (1804, withdrawn) 499; Scottish Record Office, CS. 5/16, ff. 34v. and 65r. For evidence on the management of Leuchars by Baldred and Margaret, see *ADC*, i, 249. Deteriorating relations between Baldred and Thomas and Andrew Wemyss in the 1490s, perhaps caused by his active control of the long-lived Margaret's lands, are shown by *ADC*, i, 110, 251, 349, 359, 362, and *ADA*, 188.
[65] *ADC*, i, 314, 420. The dating of this latter entry is not affected by the observations of A. A. M. Duncan and M. P. McDiarmid anent the printed record for November 1495: 'Some wrongly dated entries in the Acts of the Lords of Council', *SHR* 33 (1954), 86-8.
[66] *ADC*, ii, 184. For the appointment of James Stewart Duke of Ross as Archbishop of St. Andrews in 1497, see R. Nicholson, *Scotland: The Later Middle Ages* (Edinburgh, 1975), 558.

Drummond produced a charter showing that he held the lands in assedation from Margaret.[67] But in January 1500 the parties agreed that the dispute should be submitted to amicable composition, with Andrew lord Gray, one of the king's justiciars, as 'superior and odman chosin to baith the partiis'.[68] The case was briefly revived in 1501 by Margaret Wemyss, daughter of Margaret Melville and Sir Thomas Wemyss,[69] but receives no further mention in printed records. Presumably Margaret Melville too had died by this time and her various liferents and terces, which would not pass to either her husband or her descendants, would then have ceased to trouble the Forbes possessions.

In his declining years Arthur Forbes appears to have fallen into debt; at any rate he defended a number of actions of payment.[70] In February 1495 the lands of North Falfield, part of the barony of Reres, were apprised by the sheriff for his failure to find 100 pounds as caution against his non-compearance at a justice-ayre in Perth. (His liability for suit there presumably stemmed from the lands of Strathibois and Nether Pirny in Strathearn). The apprised lands were subsequently sold to Andrew Wood of Largo, although it was provided that if Arthur paid the 100 pounds together with expenses within the *septennium* provided for in the act of 1469 anent apprising, he should have full regress to the lands.[71] In 1505 Arthur's heir, William, not only sold North Falfield outright to Wood of Largo and his wife (implying that there had been a re-entry by Forbes within the *septennium*), but he also sold them the lands of Frostleys.[72] Wood was to hold both of William in blench ferme. In 1512 the king confirmed the transaction and it was stated that Wood would hold directly of him in fee.[73]

The death of Arthur Forbes was followed by an inquest before the Fife sheriff court serving his son William as heir to Reres and Leuchars Wemyss as though Arthur had been the heritable proprietor. But Thomas Wemyss of Pittencrieff, son and heir of Arthur's old protagonist John, did not allow this to pass. His action of error against the sheriff and inquest, and William for his interest, came before the lords of council in February 1505, and clearly the familiar objection about the lords' lack of jurisdiction to determine questions of heritage was given another airing. However William and Thomas were persuaded to agree to the lords acting to determine the ground right between them and not to except to their jurisdiction.[74] The hearing was fixed for July 1505, but unfortunately, if it was held the record has not survived, as there is now a gap in the acts of council between May and November of that year. The 1543 record refers to an agreement of July 1506 between William and Thomas, possibly an error for 1505. However, that there was a compromise rather than a judicial determination appears from a royal confirmation under the great seal, made in February 1507, of a charter

---

[67] *ADC*, ii, 190.
[68] *ADC*, ii, 356. For Andrew lord Gray as justiciar from 1497 to 1513 see *RMS*, ii, reign of James IV, witness no. 48; *Exch. Rolls*, xi, 353*; *APS*, ii, 273; *Registrum Episcopatus Glasguensis* (Bannatyne and Maitland Clubs, 1843), no. 488.
[69] *ADC*, ii, 500.
[70] See e.g. *ADC*, i, 328 and *ADA*, 186, 201 (all 1494).
[71] *RMS*, ii, no. 2231. For the 1469 act, see *APS*, ii, 96, c. 12.
[72] *RMS*, ii, no. 2824.
[73] *RMS*, ii, no. 3700. See also *Fife Court Bk.*, 253.
[74] Scottish Record Office, CS. 5/16, ff. 76r.-77r. See also CS. 5/12, ff. 165r.-165v.

dated 28 January 1507 by which William gave Thomas the lands of South
Falfield and an annual rent of eight marks in Reres 'for the renunciation of his
rights' to the lands of 'Reras, Fawfeildis, Frostleys, Bowhill, Cabiris-willis and
Lucheris Wemys'.[75] Thus Thomas appears finally to have abandoned his father's
claim. The terms of the agreement show that the Forbeses were reluctant to
undergo the lengthy procedures which would be necessary to establish their
rights at law; on the other hand they had a strong case and only seem to have
needed to make relatively minor concessions to buy off the Wemyss claim.

From this time the barony of Leuchars seems to have become known as
Leuchars Forbes rather than Leuchars Wemyss, confirming that entrenchment
of the Forbes position had been achieved by the agreement of 1506.[76] However, it
would seem that no title to the lands of Reres was made up until 1537, some sixty
years after the original grant by the king to Arthur Forbes. It appears from a case
of 1533 that Reres had been in non-entry since the death of Sir Thomas Wemyss.
At that time the lands were in the ward of the Archbishop of St. Andrews
following the death of William Forbes ten years previously.[77] The records of the
1543 litigation tell us that the Arthur Forbes who defended that action was
William's grandson and heir,[78] and that he made up titles to Reres on 13 April
1537. Presumably this was after he attained his majority.

On the Wemyss side, we find Thomas of Pittencrieff being succeeded by his
son David, who was followed, in 1517, by his uncle, Patrick, brother of Thomas,
and thus a son of John Wemyss. Patrick was to be the pursuer in 1543. He seems
to have been a familiar at the court of James V and was captain of Inch Garvie
castle in the Firth of Forth as well as a royal ambassador abroad.[79] There is no
sign in any of the records in print that these Wemysses pressed any claim to the
lands which Sir Thomas had held in the mid-fifteenth century, and we must ask
what prompted the apparent revival of the dispute in 1543.

A clue may be provided by the gift which James V made in February 1540 to
David Beaton the Cardinal and Archbishop of St. Andrews, of the non-entries,
maills, fermes, profits and duties of the lands of 'Reras, Fawfields, Frostleys,
Bowhill, Caberiswallis, Leuchars-Wemyss, Netherpirny and Strathibois'. In the
document embodying the gift it is stated that these lands had been in the hands of
the king and his predecessors for non-entry since the deaths of Thomas Wemyss
of Reres, Michael Wemyss and Arthur Forbes, and that Beaton is to have all the
monies due from the lands for this period until the lawful entry of the rightful heir
or of heirs of lawful age.[80] Now if Arthur Forbes had entered the lands of Reres in
1537, then this gift of the king was in part at least illegal. Questions must remain

---

[75] *RMS*, ii, no. 3052. This enabled Forbes to exercise an unquestioned right of superiority over the
   Ramsays of Brackmont: see *RMS*, ii, no. 3834.
[76] See *RMS*, ii, no. 3499.
[77] *Acta Dominorum Concilii et Sessionis 1532-33*, ed. I. H. Shearer (Stair Society, 1951), [*Acta
   Sessionis* (Stair)], 53. This refers to the death of *John* Wemyss of Reras, knight, sixty years
   previously: it seems clear that this is a slip for Thomas.
[78] William had a son David, who must have predeceased him: see *Fife Court Bk.*, 139, 146, 147.
[79] *Fife Court Bk.*, 86; *RSS*, i, no. 3508; *RMS*, iii, nos. 1744 and 1838; *Acts of Council (Public Affairs)*,
   ed. R. K. Hannay (Edinburgh, 1932), 314, 322 and 505-6; *APS*, ii, 311; *Dunfermline Court Bk.* 156-
   8; Fraser, *Wemyss*, i, 61.
[80] *RSS*, ii, no. 3374.

about the lands of Leuchars, Nether Pirny and Strathibois however. These had been the heritage of Elizabeth Wemyss and there is no record of any formal entry by her Forbes heirs. The casualty to be paid for non-entry was a heavy one, increasing with each year in which the heir failed to enter. As such it was ruthlessly exploited as a source of revenue by the later medieval Scottish kings.[81] The death of James V on 14 December 1542 and the accession of the infant Mary as queen may have encouraged Forbes to seek entry to Leuchars in the hope of avoiding or minimising his liability for the casualty.[82] He would also know that Patrick Wemyss would no longer have the support of his royal patron. Patrick's

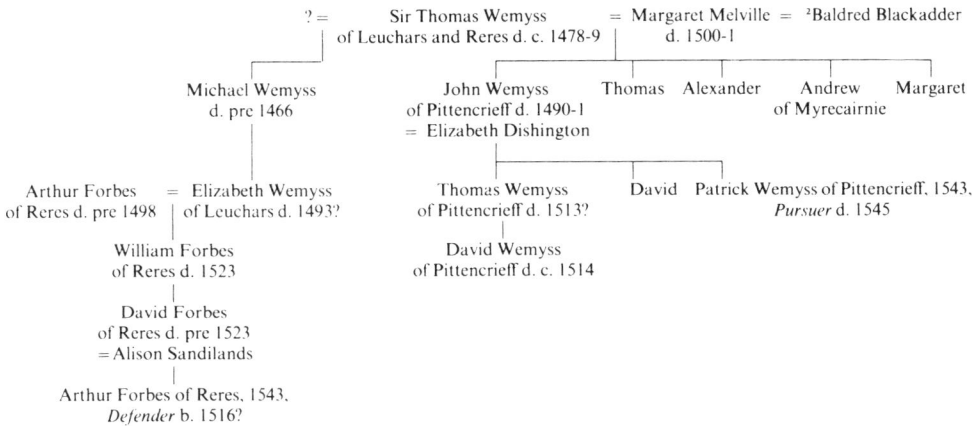

```
                          ? =    Sir Thomas Wemyss        = Margaret Melville =  ²Baldred Blackadder
                                 of Leuchars and Reres d. c. 1478-9    d. 1500-1
             ┌──────────┘          └─────────────┬──────────────┬────────┬─────────────┬──────────┐
       Michael Wemyss              John Wemyss          Thomas   Alexander      Andrew      Margaret
        d. pre 1466            of Pittencrieff d. 1490-1                      of Myrecairnie
                                 = Elizabeth Dishington
                                          ┌───────────────┬─────────┐
   Arthur Forbes   = Elizabeth Wemyss   Thomas Wemyss     David   Patrick Wemyss of Pittencrieff, 1543,
  of Reres d. pre 1498 | of Leuchars d. 1493?  of Pittencrieff d. 1513?         Pursuer d. 1545
        William Forbes                   David Wemyss
        of Reres d. 1523             of Pittencrieff d. c. 1514
        David Forbes
       of Reres d. pre 1523
       = Alison Sandilands
    Arthur Forbes of Reres, 1543,
       Defender b. 1516?
```

(This table is based on Fraser's *Wemyss*, Dickinson's *Sheriff Court Book of Fife*, Duncan and Webster's *Regality of Dunfermline Court Book*, and the discussion in the accompanying text.)

Table — *WEMYSS* v. *FORBES*, 1543.

action before the lords of council and session may also have been prompted by the death of James V. He may have felt that his position was thereby made less secure and that he could best protect himself by regaining the old family lands. On the other hand, the action may be wholly unrelated to contemporary political events and be merely another example of medieval persistence in the pursuit of claims to land. As son of John Wemyss, Patrick was very likely to recall the existence and nature of his right.

It is clear however that the nub of the action was competing claims of right to land such as might have been determined in earlier times by a brieve of right. Certainly in the fifteenth century the council would have declined to hear the case on the ground that it concerned fee and heritage. We can see that happening in the litigations between the first Arthur Forbes and John Wemyss in 1479, which council referred to the judge ordinary on those grounds. That the action of 1543

[81] See R. Nicholson, 'Feudal developments in late medieval Scotland', *JR* 18 (1973), 1-21, especially at 19-20; C. Madden, 'Royal treatment of feudal casualties in late medieval Scotland', *SHR* 55 (1976), 172-94, especially at 181-4; Donaldson, *James V*, 53.

[82] The attention of Scottish royal government was occupied firstly with the need to provide for a minority, and secondly by what Donaldson describes as 'a political revolution' in late January: *James V*, 63-4.

threatened the second Arthur's title to his lands is shown by the fact that he was permitted to 'call his warand' in his defence. The case is therefore an excellent indicator of an extremely important change in the nature of the court over the lifetime of the dispute between the two families.

The record of the case in 1543 is extremely accurate in its references to the events which had led up to it. This gives greater confidence in its reliability where the information it contains cannot be confirmed from another source: for instance, the infeftment of Arthur Forbes in Reres in 1537. The pleadings show that the prolocutor for the lord of Reres did take objection to the competency of the court on the ground that the case concerned an old infeftment. There is no reference to the brieve of right, but in other respects Sinclair's report of this point is borne out by the record. As has already been suggested, the dispute was one in which a brieve of right might have provided an appropriate remedy, and it is certainly possible that reference might have been made to this point in the course of the pleading. It seems likely, therefore, that *Wemyss* v. *Forbes* was a case in which the court was reminded of earlier limitations upon its jurisdiction which would have prevented them dealing with this particular dispute, but that this aspect of the matter was rapidly set aside.

Caldwell v. *Mason*[83]
Ff. 18r.-18v. (20 March 1545/6)

> Anent our soverane lordis lettres purchest at the instance of Schir James Caldwell aganis Schir Jhone Maison: that quhare the said Schir James has ane tenement of land lyand within the cietie of Glasgu on the west syde of the grete streit passand fra the wynd hed to the Blak Friars of the sammyn betuix the landis of Sanct Nicholace on the south part, the commoun wenale on the north part, the hie gait on the eis part, and the landis of umquhill Donald Lyoun on the west part, pertening to the said Schir James in heretage be resignatioun maid thareof in the handis of ane of the baillies of the said cietie be Maister Patrik McClane in favour of the said Schir James, as his seising thareof purportis; be virtu of the quhilk he hes broukit peciablie the said tenement and bene in possessioun thareof without interuptioun be the space of v yeris or thareby last bypast; nevertheles, the said Schir Jhone Maison, allegiand him cessionare and assignay to the said Schir James tenement forsaid, constitut be Schir David Maison his brother allegit heritour thareof, hes menit him to the provost and ballies of the said citie of Glasgu, quha hes direct thare precept and tharewith causit summound the said Schir James, and all utheris havand interess, to the said tenement to compeire befor thaim the xvi day March last bypast, to heir and se the said Schir James' instrument of seising of the said tenement, and the said Maister Patrik's instrument of seising quha resignat the sammyn in favour of the said Schir James, and als the instrument of seising of the sammyn tenement of the said umquhill Donald Lyoun, and ilk ane of thame, to haif bene fra the begynning of nane avale, fors nor effect, and the sammyn to be retretit, rescindit and reducit be

---

[83] Scottish Record Office, CS. 6/20, ff. 18r.-18v. I have followed the same editorial principles here laid out in note 18, above.

decrete of court with all that folowand thareupoun; and the saidis provost and ballies intendis to proced tharein, howbeit thai ar na jugis competent thareto be ressoun that the lordis of counsal usis to tak the decisioun of all actiounis of retretting of infeftmentis, evidentis or seisingis to thaim selfis and to remit the same to na uther jugis. And anent the charge gevin to the said Schir Jhone to bring with him and produce befor the lordis of counsale the said precept purchest be him in the said mater and to heir and se the said actioun advocat, and the saidis provost and ballies dischargit thareof for the caussis forsaid, or else to schawin ane ressonable cause quhy the sammyn suld nocht be done, as at mair lenth is contenit in the saidis letrez, the said Schir James Caldwell being personaly present, and the said Schir Jhone Maison being lauchfully summounde to this actioune oftymes callit and nocht comperit, the lordis of counsale advocatis the said mater to thame selfis, to be procedit befor thame siclik and in the sammyn maner as it aucht or sulde have been procedit befor the saidis provost and ballies of Glaisgu, becaus thai ar in use to tak the decisioun of all actiounis of retretting of infeftmentis, evidentis or seisingis to thame selfis; and tharefor dischargis the saidis provost and ballies of all furthir proceding in the said mater, and dischargis thame thareof and of thare offises in that part for the caussis forsaid. And letres to be direct gif nede be in form as efferis.

The official record of this case is to be found only in the series now known as the *Acta Dominorum Concilii et Sessionis*. As stated in Balfour's *Practicks*, it was decided on 20 March 1545/6. There is accordingly no record of it in the acts and decreets, as there is a gap in that series from 11 May 1545 to 1 April 1549.[84] John Sinclair does appear on the sederunt,[85] so that it is perhaps surprising that there is no report of the case in his *Practicks*.

Details of the background to this case cannot be found in any of the sources used in our discussion of *Wemyss* v. *Forbes*. On the face of the record, however, the case is not dissimilar to *Wemyss* in that it involves reduction of an infeftment. The action of reduction was raised by Sir John Mason in the burgh court of Glasgow on 16 March 1546. The argument raised by Sir James Caldwell in defence of his right to the lands was that the burgh court had no jurisdiction in actions of reduction, which pertained only to the lords of council and session. His action before the lords was an attempt to have the reduction 'advocated', or transferred, to them from the burgh court. In this he was successful. The record states that the lords 'ar in use to tak the decisioun of all actiounis of retretting of infeftmentis, evidentis or seisingis to thameselfis'. As in *Wemyss*, therefore, there is no explicit statement about jurisdiction in heritage: the case is rather an assertion of jurisdiction in actions of reduction.

Caldwell thus appears to be one of what were in fact a number of cases in the mid-sixteenth century in which the lords of council and session established a general and exclusive jurisdiction in actions of reduction for themselves. Thus for example in 1532 they declared themselves to be the only judges competent to reductions of nineteen year tacks,[86] while in 1550, in an action for reduction of a

---

[84] See note 19, above.
[85] Scottish Record Office, CS. 6/20, fo. 18r; Scottish Record Office, RH 2/1/9, p. 78.
[86] *Acta Sessionis (Stair)*, 43-4; Balfour, *Practicks*, i, 269.

liferent of teinds, it was stated that 'the lordis sufferis na uthir juge within this realm to proceid tharupoun bot thame selfis allanerlie'.[87] In both cases the action had been initiated in the court of the Official of St. Andrews. It is difficult to judge how much, if anything, this development owed to the act of 1532: certainly actions of reduction had been competent in the conciliar courts in the fifteenth century, but it was never said then that the jurisdiction was an exclusive one.[88] In 1532 and 1533 however, there was perhaps some doubt as to whether reductions of infeftments could be taken by the lords, for in two such cases from that period it was argued that they had no jurisdiction.[89] The exception was repelled in both cases. In 1535 it was apparently accepted that the lords could not reduce 'old infeftments'.[90] Thus it may be that *Wemyss* v. *Forbes* has some significance in the development of the court's jurisdiction in reduction: it will be recalled that Sinclair's report of the case is headed, 'That reductioun of auld infeftmentis pertenis to the lordis of sessioun', and that the exception pleaded on behalf of Forbes was that the lords were not competent judges on old infeftments. But if Sinclair is to be believed, *Wemyss* was not the first case which the lords had taken in this way, as 'divers sic interlocutoris' had been given previously.

The doubts as to the lords' jurisdiction to reduce infeftments must have arisen because such actions touched heritage. Reduction of an infeftment would destroy a title to land. Thus in *Dudingstoune* v. *Dudingstoune* in 1533, the lords declared themselves to be competent judges in reduction of infeftments, but then went on to hold that, as the defender was a minor, there could be no proceedings against his heritage until he was of full age.[91] In 1539, it was decided that 'all summondis rasit for reductioun of infeftmentis be privilegiat, tablit and callit be the Monundayis table wolkly becaus the samin concernis tinsale of heritage'.[92] We can see an important change here. In 1533 there was still room for debate as to whether the lords could take cases which might involve depriving a man of his heritage; in 1539, the jurisdiction has been established and the action is to be a privileged one.

There was then clear recognition in the 1530s that, by taking jurisdiction to reduce infeftments, the lords were establishing for themselves a jurisdiction in heritage. Neither *Wemyss* v. *Forbes* or *Caldwell* v. *Mason* can therefore be regarded as cases in which the lords created this jurisdiction for themselves. Rather they both appear to be steps in a process whereby the lords expanded the jurisdiction and made it exclusive to themselves. Thus, as we have seen, the lords initially did not reduce old infeftments: *Wemyss* is part of the process of expansion in this regard. As late as 1567 it was doubtful whether the lords could reduce infeftments which had been confirmed by parliament.[93] The jurisdiction in heritage of the lords of council and session seems therefore to have been developed over a period of years, rather than in any one particular case.

A similar observation undoubtedly holds good for jurisdiction in reductions.

---

[87] *Acts of Council* (*Public Affairs*), 605.
[88] See e.g. *ADC*, i, 57, 215, 216, 238, 244, 254; *ADC*, ii, 388, 434.
[89] *Acta Sessionis* (*Stair*), 17, 43-4; *Wigtownshire Charters*, ed. R. C. Reid (SHS, 1960), 143.
[90] *Acts of Council* (*Public Affairs*), 440.
[91] *Acta Sessionis* (*Stair*), 43-4.
[92] *Acts of Council* (*Public Affairs*), 478.
[93] A doubt resolved in favour of the lords' jurisdiction: *APS*, iii, 29, c. 22.

The move to what is still the position today, that actions of reduction in general pertain exclusively to the Court of Session,[94] seems to have been a piecemeal one, with a number of separate decisions on specific situations such as tacks, liferents and infeftments, rather than being the result of any initial general principle. *Caldwell* is one such decision, relating to reduction of infeftments. However it may not have been the first decision on the point. Sinclair reports a case of 1543, *Wachtoun* v. *Sinclair*, as holding that '*de iure et practica Scotie* thair is na juge spirituall nor temporall to reduce heretabill infeftment or cognitioun in materis of heretage bot the lordis of counsall alanerlie'.[95] *Caldwell* may then be one of a chain of decisions which established the 'practick' of the court; it certainly seems from much of the foregoing that one case would not be enough for that.

The fact that the court took exclusive jurisdiction to reduce infeftments seems likely, then, to have been because such actions affected heritage rather than because it was the only court in which reduction was competent. I have noted elsewhere that by 1532 it was being argued that the lords were the most appropriate judges to try causes of heritage;[96] certainly by the end of that decade they were prepared to determine such questions even where reduction of an infeftment was not involved.[97] What we have are two areas of law, heritage and reduction, in both of which the court was gradually asserting an exclusive jurisdiction. These developments clearly overlap but we cannot explain either by reference only to the other, for that is to beg the fundamental question. Why was it that, in the decades after 1530, the lords of council and session began to regard certain business as competent to their court only?

The role of advocation in enforcing their views may have been important. Thus, in the case involving the reduction of a nineteen year tack in 1532, the lords advocated the matter from the Official's court to be determined by them as the only competent judges.[98] Similarly in *Caldwell* v. *Mason* the lords asserted their exclusive jurisdiction in reductions of infeftments by an advocation from the burgh court of Glasgow. Such evidence as there is in print concerning the lords' power of advocation suggests that it was sometimes used to bring cases before them which strictly pertained to the jurisdiction of another court. A particularly prominent example of this in the 1540s concerned the Admiralty court, from which there were numerous advocations despite the protests of the Admiral.[99] There may have been some development of the procedure after 1532, when it seems only to have been competent if consented to by both parties.[100] The principal ground seems to have been, speaking generally, the incapacity of the judge in the other court, as shown by his enmity to a party or his failure to execute justice. But Balfour notes decisions in the early 1540s which enabled the lords to advocate cases *ex officio* if they concerned large sums of money or 'uther wechtie

---

[94] See D. Maxwell, *The Practice of the Court of Session* (HMSO, 1980), 92. Reduction is only competent in the sheriff court where a defender *ope exceptionis* challenges a deed or writing relied upon by the pursuer.

[95] Edinburgh University Library, Laing MS. III 388a, c. 322.

[96] MacQueen, 'Brieve of right', 66.

[97] See *Acts of Council* (*Public Affairs*), 484, 486.

[98] *Acta Sessionis* (*Stair*), 43-4.

[99] See *APS*, ii, 449-50; *Acts of Council* (*Public Affairs*), 539, 540, 608, 626, 633; Murray, 'Sinclair's Practicks', 98-9.

[100] See *Acta Sessionis* (*Stair*), 104, 155; also introduction, p. xx.

materis of greit importance'.[101] Litigants were in any event often willing to submit disputes over heritage to the judgement of the lords.[102] The extension of the power to advocate must have enabled the court to develop its jurisdiction in this field, had it wished to do so.

The extent of the lords' jurisdiction to advocate seems to have caused some concern in the second half of the sixteenth century. In 1555 parliament passed an act concerning procedure for the warning of tenants to flit and remove.[103] After a lengthy narrative, the act concludes:

> And als that na advocatioun of causis be takin be the Lordis fra the Juge Ordinar except it be for deidlie feid or the Schiref principall or the Juge Ordinar be partie ui the causis of the Lordis of counsall and thair Advocattis Scribis and members.

There is some debate as to whether this part of the act was to be read separately from the rest and was thus a general restriction on advocations, or whether it merely limited the power to advocate in cases of removing.[104] However that may be, the act does show some attempt being made to restrict the scope of advocation. In 1567 it was suggested in parliament that all complaints should be heard first before the judge ordinary and only taken by the session or privy council if there was refusal of justice, delay or manifest iniquity. The session and council were to hear 'onlie actionis propirlie appertening to thame etc, and thai to be qualifiit and specialie expressit'.[105] There is more than a suggestion here that the central courts were appropriating matters outwith their customary jurisdiction.

Twenty years later, parliament referred 'ane article aganis advocationis' to the lords of council and session for their consideration.[106] But it seems to have been only in the seventeenth century that limitations were placed upon the procedure in a series of parliamentary enactments.[107]

Conclusions

We began this paper with a brief discussion of the significance of the act of 1532 in the history of the Court of Session. We have seen that there were some important developments in the jurisdiction of the court after that date. To what extent we can attribute these developments to the act of 1532 is however doubtful, since there is little express reference to it in the sources examined here. The same observation would hold good for the confirming acts of 1541 and 1543. We also need to know more of what was happening in the court before 1532. It can, I think, be accepted that the acts were not intended to be of particular significance,

---

[101] Balfour, *Practicks*, ii, 340-2.
[102] See note 100 above.
[103] *APS*, ii, 494, c. 12.
[104] See *Habbakuk Bisset's Rolment of Courtis*, ed. P. J. Hamilton-Grierson (Scottish Text Society, 1920-6), iii, 88-9.
[105] *APS*, iii, 44.
[106] *APS*, iii, 448, c. 26.
[107] *APS*, iv, 430, c. 8; *APS*, v, 420, 603, 606; *APS*, vii, 451, c. 3; *APS*, viii, 83, c. 40 and 351, c. 82. See also Stair, *Institutions*, IV, 37.

or to change the character of the court, at the time they were passed; but nonetheless as acts of the Scottish parliament they could be used to give legal authority to what clearly appears as an expansionist attitude of the court to its jurisdiction in the 1530s and 1540s.

It may also be accepted that an important field into which the court extended its jurisdiction was heritage. The evidence suggests that neither *Wemyss* v. *Forbes* nor *Caldwell* v. *Mason* was the decisive case in this particular development, although both were part of it. Why then were these cases given such prominence by Skene and Balfour respectively? For Skene, the answer must surely lie in Sinclair's report of *Wemyss* v. *Forbes* and its reference, whether or not authentic, to the brieve of right. Skene's knowledge of Scottish legal history must have given this a particular significance in his eyes. It is less easy to explain Balfour's citation of *Caldwell* v. *Mason*. It may have been the most recent case on the point, or the last in a concurring series of decisions which established the 'practick' of the court. If then the cases are of a somewhat lesser significance than has previously been thought, nevertheless, both give guidance as to the paths which future research on this subject could follow, with profit for our understanding of the history of the Court of Session.

Acknowledgements

In preparing this paper I have incurred a considerable debt of gratitude to Dr. A. L. Murray of the Scottish Record Office, who guided a 'prentice hand through the intricacies of the council and session records and corrected my transcripts of the cases in which I was interested. He also made available to me relevant parts of his transcript of the Edinburgh University Library Laing MS. III 388a and gave advice on other MSS. of Sinclair's *Practicks*. I am also grateful to Mr. I. A. Fraser of the School of Scottish Studies at Edinburgh University for invaluable assistance in locating several of the places mentioned in *Wemyss* v. *Forbes* (see notes 26 to 28). I owe much to discussions of an earlier draft with my colleague Mr. David Sellar. Publication of extracts from the Court of Session records is made with the approval of the Keeper of the Records of Scotland.

DISCOURS PARTICULIER D'ESCOSSE, 1559/60

Edited, with an Introduction, by PETER G. B. MCNEILL, M.A., LL.B., PH.D.,
Sheriff of Lothian and Borders

INTRODUCTION

Context

On 11 January 1560 the clerk register and the justice clerk of Scotland had prepared, at the command of Mary of Guise, the queen regent, a report on Scotland which dealt with the patrimony of the crown, the courts and the law of treason in Scotland. The document was possibly written in French: the copy which is best known is entitled '*Discours Particulier d'Escosse*'; a contemporary copy probably made in France is called '*État et Constitution du Royaulme d'Escosse*'. The bibliography of the documents is discussed later.

The content of the *Discours* does not amount to an exhaustive or systematic account of the workings of the whole government in Scotland in 1560: rather, it is a very selective description of certain Scottish institutions; its content is, no doubt, governed by its genesis. It was written by the express command of the queen regent for the use of Mary and Francis, the monarchs of Scotland and France at the time when the French were reducing Scotland to a mere province of France and were also seeking to extirpate heresy there.

In the previous decade the French had been quietly taking over the Scottish state.[1] The young Queen was half French and had spent almost all her life in France. She had married the heir to the French throne, and on 10 July 1559 on the accidental death of Henry II the couple became king and queen of France as well as of Scotland. Since 1554 Mary's French mother had been regent of Scotland. Shortly thereafter, many of the Scottish officers of state were appointed anew. Some of the offices were filled by Frenchmen: de Rubay[2] had the great seal (although Huntly remained titular chancellor), and Villemore[3] became comptroller. In addition, Bonot[4] was stationed in the Orkneys for a descent on Ireland; and — the last word in subservience — d'Oysel,[5] the roving ambassador of the French court, took to appearing at the Scots privy council. Native Scottish ministers such as McGill[6] and Bellenden[7] — the authors of the *Discours* — and John Spens,[8] the queen's advocate, worked along with the Frenchmen.

[1] G. Donaldson, *Scotland: James V-James VII* (1965), 80-9.
[2] Yves de Rubay, conseiller du Roi, Maistre des Requestes Ordinaires de son Hostel, Garde des Sceaulx d'Ecosse.
[3] Bartholomew de Villemore.
[4] Otherwise Bonnauld or Bonault, bailie of Orkney.
[5] Henri Cleutin, sieur d'Oysel et de Villeparisis Aignan.
[6] James McGill of Nether Rankeilor, clerk register 1554-66 and 1567-79.
[7] John Bellenden of Auchnoul, justice clerk 1555-73.
[8] John Spens of Condie, Queen's advocate 1555-73.

86

It was probably inevitable in the state of the limited administrative development which existed in sixteenth-century Europe that the French should merely capture and perfect the existing Scottish institutions and fill them with Frenchmen or Francophil Scotsmen, rather than impose new institutions as did the British parliament after the Union of 1707. A similar approach was adopted in other lands which came into French control. Thus, for example, after the acquisition of Brittany, a governor was appointed to represent the monarch while the Breton institutions such as the court of parliament (which was drawn from the estates) and the exchequer remained. Later, in an era of more sophisticated administration, intendants with a network of subdelegates (subsequently prefects) were intruded. In other lands, such as Bourbonnais and Burgundy, similar developments took place. In Scotland, in the 1550s the French limited themselves to rehabilitating a somewhat derelict estate. It was during the regency of Mary of Guise that there was an attempt to stent the Scots to pay for a non-feudal standing army. At the same time the existing administration was tightened up with emphasis on the creation of revenue. The court of session began to receive its due contribution out of the church revenues. There were schemes to extract money from the church and laity;[9] and French coinage was introduced. It is not surprising therefore that the *Discours* deals with the patrimony of the crown.

At the same time the French administration had for political reasons, and also because of the animosity of the French crown to heresy, to deal with the uproar for religion which had taken on the aspect of a rebellion. On 17 July the king and queen had written separate personal letters to the duke of Châtelherault seeking his continued support;[10] in his letter, Francis said that the bearer would report the position (*faict*) of Châtelherault's son, the earl of Arran, who had gone to France in 1548 as security for the military aid to be sent by Henry II to deal with the English occupation of parts of Scotland, but thereafter he was detained in France virtually as a hostage for the duke's good behaviour.[11] The view of Francis, and of Mary of Guise, was that the rebels were merely using religion as a pretext for their political disobedience.[12] In September, almost as soon as the earl of Arran had arrived safely in Scotland, the duke joined the rebels and became party to a variety of acts of treason. If the French were to proceed against him for treason it would be necessary for the French to know the state of the law of treason in relation to these acts and the effect of a conviction for treason on the potential accused, who was the next entitled to succeed to the throne. These matters are dealt with in the latter part of the *Discours*: this and other items in the *Discours* are in terms which suggest that they were answers to specific questions on these topics raised by the French government.

---

[9] 'Suggestions for augmenting the queens dowagers revenue without grudge, hurt or feiling of the people': Adv. MSS 34.2.17. *f.* 124.

[10] *Négociations etc rélative au Règne de François II* (Paris, 1841), 17, 18.

[11] It had been said that in 1543 the Catholic clergy and the French connection turned the governor away from protestantism and the English alliance by threatening to use the church courts to declare him to be illegitimate (R. Keith, *History of the Affairs of Church and State in Scotland* (Spottiswoode Society, 1844), i, 95), but that danger if it ever existed was surely spent by 1559.

[12] *Négociations*, 17; Knox, *History*, ed., W. C. Dickinson (1949), 173, 192-3.

Royal authority

The first topic which the authors of the *Discours* dealt with was whether the rulers of Scotland had absolute power over their subjects, or were subject to any other monarch. It would not be altogether surprising that such a question were raised. The French lawyers would, no doubt, have been interested to know what their king had achieved by virtue of Mary's assignation in 1558 of her realm to him in the event of her dying without issue: he could not acquire any higher right than Mary had had; *assignatus utitur iure auctoris.*[13] Also the French would be well aware of the English claims over the centuries to overlordship of Scotland: as late as 1515 Henry VIII had written to the holy see in the style of protector and governor of Scotland[14] and in 1548 the protector Somerset told the French ambassador that the king of England had a just title to the sovereignty of Scotland;[15] by force of arms and by treaty Scotland had maintained her independence against England which was the only power seeking to challenge it; and earlier she had successfully asserted her ecclesiastical and political control of the northern parts against the claims of Norway. On a smaller scale, by the act 1496 c. 6 the power of imperial notaries was brought to an end, although the right of papal notaries to act was preserved.[16] That act provided that the king had full jurisdiction and 'fre impire within his Realm' to make notaries: it may be that the word empire cannot in that context bear the meaning of sovereignty.[17] The *Discours* did not mention the authority of the papacy which subsisted until after the reformation.[18]

At the same time, as has been noted by Dr. Wormald, James III affected an imperial rather than a royal crown.[19] The words of this first paragraph are similar to Mackenzie's paraphrase of the acts 1606, c. 1 and 1661, c. 6: 'The King is the Author and Fountain of all Power, and is an absolute Prince, having as much Power, as any King or Potentate whosoever, deriving his power from God Almighty alone.'[20]

Dues and estate of the crown

The paragraphs dealing with the royal patrimony merely state what the rights of the crown are but with little comment. However, a contemporary document, whose date must lie between the accession of Queen Elizabeth (17 November 1558) and the death of Mary of Guise (10 June 1560), deals with some of the royal patrimony but also suggests ways in which the revenue could be augmented.[21] It proposes that the great abbeys, wards and marriages be retained in the queen's

---

[13] Hay Fleming, *Mary, Queen of Scots* (1897), 23; Trayner, *Latin Maxims and Phrases* (3rd ed. 1883).
[14] *ADC (Public)*, 40.
[15] *Calendar of State Papers, Scotland*, i, 170-1.
[16] *APS*, ii, 95.
[17] See Norman Macdougall, *James III* (1982), 98; a more likely meaning is capacity or jurisdiction.
[18] 'That the bischope of Rome haif na Jurisdiction or autoritie within this realm in tymes cuming': 1560 c. 2 (*APS*, ii, 534), 'ratified' in 1567 (*APS*, iii, 36).
[19] *Court, Kirk and Community — Scotland, 1470-1625* (1981), 19.
[20] *APS*, iv, 281; vii, 10. *Institutions* 1.3.1 — then the competing claims came from 'the People' not other monarchs.
[21] 'Suggestions for augmenting the queens dowagers revenues': Adv. MSS 34.2.17, *f.* 124.

hands 'like other princes do'; and that the crown should look to the coinage and the mines for greater profit.[22]

The *Discours* states that a great part of the lordships and lands of the crown are set in feu; while the other part is set in tack (*a ferme*) for three, five, seven or nine years with the result that tenants 'do not make any building, plantations or other improvements for fear of being ejected from them'.[23] The suggestion of an almost precarious tenantry cannot be typical of the whole country or of all tenants: many tenants had safeguards by operation of law and by the benevolence of landlords or the custom of the area. Thus as early as 1449/50 an act had been passed 'for the sauftie & favour of the puir pepil that labouris the grunde' whereby if certain conditions were satisfied 'the takaris sall remayn with thare takis on to the ische of thare termis' even although the landlord alienated the land.[24] By legislation passed only five years before the *Discours* was written, the right of a landlord had been modified by imposing upon him an obligation to give forty days' warning to remove at the term; and thereafter if the tenant did not remove, the landlord had to seek a decree of court in order to have the tenant removed.[25] Further, at common law, a lease did not necessarily come to an end when its term arrived, but it could be continued by tacit relocation.[26] Long leases did exist, even for life or lives; and often at the end of the lease or at the death of the tenant, leases were often renewed in favour of the old tenant or his kin.[27] In addition leases were also being converted into feus in favour of sitting tenants.[28]

Similarly, the authors baldly state that avail of marriage is valued 'at far too great a price in this country and almost the value of the lands';[29] but it seems clear that this burden was becoming less onerous. According to Craig, writing almost fifty years later, in assessing the amount of a single avail, account had to be taken not only of the value of the estates held of the superior but of the worth of the whole means possessed by the vassal whether these consisted of money, cattle, blench feus, or feu-farms, inclusive of teinds. In short, the liability of the vassal is fixed with relation to his means of living, and his whole resources must be set out in a summons proved so that the court of session can ascertain the true amount of the avail.[30] Balfour and Skene speak with one voice: 'to be modifyit and taxt be the Judge eftir the zeirlie rental, avail and quantitie of the lands and living pertening to the air'.[31] By the time of Stair (1681), 'since personal debts came to be so frequent, the avail of marriage is only in relation to the free estate . . . about two years' free rent'; and in relation to double avail Stair says 'I never observed, since the institution of the College of Justice, the double avail to be found due'.[32]

[22] Cf. *Discours*, para. 12.
[23] Para. 8. Similar views expressed by John Major in 1519 are doubted in M. H. B. Sanderson, *Scottish Rural Society in Sixteenth Century* (1982), 47 *et seq.*
[24] 1449, c. 6: *APS*, ii, 35.
[25] 1555, c. 12: *APS*, ii, 494.
[26] Balfour, *Practicks*, 208-9.
[27] M. H. B. Sanderson, *Scottish Rural Society in the Sixteenth Century*, 41 *et seq.*
[28] *ibid.*, 77 *et seq.*
[29] Para. 14.
[30] Craig, *Jus Feudale*, 2.21.21.
[31] Balfour, *Practicks*, 246-7; Skene, *De Verborum*, sv 'Maritagium Haeredes'.
[32] *Institutions* (2nd ed.) II.4.47. Ward holding was abolished by the Tenures Abolition Act 1746 (20 Geo. 2, cap 50).

If the *Discours* did overstate the position, the authors may have sought to dissuade the French from seeking to raise the crown income in this way.

Civil causes

In the part of the *Discours* which deals with the manner of proceeding and doing justice in civil causes the authors again seem to simplify the state of the law — at least in relation to the burghs. It is stated that the provost and bailies have jurisdiction — without specifying whether civil or criminal — over the inhabitants of the burgh in all respects the same as that of the sheriff.[33] However, Mackenzie says that the royal burghs are *not* sheriffs in themselves 'except the King grant them the Privilege by a special Concession'.[34] Balfour has in his list of sheriffs a marginal note, '*Nota*, that the burrows of Edinburgh and Stirling ar Scheriffis within thameselfis';[35] and Hope writing half a century later names Edinburgh, Lanark, Perth and Stirling as having the privilege specially granted to them.[36]

Criminal causes: lords of regality

In the section dealing with the manner of proceeding and doing justice in criminal causes, the paragraph dealing with the judges of regality calls for comment.[37] Several modern works state or imply mostly without clear contemporary authority that the lords of regality had a criminal jurisdiction equal to that of the justiciar.[38] Hume[39] is to the same effect: this is especially surprising because Hume not only knew of the *Discours* but actually quoted from it in relation to the tenure of the justice general.[40] The unanimity and authority of these works makes one hesitate to call the statement in question.

Perhaps the matter can best be approached by clearing away the areas where there can be little or no dispute. In civil matters no one seriously suggests that the jurisdiction of the lords of regality was not the same as that of the sheriff; and this is what the *Discours* says.[41] In criminal jurisdiction it could hardly be contended with any conviction that the lord of regality could try a case of treason against the Crown: the authorities all point to the proposition that only parliament[42] or the

---

[33] Para 30.
[34] *Institutes*, I.4.4.
[35] *Practicks*, 16.
[36] *Major Practicks*, 1.5.7. Perth had been granted this privilege by 1394: Nicholson, *Scotland: the Later Middle Ages* (1974), 263.
[37] Para. 38.
[38] e.g. *Sources and Literature of Scots Law* (Stair Society, 1936), 375; *Introduction to Scottish Legal History* (Stair Society, 1958), 378; Willock, *Jury in Scotland* (Stair Society, 1966), 45; Walker, *Oxford Companion to Law*, sv 'regality' but cf. Walker, *Stair Tercentenary Studies* (Stair Society, 1981), 74; *Crime and the Law* (ed., Gatrell and others) 141; R. Nicholson, *Scotland: The Later Middle Ages* (1974), 24; Bruce Lenman, *The Jacobite Risings in Britain 1689-1746* (1980), 278; and J. MacKinnon, *Constitutional History of Scotland* (1924), 193.
[39] *Commentaries* (1819), ii, 30-1.
[40] *ibid.*, ii, 14.
[41] Para. 28.
[42] e.g. 'Since Parliament is the Supream Judicatory, it may certainly cognosce all Causes', Mackenzie, *Matters Criminal*, 364.

justice court[43] could try treason. Again the *Discours* also says so.[44] With the less serious crimes including those which were competent to be tried before the sheriff, it would be generally accepted that the lords of regality could also try them. It is in relation to the remaining crimes, between these two extremes, that the problem exists.

The *Discours* says that 'the judges of regality have the privilege and full jurisdiction in their lands, to punish all crimes as well old ones as recent' but the authors go on to make a significant qualification 'except the crime of lese majesty and the four pleas of the crown: which are ravishing of girls and women, public robbery with resistance, fire-raising, and secret homicide which has not been confessed'.[45] That qualification in so far as it relates to the pleas of the Crown is inconsistent with the works already noted which equiparate the jurisdiction of a lord of regality with that of the justiciar. Of these works only MacKinnon (who was writing in 1924) gives authority for his view that the jurisdiction of the lords of regality did include the pleas of the crown; and his work is probably the direct or indirect source which the other authors relied upon. MacKinnon refers to Green's *Encyclopaedia of Scots Law* (1898) in which the title 'Regality' was written by J. H. Tait, advocate, who in turn relied upon Erskine. Erskine[46] states that 'the jurisdiction of the lord of regality was truly royal; for he might have judged in the four pleas of the crown; whereas the Sheriff was competent to none of them but murder. It was even as ample as that of the Justiciary as to every crime except treason: Mackenzie, Crim. Tr. part 2, t.ll § 5'.[47] That is a categorical statement; but what Mackenzie says is the very reverse of that: 'The Justices are (the) only judges competent to these crimes which are call'd *placita coronae*, the Pleys of the Crown which are four with us, wilful Fire raising, ravishing of Women, Murther, and Robbery, or Reif, 1. Malcol. 2. cap.13'.[48] Skene says the same as Mackenzie;[49] and Balfour[50] and Hope[51] are consistent with Mackenzie. Skene and Mackenzie also give as a reason for this state of affairs, namely, the fact that the lords of regality exercised an inferior jurisdiction — that is unlike the superior courts their jurisdiction did not extend to all of Scotland — and accordingly they could not have the ample jurisdiction of a superior court such as the justice court.[52]

However, many, and probably most, of the regality courts did in fact have power to deal with the pleas of the crown and did have a grant to that effect in their charters, *et cum placitis quatuor punctorum corone nostre*.[53] Other writs excluded the jurisdiction expressly, *reservatis tamen nobis et successoribus nostris*

---

[43] e.g. *ibid.*, 403-4.
[44] Paras. 40 and 43.
[45] Para. 38. Traditionally, these were the four pleas of the crown as set forth in the assize of 1180 (*APS*, i, 375), but there were other reserved pleas: Duncan, *Scotland: The Making of the Kingdom* (1975), 202.
[46] *Institutes* (ed. Nicholson), I.4.7-11.
[47] that is, in the edition of 1678, pages 403-5; cf. 427-8.
[48] *ibid.*, 427.
[49] *De Verborum*, sv 'Murthrum' and 'Placitum'.
[50] *Practicks*, 289.
[51] *Major Practicks*, 5.3.1.
[52] Mackenzie, *Matters Criminal*, 402, 427-8; cf. Mackenzie, *Institutions*, 1.2.10.
[53] *RMS*, i, no. 399.

quatuor punctis precipuis ad coronam nostram spectantibus.[54] In some cases the charter was silent,[55] and yet others defined the rights of the lord of regality by reference to the extent of the holding of a predecessor in title,[56] or *in adeo liberam regalitatem sicut aliqua regalitas per totum regnum nostrum possidetur seu tenetur.*[57] The varying styles suggest that the grant of the pleas of the crown was not an attribute of the right of regality. Mackenzie concedes that '*de facto*, Lords of Regality do ordinarily judge upon these crimes without any Commission'.[58] In his lesser work,[59] Mackenzie says that jurisdiction of a lord of regality is 'equal to the Justices in Criminal Causes'; but this bald statement is qualified in the next title: the lords of regality can repledge from other courts including the justices in all cases except treason and the four pleas of the crown. It appears then that the inclusion of the pleas of the crown was not of the nature of the jurisdiction of a regality, but could properly be the subject of a special grant: 'nor can any other judge proceed to judge these Crimes except they be particularly warranted by a Gift from his majesty to that effect';[60] 'except the samin be specially granted to him be the king';[61] 'the right of holding court is one which never appertains to a vassal unless it has been specially granted by the superior'.[62] This would accord with the law relating to conveyancing which only permitted a prescriptive title to heritable property on the basis of a habile title.[63]

The most satisfactory statement of the position is that of Professor Barrow and Dr. Grant[64] that the mark of a regality was the exclusion of the royal officers: some regalities had a separate chancery to which writs could be retoured.[65] Quite 'extra to the concept of regality' there might be an express grant of the pleas of the crown.[66] Such a view would be strictly in accordance with the statement in the *Discours*; but the bald statement is misleading, because so many lords of regality did also have grants of jurisdiction to try pleas of the crown. Professor Pryde had noted over a thousand baronies before 1560, of which fifty four were regalities:[67] and in the judicial proceedings following the abolition of the heritable jurisdictions, the lords of session 'adjudged the claimants to be lawfully possessed of those several jurisdictions' set forth in the Act of Sederunt of 18 March 1748:[68] they amounted to forty seven lords of regality, and twenty seven bailies of

[54] *RRS*, vi, no. 194.
[55] e.g. *RMS*, i, nos. 414, 590, 847.
[56] e.g. *RRS*, vi, no. 187: similarly, the act which annexed the temporalities of church-lands to the crown preserved the rights of the bailies of regality in criminal cases 'in all maner of crymes quhairin the lord or baillie of the regalities wes accustumat to be judge in tymes bypast': 1587, c. 8: *APS*, iii, 435.
[57] *RRS*, vi, no. 39.
[58] *Matters Criminal*, 404.
[59] *Institutions* (1684), 1.4.5.
[60] Mackenzie, *Matters Criminal*, 428.
[61] *De Verborum*, sv 'Murthrum'.
[62] *Craig, Ius Feudale* (ed. Clyde) 2.8.30.
[63] 1617, c. 12 (*APS*, iv, 543-4).
[64] G. W. S. Barrow, *Robert Bruce* (2nd ed. Edinburgh, 1976), 397; Dr. A. Grant by letter.
[65] Erskine, *Institutes*, I.4.7: Hector McKechnie, *Pursuit of Pedigree* (1928), 18; 'ane haill and free Regality with free Chapell and Chancellery': regality of Grant, 1694: *APS*, x, 93; cf. Helen Cam, 'The Medieval English Franchise', *Speculum* xxxii (1957), 434-5 (Archbishop Gerard of York).
[66] cf. Professor Donaldson, *Scotland: James V to James VII* (Edinburgh, 1971), 5: W. C. Dickinson, *The Court Book of the Barony of Carnwath* 1523-42 (Scottish History Society, 1937), xi-xli.
[67] *Court Book of Burgh of Kirkintilloch*, ed. G. S. Pryde (Scottish History Society, 1963), xli.
[68] *Acts of Sederunt, 1553-1790*, ed. A. Tait (Edinburgh, 1790), 415-33.

regality — a total of seventy four: of those jurisdictions only seven life clerkships were so adjudged.[69] The authors of the *Discours* would have given a more realistic account of the jurisdiction of the lords of regality if they had said that although they can try all crimes except the pleas of the crown such a jurisdiction can be granted, and commonly is.[70]

Treason is to this day a matter exclusively for the high court of justiciary; but of the four traditional pleas of the crown only two, murder and rape, must still be indicted in the high court. The other two, wilful fire-raising and robbery, may since 1887 proceed before a sheriff and jury;[71] and now may also be tried summarily before a sheriff sitting without a jury.[72]

Tenure of judges: justice general

Another persistent topic in the *Discours* is whether the administration of justice could be controlled by the crown. In relation to most of the various judges the *Discours* deals with the nature of their tenure. The sheriffs — apart from those of Orkney and Shetland which are held 'at pleasure' — hold their offices 'in fee, from father to son and from degree to degree'[73] as do the barons.[74] The provost and bailies of the burghs are elected each year.[75] The paragraphs dealing with the lords of session do not touch on the mode of their appointment or their tenure. According to the *Discours* the holders of the office of justice general are appointed '*ad nutum principis*',[76] which would be referred to otherwise as *ad beneplacitum*. The records of the appointments to the office are deficient for this period; but by 1560 three generations of the Argylls had held the office. By 1514 Colin, 3rd earl of Argyll was appointed justice general for the whole kingdom.[77] Archibald, 4th earl was also justice general; he died in late 1558. By 13 March 1560 — a few months after the date of the *Discours* — Archibald, 5th earl is noted as being in office.[78] Mackenzie, writing a century later, noted that the office 'is constitute by a Gift under the great Seal, either *ad vitam*, or by a temporary commission, but still under the great Seal'.[79] By then, however, there had been considerable changes: since 1628 the jurisdiction of the Argyll family as justice general had been limited to the sheriffdom of Argyll and the Isles; and this area was until the abolition of the heritable jurisdictions in 1748 excluded from the commission of justiciary which was set up in 1672.

---

[69] cf. also Bruce Lenman, *The Jacobite Risings in Britain*, 278-80.

[70] 'And there are but very few Abbacies in Scotland which were not erected in Regalities': Mackenzie, *Matters Criminal*, 405.

[71] Criminal Procedure (Scotland) Act 1887, section 56.

[72] Criminal Procedure (Scotland) Act 1975, section 291(3); and Criminal Procedure (Scotland) Act 1980, section 38.

[73] Para. 24.

[74] Para. 27.

[75] Para. 30.

[76] Para. 39. The copyist of the manuscript in the National Library of Scotland has rendered the phrase as *ad initium principis* and a later hand has inserted beneath the line the word *libitum*. Hume says that on the basis of the *Discours* the tenure of the justice general is *ad Initum (supposed Libitum) Principis*: *Commentaries*, ii, 14.

[77] *Scots Peerage*, i, 337.

[78] *RMS*, iv, no. 1592.

[79] *Matters Criminal*, 424.

If the earl of Argyll was in fact justice general from the time of his father's death in 1558, the nature of his tenure of the office would have been of importance in any prosecution of the duke of Châtelherault or any others for treason. One possible forum was parliament; but any parliament was liable to be unpredictable. Recent parliaments had not wholly fallen in with the wishes of the regent; the nobles were not anxious to agree to any scheme for taxing them; and the reformers were ready to put the question of religion to parliament. The 'parliament' of 1560 purported to deal with religion contrary to the express reservation of that topic by the crown in the concessions attached to the treaty of Edinburgh which ended the French occupation. Even in a prosecution for treason in parliament, the accused was 'summoned to appear before his majesty and his justice general at the parliament'.[80] The only other competent forum to try a case of treason was the justice court. For some months the earl of Argyll had been an adherent of the reformed faith; and after the duplicity of the queen regent over the occupation of Perth he deserted her and joined the rebels.[81] If Argyll's office were *ad beneplacitum*, presumably he could be replaced by a more amenable judge; if his office were hereditary or even *ad vitam*, it is difficult to see how he could be by-passed unless the trial were to be presided over by one of his deputes, or unless he were removed from office perhaps also on a charge of treason or because of some *culpa* such as mentioned elsewhere in the *Discours*: for example 'if the said sheriffs, bailies, stewards or other judges holding heritable office, do not carry out due execution and justice on the said criminals, they thereby lose their offices, and are punished in their bodies and goods, according to the quality of the criminal and the crime committed by him'. Long absence from office was relied upon by the crown in its attempts some years later to remove lords of session whose tenure was *ad vitam*.[82]

The authors also point out that the various judges cannot take anything from the litigants because they hold their offices in fee:[83] that the right of appeal against their decisions is in general very restricted; and that — in a paragraph coming immediately after the one dealing with trial for treason before the justice general and an assize — if the assize assoilzie a person who merited conviction it can be proceeded against, but the accused cannot have or thole another assize.[84] It may be that this information was sought to see how far the crown could control the administration of justice.

Treason

Similarly, the text at paragraphs 46 to 59 suggests that the French government wanted to know the law of Scotland in relation to treason and in particular (a) the mode of procedure for the execution of the crime of treason; (b) the definition of treason and lese majesty; (c) whether a charge of treason could be made against the highest in the land — such as the duke of Châtelherault; and (d) the effect of a conviction for treason on succession to property and honours.

[80] Para. 40.
[81] Knox, *History*, i, 179 *et seq.*
[82] Para. 45; McNeill, 'Independence of the Scottish Judiciary', 1958, J.R. 134.
[83] e.g. Para. 27.
[84] Para. 40.

It is most probable that this part of the *Discours* is linked with the proceedings for treason against the duke of Châtelherault which had been ordered by the government in France on 10 November 1559 which is contained in the 'Report by de la Brosse and d'Oysel on conditions in Scotland in 1559 and 1560'.[85] The preparation of the case — or as it is called the *Information* — against the duke was to be carried out *'secretement'*;[86] the *Information* including the statements of the witnesses was sent to France. The chronology suggests the connection between the two documents — the *Discours* and the *Information*. The date of the duke's first treasonable act — the convocation at Hamilton — was mid-September; and this is the date of the first charge in the articles against him. On 24 January 1560 the duke and others wrote the letter which is included as a production in the process as a treasonable item. On a date towards the end of December 1559 the king and queen in France asked the government in Scotland for the information which resulted in the preparation of the *Discours*. In the course of February the Scottish officers carried out the taking of statements from the witnesses; and thereafter the *Information* was translated into French and transmitted to France.[87] Meantime on 13 February the queen regent asked the French authorities to send her a copy of it.[88]

Procedure

As has been noted treason could be prosecuted either in parliament or in the justice court. When the prosecution was in parliament, the king ordained that the three estates be assembled in parliament, and the king's advocate had the accused summoned before his majesty and his justice general at the parliament.[89] In this procedure it was competent to have probation in the absence of the accused.[90] This is contrary to the normal rule of Scots law and civil law. On the other hand where the prosecution took place in the justice court,[91] and the accused was in custody, the king's advocate proceeded by way of accusation before the justice general and had the accused put to the knowledge of an assize. If the accused was not in custody, the advocate raised criminal letters charging the sheriffs and other royal officers to have the accused cited to appear before the justice general: the accused was ordained to find caution within six days after the charge that he would appear on the diet of trial assigned to him.[92] If the accused failed to find caution, or if having found caution he failed to appear at the diet, he was put to the horn: there was then no procedure for trial in absence. If the accused appeared at the diet, trial and conviction took place on that day. In neither mode

---

[85] The Report is edited by G. Dickinson in *Scottish History Society, Miscellany* x (1965), 87-125.
[86] *ibid.*, 89, 125.
[87] *ibid.*, 98-124.
[88] Archives of Foreign Office, Quai d'Orsay, Paris, *Mémoires et Documents: Angleterre: Régie* 15 (13), folio 61.
[89] Para. 40.
[90] This rule was extended to prosecutions in the justice court also in 1667: Mackenzie, *Matters Criminal*, 55-9.
[91] Para. 43.
[92] Mackenzie, however, states that the accused 'should be immediately committed to prison': *Matters Criminal*, 51.

of trial was there any appeal; although the heirs could seek to reduce the decree by simple complaint.[93]

Sources of the law of treason

The authors regard treason as being comprehended within the brocard *proditio in regem, regnum et exercitum* and seek their authority in legislation and 'sentences pronounced by parliament against traitors', that is, 'express law or sufficient custom'. The succeeding paragraphs of this part of the *Discours* narrate the statutes and decisions which define the limits of treason: thus the law was not arbitrary but accorded with the maxim *nullum crimen sine lege*. The examples which they cite come from 'the books of the register of parliament'.[94] The authors state that after the conviction of James, earl of Douglas (in 1455) an ordinance was made in relation to him to the effect *inter alia* that no person 'procreated to any of those who have been condemned in parliament (*audit parlement*) shall succeed to any heritable property in the kingdom';[95] and that ordinance was commonly and invariably practised and observed as law in the kingdom.[96]

Duke of Châtelherault

The authors point out that treason has been rigorously executed 'against some very great personages of this kingdom; as, for example, the earl of Douglas, earl of March, earl of Atholl, earl of Ross and the lord of the Isles who for the crime of lese majesty and rebellion against the kings, were convicted and their lands taken to the crown up to this very day'.[97] The authors do not mention the proceedings against Alexander, duke of Albany, who had been the second son of the king: they do mention earlier in the *Discours*, the earl of Lennox[98] whose line also had a claim to the throne. In the proposed proceedings for treason which were envisaged in the concurrent *Information* the principal accused was the duke of Châtelherault — although in the *Information* he is referred to as the earl of Arran, as if he had already lost the dukedom. During Mary's minority he had been the next person entitled to succeed to the throne, and after a false start had held the governorship of the realm during Mary's pupillarity by virtue of that pro-pinquity. There could be no question of sovereign immunity in the case of a former governor in respect of acts done long after he had ceased to be in office. The duke was in his own right an important nobleman in Scotland: and much of the crown wealth had passed through his hands during his rapacious stewardship of the realm.[99] In 1548 he had been granted the valuable French dukedom of

---

[93] Para. 42.

[94] The printed 'Black Acts' were not published until 1566.

[95] Para. 53.

[96] Later, Mackenzie made a more systematic and elaborate division between high treason and 'Statutory Treason which is not Treason properly of its own nature, but is declared to be so by a particular Statute': *Matters Criminal*, 39-40.

[97] Para. 46.

[98] Para. 7.

[99] Indeed in 1542/3 the comptroller appealed in vain against his extravagant claims on the royal revenues: *APS*, ii, 424; and by November 1543 he had, according to de la Brosse, 'recklessly squandered the entire personal estate of the late King, valued at more than three hundred thousand livres': *Two Missions of Jacques de la Brosse, 1543 and 1560* (Scottish History Society, 1942), 19.

Châtelherault on the Vienne in Poitou. When he surrendered the governorship before the end of Mary's pupillarity he was not called to account for his intromissions with the royal estate.[100]

There is further support for the connection between the *Discours* and the *Information*: the authors of the *Discours* expressly limit themselves to a selection of the laws and sentences, 'an extract of some of those which are more suitable for the punishment of crimes committed today'.[101] The use of the word 'today' suggests not merely nowadays, but the contemporary actings of the rebels of whom the duke of Châtelherault was the most significant. The rebellion had been in progress since May 1559, but the *Information* only deals with the illegal actings from September which saw the beginning of the duke's involvement: once his son was safely back in Scotland he attended the illegal convocation at Hamilton. Further, the selection of the categories of treason which the *Discours* deals with has some congruence with the various items which the rebels were committing and with the sundry articles of charge against the duke which are set forth in the *Information*: the precise terms of the charges would of course be governed by what the witnesses were prepared to say in their statements. The charges which are common to the *Discours* and the *Information* are illegal convocation and assembly,[102] treasonable actings against a regent,[103] rebelling against royal authority,[104] the purported suspension of the regent and coining without royal authority.[105] The *Discours* pointed out that it was still treason even if the acts were directed against a regent[106] such as Mary of Guise; and it did not matter whether the monarch was young or an adult.[107]

Succession to Crown

If the duke of Châtelherault, alone or with his son, were to have been convicted of treason his line would have been incapable of succeeding to heritable property which presumably included the dues and estate of the crown, or to any honour or title, which presumably included the crown itself.[108] In the previous reign, the forfeiture of the duke of Albany had had to be rescinded to enable his son John to become governor to the infant James V.[109] If the Hamilton line had been excluded from the succession by a conviction of the duke on a charge of treason it would be a nice point to say who was next entitled to succeed to the throne; because the representative of the rival Lennox line had been forfeited in 1545 and was not to be restored until 1564,[110] and on 30 April 1558 the young queen had by

---

[100] *APS*, ii, 517, 518, 600-4.
[101] Para. 46.
[102] *Information*, articles i, ii, iii: *Discours*, paras. 55, 56, 57.
[103] Article iii; paras. 52, 54, 56.
[104] Articles i, vi, vii; *Discours*, para. 48.
[105] Article ix; para. 51: and by extension, counterfeiting the royal signet: articles vi, vii.
[106] Para. 56.
[107] Para. 50.
[108] Para. 53.
[109] *Handbook of British Chronology* (2nd ed.), 467 puts the earliest date for his restoration as 8 April 1515; elsewhere it is said that 'long before his arrival, James IV had restored the Albany title': Norman Macdougall, *James III* (1982), 279; but as late as 5 Dec. 1512 he was still seeking restoration: *Flodden Papers* (Scottish History Society, 1933), 65.
[110] *Handbook of British Chronology*, 480.

secret documents assigned *quantum valeat* her kingdom in the absence of issue to the French king. The position is further complicated by reason of the public documents granted on 15 April by Henry II and by the queen and dauphin to the contrary effect — namely, preserving the liberties of Scotland and the rights of Châtelherault to succeed to the Scottish throne.[111]

Although the statements of the witnesses in support of the information against the duke of Châtelherault were taken in February the prosecutions for treason did not proceed: the intervention of the English on the side of the rebels first with money, then with the fleet (22 January) and finally with the army (April) brought the French power in Scotland to an end; and the death of the tenacious queen regent in June 1560 made possible a diplomatic settlement (July). At the same time as the treaty of Edinburgh was entered into between England and France the king and queen conceded through the agreement of their deputies 'that in the ensuing Parliament the States shall form, make, and establish an act of oblivion, which shall be confirmed by their Majesties the king and queen, for sopiting[112] and burying the memory of all bearing of arms, and such things of that nature as have happened since the 6th day of March (1559)'.[113] The promise contained in that concession was fulfilled in the legislation of the Scottish parliament in 1563 when a most ample and meticulous act of oblivion was passed.[114]

Bibliography

The *Discours* — the original document was said to run to thirteen and a half pages — was written in French or, more likely, translated into French: the indications are that McGill, Bellenden and Spens as well as some of the lords of session were at ease in that language.[115] It seems probable that at least two copies were sent to France, one of which had a few lines omitted from it in the copying.[116] One copy at least went into the French archives and was ultimately included in a collection of treaties and other documents entitled 'Traittez entre les Roys de France et les Roys d'Escosse'. According to the preface to the Bannatyne edition of the *Discours*, this compilation was made from originals in the French archives by the order of Louis XIV and presented by him to Richard Graham, viscount Preston, a Scot who had been British ambassador at the French court from 1682 to 1685;[117] and according to Keith, the ambassador had accepted this collection instead of the more usual gift of gold.[118] One copy of the collection was deposited in the Harleian manuscripts and another in the Advocates' Library[119] and it was referred to by Keith in 1734 (but without any reference to the *Discours*), and by Hume in 1819[120] who does rely on the *Discours*. It was from this

---

[111] Hay Fleming, *Mary, Queen of Scots* (London, 1897), 23.
[112] Putting to sleep or settling, *Oxford English Dictionary*.
[113] Keith, *History*, i, 302; Knox, *History*, i, 327.
[114] *APS*, ii, 535-6; see also 'Legal aspect of the Scottish Reformation', 1962 SLT (News) 84.
[115] *Information* 89; *ADC (Public)* lxii, 637.
[116] Para. 33.
[117] *Dictionary of National Biography*.
[118] Keith, *History*, i, 169.
[119] Adv. MSS 35.1.5.
[120] *Crimes* (2nd ed.), 14.

seventeenth century manuscript that Thomas Thomson prepared his edition for the Bannatyne Club.

Meanwhile, at least one copy of the original manuscript was made, and it came into the hands of Sebastien de l'Aubespine, Bishop of Limoges, almost contemporaneously. The bishop was engaged in diplomatic business and was in frequent correspondence with the Guise family. He became French ambassador at Madrid. No doubt the bishop acquired a copy of the *Discours* in the course of his diplomatic business; but he was also a collector of public documents. Part of his collection was lost with the ship that was taking his property to Spain; but others including his copy of the *Discours* were not on board: the portfolio of his documents remained until the death of the last count of l'Aubespine when they lay forgotten in the attic of the castle of Sully. They came to light in 1833 and selections of them were printed in 1841 under the title *Négociations, Lettres et Pièces Diverses rélative au règne de François II*.[121] The document which we know as the *Discours Particulier* appears in that volume;[122] it is also in French but is entitled *État et Constitution du Royaume d'Escosse*. It is reasonable to assume that the *Discours* was written in Scotland in French or translated from Scots into French and sent to the French court.[123] The *État* has some persistent differences from the *Discours*: for example, it usually renders '*sieurs*' as '*seigneurs*'. The fact that some proper names are transcribed wrongly — such as 'Erhany' for 'Orkney' and 'd'Alveris' for 'Balnevis' would tend to indicate that the *État* was possibly produced by dictating the *Discours* to a scribe who was unfamiliar with Scottish names. And other variations suggest that the *État* was transcribed from a copy different from the one which went into the French archives.

Acknowledgements

I am most grateful to Dr. A. Grant, Lady McCluskey, Dr. M. Merriman, Dr. A. L. Murray, Dr. T. I. Rae and Mr. David Sellar for the valuable assistance which I have received from them in the preparation of this work.

---

[121] Edited by Louis Paris and published by the Imprimerie Royale at Paris: see Notice Bibliographique at page xlv.

[122] At pages 225-42.

[123] Limited research in the archives of the French Foreign Office failed to turn up the original *Discours*, the *État*, the collection of treaties of the 1680s or the Aubespine papers. I have referred to the texts as follows: A, Adv MSS 35.1.5: E, *État*; and D, *Discours*.

[a]DISCOVRS PARTICVLIER D'ESCOSSE.[a]

[b]XI IANVIER M.D.LIX.[b]

LE[c] ROY ET ROYNE[d] d'Escosse noz souuerainz, ont en ce leur royaume telle préeminance et authorité royalle, comme et autant que autres [e]roys[e] chrestiens ont ou peuuent auoir sur leurs suietz, ne reconnoissant autres superieurs que dieu, roy des roys.

Et quant aux droicts et estats de la couronne, ilz consistent en la charge de deux officiers; sçauoir est, le controlleur et tresorier.

Le controlleur est [f]receuueur[f] general des droictz appelléz le proprieté; la quelle gist ez fruits, rentes et reuenus ordinaires des duchéz, comtéz et autres terres et seigneuries qui sont propres a la couronne, soient vniz ou non vniz à icelle; le reuenu des quelles est contenu ez roolles de l'eschequier. Lequel controlleur a en chascune contrée, certains commis particuliers receuueurs, pour reçeuoir les dits droictz et en tenir compte. Aussy est ledit controlleur et receuueur[g] general de toutes les grandes coustumes de toutes et chascunes villes, portz et haures de ce royaume. Et pareillement a ledit controlleur particuliers receuueurs en chascune des dictes villes, pour illec reçeuoir lesdictes grandes coustumes. Les quelles grandes coustumes consistent en ce que les marchands payent, pour transporter leurs marchandises non deffendues, comme harenc, saulmons, laynes, cuirs, draps, et autres semblables; le prix desquelles marchandises est contenu ez dictes roolles et ordonnances de l'eschequier.

Et pour le payement des droictz que dessus, ledit controlleur peut proceder par trois manieres. L'vne est l'arrest de tous et chascuns les biens estans sur le fond, [h]et vente[h] consequemment d'iceux iusques au plein payement.

L'autre est de mettre les debiteurs[i] en prison jusques audit payement.

La tierce est de les mettre à l'horne, dite rebellion, [j]et[j] exil du royaume; de la quelle s'ensuit confiscation de tous leurs biens meubles, pour fault dudit payement; et ce sans deduction de la principale debte.

---

a—a *État et Constitution du Royaulme d'Escosse:* E.
b—b 11 *Janvier* 1559: E.
c *Les:* E.
d *Reyne:* A.
e—e omitted from E.
f—f *général recepveur:* E.

g *recepveur:* E.
h—h *ne i rent:* E.
i *créditeurs:* A, E.
j—j omitted from E.

Special Survey of Scotland

11 January 1559[1]

[*1. King and Queen*]
The king and queen of Scotland,[2] our sovereigns, have in this their kingdom such and as much pre-eminence and royal authority as other christian kings have or could have over their subjects, not recognising any superiors other than God, the king of kings.[3]

[*2. Estate of the Crown*[4]]
And as for the dues and estates of the crown they are in the charge of two officers; known as the comptroller and the treasurer.

[*3. Comptroller*]
The comptroller is receiver general of the rights called the property; which consist of the fruits, rents and ordinary revenues of duchies, earldoms and other lands and lordships which appertain to the crown, be they annexed to it or not. The revenue of these is contained in the rolls of the exchequer. The comptroller has in each district certain special receivers to receive the said duties and keep an account of them. Also, the said person is comptroller and receiver general of the great customs of all and every burgh port and harbour of this kingdom. And likewise the said comptroller has special receivers in each of the said burghs there to receive the said great customs which customs consist in what the merchants pay to export their goods (such as are not prohibited[5]) such as herring, salmon, wool, hides, cloths and other such things; the price of such goods is contained in the said rolls and ordinances of the exchequer.

[*4. Poinding of the ground*]
And to receive payment of these duties the said comptroller can proceed in three ways. One is the arrestment of all and sundry goods being on the ground and subsequent sale of them up to full payment.

[*5. Imprisonment*]
The other is to put the debtors in ward until said payment.

[*6. Horning*]
The third is to put them to the horn, otherwise 'rebellion', and exile from the kingdom;[6] from which follows escheat of all their movable goods in default of payment; and this without deduction of the principal debt.

---

[1] That is 1560 in the modern computation.
[2] Francis, king of Scotland, 1558-60, king of France, 1559-60; Mary, queen of Scots, 1542-67, queen of France, 1559-60.
[3] See Introduction, 88.
[4] See Introduction, 88-90.
[5] Para. 9.
[6] Para. 23.

Et pour l'intelligence des parolles 'vniz ou non vniz,' est^a à sauoir qu'il^b y a des terres au^c roy qui sont vniz, lesquelles ne peuuent estre alliennées, ny baillées à ferme perpetuelle, dicte emphiteose, sans le consentement des trois estats. Il y a aussy des terres non vnies; comme la comté de Murray, qui nagueres est escheue à la couronne, pour ce que le dernier heretier d'icelle estoit bastard; et pareillement les terres du comte de Lennox et d'autres, qui pour auoir esté condamnéz de leze maiesté, ont perdu leurs terres; et icelles confisquées a la couronne; et le roy peult faire alliénation et disposition de ces terres, sans l'aduis ou consentement desditz trois estatz.

Et desdites seigneuries et terres appartenans^d à la couronne, vne grande partie est baillée à ferme perpetuelle; autre partie, à ferme pour trois, cinq, sept ou neuf ans. Et est à notter, que les tenans d'icelles qui sont pour vn certain temps, ne font aulcun bastiment, ne plants ou autre police sur les dites terres, pour crainte d'estre eiectéz^e d'icelles.

Il y a certaines marchandises prohibées et deffendues d'estre portées hors de ce royaume, sur peine de confiscation d'icelles; comme bledz, orge, auoyne, et autres grains, chairs et gresse, poisson blanc, scauoir morue et merlue.

Le tresorier a generalle intromission et charge sur les casualitéz; lesquelles consistent ez droictz et proffitz que^f par accident et aduenture viennent à la couronne; comme wardis,^{g} relieffis, non-entrées aux terres vaccantes, ^{h}proffitz^h les mariages.

Item compositions données de par le roy, pour infeudations au^i terres vendues ou resignées entre les habitans de ce royaume ez mains du roy; aussy tout le reuenu des biens meubles escheuz à la couronne par confiscation, et execution de iustice en cas criminel; pareillement les compositions faictes pour remissions et pardons des crimes commis; mesmes les biens des bastardz non legitiméz, et autres ^{j}qui decedent^j sans hoirs.

Item les fruitz et reuenus temporelz des ueschéz, iceulz vaccans, et iusques à l'intimation des bulles de la prouision d'iceux. Finablement les profittz qui peuuent venir des mines et du coing: et est à entendre que toutes les mines d'or ou

---

a *ce est:* E.   f *qui:* E.
b omitted from E.   g *wardie:* E.
c *du:* E.   h—h *par décetz:* E.
d *appartenant:* E.   i *aux:* E.
e *déjéctés:* E.   j—j *décedentz:* E.

[7. *Annexed and unannexed land*]

And in order to understand the words 'annexed or unannexed' it is necessary to know that there are lands of the king which are annexed, which cannot be alienated nor set in perpetual feu (otherwise called emphyteusis[7]) without the consent of the three estates. There are also unannexed lands; such as the earldom of Moray, which recently was escheat to the crown because the last heir of it was a bastard,[8] and similarly the lands of the earl of Lennox and others, who having been convicted of treason have lost their lands;[9] and the same were confiscated to the crown; and the king can alienate or dispone these lands without the advice or consent of the said three estates.

[8. *Feus*]

And of the said lordships and lands pertaining to the crown a great part is set in perpetual feu; the other part in tack for three, five, seven or nine years. And it is to be noted that the tenants of these leases, which are for a specified time, do not make any building, plantations or other improvement on the said lands for fear of being ejected from them.[10]

[9. *Prohibited exports*]

There are certain goods whose export is forbidden on pain of confiscation; such as wheat, beir, oats and other grains, meat and tallow, white fish, that is, cod and hake.

[10. *Treasurer*]

The treasurer has general intromission and charge over the casualty which consists of the duties and profits that come to the crown by accident and chance; such as wards, reliefs, non-entries to vacant lands, profits of marriages.

[11. *Compositions*]

Also compositions given by the king for entry to lands sold or resigned by the inhabitants of this kingdom into the hands of the king;[11] also, all the revenue of movable goods escheat to the crown by confiscation and execution of justice in criminal causes;[12] similarly compositions made for remissions and pardons for crimes already committed; likewise the goods of bastards who have not been legitimated and others who die without heirs.

[12. *Other revenues*]

Also the fruits and revenues of temporalities of bishoprics *sede vacante* and until intimation of the bulls for the provision thereof.[13] Finally, the profits which may come from the mines and the coinage;[14] and it should be understood that all

---

[7] A Greek word for a Roman invention so similar to the Scottish feu farm that Craig and other writers apply the word to the feu-right.
[8] *Scots Peerage*, vi, 311-2.
[9] *Scots Peerage*, v, 353.
[10] See Introduction, 89.
[11] Para. 21.
[12] Para. 22.
[13] Balfour, *Practicks*, 23.
[14] 1424, c. 13 (*APS*, ii, 5).

d'argent de ce royaume appartiennent au roy, mesmes celles de plomb, duquel en l'affinant l'on peut tirer et extraire argent, comme et quel est tout le plomb de ce pays; et ce sans donner aucun droit ou composition au sieur de la terre ou sont scituées les dites mines.

Il est à notter que toutes terres de ce royaume sont tenues[a] du roy par ses suiets en cinq manieres: sçauoir est, warde[b], dicte en françois, guarde; la seconde est dicte blancheferme; la tierce est appellée en bourgeosie; la quarte[c] est dicte en omosne; la cinq[e] est à ferme perpetuelle, ou à certain temps, comme est declaré en l'article de la proprieté.

Warde est, quant les possesseurs d'icelles terres meurent, leurs heriteurs ne peuuent auoir possession, dicte en escossois saisine, et entrée ez dites terres, iusques à ce qu'ils sont[d] d'age de vingt vn[e] ans complets, quant aux masles, et quant aux femelles, xiiij ans complets; durant lequel temps, le roy tient lesdictes terres en sa main. Et à l'entrée ausdites terres, appellées saisine, les heritiers sont tenus d'aduancer les fruitz d'vne année au roy pour leur entrée; ce qui est appellée relief. Et au cas que les heritiers d'iceulx tenans terres du roy en[f] warde ne soient mariéz, ilz sont tenus de se[g] marier au plaisir et volonté du roy, auec toutesfois de[h] personnes de bonne renommée et pareil estat; sur peine s'ilz y sont masles, et requis de par le roy a eux marier, de payer le double du proffit qu'ilz auroient ou pouroient auoir pour ledit mariage; et s'ilz ne sont à ce requis, de payer ledit proffit. Et s'ilz sont femelles, requises pour le dit mariage comme dessus, et se marient à autres personnes que à celles nommées de par le roy, elles payent pareillement le double du proffit de leur mariage; lequel mariage est estimé plus que trop chair en ce pays, et presque à la valleur des terres: Et sy elles ne sont requises, elles payent seulement la valleur de leurs mariages. Et ou[i] cas qu'elles ayent [j]à faire[j] charnellement auec aucun, sans estre auec luy mariée,[k] elles perdent la succession dudit heritage; et sy celle qui a [j]à faire[j] charnellement sans mariage a sœur, les terres qu'elle perd pour ce, sont escheues et deuolues à icelle sa sœur.

Et combien que le tenant desdites terres en warde tient[l] aussy autres terres d'autres seigneurs aussy[m] en warde, de quelque valleur qu'elles soient, il ne doit rien ausdits[n] seigneurs desquels il tient aussy lesdites terres, pour raison de son mariage; mais seulement au roy est tenu de payer tout le proffit.

a *terres:* E.
b *Wardis:* A.
c *quatrième:* E.
d *soient:* A and E.
e xxj: E.
f *à:* A and E.
g *soi:* E.

h omitted from E.
i *en:* E.
j—j *affaire:* E.
k *mariées:* E.
l *tienne:* E.
m omitted from E.
n *aux susdits:* E.

the gold or silver mines of this kingdom pertain to the king, and similarly lead mines from which, by refining, one can extract silver, and such is all the lead of this country; and this without giving any dues or composition to the lord of the land where the said mines are situated.

[13. Land-holding]

It should be noted that all the lands of this country are held of the king by his subjects in five ways: viz., ward, called *guarde* in French; the second is called blench farm; the third is called burgage; the fourth is called alms; the fifth feu farm, permanent or for a certain time,[15] as is explained in the article on the property.[16]

[14. Ward[17]]

Ward arises when the possessors of these lands die, their heirs cannot have possession (called sasine in Scots) and entry to the said lands until they have reached the age of twenty one years complete, in the case of males, and in that of females fourteen years complete; during which time the king holds the said lands in his hands. And at entry to the said lands (called sasine) the heirs are bound to pay in advance the fruits of one year to the king for their entry; which is called relief.[18] And in the case where the heirs of these lands held in ward are not married,[19] they are bound to marry at the pleasure and will of the king with, however, persons of good repute and like estate; on pain of paying, if they are males and required by the king to marry, double the profit that they would or could have had by the said marriage; and if they are not required to do so, of paying the said profit. And if they are females, required to marry as described above, and if they marry persons other than those nominated by the king they pay likewise double the profit of their marriage; which marriage is valued at far too great a price in this country and almost the value of the lands.[20] And if they are not required to marry they pay only the value of their marriage. And in the case where they have carnal copulation with anyone without being married to him, they lose the succession to the said heritage; and if the one who has the carnal connexion without marriage has a sister, the lands which she loses through this are escheat and devolve upon her said sister.

[15. Double tenure]

And whenever the tenant of the said lands in ward also holds other lands of other lords also in ward, of whatever value they be, they owe nothing to the said lords from whom they also hold the said lands because of his marriage: but he must only pay the whole profit to the king.[21]

---

[15] i.e. tack not feu: see para. 8.
[16] Para. 3.
[17] Balfour, *Practicks*, 250-4.
[18] Balfour, *Practicks*, 255-7.
[19] Balfour, *Practicks*, 243-50.
[20] See Introduction, 89-90.
[21] But see Balfour, *Practicks*, 245.

Et est à notter que les possesseurs des dites terres ainsy tenues, ne les peuuent vendre, ne donner, en tout ny pour la grande partie d'icelles, sans congé[a] du roy: et s'ilz les vendent en tout ou plus grande partie, les vendeurs et achepteurs d'icelles perdent les terres, et sont confisquées entre les mains du roy.

Blanche ferme est la plus noble et franche manière de tenir terres en ce royaume; car les possesseurs des terres ainsy tenues ne sont tenus si non de payer annuellement, comme en la feste St Jean Baptiste, vne rose, ou vne paire de gands, ou autre semblable chose, en signe de liberté, comme appert par les lettres de leurs infeudations sur ce faites.

En Bourgeosie consiste en ce, que le roy a donné certaines terres de villes et bourgages, aux habitans pour le temps ez dites villes et bourgages, pour illec faire bastir maisons; [b]pour lesquelles maisons[b] est payé chascun an au roy, certaines petites sommes contenues en [c][rooles de][c] l'eschequier.

En Omosne est, que le roy a donné à l'eglise certaines terres pour faire prieres et oraisons à perpetuité.

Nonentrée. Il convient entendre que, par las coustume de ce royaume, le mort ne saisit le vif en terres et heritages; car le possesseur trespassé, son heritier ne peut, de son[d] propre auctorité, prendre possession des terres du trespassé, sy en prealable ne obtient lettres de la chancellerie, addressantes[e] au seneschal, steward ou bailliff du pays ou sont scituées les dites terres, à cet effect de s'enquerir qui est le vray heritier dudit deffunct; et l'inquisition faite de par le dit seneschal, et reproduite en la chancellerie, le dit heritier impetre autres lettres de la chancellerie, addressantes audit[f] seneschal, steward ou bailiff, pour le mettre en possession d'icelles terres; pendant lequel temps, le roy a lesdites terres en sa main, ce qui est appellée nonentrée: et ce droit de nonentrée a lieu en terres tenues du roy en chacune de trois manieres de tenir terres dessusdites, qui font, warde, blancheferme, et ferme perpetuelle, dite emphiteose.

Et pour plus facilement entendre l'article, 'des compositions données pour les infeudations aux terres vendues, ou resignées entre les habitans de ce royaume ez mains du roy,' faut entendre que le roy n'est tenu reçeuoir aucunes resignations, [g]n'autres[g] dispositions desdites terres, si non à son bon plaisir, et pourtant pour ce composition que reçoit son tresorier.

---

a *congié:* E.
b—b omitted from E.
c—c omitted from A.
d *sa:* E.

e *addressées:* E.
f *susdit:* E.
g—g *n'y aultres:* E.

[*16. Alienation of land*]

And it should be noted that the possessors of the said lands held in this manner cannot sell them nor give them, in whole or in great part, without leave of the king; and if they sell them wholly or the greater part, the seller and buyer of them lose the lands and they are confiscated into the hands of the king.

[*17. Blench*]

Blench farm is the most noble and free way of holding lands in this kingdom; for the possessors of the lands thus held are obliged only to pay annually as, at the feast of St. John the Baptist, a rose, or a pair of gloves, or other similar things as a token of liberty, as appears from the writs or their infeftments made thereupon.

[*18. Burgage*]

Burgage consists in this, that the king has given certain lands of towns and burghs to the inhabitants for the time in the said towns and burghs to have their houses built there; for which houses is paid each year to the king certain small sums contained in the rolls of the exchequer.

[*19. Alms[22]*]

Alms occur when the king has given to the church certain lands in perpetuity for saying of prayers and orisons.

[*20. Nonentry[23]*]

Nonentry. It is fitting to explain that by the custom of this kingdom, the deceased does not seise the living in lands and heritages; for the possessor being deceased his heir cannot by his own authority take possession of the lands of the deceased unless he first obtain brieves of chancery direct to the sheriff, steward or bailie of the district where the said lands are situated, to the effect of enquiring of them who is the true heir of the deceased; and the inquest having been made by the said sheriff and retoured to chancery the heritor obtains further brieves of chancery addressed to the said sheriff, steward or bailie to give him possession of these lands. During this time the king has the said lands in his hands which is called nonentry; and this right of nonentry arises in lands held of the king in each of the three ways of holding the above mentioned lands, which are ward, blench farm and perpetual feu, called emphyteusis.

[*21. Composition*]

And the more easily to understand the article 'of composition given for infeftments of lands sold or resigned by the inhabitants of this kingdom into the hands of the king'[24] it should be understood that the king is not obliged to receive any resignations, or other dispositions of the said lands except at his good pleasure and in so far as his treasurer receives composition.

---

[22] Balfour, *Practicks*, 142.
[23] Balfour, *Practicks*, 257-64.
[24] Para. 11.

Et pour l'intelligence de l'article, 'aussy tout le reuenu des biens meubles escheuz à la couronne par confiscation et execution de iustice en cas criminel,' *a*est à sauoir*a* que combien que aucun soit mis à mort, et executé par iustice, pour quelque cas que ce soit, il ne perd pour ce ses terres et heritages, si non en de crimes de leze maiesté. Et par les actes de parlement dernierement faits par feu de bonne memoire Jacques roy d'Escosse cinq*e*, est dict et enjoint que aucun n'ayt a brusler gerbes de bledz ou autres grains, ou faire meurtre de conseillers de la session de ce royaume, sur peine de leze maiesté. Pour autres crimes, et condemnations de corps ensuiuyes, n'y a perte ny confiscation, si non de leurs biens meubles.

Et pour l'intelligence de l'article, horne, dite rebellion, est à notter que sy aucun demeure en icelle an et iour, toutes ses terres sont confisquées pour ce ez mains du roy, la vie durant dudit rebelle; après la mort du quel, son heritier peult succeder à icelles. Et en cas que le roy succede, pour cause de delit et crime, ez biens d'aucuns criminelz, *b*encores que leurs debtes fussent liquidées par sentence ou autrement*b*, le roy n'est tenu payer aucune chose aux crediteurs d'iceux criminelz.

Et quant à la maniere de proceder et faire la iustice ez causes ciuilles, faut entendre que le royaume d'Escosse est diuisé en plusieurs vicomtéz et seneschasséz*c*; y a vn seneschal qui est iuge ordinaire du pays, ayant iurisdiction et connoissance en toutes causes ciuilles en la premiere instance, hors mises les matieres des terres et heritages, quant au petitoire d'icelles, en quoy ledit seneschal n'a aucune iurisdiction: Tous lesquels seneschaulx ont leurs offices en heritage, du pere au filz, et aussy*d* de degré en degré; reservé Orknay*e* et Zetland, les quels deux seneschaux sont ad nutum. Et lesdits seneschaux sont tenus faire iustice à vn chacun, sans prendre ny exiger pour l'administration de iustice aucune chose des parties. Et en la seneschaussée d'Air y a trois baillages, en chacun desquels les baillifs, et chacun d'eulx, ont iurisdiction comme le seneschal, exerceans leurs offices comme luy; lesquelz sont semblablement en heritage. Et en la seneschaussée de Perth, y a deux officiers ditz 'stewartz,' lesquelz ont tel pouuoir comme les dits baillifs; et n'y a aucune difference desdits offices de stewarts et baillifs, si non de nom tant seulement; lesquels baillifs et stewarts ne peuuent semblablement prendre ny exiger aucune chose pour l'administration de

a—a c'est assavoir: E; est assavoir: A.
b—b transported to end of paragraph in E.
c en chascune desquelles sénéchaussées supplied from E.
d ainsi: E.
e Erhnay: E.

[*22. Escheat*]

And for understanding of the article 'also all the revenue of moveable goods escheat to the crown by confiscation and execution of justice in a criminal cause'[25] it should be understood that if someone is put to death and executed according to justice, for any cause whatsoever, he does not lose his lands and heritage unless in crimes of lese majesty. And by the acts of parliament lately passed by the late king James the fifth of Scotland of good memory it is said and enjoined that no one must burn sheaves of wheat or other grain[26] or murder the councillors of the session of this kingdom[27] on pain of lese majesty. For other crimes, and capital convictions, there is no loss or confiscation except their moveable goods.

[*23. Life-rent escheat*]

And for understanding of the article on horning (called rebellion[28]) it is to be noted that if any one remains in this state for a year and a day, because of that all his lands are confiscated into the hands of the king during the life of the said rebel; but after his death his heir can succeed to the same. And in the case where the king succeeds on account of offence or crime to the goods of any criminals, although their debts have been made liquid by decree or otherwise, the king is not bound to pay anything to the creditors of these criminals.

[*24. Sheriffs*]

And as for the manner of proceeding and doing justice in civil causes it should be understood that the kingdom of Scotland is divided in several sheriffdoms and stewartries: (in each of which sheriffdoms[29]) there is one sheriff who is judge ordinary of the country having jurisdiction and cognizance in all civil causes in the first instance, except matters concerning lands and heritages, as for claims for the same in which the said sheriff has no jurisdiction:[30] all these sheriffs have their offices in fee, from the father to the son and also from degree to degree; except Orkney and Zetland, which two sheriffdoms are at pleasure. And the said sheriffs are bound to do justice to each one without taking or exacting anything from the parties for the administration of justice. And in the sheriffdom of Ayr there are three bailiaries[31] in each of which the bailies and each of them have a jurisdiction like the sheriff and they exercise their offices like him; these are similarly hereditary offices. And in the sheriffdom of Perth there are two officers called stewards[32] who have the same power as the said bailies; and there is no difference between the said offices of 'steward' and 'bailie' unless in name only. These bailies and stewards can likewise take or exact nothing for the administration of justice

[25] Para. 11.
[26] 1526, c. 10 (*APS*, ii, 316).
[27] Cf. *APS*, ii, 445. Robert Galbraith, parson of Spott, was murdered between 17 December 1543 and 13 February 1544: Brunton and Haig, *Senators of the College of Justice* (1832), 57-8. After the Union the English law of treason superseded the Scots law, but by a new statute of the Union Parliament it was again declared to be treason to murder a judge of the supreme court: Treason Act 1708 (7 Anne c. 21) section 9; Hume, *Commentaries*, i, 522 and note 2.
[28] Para. 6.
[29] Supplied from E.
[30] Balfour, *Practicks*, 19.
[31] Kyle, Carrick and Cunningham.
[32] Strathearn and Menteith.

iustice, comme dit est des seneschaux[a]. Toutesfois les sentences de par eulx et chascun d'eux données, sont non retractables, et sans appel ausdits seneschaux ou autres, sy non immediatement ausdits sieurs de la session.

Est à notter qu'il est permis à la partie actrice de plaider sa cause deuant le iuge ordinaire, ou sy mieux luy plaist, deuant les sieurs de la session immediatement à la premiere instance, sans que la partie deffendante puisse demander renuoy; hors mises les causes de petite consequence, et dessous la valleur de quatre vingtz[b] liures tournois.

Et n'y a aucune appellation des sentences données de par les seneschaux. Toutesfois peult la partie condamnée se plaindre aux sieurs de la session, de la sentence donnée contre elle par le dit seneschal; lesquels sieurs de la session pourront pourtant connoistre de la cause, par la voye de complainte; la sentence, toutesfois et ce nonobstant, dudit seneschal demourant entiere et executée, iusques a la decizion desdit sieurs de la session au contraire; si non en cas qu'il apparoisse notoirement et de prime face, ausdits sieurs de la session, de la notoire iniustice dudit seneschal; ou qu'il ayt iugé et cognu en chose ou il n'avoit aucune iurisdiction, comme en matiere de petitoire de heritage[c]; et en ce cas, lesdit sieurs de la session suspendent et rompent l'execution de la sentence dudit seneschal.

Aussy tous barons de ce royaume tenans terres de baronnies[d], ont iurisdiction au dedans desdits terres, sur leurs subiectz illec demourans, ez cas de petite consequence; comme de iniures verballes, prinses et usurpations d'aucuns biens meubles, et autres petites choses et altercations auenantes iournellement entre viosins; et ce sans appellation, si non par voye de complainte ausdits sieurs de la session, comme dessus est dit des sentences des seneschaux; lesquelz barons ne leurs deputéz ne peuuent [e]n'en[e] prendre des parties pour l'administration de la iustice, pour ce qu'ilz ont leurs offices en heritage[f].

Aussy y a certains prelatz d'eglise, et autres seigneurs temporelz, qui ont priuilege et iurisdiction de regalité en leurs terres; les iuges desquelz regalitéz ont telle et semblable iurisdiction de cognoistre ez causes ciuilles comme les seneschaux. Et auenant que aucuns des habitans de leurs terres soient adiournéz pour comparoistre deuant les ditz seneschaux, baillifs, stewarts ou autres iugez,

a *et combien que les baillifs et stevards soient juges inférieurs des sénéschaulx* supplied from E.
b iiii[xx]: E.
c *d'héritage:* E.
d *baronnye:* E.
e—e *riens:* E.
f *héritaiges:* E.

(as in the case of the said sheriffs), although the bailies and stewards are judges inferior to the sheriffs. Always the judgments give by them and each of them are final, and without appeal to the said sheriffs or others, except immediately to the said lords of session.

[25. Choice of forum]

And it should be noted that it is permitted to the pursuer to plead his cause before the judge ordinary, or if it pleases him better, before the lords of the session directly in the first instance without the defender's being able to demand remit to another judge except in causes of little consequence and under the value of eighty livres tournois.[33]

[26. Appeal]

And there is no appeal from decreet given by the sheriff. Yet, it is possible for the unsuccessful party to complain to the lords of session of the decreet given against him by the said sheriff; the lords of session would be able however to cognosce the cause by way of complaint; nevertheless and notwithstanding this, the sentence of the said sheriff always remaining entire, and executed, until the decision of the said lords of session to the contrary; unless in the case where there appears plainly and *prima facie* to the said lords of session manifest injustice on the part of the said sheriff; or that he has judged and cognosced in a matter where he had no jurisdiction, as in matters of claim to ownership to heritage; and in that case the said lords or session suspend and reduce execution of the decreet of the said sheriff.

[27. Barons[34]]

Also, all barons of this kingdom holding their lands in barony have jurisdiction within the said lands, over their vassals living there in causes of small consequence; such as verbal injuries, spuilzie, prises, and usurpations of any movable goods; and other small matters and quarrels occurring daily among neighbours; and this without appeal, unless by way of complaint to the said lords of session, as is said above of decreets of the sheriffs. These barons or their deputes cannot take anything from the parties for the administration of justice, because they hold their offices in fee.

[28. Regalities[35]]

Also there are certain prelates of the church and other temporal lords who have the privilege and jurisdiction of regality in their lands; the judges of which regalities have the same sort of jurisdiction to cognosce civil causes as the sheriffs. And in the event of any inhabitants of their lands being called upon to compear the said sheriffs, bailies, stewards or other judges, the said lords, prelates of the

---

[33] £40 Scots: Hope, *Major Practicks* (Stair Society), 5.6.21; cf. Balfour, *Practicks*, 664, a similar limit in the commissary court in 1564.
[34] Balfour, *Practicks*, 38-42.
[35] Balfour, *Practicks*, 289.

lesdits sieurs prelatz d'eglise et sieurs temporels, replegent lesdits habitans de leurs terres; c'est à dire, demandent et obtiennent renuoy des ditz leurs subiectz deuant eux ou leurs deputtéz, en donnant caution au seneschal de faire et administrer la iustice aux parties.

Toutesfois sy les ditz habitans de regalité sont conuenus et adiournéz par deuant les ditz sieurs de la session, ladite replegiation ou renuoy n'a lieu en ce cas. Les quelz sieurs de regalité ne peuuent prendre ny exiger aucune chose pour l'administration de la iustice; et n'y a aucune appellation de leurs sentences, si non et comme dessus est dit des seneschaux, par voye de complainte deuant lesdits sieurs de la session.

Et en chascune des villes franches de ce royaume, y a un preuost et quatre baillifs; qui sont par chascun an esleuz des habitans des dites villes, en la feste de St Michael communement; lesquels preuost et baillifs ont iurisdiction ez habitans desdites villes, telle et en toute semblable comme celle des ditz seneschaulx.

Les derniers et supremes iugez en ce royaume ez matieres ciuilles^a, sont les sieurs de la session, autrement nomméz le college de la iustice; lesquelz ont pleine connoissance en toutes causes ciuilles, tant en premiere qu'en seconde instance; la iurisdiction desquelz est si grande, qu'ilz peuuent euocquer^b à soy toutes causes dependantes deuant tous les autres iuges de ce royaume, et leur faire inhibition et deffenses de ne proceder outre ez dites causes, sur peine de nullité de procèz et perte de leurs offices: Laquelle inhibition et deffense n'ont accoustumé de faire lesdits sieurs, sy non en cas concernans le fait et estat du parlement de ce royaume, ou quand les parties, ou vne^c d'icelles, ne ozent comparoistre par deuant ledit seneschal, ou pour autres grandes et vrgentes causes et raisons; et ce, ante litis contestationem, et in statu in quo erat lis apud ^{d}iudicem a quo^d. Lesdits sieurs procedent en toutes leurs causes sommairement; et combien que la citation soit par escrit, et la coppie d'icelle baillée à la partie deffendante, ce neantmoins, sur toute la reste du procèz, les partyes sont contraintz de respondre et repliquer par viue parolle, sans ce qu'il leur soit octroyé delay aucun pour soy aduiser; si ce n'est pour auoir inspection des droitz des parties et escriptures produittes, à quoy on leur assigne le lendemain.

Les dits sieurs sont nombre de quinze; sçauoir est, vn president, et autres sept tousiours de l'estat spirituel, et sept autres gens laiques. Et pour leur estat et entretènement, leur a esté accordée^e de ^{f}II^m VIII^{cf} liures tournois^g, imposée par le feu pape Clement VIIe sur les prelatz de l'eglise de ce royaume; et est distribuée en maniere de distributions quotidianes, aux residentz et non à autres; car les

a *criminelles:* E.
b *avocquer:* E.
c *l'une:* E.
d—d *judices aequos:* E.
e *pension* supplied from E.
f—f *deux mil huit cent livres:* E.
g omitted from E.

church, and temporal lords repledge the said inhabitants to their lands; that is to say, they demand and obtain the remit of their said subjects before them or their deputes, giving caution to the sheriff that they will do and administer justice to the parties.

[*29. Regalities and the lords of session*]

Always, if the said inhabitants of regality are convened and called upon before the said lords of session the said repledging or remit has no place. These lords of regality cannot take or exact any thing for the administration of justice; and there is no appeal from their judgments unless, as is said above of the sheriffs, by way of complaint before the said lords of session.

[*30. Burgh Court*[36]]

And in each of the free burghs of this kingdom there is a provost and four bailies; who are each year elected by the inhabitants of the said burgh, usually at the feast of St. Michael;[37] and the provost and bailies have jurisdiction over the inhabitants of the said burghs in all respects the same as that of the said sheriff.[38]

[*31. Lords of session*[39]]

The last and supreme judges in this kingdom in civil matters are the lords of session, otherwise called the college of justice; and they have full cognizance in all civil causes both in the first and in the second instance. Their jurisdiction is so great that they can advocate to themselves all causes depending before all other judges of this kingdom and inhibit and forbid them from proceeding further in the said causes, on pain of nullity of process and loss of their offices. The said lords have not been in use to make this inhibition and prohibition except in cases concerning the business and condition of the parliament of this kingdom, or when the parties or one of them dare not compear before the said sheriff or for other and great and urgent causes and reasons; and this *ante litis contestationem et statu quo erat lis apud iudicem a quo*. The said lords proceed summarily in all their causes; and although the citation is by writ and the copy of the same is served on the defender, nevertheless, on all the rest of the process the parties are compelled to reply and defend orally without there being permitted to them any delay to advise themselves; unless for having inspection of the titles of parties and writs produced for which they are assigned the next day.

[*32. Composition and remuneration*]

The said lords are fifteen in number, that is, a president and other seven always of the spiritual estate, and other seven laymen. And for their remuneration and maintenance there was accorded to them a pension of 2,800 livres tournois[40] imposed by the late Pope Clement VIII on the prelates of the church of this kingdom; and it is distributed by way of daily payment to those in

---

[36] Balfour, *Practicks*, 42-4.
[37] 29 September.
[38] See Introduction, 90.
[39] Balfour, *Practicks*, 265-72.
[40] £1400 Scots: Keith, *History* (Spottiswoode Society, 1844), i, 469.

absens, soit par cause de maladie, ou pour la republique, ou autre cas tant que peut estre necessaire, ne sont aucunement participans des dites distributions.

Les dits sieurs viennent et se assiessent à la session, chacun iour ouurable au matin, trois heures deuant disner; et ont vaccances depuis le dernier iour d'Aoust, iusques a l'vnziesme de Nouembre; et depuis[a] la veille de Pasques fleuries, iusques au dimanche de Kasimodo[b]; et du mercredy precedant la feste de Pentecouste, iusques au iour et feste du dimanche de la Trinité.

Et quant à l'administration de [c]iustice ez[c] causes criminellez, lesditz seneschaulx, baillifz et stewartz ont, chacun en leurs pays, iurisdiction et puissance de punir homicides et mutilations nouuellement faites; c'est à sauoir, dedans trois iours après le crime commis. Car lesditz officiers sont tenus d'apprehender les meurtriers et mutilateurs incontinent après le fait, et faire de ce soudaine et briefue iustice, tellement que s'ils ne le font dedans ledit temps de trois iours, leur iurisdiction est pour ce expirée; et partant sont tenus de mettre ez mains de la supreme iustice, lesdits meurtriers et mutilateurs.

Pareillement lesdits officiers ont iurisdiction de punir les larrons qu'ilz trouuent saisiz de larçin, et les recepteurs[d] d'iceulx; de quoy sont aussy tenuz de faire briefue et soudaine iustice. Aussy lesditz officiers ont iurisdiction de punir tous qui frappent et blessent aucuns, et font effusion de sang, ou font autres iniures corporelles, et à[e] tant soudainement et de[f] brief, que de long temps après le crime faict.

Aussy lesditz barons qui tiennent leurs terres en baronnie, ont iurisdiction criminelle sur les habitans de leurs terres, comme et autant que lesdits officiers ont iurisdiction de punir tous qui frappent et[g] blessent aucuns, et font effusion de sang, ou font autres iniures corporelles, sy mort ou mutillation pour ce ne s'ensuit.

Semblablement, pour ce que larcin est fort commun en ce royaume, et à ce euiter, les dits barons ont semblable pouuoir de punir les larrons et recepteurs[h], comme ont les ditz seneschaulx; et pour ce faire, ont authorité d'eriger en leurs iurisdictions, tant de potences qu'il leur plaist.

---

a la veille saint Thomas, avant Noel jusques au lendemain du jour des Roys et depuis supplied from E.
b Quasimodo: E.
c—c la justice: E.
d recelleurs: e
e ce
f omitted from E.
g ou: E.
h recelleurs: E.

residence and not to the others: for the absentees, be it because of illness, or state business, or other necessary reason, get no share at all of the said distributions.[41]

[33. Sittings]

The said lords come and sit in the session every weekday in the morning; three hours before dinner. And they have vacation from the last day of August until the eleventh of November; (and from the eve of St. Thomas before Christmas[42] to the day after the day of the Kings[43]) and from the eve of Palm Sunday until Low Sunday.[44] And from the Wednesday preceding Whitsunday until the day and feast of Trinity Sunday.[45]

[34. Criminal jurisdiction of sheriff[46]]

And as for the administration of justice in criminal causes the said sheriffs, bailies and stewards have, each in their own districts jurisdiction and power to punish homicide and mutilation recently committed, that is within three days after the commission of the crime. For the said officers are obliged to arrest murderers and assailants incontinent after the event, and to do speedy and summary justice thereon, so that if they do not do so within the said space of three days, their jurisdiction in this matter expires. And consequently they are obliged to put the said murderers and assailants into the hands of the supreme justice.

[35. Theft]

Similarly, the said officers have jurisdiction to punish thieves whom they find possessed of the stolen goods, and also the resetters of the same. Upon them they are also obliged to do summary and speedy justice. Moreover the said officers have jurisdiction to punish all those who attack and wound anyone, to the effusion of blood, or inflict other bodily injuries, if death or mutilation do not ensue.

[36. Barony[47]]

Also, the said barons who hold their lands in barony exercise criminal jurisdiction over the inhabitants of their lands as the said officers have jurisdiction to punish all those who strike and wound anyone to the effusion of blood, or commit other bodily injuries if death or mutilation do not ensue.

[37. Theft]

Similarly, since theft is very common in this kingdom and in order to suppress it, the said barons have similar power to punish thieves and resetters, just as do the said sheriffs; and in order to carry this out they have authority to erect within their jurisdiction as many gallows as they please.

[41] McNeill, 'Senators of the College of Justice, 1569-1578', 1960 Jur. Rev. 120.
[42] 21 December.
[43] Twelfth night, 6 January. The passage in brackets is supplied from E.
[44] Sunday next after Easter.
[45] Later altered to 10 July to 20 October with a fortnight's vacation at Yule and Easter: 1567, c. 29 (*APS*, iii, 32).
[46] Balfour, *Practicks*, 503.
[47] Balfour, *Practicks*, 39.

Mesmes lesditz iuges de regalité ont priuilege, et pleine iurisdiction en leurs terres, de punir tous crimes, tant vieux que nouueaux, hors mis les crimes de leze maiesté, et les quatre cas reseruéz à la couronne; qui sont, rauissement des filles et femmes, et rapine publicque auec resistence, bruslement, et homicide ªsecret non confesséª. Lesquelz iuges de regalité, auenant que leurs suietz soient conuenus[b] par deuant autres iuges, ils les replegent; c'est à dire, demandent et obtennent renuoy de leurs dits suietz deuant eulx, pour crimes par eulx commis ez terres de la regalité; en donnant par iceulx iuges de regalité, caution de faire et administrer iustice.

Et aussy y a en ce royaume, iustice generalle, laquelle a puissance de cognoistre en tous crimes. Et combien que pour ce iourd'huy n'y en ayt qu'vn[c], toutesfois le temps passé y en auoit deux; l'vn[d] estoit par de là la riuiere ᵉde Forthᵉ tirant vers le north; et l'autre, de l'autre coste de la riuiere tirant vers le south[f]. Sur quoy conuient entendre, que ez sentences criminelles, tant données de par les seneschaulx, iuges de regalité, barons et autres iuges, n'y a aucun appel, mais d'elles s'ensuit incontinent l'execution; et en cas que les heritiers de celuy mis a mort, voyent que le iuge ait mal procedé contre luy, ilz peuuent, par voye de simple querelle, se plaindre au roy, et aux troix estatz de ce royaume, estans assembléz en plein parlement, et demander reduction et rescizion dudit procèz. Sur quoy faut notter, que tous et chacuns les officiers ont leurs offices en heritage, c'est à dire du pere au filz, et de degré en degré, excepté seulement l'office de la iustice generalle dessusdit, les officiers de la quelle sont ad nutum principis; tous les quelz officiers ne peuuent exiger ne prendre aucune chose des parties pour l'administration de la iustice criminelle.

Et quant à l'execution et punissement des crimes de leze maiesté, communement appellé en ce royaume, trahison, il y a deux manieres d'y proceder. L'vne est que quant aucun est suspect dudit crime, le roy ordonne que les trois estatz de son royaume soient assembléz en parlement, et son aduocat fait adiourner le criminel pour comparoir deuant sa maiesté et sa iustice generalle audit parlement, pour illec respondre aux crimes continus en la citation. Et à icelle fin que ledit criminel, au iour à luy assigné, soit prest de promptement respondre aux pointz et crimes[g] de la dite citation, le double d'icelle luy est baillé ou offert; car au premier iour il est tenu de comparoir, et vser de toutes ses deffenses. Et s'il ne compare au iour a luy assigné, on procede ʰin pœnam contumaciæʰ; receuans toutes probations, et autres choses necessaires pour la deduction[i] du procèz allencontre de luy, tout ainsi que s'il auoit personallement comparu; et selon les merites de la cause, donnent sentence absolutoire ou condamnatoire. Et s'il est condamné d'auoir commis crime de trahison et de leze

a—a secrets non confessés.
b amenés: E.
c que une: E.   f sud: E.
d une: E.   g preuves: E.
e—e du Fort: E.   h—h au procès en contumace: E.
                                            i reduction: E.

[*38. Regality*[48]]

Likewise the said judges of regality have the privilege and full jursidiction in their lands, to punish all crimes as well old ones as recent, except the crime of the lese majesty and the four pleas of the crown: which are ravishing of girls and women, public robbery with resistance, fire-raising, and secret homicide which has not been confessed. These judges of regality in the event of their subject being convened before other judges, repledge them: that is to say, they demand and obtain the remit of their subjects before them, for crimes committed by them in the lands of regality: while these judges of regality give caution that they will do and administer justice.

[*39. Justice General*]

And there is also in this kingdom a justice general who has the power to cognosce all crimes. And although there is today only one, in former times there were always two; one was for the region extending north of the river Forth; and the other, from the other bank of the river extending towards the south. At this point, it is fitting to explain that in criminal sentences, pronounced by the sheriffs, judges of regality, barons and other judges there is no appeal; immediately thereupon follows execution; and in the case where the heirs of the person put to death see that the judge had proceeded with malice against him, they can, by way of simple complaint, complain to the king and to the three estates of this realm being assembled in full parliament, and demand reduction and rescission of the said process. On this head, one should note that each and every one of the officers hold their office heritably, that is, from father to son, and from degree to degree, except only the office of the justice general above mentioned, the holders of which office are appointed *ad nutum principis*.[49] All these officers cannot exact or take anything from the parties for the administration of criminal justice.

[*40. Treason: prosecution in parliament*]

And as for the execution and punishment of crimes of lese majesty, commonly called treason in this kingdom, there are two modes of procedure. The one is that when anyone is suspected of the said crime, the king ordains that the three estates of his kingdom be assembled in parliament, and his advocate has the criminal summoned to compear before his majesty and his justice general at the said parliament, to answer there to the crimes contained in the summons. And to the end that the criminal, on the day assigned to him, shall be ready to answer promptly to the points and crimes of the said summons, a copy thereof is delivered or offered to him; for he is obliged to compear and use all his defences on the first day. And if he does not compear on the day assigned to him, there is procedure *in poenam contumaciae*; receiving all probation and other things necessary for the deduction of the process against him in just the same way as if he had personally compeared; and according to the merits of the cause, they pronounce sentence of absolvitor or condemnator. And if he is convicted of having committed the crime of treason and of lese majesty by the sentence

---

[48] See Introduction, 90-93.
[49] See Introduction, 93-94.

maiesté, par la sentence donnée contre luy, il forfaict au roy et perd ses vie, terres, heritages et biens quelconques; et à iamais est incapable d'office honneur et dignité en ce royaume, et le memoire de luy est et doit estre abolie et exteincte. Et comme les ditz traistres sont destituéz et priuéz de toutes heritages et tiltres, leurs aduenans par succession de leurs progeniteurs et ancestres; pareillement leurs heirs et posterité descendans d'eux, sont repousséz^a de toute succession d'heritages, offices et biens quelconques qu'ilz pourront acclamer, demander, et dire leur estre deues, pour auoir esté procréez et engendréz ^{b}dudit traistre^b, soit en ligne droite^c, ou a latere dudit traistre; et ce pour ce que le dit traistre est comme l'arbre secq et pourry, par le quel nul humeur ny nourriture peult venir aux branches et fruicts d'icelluy; et est tamquam inhabile medium disiungens extrema. Et est commandé à tous seneschaulx, et officiers quelconques de ce royaume, de poursuiure, chercher^d et apprehender ledit traistre, et de l'amener à la iustice pour estre executé comme il appartient.

La maniere de l'execution est communement de les^e pendre, decapiter, et mettre leurs corps en quatre quartiers, et faire mettre et attacher leurs membres ez lieux publicques, pres le lieu ou a esté faite la dite execution.

Et des dites sentences de forfaictures données par le parlement, n'y a aucune appellation, sy non que les heritiers dudit traistre peuuent, par la voye de simple querelle, se plaindre au roy et trois estatz de ce royaume estans assembléz en plein parlement, et demander rescizion^f et reduction dudict procèz; la premiere sentence demeurant tousiour entiere iusques à la reduction d'icelle.

La second maniere de proceder en crime de leze maiesté est, sy ceulx qui sont suspectz dudit crime sont apprehendéz et constituéz prisonniers, l'advocat du roy peult proceder par voye d'accusation deuant ladite iustice generalle, et faire mettre le criminel en la connoissance d'vne assize de treize, quinze ou plusieurs personnes non suspectz, qui sans suspicion peuuent connoistre de la cause. Et sy ledit prisonnier est declaré par ladite assize coupable, le iuge le fait condamner, et donne sentence allencontre de luy, toute telle que sy ladite sentence eust esté donnée en parlement; et^g a semblable force et vigueur comme si^h celle estoit donnée en parlement, et n'est retractable sy non par voye de simple querelle, comme dict est. Et sy le criminel n'est apprehendé, l'aduocat du roy peult leuer lettres et commandement, addressantes^i aux seneschaulx et autres officiers du roy, pour le faire adiourner^j comparoir deuant ladite iustice generalle, pour illec respondre aux crimes continus en la citation; auquel criminel est commandé de donner caution, dedans six iours après le commandement, qu'il comparoistra au

a *repulsez:* E.

b—b *desdites traistres:* E.

c *directe:* E.

d *sercher:* E.

e *faire* supplied from E.

f *décision:* E.

g *laquelle sentence* supplied from E.

h omitted from E.

i *addressé.*

j *à* supplied from E.

pronounced against him he forfeits to the king and loses his life, lands, heritage and goods whatsoever; and is for ever incapable of office, honour and dignity in this kingdom, and his memory is and should be abolished and extinguished. And as the said traitors are stripped and deprived of all their heritage and titles, coming to them by succession from their progenitors and ancestors; similarly their heirs and posterity descending from them are all excluded from all succession to their heritage offices and goods whatsoever they could claim, demand, and say to be owed to them, for having been procreated and begat by the said traitor, be they of lineal or collateral descent from the said traitor; and this is because the said traitor is like the dry and rotten tree up which no moisture or nourishment can come to its branches and fruits: *et est tanquam inhabile medium disiungens extrema*. And all the sheriffs and officers whatsoever of this kingdom are commanded to pursue, seek out and arrest the said traitor and to bring him to justice to be executed as is appropriate.

[*41. Manner of execution*]
The manner of execution is commonly hanging, beheading and quartering their bodies; and having their limbs put and attached in public places near the place where the said execution has been carried out.

[*42. Appeal in treason*]
There is no appeal from the sentence of forfeiture pronounced by the parliament except that the heirs of the said traitor may by way of simple complaint, complain to the king and three estates of this kingdom being assembled in full parliament, and demand rescission and reduction of the said process. The first sentence remains entire until it is reduced.

[*43. Treason: prosecution before justice court*]
The second manner of proceeding in the crime of lese majesty is, if those suspected of the said crime have been arrested and made prisoners, the king's advocate can proceed by way of accusation before the said justice general and have the criminal put to the knowledge of an assize of thirteen, fifteen or more unsuspect persons who can cognosce the cause without suspicion. If the said prisoner is declared by the said assize to be culpable, the judge has him condemned and pronounces sentence against him just as if the said sentence had been pronounced in parliament. And it has the same force and vigour as if it had been given in parliament, and is not retractable unless by way of simple complaint, as said is. And if the criminal is not arrested, the king's advocate can raise letters and command charging the sheriffs and other officers of the king to have him cited to compear before the said justice general to answer for the crimes contained in the citation: this criminal is ordained to find caution within six days after the charge that he shall compear on the day assigned to him under pain of

iour a luy assigné, sur peine de rebellion dite la horne; et à fault de donner la dite caution, ledit aduocat le peult faire declarer rebelle, que l'on dit mis à la horne. Et s'il donne caution et comparoist, il est tenu d'vser toutes ses deffenses au premier iour, et endurer le iugement de ladite assize, et receuoir sentence condamnatoire ou absolutoire comme dessus. Et au cas qu'il donne caution et ne comparoisse, sa caution est iugée de payer amende pecuniaire; et le criminel est mis à la horne pour cause de sa contumace. Et ne peult ladite iustice faire autre voye de proceder, si non celle que dessus, pour raison de l'absence dudit criminel.

Et est à notter que, si l'assize purge et absoult l'accusé qui a merité estre condamné, en ce cas l'aduocat du roy peult faire ladite assize endurer le iugement et sentence d'vne plus grande assize; laquelle doit estre, pour le moins, de vingt cinq[a] personnes, doublant le nombre de la premiere assize: et s'il est trouué par la grande assize, que la premiere ait erré, ceulx qui ont fait ladite premiere assize sont condamnéz d'estre perjures, et punis comme il appartient. Et fault entendre que pour auoir condamné[b] ledit accusé par ladite premiere assize, il ne s'en peult auoir ny faire autre assize, soit a l'instance dudit aduocat ou de la partie, mais ledit iugement tient inuiolablement. Et cet[c] ordre, que la premiere assize doit souffrir le iugement d'autre plus grande[d], pour raison[e] de leur iniuste absolution, c'cst[f] fait et est commung en toutes causes criminelles, là ou est procedé par voye d'assize.

Est[g] à notter que, si les dits seneschaux, baillifs, stewartz, ou autres iuges ayans leurs offices en heritage, ne font deue execution et iustice desditz criminelz, ils perdent pour ce leurs offices, et sont punis en leurs corps et biens, selon la qualité du criminel et des crimes par luy commis. Et aussy, sy les sentences desditz iuges données en cas ciuil sont reduites, et retardées[h] par les sieurs de la session, pour l'iniquité et iniustice des iuges; s'ilz ont leurs offices en heritages, ils perdent l'administration d'icelles pour trois ans, et leurs corps sont imprisonnéz par l'espace d'vn an, et plus si au roy plaist, outre l'interest de la partie greuée; et ce pour la premiere sentence. Et sy deux de leurs sentences sont annullées pour l'iniquité d'iceux iuges, ilz perdent leurs offices leurs vies durantes, et sont punis par l'emprisonnement de leurs personnes, et perdent leurs biens meubles au vouloir du roy. Et sy trois de leurs sentences sont cassées et annullées comme dessus, ils perdent leurs offices pour iamais, outre l'emprissonnement, la perte de leurs biens, et l'interest de la partie comme dessus. Et s'ilz n'ont leurs offices que pour leur vie durant, pour auoir une fois mal iugé et condamné, ils perdent leurs offices, et sont punis par corps et biens, comme dict est de ceux qui ont leurs offices en heritage.

a xxv: E.   e d'erreur supplied from E.
b pardonné: E.   f se: E.
c c'est: E.   g c'est: E.
d assise supplied from E.   h rétractées: E.

rebellion *viz.* horning, and if he fails to find the said caution, the said advocate can have him denounced rebel, that is, put to the horn, and if he finds caution and compears, he is bound to use all his exceptions on the first day to thole the judgment of the said assize and undergo sentence condemnator or absolvitor, as above. And in case he finds caution and does not compear, his cautioner is decerned to pay a pecuniary fine and the criminal is put to the horn because of his contumacy. And the said justice cannot act in any other way than that described above by reason of the absence of the said criminal.

[*44. Perverse assize*]

And it should be pointed out that if the assize purge and assoilzie a person who merited condemnation, in that case the king's advocate can make the said assize thole the judgment and sentence of a larger assize, which ought to be of at least twenty-five persons, doubling the number of the first assize. And if it is found by the grand assize that the first has erred, those who composed the first assize are condemned as perjurers and punished as is appropriate. And it should be understood that for the said accused to have been condemned [*lege* 'acquitted'] by the first assize, it is not possible for him to have or thole another assize, be it at the instance of the said advocate or of the party, but the said judgment remains inviolable. And this procedure, that the first assize ought to thole the verdict of another grand assize, by reason of this unjust acquittal, is followed and is common in all criminal causes, where procedure has been by way of assize.

[*45. Negligent judges*]

And it should be noted that if the said sheriffs, bailies, stewards or other judges holding heritable office, do not carry out due execution and justice on the said criminals, they thereby lose their offices, and are punished in their bodies and their goods, according to the quality of the criminal and the crime committed by him. And also if the sentences of the said judge pronounced in civil cases are reduced and retreated by the lords of session because of the iniquity and injustice of the judges, if they hold their offices heritably, they lose the administration thereof for three years, their bodies are imprisoned for the space of one year, and more if the king pleases, besides the interest of the party grieved, and that for the first sentence. And if two of their sentences are annulled because of their iniquity they lose their offices during their lives, and are punished by imprisonment of their persons and they lose their moveables at the will of the king. And if three of their sentences are cassed and annulled as abovementioned they lose their offices for ever in addition to imprisonment, the loss of their goods and the interest of the party, as abovementioned. And if they only held their office for life, for having on one occasion judged and condemned with malice, they lose their offices and are punished in person and goods, as said is of those who hold their offices heritably.

Le crime de trahison, autrement appellé en ce royaume leze maiesté, consiste en trois especes; c'est à savoir*a*, proditio in regem, regnum, et exercitum; lesquelz trois pointz sont sy amplement interpretéz et extendus, que toute maniere et espece de leze maiesté se peult comprendre es dites trois manieres. Car*b* par les statuts, loix, actes et ordonnances de ce royaume, et sentences données par le parlement d'icelluy contre les traistres, on peult connoistre et entendre, que les pointz de trahison sont presque du tout telz et tellement esteintz, comme est en droit commun; tellement qu'il est quasi impossible que cas de leze maiesté puisse aduenir, qu'il n'ait loy expresse, ou coustume, suffisante*c* pour la punition d'icelle. Et pour ce que le crime de leze maiesté est de soy meme fort detestable et horrible, ainsy de temps passé la iustice sur la punition desditz crime a esté fort rigoureusement executée allencontre des plus grands personnages de ce royaume; comme le Comte de Douglas, le Comte de la Marche*d*, le Comte d'Athol, le Comte de Rosse, et le Seigneur des Isles*e*; qui, pour crime*f* de leze maiesté et rebellion faicte contre les roys, ont esté par sentence condamnéz, et leurs terres possedées iusques a ce iour par la couronne. Et pour ce qu'il seroit trop long de mettre par escrit toutes les dites loix et sentences, il souffira, pour le present, faire extraict d'aucunes d'icelles que, pour la punition des crimes auiourd'huy faictz, sont plus conuenables: car quant a la reste, elles sont aysées a trouuer dedans les loix, ordonnances, sentences et coustumes escrites, et continues au long aux liures du registre du parlement.

En l'acte et ordonnance 3*e* de parlement faict par le feu roy Jacques premier de ce nom, et ez actes xxv et xxvi du dit roy, est declaré et determiné, que sy aucun manifestement ou notoirement rebelle contre le roy, il encourt la peine de forfaicture, qui est, perte de ses vie, terres, heritages et biens quelconques.

Item*g*, en l'acte vingt*e* du roy Jacques le second, est statut et ordonné, que nul ne fait*h* rebellion contre la personne du roy, ny contre son authorité, et sy aucun est trouué sy temeraire de ce faire, il soit puny selon la qualité de la rebellion, par l'aduis des trois estatz du royaume. Et en cas que aucun en ce royaume, publicquemeut ou notoirement rebelle contre le roy, ou face la guerre contre les suiets du roy, estant prohibié de ce faire, le roy, ayant l'assistance de tout son royaume, le doit inuader, poursuiure, et auec toute rigueur en faire punition, selon la qualité du crime: surquoy fault notter, que la peine est arbitraire, ayant respect à la qualité et quantité du crime.

---

a assavoir: E.   *e Destiles:* E.
b omitted from E.   *f crimes:* E.
c suffisant: E.   *g Et:* E.
d Lamarche: E.   *h face:* E.

[*46. Meaning of treason*[50]]

The crime of treason, otherwise called lese majesty in this kingdom, exists in three types: that is to say, *proditio in regem, regnum et exercitum*. These three points are so embracingly interpreted and extended that all manner and kind of lese majesty can be comprehended in the three types. For by the statutes, laws, acts and ordinances of this kingdom, and sentences pronounced by the parliament against traitors, one can know and understand that the points of treason are almost such and so embracing as is in common law so that it is wellnigh impossible that a case of lese majesty could arise for the punishment of which there was not an express law or sufficient custom. And because the crime of lese majesty is in itself very detestable and horrible, in times gone by, the prosecution for the punishment of the said crime has been very vigorously carried out against some very great personages of this kingdom: as, for example, the earl of Douglas,[51] earl of March,[52] earl of Atholl,[53] earl of Ross and the lord of the Isles,[54] who for the crime of lese majesty and rebellion against the kings, were convicted and their lands possessed by the crown up to this very day. And since it would be too tedious to put into writing all the said laws and sentences, it will suffice, for the present, to make an extract of some of those which are more suitable for the punishment of crimes committed today, because, as for the remainder, they are easily found among the laws ordinances, sentences and customs, written and contained at length in the books of the register of parliament.

[*47. Rebellion*]

In the 3rd Act and ordinance of the parliament made by the late King James, first of this name,[55] and in the 25th and 26th acts [*lege* 'years'?] of the said king, it is declared and determined that if anyone openly or notoriously rebels against the king, he incurs the pain of forfeiture, that is, loss of life, land, heritage, and all goods of all description.

[*48.*]

Item, in the twentieth act of King James the second[56] it is statute and ordained that no one shall rebel against the king's person or against his authority, and if anyone is found so rash as to do this, he shall be punished according to the quality of the rebellion, by the advice of the three estates of the realm. And in case anyone in this realm rebel openly or notourly against the king, or make war against the king's lieges, being prohibited from doing this, the king, with the assistance of all his kingdom, ought to invade and pursue him, and exact punishment with all vigour, according to the quality of the crime; on this point we must note that he penalty is arbitrary, having respect to the quality and magnitude of the crime.

[50] See Introduction, 96.
[51] James, 9th earl, forfeited 10 June 1455.
[52] Alexander Stewart, duke of Albany, second son of James II, forfeited 27 June 1483.
[53] Walter Stewart, forfeited 26 March 1437.
[54] John Macdonald, forfeited 1475.
[55] 1424, c. 3 (*APS*, ii, 3).
[56] 1449, c. 3 (*APS*, ii, 35).

Item, en l'acte cent cinquant^e dudit roy Jacques le premier, et audit acte vingt^e de Jacques le second, et plusieurs autres, est declaré que ceux qui volontairement recettent^a, maintiennent, font faueur, ou^b donnent assistance, conseil, confort, fortification, supply ou ayde aucune, à ceux qui pour crime de leze maiesté sont condamnéz, forfaitz ou bannis, qu'ilz soient condamnéz, ^{c}forfaictz, et^c estre punis comme le principal, et encourent toute et telle peine pour ce faire comme le dit criminel principal.

Item, en l'acte cent vingt neuf^e dudit roy Jacques le second, est dit, que sy aucun ayt commis^d trahison contre la personne du roy, ou contre sa maiesté, ou se leue ou^e se mette en armes en maniere de guerre, alencontre de luy, ou qu'il mette les mains en sa personne violentement, de quelque age que le roy soit, ieune ou vieil, ou qu'il recete^f aucuns qui ayent commis le crime de trahison, ou qu'ils leur portent ayde ou supply, soit par conseil, confort ou autrement^g, ou qu'ilz garnissent las maisons dudit rebelle de victuailles, ou autre choses à l'aduantage desdits rebelles, ou qu'ilz assaillent chasteaux et places ou le roy sera pour le temps, sans le consent et aduis de trois estatz, ils seront punis comme traistres, et commettans crimes de leze maiesté.

Item, faire faulse monnoye est crime de trahison, et nul en ce royaume n'a puissance de forger, ou faire imprimer monnoye, soit d'or, d'argent, ou autre monnoye d'alloy, s'il n'a commission du roy pour ce faire, sur peine de trahison; comme est declaré en l'acte xxiiii^c du dit roy Jacques le second, et plusieurs autres.

Item, il n'est permis à aucun de ce royaume tenir maison ou fortresse contre le roy, estant requis et commandé de laisser ladite maison pattente et vuide, au nom du roy, dedans six heures; lesquelles complettes apres commandement fait, et ne la laisse pattente et vuide comme dessus, il commet crime de trahison, et perd la vie, terres et biens quelconques: comme fust pratiqué contre le Lord Crichton^h, et aussy contre Normant^i Lesly et Me Henry Balneuis^j, durant le temps que Monsieur le Duc tenoit l'authorité de ce royaume.

a *recèlent:* E.
b omitted from E.
c—c *à:* E.
d *connoist:* E.
e *et:* E.
f *recèle:* E.
g *aultres:* E.
h *Creychtrux:* E.
i *Normanl:* E.
j *Alveris:* E.

[*49. Resetting of those condemned of treason*]

Item, in the one hundred and fiftieth act of the said King James first[57] and in the said twentieth act of James the second[58] and several others, it is declared that those who voluntarily, reset, maintain, do favour, or give assistance, counsel, comfort, asylum, fortification, supplies, or any help to those who are condemned, forfeited or banished for the crime of lese majesty, shall themselves be condemned forfeited and punished in the same manner as the principal, and incur just the same penalty for doing this, as the said principal criminal.

[*50. Taking up arms, etc.*]

Item, in the hundred and twenty ninth act of the said King James the second[59] it is said that if anyone has committed treason against the king's person, or his majesty, or rises or takes up arms in a warlike manner against him, or lays violent hands upon his person, no matter what age the king be, young or old, or resets anyone who has committed the crime of treason or who has carried help or supplies to them, whether it be by counsel, comfort or otherwise; or stock the houses of the said rebels, or attack castles and places where the king is for the time being, without the consent and advice of the three estates, they shall be punished as traitors, and as having committed the crime of lese majesty.

[*51. Coining*]

Item, to counterfeit coin is the crime of treason, and no one in this kingdom has power to make or have money struck, whether of gold or silver or other coin of alloy, unless he have commission from the king to do so, under the pain of treason; as is declared in the 24th act of the said King James the second,[60] and several others.

[*52. Maintaining fortalices*]

Item, it is not permitted for anyone in the kingdom to maintain a house or fortress against the king, having been requested and commanded to leave the said house open and empty in the name of the king, within six hours.[61] If this period having passed after the command has been made, he does not leave it open and empty as abovementioned, he commits the crime of treason and loses his life, lands and goods whatsoever, as was practised against Lord Crichton[62] and also Norman Leslie[63] and Mr. Henry Balnavis[64] during the time that M. le Duc held authority in this kingdom.[65]

---

[57] 1424, c. 15 (*APS*, ii, 8).
[58] 1449, c. 3 (*APS*, ii, 3).
[59] 1449, c. 12 (*APS*, ii, 35).
[60] 1449, c. 17 which merely provides for punishment 'as law will': *APS*, ii, 37.
[61] 1449, c. 16 (*APS*, ii, 37) which refers back to 'the alde law & Statute maid therapoun of befoir'; c.f. *APS*, ii, 323b.
[62] William, third lord Crichton, forfeited 24 February 1483/4.
[63] Eldest son of George, fourth earl of Rothes.
[64] Lord of session 1539-47 and 1564-70: McNeill, 'Senators', 1960 Jur. Rev. 120.
[65] James, earl of Arran, later duke of Châtelherault, governor 1543-54.

Item, après que le feu Jacques Comte de Douglas fust condamné de trahison, en plein parlement, pour auoir rebellé contre le roy et son authorité publicquement, et attaint des autres crimes de leze maiesté, du temps de Jacques le second; a esté fait ordonnance continue en l'acte cent cinq^te quat^e dudit roy, que aucun de quelque estat ou condition qu'il fust, ne recoiue, ny loge, ny fasse faueur, fortification ou supply par quelque voye que ce soit, au dit Jacques Comte de Douglas, ses freres, complices et compaignons, sur peine de perdre leur vie, terres, et biens quelsconques, ipso facto; et aussy que nulles personnes procrées de ceux qui auoient esté condamnéz audit parlement, ne^a succedassent a aucuns heritages en ce royaume; laquelle ordonnance est communement et inuiolablement^b practiquée et obseruée pour loy en ce royaume.

Item, le sept^e jour d'Auril l'an 1522, monsieur le duc d'Albanie, lors gouuerneur en ce royaume, les trois estatz estans en parlement assembléz, sentence de forfaicture fust donnée contre Jehan Summerwell sieur de Camnetham^c, qui^d pour auoir commis les crimes qui s'ensuiuent, il auoit encouru le crime de trahison de leze maiesté, et tous ses biens pour ce furent confisquéz; qui sont, pour auoir par le dit Jehan fait cruelle et traisonnable enuasion sur les personnes de tres reverend pere en dieu Jacques archevesque de Glasgow, chancellier, et Jacques comte d'Arran, deux des regens de ce royaume, constituéz en l'absence dudit duc d'Albanie gouuerneur; les ditz archeuesque et comte allans^e de leur^f maison^g dedans la ville d'Edinbourg, au pretoire de la dicte ville, pour l'administration de la iustice, le lundy dernier iour d'Auril l'an 1520; contre lesquelz regens, ledit Jean auec ses complices, en ordre de bataille, sur le grand chemin, traisonablement venit^h auec armes inuasibles; et pour auoir traisonnablement fait expulsion et deiecté les dits regens, et la reste des seigneurs, hors de ladicte ville, eulx estans deputtéz pour l'administration de iustice en icelle; et pour auoir fait traisonnable resistance et empeschement ausdits regens et seigneurs estans auec eulx, tellement qu'ilz ^ine peuuent^i faire ny administrer la iustice au suietz du roy; parce qu'ilz auoient esté contraintz par ledit Jehan et ses complices, par la voye d'armes, sortir de ladicte ville.

Item, pour auoir traisonnablement faict conuocation et assemblée d'aucuns traistres et rebelles de ce royaume, et signantement de ^jDauid Hume de Waderbourn^j et ses freres, auec vne grande compagnie des larrons et autres malfaicteurs, le premier iour de [May] l'an 1520, les mettant en ordre de battaille et guerre, en l'adeu do nostre souuerain, sur vne terre dit Burrow-muire près Edinbourg; et pour auoir traisonnablement conuoqué et assemblé les suietz du roy^k en battaille, en l'adeu dudit souuerain, aux villes de [Linlithgow]^l et

a n'y: E.
b lege 'invariablement'?
c Camnethex: E.
d que: E.
e Albani: E.
f leurs: E.

g maisons: E.
h vint: E.
i—i n'ont peu: E.
j—j Daniel Hirme de Waderbourg: E, A.
k passant supplied from E.
l Lecqnih: E.

[53. Accomplices of James ninth earl of Douglas]

Item, after the late James, earl of Douglas, was condemned of treason in full parliament, for having rebelled publicly against the king and his authority; and arraigned for other crimes of lese majesty in the time of James II, there was made an ordinance contained in the hundred and fifty fourth act of the said king[66] to the effect that no one of any estate or condition shall receive, put up, give favour, fortification or supply in any way at all, to the said James, earl of Douglas, his brothers, accomplices and companions under the pain of losing their lives, lands and goods whatsoever, *ipso facto*, and also that no persons procreated of those who had been condemned in the said parliament shall succeed to any heritable property in this kingdom. This ordinance is commonly and inviolably [*lege* 'invariably'] practised and observed as law in this kingdom.

[54. John Somerville of Cambusnethan]

Item, on the seventh day of April in the year 1522 when the duke of Albany was governor of this realm, and the three estates were assembled in parliament, sentence of forfeiture was pronounced against John Somerville, laird of Cambusnethan who having committed the following crimes, had incurred the crime of treason and lese majesty, and for this all his goods were confiscated: these were for having been art and part in the cruel and treasonable invasion of the most reverend father in God James, archbishop of Glasgow, chancellor, and James, earl of Arran, two of the regents of this realm, in the absence of the said duke of Albany, governor. The said archbishop and earl were going from their homes in the town of Edinburgh, to the tolbooth of the said burgh to administer justice on Monday the last day of April 1520 against those regents, the said John, with his accomplices in battle order, treasonably came on the public street with offensive weapons; and for having treasonably expelled and ejected the said regents and the rest of the said lords out of the said burgh, they being depute to administer justice in it; and for having treasonably resisted and obstructed the said regents and lords being with them, to such an extent that they could neither do nor administer justice to the subjects of the king, because they had been forced by the said John and his accomplices by means of arms to leave the said town.[67]

[55. David Hume of Wedderburn]

Item, for having treasonably made convocation and assembly of some traitors and rebels of this kingdom, and particularly of David Hume of Wedderburn and his brothers, with a large company of thieves and other malefactors on the first day of May in the year 1520, putting them in order of battle and war, in the sight of our sovereign on a piece of land called Burrow-muire near Edinburgh; and having treasonably convoked and assembled the subjects to the king (passing[68]) in battle, in view of the said sovereign to the towns

---

[66] 1455, c. 14 (*APS*, ii, 43).
[67] *APS*, ii, 43.
[68] Supplied from E.

Stirling[a], nonobstant que ledit Jean et ses compagnons auoient estéz admonestéz et inhibéz de par le roy, de soy desister de ce faire sur peine de trahison.

Item, ledit Jean, à son retour, pour auoir traisonnablement mis ses gens en ordre de bataille, contre ledit Jacques comte d'Arran, et l'auoir inuadé; laquelle inuasion fust reputtée comme contre la personne de nostre souuerain, pour ce que ledit comte d'Arran estoit pour lors un des regens de ce royaume, et lieutenant pour le roy en la marche orientale vers Angleterre; et ledit Jean et ses complices ont tué diuers suietz du roy, estans sous la charge dudit comte d'Arran.

Item, le cinq[e] iour de Septembre l'an 1528, sentence de forfaicture fust donnée en parlement contre le feu comte d'Angus, pour auoir commis le crime de trahison qui ensuit; à sauoir[b], pour n'auoir obey au commandement du roy, fait et deuisé par les sieurs de son conseil; et pour auoir faict conuocation et assemblée des suietz de ce royaume dedans la ville d'Edembourg, par l'espace de huict iours continuellement; et pour auoir muny et garny les chasteaux de Tamtallon et Newerk, auec gens, artillerie et enuictuaillement, contre la maiesté du roy; et pour auoir fait assistener[c] et maintenir[d] au laird de Johnston, à piller et brusler les suietz de ce royaume, de iour et nuict, auec compagnies de larrons; et pour auoir detenu la personne du roy contre sa volonté, continuellement par l'espace de deux ans, contre le decret de messieurs de son conseil[e].

Item, le xiiii[e] iour de Mars 1540, feu Jacques Coluil[f], sieur de Easterwyms, pour auoir fait certains crimes de leze maiesté en sa vie, il eust sentence de forfaicture contre luy, aprés sa mort, ses femmes et heritiers à ce appelées, et les parolles condamnatoires de la sentence sont telles: La cour de parlement ordonne et declare, que pour autant qu'il est trouué et entendu par le dit parlement, que feu Jacques Coluil de Easterwyms cheuallier, a incouru les peines de crimes de leze maiesté, pour auoir traisonnablement desobey et refusé de faire le commandement du roy, par lequel luy fust commandé de se constituer prisonnier au chasteau de Blaknesse[g]; passant hors de ce royaume à la compagnie d'Archibald feu comte d'Angus, et George Douglas son frere, traistres et rebelles, et traictant et communiquant[h] auec eux la ruine de sa maiesté, de ses suietz et de son royaume: Pour lesquelles caufes la cour ordonne et decerne, que la memoire dudit Jacques soit du tout abolie et esteinte; et que tous ses biens meubles et immeubles[i], tant terre[j] qu'autres biens quelconques, appartenant audit Jacques, lors et depuis iusques à son trespas, feussent au roy consisquéz; et demeurer ez

a Steelnig: E.   f Solvie: E.
b assavoir: E and A.   g Blashues: E.
c assistance: E.   h pratiquant: E.
d maintenance: E.   i non meubles: E.
e parlement: E.   j terres: E.

of Linlithgow and Stirling, notwithstanding that the said John [lege 'David'] and his companions had been admonished and forbidden by the king, to desist from doing this under pain of treason.[69]

[56. *Treasonable acts against a regent*]

Item, The said John [lege 'David'] on his return for having treasonably put his people in order of battle against the said James, earl of Arran, and for having invaded him which invasion was reputed as against the person of our sovereign because the said earl of Arran was then one of the regents of this kingdom and lieutenant for the king in the east march against England; and the said John [lege 'David'] and his accomplices have killed diverse lieges of the king who were under the charge of the said earl of Arran.[70]

[57. *Earl of Angus*]

Item, on the fifth day of September in the year 1528 sentence for forfeiture was pronounced in parliament against the late earl of Angus for having committed the following crime of treason: that is, for not having obeyed the command of the king made and devised by the lords of his council, and for having convoked and assembled subjects of this kingdom within the burgh of Edinburgh for the space of eight consecutive days; and for having fortified and garrisoned the castles of Tantallon and Newark with people, artillery and food against the king's majesty; and for having given assistance and maintenance to the laird of Johnston, to pillage and burn the lieges of this kingdom by day and night with bands of robbers; and for having detached the person of the king against his wish continually for the space of two years, contrary to the decree of the lords of council.[71]

[58. *James Colvile of Easter Weymss*]

Item, on the 14th day of March 1540, the late James Colvile, laird of Easter Wemyss, for having committed certain crimes of lese majesty in his life had sentence of forfaulture after his death, his women folk and heirs being called to hear this, and the words of condemnation in the sentence are as follows: the court of Parliament ordains and declares that for as much as it is found and understood by the said parliament that the late James Colvile of Easter Wemyss, knight, has incurred the pains of crimes of lese majesty for having treasonably disobeyed and refused to perform the command of the king by which he was commanded to render himself prisoner at the castle of Blackness, passing outwith this kingdom in the company of Archibald late earl of Angus, and George Douglas, his brother, traitors and rebels, treating with the destruction of his grace of his lieges and his realm. Wherefore the court ordains and decerns that all his property, moveable and immovable, land as well as other goods of any description, belonging to the said James before and up to the time of his crimes, are confiscated to the king to remain in the hands of the king as his property for ever

---

[69] *APS*, ii, 298.
[70] *APS*, ii, 298.
[71] *APS*, ii, 326.

mains du roy tousiours comme sa proprieté, auec tous autres biens par ledit Jacques disposéz, tant à sa femme que à ses enfans, depuis qu'il a commis ledit crime; encore que lesdits biens soient de par eux possedéz, neantmoings ayent a demeurer auec le dit nostre souuerain doresnauant en temps aduenir.

Item, le premier iour de Juillet 1549[a], durant le temps que Monsieur le duc de Chastellerault auoit le gouuernement de ce royaume, sentence fust donnée en parlement contre les heritiers de feu Georges Cockburne, en son viuant habitant à[b] petit Leyth, pour autant que ledit Georges auoit commis faict de trahison contre nostre souueraine dame, son authorité et son royaume, par plusieurs [c]manieres contenues[c] en ladite sentence; par laquelle fut dit que la[d] dit Georges auoit forfaict tous ses biens meubles et non meubles, terres, heritages, et biens à luy appartenans, tant le temps de son deçedz que tous autres, et quelconques ses biens et terres, alliénez ou disposéz par aucune voye que ce soit, et à quelconques personnes, depuis et après la perpetration desdits crimes; et qu'ilz appartenoient doresnauant à nostre souueraine dame comme son propre; et aussy que le nom et renommée dudit feu Georges soient totallement abolliz, esteintz et oubliéz de tout temps futur.

Plus est à entendre, que les seneschaux, bailifz, stewartz, conseillers de la session, officiers de la iustice royalle generalle, et autres officiers susditz, n'ont aucun estat ny entretenement du roy pour l'administration et exercice de leurs ditz offices.

Ce iourd'huy xie Januier, mil cinq cens cinq[e] neuf, par commandement et ordonnance de la royne douairiere et regente de ce royaume, auons signé ce present cahier, contenantz treize feuilletz et demy, escritz paraphéz par nous, M[rse] Jacques Makgill, clerc du registre, et Jean Bellenden, clerc de la iustice de ce royaume d'Escosse, pour estre enuoyé au roy et royne nos souuerains.

[f][J. MAKGILL.]
J. BELLENDEN.[f]

---

a M. V[c] LIX: E.
b au: E.   *d le:* E.
c—c mains de ce contenir: E.   *e maistie:* E.
f—f J. Makgill, *Cler-Reg[re]* J. Bellenden, *Justice-cleric:* E; *J. Bellenden* which may represent a copy of his signature followed by abbreviation possibly 'JC': A.

along with all other goods disponed of by the said James to his wife as well as to his children since he has committed the said crime, even although the said goods are possessed by them, nevertheless having to remain with our said sovereign henceforth in time coming.[72]

[59. *George Cockburn*]

Item, on first day July 1549 during the time that M. le Duc of Châtelherault held the government of this kingdom, sentence was pronounced in Parliament against the heirs of George Cockburn, in his lifetime living in Leith, for as much as the said George had committed an act of treason against our sovereign Lady, her authority and her kingdom in several ways contained in the said sentence;[73] by which it was said that the said George has forfeited all his goods, movable and immovable lands, heritages and goods belonging to him as much at the time of his decease as all others, and his goods and lands of whatever kind, alienated or disponed in any way at all, and to whatever persons since and after the perpetration of the said crimes; and that they pertain thenceforth to our sovereign lady as her own; and also that the name and reputation of the said late George be totally abolished, extinguished and forgotten in all time coming.

[60.]

Furthermore it is to be understood that the sheriff, bailies, stewards, councillors of session, officers of the king's justice general, and other officers above spoken of, have no renumeration or maintenance from the king for the administration and exercise of their said offices.

[61.]

This day 11th January one thousand five hundred and fifty nine, by command and ordinance of the queen dowager and regent of this kingdom (we) having signed this present memorandum containing thirteen leaves and a half, written and initialled by us, Mr. James Makgill, clerk of register and Mr. John Bellenden, justice clerk of this realm of Scotland, to be sent to the king and queen our sovereigns.

[J. Makgill]
J. Bellenden

---

[72] *APS*, ii, 368.
[73] By March 1548/9 the lands of the late George Cockburn had come into the hands of the crown because he 'past in the realme of Ingland and thair remanit be the space of ane yeir with the mair in tyme of weir, assistit, fortefeit and suppleit the auld inymeis thairof with his counsale, support and help and tuke plane part with thame aganis hir grace, hir realme and leiges, and is now decessit at the faith of Ingland amangis the saidis auld inymeis': *Register of Privy Seal*, iv, 154.

A GAELIC CONTRACT OF LEASE, c. 1603 × 1616

Edited, with Introduction and Commentary, by
Ronald Black, M.A.
Department of Celtic, University of Edinburgh

Introduction

In compiling his *Celtic Law* (London, 1937), John Cameron necessarily made much of three Scottish legal documents written in Gaelic, namely some twelfth-century notes on grants of land to the monastery of Deer,[1] a charter of 1408 from Islay probably written by a physician, Fergus MacBeth,[2] and a contract of fosterage of 1614 from Skye written by the poet Toirdhealbhach Ó Muirgheasáin.[3] No-one would have any way of guessing from these odd and meagre remnants that the Lords of the Isles and some of their successors were comprehensively served by hereditary legal families trained and literate in Gaelic (and indeed the representative of such a family witnesses the Islay charter with his mark!) yet such I believe to have been the case. Set against other types of material — I have calculated, for example, that twenty-nine of the eighty-three surviving Gaelic manuscripts of pre-1700 Scotland are medical — the paucity of this survival suggests to me the destruction or perishing of Gaelic legal documents on a wide scale; Dr. John Bannerman, on the other hand, argues that it reflects the strongly oral character of Gaelic law.[4]

Let us compare the Irish situation. There, too, the medical survival was large, in fact over thirty Irish medical manuscripts survive from the sixteenth century alone, more than any other single category.[5] But from Ireland we also have the whole system of Brehon Law, with a sizeable corpus of late commentaries, decisions, agreements, deeds, wills and pleadings in court.[6] Virtually the only Brehon Law text preserved in Scotland is a commentary on aspects of the law on sick-maintenance, noted by a physician on what look like the excised margins of

---

[1] *Celtic Law*, 199-211, 229-42; re-edited in Kenneth Jackson, *The Gaelic Notes in the Book of Deer* (Cambridge, 1972). The original is Cambridge University Library MS. I.i.6.32.

[2] *Celtic Law*, 212-9, 242-6; see also W. D. Lamont, 'The Islay Charter of 1408', in *Proceedings of the Royal Irish Academy*, vol. 60 (Dublin, 1959-60), Section C, 163-87. The original is SRO RH 6/218.

[3] *Celtic Law*, 220-5, 246-7. The original is SRO RH 9/17/35.

[4] See his 'The Lordship of the Isles', in Jennifer Brown (ed.), *Scottish Society in the Fifteenth Century* (London, 1977), 228.

[5] Brian Ó Cuív, 'The Irish Language in the Early Modern Period', in Moody, Martin and Byrne (edd.), *A New History of Ireland* (Oxford, 1976), 518.

[6] *Ibid.*, 514. The text of the Brehon Laws is now available in a diplomatic edition, D. A. Binchy, *Corpus Iuris Hibernici*, 6 vols. (Dublin, 1978). For examples of the later Irish documents see Standish H. O'Grady, *Catalogue of Irish Manuscripts in the British Museum*, vol. 1 (London, 1926), 149-57, and G. Mac Niocaill, 'Seven Irish documents from the Inchiquin Archives', in *Analecta Hibernica* 26 (Dublin, 1970), 47-69.

GAELIC CONTRACT OF LEASE, c. 1603 × 1616

an illuminated mass-book and bound into a collection of medical texts.[7] We may add such other ephemera as the grades, rights and privileges of the poets,[8] the law of Sunday in the Celtic Church,[9] a note of the signs of good and bad pleading,[10] some seventeenth-century Gaelic endorsements on MacLeod receipts,[11] and one treaty, that of 1555-60 between Argyll and O'Donnell.[12] It would certainly seem on the face of it that the extant Gaelic legal documents of Scotland were written not by lawyers but by members of other professions. Dr. Bannerman may therefore have a point, as far as Scotland is concerned — in which case we would seem to have evidence for the greater archaism of our legal tradition and its distinctness from that of Ireland.

This being *l'état de la question*, it is with pleasure that I now throw into the ring one further Scottish legal document written in Gaelic. It is Advocates' MS. 72.1.31 (Gaelic MS. XXXI), f. 8, in the National Library of Scotland.

The Manuscript

Adv. 72.1.31 is the detritus of the Kilbride Collection, an important collection of Gaelic manuscripts made by the MacLachlans of Kilbride in the island of Seil in Lorn.[13] The bulk of the manuscripts, including the present item, passed in the early nineteenth century into the hands of Hugh Kerr, a Glasgow solicitor who represented the last member of the family. He wrote 'No. 31. H. Kerr' on f. 8r; the number refers to his inventory, a copy of which is now Adv. MS. 73.2.10, ff. 200-4. In 1844 the manuscripts were said to be in the library of the Royal Faculty of Procurators in Glasgow; as the collection appears to have shed items at various stages, it would be very useful to have detailed evidence of this from the Faculty's records, but none has so far come to light. On Kerr's death the collection passed (seemingly in 1851) to the Advocates' Library, Edinburgh, where it received the shelfmarks which it bears in the National Library to this day — Adv. MSS. 72.1.5-72.1.31, also known as Gaelic MSS. V-XXXI.[14]

F. 8 is referred to simply as 'A torn scrap of paper, with writing, marked H. Kerr. xxxi' in Professor Donald Mackinnon's *Descriptive Catalogue of Gaelic Manuscripts in the Advocates' Library, Edinburgh, and elsewhere in Scotland* (Edinburgh, 1912), p. 91. This explains why it was overlooked by Cameron. It is described as Adv. 72.1.31 'Fragment D' in Rev. John Mackechnie's *Catalogue of*

[7] Adv. 72.1.2, ff. 107rl-111v6. See Mackinnon, *Catalogue*, 14; D. A. Binchy, 'Bretha Crólige', in *Ériu* 12 (Dublin, 1938), 1-77, and 'Sick-Maintenance in Irish Law', *ibid.*, 78-134.

[8] Adv. 72.1.7, ff. 6r-8v. See Mackinnon, *Catalogue*, 177-8.

[9] Adv. 72.1.40, pp. 72-5. See Mackinnon, *Catalogue*, 95-6; V. Hull, 'Cáin Domnaig', in *Ériu* 20 (Dublin, 1966), 151-77; Donald MacLean, *The Law of the Lord's Day in the Celtic Church* (Edinburgh, 1926).

[10] Adv. 72.1.7, f. 8v; see Mackinnon, *Catalogue*, 178.

[11] John Bannerman, 'Gaelic Endorsements of Early Seventeenth-Century Legal Documents', in *Studia Celtica* vol. 14-15 (Cardiff, 1979-80), 18-33. Dr. Bannerman identifies the writers as (a) Thomas 'Donaldson', possibly a Beaton physician; (b) possibly John Beaton; (c) unknown.

[12] Rev. John Mackechnie, 'Treaty between Argyll and O'Donnell', *Scottish Gaelic Studies* 7 (Aberdeen, 1951-3), 94-102. The original is now regrettably missing from its place in the archives at Inveraray Castle.

[13] Not to be confused with the church and parish of Kilbride on the Lorn mainland, referred to *infra*.

[14] John Bannerman, 'The MacLachlans of Kilbride and their Manuscripts', in *Scottish Studies* 21 (Edinburgh, 1977), 2-3.

Gaelic Manuscripts (Boston, 1973), vol. 1, p. 172. It is a lozenge-shaped fragment of paper measuring roughly 16 cms. across by 14 cms. down. The verso is blank save for pen-marks. No watermark is visible, and the paper is torn off, mouse-eaten or otherwise perished on all four sides. It has been folded or crushed in places and bears stains of various kinds, including the encroachment of damp at the top, where it has become extremely fragile and tattered. Since the text occupies only the upper third of the leaf, it is defective at the beginning and end of every line, and even what remains of the first four lines is largely illegible. The shape of the leaf at bottom left, the fact that only 'Dunc' remains of what might

Text

The 12 lines of text are reproduced below as diplomatically as possible. *Square brackets* represent the edge of the paper. *Dots*: illegible text. *Round brackets*: attempted restoration of missing, illegible or semi-legible text. *Italics*: expansion of all contractions except those for *m* and *n*, which are expanded silently.

The text has been checked under ultra-violet light.

1   ] . . g . . . . (donnc)h*adh* m*ac*
   dubhghaill ta . . . . [
2   ] . . . . an marg . . . .
   . . . . [
3   ] . . . . 7 ise paig . . . . (m)arg ata
   . . . . ag . . . . ata se . . . . g . . . . g . . . . [
4   ] . . . . bolla mine . . . . 7 ~~ndiaig~~o gach uile ni
   7 m*ar* paigis f*ear* (2 m)airg . . . . [
5   ]7   giodh   be   a*ca*   f . g . . o   tacair   each   foghn*as*
   do d*e*arg*adh* an da marg an f*ear* ele do t[(habhairt)
6   ]tigh 7 dfhiacuib ar donnch*adh* fios dho thab*hair*t da oglach
   faoi la feil eoin ma bhis e(a)[
7   ]7 da mb*eith* barr si(1) ag donnch*adh* rena tab*hair*t da
   oglach ata iasacht sin aige re bliadn[(a)
8   ](at)a dfhiacuibh   ar   an   og*lach*   donnch*adh*   dainiaca
   a gcuid oidhchi 7 dfiacuibh ar donnch[(*adh*)
9   ]an   fiacadair   saor   o   uile   obair   noch   bhuain*eas*   don
   2 marg thaoibh m*hic* dubghaill 7 (d)[
10   (1)]leas*ach*a   laimhe   7   leas*ach*a   ele   an   da   mharg
   7 g*ach* ni bhuin*eas* doiph do chrann diarann[
11   ]*ch*t   butalla   amhain   iad   so   an   fiaghn*uise*
   eogan m*ac* eoin vich eogain[
12   ]
                          Dunc[(an)

have been the signature 'Duncan MacDougall' at the right, and the complete absence of any further signatures on the right, would seem to suggest that as much as half as much again of the text may be missing, part at one side of the page and part at the other.

As with all the documents mentioned above, the script is Gaelic (save for 'Dunc' and the *v* of *vich*, 1. 11). The language is basically the classical Gaelic shared to the seventeenth century by the learned men of Scotland and Ireland, although certain terms are unknown from other sources; these are discussed in the notes.

Translation

    Italics here represent particularly doubtful or ambiguous text.

1   ] . . . . Duncan MacDougall . . . .[

2   ] . . . . the merk*land* . . . .[

3   ] . . . . .and pays . . . . merk*lands* which . . . . .he is . . . .[

4   ] . . . .boll*s* of meal . . . and ~~after~~ from everything whatsoever and as the *tenant* of 2 merklands pays . . . .[

5   ]and whichever of them . . . . .a supply of horses sufficient to plough the two merklands, the other is to *give*[

6   ]house and an obligation upon Duncan to give notice to his óglach around St. John's Day should *a horse* be[

7   ]and should Duncan have a surplus of *seed* to give to his óglach he has the loan of that for a year[

8   ]there is an obligation upon the óglach to *indemnify* Duncan in cuddich and an obligation upon Duncan[

9   ]the debtor free from all work that pertains to the 2 merklands. As for MacDougall and *Duncan*[

10   ]improvement by hand and other improvement of the two merklands and *of* everything that appertains to them by way of plough, of iron[

11   ]*except bottles* only.   These are witness: Hugh son of John son of Hugh[

12   ]

            Dunc[an

Notes on the Text

The language is classical Gaelic (i.e. 'Early Modern Irish' or, occasionally, 'Middle Irish') except where stated. Sc. G. = vernacular Scottish Gaelic.

Line

1   *ta . . . . : ?*

2   *marg*: in Ireland, a mark; in Scotland, a merk or merkland, see Cameron, *Celtic Law*, p. 243. Also *passim*.

3   *paig . . . . :* i.e. presumably *pháigheas*, written *paigis* at l. 4, a relative form of the Sc. G. verb *pàigh*, derived from English 'pay'.

4   *bolla*: boll (= 16 pecks). Used in the singular after numerals which otherwise require the plural, cf. for example the saying

> *Cuiridh aon uair de chathadh Gearrain*
> *Seachd bolla sneachd troimh tholl-tora*

'One hour of drifting in early spring will put seven bolls of snow through a wimble-hole', A. Cameron, *Am Bard* (Edinburgh, 1926), p. 56.

paigis: see l. 3.

fear (2 m)airg, 'the tenant of 2 merklands'. *Fear* 'man' followed by a genitive (as here) is common in Scotland in the sense of 'goodman, tenant, tacksman', and is popularly translated 'laird', e.g. *Fear Chille-Brighde* 'the Laird of Kilbride'. See Bannerman, 'Gaelic Endorsements', p. 27.

6   *dfhiacuib ar* 'an obligation upon': i.e. *d' fhiachuibh ar*. The phrase is a common one. It occurs twice at l. 8 and once in the Argyll-O'Donnell treaty, SGS 7, p. 98. *Fiachuibh* is dative plural of *fiach*, cf. *dainiaca* (below, l. 8).

oglach: see below, l. 8.

la feil eoin: i.e. *Lá Féill Eoin*, the Feast of St. John (the Baptist), 24 June. This day traditionally marks midsummer, and is associated with the equalising of stock for grazing purposes: see my forthcoming *Highland Year* (Mercat Press, Edinburgh).

e(a)[: *e* is certain, *a* doubtful, the rest missing, so *each* 'a horse' is a mere guess.

7   *barr*: a crop or surplus.

oglach: see below, l. 8.

re: i.e. *ré*, a space or period of time, used prepositionally (as here) in Sc. G.

8   *oglach*: i.e. *óglach*. Derived from *óg* 'young', hence it means 'a young man, warrior', but in the later classical language, which is what we are dealing with here, its principal meaning is 'attendant, servant, vassal' (Royal Irish Academy's *Contributions to a Dictionary of the Irish Language*, fasc. N-O-P, col. 93); in Sc. G. the meaning 'servant' predominates. Its use with the article ('the') suggests that it has legal force. 'Vassal' would be inappropriate in the present context. 'Sub-tenant' is clearly what it implies here, but as it is not otherwise recorded in that specific meaning I am content to leave it untranslated.

dainiaca: I take this to represent a verb-noun phrase *d' ainfhiachadh* with dialectal loss of final -dh as in *leasacha*, l. 10. The root is certainly *fiach*, originally 'a debt', now in Sc. G. usually 'value, price, worth', in Irish 'a fine, a duty'; it has retained its original meaning in the plural. The intensive *ainfhiach*, found in classical Gaelic as 'a great debt, liability', has replaced it in the meaning 'debt' in Sc. G. Verbal derivatives of *fiach* are not common, but *fiachaigid* is found in the Brehon Laws with the meaning 'makes liable, makes a claim (on or against)', and it has a verbal noun *fiachugud* 'fining, making liable'. (Royal Irish Academy's *Dictionary of the Irish Language*, fasc. F-fochraic, col. 110.) Unfortunately this meaning seems inapplicable in a context such as the present where the contract is requiring the sub-tenant to do this to the tenant. It is probably more realistic to relate *ainfhiachadh* to the attributive genitive *ainféich* 'free of obligation or debt' (*Contributions*, fasc. A, col. 144: another Brehon Law term), where the prefix *ain-* is privative this time rather than intensive, and to Sc. G. *fiachaichte*, used by the nineteenth-century evangelical poet John Morison with the theological meaning 'ransomed'. (G. Henderson (ed.), *Gobha na Hearadh* (Glasgow, 1896), vol. 2, p. 335.) This last suggests a Sc. G. verb *fiachaich* or possibly *ainfhiachaich*, and a verb-noun *fiach(ach)adh* or *ainfhiach(ach)adh*, 'ransoming', hence our *d' ainfhiachadh*, 'to indemnify, to free from debt'.

cuid oidhchi: i.e. *cuid oidhche*, literally a 'night's portion' (of hospitality to the chief and his retinue as they travelled about his territories). This exaction, called cuddich, formed a substantial proportion of the rents payable in many parts of the West Highlands and Islands, at least until proscribed by the Statutes of Iona of 1609 and the ensuing Privy Council regulations of 1616. As late as 1719-20 tenants in Atholl were paying 'cudeichs' of corn and straw. See Frances J. Shaw, *The Northern and Western Islands of Scotland: Their Economy and Society in the Seventeenth Century* (Edinburgh, 1980), p. 154; Derick S. Thomson, 'Gaelic Learned Orders and Literati in Medieval Scotland', in *Scottish Studies* 12 (1968), p. 58; Kenneth Nicholls, *Gaelic and Gaelicised Ireland in the Middle Ages* (Dublin, 1972), pp. 34-5.

9 *fiacadair*: i.e. *fiachadair*, another derivative of *fiach* 'debt'. The meaning 'debtor (in an obligation)' is clear enough, but the word does not seem to be otherwise recorded in this form; the ending *-air* is Sc. G. rather than classical Gaelic, in which it would have appeared as *fiachadóir* as in modern Irish (N. Ó Dónaill, *Foclóir Gaeilge-Béarla*, Dublin 1977).

bhuaineas 'pertains': see *Contributions*, fasc. B, cols. 72, 73, 226.

(*d*)[: only a single stroke of what might be a *d* remains.

10 *leasacha*: I take this to represent *leasachadh*, with dialectal loss of final *-dh* (cf. *dainiaca*, 1. 8). The word means 'improvement', 'cultivation' and 'manuring' in both classical Gaelic and Sc. G., and additionally 'feeding' (of animals) in classical Gaelic.

gach ni 'everything': this phrase does not show case in Gaelic, so it is not possible to say whether it should be preceded in English by 'of'.

11]*cht*: MS.]*st*, but in Gaelic palaeography *s* with a suprascript stroke (which can be misplaced or omitted by mistake) signifies *acht* 'but, except' or the associated sounds *ach* or *cht*. The word here may therefore be *acht* or possibly *ocht* 'eight', depending on the sense in which *butalla* is intended.

butalla: the plural of classical Gaelic *buidéal* 'a bottle', Sc. G. *buideal* 'a keg, cask, anker or bottle', or Sc. G. *botul* 'a bottle'. 'Bottle' is possibly to be understood in its lesser-known sense of 'a bundle (of hay)', in which case we should read *ocht butalla amhain*, 'eight bottles only', much as in a late seventeenth-century tack in which the last items of rent are declared to be 'nyne pecks oats and of straw and hay ane hundred and eight bottles' (SRO GD 112/10/7, f. 423v). 'Bottle' in this sense is usually *boitean* in Sc. G.

iad so an fiaghnuise: this is also the phrase used in the Argyll-O'Donnell treaty, SGS 7, p. 99.

vich: this spelling of *mhic* is common in records not written in Gaelic and probably reflects the preaspiration of *c* in Sc. G.

The Scribe

The hand of the document (i.e. all except 'Dunc') is known from other sources and can be identified as that of Hugh MacPhail (fl. 1603-38). Identification on calligraphic criteria alone is notoriously risky when, as here, the hand is not exhibiting strongly distinctive features, but in this case there is a corroborating factor: the forename of the first witness.

Hugh MacPhail comes to the notice of the public records of Scotland in 1619 when, as Ewne or Ewane McPhaill, servant and tenant of Mr. Donald Campbell of Barbreck, he is described as having been captured by a number of men who had besieged Barbreck's house and 'expelled him from his lands and possessions'. They were put to the horn on 21 April 1619 but found sanctuary with MacDonald of Clanranald.[15] As Professor Derick Thomson has pointed out, Hugh (or a son of his?) is also likely to be the Eoghan Óg MacPhail described as 'mediciner and servitor' to Sir Donald Campbell of Ardnamurchan in 1631-2.[16] A John McDougall VcPhaill is described in November 1620 as servant to Sir John MacDougall of Dunollie.[17]

In an appendix on the MacPhails in his forthcoming study *The Beatons* Dr. John Bannerman sees them as a family of ecclesiastics, associated with the parish of Muckairn and the priory of Ardchattan, who also became physicians and servitors to the Campbells of Cawdor and Ardnamurchan after the former acquired Muckairn in 1532.[18] This pattern of general professional service was not uncommon in Gaelic society, and the range of Hugh's interests — and patrons — is revealed in the following chronological list of writings in his hand.

Adv. 72.1.34. A 48-page paper manuscript containing: traditional tales (pp. 1-38);[19] satirical verse addressed to the well-known Irish poet Fearghal Óg Mac an Bhaird, who visited Scotland in 1581 (p. 39);[20] a letter, partly in Scots, to the Lorn physician John MacConnacher (Eoin Ó Conchubhair), explaining his lack of progress in copying an unnamed book and signed Eouin Mak

---

[15] *R[egister of the] P[rivy] C[ouncil of Scotland]* , xi, 643; xii, 635-6, 661-2; xiii, 11-12.

[16] 'Gaelic Learned Orders', 64, 76.

[17] RPC, xii, 698.

[18] I am grateful to Dr. Bannerman for this information, and would like to acknowledge here that I have drawn upon it in correcting a proof of my article on the MacPhails in D. S. Thomson (ed.), *The Companion to Gaelic Scotland* (Oxford, 1983).

[19] See Alan Bruford, *Gaelic Folk-Tales and Mediaeval Romances* (Dublin, 1969), 251.

[20] Tomás Ó Concheanainn, 'The Poetry of Fearghal Óg Mac an Bhaird', in *Éigse* 15 (Dublin, 1973-74), 249; SRO Treasurers' Accounts E 21/62, f. 131 (Maii 1581), 'item to Fergall og Irische poet jᶜ lib.' I am grateful for these references to Pádraig Ó Macháin and John Durkan.

Phaill, Dunstaffnage, 22 October 1603 (p. 41); an incomplete letter in Scots on certain legal matters, in which MacPhail advises the recipient to communicate with a special friend such as the Laird of Grant, and asks him to accede to a request made by his (MacPhail's) father (p. 42); a medical receipt 'to heal banes that ar broken' in Scots (p. 45); and a fragment of religious verse by another Irish poet, Tadhg Óg Ó Huiginn (p. 46).

Adv. 72.2.2, ff. 7-11. These leaves are detached from Adv. 72.1.34, where they belong between pp. 38 and 39 in this order: 7, 8, 10, 11, 9. They contain: an Ossianic ballad (ff. 7v-8r); a poem on Archibald Campbell, 7th Earl of Argyll 1584-1638, with one stanza to the Earl's wife Anne Douglas (m. by 1594, d. 1607) and another dedicating a book to *mac Radnaill*, the son of Ronald (ff. 8v, 10, 11r); some verse on courtly love, and two triads (ff. llv, 9).[21]

Adv. 72.1.31, f. 8. The present manuscript. Given the broken-up condition and size (19 × 14 cms.) of the preceding two items it is not impossible that our document is another fugitive from Adv. 72.1.34; this would suggest a dating c. 1603.

Adv. 72.2.10, pp. 144z-146, 149-151 1. 2. MacPhail here helps the Skye physician Angus Beaton to copy a Gaelic version of the *Regimen Sanitatis Salernitanum*. Most of the writing of this and the other texts in the manuscript was done by Beaton on circuit in the contiguous Lorn parishes of Lismore, Ardchattan, Muckairn and Kilbride; he was much in the Dunollie area of Kilbride in the company of MacDougall's physician Donnchadh Ó Conchubhair (1571-1647), of whose very considerable experience in Ireland and Scotland he was no doubt taking advantage. At p. 146 Hugh writes: *Sin duit Aonguis 7 mo bendacht leis o Eoghan Mac Phoil*, 'There you are Angus and my blessing with it from Hugh MacPhail'. The manuscript as a whole was written in 1611-14, MacPhail's contributions between 23 August and 5 November 1612.

Adv. 72.1.9. A single folio, no signature. Bears the conclusion of a tract dealing here with medical prognosis; the pedigree of Alasdair Mór MacDougall of Dunollie (fl. c. 1625 — c. 1650); and a covering note addressed to *a brathair inmuin*, 'my dear brother'.

Trinity College, Dublin, MS. 1362a, ff. 1r-2r (formerly in MS. 1298). A poem to Archibald, 8th Earl of Argyll, on his accession in 1638. Unsigned. (Photographs: N.L.S. MS. 14901.)

It is also worthy of note that a possible forebear of the family, Dubhghall Albannach mac Mhic Pháil, wrote religious texts (Adv. 72.1.1, ff. 2-9) in Munster in 1467. These were embellished for him with the measurements of Christ's feet (ff. 4r-5r) in the house of MacEgan, brehon of Ormond. Later he jotted on the cover (f. 1) the genealogies of those Highland clans who had accepted the authority of Donald, Lord of the Isles c. 1400 — the celebrated '1467 MS.'.

To sum up, it will be recognised that Hugh MacPhail was a most versatile young doctor; while no brehon, he was no stranger to the law either. Our manuscript is the unique source for the name of his father and grandfather, and thus provides the genealogical link which connects him with the MacPhails of Muckairn and Ardchattan.

[21] Henry Mackenzie, *Report of the Committee ... appointed to inquire into the nature and authenticity of the Poems of Ossian* (Edinburgh, 1805), Appendix, 295.

Commentary

It seems to me that the document concerns three individuals, landlord, tenant and sub-tenant. The syntax of *thaoibh mhic dubghaill 7 (d)* in 1. 9 strongly suggests (while breaking off tantalisingly short of final confirmation) that *Mac Dubhghaill* and *Donnchadh* are different people. It is unlikely in any case that the same person would be referred to by different names in the course of the document. The designation *Mac Dubhghaill* (of which *mhic dubghaill* is a form of the genitive) could only be held by the chief of that name. Conversely, a chief was most unlikely to be referred to by forename alone. *Mac Dubhghaill*, then, may be taken as landlord, and *Donnchadh* his tenant. The *(donnc)hadh mac dubhghaill* of 1. 1 may refer to either, and may include either surname or patronymic, i.e. it can be read as Duncan MacDougall or Duncan son of Dougall. But in any event the chief of the MacDougalls of Dunollie from 1590 × 91 to 1616 was called Duncan, his father's name was Dougall, and he is known as a patron of Gaelic physicians, notably Donnchadh Ó Conchubhair, who records his death in the following terms:

'Aois an tigherna an ta(n) fuair Donnchadh Mac Dubhghaill tigherna Dhunolamh bas annsa chodaltai bhreac an Dunollamh .i. mili 7 6 c. bliadhna 7 se bliadhna deag nisa mho, an la deighinach d'Agus(tus) 7 do hioghladh a gCilli Bhridi he annsa chisti chloidhe is neasa don dorus air taoibh cuil an teampaill & a Dhia athair cuir uair mhaith chugum go cass na dhiaigh maille trocaire dom anmuin. Misi Donnchadh O Concubhair do sgriobh so le droc penn.

Uch a Dhia on uch a Dhia
Is mairg ata anocht gan triath
Ni fada bheris me beo
Mo chraidhe da bhreo na dhiaig.'[22]

'The age of the Lord when Duncan MacDougall Laird of Dunollie died in the speckled bedchamber in Dunollie was 1616, the last day of August, and he was buried in Kilbride in the stone coffin nearest the door at the back of the church & God the father send me good fortune without delay after him, with mercy to my soul. I am Duncan MacConnacher who wrote this with a bad pen.

Och O God and och O God
Woe to him who is tonight without a chief
Not long will I remain alive
My heart is anguished after him.'

Duncan MacDougall of Dunollie, then, is the most obvious candidate to be the landlord in question. Research into MacDougall landholdings may shed further light on the matter, but is not within the scope of the present study.[23]

---

[22] Adv. 73.1.22, f. 257v. The verse is likely to be old. The metre is what Miss Knott called *rannaigheacht ghoirid*, with a trisyllabic first line *Uch a Dhia*; Ó Conchubhair falls into her category of 'later scribes' who 'misunderstand the intention, and spoil the effect by repeating the line with *ón* prefixed, in order to obtain the usual seven syllables' (Eleanor Knott, *Irish Syllabic Poetry* (Dublin, 1957), 14).

[23] A serious history of the MacDougalls in all periods remains to be written. In the meantime we have Lord Archibald Campbell's *Records of Argyll* (Edinburgh, 1885); *The Galley of Lorn* (Sheffield, 1909-14); and Michael Starforth's recent *A short History of the Clan MacDougall* (? Glasgow, 1976).

The third person involved in the contract is the *óglach* or sub-tenant. Tenant and sub-tenant appear to have a well-balanced relationship. If one of them can provide sufficient horses to plough the two merklands, the other must give something else (1. 5). The sub-tenant is entitled to warning about something, perhaps the future need of a horse for gathering peats, around midsummer (1. 6), and should the tenant have a surplus of seed-corn for him he has a year in which to make good the loan (1. 7). The burden of paying the landlord's cuddich falls ultimately on the sub-tenant, but the tenant agrees to something in exchange (1. 8). This something appears to be what is in 1. 9, i.e. that the debtor in the obligation is to be relieved by the creditor of all work that pertains to the two merklands. This is a reference to services — not merely the working of the land but something like the 'oisting (hosting), hunting, stenting (tax assessment), ariage (transport), cariage and all utheris dew services' which the tenant of Balliveolan in Lismore was bound to perform for his landlord, Campbell of Glenorchy, in 1629.[24] I am surprised to find the word *obair* 'work' used in this context, rather than *feidhm* 'service' as in Glenorchy's elegy of 1631:

> Dob iomdha um nóin a mbrugh Bhealaigh
> brughaidh, biatach, barún ríogh,
> ag feitheamh ar fheidhm thriath Tatha —
> seinm 'na iath, flatha agus fíon.[25]

'Numerous at evening in the mansion of Taymouth were the farmer, the yeoman and the king's baron, waiting upon the service of the lord of Tay — in his land were music-making, princes and wine.'

The final clause (11. 9-11) appears to refer to the terms of the original tack granted by the landlord to the tenant. It is reminiscent of steelbow tenure, which, as Dr. Frances Shaw has pointed out, was more in evidence in this period in the islands off the coast of Nether Lorn than in any other part of the Hebrides.[26] Steelbow was an arrangement whereby the proprietor provided the incoming tenant with some or all of the livestock, grain, implements and even money required for the land; Cosmo Innes called it 'a system which must, in all likelihood, have been the earliest mode of land tenancy everywhere', and it certainly reflects the situation in Brehon Law whereby the chief's claim to rent depended on his being able to supply stock to the occupier of the land.[27] It was particularly common in tacks granted by Glenorchy — the above-mentioned Balliveolan tack notes the steelbow goods on his lands as being listed in the 'steilbow buikis'.[28] John MacDougall of Rara got a steelbow tack of the island of Torsay by Seil for three years from Lady Argyll in 1640 or shortly before; for this he paid a rent of thirty-two bolls of meal and sixteen bolls of bear, and obliged himself at the expiry of his tack to leave the land adequately worked and in good order and to return the capital of fifty- two bolls of seed oats, six bolls of seed bear

[24] Shaw, *Northern and Western Islands*, 52.
[25] SRO RH 13/40. Ascribed to Neil MacEwen. Ed. W. J. Watson, 'Marbhnadh Dhonnchaidh Duibh', in *An Deò-Gréine* 12 (Glasgow, 1916-17), 132-4 and 149-51. For further references see John Bannerman, 'Literacy in the Highlands', in I. Cowan and D. Shaw (edd.), *The Renaissance and Reformation in Scotland* (Edinburgh, 1983), 228, n. 87.
[26] Shaw, *Northern and Western Islands*, 56.
[27] Cosmo Innes, *Sketches of Early Scotch History* (Edinburgh, 1861), 190; Cameron, *Celtic Law*, 74.
[28] Innes, *op. cit.*, 384-6; Shaw, *op. cit.*, 56-7.

and 200 merks in money.[29] Seventeenth-century steelbow tacks from Orkney mention not only crops and animals but also, as in our document, agricultural implements — ploughs in particular, with harrows, forks, flails and creels.[30] Elsewhere, certain profits of the land and stock, such as grain, butter, cheese and the young of the animals, might have to be rendered, and this may be reflected in the phrase 'improvement by hand and other improvement of the two merklands' (1. 10).[31] From the tenant's point of view steelbow was a way of allowing a young man with little capital to obtain a lease of land, while the landlord probably saw it as a way of dealing with newly cultivated land.[32]

The formula of the document is broadly similar to that of contemporary contracts in Scots. The signing of writs by contracting parties had been customary since the fifteenth century, and was made compulsory by Act of Parliament in 1540; customs regarding witnesses were mixed in our period, but it is usual to find the writer (who could not himself be a contracting party) signing his name as first witness, followed by the grantor and other party or parties on the right and additional witnesses on the left.[33] One person with whom the óglach can certainly not be identified, therefore, is Hugh MacPhail.

Now, it is perhaps legitimate to ask the question, why is the document written in Gaelic? It is later by two centuries than the Islay charter. MacPhail was literate in Scots. And unlike the contract of fosterage of 1614, our document does not refer to any exclusively Gaelic law or custom except, briefly, cuddich; indeed, I have expressed my surprise that the word *feidhm* is not used for 'services'. (On the credit side, it has to be said that MacPhail handles terms like the *fiach* derivatives quite smoothly, and stock phrases like *iad so an fiaghnuise* show him to be au fait with the basic conventions of Gaelic legal phraseology.)

The answer must simply be, then, that it was written in Gaelic because the persons involved were more capable of reading that language than they were of reading Scots. Dr. Bannerman has presented evidence for widespread literacy in Gaelic among the aristocracy of the Highlands in the period up to and including our own, and his conclusion is particularly notable: 'The ruling grade of society, that is, the heads of important kindreds and their immediate families, cannot easily have avoided being literate in the language and there is some evidence that literacy therein might extend downwards to include lesser people, specifically perhaps the *daoin-uaisle* or gentlemen of individual kindreds.'[34]

It may safely be inferred, then, that MacDougall could read Gaelic. What about the identity of Duncan, the middle man? *Daoin-uaisle* apart, one possible candidate has already presented himself — Duncan MacConnacher, MacDougall's physician, who had been sent by his patron to study at the Ó Conchubhair medical school in Ossory, Ireland, and who wrote most of Adv. 73.1.22 there during 1596-1600.

[29] SRO RH 11/6/2, f. 173v; Shaw, *op. cit.*, 56.
[30] Shaw, *op. cit.*, 101.
[31] Margaret Sanderson, *Scottish Rural Society in the Sixteenth Century* (Edinburgh, 1982), 22.
[32] Shaw, *op. cit.*, 57; Sanderson, *op. cit.*, 22.
[33] Grant G. Simpson, *Scottish Handwriting 1150-1650* (Edinburgh, 1973), 9; Bannerman, 'Literacy in the Highlands', 215; additional information from Dr. Bannerman.
[34] 'Literacy in the Highlands', 235.

Conclusion

The document was written by Hugh MacPhail (fl. 1603-38). It may be seen as a subtack or sub-lease by which two merklands in Lorn are set by a certain Duncan to a sub-tenant. Duncan appears to hold the land in steelbow from his superior, probably Duncan MacDougall of Dunollie. The document may be tentatively assigned to the period from c. 1603 (the beginning of MacPhail's floruit, and the date of Adv. 72.1.34, from which it may have come adrift) to 31 August 1616 (MacDougall's death). As the document is in Gaelic, it may be speculated that Duncan the tenant is MacDougall's physician Duncan MacConnacher.

With regard to the question of the nature of the legal tradition of Gaelic Scotland (as outlined in my introduction) the evidence of the document is equivocal. On the one hand it was written by a man who was not a hereditary lawyer, it contains many minor vernacularisms, and it fits comfortably into a Scots legal context: this hints at a distinct Scottish tradition preserved by oral transmission. On the other hand its phraseology belongs securely to a shared Gaelic tradition, and in general nature it fits well into the corpus of decisions, agreements, deeds, wills and pleadings in court extant from contemporary Ireland: this suggests a written tradition like the known Irish one, differing from it merely in being influenced by Scots rather than English law.

Acknowledgements

I wish to thank Dr. John Bannerman, Dr. Frances Shaw and Mr. David Sellar, all of whom kindly read this article in a first draft, for help and advice. I am also grateful to the Trustees of the National Library of Scotland for permission to publish the document.

Additional Note

Mr. William Matheson has pointed out to me that the practice of steelbow tenure (métayage) survived in the Outer Isles at least to the end of the eighteenth century, and that it is referred to as having land *air leathchois*, 'in tandem' — literally 'by one foot', as the possessor provided the land and the seed, while the tenant cultivated the ground and divided the produce equally between them. Fr. Allan MacDonald (1859-1905) noted the expression *Tha sinn ag obair air leathchois*, 'We are working by steelbow' (J. L. Campbell (ed.), *Gaelic Words and Expressions from South Uist and Eriskay* (Dublin, 1958), 162). Its use by this late period was occasional and no doubt reflected difficult economic circumstances — the need to bring waste land under cultivation, to relieve population pressure, or perhaps to bind an individual with an exacting lease. One instance from the period 1750-1800 is that of Luskentyre, Harris (W. Matheson, 'The Morisons of Ness', in *Transactions of the Gaelic Society of Inverness*, vol. 50 (1976-8), p. 78, n. 25). Another is that of the outby district called Paiblesgarry in North Uist, held by Hugh MacDonald as steelbow tenant from Donald MacDonald of Balranald ('List of the Inhabitants of North Uist, May 1799', SRO GD 221/153/1). See also A. and A. Macdonald, *The Clan Donald*, vol. 3 (Inverness, 1904), 139–40; Dwelly, *Illustrated Gaelic-English Dictionary*, s.v. *leth-chois*; Alexander Carmichael, *Carmina Gadelica*, vol. 6 (Edinburgh, 1971), 96.

THE COMMISSARY COURT OF ABERDEEN IN 1650

By DAVID STEVENSON, B.A. PH.D.,

Department of History, University of Aberdeen

Traditionally the commissary court of Aberdeen met in a room in St. Machar's Cathedral in the little ecclesiastical burgh of Old Aberdeen, a mile and a half to the north of the much larger royal burgh of 'New' Aberdeen. As it was a church court under the control of the bishop of Aberdeen it was natural that it should meet at the centre of the diocese. However, some considered that it was inconvenient and anomalous that the court was not based in the main legal, social and economic centre of the region, Aberdeen itself. None felt this more strongly than the citizens of Aberdeen: economic advantages could be expected if the court was transferred to their burgh and those with business before the court resided there, and the court's presence would emphasise further Aberdeen's pre-eminence in the North East.

An opportunity for Aberdeen to make a take-over bid for the court was provided by the success of the covenanters in gaining control of the country and abolishing episcopacy in 1638; if there were no longer any bishops, there was no longer any logical reason for the court to sit in Old Aberdeen. On the other hand, however, the weight of tradition was not easy to overcome, and the strength of episcopalian sympathies in Aberdeen may have led to a reluctance to exploit a position that had been created through the fall of the bishops. But after the radical 'kirk party' faction of the covenanters seized power in 1648 Scotland had a regime much more willing to push through reforms in defiance of tradition than the earlier covenanting regime, and this new atmosphere stirred those favouring change into action. On 16 March 1649 parliament passed an act relating the incovenience of having the commissary court meet in 'ane village', as Old Aberdeen was disparagingly called. None of the procurators who pleaded before the court lived there, and attending was inconvenient both for them and for others who had to appear before it. The commissioners who sat in parliament for both the shire and the burgh of Aberdeen had earnestly desired that the court be moved to Aberdeen, and parliament agreed to this.[1]

The court was at this point dominated by a prominent dynasty of Aberdeen advocates. Mr. Thomas Sandilands was commissary, and his brother Mr. James Sandilands taught civil law in King's College, Old Aberdeen, as well as acting as commissary clerk.[2] Aberdeen burgh council had doubtless negotiated with the

[1] *The Acts of the Parliaments of Scotland [APS]*, ed. T. Thomson and C. Innes (12 vols., 1844-75), VI, ii, 320; *Extracts from the council register of the burgh of Aberdeen. 1643-1747 [Aberdeen records]*, ed. J. Stuart (Scottish Burgh Record Society, 1872), 94-5.
[2] J. A. Henderson, *History of the Society of Advocates in Aberdeen* (New Spalding Club, 1912), 315-17.

144

Sandilands to gain their support for the move. Just a few weeks before the act was passed James Sandilands had the post of town clerk added to his other responsibilities, the timing suggesting that this was more than mere coincidence.[3] Thomas Sandilands was evidently promised that the burgh council would finance the move; on 9 May 1649 the council ordered the dean of guild to repair and adapt St. Ninian's Chapel on Castlehill. He was to 'caus big partitioun wallis, barres with ane seat for the judge and clerkis, strick out lightis and ane entrie' and lay a floor. This was then to be the seat of the commissary court. Moreover, as Thomas Sandilands had 'gratified the toun in condescending willinglie to the transportatioun of the said commissariot' the town agreed to provide him with 'ane comodious chamber' for storing the court's registers.[4]

Though bishops had been abolished the basic regulations for the commissary courts seem to have remained those agreed on by the archbishops and bishops of Scotland at a meeting in Edinburgh on 2 March 1610; consistorial jurisdiction had been restored to the bishops the previous year,[5] and they had hastened to act to define the competence of the courts, to regulate their procedures, and to detail fees to be charged.[6] However, Thomas Sandilands evidently decided, on taking over his new court house in Aberdeen, to introduce some regulations of his own, adding to those of 1610 or repeating old rules which had not been enforced (such as that ordering procurators to wear gowns). The result was the document transcribed below.[7]

Any document relating to Aberdeen commissary court before 1721 is given particular interest by the fact that all the court's early records were destroyed by fire in that year.[8] The survival of a copy of the 1650 regulations is the chance result of the interest taken in his work by Robert Burnett, ws, who was nominated commissary of Peebles by his first cousin, Alexander Burnett, archbishop of Glasgow, in 1679.[9] Robert Burnett took his new duties seriously enough to acquire copies of both the 1610[10] and Aberdeen 1650 regulations, and another indication of his conscientiousness may be that the earliest surviving registers of testaments for Peebles date from his time as commissary.[11]

[3] *Aberdeen records*, 94.
[4] *ibid.*, 95.
[5] *APS*, iv, 430; G. Donaldson, 'The church courts', *Introduction to Scottish Legal History* (Stair Society, 1958), 370.
[6] Sir James Balfour of Pittendreich, *Practicks* (Edinburgh, 1754; facsimile reprint, 2 vols., Stair Society, 1962-3), 664-70. These 1610 regulations seem to be virtually unknown to historians, partly no doubt because they form one of a few later papers in a work otherwise completed in the early 1580s.
[7] Scottish Record Office [SRO], RH.15/15/12, Papers of Robert Burnett. In the transcript abbreviations have been extended and punctuation and capitalisation have been modernised. Transcripts of Crown-copyright records in the Scottish Record Office appear with the approval of the Keeper of the Records of Scotland.
[8] W. Kennedy, *Annals of Aberdeen* (2 vols., Aberdeen, 1818), ii, 260.
[9] Both men were grandsons of William Burnett of Barns, Peeblesshire; Hew Scott, *Fasti ecclesiae Scoticanae* (8 vols., Edinburgh, 1915-50), ii, 125-6; *A history of the Society of Writers to the Signet*, ed. R. K. Hannay (Edinburgh, 1936), 29. Robert Burnett's appointment as commissary was renewed by Archbishop Arthur Rose, Alexander Burnett's successor, in 1680. Incomplete copies of both gifts are at SRO, RH.15/55/51/13-16.
[10] SRO, RH.15/55/15/18.
[11] *The commissariot record of Peebles. Register of testaments, 1681-1699*, ed. F. J. Grant (Scottish Record Society, 1902).

The refurbished St. Ninian's Chapel was not destined to house the commissary court of Aberdeen for long, however. In 1660, after the years of conquest and English republican rule in the 1650s, monarchy was restored, and this was followed in 1661 by the restoration of bishops. The threat posed by these developments to Aberdeen's hold on the commissary court was obvious, but at first it was countered successfully; in 1661 a new act of parliament confirmed that the court should sit in Aberdeen. But Old Aberdeen had seen the opportunity — as well as the potential danger of a further reduction in its place in public affairs if action was not taken. It seems to have been feared that the new bishop might follow the court by deserting Old Aberdeen. Efforts were therefore made to persuade Bishop David Mitchell to reside in Old Aberdeen, with offers of accommodation to replace the bishops' palace which had been destroyed under the covenanters. The general atmosphere of the time, dominated by a desire to undo all innovations made in the years of revolutionary turmoil and to uphold tradition, was on Old Aberdeen's side. The bishop confirmed that the 'village' would remain the centre of his diocese, and now that episcopal jurisdiction over the commissary courts had been again restored it was agreed that the Aberdeen court should return to its old home. Parliament accepted this by an act of 1662, reversing those of 1649 and 1661.[12]

Ultimately, however, Aberdeen was to triumph. In 1690 bishops were finally abolished and, as under the covenanters, this was taken as justifying moving the commissary court — though parliament claimed (by an adroit reversal of the facts) to be acting in favour of tradition. Its act asserted that the court was 'always in use' to sit in Aberdeen as the head burgh of the shire until it had been moved to Old Aberdeen by the 1662 act![13] Thus the facts of relative population and importance were given the support of ficticious history in finally depriving Old Aberdeen of the court which, along with the cathedral and King's College, had supported her claim to be more than a mere village.[14]

> The heids concludit betuixt the commissar, clerk, phiscall and procurators in the auditorie of the commissariot of Aberdeen upon the tuentie thrid of May 1650 yeiris.

In the first it is statute and ordainet anent the ordering of the hous that the bell be rung be the officir at evrie day in tyme of sessioune at halff elevine houres and to ring ane quartir of ane hour, and the consistorie dore to be opint at that tyme under the paine of deprivatoune of the officir.

2. It is ordainet anent the cariage of the hous that the commissarie keip preceislie and sit doune in judgment at elevne hours.

3. That the haill procurators keep thir seattis, and non of them to stand at the barr except in tyme of pleading thair actiones; and quhen the procurator gives in his sumounds that he breifflie rehears his caus at the ingiveing thairof.

[12] *APS*, vii, 329; *Records of Old Aberdeen*, ed. A. M. Munro (2 vols., New Spalding Club, 1899-1909), i, 101, ii, pp. xv-xvi.
[13] *APS*, ix, 204.
[14] Some further information concerning commissary clerks of Aberdeen in the seventeenth century appears in my forthcoming article 'Who was John Spalding', *Aberdeen University Review* (1985).

4. That the judge, clarks and procurators sall all use thir offices in gounes, and they that wantis to have them in readienes against the first of Junii nixt and that thes who beis not investit with thir gounes sall have no somonds nor actione callit in thir favours quhen evir they want them.

5. That the procurators at the calling of interloquitor in thir causs, they resume the haill defenss, answers, eiks and replyes made thairto.

6. That the procurators reasone the causs modestlie, calmlie in terminos juris without any intiruptione to be maid to the ane quhill the uthir be done.

7. That no sumounds of improbatioun be formit or lybellit bot onlie be the procurator phiscall, and als deforcementis and brak of arreistments in lyk maner, the phiscall always tackand the compleantes aith give he wes sumondit or not in the improbatiounes.

8. That no sumonds be callit be the clark but sic as the procurator or his servand in his absence, settis to his name.

9. That no executioune of any somounds quhatsumevir be valid heraftir except the officir and witness names be designit.

10. That Thomas Merser and his successores, keeperes of the registers, procure in no caus of registratioune, and that he keip the utir bar as ane procurator except quhen he uses his awne office of registratioune.

11. That no man be latt in within the utir barr but at the commissaries comand quhen they ar callit, and incaise the officirs lett any man [in] without comand, the officir to tyne his wages that day; and being thryse in on day fund in that fault, to be depryvit.

12. That no day be assint to defend againes any claime within tuentie pund and that the procurators have thir claimes formit in thir hands; and if any defence be, that it be presentlie exponit in that caice.

13. That no pairtie gett ane day to advyse with thir aithes except they depone that they ar not able nor resolvit presentlie to give thair aithes; and if the pairtie be sumounit to give his aith and be present at the bar and be put away be the procurator, that that [sic] they sall get ane new day to depone and the procurator to be unlawit.

14. That the haill procurators convene preceislie at elevin hours quhen the commissarie sitts doune, and incaice they conveine not at the said hour thir sumounds not to be receavit not callit.

15. That the perseuares give thir aithes that the day they sumound the defendares to is the just day they were sumoundit to.

16. That no pairtie be obleist in drink money but onlie to the principall deput [clerk?] except it be voluntarlie givin.

17. That no wreitts be givin up be the clerk or his deputis but onlie to the procurator or his parties produceres.

18. It is ordainet that in tyme hereaftir that the promuting of all decreitts be ten shillingis of sentance silver and the officir to have two shilling of evrie wreitt, 13s 4d of evrie interloquitor and desolvitur for his servace.

Endorsed 'Injunctiounes anent the comissariott of Aberdeen'.

THE LIFE AND CAREER OF JOHN SNELL (c. 1629-1679)

By Lionel Stones, F.B.A., F.S.A.,

Professor Emeritus, University of Glasgow

dedicated

to

Professor Robert Rankin
who inspired this new investigation of John Snell

CONTENTS

INTRODUCTORY NOTE

The occasion was provided for beginning a new study of the life of John Snell by the celebrations which took place, at Glasgow and at Oxford, of the third centenary of his death, in 1979. I am grateful to both the University of Glasgow and Balliol College for their help and encouragement in this task of piety, and especially to Professor Robert Rankin, then Clerk of Senate at Glasgow, and Dr. Anthony Kenny, Master of Balliol. My incursion into a period of history in which I am inexpert would have been impossible without the ready help of a large number of friends. Many specific acknowledgments are made in the text and notes below, but I have a more general debt to those now to be named. From the outset, Professor John Roskell has given me advice, and towards the close he was kind enough to read the whole typescript most carefully, and to suggest many corrections and improvements. Dr. Gerald Aylmer has given expert counsel on many points, as well as general encouragement, and Mr. David Yale has helped very materially with the legal background. In Glasgow University Archives, Mr. Michael Moss and Dr. Irene O'Brien have answered my numerous queries with extreme patience, and I owe to Mr. Moss my knowledge of the relics of Sir Orlando Bridgman (the seal bag and silver cup) at Weston Park, Staffordshire, as well as my introduction to the records in the Staffordshire Record Office. At that office, in Stafford, Mrs. Randall, the assistant archivist, has not only helped me by supplying photocopies, and by obtaining permission from the earl of Bradford to publish certain documents, but she is to be credited with the discovery of one of the most important of all the new documents on Snell to be found below (see p. 200). At the Public Record Office, Dr. Roy Hunnisett, as often before, has eased my task in many ways. So also has Miss Jane Fowles, at Longleat House. To Mr. Vincent Quinn, sometime librarian of Balliol, and now keeper of the college's Special Collections, I owe both encouragement, and the communication of a great many facts otherwise unknown to me. Dr. Arnold Taylor, who has a special felicity in historical discovery on behalf of his friends, has always been at hand in this, as in my researches for many years. At Glasgow University Library, Mrs. Barbara Fletcher's *ad hoc* catalogue of *Snelliana*, made for the celebrations of 1979, has proved invaluable. Concerning Snell's gifts of books to Glasgow, I have most generously been given bibliographical information, much of it, I fear, laborious to assemble, by Mr. Jack Baldwin and Dr. John Durkan. Mr. Bruce Webster, himself formerly one of Mr. Snell's exhibitioners, has very kindly read my proofs with great care. Lastly, I have been helped, in various ways, by Mr. T. H. Aston, Mr. Peter Asplin, Dr. Robert Donaldson, Mr. Norman Evans, Dr. Donald Galbraith, Professor K. H. D. Haley, Mr. K. Hall, Miss Inez Hamilton, Dr. John Imrie, Dr. John Jones, Dr. John Maddicott, Professor Neil McCormick, Mr. Peter McNiven, Dr. Doreen Milne, Dr. Ian Rae, Mrs. Jean Robertson, and Professor David Walker. None of those mentioned, of course, are responsible for my mistakes.

I cannot pretend to have searched the possible sources beyond modest limits. My search of the State Papers, for example, has been confined to an examination of the original letters suggested by the indexes of the printed *Calendars*. Any references to John Snell in the originals, which are not noted in the *Calendars*, will not have come to my attention. I have not been able to examine in person either the Bridgman papers at Stafford, or the Buccleuch papers in the Scottish Record Office. It will be no surprise if further discoveries are made. Yet I hope that the present essay will, within its limits, be of interest not only to former Snell exhibitioners, and to others who belong both to Glasgow and to Balliol, but also to a wider public.

Formal acknowledgments of permission to publish documents are given on p. 194 below, at the beginning of the section devoted to original sources.

E. L. G. Stones

Table of the chief recorded events in John Snell's life

c. 1629	Born, presumably in parish of Colmonell, Ayrshire.
1642-3	First session at University of Glasgow.
1644	Signs a text of Solemn League and Covenant, at Glasgow.
1651 (Sept.)	Alleged to have fought at battle of Worcester.
c. 1653	Enters household of Lady Hoghton.
c. 1654	Enters private service of Sir Orlando Bridgman.

1660	Appointed crier in Bridgman's court.
1661 (June?)	Makes first gift of books to University of Glasgow.
(Sept.)	Visits Colmonell, and leaves 100 marks for the poor.
1662 (May)	Married to Joan Coventry, in St. Clement Danes, London.
1662	Receives M.A. diploma from University of Glasgow.
1663 (March)	Death of his father, Andrew.
1663	Birth of daughter, Dorothy.
1664 (Oct.)	Erects gravestone of father, at Colmonell.
1667 (autumn)	Appointed 'seal-bearer' to Bridgman.
1669 (autumn)	Visits Scotland (Edinburgh, and the west).
1670 (March)	Promises another gift of books to University of Glasgow.
(May)	Mentioned by Gilbert Burnet, as desiring to settle Scottish students in Oxford.
1672 (Nov.)	Bridgman leaves chancery; succeeded by Shaftesbury, who continues to employ Snell as seal-bearer.
1673 (Nov.)	Shaftesbury leaves chancery.
1673	Snell gives copy of Jackson's *Works* to University of Glasgow in, or after this year.
1674 (Feb.)	Witnesses Bridgman's will.
(May)	Witnesses codicil to Bridgman's will.
(June)	Death of Bridgman.
(Oct.)	Made an M.A. of Cambridge, possibly a sign of his now being in service of Monmouth.
(Michaelmas term)	Completes purchase of Ufton estate, Warwickshire.
(Nov.)	Death of his mother.
1675 (May)	Makes deposition before enquiry into will of duchess of Somerset.
(Oct.)	Death of his friend Thomas Ross, librarian to Charles II.
1676	His employment by Monmouth first recorded in official documents. Latest volume given by Snell to Glasgow published in this year.
1677 (Oct.)	Allowed access to Shaftesbury in the Tower.
(Dec.)	Draws up his will.
1679 (Jan.)	Messenger from Monmouth to archbishop of Canterbury (?) concerning parliamentary election in Cambridge University.
(6 Aug.)	Revises and re-affirms will, and dies at 31 Holywell, Oxford.
(8 Aug.)	Buried at St. Cross, Oxford.

Some important posthumous events

1682 (Feb.)	Marriage of Dorothy Snell to William Guise of Winterbourne, Gloucestershire.
1682	Publication of first volume of Bridgman's *Conveyances*.
1697	Death of Joan Snell, John's widow.
1699	First Snell exhibitioners enter Balliol College.
1738	Death of Dorothy Guise, *née* Snell.

THE LIFE AND CAREER OF JOHN SNELL (c. 1629-1679)

Whatever else is uncertain about John Snell, we know that he died in 1679; and the third centenary was splendidly celebrated in Glasgow and in Oxford in 1979. A fortunate result was the discovery that many important documents are now available which were unknown to his earlier biographers: W. I. Addison (1901), G. W. Campbell (the contributor to the *Dictionary of National Biography*, about 1902) and A. Milroy (1923).[1] Careful and diligent as they were, they did not go to the *State Papers, Domestic* of the time of Charles II for evidence of Snell's work as a minor civil servant, nor did they have access to certain private archives where some important new material is to be found. Our object here is to set forth the texts of both the traditional and the new sources for Snell's life, and to provide an introduction (not by any means exhaustive) which will explain the present state of knowledge, and show where the evidence fails us at the moment. It is likely that some of the gaps will be filled by further discoveries. Certain limitations must be stated here. We deal chiefly with the events of Snell's own life, so limiting discussion of the origin of his family, except in the merest outline, and of the circumstances of the foundation of the exhibitions at Balliol, some twenty years after his death, and excluding altogether the legal controversies which have arisen from his bequest.[2] When we focus attention thus on the man himself, it becomes clear that he is no pallid benefactor, as so many pious founders are made to seem, but a creature of like passions with, let us not venture to say ourselves, but with the vigorous full-blooded Londoners of Samuel Pepys's day, among whom dull men were not likely to thrive and make fortunes as Snell did. The contemporary who accused him of 'arrogancy' (see below, p. 201) was a fellow-servant in a great household, who probably resented the rapid rise of a Scotsman to favour, but he need not have been jealous of a man who did not impress others by enterprise and ambition.

Lest any reader ask why Snell should be given hospitality by the Stair Society, we must say at once that, in his mature years, he confessed himself with pride to have been a pupil of Stair, when Stair, then James Dalrymple, was a regent at the University of Glasgow. It is easy to see why Snell, as a student, became attached

---

The following abbreviations are used in the notes: Addison, *D.N.B.*, and Milroy, for the first three works named in note 1 below; *Munimenta*, for *Munimenta Alme Universitatis Glasguensis* (ed. Cosmo Innes, 4 vols., Maitland Club, Edinburgh, 1854); P.R.O., for Public Record Office, London.

[1] The details of these works are (1) W. Innes Addison, *The Snell Exhibitions* (Glasgow, 1901), some copies having a double leaf loosely inserted, with the date February 1902, giving the substance of new evidence from Anthony Wood published in 1899, and of some other then recent discoveries; (2) *Dictionary of National Biography*, article 'Snell, John', by George W. Campbell of Leamington, shown by its bibliographical note to be not earlier than 1902; (3) A. Milroy, *John Snell, his Schools, Schoolmasters and Scholars* (Ayr, 1923, reprinted from the *Ayr Advertiser*). Mention should also be made of the articles by W. Fergusson Irvine, 'Dr George Snell, archdeacon of Chester', in *The Cheshire Sheaf* of 16 September 1896, 83-6, and by George W. Campbell, 'John Snell of Ufton and the Snell Exhibitions', in *Transactions of Glasgow Archaeological Society*, New Series, ii (1896), 271-86.

[2] On these controversies see Addison, 18-26.

thus to Dalrymple, an Ayrshire man like himself, and only about ten years older, who already had a fine academic record, a commission in the Scots army, and a notable place in University affairs. Our tribute here to Snell is assuredly an indirect tribute to his master, but the colleges of Glasgow and Balliol would doubtless wish to express their gratitude to the Stair Society, for making it possible to publish this account of their benefactor in the pages of the present series.

(i)

John was the only son of Andrew Snell, blacksmith, of the parish of Colmonell, Ayrshire, and his wife Margaret Carnahan.[3] The date of his birth cannot be given more exactly than 'about 1629', because the only two indications which we have of his age cannot be reconciled with each other.[4] John had a sister who married a John Muir, but there are references to grandsons of Andrew and nephews of John with the surname Stewart, so that if there was not a second sister who is otherwise unrecorded, it may be that Isabel had another marriage to a man of that surname.[5] There have been suggestions that Andrew Snell's forebears may have been Englishmen settled in Scotland not long before. The grounds for this view are John's use of the arms of the English Snells on his seal, and on his own and his father's tombstones,[6] and the connexions between certain English Snells and his great patron, Orlando Bridgman.[7] It has been supposed that Dr. George Snell, archdeacon of Chester, who married into the Bridgman family, and died in 1653, was the means whereby John was introduced to Orlando's service, as a known kinsman. But though we are ignorant of Andrew Snell's pedigree, the facts can all be explained without depriving him of his Scottish ancestry. It is enough to assume that when John settled in England, he found it convenient to claim kinship with the English Snells, and to assume their arms, steps which they would perhaps not resent when taken by a man of substance, and of some status in the public service. For such irregularities there are many parallels. The assumption that the Snells helped John to enter

---

[3] Andrew Snell's tombstone at Colmonell names John as the only son (Addison, p. 1); and for Margaret see below, p. 218, evidence of Wood.

[4] The inscription on John's tomb makes him die 'anno aetatis 50' on 6 August 1679; and John himself, in his deposition printed below, p. 212, says that on 20 May 1675 he was aged 47, or thereabouts. The former gives limiting dates for his birth of 7 August 1629 to 5 August 1630. The latter is too vaguely expressed to be of much use, but if taken to mean that he was then between 46 years and a day and 48 years less a day, it gives a range between 21 May 1627 and 19 May 1629, which does not overlap the range derived from the tomb. Further evidence is needed for a precise answer. We are grateful to Dr. D. Martin for advice on this point.

[5] For the Stewart nephews see John's will (below, p. 189), and for Isabel see Milroy, 128, 137-41.

[6] Below, pp. 186 (seal), 161 and 218 (tombs).

[7] The case for a connexion with the English Snells is well set out by Addison, 8, and in the *Cheshire Sheaf* article referred to above. The arms are found on the gatehouse roof at Exeter College, Oxford, where they commemorate a benefaction by a John Snell of the city of Exeter late in the seventeenth century, but no link is known between him and our John. We are grateful to Dr. John Maddicott of Exeter College for help with this point. Such 'adoption' of arms was, of course, discouraged by the heralds, but never with complete success. Sir Anthony Wagner's advice on all this has been very valuable to us, but he is not to be committed to any specific view on the Snell pedigree.

Bridgman's service is now altogether superseded by the certain evidence, which came to light in 1899, that John's true saviour was Lady Hoghton.[8] To return for a moment to Colmonell: Dr. Milroy has printed a number of documents to illustrate the social and ecclesiastical life of the village in John's youth. He gives Andrew's will,[9] the inventory of his widow's goods after her death,[10] and passages from session records about an assault on her with an axe, avenged on the spot by her sister with a knife.[11] He also shows that in 1641, and perhaps earlier, there was a graduate session-clerk in the parish, one Anthony Kennedy, who may have been John's first teacher.[12]

John's name first appears in the records of the University of Glasgow as a student enrolled for the session of 1642-3, when he would have been aged about thirteen.[13] His age at entry was, for that date and long after, not exceptionally low. The medieval habit long survived; Adam Smith matriculated at Glasgow when aged fourteen, and Henry Philpotts (1778-1869), later bishop of Exeter, entered Oxford at thirteen.[14] John was also present in the next session, though our only evidence is his signature in a volume containing subscriptions to the Solemn League and Covenant, preserved in Glasgow University Library.[15] As we have seen, his 'regent', or tutor, was James Dalrymple (1619-95), who held the post from 1641 until 1647.[16] Addison has constructed a very useful list of Snell's fellow-students. It includes a future earl of Argyll, born in 1629 and executed in 1685, two grandsons of James Law, archbishop of Glasgow, a John Colquhoun who became the second baronet of Luss, Alan Cathcart, who already held the title of Lord Cathcart, Matthew Brisbane, a future rector of the University, and (as well as many other Scots with no notable future that we know of) a few obscure English and Irish.[17] In the two sessions of 1642-4, Snell must have grown up to understand much which prepared him for a career in the confidential service of the great. Thereafter we lose him altogether in contemporary records until after the great Civil War, and the era of the Commonwealth, were over. We have to fill a gap from 1644 until 1661 by using reminiscences set down thirty years or more after the gap was ended. The ground under our feet is often unsure,

[8] Below, p. 155.
[9] Milroy, pp. 125-30, dated 10 March 1663, the date of his death as given on the Colmonell gravestone. The year here is 1663, not 1663/4, because in Scotland the 'new style' beginning of the year was introduced in 1599.
[10] *ibid.*, 139-40.
[11] *ibid.*, 26-7.
[12] *ibid.*, 33-4.
[13] *Munimenta*, iii, x, 97-8.
[14] Cf. H. Rashdall, *Medieval Universities* (ed. Powicke and Emden, 3 vols., 1936), i, 125 n.
[15] The book is entitled *A Solemn League and Covenant for Reformation and Defence of Religion* (etc.), published at Edinburgh in 1643. The last 14 pages are headed 'Subscribers of the League and Covenant', and John signs among the students of the second year. His presence in 1643-4 seems to be corroborated by Principal Baillie's cautious words in 1661, see below, p. 196.
[16] On the role of regents see J. D. Mackie, *The University of Glasgow 1451-1951* (Glasgow, 1954), 68, 74-7. Dalrymple's *Theses Logicae*, used in his courses at the University were printed at Glasgow in 1646. On Dalrymple, see G. M. Hutton's article in *Stair Tercentenary Studies* (Stair Society, vol. 33, 1981), 1-68, and D. M. Walker's introduction to Stair's *Institutions* (6th ed., 1981), 1-10. We may suppose that Snell's interest in law was first aroused by Dalrymple's Glasgow teaching, for though Anthony Wood calls Dalrymple 'professor of philosophy' (below, p. 216), his more correct title of 'regent' implies a much wider responsibility in instruction. See J. D. Mackie, *op. cit.*, 166.
[17] Addison, 4-6.

and caution is wise before we accept some of the conjectures that have not unnaturally been made.

The record of 1661 which ends the blank period (it is printed below at page 195) is a letter from Snell, now settled in London, to Robert Baillie, principal of the University of Glasgow, who had been a professor there in Snell's student days. Snell tells Baillie to expect the six volumes of Brian Walton's Polyglott Bible, published in 1657, as a gift to the 'publiq library' of the University, this being 'the first fruits' of his affection towards a place where he had been educated 'under the tutorage of the truly honourable and eminent Sir James Dalrimple'. This magnificent work[18] would have cost Snell not less than the then very large sum of £50, unless he had obtained a copy more cheaply from one of the subscribers. Great though his gratitude to the University must have been, this amount can hardly have been his entire capital. One may note that in the same year 1661, making a journey to Colmonell, he was able to afford a gift of 100 merks for the poor there,[19] perhaps not his only local benefaction. By now, at the age of 32, he had become well-off. How did this come about?

Thanks to the Oxford antiquary Anthony Wood (1632-95), to whom Snell must surely have told the tale himself in later life, we know the substance of the story, though to give exact dates to its early stages is not possible. Wood's narrative survives in three rather different forms, which complement each other, and seem to be equally authentic in details, though on critical grounds it would be wrong to combine them together in a conflated version. We print them all separately below, at pages 215-19. Only one of the three, however, that being the first given below, was published in Wood's *Athenae Oxonienses* of 1692 (a date within Wood's lifetime). The others were unprinted until late in the nineteenth century,[20] and were unknown to Addison until shortly after his book was published, an unfair stroke of fate towards so assiduous a searcher. The story begins with Snell leaving Glasgow in the 1640s without a degree. This may be inferred from Wood's clear statement that he had seen Snell's M.A. 'testimonie', or diploma, dated 1662. Evidently the University conferred the degree at a decent, though short, interval after the first gift of books in 1661.[21] Presumably, then, he departed from Glasgow at some date not long after the session 1643-4. It may be remembered that a Scottish army crossed the Tweed early in 1644 to take part in the Civil War, and that in 1645 the University was driven by plague to leave Glasgow for Irvine. In these disturbed times Snell may well have done any one of so many things that conjecture is futile. We lose all trace of him until early in the 1650s, and when he reappears, we are on treacherous historical ground. Anthony Wood tells us that he came into England 'in a very meane condition', and in 'the time of Oliver Cromwell'. But there is also a tradition (recorded in the

[18] See the editorial remarks on Snell's letter of 1661 (below, p. 195). For the figure of £50, see *D.N.B.*, under 'Walton, Brian'.
[19] Milroy, 121-2.
[20] In 1892 and 1899, see below, p. 216.
[21] There is no record of the conferment of the degree in the University of Glasgow records. Addison (p. 4 of the supplementary leaflet to this book) speculates on the possible reason, but it is well known that every system of official registration occasionally fails to record a genuine grant of this sort.

prefatory materials to Orlando Bridgman's *Conveyances*, and printed in full on pp. 219-20 below) that Snell fought on the royal side in 'several engagements till the defeat at Worcester, from whence narrowly escaping he sheltered himself in the family of a person of quality in Cheshire'. The fight at Worcester, after which prince Charles himself so narrowly escaped, was in 1651, and if we seek for at least one earlier battle to justify the 'several engagements', we may well include the affair at Preston, when Cromwell defeated a Scottish army under the duke of Hamilton, chancellor of the University of Glasgow (1648). It has often been readily assumed that Snell's 'coming into England in a very mean condition' (Wood) can be taken to mean the same thing as his escape from Worcester. That is not so. The coming in a mean condition was said to be 'in the time of Oliver Cromwell', and it is not too pedantic to think that this must imply a date after beginning of the Protectorate in 1653; in the later seventeenth century men were not so vague on such a matter as most of us now are. Again 'coming into England' is a very inappropriate phrase for escape from the battle of Worcester. We ought not, however, to dismiss the narrative of the *Conveyances* preface, late though it is (some time near to the end of the seventeenth century),[22] because, as we shall see,[23] it probably rests on a family tradition of the Guises, who were connected with Snell by marriage. We must, therefore, seek to reconcile the two accounts without assuming that they both refer to events of 1651. We can do so by allowing Snell to fight on the royal side from an unknown beginning until the battle of Worcester, in 1651, to escape thence to Scotland (a rare feat, since Sir Charles Firth notes that 'not a single [Scottish] regiment or troop reached their home'),[24] and at a later date to come south again, not in the ranks of an army, but 'in a very mean condition' as a lone individual. Before we consider the likely date of his return south, we have to note, as a slight difficulty in this theory, that Wood makes no mention of the battle of Worcester, nor, indeed, of any campaigning by Snell. Assuredly there was no need, after 1660, for Snell to keep quiet about this part of his life. It would have been a cause for satisfaction and pride, and a thing which he might have been expected to recall, when talking to Wood, with all the garrulity of an old soldier. We have no answer to this except that one should remember that negative evidence — the mere absence of a reference — does not prove the non-existence of an event. Wood may perhaps have forgotten what he had heard, or mislaid part of his notes. If, however, this objection be set aside, we are free to consider a likely date for Snell's re-entry to England.

Our evidence here has to be indirect. The circumstances of Snell's return (if we may now assume that he escaped to Scotland after eluding the pursuers of the Worcester fugitives) are given by Wood. 'In his journey through Lancashire', Snell presents himself at Walton, near to Hoghton Tower, is taken in by the Scottish Lady (Margaret) Hoghton, enters her household staff and, about a year later, is recommended to Sir Orlando Bridgman, the lawyer, in whose service he will spend much of his life, and make his fortune. Lady Hoghton was indeed his

[22] The reference there to Snell scholars at Balliol (below, p. 220) shows the text to be not before the 1690s (below, p. 174), but of course Wood's narrative itself cannot be earlier than the 1680s.
[23] Below, p. 180.
[24] C. H. Firth, *Oliver Cromwell* (1901), 292. Note his remark that 'the country people hunted down the fugitives with merciless ferocity'.

fairy godmother. When did this romantic call at Hoghton Tower take place? In giving evidence on a disputed will in 1675, Snell declared that he had been in Bridgman's service for 'twenty years or thereabouts' (below, p. 213). Bridgman died in 1674. Roughly speaking, then, Snell joined Bridgman about 1654. Subtract Wood's 'about a year' spent at Hoghton before going on to Bridgman, and we have him coming into England 'in a mean condition', which means certainly in poverty, but not otherwise in distress, about 1653. That year, we may note with a touch of satisfaction, was the beginning of (in the strict sense) 'the time of Oliver Cromwell'.

This version of events enables us to reconcile our two sources, save for one detail not so far discussed. The *Conveyances* preface, as we have cited it above, says that after Worcester, Snell sheltered in the family of a person of quality in Cheshire, but goes on to say, in a so far unquoted passage, 'where he had the opportunity of being known to Sir Orlando Bridgman, who was a native of that country'. Thus Wood's story makes the association with Bridgman come later, and through Lady Hoghton (in fact, through Lady Hoghton's introducing Snell to her daughter, Lady Calveley); but the *Conveyances* make it come earlier, through an unnamed family in Cheshire. Here we can have no certain guidance. There is no difficulty in believing that Snell sheltered in Cheshire in 1651 (if he fought at Worcester), for he would almost certainly have passed through the country in his northward flight from the battle. Further, Professor Roskell has pointed out to us that, since Lady Calveley was the wife of Sir Hugh Calveley of Lea, Cheshire, Lea may even have been the house where Snell took refuge in his flight. To go further, and accept the statement of the *Conveyances* that Snell came to know Bridgman as early as 1651, is not only inconsistent with the statement of Wood, but also objectionable because, as a fugitive, Snell is not at all likely to have wished to draw any attention to himself. Yet it is at least an attractive possibility that Snell, if succoured by Lady Calveley in 1651, derived from her that knowledge of her mother to which he laid claim a few years later, when he called at Lady Hoghton's door and alleged that he had heard that 'a gude lady, his countrywoman, lived there'.

This discussion of Snell's career between his student days and his settlement in England has, unfortunately, been intricate, but we are left with little doubt that his career as a soldier was separated from his entry upon a civilian life in England by a space of a couple of years spent, most probably, in Scotland. That Lady Hoghton set him on the road to success is certain, though precisely at what stage he first met her daughter is not. Before we leave Lady Hoghton, a tribute is surely due to her, as one who — one may say without undue extravagance — helped to make possible the Snell exhibitions. Her portrait[25] may be seen at Hoghton Tower, where now resides her direct descendant, Sir Bernard de Hoghton, baronet. A visit to the Tower should be an act of piety for former exhibitioners, and for all those who prize the ancient association between Glasgow and Balliol. Lady Hoghton was, as Wood tells us, a daughter of Sir Robert Ashton, barber to James VI and I and, later, master of the robes. The most famous event in the history of the Tower is the visit of James in 1617, when he knighted the loin of

---

[25] It is attributed to Van Dyck.

beef.[26] At the date when Snell may have supposed to have arrived (he was then about 25) she was a widow,[27] living, it seems, not at Hoghton Tower itself, up on the hill, but at Walton Hall (Wood's 'Walton near Hoghton Tower'), three or four miles lower down, to the north-west. In her widowed state she would certainly have found it useful to keep young Snell in the house to manage the accounts, wait on her, and say prayers. She may have found it hard to part with him, but by her way of so doing she ensured his future prosperity.

Who was the Orlando Bridgman whose service was so profitable that in only six years Snell was changed from a lady's domestic, to a man of affairs wealthy enough to give lavishly to his University? He was one of the many lawyer-statesmen who richly deserve a modern biography. His papers, which survive in the possession of his descendants, the earls of Bradford, are now kept in the Stafford County Record Office. He was born about 1607,[28] the eldest son of John Bridgman, who became bishop of Chester in 1619. Though a royalist, Orlando established so great a reputation by the end of the Civil War, that he was employed as a conveyancer by Cavalier and Roundhead alike, 'his very enemies', it was said, 'not thinking their estates secure without his advice'.[29] He was not then allowed to live in London, and from 1650 onwards seems to have resided at Beaconsfield, though coming to London occasionally on business. Anthony Wood tells us (below, p. 218) that Snell 'was taken into the service of Sir Orlando Bridgman who, having much chamber-practice, Snell did write several conveyances for him, and was so diligent a servant to him and to his lady, that whenever the said knight was afflicted with the gout, he was the onlie person who was entrusted to attend him'. This sounds like a humorous tale told by Snell to Wood, and we need not imagine that the gout played as much part in Snell's success as did the conveyances. Moreover, Snell's success with women, seen already with Lady Hoghton, and later with the duchess of Somerset (below, p. 171), is likely also to have been an important element dealing with Bridgman, whose second wife was 'a most violent intriguess in business'.[30] The picture can readily be imagined. Bridgman takes Snell to Beaconsfield as a general factotum. At the age of nearly fifty in 1655, Bridgman is feeling his years, and the gout. Snell is more than twenty years younger, has the advantage of a good Scottish education, can write conveyances from his master's briefest hints, and deal tactfully with clients in his absence. Perhaps also, in the perilous years between 1654 and 1660, Snell can visit people and places which were inaccessible to so well-known a man as Bridgman, and do business for him. Precisely how Snell gained so much money between 1654 and 1661 we cannot tell, for until 1660 he is not known to have held, and in the circumstances cannot have held, any public office. The money must have come, directly and indirectly, from Bridgman's wealthy clients; directly when Bridgman paid Snell out of his own fees, indirectly when clients

---

[26] Victoria County History, *Lancaster*, vi (1911), 40; and on the Tower in general, with plans and illustrations, see *ibid.*, 41-6.
[27] Her husband, Sir Gilbert Hoghton, died in or before 1646 (V. C. H., *Lancaster*, vi, 40).
[28] *D.N.B.*, under Bridgman, Orlando.
[29] *ibid.*
[30] *D.N.B., art. cit.*, quoting Roger North.

recompensed Snell the clerk for his trouble, or 'tipped' him to gain Bridgman's ear when he was busy, or indisposed.

The Restoration of the monarchy took Bridgman to the post of chief baron of the exchequer, the president of the court of exchequer. (He was well known to Charles II from of old, having been his solicitor-general when Charles was Prince of Wales.) Snell now received the appointment, according to Anthony Wood, of 'crier' of the court. At this point, where it is necessary that we discuss Snell's court-work, we find that the details of the management of the seventeenth-century English courts have many obscurities.[31] Our best near-contemporary authority on the court of exchequer (in fact it is some twenty years earlier) is the treatise of Lawrence Squibb, published in 1975, on the officers of the court.[32] It is disquieting to find there the statement that the officials called criers in other courts are in the exchequer called ushers.[33] This, however, is a mere technicality of the exchequer; its ushers may have been called criers by the common herd, and Snell may have adopted the term in talking to Wood, or Wood may have misheard him and substituted the more familiar term. A greater difficulty is that Squibb talks of a chief usher with four ushers under him.[34] The chief held his place 'by inheritance from Edward the Second's time', and his name in Squibb's day was Clement Walker. He appointed the four subordinate ushers. It is not clear how Bridgman can have overridden the rights of the Walker family, if it survived, in appointing Snell, or whether Snell held the principal post, or one of the subordinate crierships. Since further evidence may come to light, we shall not speculate about Snell's rank in the exchequer court, but Wood's wording 'Snell was made the crier of that court' does not sound appropriate to a post as a subordinate crier, or usher. No record of his appointment, or of payments made to Snell, has so far been found in the Public Record Office. Either such record might settle the matter, but at the moment it seems likely that Snell was paid by Bridgman himself, or by fees gained from litigants, a possibility to which we shall recur shortly.

Bridgman was chief baron of the exchequer for only a little over four months (1 June to 21 October 1660) and was then promoted to be chief justice of the common pleas, and so the head of the busiest court in England. Snell went with him, according to Wood, as crier.[35] Here again we have the problems caused by the absence of any official record of appointment, or of payment, and by the present obscurity of the detailed administration of the court. For what it is worth, we have some help concerning the post itself from the medieval records. Professor Sayles' tireless work on the king's bench has revealed that the medieval court had a chief crier and subordinate criers, and that the chief crier was allowed to perform his duties by deputy. His remuneration came from 'the profits of

[31] Without committing them to any of our statements, we must acknowledge the kind help in these problems of Mr. D. E. C. Yale and Mr. Hamilton Bryson.
[32] Lawrence Squibb, *A Booke of all the Severall Officers of the Court of the Exchequer* (1642), ed. W. H. Bryson in *Camden Miscellany xxvi*, 1975.
[33] Squibb, 126: '[Ushers] are in the nature of cryers of other courts'. Details of their duties follow.
[34] Squibb, 126.
[35] This move is made clear in Wood, version A (below, p. 216), and in the preface to *Conveyances* (below, p. 219), but is obscured in Wood, versions B and C, by the phrase 'in which office he continued', which is ambiguous.

justice' rather than from a salary, partly, it seems, by his receiving a portion of the 'damages-cleer', the sum paid in by a successful plaintiff, and partly (it may be) by a customary direct fee from litigants. Professor Sayles observes (he is speaking of the early fourteenth century) that 'there can be no doubt that the manifold perquisites of office were highly remunerative, especially to an unscrupulous man'.[36]

For the court of common pleas itself, we have information a century nearer to Snell's time, in the treatise by Dr. Margaret Hastings, *The Court of Common Pleas in the Fifteenth Century* (1947). She prints a table of fees, showing that 'the cryors' were allowed 4d for every judgment and nonsuit, 8d for every fine (presumably meaning final concord), 12d for every final judgment, and that in addition they expected, though not of right, but of courtesy, a payment 'at the pleasure of the party' for taking custody of a jury.[37] This last, Dr. Hastings suggests, means looking after juries while they considered their verdict.[38] All this helps to show whence a crier might expect to receive his income, and Dr. Hastings remarks that from Edward IV's time, the criers also acted as 'common vouchees' in common recoveries, and probably received liberal gratuities for this service as well.[39] It is clear that the method of payment by fees in court precludes any hope of finding regular notes of salary payments to Snell in the exchequer records. Dr. Hastings also finds (not surprisingly) that the hereditary nature of the office, which rather perturbed us in the exchequer court, was in some complex fashion applicable, in her period, to the criership of the common pleas.[40]

This discussion, we fear, may merely have darkened the subject of Snell's rise to affluence, for however well he did in fees and 'pourboires', the space between his first appointment to the exchequer in June 1660, and his gift of costly books to Glasgow, is only one year, and there may be some other explanation of his immediate enrichment which is veiled from us. The confusion between chief criers and their subordinates, and the uncertainty whether Snell performed his office in person or (whether wholly or partly) by deputy, make any speculation about his official routine rather hazardous. We may take it, however, that even the assistant criers had a social status which was not of the lowest. Little as we seem to know of these men in general, we may note that one of them, Robert Hellier, who died in 1630, is commemorated in a mural tablet in St. Cyriac's church, Lacock, Wiltshire, as 'late one of his Majesty's cryers to the Courts of the Common Pleas in Westminster'. Evidently the appointment was held to enhance the reputation of a gentleman.

(ii)

Snell's two appointments as crier (first in the exchequer, then in the Common Bench) stretch from 1660, until his master left the bench in 1667. Our surviving documents reveal nothing of the detail of his official work in these years, and we

---

[36] *Select Cases in Court of King's Bench under Edward III*, vol. 5, ed. G. O. Sayles (Seldon Society, vol. 76, 1958), xvii-xx.
[37] Hastings, *Common Pleas*, 255.
[38] *ibid.*, 152.
[39] *loc. cit.*
[40] Hastings, 98, and cf. 152.

do not even know for certain, though it is a likely assumption, that he helped
Bridgman in the great trials of the regicides, at the Old Bailey, from 9 to 16
October 1660. What information we have concerns his private life, and his
position as confidential adviser and helper to people in high places. Some time
before the end of 1666 he is known to have had quarters in London, in the parish
of St. Clement Danes,[41] the more easterly of the two churches which now stand
on island sites in the Strand (though neither of the present buildings, of course,
were there in Snell's day). He would thus be near to Bridgman, who lived at Essex
House,[42] on a site roughly shown by the present Essex Street, and he was far
enough from the City to escape the destruction of the Great Fire. (During the
plague of 1665 he may well have spent some time out of London with
Bridgman.)[43] Yet, since he was married in St. Clement Danes church on 8 May
1662,[44] there is every likelihood that his settlement in the parish dates back to his
first arrival in London after the Restoration. His wife was described by Wood as:

> 'A servant maid in the family of Sir Orlando Bridgman, named Joane,
> daughter of Vincent Coventrie, rector of Begbrooke, neare Woodstock in
> Oxfordshire, sister to the wife of Benjamin Cooper, registrarie of the
> Universitie, in whose house, in Holywell, Snell died.'[45]

Joan's father was a member of Trinity College, Oxford, and a 'praelector'
there.[46] Her sister's Christian name was Silvester, and her sister's husband,
Benjamin, was a member of Merton.[47] Thus by marriage Snell gained a foothold
in University circles in Oxford, and had a *pied-à-terre* in Benjamin's house, now
right in the city, but then, of course, just outside the walls, and strictly 'in a
suburb', as one version of Wood's account says.[48] The site of the house can be
identified with some certainty as that now occupied by no. 31 Holywell.[49] The

---

[41] Below, p. 198.
[42] Bridgman's letters to the Duchess of Somerset, written from Ampney Crucis on 11 December 1665
and 3 January 1666, show that he has a house within 'the great compass of ground' at Essex House,
for which he is paying what he regards as an excessive rent (Historical MSS. Commission, 58, *Bath
iv*, (1968), 255-6).
[43] The first letter mentioned in the previous note speaks of a case of plague at Essex House, and the
fears caused thereby. Snell is not mentioned, but one may guess that he would not be far from
Bridgman, at Ampney Crucis (*op. cit.*, 255).
[44] St. Clement Danes, London, Registers, vol. iii, 84, a reference kindly found for us by Dr. A. J.
Taylor.
[45] Below, p. 218.
[46] Mrs. Bryan Stapleton, *Three Oxford Parishes, a History of Kidlington, Yarnton, and Begbroke*
(Oxford, 1893), 334. We take this reference from the leaflet-supplement to Addison.
[47] J. Foster, *Alumni Oxoniensis*, i (1891), 324. Dr. Roger Highfield has drawn our attention to entries
concerning Cooper in A. J. Bott, *Baptisms and Marriages at Merton College* (Oxford, 1981). He
was University registrar from 1659 to 1701, and Bott (117) gives proof that he became chaplain of
Merton in 1649, and (13) that he was at a baptism in 1655, when Anthony Wood was also present.
Here is evidence, perhaps, of a link which brought Wood into touch with Snell.
[48] Below, p. 216.
[49] We owe this identification to the researches of Dr. Roger Highfield, and of Mr. R. B. C. Hodgson,
Estates Bursar of Merton College, which owned the house in Snell's time, and leased it to Cooper.
See Merton Register 6:3, 370-2, which calls the house 'no. 23rd'. Merton Register 5:23, a survey of
Holywell, shows that in 1758, no. 23 was on the north side of the street, bounded directly on the
west by Wadham land. Dr. Highfield observed old Roman numerals on the lintels of some houses,
from which he was able to calculate that the old no. 23 was the present 31; and the Estates Bursar
provided a map of Holywell in 1758, which showed that the present 31 occupies the position
required by this identification.

present house has all the appearances externally of eighteenth-century construction,[50] but its core may well have earlier work in it, and from the appearance of nearby houses, which have suffered less drastic change, one may picture the building as it was when, perhaps, Anthony Wood called occasionally for a talk with John Snell, and took notes for *Athenae Oxonienses*.

It seems very likely that Joan Coventry entered the household of Bridgman because of family poverty, after the death of her father, Vincent, in February 1660.[51] But we must not take the term 'servant maid', as used in a wealthy household like Bridgman's, to imply a lower social status than Snell's own. Joan was literate, though her handwriting was unpractised, and her spelling erratic (see her letters below, p. 206), and she brought up a daughter refined enough to marry into the ancient family of Guise of Elmore. This daughter, Dorothy, was probably named after Bridgman's second wife, Dorothy Saunders, who may have been a god-mother. She died on 12 June 1738, aged 76, as is recorded on the fine memorial at Elmore church, Gloucester, printed by Addison (p. 216); and in the absence of any known baptismal record, but in view of the date of her parents' marriage, we must assume that she was born in the spring of 1663.

Snell's father died, according to the inscription on his tombstone at Colmonell, on 10 March 1663. John had the stone erected on 29 October 1664. Originally, as Mr. John Dunbar has pointed out to us, the tomb was a 'table-tomb' of a well-known Scottish type, but only the top of it survives, giving the appearance of a recumbent slab.[52] The inscription was recut about 1890, when part of it was illegible, this being represented by the square brackets below. It now reads:

HEIR IS BURIED ANDRO SNELL SMITH [
                    ] DIED MARCH 10 1663 aged 72

(*the above words run round the margin. In a central panel are the Snell arms of a cross fleury, and the following words, in smaller letters than those in the margin*):

BY Mr JOHN SNELL ONELY SON TO THE FORENAMED IN TESTIMONIE OF HIS FILIAL RESPECT TO THE MEMORY OF HIS PARENTS WAS THIS GRAVESTON ERECTED OCT^r 29 1664

There has been some speculation whether this stone was made in England, at John's order, but the suggestion is both needless and unlikely. The design and the buff-coloured sandstone are probably both local, and Mr. Dunbar has noted that we even have, in the nearby McConnel burial aisle, the name of an Ayr mason who was at work in the kirkyard in 1663, one Dickson. Snell probably commissioned him, or some other local man, to do the work. The missing words in the

---

[50] Royal Commission on Historical Monuments, England, *City of Oxford* (1939), 180, item 200. For an adjacent house of older appearance, no. 29, see *ibid.*, item 202, ascribed to *c.* 1600.

[51] Mrs. Stapleton, *ut supra*, note 46.

[52] Mr. Dunbar, secretary of the Royal Commission on Ancient and Historical Monuments, Scotland, kindly visited Colmonell and made a special examination of the stone at our request, and subsequently obtained a geological report, but he is not responsible for any errors in what we say here.

marginal inscription may have recorded either Andrew's parentage, or his domicile.

Four documents printed below (pp. 198-201) illustrate John's associations with his patron-in-chief Bridgman, and with others who found him useful, during these seven years as crier. For a transaction of December 1666 he engrosses a document in which he appears, nominally at least, as a party with members of the Bridgman family, and in 1667 he acts twice on behalf of the dowager duchess of Somerset, a great lady descended both from Sir Francis Walsingham and from the earl of Essex, executed in 1601. She was a friend and client of Bridgman (see below pp. 212-14), and Snell, so obviously skilled in dealing with eminent ladies, attended to her business in the House of Commons (receiving £20 for his trouble). A letter which he wrote to her a couple of months later (April 1667) bears an undamaged example of his seal, and is the first evidence, apart from the coat on the tomb of his father, of his use of the arms probably assumed from those of the English Snells. Far the most interesting private document of these years, however, and unique in the picture given of him, is a letter now in the papers of the earl of Bradford, written by Snell, on 12 January 1664, to John Bridgman, the son and heir of Orlando. (It bears no address, but the internal evidence leaves no doubt.) Snell writes in familiar terms, and scandal is joyously rehearsed: 'my lord Cholmondley and my lady [i.e., Orlando Bridgman's wife] are falne out about his drinking of her syder and bere' (a tale confirming the alleged 'violence' of the lady's nature); and, though this indeed is related with a purpose, the son is candidly told that his father's advice had caused the eminent physician, Sir Edward Alston, to be 'foold out of £10,000 for faire promises and nothing else'. The main objects of the letter thus adorned with tales are to let young Bridgman know that his father would like him to sit in the commission of the peace, and to tell him that a bill for £50 will shortly be honoured. Reading this letter we can understand why Anthony Wood seems to have come to know Snell in Oxford; two gossips like these would have much to talk about. Wood, like Snell's brother-in-law the University registrar, was a Merton man, and 31 Holywell was a Merton property. Doubtless Snell also visited Wood at his house, Postmasters' Hall in Merton Street.

On 30 August 1667 a political era came to an end with the dismissal of the great earl of Clarendon from the chancellorship of England. The chancellorship was left vacant, but the duties of the office were committed to Bridgman, with the lesser status of Lord Keeper of the Great Seal. Snell's long attachment to Bridgman made it inevitable that he should go with him in some capacity, but one is a little puzzled by the way in which Wood reports the event:

'When Sir Orlando was made Lord Keeper, [Snell] was, at the instance of John, duke of Lauderdale, employed to be the seal-bearer' (below, p. 218).

It may be that Bridgman could not himself contrive the appointment which he must have desired for his faithful servant, and had to secure help. Lauderdale, of course, was one of the Cabal, and immensely powerful, and his knowledge of Scotland and Scotsmen so great that he is not likely to have failed to note Snell's talents; but precisely why he should have cared to intervene is, and probably always will be, unknown. Yet Snell must have taken the intervention as a compliment, and have spoken of it to Wood with some pride. The next period in his life runs from his move to the Chancery until Bridgman ceased to be Keeper, in 1672. We hear no more of Lauderdale's influence, but we must add him to the already interesting list of notables whom John had impressed. An earl and a second duke have still to come, before the end.

Snell's new post as seal-bearer was very much more important in status than that of crier. Formally it meant that he was in charge of the two matrices of the Great Seal (the engraved silver moulds used to cast the wax seal appended to the most formal royal letters). It will be remembered that when James VII and II fled from England, he dropped his matrices into the Thames, hoping to embarrass the administration by leaving behind no means of issuing properly authenticated letters in his name; a good illustration of the importance of the matrices. Here we are more fortunate than we were with the work of the criers, because Sir Henry Maxwell-Lyte's famous *Historical Notes on the Use of the Great Seal of England* (1926) has a good deal to tell us, based on unpublished records. Snell would be present when the seal was attached, and would draw fees from those who had letters sealed on their behalf. Furthermore, though we have not evidence from his time, we know that in 1740 (and things would not be very different, in so conservative an office, in Snell's day) the seal-bearer had 'to receive all warrants or writs of privy seal, and lay them before the Chancellor, Lord Keeper, or Commissioners of the Great Seal'.[53] This means that Snell would be a secretary in control of the incoming letters which authorised the placing of the Great Seal on royal letters issuing from the chancery. As such he was, though the term was not yet used, a civil servant, and though in theory without discretionary power, in practice he must have had the 'marginal' scope which comes to administrators after experience of the system. Luckily we have a surviving letter to illustrate this (below, p. 205). In a case where Bridgman will not grant a 'breife' to a poor petitioner without order from king or council, Snell writes that if the clerk to the Secretary of State should 'think fit to doe the poore woman any kindness [in the matter], I will bee sure to give her all the assistance in the power of, sir, your most obliged servant, John Snell'. Of his familiarity with all that went on in Whitehall (and this is no anachronism, since the letter just quoted is addressed to 'Joseph Williamson, Esq., Whitehall'), there is ample evidence. In January 1671 he writes that he has 'made search at the Petty bagg, the severall offices of the six clerkes in Chancery, and at the crowne office, and cannot in all those places finde the least footstep [*a vivid touch this*] of any commission to Sir Thomas Moddyford, no, not so much as a docquet, which makes me conjecture that it came from the secretaries signed by his Majesty, and by warrant immediately passed under the great seale, in which case there is nothing remayning with any officer in Chancery, save only the warrant which remaynes with the seale-bearer, who was at that time one Mr. Kipps, and is not now in London' (below, p. 212). Surely the letter of a man who knew his business, enjoyed it, and could write about it without jargon or padding, in a way of which Sir Ernest Gowers would have approved.

The matrices were kept in an embroidered bag (whence the name 'purse-bearer' often given to the seal-bearer), and happily Bridgman's bag, which Snell would have carried before him on formal occasions, still survives in the

---

[53] Maxwell-Lyte, *op. cit.*, 264.

possession of Lord Bradford, with a silver cup made from the silver of the matrices after they ceased to be used.[54] Snell was not ultimately responsible for safe custody of the matrices, as we know from an episode of 1677 (a little after his period as seal-bearer, but proof of the custom) when a thief tried to steal them for under the Keeper's pillow,[55] but his post was described, and no wonder, as being one of great trust, requiring 'an honest-bred, understanding man'.[56] No record has been found of the payment of a regular salary, but we may assume that an ample income was available in fees and perquisites. By coincidence, Snell's predecessor, the Mr. Kipps mentioned a few lines above, can help us a little here. He was a friend of Samuel Pepys, who remarked on his appointment that 'with him the world is well changed, he being now a seal-bearer to the Lord Chancellor' (*Diary*, 25 June 1660). When Pepys sought the necessary patent for his appointment as Clerk of the Acts, he had to procure the *recepi* for his warrant from Kipps, and though he does not tell us how much the tedious process of the *recepi* cost, the total expense of his patent was £40, and he was very mournful about 'the great debts which he had to the secretary, Mr Kipps, and Mr Spong' for procuring it (*Diary*, 13, 15, 18 July 1660). Now it is certain that by Snell's day the *recepi* was added to all warrants received in Chancery, and that the work was supervised by the seal-bearer.[57] We know that from 1706 the range of fees for this was between £1 6s 6d and £5 5s on each occasion. Maxwell-Lyte gives us other examples of a seal-bearer's fees, and though they belong to later times than Snell's, they give some general guidance. In the middle of the eighteenth century a newly-elected bishop paid the seal-bearer £2 12s 6d for each of the three instruments necessary for his appointment. A new baronet paid the same sum once.[58]

It is tempting to think that we might so follow up the tale of Mr. Kipps as to discover some details, in the chancery records, of Snell's daily work, and perhaps to calculate his income from the adding of the *recepi*. The warrants for the Great Seal in this period (classified in the P.R.O. as C 82) are made up in monthly files, and the files relevant to the Bridgman epoch are nos. 2364 to 2432 (Sept. 1667 to Nov. 1672) a total of 69 files. A full examination of even part of these has not been possible, but in general we may say that each monthly file contains between fifteen and twenty warrants, whose average dimensions are about two feet wide and eighteen inches high. On the front there is a mandate, in Latin, from the king to Bridgman, ordering him to issue under the Great Seal a letter whose purport is given in full detail in the mandate. Below, in another hand,[59] which seems never to be Snell's, is the word *recepi*, followed by a date, which is sometimes so much later than the date of the mandate as to show that Pepys's troubles in finding

---

[54] We are indebted to Mr. Michael Moss for our knowledge of these survivals, and for providing photographs. Maxwell-Lyte, *op. cit.*, 318 ff., traces the history of the provision of such bags, and shows that considerable expense was incurred by the exchequer in paying for them; it seems that after about 1501 a new bag was made each year, and that Snell must have handled several different bags during his term of office.

[55] Maxwell-Lyte, 316.

[56] *ibid.*, 264.

[57] *ibid.*, 263.

[58] *ibid.*, 337, 351 (case of Lloyd Kenyon in 1784).

[59] In G. E. Aylmer, *The States' Servants, 1649-60* (1973), 463-7, there is printed a document of *c.* 1653 which states that the *recepi* was, in the time of Charles I, written only by the Lord Keeper himself.

Kipps were not exceptional. On the reverse, usually near to the point where the filing thong runs through the parchment, we often find a brief description of the content of the mandate, and in some of the files that we have examined, the hand is, almost beyond doubt, that of Snell. He writes, for example, in file C 82/2367 (December 1667, soon after he took office): 'Lord Halifax' patent of creation' (this, of course, is the famous 'Trimmer', George Savile), and 'A commission of lieutenancy to the Lord St. John of Basing for the county of Southampton'. One can see that though the simple routine writing of *recepi* on the warrant might safely be left to a mere clerk, the summarising of the text of a long Latin document might best be done by a man with Snell's good knowledge of Latin and of law. A later file, no. 2401 of June 1670, has the same features. In no file that we have seen does Snell endorse every warrant, and a much more detailed examination is needed before one can generalise, but at least we have here, if not the personal detail that we were seeking, at least the sense of finding (to echo a phrase of Snell's own), a trace of his footsteps.[60]

As for fees, if he collected even the apparent minimum figure of £1 6s 6d on as many as ten warrants a month, he was receiving from that source alone some £150 a year, and it is obvious that fees for the *recepi* were only one source of his official income. All in all he must have been now tolerably well-off, if not even 'passing rich'.

The privilege of bearing the embroidered bag before the Lord Keeper must have brought him into the public eye, and when we read how Pepys 'got in with ease to Whitehall chapel by going before the Lord Chancellor with Mr. Kipps [and] heard very good music' (*Diary*, 8 July 1660) we can appreciate both the power which he would have to oblige his friends, and the opportunities that he had to enjoy public ceremonies. His love of liturgical worship, shown in the only remark of his that has been preserved, that he loved to hear Bridgman's chaplain 'read the prayers of the church distinctly and with reverence'[61] could now be indulged to the full when he was by duty bound to escort the Lord Keeper to worship in the best appointed churches and chapels of London, in the age when organs and choirs were coming back, after the dark days of the Puritan period. We can perhaps safely assume that when Bridgman went with the seal to the chapel-royal for the first time, on 1 September 1667, as Pepys noted on that day, Snell bore the purse before him. It seems that no successor was appointed to

---

[60] See Snell's letter of 24 Jan. 1670/71, below, p. 212.

[61] This reminiscence of a saying by Snell was cited by Addison, p. 13, but deserves to be given in full here. It comes from the *Life of Robert Frampton, bishop of Gloucester*, ed. T. Simpson Evans, 1876, 234. The original MS. is now in the London Library. Frampton lived from 1622-1708, was one of the seven bishops tried in 1688, and was later deprived as a non-juror (see *D.N.B.*). The relevant passage reads thus: 'So moving was [Frampton's] repeating the prayers of the church that when he officiated in the Lord Keeper's Chapel, his seal-bearer [*i.e. Snell*] told him one day, "Mr Frampton, I had rather hear you, or anyone doing as you do, read the prayers of the church distinctly and with reverence, than hear the best sermon that was ever preached". Now 'tis to be noted that this gentleman was a Scot, yet so truly Episcopal, that he left as a legacy near £500 per annum for the mayntainance of some of his nation in the University of Oxford for some years, having been of some University before in Scotland, and to return thither to promote Episcopacy.' We ought to add that despite Snell's apparent slur upon sermons, Frampton was also a very celebrated preacher, and Pepys says that from him he heard 'the best sermon, for goodness and oratory, that I ever heard in my life . . . he preaches the most like an apostle that I ever heard man; and it was much the best time that I ever spent in my life at church' (*Diary*, 20 Jan. 1667/7).

Bridgman as chief-justice until May 1668, and that until then, Bridgman held both that office and the keepership of the seal, but whether Snell also had his post as crier as well as at the chancery we cannot tell. At Bridgman's first meeting of the council, at Whitehall, Pepys was present, and 'observed the Lord Keeper to be a mighty able man' (*Diary*, 4 Sept. 1667), an opinion which he changed next year when, with Christopher Wren and the Duke of York, he read a 'silly' and 'ridiculous' paper by Bridgman on the faults of the Royal Navy, but on that subject, of course, Pepys may have been hasty (*Diary*, 28 August 1668). It is obvious that Snell, enjoying Bridgman's confidence as he evidently did, must have been in close touch with many of the great men, and important events and secrets, of a period when, according to Pepys, all power was in the hands of a group consisting of the king, Buckingham, Bridgman, Albemarle, and John Robarts, the Lord Privy Seal (*Diary*, 21 December 1667). He would surely not be left out of the preliminary discussion of Bridgman's abortive scheme of 1668 for religious comprehension, nor have been unconcerned about the plan (current at the same time) for a union between England and his native Scotland.[62]

A document unexpectedly found in 1982, among the Bradford papers, by Mrs. Randall, is unique in giving the views on Snell of another member of Bridgman's household (below, p. 200). Unluckily we cannot date it more closely than to the years when Snell was seal-bearer to Bridgman (1667-72). The writer, Mr. J. Eddowes, takes an unfavourable attitude both to Snell's character (accusing him of 'arrogancy'), and to his paper-work, finding his accounts to be incompetently kept, and perhaps suggesting that he has concealed some of his receipts as seal-bearer, though it may be that the charge is only of carelessness, and of being too busy with other things to attend to such details. Two points must be borne in mind here. First, that Bridgman did not cease to employ Snell after this criticism. Even if it be as late as 1672, when Bridgman departed from public life, he continued to employ Snell privately until his death two years later, in such delicate services as the making of his will (below, p. 171), and took him into his confidence in the affairs of the duchess of Somerset (below, p. 212). Second, we must allow for jealousy on the part of Eddowes. We hear of him once previously, in 1664, when Snell mentions him in his letter to John Bridgman, and the two references, that of 1664 and the present one, together suggest that he was a steward, or the like, responsible for the finances of Bridgman's household. He may very well have disliked Snell, both as an individual, and (it may be feared) as an instance of the intrusion of able Scotsmen into English pastures. Beyond this, there is an obvious contradiction between Eddowes' picture of Snell as a man incompetent with accounts, and his actual record, from the time when he was given charge of Lady Hoghton's family accounts, to the day when he died a wealthy man. The rather incoherent composition of parts of Mr. Eddowes' letter suggests that he was in an angry mood; and he even forgot to put a date on it. Nevertheless the document is a useful reminder that Snell must have encountered critics, as well as helpers, on his road from Colmonell to the Savoy.

Of Snell's private life during these years as seal-bearer to Bridgman we have some glimpses in the documents, and may perhaps hope, in time, to gain more.

---

[62] Cf. *D.N.B.*, 'Charles II' (22 vol. ed., 96, col. 1).

When he went on a visit to Scotland, in the summer of 1669, he wrote a letter to Whitehall which has fortunately been preserved, as have also been two letters from his wife to the office, asking to have enclosures forwarded to him. His own letter, written to Robert Francis,[63] clerk to Joseph Williamson, in Whitehall, was composed at Edinburgh after he had already been to 'the west', though whether that means Glasgow, or Colmonell, or both is unknown. He tells a weird tale of the ravages, in the west, of a malady caused by darnel-seeds in oats and barley, by which men are fuddled and stupefied (below, p. 207). Modern agricultural science entirely confirms his account. He also asks whether his wife is living at Ampney Crucis, Gloucester, or with her brother-in-law, Cooper, in Oxford. We know from Joan Snell's letters of the same period that she was in fact living 'at Mr Pleadal's house at Halyrood Ampney [Ampney Crucis], neer Sisester in Glostershire'. This Gloucester connexion is interesting, and suggestive. Ampney Park house lies immediately west of Ampney Crucis church, and it had belonged to the Pleydells for a century: indeed much of the house where Joan was then staying still survives. Her host would be the Robert Pleydell who died, according to the memorial in the church, 'between 2 and 3 a.m. on 29 January 1675', and who is described in the same tribute as hospitable (φιλόξενος). Snell's daughter, Dorothy, was later to make an excellent marriage into another well-known Gloucester family, the Guises of Elmore, and the John Guise who published Bridgman's *Conveyances* from Snell's manuscript may have been connected with them. It is clear that Snell was becoming established in the company of the country gentry, as well as in the 'civil service'.

The next year, 1670, is of special interest. In a letter known only from a partial transcript, Snell tells the University of Glasgow that he is sending the first volume of Matthew Poole's *Synopsis Criticorum* (published in 1669) and that he will send the whole work when finished, which means that in fact the gift was not complete until 1676 (below, p. 208). The whole work is still extant in the University library, in five volumes. Matthew Poole (1624-79) was a strong Presbyterian[64] who, because of his eminent scholarship, won favour and encouragement from many eminent Anglican divines, including William Lloyd, bishop of Worcester, Tillotson and Stillingfleet. His work was a survey of biblical commentators, and it is said that four thousand copies were quickly sold. Snell would rejoice to give such a book to his University. There is one odd feature about the Glasgow copy, which is not found in either of the British Library copies, nor, apparently, in any copies save that at Glasgow. In the first and the last volumes there is bound in, as frontispiece (not a bookplate, as stated by Addison, p. 13), an engraving, by the elder William Faithorne, of Sir Orlando Bridgman. Snell would have had no difficulty in procuring some 'pulls' of the engraving. It was in existence as early as 1666, when it appeared in Dugdale's *Origines Juridiciales*, and Faithorne's shop was near Temple Bar, and close to Snell's presumed place of work at the Chancery. We know from Pepys that Faithorne did a brisk trade there.[65]

---

[63] It is curious that Snell styles him 'cosen Francis', and that Joseph Williamson, putting an endorsement on Snell's letter of 22 April 1669, writes 'cousin Snell'. In neither case do we know of any relationship by blood or by marriage.

[64] See *D.N.B.*, under 'Poole, Matthew'.

[65] See index to Pepys, ed. Wheatley, under 'Faithorne'.

Presumably Snell, who certainly took delivery of Poole's book in loose quires and had them bound up, arranged the insertion of the frontispieces to commemorate his patron.[66]

It is possible that Snell visited Glasgow in the year of this gift (1670), but the document which would have settled this has disappeared since 1850, and the alleged reference in it may only have been to the visit in 1669.[67] We should say here that Snell gave many books to Glasgow which are not mentioned in his letters of 1661 and 1670; we shall deal with the whole of his gifts at a later point (Appendix I, below, pp. 183-5). The most remarkable episode of 1670 is one which has come to light only in 1977, thanks to the researches of Mr. J. Donnelly, in the Aikman papers at Hamilton. Mr. Donnelly found there two letters of 26 May and 28 May 1670 (printed below, pp. 209-11) which, at a stroke, transformed all previous ideas of Snell's benefactions in aid of young scholars. Hitherto, apart from a hint in Addison (p. 12) that Snell had already, by 1670, 'got at least one young Scotsman placed as a student at Oxford, and was desirous that others should be sent to him for the same purpose', a hint based on the document now lost, one had thought of Snell as only a posthumous benefactor of the young. It is clear now that the foundation of the exhibitions was an extension, to come after his death, of educational benevolence begun ten years or so before it. The letter of 26 May, from the famous Gilbert Burnet, later bishop of Salisbury, but in 1670 professor of Divinity at Glasgow, shows that Snell had recently asked Glasgow, Edinburgh, and St. Andrews, each to supply one young man of promise for Snell to settle in England. (One wonders why poor Aberdeen was excluded from consideration.) The second letter, of 28 May, from the Principal of Glasgow to the Principal of Edinburgh University makes explicit the hint already noted, saying that Snell had already 'setled a young man at Oxfuird upon our desire'.

It would be pleasant if this young man, and the others chosen in 1670, could be identified, for they would then be the earliest known Glasgow men sent to Oxford by Mr. Snell's generosity; but at present they remain anonymous. Snell did not make his famous will until the very end of 1677, but we now know that he then had seven years or more of experience to guide him. One wonders if the restriction which the will imposed, binding exhibitioners to return to Scotland, was imposed also during Snell's lifetime upon his young men of promise, or whether it was rather suggested to him by finding that, in the experimental period, most of them stayed in England. It is interesting to find that in 1670, though he found his candidates through the agency of Glasgow, he was ready to accept them from other Scottish Universities, even if they had not spent the minimum of one year at Glasgow, which was to be demanded in the will.

(iii)

In November 1672 Orlando Bridgman, after some considerable disagreements with Charles II, lost the Keepership of the Great Seal, and was suceeded

---

[66] Such inclusion of portraits from other sources is not without parallel in this period, but they are usually of some relevance to the volume, or depict the ruling sovereign. Mr. R. K. Browne of the British Library has kindly helped us here, but is not responsible for our statement in the text.
[67] See preliminary note to Snell's letter of 26 March 1670, below, p. 208.

by Shaftesbury, who was given the full rank of Chancellor, but held office only for the year between November 1672 and November 1673. The preface to Bridgman's *Conveyances* says that Bridgman 'recommended Mr Snell to his successor, the earl of Shaftesbury, as a person of known fidelity and diligence' (below, p. 219). Whatever Bridgman's part was, there is evidence, in the great seal warrants, that Snell did serve Shaftesbury as seal-bearer. For example, C 82/2433, of December 1672 seems to have Snell's endorsements on membranes of 14 and 24 December.[68] It is entertaining to imagine him carrying his seal-bag on horseback, as he almost certainly did, during the famous cavalcade of judges from Exeter House to Westminster Hall, a disused custom revived by Shaftesbury, in January 1673, to the confusion of poor horsemen.[69] Snell's prominent position in front of the chancellor made skill in riding, on this occasion, very needful. If the anecdote is true, and the new chancellor was, at another time, greeted by King Charles with the audible aside 'here comes the greatest whoremaster in England', to which Shaftesbury countered with 'of a subject, Sire', then, it seems, Snell was present to witness the exchange.[70] To return to the *Conveyances* preface: it says that when Shaftesbury resigned the seal (Nov. 1673) he 'took care to help Snell into the service of the duke of Monmouth, whose secretary he was, and commissioner for the management of his grace's estate in Scotland' (below, p. 220). Anthony Wood, while agreeing that Snell was employed by both Shaftesbury and Monmouth, is confused in his sequence (below, pp. 215-19). He can be read as suggesting that Monmouth took Snell into his employment before Shaftesbury did. But any 'employment into Scotland' for Monmouth, who, by marriage to the duchess of Buccleuch in 1664 had acquired great landed interests in Scotland, would have meant long absences from London hardly compatible with the work of seal-bearer. Hence we must suppose that Snell did not work actively, if at all, for Monmouth, until after the fall of Shaftesbury. Yet he retained some connexion with Shaftesbury after his fall, for in October 1677 he was given permission to visit him in the Tower, on business unspecified.[71]

One must observe the political flexibility of Snell, who had in his time signed the Scottish covenant, yet probably fought at Worcester, and served in Cavalier households such as those of Lady Hoghton and Bridgman; then at the end of his days elected to serve Absalom (Monmouth), and the very arch-Whig Achitophel (Shaftesbury). Yet we should not regard him as a vicar of Bray. Many are the examples, even before the emergence of a non-political civil service in modern times, of the readiness of able men, at all periods, to work for either side, and of their ready acceptance by either side. For Snell in the 1670s, as his thoughts turned more to the endowment of learning, the problem may have been negligible. When we contemplate what he might have thought of the effect of the Revolution of 1688 on his scheme, laid down in his will, for strengthening episcopacy in Scotland, we may remember that his own life shows him not to have been fanatical in his allegiances.

---

[68] See also Snell's own remark, in 1675, that he was, after Bridgman's time, 'recommended to the now earl of Shaftesbury' (below, p. 213).

[69] K. H. D. Haley, *The First Earl of Shaftesbury* (Oxford, 1968), 308-9.

[70] *ibid.*, pp. 214-5.

[71] *Cal. State Papers, Domestic, Charles II*, March 1677-Feb. 1678 (1911), 688.

We may best consider the remaining years of Snell's life (1673-9) under the heads of public career, private affairs, and academic benefactions. There is no evidence of his employment at the great seal after the fall of Shaftesbury in November 1673, and one may suppose that after then his income came mainly from Monmouth. Of his connexion with Monmouth only a very few 'footsteps' (as he himself might have said)[72] now survive. In 1676 he recommends that a tenant of Monmouth be allowed to pass the Scottish border (this is equivalent to signing a passport application);[73] and in the same year he is named as having authority to act on Monmouth's behalf in matters concerning Rockingham forest.[74] A portrait of Monmouth now at Elmore Court (as Lady Guise has kindly informed us) may perhaps have belonged to Snell, and come there by inheritance through Snell's daughter Dorothy. The chief known instance of his work for Monmouth was at the general election of 1679, the first since 1661, when Monmouth, as Chancellor of the University of Cambridge, was anxious to secure the election of another of his 'secretaries', one Mr. Vernon, as member for the University. He sent Snell to explain this to a person who cannot be certainly identified, but was probably the archbishop of Canterbury (below, p. 215). We can hardly tell if the task was a particularly delicate one, though *a priori* one may think that archbishop Sancroft, himself a celebrated Cambridge scholar, might have preferred an appointment with other recommendations than mere approval by Monmouth.[75] It may perhaps have been a desire by Monmouth to give Snell status at Cambridge, for acting on his behalf, that caused Snell to be made an M.A. of the University by royal command in 1674:[76] an honour that he did not have, and had no reason to have, from Oxford. We may indeed wonder how Snell did acquire the influence that he seems to have had in so clannish a society as that of Oxford, being well able, it seems, to see that any Scots lad sent to him was 'well-placed' at the University. Merely to be wealthy, and to be brother-in-law of the registrar, was perhaps enough, and there seems to be nothing in either University or college records to show that he had any other connexion. This, however, is an unfruitful speculation. The Cambridge University parliamentary election came only a few months before Snell's death. Monmouth secured his wishes, James Vernon being one of the two members returned. The election is the last known episode in Snell's public career. When he died at Oxford, in his brother-in-law's house, he can hardly have been at ease (despite his political flexibility) concerning the world outside. He died in August of the year which had already seen the publication of Titus Oates's 'True Narrative' of the popish plot (April), the beginning of the Exclusion Bill in parliament (May), designed to exclude the duke of York, but (if it were passed) leaving Snell's patron

---

[72] For the phrase see above, p. 163, and below, p. 212.

[73] *Cal. S.P. Dom., Charles II*, March 1676-Feb. 1677 (1909), 245.

[74] *ibid.*, 415.

[75] Professor Roskell has drawn our attention to a singularly heavy-handed letter from Monmouth to the vice-chancellor of Cambridge on his wishes in this election (C. H. Cooper, *Annals of Cambridge*, [1842-1908, 5 vols.], iii, 577).

[76] The royal mandate is dated 13 October 1674, see Cambridge University Archives, UA Grace Book θ, 1668-1718, 101, 103, the degree being taken by proxy. We owe these details to Dr. Dorothy Owen. The degree comes so soon after Monmouth's appointment as chancellor of Cambridge, in July 1674, that one can hardly doubt the connexion.

Monmouth as a possible heir, and the murder of Archbishop Sharp (May), followed by the Scottish rebellion against which Monmouth took command. Like many other men he may have fancied that he was threatened by the frenzy of Oates and his followers: it was on 22 May 1679 that the innocent Samuel Pepys was sent to the Tower, and perhaps Snell went to Oxford to escape from the furore in London. Certainly fears for the future of Scotland can hardly have been far away from his mind in those last days at Oxford.

In a private capacity, Snell remained in Bridgman's circle until Orlando died, in June 1674. The original of Bridgman's will bears interesting marks of Snell's presence.[77] The document is long and complex, with sundry codicils. The main body of it is in Bridgman's hand, dated 19 February 1674, and it was apparently on that date that Snell witnessed an appended request by the testator to his son. Snell also added, in his own hand, the whole of a codicil of 1 May, and witnessed it. He likewise witnessed a note signed by Bridgman, on 31 May, in a hand so feeble as to suggest a death-bed provision. On 4 June, Snell wrote a memorandum of a declaration, made verbally by Bridgman, about an annual grant to Bridgman's daughter, adding the words 'which for this deponent's [*i.e.* Snell's] better memory, hee did sett it downe in his Almanack in these words ... [the declaration follows] and after the deponent had written these words in his Almanack, hee gave the booke into my Lord's hands ... and his Lordship did read the words and said that that was according to his mynde and will'. He was present when the will was proved. Bridgman seems to have made no gifts to Snell in the will, but of course he may have provided for him in some other way, and it may be no mere coincidence that Snell bought the estate of Ufton in Warwick, from which the exhibitions were to be endowed, later in the year of Bridgman's death.[78] We may perhaps presume that Snell intended himself to publish his patron's formula-book of conveyances, did not have time to work on it until he left the chancery, and in the years 1673-9 managed to complete the text, but not to prepare it finally for publication. But to this we must return later.

While Bridgman was spending his last days in will-making, a close friend of his died under mysterious circumstances, which were to cause some concern to Snell. This was the dowager duchess of Somerset, whom we have already encountered. The effigy upon her tomb in Great Bedwyn church, Wiltshire, testifies to the vigour, and strength of mind, by which she ruled her large estates during fifteen years of widowhood. It is fortunate for the biography of Snell that a dispute arose about her will, causing a formal enquiry, in which Snell gave evidence. The dispute was about the duchess's state of mind in her last days, when she was alleged to have executed a codicil. At the material time, as lawyers say, Bridgman, Snell, and the duchess were all in London, but on the day of the signature of the disputed codicil, 21 April 1674, Bridgman, the enquiry records, was confined to his room with gout, so confirming Wood's report of his tendency to the disease. Snell's view was generally hostile to the codicil. He said that he had written down many wills for the duchess, all drafted by Bridgman, and that whenever she altered her will, he, Snell, wrote out a new one and saw to the cancelling of the old (see below, p. 213). Moreover Snell declared that after the

---

[77] The will is now Public Record Office, PROB 10/1059, proved 15 July 1674.
[78] Date (Michaelmas term, 1674) from Victoria County History, *Warwickshire*, iv (1951), 245-6.

duchess's death, Bridgman protested to him that if she had been herself, she would never have acted so, without his advice. The points on which this enquiry gives us personal information are numerous, and many of them have already been incorporated above, but perhaps as interesting as anything is the evidence of Snell's easy movement among the aristocracy, as a trusted confidant and adviser. We ought to add that the enquiry is preserved at Longleat House,[79] and its bearing on Snell would have been unknown to us, without the good offices of the then secretary of the Royal Commission on Historical Manuscripts, Dr. Godfrey Davis.

The enquiry gives Snell's address, in 1675, as the parish of St. Mary Savoy in the Strand, and in his will he bequeaths to his wife his house in the Savoy, the area now occupied by the Savoy hotel, the street called Savoy Hill, and the chapel of the Savoy, all of them taking the name originally from the occupation of the site by Peter of Savoy in the thirteenth century. It was certainly not a home for any but the well-to-do.[80] We may wonder what part the estate of Ufton in Warwickshire, acquired by Snell in 1674, played in his life. Did he ever live there, or was it bought essentially as an endowment for his academic plans? There is no means of knowing. In his will he leaves money to repair Ufton church, and for the poor of the parish, and secures the annuities for his widow and daughter on the estate, but there is no suggestion that either he or they had lived there, or that the widow and daughter were to do so after his death (see the will, as printed below, pp. 187-93). On the whole, especially in view of Snell's connexions in London and Oxford, it seems likely that he did not habitually live at Ufton at any time between its purchase, and his death five years later.

Snell continued to give books to Glasgow after 1670, but no correspondence survives about these later benefactions. The dates of publication of the books are our only guide. Volume i of the *Works* of Henry Hammond came out in 1674, and the fact that Glasgow has no more of the series may be a result of Snell's death; but the three volumes of Thomas Jackson's *Works* (1673) are there, and all of the five volumes of Poole's *Synopsis* (1669-76). After 1675 it may have been less easy for Snell to keep in touch with new publications, for in October of that year died his friend Thomas Ross, who had been librarian to Charles II since 1661,[81] the year of Snell's first gift of books to Glasgow. It is one of the achievements of Dr. Milroy to have noticed this connexion with Ross, though he mentions no source for his knowledge. Ross's will, of which the original survives,[82] describes him as library keeper to His Majesty, and appoints as joint executor 'my worthy deare friend John Snell Esquire, of the Savoy' to dispose of his 'monies and arrears', the latter being, as anyone acquainted with the methods of Charles II's government would readily understand, the large sum of '£1000 due in the

---

[79] See the text printed below, pp. 212-14.
[80] It seems that some details about Snell's dwelling in the Savoy might be discovered by search in the Duchy of Lancaster Records in the P.R.O., especially since it was inherited by Snell's widow. Sir Robert Somerville has suggested to us that search might be made in the Savoy manor court books (DL 30/1372 and 1273), the leases of hospital property (DL 47/4, 5, 6), the Land Revenue records (LRRO 5/13/31-56), and in the rentals (LRRO 60/1703). We are grateful to Sir Robert for his help, and think it right to record these suggestions for further investigation.
[81] See *D.N.B.*, under 'Ross, Thomas'.
[82] P.R.O., PROB 10/1071, proved 10 Dec. 1675. Cf. Milroy, 119.

exchequer'. Probably Ross could not have found any friend better qualified than Snell to prise this amount from the royal coffers; he was certainly present when the will was proved at London on 10 December 1675. Ross's origins are unknown, but he was tutor to the young James Scott, later duke of Monmouth, when Charles II was in exile, and after the Restoration, was concerned in the attempt to prove that the duke was really legitimate. One glimpses here something of the political stresses amid which Snell's friends were moving, and through which he can hardly have avoided some excitements on their behalf, even if he himself never took any risks.

We give below a more detailed account of the whole Snell collection at Glasgow. One other gift made to Glasgow in his lifetime has to be recorded, though unfortunately we do not know the date. When the royal commissioners visited the University in 1690, they were given a list of 'mortifications' made to the college since the year 1664, and it included a gift 'by Mr. Snell, thrie thousand merks impendit on the building of the steeple'.[83] The money if converted to English currency would be about £167, and the steeple was that of the 'Old College', so familiar from the Slezer engraving of 1693. The sum can be given comparative value if we note that the Town Council of Glasgow had given only two-thirds of that amount, and that a Scots merchant in London, presumably a wealthy man, gave £100, both sums being for general building costs, and not specifically for the steeple.[84] Indeed, the wording of the record of Snell's gift may mean that his 'mortification' was not tied to any special purpose, but was directed by the college to help with the steeple. For this reason it is idle to calculate the date of the gift by the date of erection of the steeple, which is (in any case) an ambiguous term, meaning either tower or spire, though in this case, spire is probably the sense.

The famous will, indeed, comes as the climax of all this well-doing. Happily, the original holograph document survives, in the Public Record Office,[85] revealing much detail of drafting not detectable in the printed versions. It was originally written and signed on 29 December 1677, but on the day of his death in 1679, Snell confirmed it, in the presence of witnesses, and declared that all the interlineations and alterations made, apparently, on his death-bed, were in his own hand. The document was admirably photographed by the Public Record Office in 1981, and prints will be deposited eventually both in Balliol College, and in Glasgow University archives. Further details are given in Appendix II (below, p. 186), but it will be as well to remark here on a common misunderstanding of Snell's directions. Neither Balliol, nor any other college in Oxford was named in his will as the beneficiary of the endowment, and it was not assigned to Balliol until nearly fourteen years after Snell's death, and then by a court award. Snell did not single out any Oxford college; his intention was to do service not to a college, but to Scottish scholars, and principally to men from the University of

---

[83] Glasgow University Archives 26637 (CP 25), entry of 29 August 1690, cited by Adddison, p. 13, with no reference, whence very warm thanks are due to Dr. Irene O'Brien for locating it.

[84] J. D. Mackie, *The University of Glasgow, 1451-1951* (1954), 96-7.

[85] P.R.O., PROB 10/1103, proved 13 Sept. 1679. The will is printed in full below, pp. 187-93, and by Addison, pp. 197-202. Mrs. Jane Cox of the P.R.O. gave us indispensable help in connexion with access to the original.

Glasgow. His executors were told to convey the residue of his estate, after provision had been made for his wife and daughter, and for specific legacies to many others, to trustees, who would arrange to educate and maintain Scottish students in some Oxford college of their choice. The wording would, it seems, not prevent the trustees from selecting different Oxford colleges from time to time, if they had sufficient reason. We do not know why the Lord Keeper, in 1693, closed the issue by directing that the Snell estate be conveyed to Balliol.[86]

The Lord Keeper's reasons may never come to light, but it may well be the poverty of Balliol that made her a deserving candidate. Of her poverty, in the later seventeenth century, there is, indeed, no doubt. At Longleat House there is a petition from the Master and Fellows which, though it is undated, must belong to the 1670s, since it is among the papers of Henry Coventry, secretary of state (southern) from 1674 to 1680.[87] The college declares that its financial troubles may force a closure of its gates, unless the king will come to its aid with a gift of benefices, as his royal father had done for the Queen's College. This evidence, though the most striking, is not the only indication of the low state of the college's finances.[88] Now the Snell trustees included the Master of Balliol, who would be well able to put his own college's case to the Lord Keeper. It is true that the acceptance by Balliol of the Snell estate would bring the college only the difference between the income of the foundation, and the cost of paying stipends to the exhibitioners, and that for many years the college had the burden of paying an annuity to Dorothy Snell, who lived until 1736 (recently the college has found her receipt for such a payment in June 1729).[89] One can well see why H. W. C. Davis, in his history of the college, declared that the Snell exhibitions 'did nothing to relieve the pecuniary embarrassments of the college'.[90] It may be so, and we do not have the necessary financial information to prove him wrong. The point at issue, however, is not whether Balliol did gain, but whether the Lord Keeper (to use the kind of wording beloved of lawyers) 'might reasonably suppose' that Balliol would gain; and however little he expected the gain to be, the benefaction might best be allowed to a notoriously poor college, which would find a small subsidy proportionally more valuable than would a richer one. Moreover an Oxford college, even if burdened with an annuity of £100 a year to Snell's daughter, enjoyed, in the seventeenth and eighteenth centuries, a freedom in handling 'scholarship' income which had largely disappeared by the era of Victorian rectitude in which Davis lived. We shall see below (p. 178) that the epitaph on Snell's daughter goes out of its way to allege that the Snell foundation would support more exhibitioners than the number then 'partaking' of the endowment. At much the same date (1738), the University of Glasgow alleged that at least £50 per annum was being spent from the fund on 'the uses of Balliol

---

[86] Addison, 19.
[87] Longleat House, Coventry papers, vol. vii, f. 346. Apparently this is the original document, not a copy. It is now printed in *Archives*, xvi (1983), 131-6.
[88] H. W. C. Davis, *History of Balliol College* (revised ed., 1963), 142 ff.; Victoria County History, *Oxfordshire*, iii (1954), 83-4.
[89] Balliol College Archives, Book of Final Accounts, 1672-88 (*sic*), a text found by Dr. John Jones of Balliol. For the annuity to Dorothy, see Addison, 14.
[90] Davis, *op. cit.*, 142.

College'.[91] Whether or not these statements are true is hardly relevant here; but they show that such dealing with trust funds was suspected, and we may hardly doubt that in the Lord Keeper's mind, in 1693, it was anticipated, and allowed for. In fact the Keeper had specifically permitted Balliol to keep the 'overplus' of the fund, and argument could properly arise only if this 'overplus' was held to be excessive; a matter on which an 'average reasonable man' might hold different opinions if he were at one time an impoverished exhibitioner, at another time a fellow of Balliol, and perhaps later still became principal of the University of Glasgow.

Thanks to the delays caused by the need to pay Snell's outstanding obligations, and the annuities for his widow and daughter, and by the legal disputes which arose over his will, there was an interval of twenty years between his death and the appearance (in 1699) of the first exhibitioners at Balliol. They were Robert Carnegie, Robert Duncan, Charles Gregory (one of the famous family of mathematicians, who himself became professor at St. Andrews), and James Munro (later F.R.C.S., and ancestor of a number of well-known medical men).[92]

Though we can only speculate on the point, we may suspect that Snell discussed his proposed foundation with two sagacious and experienced men, with whom he had every opportunity of so doing. One was Orlando Bridgman. Though Bridgman died in 1674, three years before the will was made, he had been chief executor of John Warner (1581-1666), bishop of Rochester, who had bequeathed £80 a year to Balliol College for the foundation of awards to be held by Scotsmen so that 'there may never be wanting in Scotland some who shall support the ecclesiastical establishment of England'.[93] It seems very likely that in 1666 Bridgman would have told his Scottish 'crier' of Warner's foundation, and perhaps even have encouraged him to think of doing likewise.[94] Certainly the presence of the Master of Balliol among the trustees named in Snell's own will may have been due to the existence of the Warner foundation in that college. The other influence was, perhaps, that of Gilbert Burnet, who was settled in London from 1675 until after Snell's death, and was chaplain at the Rolls, where Snell must surely have attended sometimes, even after leaving the seal-office. The two men had much in common, not least an education in a Scottish University combined with an interest in English Universities. We have noted that, as early as 1670, Burnet was well aware of Snell's desire to see young Scots well settled in Oxford or Cambridge, and in every way he was the most obvious person in London, after Bridgman's death, with whom Snell might discuss his plans.

Some personal details of the will raise problems. One of the executors is a William Bridgman, but Orlando had no son of that name by either of his marriages,[95] and this William is at present not identifiable. And one of the

[91] Addison, 20.
[92] *ibid.*, 29-33.
[93] Warner's will is in Anthony Wood's *Athenae Oxonienses* (3rd ed., 1813-20), iii, column 732.
[94] For Orlando's pedigree see the earl of Kerry's article 'King's Bowood Park' in *Wilts. Archaeological Magazine*, xli (1922), 503, a reference kindly supplied by Miss D. M. Slatter.
[95] Dr. Barratt has found among the Warner Papers in the Bodleian library an agreement between Bishop Warner and Sir Patrick Warwick, dated 21 June 1666, to which Snell was one of the witnesses (Bodley MS. Top. gen. c. 75). Evidently Snell may have come to know Warner in some such manner, and have learned of his proposed benefaction even in Warner's lifetime.

witnesses to Snell's death-bed confirmation is a Thomas Snell. No such person is known in the Colmonell family, and the possible explanation is that this Thomas was one of the English Snells, whose arms we have supposed John to have assumed after he came south. We know that Dr. George Snell, archdeacon of Chester, who was married to an aunt of Orlando Bridgman, had a son Thomas, born in 1620, of whom nothing else seems to be known.[96] The question must be left open, but if the witness is George Snell's son, and he was with John at his death in Oxford, the acquaintance between John and his English namesakes was closer, by the end of his life, than we have perhaps imagined. Of the remaining executors, Benjamin Cooper, Snell's brother-in-law, needs no comment, but Thomas Newcombe, 'citizen and stationer of London' is probably the 'king's printer' (1627-81, see *D.N.B.*), printer of the *London Gazette*, and of the third volume of Dugdale's *Monasticon* (1673). Like Snell, he lived in the Savoy. He was an important personality in the book-trade, and presumably (as was Thomas Ross) a source of Snell's knowledge of new publications. William Hopkins was an Oxford attorney, who died in 1681, leaving £100 for charitable uses, which was used to pave the upper end of the chancel of St. Mary the Virgin, Oxford. He had many connexions in the University, and Benjamin Cooper was one of the overseers of his will, of which there is a copy in the Bodleian.[97] Snell originally named Sir John Bridgman, eldest son of Orlando, as his first executor, but, for whatever reason, the name was struck out at some time after the will had been completed.

John died on 6 August 1679, in his brother-in-law's house in Holywell, and was buried in St. Cross church, a few hundred yards away, on 8 August. His right to be buried there has been rather taken for granted, since he was not even a parishioner, much less so prominent a one as to be entitled to burial in the chancel. It may be that he was given this place by right of his brother-in-law Cooper, registrar of the University, whose son Charles and mother-in-law Elizabeth were buried in the chancel.[98] According to Anthony Wood, Snell lay under a black marble slab, 'at the upper end [of the chancel], neare the north wall' (below, p. 218). His arms are given by Wood as well as the epitaph, and we know from another source that they are without tinctures.[99] Such a black slab, with arms in low relief, is of a type very familiar in this period (several fine examples may be seen, for example, in Winchester cathedral). Unhappily Snell's does not survive. It was seen as late as 1837, but vanished during the Victorian restoration. In the years 1910-12, when arrangements were in train for placing the present brass plaque in the church, which records Snell's burial, there was some correspondence between the then Master of Balliol, J. L. Strachan-Davidson, and C. L. Stainer, the vicar's warden, about the fate of the slab. The opinion then was that it had been buried under the Victorian pavement, though it seems strange that other slabs had, at that same time, been carefully removed from the

[96] *The Cheshire Sheaf*, 83.
[97] *Wood's City of Oxford*, ed. A. Clark (Oxford Hist. Soc.), iii (1899), 122; Bodley MS. D. D. Par. Oxford, St. Mary the Virgin, c. 25, no. 4, a reference supplied by Dr. D. M. Barratt.
[98] *Wood's City of Oxford*, iii, 190.
[99] *The Anterior and Present State of the City of Oxford, chiefly collected by Anthony Wood, with additions by Sir John Peshall* (1773), 24.

chancel, and laid in the body of the church. An alternative possibility was that the stone had become too badly worn to be recognised, but why should this happen to a stone laid originally near to the wall in the chancel, where there would be very little reason to tread on it?[100] There must rest, for the time, at least, the question of the fate of Snell's tomb. Happily he is not without other memorials, truly more lasting than marble.

(iv)

A sign of Snell's success in life is manifested soon after his death, in the excellent marriage of his daughter, Dorothy. Late in February 1682 she was married, at St. Mary-le-Strand, London, to William Guise of Winterbourne, Gloucester (often then called Winterborough, as it is in the marriage-licence).[101] William (1649-1716) was on the younger side of the distinguished family of the Guises of Elmore. The senior branch, who held a baronetcy, lived at Elmore Court, an Elizabethan house 'beautifully set in the first loop of the Severn below Gloucester, on land that has belonged to the Guise family since the thirteenth century'.[102] This house was destined to come to Dorothy's descendants in 1783, and it is still in their hands. William's house at Winterbourne, of which she became the mistress in 1682, has not been identified, and it is clear that William retained close links with Elmore, though it lay some twenty-five miles away, because he and Dorothy were buried there, and their monument is in the chancel of the church.[103] Marriage into such circles was certainly a rise in social status for Dorothy, and it would scarcely have been possible without her dowry of £2000.[104] It is to be feared that if Snell had had a son, or the hope of one, there would have been no exhibitions, since he could hardly with justice have deprived a son of the Ufton estate. As it was, his fortune sufficed both to found the exhibitions, and to buy his descendants a place among the English county gentry, and perhaps, had he lived to see the result, he would have preferred the compromise. Nor can we be sure that he did not anticipate the possibility of the Guise marriage. As we have seen, he had friends in Gloucester at Ampney Crucis, and shortly we shall be considering a possible connexion, in John's lifetime, with a lawyer Guise from Gloucestershire.

The lengthy epitaph of William and Dorothy at Elmore deserves a word. It was compiled by their youngest son, Henry Guise (1698-1749). Dorothy is praised, in lavish but conventional terms, for her charity and engaging courtesy,

---

[100] The Strachan-Davidson and Stainer correspondence is now represented only by the letters of the latter to the former, preserved in Balliol College, and kindly shown us by Mr. Vincent Quinn.

[101] Licence in *Allegations for Marriage Licences Issued from the Faculty Office of the Archbishop of Canterbury, London, 1543-1869*, extracted by J. L. Chester and ed. by G. J. Armytage (Harleian Society, 1886), 159. The date is 21 Feb. 1681/2 but the wedding would have to take place before Lent began on 1 March. Dorothy's eldest son, John, was baptised on 5 Dec. 1682 (*Trans. Bristol and Glos. Arch. Soc.*, iii (1878-9), 74-5, where note that the baptism of her son Henry is placed in 1678, instead of 1698). We owe these references, and helpful comment, to Mr. Christopher Currie, deputy-editor of the *Victoria County History*.

[102] N. Pevsner, *Buildings of England, Gloucestershire* ii (by David Verey), 1970, 180.

[103] Inscription printed in Addison, 216-7.

[104] Snell's will, below, p. 188.

but the attainments of her eldest son, John (1682-1703), who was 'eminently studious' and had a 'perfect knowledge of all the polite languages ancient and modern', may not be a pure invention of fraternal affection, but a sign of John Snell's talents appearing in a grandson. A rather strange feature of the inscription (we have already mentioned it above) is its excursus upon the Balliol exhibitions:

'She [Dorothy] was the only daughter[105] of John Snell Esq., Lord of the manor of Uffeton in the county of Warwick, which manour with lands to the value of near a thousand pounds a year he gave by will to support the interest of episcopacy in Scotland; but this application of his intended benefaction being defeated by the Union, a decree was obtained in the High Court of Chancery for settling the estate on Baliol College in Oxford for ever, to maintain, support, and educate certain scholars to be sent thither by the University of Glasgow, allowing to each fifty pounds a year for ten years only; eight partake at present of these exhibitions, though the estate may be deemed to be capable of supporting a greater number.'[106]

There are many curious points here. £1000 a year seems far too large a figure for the total bequest since in 1738, not far from the date of this epitaph, Glasgow College, whose interest at that point would have been best served by naming a high figure, stated the value as only £600.[107] To say that the benefaction was to support the interest of episcopacy in Scotland, though a one-sided statement, was perhaps allowable, because the Guises had tried to upset the will on the grounds of frustration of the testator's wishes, but to blame the Union for this, instead of the revolution of 1688, is absurd. Stranger still, perhaps, it was for the Guises to describe with such relish the very foundation which not many years since they had striven to frustrate; but at least we have proof here that before the death of Henry Guise, in 1749, the Snell exhibitions were well enough known to be a cause of family pride and satisfaction. It is worth noting that Adam Smith was in residence as an undergraduate at Balliol from 1740 to 1746, at a time when the epitaph must have been newly placed on view. Strangest of all is the apparent complaint that the foundation should be able to support more exhibitioners than eight. The complaint might be reasonable, but why give vent to it in an epitaph? However this may be, we have evidence of another kind, at about the same time, of the growing fame of the foundation. We owe our knowledge of it to Mr. Robin Gibson of the National Portrait Gallery, London. The *Oxford University Almanac* for 1742 (of which Mr. Vincent Quinn of Balliol has kindly sent us photocopies from the college collections) has an engraving of a design for new buildings at Balliol. Below the design are groups of benefactors of Balliol among whom, very prominent in the front row, beside the famous Dr. Busby of Westminster School, stands John Snell. Busby's likeness is taken from a known painting, but Snell's dress is so very much after the manner of 1742, that this picture of him is almost certainly imaginary. Indeed no contemporary portrait has ever been said to exist.

---

[105] 'Only daughter' rather than 'only child' may perhaps suggest that Snell had a son who died very young?
[106] Addison, 216.
[107] Addison, 20.

We come now to the problem of the publication of his master Bridgman's *Conveyances*. We have seen already that the work purports to be in part printed from Snell's manuscript, but the bibliography of the publication is complex and obscure, and needs investigation by an expert in such matters. What is said here should be taken as a preliminary statement, subject to correction when that investigation is made. Meanwhile we are grateful to Mr. R. K. Browne, of the rare book department, British Library, and to Mr. David Yale, for their assistance. Mr. Browne drew our attention to the information in W. H. and L. F. Maxwell, *A Legal Bibliography of the British Commonwealth of Nations* (London, 5 vols., 1955-7) i. 479-80, and reference should also be made to D. G. Wing, *Short Title Catalogue . . . 1641-1700* (3 vols., London, 1945-51), and its supplements.

A single volume of *Sir Orlando Bridgman's Conveyances* appeared in 1682, three years after Snell's death. It is now somewhat rare, there being no copy in the British Library, and has to be sought at the Bodleian, Lincoln's Inn, the Middle Temple, the Law Society, and the Law Faculty Library at Cambridge.[108] There is no mention in the preliminaries, or on the title page, of Snell. The dedication is to Sir John Bridgman, Bt., son of Orlando, dated 'from my chamber in Thavies Inn, June 24, 1682', and signed 'Thos. Page Johnson'. There follows an address 'To the Reader' of one and a half pages, which bears the same signature. Of this Johnson we have no other knowledge. There is a second edition in 1689, of which the British Library does have a copy, and a number of later editions. In 1699 there first appeared (so far as we can tell) a second volume, of which Glasgow University Library has a copy. It has a new preface, signed by a certain 'N. E.', and there we find, *inter alia*: the statement that 'the whole was copied by Mr Snell, for his private use'; the biography of Snell printed below, on pp. 219-20; and the remark that Snell's 'books etc. came to be sold', so that the manuscript of the *Conveyances* came, amongst others, into the writer's hands. He adds that one of the other papers so acquired was the copy, in Snell's writing, of Bridgman's congratulatory letter from Cambridge, on the occasion of his becoming Lord Keeper, which he prints from Snell's papers at the end of his preface. It is of particular interest to see that he treats the existence of the Snell foundation at Balliol as an established and well-known fact; he is writing not later than 1699, the year when the first group of four Snell exhibitioners was elected (see above, p. 175). Though he gives Anthony Wood as authority, Wood naturally does not attach the gift to Balliol, because he published *Athenae Oxonienses* in 1692, seven years before the Lord Keeper assigned Snell's bequest to the college.

The relation, if there is any, between Snell and the first volume of *Conveyances* is unknown, though we cannot exclude the possibility that another of his manuscripts, covering different ground, was the source of it. Perhaps, since it is hard to think of any other source which is so plausible, the balance of probability is that Snell did provide, posthumously, the 'copy' for volume i. But we have not come to the end of the puzzle. When the librarian of Balliol College, Mr. Vincent Quinn, was searching, in 1979, for a copy of the *Conveyances* to be

---

[108] Thanks are due to the librarian of the Law Society for allowing examination of his copies of various editions of the *Conveyances*, and to Mr. David Yale for sending a photocopy of the title-page of the Cambridge Law Faculty copy of the 1682 edition.

presented to the college by the Snell exhibitioners, he was offered, and bought, an edition of volume ii, dated 1710, on the title page of which were the words:

'Published (from an Original Manuscript of Mr John Snell, Purse-Bearer to Sir Orlando) by John Guise, of the Inner Temple, Esq.'

The preface to this edition is the same as the 'N. E.' preface of 1699, and is subscribed with the same initials, with no reference made to Guise. Conceivably the initials 'N. E.' were fictitious, and Guise was the real author of the preface? Who can this Guise have been? The Inner Temple, as their librarian kindly informed us, has no record of such a man, but the Middle Temple has, in an entry brought to our notice by Mr. David Yale. A John Guyse, son and heir of John Guyse of Gloucester, Esq., was admitted on 22 June 1655, and called to the bar on 13 June 1662.[109] The difficulty concerning which Temple Guise belonged to may be met by supposing that he had chambers in the Inner Temple, but was a member of the Middle Temple, a not uncommon situation. The possibility of Snell's coming to know John Guise in the 1660's when Snell was crier in the Common Pleas, and Guise a young barrister, is obvious. Guise would be a younger man than Snell (we might guess that he was born about 1640). Any further speculation is hazardous, but one must wonder if Snell's connexions in Gloucester arose through Guise, and culminated in Dorothy's marriage. Moreover John Guise may have been 'N. E.', have died before the 1710 issue of the book, and then been revealed publicly on its title-page. Such a family connexion would explain why 'N. E.' had enough knowledge of Snell's life to enable him to write so full a biography in his preface.

Another way in which it would have been possible for Snell to meet the Guises is through William Guise (1653?-1683; see his notice in *D.N.B.*). He was beyond doubt a member of the Elmore family (which cannot be said with confidence of the John Guise discussed above), and seems to have resided in Oxford, from 1669 until his death, as an undergraduate at Oriel, and a fellow of All Souls. He was a very learned man, and one cannot doubt that Snell would know of him, especially since Anthony Wood, who later included Guise among his Oxford worthies described in *Athenae Oxonienses*, might well have spoken to Snell about him.

(v)

John Snell's life, taken as a whole, is an intriguing study in social and economic advancement, to use modern terms for aspects of history that are of particular interest to present-day historians. To compare his career with those of other men of his day in detail is a task for experts in these matters, but we ought not to close our biography without a few general remarks, for many details of which we are indebted (without committing him to any of our conclusions here) to Dr. Gerald Aylmer. Seen from the social standpoint, Snell begins as the son of a Scottish blacksmith, and rises to be an esquire, a country gentleman by purchase of an estate in Warwickshire, and a man whose daughter finds a match

[109] *Register of Admissions to the Hon. Society of the Middle Temple* (etc.), ed. H. A. C. Sturgess (3 vols., London, 1949), i, 156.

in an ancient and highly reputed family in Gloucestershire. He has a London house, in a rather exclusive part of the suburbs of the city, he is an M.A. of Cambridge and of Glasgow, and is well known, and influential, in Oxford. On the financial side, we have very few figures to go upon, except that the annual value of his country estate in Warwickshire is estimated at £450 a year,[110] and that he had been able to buy it in 1674, despite the expense of acquiring, by purchase or lease, the house in the Savoy, and despite his generosity in paying to send young Scots to English Universities, in buying books of the most expensive kind for Glasgow, in giving money to the poor at Colmonell, in helping to pay for the college steeple at Glasgow, and, we can hardly doubt, in subscribing generously and regularly, on a similar scale, to other good causes of which we know nothing. All this is impressive; and we would wish to know how common was such advancement among his contemporaries. The answer seems to be that it was certainly not without parallel, but on the other hand was not common. It should be remembered that not every man whose career began during the interregnum of 1649-60, was able to continue it as successfully as Snell did after the Restoration. That political convulsion naturally reduced the number of possible rivals to Snell's achievement. We are seeking for lawyers, or men like Snell serving the legal profession as what would now be called 'legal executives', who made their fortunes by attaching themselves to 'the great'. Without straying beyond those whose careers are given in the *Dictionary of National Biography*, we can give several examples. Sir William Clarke (1623?-1666) is well known because of the survival of the 'Clarke papers'.[111] Of 'obscure parentage', he became a barrister, and, after twelve years as secretary to General Monck, rose to be secretary at War. He made an excellent marriage, but his career was prematurely ended by death in a naval battle, which he 'attended in his official capacity'. His son, George, became very wealthy, and a benefactor of Oxford on a considerable scale. Another man, John Rushworth (1612?-1690), gains some special interest for us, because when Bridgman became Lord Keeper, he appointed him his secretary, and so Snell and he must have been well acquainted. Rushworth began his career as solicitor to the town of Berwick-upon-Tweed in 1638. He served parliament indefatigably during the Civil War, was a secretary to Cromwell himself in 1650, but was able to enter royalist service before the Restoration, and established himself readily after it. He differed from Snell in allowing his financial affairs to fall into confusion, so that he ended his life in prison, but in other respects his career shows the same ability to rise, despite the stresses of political change. A third example is John Creed, who died in 1701.[112] His career before the Restoration is so obscure that we cannot tell if he began with any legal experience, and it may be the prejudice of Pepys which gives us the impression that his origins were very humble indeed. Yet it is unlikely that he began life with any great advantages, and before he emerges into the light of day he seems to have been in the retinue of Edward Montagu, later earl of Sandwich. The year

---

[110] So estimated in preface to *Conveyances* (below, p. 220), but at £429 in the Lord Keeper's judgment (Addison, p. 19). The life of bishop Frampton, quoted above at note 61, speaks of the amount as 'near £500 per annum'.

[111] At Worcester College, Oxford; edited, in 4 vols. by C. H. Firth, 1891-1901.

[112] See *D.N.B.* under his wife's entry (Creed, Elizabeth), and Pepys's *Diary* (ed. Wheatley), i, 72 n.

1660 brought him the deputy-treasureship of the Fleet, as it brought Snell the criership of Bridgman's court, and he was soon an F.R.S., and secretary to the commissioners for Tangier, and married to Sandwich's niece. His epitaph at Tichmarsh, Northants. may naturally err on the side of generosity, but, for what it is worth, it speaks of his service to King Charles 'in divers honourable employments at home and abroad'. He had certainly risen to be a well-to-do country gentleman, and as early as 1664 Pepys had heard that he was worth £10,000, and was 'very rich' (*Diary*, 6 December).[113] And indeed we should be rather blind to an obvious case, already known to us in Snell's own circle, if we ignored his Whitehall correspondent Sir Joseph Williamson (1633-1701), who has earned ten columns in the *Dictionary of National Biography*, but began his career as clerk to an M.P., and rose through a 'not lucrative' post with the secretary of state, where 'he showed himself no backward pupil in the art of exacting gratifications from all kinds of suitors and petitioners'. Like Snell, in later life he helped young men of promise in their careers, and his legacies for educational causes were very lavish.

As a Scottish immigrant Snell is in a rather different category from these and other examples, and it would be interesting to have him compared with any of his countrymen who followed a similar career in England at the same period. Whether his Scottish origin made his task easier or harder one can scarcely say, though it may have commended him to Lauderdale, and it surely was an advantage in his connexion with Monmouth's Scottish interests. On this note of uncertainty we may well leave him, for he comes to life more surely in the documents which follow than he can in the words of a biographer.

---

[113] It is hardly necessary to say that for a detailed study of the official classes of the earlier part of this period, the reader should turn to Dr. G. E. Aylmer's *The King's Servants, 1625-42* (revised ed., 1974) and *The State's Servants, 1649-60* (1973).

APPENDIX I

Books given by John Snell to the University of Glasgow

No attempt seems to have been made to print a list of Snell's gifts of books to Glasgow. With much help from Dr. John Durkan and Mr. Jack Baldwin, we have attempted here to provide one, but any errors in it are to be attributed to us, and not to either of them. We have mentioned above Snell's two letters of 1661 and 1670, in which he writes to Glasgow describing books which he is about to send (above, pp. 154, 167; the texts of the letters are given below at pp. 195, 208). We have other evidence, in an incomplete list in Glasgow University Archives, printed in *Munimenta Alme Universitatis Glasguensis* (ed. Cosmo Innes, 4 vols., Maitland Club, Edinburgh, 1854), iii. 434, in a few *ex dono* inscriptions in the actual books by the University, and in the old press-marks in the books. The best evidence of all, however, does not seem to have been used until Dr. Durkan worked on the problem; it is that of the manuscript catalogue of the University library of 1691, now MS. Gen. 1313. We shall use this (Mr. Baldwin having kindly given us a photocopy of the appropriate portion, folios 248-9), as the basis of our list.

The catalogue heads folio 248 with the letters AP, in majuscules. These letters are the sign of the Snell 'press', a word still current in Scotland for any shelved cupboard, but now known in England, in this sense, only in the first element of the word 'pressmark'. The catalogue next has the words EX DONO D: JO: SNELL (the abbreviations stand, of course, for 'domini Johannis'), and in the next line 'In forulo primo' (on the first shelf). The first book on that shelf would be pressmarked AP 1, 1, and the press had four shelves. We shall not reproduce here the catalogue entries as they stand, for it will be more helpful to give titles and dates in the modern form, but we give the books in the order of the catalogue, and add the old pressmarks, and also note which of the books themselves were given *ex dono* inscriptions.

Pressmark	Author and Title *(first shelf)*	Whether Inscribed
AP 1,1 to 1,11	Blaeu, Jan: *Geographia Blaviana* (11 vols., Amsterdam, 1662). [The most magnificent of the books given by Snell.]	No
	(second shelf)	
AP 2,1 to 2,5	Poole, Matthew: *Synopsis Criticorum aliorumque S. Scripturae Interpretum* (5 vols., 1669-76). [First and last vols. of this contain portraits of Bridgman, see above, p. 167.]	No
AP 2,6	Cressy, H. P. de: *Church History of Brittany, or England* [*etc.*] (Rouen, 1668). [Perhaps a doubtful candidate for inclusion, since inscription on title-page says that book was acquired by purchase at the University's expense. That, however, may be a mistake.]	No
	(third shelf)	
AP 3,1 to 3,6	*Biblia Sacra Polyglotta*, ed. Brian Walton (6 vols., 1655-7).	Yes

(fourth shelf)

AP 4,1	Castell, Edmund: *Lexicon Heptaglotton* (1669).	Yes
AP 4,2	Castell, Edmund: *Lexicon Heptaglotton* (1669).	Yes
	[These two identical volumes are both incomplete copies of the *Lexicon*, giving only columns 1 to 1656 of the text. For the probability that this is the work asked for by Principal Baillie in 1661, see below, pp. 196-7. It seems possible that by some mistake, Glasgow was given two copies of the first part, instead of a set of the complete work.]	
AP 4,3	Hammond, Henry: *Paraphrase and Annotations upon all the Books of the New Testament* (2nd. ed., 1659).	No
AP 4,4	Hammond, Henry: *Paraphrase and Annotations upon the Books of the Psalms* (1659).	Yes
AP 4,5	Hammond, Henry: *Works*, vol. i only (1674), of the 4 vol. edition of 1674-84.	No
AP 4,6 to 4,8	Jackson, Thomas: *Works* (3 vols., 1673).	No

A little information about the state of Glasgow University Library in the seventeenth century will help to show the relative importance of Snell's gift. (For a fuller account, see a paper by Dr. John Durkan, entitled 'The Early History of Glasgow University Library', in *The Bibliotheck*, viii (1977), 102-26). Not long after Snell's student days, an English visitor, Sir William Brereton (c. 1636) saw the library, and described it as 'a very little room, not twice so large as my old closet' (Durkan, 104), and the Parliamentary commission of 1664 found it 'verie small for an Universitie, and having no considerable ways to better the samen by the Universities awin cair' (*Munimenta*, ii, 480). By the 1690s it has been estimated that the total stock of books was about 3,000. This may be small compared with the 12,000 or so of the Bodleian in or about 1650,[114] but is so like the 2948 of Chetham's library, Manchester, in 1685,[115] as to suggest that until the first copyright act of 1709 provided an automatic flow of accessions, Glasgow was developing on the modest scale to be expected in a typical collegiate library of the time, situated in a major city. Against this background, we can see that Snell's gift of over 30 volumes of great intrinsic value was both timely and important. Doubtless in making it he had in mind the poor state of the library as he knew it in his student days. One final scrap of evidence makes a pleasant close to this survey. In 1677, two years before Snell's death, a Mr. John Lees was paid by the University to 'write a broad [a Scots form of the word 'board'] for Mr Snell', a task which Dr. Durkan thinks to be the preparation of a commemorative plaque of some sort, above the bookcase numbered AP, containing Snell's gifts (Durkan, 120). Presumably this case may have survived until the move of Glasgow College to Gilmorehill in 1870.

The inscription placed by Glasgow in some of Snell's presented volumes reads as follows:

> Ex dono clarissimi D[omini] Joannis Snellij, qui, emenso humaniorum literarum et philosophiae in hac Academia stadio, testandae in almam matrem gratitudinis ac animi in rem literariam propensi ergo, hoc volumen cum [   ] alijs Universitati in communi Bibliotheca reponendum donavit.

---

[114] W. D. Macray, *Annals of the Bodleian Library, Oxford* (2nd ed., Oxford, 1890) p. 107, listing folios, 5889, quartos 2067, octavos 4918.

[115] *ex. inf.* Professor J. S. Roskell, who gives the figures: 1994 folios, 954 quartos and octavos.

Three small comments have to be made. First, that the blank space in the inscription was obviously meant to specify in figures the total number of books given by Snell, when it was certain, which could only be after his death, that there were no more to come. Like many good ideas, this one proved too difficult to carry out, and the library neglected even to insert the inscription itself in the majority of the books. Second, that the stream of books from Snell may have been broken by his death in 1679, because the library received only the first volume of Henry Hammond's *Works*, published in 1674. We seem not to know the details of the publication dates of the remaining three volumes, but the set was not completed until 1684. Lastly, the elegant remark in the inscription that Snell had 'measured out' (*emenso*, perhaps meaning more idiomatically 'traversed') the course (*stadium*) in humane letters and philosophy at Glasgow was not strictly true of one who, even if his second undergraduate year (1643-4) was not cut short by war, had completed only two years of study. But on this matter it would be too curious to enquire more deeply, and the University cleared all doubts in 1662, if Anthony Wood's date be correct, by giving him his M.A. diploma.

APPENDIX II

The holograph original of Snell's will

The text of the will has been in print for many years, but even Addison's book, where it is given on pp. 197-202, is not very widely available, and his text is based on a transcript, which is textually accurate, but does not keep Snell's spelling (often a little idiosyncratic), and gives no clue to the alterations made by Snell on his deathbed (above, p. 173). There is no adequate way to supply the evidence now available, except to print the will in full from the holograph, indicating in footnotes the differences between the original will of 1677, and the will as revised in 1679 (we use the dates themselves to distinguish the two versions in the notes).

The will is now in the Public Record Office, with the reference PROB/1103/3 Sept. 1679. It consists of six sheets, measuring nineteen inches by fourteen inches, with traces of gilt on the edges, and held together at the top centre by strings secured with Snell's seal, which appears also after his signatures on each sheet, at the foot. The 1677 text is in a clear and bold hand, but most of the alterations show signs of physical weakness. Those which do not, we have taken to belong to the original writing of 1677.

Very briefly we draw attention here to the effect of the changes in 1679. (1) Joan Snell's legacy is raised from £50 to £100 (p. 188). (2) Dorothy's possible marriage without the consent of the executors[116] will not (it is now made clear) deprive her of her annuity of £100, but only of £1500 out of her dowry of £2000 (p. 188). (3) Snell's nephew James Stewart is now given £20 to bind him to a trade, but the two Mason nephews receive only £10 each instead of £20 (p. 189). (4) Snell cannily adds words to make clear that the gift of £10 to each executor to buy mourning must not go to any person named who declines to be an executor (p. 189). (5) Possibly in 1679, though the writing here is not decisive, Snell altered to £500 the penalty to be forfeited by Snell scholars who accept spiritual offices in England or Wales, and added words obliging them to take Holy Orders, this being the only place in the whole will where that celebrated demand was explicitly stated. The near-silence on this point is perhaps due to the fact that ordination was still almost universal among candidates for an academic career[117] (p. 190). (6) The long marginal addition given on p. 191 below, though more boldly written than some of the changes, seems likely to belong to 1679. It lays down minimum payments to Snell scholars, and requires (not merely allows) these to be raised, if the revenue be sufficient.

However weak Snell was in body on his deathbed, his mind was very clear, though of course he may have meditated beforehand about the changes. His

---

[116] For remarks on these executors, see above, pp. 175-6.
[117] The few notable exceptions, such as Sir Isaac Newton, tend to stand out as requiring explanation: in his case, religious heterodoxy.

motives are generous: he doubles the payment due to his widow within a month of his death, he is anxious to make clear beyond any possible doubt that a rash marriage will not cause his daughter to lose her annuity, and he shows fears that his scholars may not receive an adequate stipend. He also remembers his young nephew, who has to be bound to a trade. Our last thought, however, as we read the will, may be that it is a fine tribute to Lord Stair. Snell, despite his long service to lawyers, was only a layman, yet he wrote a will which, despite every effort by the Guise family, the University of Oxford, and the Scottish Episcopal Church over a century and a half, was never upset. Had he lived to know it, the man of business in him would have been well pleased.

In the footnotes to the text which follows, we use '1677' for the original text of the will, with contemporary changes; and '1679' to indicate alterations apparently made on his deathbed.

IN THE NAME OF GOD AMEN.^{a} I John Snell of Uffeton in the County^b of Warwick being in health of body^b and of Perfect Memory and understanding (God bee Praysed for the same and for all other his great Mercies bestowed upon mee) yett considering my mortality and the certainty of my Death, but the uncertainty of the tyme thereof, And being minded to settle and dispose of that Estate wherewith it hath pleased my most gratious and bountifull God to blesse me in this world. DOE make and ordayne this my last will and testament, as followeth, I desire to bee decently buryed at the discretion of my Executors herein after named. AND whereas I have purchased to Mee and my heyres of William Spencer Esq. the Mannor of Olufeton alias Ulveton alias Uffeton with the appurtenances in the said County of Warwick and diverse lands and tenements thereunto belonging in the same County, And whereas by a note all written with my owne hand bearing even date with this my will, and left under a cover, sealed with the same, it doeth appeare what debts are owing to mee and by whome, and what debts I doe now^c owe and unto whome I DOE will and appoynt my executors hereafter named to satisfy and pay all my Debts which I shall owe at the tyme of my Death, and all such legacies as by this my Will are given and bequeathed to any Person or Persons together with my funeral charges out of my Personall Estate, so farr as the same shall bee sufficient to pay and discharge the said debts, But because my Personall Estate, may fall shorte for that purpose, It is my Will and pleasure, And I doe appoynt my said executors, by lease, or leases, or sale of any part, or parts, of my said Manor and lands of Uffeton, at their discretions to pay and discharge the rest and residue of my debts and legacies not payd by my Personall Estate. AND I doe give and devise to my deare and loving Wife Johanna Snell one annuitie or yearely rent charge of one hundred pounds of lawfull money of England, to bee issuing and payd unto her yearely out of my said Mannor and lands of Uffeton dureing her naturall life, at the place of her dwelling and habitation for the tyme being at two payments in every yeare, that is

---

a Capitals here and elsewhere in the will represent majuscules in MS.

b Text in Addison spelt with final -ie, and so with such words throughout. Such variations hereafter not noted.

c now *interlineated probably in 1677.*

to say, upon the five and twentieth day of June and the five and twentieth day of December, the first payment thereof to bee made at such of those dayes which shall first happen next after my Death. And I doe further give and bequeath unto her the summe of one hundred^d pounds of lawfull money of England to bee payd unto her within one Moneth after my death, And my will is, and I doe appoynt that my said Wife shall have and enjoy my now dwelling house in the Savoy, and the use of all my household stuffe, plate, and jewels therein during her Widdowhood. And I doe hereby declare, that what I have given and bequeathed to my Wife shalbee^e in full Satisfaction and barr of all Dower and thirds which shee may clayme out of my Reall and Personall Estate. AND I doe give and bequeath unto my Daughter Dorothy Snell the summe of two thousand pounds of lawfull money of England to bee payd to her, at her Age of Eighteen yeares, or day of Marriage, so as shee doe marry with the consent of my Executors or of the survivors or survivor of them, but in case she shall Marry without such consent, if they or any of them bee then living, I doe declare will and appoynt, that the said legacy of two thousand pounds by mee hereby devysed unto her shall cease and become voyde, and shall not bee payd unto her, But in lieue [sic] and stead thereof I doe onely give and bequeath unto her my said daughter five hundred^f [folio 2] pounds of lawfull money of England to bee payd unto her within six Moneths after such her Marriage without their consent as aforesaid, And I doe further give and bequeath unto her my said Daughter one Annuity or yearely rent charge of one hundred pounds of lawfull money of England during her naturall life, to bee issuing and payd unto her yearely out of my said Mannor and lands of Uffeton whether^g shee marry with or without any such consent as aforesaid^g And I doe hereby Will and appoynt my Executors and the survivor of them, or whosoever shall bee Possessed of my said Mannor and lands of Uffeton shalbee^h charged with the true payment of the same at the place of her habitation for the tyme being at two payments in every yeare, that is to say upon the first day of July, and the first day of January by equall payments, the first payment thereof to bee made at such of those dayes which shall first happen next after her portion^j of two thousand pounds or five hundred pounds shalbe payed^j, But I doe hereby Will and require that the said payments may constantly bee made to her owne proper hands, and not to the hands of any Husband with whom she shall marry, nor to the hands of any other Person or Persons, that may clayme the same by assignment or otherwise howsoever, but it shall bee payd and employed to and for her owne sole and separate use and mayntenance, and with which her Husband is not to Intermeddle, but her owne Receit and acquittance for the said Annuity shalbee a sufficient discharge to my Executors, or to such other Person or Persons who shall bee possessed of my said Mannor and lands and chargeable by this my Will to pay the same. AND I doe will and appoynt, that shee doe live and continue with her Mother till her age of Eighteen yeares, or day of Marriage.

---

d one hundred *1679*; fifty *1677*.

e *So spelled here and elsewhere in MS.*

f *Signature* 'John Snell' *and seal at lower right-hand corner of this folio, and similarly on ff. 2, 3, and 4*.

g—g: whether *to* aforesaid, *interlineated 1679*.

h *rectius* that they shall be.

j—j portion ... payed *added 1679 in place of* age of eighteen yeares or day of marriage (1677).

And for her support and Education during that tyme I doe give and bequeath to my said Wife to bee Employed for the Mayntenance Dyett and Apparell of my said Daughter, one other Annuity or yearely rent charge of threescore pounds of lawfull money of England to bee issuing and payable to my said Wife yearely out of my said Mannor and lands of Uffeton in manner and forme as aforesaid, but onely till the said Annuity of One hundred pounds above bequeathed unto my said Daughter shalbecome^k due and payable unto her and no longer. AND I doe give and bequeath unto my three nephews Andrew Stewart and John Stewart and James Stewart^l twenty pounds a peece to bee payd unto them severally within two Moneths next after my death besides^m twentie pounds to James to binde him to a trade^m and to my wifes nephew Edmond Mason and to her neece Elizabeth Mason I doe give and bequeath tenn^n pounds a peece to bee payd unto them as aforesaid. AND for the better performance of this my Will I Doe hereby give devyse and bequeath All my said Mannor and lands of Uffeton charged and chargeable as aforesaid, And all other my lands tenements and hereditaments whatsoever whereof or wherein I have any estate of freehold or inheritance, or whereof or wherein any other Person or Persons have or hath any estate of freehold in trust for mee, and whereof I have power to dispose and the reversion and Inheritance thereof to my said Deare Wife Johanna Snell and unto my honnored and worthy freinds^o William Bridgeman of St Martins in the feilds in the county of Middlesex, Esq., Benjamine Cooper [$f.$ 3] Register to the University of Oxford, William Hopkins of Oxford aforesaid, gent., and Thomas Newcome, Cittizen and Stationer of London, and to the Survivor of them and to their heyres and assignes, and to the heirs and assignes of the survivor of them for Ever whom I doe make Executors of this my last Will and Testament UPON trust for the performance of this my Will according to the directions herein and hereby given And I also give and bequeath unto them the said Johanna Snell^p William Bridgeman Beniamine Cooper William Hopkins and Thomas Newcomb their Executors and Administrators All my leases goods Chattells and Personall Estate whatsoever upon like trust for the performance of this my Will And I doe give to Every of them the said^q William Bridgeman Benjamine Cooper, William Hopkins and Thomas Newcomb who^r will undertake to execute this my will^r tenn pounds a peece to buy each of them mourning And I doe give unto my Sister Sylvester Cooper five pounds to buy her a ring, and to every one of her Children who shall bee living at the time of my Death twenty shillings a peece to buy them Rings And I doe give to the poore of the Parish of Uffeton aforesaid ten pounds and to the Poore of the Parishes of St Clement Danes and St Mary le Savoy in the said County of Middlesex five pounds to each Parish respectively

---

k shalbecome, *so written in MS.*

l and James Stewart *interlineated, and* three nephews *amended from original* two, 1677.

m—m besides ... trade *interlineated 1679.*

n tenn 1679, twenty 1677.

o *After* freinds *Snell has deleted* Sir John Bridgeman *of and several more words not now decipherable, but probably descriptive of Bridgeman. Bridgeman's name is deleted on several later occasions, whence it seems that the will was complete when the deletions were made, though it is not clear whether they were made as late as 1679.*

p Sir John Bridgeman *deleted after* Johanna Snell.

q Sir John Bridgeman *deleted after* said.

r—r who *to* will *added* 1679.

And I doe give fifty pounds to and for the repayring of the Parish Church of Uffeton aforesaid in case I shall not disburse the same, or a greater summe in my life tyme towards the repayre of the sayd Church AND my further Will and mynde is, And I doe hereby desire direct and appoynt, that after all my debts legacies Annuities and rent charges hereby devised and appoynted and my funerall charges shall bee all discharged satisfyed and payed, or otherwise sufficiently secured to bee payed, The sayd Johanna Snell[p] William Bridgeman Benjamine Cooper William Hopkins and Thomas Newcomb and the survivors and survivor of them and the heyres Executors and Administrators of the Survivor of them shall convey and settle All the rest and residue of my Estate which shall then remayne in their hands upon five or more Persons to bee named Trustees for that purpose and upon their heyres such as the Vice-Chancelor [sic] of the said University of Oxford, the Provost of Qweens Colledge, the Master of Baliol Colledge and the President of St Johns Colledge in the same University for the tyme being or any three of them shall nominate and appoynte UPON Trust that the profitts and produce thereof may be Employed and disposed for the mayntenance and education in some Colledge or Hall in that University to bee appointed by the said Vice-Chancelor Provost Master and President for the tyme being or any three of them and in such proportions and with such allowance and in such manner as they or any three of them shall elect think fitt and appoint, such and so many scholars borne and Educated in Scotland, who shall each of them have spent three yeares, or two at the least in the Colledge of Glascow in that Kingdome, or one yeare there and two at the least in some other Colledge in that Kingdome, as they the said Vice-Chancelor provost [f. 4] Master and President for the tyme being, or any three of them shall think fitt not Exceeding the number of twelve, nor being under the number of five at any one tyme unlesse the Revenue and profitts of my Estate for the purposes aforesaid hereby devised, by the discreet and prudent management of my Executors and Trustees shall encrease [sic] to such a condition as may beare an Allowance competent to mayntayne a greater number. And my further Will and mynde is that every such Scholar and Scholars upon Each of their Admissions to such Colledge or Hall as aforesaid shall bee[s] bound and obliged by such security as the said Vice-Chancelor Provost Master and President for the tyme being or any three of them shall think fitt, to some Person or Persons to bee by them or any three of them thereunto appoynted, that the said scholar or scholars shall respectively forfeit and pay to that Colledge or Hall whereof or wherein hee or they shall bee respectively admitted the summe of five[t] hundred pounds a peece of lawfull money of England If[u] Hee shall not enter into Holy orders and[u] if Hee or they shall at any time after his or their entring and[v] Admission take or accept of any Spirituall promotion, benefice, or other[w] preferment whatsoever within the Kingdome of England or Dominion of Wales, It being my Will and desire that every such scholar so to bee admitted, shall returne into Scotland, and there bee

---

s *After* bee *nearly three lines so deleted as to be now indecipherable, probably in drafting in 1677.*
t five *interlineated over illegible erasure, probably in 1677, but perhaps in 1679.*
u—u if *to* and *interlineated, probably in 1679.*
v entering and *interlineated, probably in 1679.*
w other *interlineated, probably in 1679.*

preferred and advanced as his or their capacity and parts shall deserve, but in no case to come back into England nor to goe into any other place, but only into the Kingdome of Scotland for his or their preferment AND my will also is, that none of the scholars to bee elected and admitted as aforesaid shall take any benefitt of this my bequest above the space of ten yeares or eleaven [sic] at the most, for after that tyme they are, And it is my Expresse Will and desire, that they shall and may bee removed into Scotland as aforesaid, And it is my further will and meaning And I doe hereby appoynt, That when any one or more of the said scholars shall bee removed or dye, that the said Vice-Chancelor, Provost, Master, and President for the tyme being and the Governor or Principall for the tyme being of such Colledge or Hall (whereof such Scholar or scholars so removed or dead shall bee a member or members) or any three of them shall from tyme to tyme for ever, as often as occasion shalbee, Have power to elect and admitt one or more other Scholar or Scholars borne and educated as is aforesaid, to succeed in the roome and stead of such scholar or scholars so removed or dead. And my further Will and mynd is, That all such schollars as shall from tyme to tyme bee Elected and admitted, shall before their Admittance bee Recommended by the Principall of the said College of Glascowe, the Professor of Divinity, the Regents and other the Cheefe officers of the said Colledge for the tyme being or three of them at the least, whereof the Principall for the tyme being to bee one, by their letters recommendatory under their Colledge Seal, And also that every such Scholar so as aforesaid to be Elected shall [f. 5] come as a Probationer to such Colledge or Hall whereunto hee shall bee appoynted as aforesaid and shall there continue at his owne charges for Six moneths at the least to give Evidence of his behavior learning and abilities before hee shall bee admitted to receive any benefitt of this my devise and will, And after those Six Moneths are Expired, Hee shall then bee allowed and admitted, or disallowed according to the discretion of the Persons before appoynted for that purpose or any three or more of them and[x] to every such Scholar I doe allowe and appoynt twentie pounds a yeare for the first three yeares after his admission and thirtie pounds a yeare after that tyme to bee payd to him half yearlie at the least, but if my estate will beare a greater allowance then what is herein expressed I desire that the schollars may have the benefitt of it, and to bee payd by halfe yearly payments at midsomer [sic] and Christmas.[x] AND I doe give and devise the summe of ten pounds of lawfull money of England yearely for ever to bee issuing and payd out of my said Mannor and Lands of Uffeton by halfe yearely payments at Midsomer and Christmasse, That is to say, To the said Benjamine Cooper during his life to commence and take effect at such of the said feasts next after it shall happen that five or more of the said scholars shalbee chosen and admitted as aforesaid, And after his death To the Register of the said University for the tyme being for ever, or unto such other Person as the Governor or Principall of such Colledge or hall where such Scholars shall bee admitted by the advice of the Vice-Chancelor for the tyme being shall think fitt and appoynt as a salary and reward[y] for the making of such bonds and securities as are hereby directed, and as shall from tyme to tyme bee requisite, and to see

x—x and to Christmas added 1679, partly between lines and partly in margin, in a very shaky hand.
y as a salary and reward interlineated, probably 1679.

them duely executed, And upon any breach of any Covenants or condicions mencioned in such bonds or Securities: that Hee or they doe sue for and recover the Moneys due upon and by the breach of such Covenants and condicions as often as Hee or they shalbee thereunto required, but the charges of suite and prosecucion I doe will and appoint to bee payd out of the moneys so to bee recovered from tyme to tyme, but the remaynder of the moneys so recovered (after the charges payd as aforesaid) shall be keept [*sic*] and preserved to bee layd out upon some good security at the discretion of the said Vice-Chancelor Provost Master and President for the tyme being or any three of them untill it shall amount to some Competent summe to purchase lands of Inheritance, to bee for an increase of the Allowance or Exhibition which shalbee appoynted for every one of the said schollars AND my further Will and mynde is, That when any three or more of the Persons (to*z* whome the Estate hereby appoynted for the Mayntenance of such Scholars as aforesaid shall be my executors be conveyed)*z* shalbee dead, That the Survivors and Survivor of them or their heyres shall convey the same to five or more such other Persons and their heires as the said Vice-Chancelor, Provost, Master and President for the tyme being or any three of them shall nominate and appoynt upon the like trusts, and Subject to the same conditions before in this my Will menconed [*sic*] and declared, directed and appoynted, and that the same course shall bee pursued, as often as there shalbee occasion for ever. AND I doe give and bequeath to the said Vice-Chancelor Provost Master and President for the tyme being five pounds of [*f. 6*] lawfull money of England yearely for ever to bee issuing and payd out of my said Mannor and Lands of Uffeton at one Entire payment upon Midsomer day: Upon this Trust neverthelesse that they the said Vice-Chancelor Provost Master and President and also the Governor or Principall of such Colledge or Hall where such Scholars shalbee admitted together with three, or more of the Senior Scholars so to be admitted, shall meet yearely upon the said day, to take the Accompts and Enquire into the right management of the said Estate, and the five pounds is to bee then spent upon a dynner that day to bee provided for them in such Colledge or Hall. And I doe will and devise to five of the Choicest and ablest Scholars of that number such as shalbee approved by the said Vice-Chancelor Provost Master and President or three of them for the tyme being five pounds a peece yearely more than what shalbee allowed to the rest of that number. And I doe devise and appoynt that my said estate shalbee subject and lyable to all reasonable charges and Expenses, in the mannagement renewing and preserving the sayd Trust, and in doing of all Acts and things which the said Vice-Chancelor Provost Master and President for the tyme being or any three of them shall think fitt. AND I doe give unto every one of my Meniall servants at the tyme of my Death*aa* one yeares wages a peece, over and above what Wages shalbee then due unto them. IN WITNESSE whereof to this my Last Will and Testament contayned in Six sheets of paper all of my owne hand Writing I have sett my hand and Seale at the bottom of everie sheet, and I doe declare this to bee my last Will and Testament this nyne and twentieth day of December, in the nyne and

---

z—z Brackets here in MS. though not in Addison's printed text.

aa After Death *four or five words entirely deleted, presumably by Snell when writing the will first in 1677.*

twentieth yeare of the Raigne of our Soveraigne Lord Charles the second by the Grace of God of England Scotland France and Ireland King Defender of the Faith etc: Annoque Domini 1677.

JOHN SNELL [seal]

Signed Sealed and published to bee the last Will and Testament of the said John Snell the day and yeare above written in the presence of us:

RICHARD TAYLER
THO. FOWLE
FRA: CANE
ROBERT FENWICKE

Republished[bb] and declared to bee the last Will and Testament of me the said John Snell the sixth day of August one thousand six hundred seventy nine and all the interlyneations and alterations are made by my owne hand and all this is done in the presence of:

RIC: LYDALL   THO: SNELL
THO: MUNDY   THOMAS ADAMS
JOHN MUNDY

[19th century endorsement of f. 6ᵛ, dating from the time when the Scottish Episcopal Church was trying to secure the benefits of the Snell foundation for Scotsmen intending to be ordained within that Church; see Addison, pp. 23-6]:

V[ice] C[hancellor] *Knight Bruce*
Wednesday the 15th day of July 1846
Att[orne]y Gen[eral] v. The Glasgow College
Produced in Court this day

H. HUSSEY Reg[istrar]

[Various notes of 1679 concerning the proof of the will are not printed here.]

---

bb *All this addition by Snell is in a very shaky hand. Before it stands the word* signe *as if someone else had wrongly begun to write* signed, *and desisted. The addition is not attested by Snell's signature or seal.*

TEXTS OF THE PRINCIPAL SOURCES
FOR THE LIFE AND CAREER OF JOHN SNELL

Grateful acknowledgment is made to the following for their giving formal permission to print here documents which are either their copyright, or in their ownership:

The Marquess of Bath, for the documents at Longleat House.

The Earl of Bradford, for the documents at Staffordshire Record Office.

Lt.-Colonel J. F. Inglefield-Watson, for the documents at The Ross, Hamilton.

The Oxford University Press, for the printed texts of Anthony Wood's memoir of Snell.

The Controller of Her Majesty's Stationery Office, for documents in the Public Record Office.

In the printing of the texts we have attempted to reproduce the original spelling, though the extension of abbreviations is not always certain. Capitals and punctuation have been modernised, except in reproducing Snell's will, where, as any good lawyer knows, there are special reasons for respecting every detail in the hand of a holograph, and in Joan Snell's artless letters, and the extracts from the *Conveyances* preface and from Wood's *Athenae*, where much of the original flavour depends on such matters. In these we have, so far as possible, kept the usage of the originals.

List of the documents printed below

Shortly before 22 June 1661	John Snell to Robert Baillie
29 June 1661	Baillie to Snell
18 Jan. 1664	Snell to John Bridgman
5 Dec. 1666	Receipt witnessed by Snell
18 Jan. 1667	Extract from letter of Thomas Gape to the duchess of Somerset
18 April 1667	Snell to duchess of Somerset
1667 to 1672	J. Eddowes to Orlando Bridgman
18 April 1668	Snell to Joseph Williamson
9 May 1668	John Tombes to Williamson
28 Jan. 1669	Snell to Williamson
22 April 1669	Snell to Williamson
7 Aug. 1669	Joan Snell to Robert Francis
14 Aug. 1669	Joan Snell to Francis
1 Sept. 1669	John Snell to Francis
26 March 1670	Snell to William Blair

26 May 1670	Gilbert Burnet to Thomas Aikman's uncle
28 May 1670	Edward Wright to William Colville
June to August 1670	Extracts from the Bridgman accounts
24 Jan. 1671	Snell to Sir Thomas Lynch
20 May and 24 June 1675	Snell's evidence concerning the will of the late duchess of Somerset
27 Jan. 1679	The duke of Monmouth to an unnamed person
undated	Versions of Anthony Wood's testimony concerning Snell
undated	Extracts from prefatory materials to Orlando Bridgman's *Conveyances*

John Snell's will is printed in full in Appendix II, at page 187.

Shortly before 22 June 1661.

John Snell to Robert Baillie, Principal of the University of Glasgow.

(Original apparently not now extant in Glasgow University Archives. Text taken here from *Munimenta*, iii. 434. It is not clear whether given there from the original or a copy. The date is inferred from that of Baillie's reply, printed below, p. 196, which says that Snell's letter was received on 22 June.)

Sir,

I have sent you by this bearer, the great Bible in the orientall languages, contayning six volumes, commonly called the Πολύγλωττα, for the use of your publiq library, gott forth by the learned Dr Walton, lord bishopp of Chester. I doe conceive that it is a book very worthy so famous an University as Glasgowe, for it is justly esteemed by all learned men to bee the best in that kinde that ever was yett extant. Sir, my education in that place, under the tutorage of the truly honourable and eminent Sir James Dalrimple, obldiges me in gratitude to wish you prosperitie, that as your religion and great learning, so also your loyaltie, may make you famous to succeeding generations . And I doe thinke it my duty to offer my small mite to promote the same, humbly beseeching you, and the rest of your brethren, the members of that honourable society, to accept this as the first fruits of my affection to you, in the quality of,

Sir,

Yours and the Universitie's
most affectionat servant
John Snell.

These to the Reverend Mr. Robert
Bayly, his most worthy freind, Prin-
cipall of the famous Universitie of
Glasgowe in Scotland.

This copy of Walton's 'Polyglott' is still in Glasgow University Library (above, p. 183). The languages represented in it are Hebrew and Greek, with various ancient translations, giving nine languages in all, though no one book appears in more than eight. The work was one of the first books to be published in England by subscription, and one of the first editions of the Bible to make use of the great 'Codex Alexandrinus', now in the British Library. There is a common misunderstanding of the second sentence of this letter, making 'it is justly esteemed to bee the best … extant' apply to the University of Glasgow, not to the Walton bible. Since this error is found in so commonly used a book as J. D. Mackie, *The University of Glasgow 1451-1951*, p. 129, where Snell is named as having this extravagant opinion of his old college, it is desirable to lay some stress on this mistake.

29 June 1661.

Principal Robert Baillie to John Snell.

(Original apparently not extant. Text given here from Addison, p. 11, where errors of transcription must be suspected. Some are here conjecturally emended, but others probably remain.)

Sir,
    Your very fair and precious gift came to our hand Jun. 22 1661. Your kind rememberance of our common mother and your mor than ordinary testimonie thirof was to us al very weelcom. Indeid that excelent, and as long I have thoughte most excelent, book is very fitt for a library: nor do I think was ever any book printit of gritter pric and worth. Great is the worlde's obligation to learnit D[r] Waltoun for his happy labours in that eminent service. I shal ever love and honor him therfor, though in my last book I debait against some part of his prolegomes [*prolegomena*?] , but in a loving, innocent, and I hope altogider in-offensive way. For a demonstration of our grit respect both to your worthy self and the con-siderable token of your affection towards us, I promise you, so sun as our new library shall be perfytit, which your trusty bearer can tel he saw farr advancit, it shall stand in the most conspicuous place of it: and in the first leaf of every volum, with a fair hand, your nam shall be written, as the bountiful donor thereof to the library. Ye[a] for thes you are pleasit to cal your first fruits, tho never mor should follow, we shall register your name in our parchment book onc mor, for as in the year 1644, if I remember right, I reid your nam under your own hand in the company of divers worthy youths, some of our prime nobility and gentrie in that considerable class of Sir James Darumple, so shall you be written over again in that same parchment register, in the catalogue of our honorable benefactours, and shall stand among them, I hope, for ever. Ther is a sevenit volum of that book, the Dictionery, yet on the presse; when it comes off, if you think expedient, it may be joinit with the rest. At this time we shall say no mor, but that we remain very sensible of your exemplary respects to our house, wishing to you, and al such publick spirits, al prosperitie and happiness, in name of the rest of the moderatours, and at their direction.

Jun. 29, 1661   R. BAILY

    Robert Baillie (1599-1662, see *D.N.B.*) was principal of Glasgow College from 1660 till 1662. He was a remarkable scholar, reputed to know thirteen languages, and so exceptionally qualified to judge Walton's 'Polyglott'. The book itself was useful to biblical students for two centuries and more, so that of all Snell's gifts it was probably the most used, and for the longest period. For further comments on it, see above, p. 154. With complete assurance, Baillie asks for the 'seventh volume', when published. This probably means, as Addison suggested, Edmund Castell's *Lexicon*, which Snell did indeed give, though it was not published until 1669. Baillie's 'last book' is presumably his *Opus Historicum et Chronologicum*, published after his death at Amsterdam (1663). The suggestion was originally made by Addison, but Dr. J. A. F. Thomson has now kindly examined a copy of this rare book in Glasgow University Library, and he confirms that it makes specific reference to Walton's *Prolegomena* at *Lib.* I, *c.* 7, as well as reference to other parts of Walton's work at various points. Even where Baillie disagrees with Walton, Dr. Thomson observes, he is at pains to show admiration for his scholarship, as at *Lib.* I, *c.* 8, where he says 'quis potest esse magis idoneus judex quam Brianus Waltonus?'

18 January 1664.

John Snell to John, son of Orlando Bridgman (1631-1710).
(Staffordshire Record Office, Stafford, Bradford Papers,
ex. D 1287/18/3.)[118]

[*holograph*]

Sir,

I have received your bill of £50 from Mr Eddowes, but was forced to goe twice before it was accepted, he pretending the first tyme that hee had no advice; it will be payd about Candlemas [*2 Feb.*] and shalbee disposed per your order. My lord Cholmondley and my lady are falne out about his drinking of her syder and bere, hee sent her some untoward message by Mr Eddowes which vexd her greivouslie. Mr Dugdale was this day with my lord from my lord chancelor, it seems it is very ill taken that you doe not sit (because of the example) in the commission of peace. I perceive my owne lord wold very fayne have you doe it, though I know hee will not over presse you beyond your owne inclinacion; hee says you may bee of the commission, and yett chuse how farr you will meddle, for *non nobis soli* [sic] *nati sumus*, and the rather hee would have you doe this because of Mr Lisle. He is unwilling that you should meddle in the match of Mr Lisle's daughter, and would have you take example by him, knowing what trouble and vexation hee has about the matching of Sir Edw: Alston's daughter [to?] my lord John Seymour, yet being keopt [*sic*] in so mean and abject a condicion, that Sir Edward thinks himself much injured, and even foold out of £10,000 for faire promises and nothing else, and all, as he says, because hee did rely upon my lord Bridgeman. Sir, I have litle at present worth your notice.

I am,
Your most oblidged humble servant,
JOHN SNELL

January 12, 1663 [*i.e., 1663/4*]

I and my wife present our most humble duty and service to your self, and my very good lady Mrs Bridgeman.

This letter has no address, but internal evidence suggests that it was written to Orlando Bridgman's eldest son and heir, the child of his first wife, Judith Kynaston. He appears in the receipt

---

[118] The Bridgman Papers, at Stafford Record Office, are being recatalogued, and in the meantime the old references are used, with '*ex*' prefixed.

of 5 December 1666 (printed below, p. 198) as 'John Bridgeman of Castle Bromwich in the county of Warwick, Esq., son and heire apparent of Sir Orlando'. On Mr Eddowes, see pp. 166 and 201-2. 'My lord Cholmondley' is Robert, Viscount Cholmondley of Kells (died in 1681) who had a London house near to St James's (G.E.C., *Complete Peerage*, [1910-59], III. 201). 'My lady', who had the dispute with him, is lady Bridgman, Sir Orlando's second wife, Dorothy, a lady with no great reputation as a peacemaker. 'Mr Dugdale' is the celebrated antiquary, and 'my lord chancellor' is Lord Clarendon. The Latin quotation is from Cicero, *De Officiis* (which Snell would have called 'Tully's offices'), I. vii. 22; but for *soli* read *solum*, the passage being in fact given in Lewis and Short's Latin dictionary as an example of *non solum* in the sense of 'not only'. It is quite possible that Snell read *De Officiis* under Dalrymple, at Glasgow.

The affair of Alston's daughter was a *cause célèbre*. Sir Edward (1595-1669) was a very wealthy physician (see *D.N.B.*). His daughter Sarah, born in 1632, was first married to George Grimston, who died in 1655. In 1661 she married John Seymour, later duke of Somerset, but lived separately from him after about 1672. The marriage certainly was arranged by Bridgman, and the £10,000 was her portion, which must have been rapidly swallowed in Seymour's debts, for Bridgman wrote in January 1666 that Seymour's 'debts do so pinch him that he is a continual prisoner'. It is fair to note that Sarah had a reputation for meanness, and was suspected of having water put, for that reason, in her second husband's wine, though perhaps another interpretation would be possible. On all this see *Complete Peerage*, XII. i. 75-6.

In writing the above notes we have been helped by Dr. L. A. Holford-Strevens and Miss D. M. Slatter. The actual letter was brought to notice, with the other documents from Stafford Record Office, by Mr Michael Moss.

5 December 1666.

Snell witnesses a receipt, written probably in his own hand, for £400, paid to Sir Robert Holt, as part of a transaction involving members of the Bridgman family.

(Staffordshire Record Office, Bradford Papers, *ex.* D 1287/3/5.)

December fifth 1666

Received, then, of the right honourable Sir Orlando Bridgeman, knight and barronet, cheife justice of his Majesty's Court of Common pleas, the summe of foure hundred pounds, being the last payment, and in full, of nyne hundred pounds, mentioned to bee the consideracion in a certaine indenture bearing date the said fifth day of December instant, and made, or menc[i]oned to bee made, betweene mee, Sir Robert Holt, barronet, of the one part, the said Sir Orlando Bridgeman, John Bridgeman of Castle Bromwich in the county of Warwick, Esq., son and heire apparent of the said Sir Orlando, Charles Bridgeman, clerke, archdeacon of Richmond and nephew of the said Sir Orlando, and John Snell, of St Clement Danes, in the county of Middlesex, gent[leman], of the other part, which said nyne hundred pounds is in full of the said consideration money.

In witness whereof I have hereunto sett my hand and seale, the day and yeare above written, annoque regni Caroli secundi xviij°.

Sealed and delivered in the   ROBERT HOLT
presence of us,
    JOHN SNELL
    VALENTINE YOUNGER

This document (apparently in Snell's handwriting) gives the first evidence concerning Snell's house in London. He is living in the parish of St Clement Danes (the church now on an island site in the Strand, by the Law Courts), in whose predecessor we know that he was married in May 1662 (above, p. 160). Later he moved to a house in the Savoy.

18 January 1667.

Thomas Gape to the dowager Duchess of Somerset.

(Longleat House, Seymour Papers, vol. vii, f. 171; summarised in Hist. MSS. Commission 58, *Bath* iv [1968], 257-8.)

[*holograph*]

(*We give only an extract from this letter, which deals with the Duchess's 'last great business' in parliament, during which 'this great concern was brought to a happy conclusion'.*)

... 'Mr Snell tells me that he layd out about £4 in money for writing, and on other occasions before my coming to towne, and although he hath bin at noe charge since, yet he hath always, when there was occasion, attended this business, both at the committee, and also at the House of Commons dore; soe that if your Grace please to order him £20 for all, I humbly conceive it will very well satisfy him'. ...

Essex House
18 Jan. 1666 [*i.e., 1666/7*]

Essex House was on the site of the present Essex Street, Strand, and had been the London house of the earls of Essex. The dowager duchess of Somerset was a daughter of the great Robert, earl of Essex, executed in 1601, after his rebellion. She used Essex House as her town-house, when in London. Bridgman was her friend and adviser, and thus Snell was concerned with her affairs on several occasions: see below, pp. 199, 212. Thomas Gape was a man of business for the duchess.

18 April 1667.

John Snell to the dowager Duchess of Somerset.

(Longleat House, Seymour Papers, vol. vii, f. 179; summarised in Hist. MSS. Commission 58, *Bath* iv [1968], 259.)

[*holograph*]

May it please your Grace,
                        It hath pleased the king's majesty to conferr upon one Mr Fifeild, clerke of the Errors to my Lord Cheife Justice Bridgeman, the reversion of the customer's place for the port of Ipswich after the death of Mr Booth, once a servant in your Grace's family, which place must bee confirmed by my Lord the Treasurer before it can pass the greate seale, but hithertoo it hath beene obstructed by Sir Philip Warwick, thereby pretending that it is out of respect to your Grace, Mr Booth being once a member of so noble a family, to whom my Lord Treasurer hath so nere a relation.

Therefore I, knowing how Mr Booth left your Grace's service, and that I doe verily beleeve your Grace will not take it at all unkindly that this revertion should bee granted to any one related to my Lord Bridgeman, both because it is not prejudiciall to **Mr Booth** in his life tyme, and also I doe humbly conceive your Grace hath no reason to befreind **Mr Booth** so much, I doe, upon that account, in all humility, presume to begg of your Grace to signe this letter here enclosed to Sir Philip Warwick in favour of **Mr Fifeild**, and as in duty bound I shall ever approve myself

Your Grace's most humble and most dutifull
servant,

April 18th: 1667   JOHN SNELL

[*draft letter in Snell's hand to Warwick attached, but not given here*]

Endorsed by Snell: To the most noble and my singular good Ladie,
Her Grace, the Duchesse of Somersett:
at her Grace's house at Walton-upon-Thames.
humbly t[hese]

John Snell's seal on verso, perfectly intact.

This is the only letter known to survive, from Snell's period as crier to Bridgman, which has even a slight relation to his employment, since it concerns a sinecure appointment for an official of the court, as a customs officer. Sir Philip Warwick (1609-83, see *D.N.B.*) was secretary to the Lord High Treasurer, and a man much admired by Pepys for his ability and honesty. The Lord High Treasurer was Thomas Wriothesley, 4th earl of Southampton (1607-67). The 'near relation' alleged between the duchess of Somerset's family and that of Southampton arose from the third marriage of this 4th earl to Frances, second daughter of William Seymour, duke of Somerset, by the dowager duchess to whom this letter was written. The letter is remarkable evidence of the rights of patronage enjoyed by the great, for the duchess is supposed to be concerned even with the fate of a sinecure once enjoyed by a former member of her household, who was no relation, and who evidently left her in circumstances that did him no credit.

Between 1667 and 1672.

Mr Eddowes to Sir Orlando Bridgman.
(Staffordshire Record Office, Bradford Papers, *ex.* D 1287/3/2A)

[*holograph*]

My Lord,

The accompts annexed my lady gave mee and toald mee it was your lordshipp's pleasure I should peruse and examine them, which I have done, and find, first, as to Mr Snell's accompt:

That whereas hee accompts for 4 Commissions of Sewers at 10^s a peece, hee did actually receive 12^s 6^d a peece for the same as secretary, besides his docquett fees as seale-bearer: £02. 10. 00
And for 7 appeales hee accompts but for 2^{li} 15^s, whereas he actually received 12^s 6^d a peece for each, being: £04. 07. 06
And whereas hee accompts for 5 denizations and saith that hee hath not yett received the same, being 6^{li} 13^s 04^d, I doe find that he hath received for one, and Mr Agar hath the fee for 4 ready to pay him when hee pleased.

And I find that Sir Richard Pigott hath the fee for 2 more which Mr Snell demanded, and Sir Richard promised to pay to him when hee made upp his Christmas accompt, soe that though hee mentions not these 2, yett they were in his view as well as the rest, being in all: £09. 06. 08
And whereas hee accompts for one pattent eleemosinary to have received 8^{li}, I find hee did receive in one entire some (besides 12^s 6^d which he remitted to the clerke of the just fee) the full some of: £10. 00. 00
soe that though hee accompts for but 19^{li} 08^s 4^d, I conceive hee ought to have accompted for: £26. 04. 02

For the master of Chancery, which your lordship mentions to be but 2^{li}, hee hath the whole fee (of which no parte belongs to him) being 5^{li} 10^s. Mr Tompson's accompt I find very right. Mr Tempest's accompt I saw not, but am sure it must be near 100^{li}.

Jo. EDDOWES

[postcript]

And for the future, as to appeales, sewers, pattents eleemosinary, and denizations, now designed for the wages of the meaner servants, and for which I dare ingage to pay to them 25^{li} each quarter, being 100^{li} per annum, I humbly conceive Mr Snell the most unfitt person in your family to meddle with ['them' *deleted*], for these reasons:

1. Because I find his imployment much more considerable then [*sic*] I thought it would have beene, and of a good value, and takes upp his whole time, hee keeping no clerke.
2. These things hee invaded, and would have imposed upon your lordshipp by a lie, they more properly belonging to any of your secretaries then to him, therefore deserves not the reputation of them, and if hee bee imployed in them but a while, hee will with confidence prescribe to them.
3. In is accompts hee hath not beene soe ingenious as hee ought to have beene, for in his first accompt given in to your lordshipp j° Decembr' I am tould hee then accompted for but 11^{li} in all, but afterwards, hearing it was enquired after hee now took it away to add something to itt and made it 19^{li} 8^s 4^d, whereas from that time to this hee hath received but j^{li} 5^s more then he then had received or knew off.
4. If hee receive these things sans fee, I know his arrogancy to bee such that shortly hee will upbraide, if not revile your lordshipp to your face.

I humbly conceive some others who have more spare time and lesse businesse, and of more meeke disposicions then himselfe, as Mr Cratford, Mr Camplisham, or others, are more fitt for these things.

For general comments on this document, see above, p. 166. Mr Eddowes must be the person mentioned by Snell in his letter to John Bridgman (above, p. 197), and one may infer that he was a member of Sir Orlando's household who took special responsibility for financial matters, under what title we do not know, but perhaps doing the work of steward. Between such a man and others in the 'family', jealousy was inevitable. There is no evidence to show whether this critique of Snell was written near to the beginning of his term as seal-bearer (1667-72), or later, but perhaps it suggests some confusion of the kind that might arise in his accounts when he was new to the work, especially since it is said that he was busy, and had no clerk. On Commissioners of Sewers, and denization, see *Guide to the Contents of the Public Record Office* (H.M.S.O., 1963), ii. 22-3, 41. Sir Richard Pigott is presumably the man mentioned in Pepys' *Diary*, 21 March 1668/9, as selling the post of Master of the Patent Office. Mr. Tempest is mentioned again below, p. 207.

18 April 1668.

John Snell to Joseph Williamson.

(Public Record Office, State Papers, Domestic [SP 29], 238, item 142; summarised in *Cal. State Papers, Domestic, Charles II, Nov. 1667-Sep. 1668* (1894), 348.)

[*holograph*]

Sir,

I have left six pounds with your servant, with Mr Howell's very great acknowledgements, and thankfullnes, for the quick dispatch you gave the letter. I doe here leave my freind Mr Spence, whome I have persuaded to accept of his Majesty's title alone, because hee thinks it is not prudence to him to expend more money in law suites to defend a patron's title, who hitherto hath borne no share of the burthen; and will therefor bee content to purchase his owne quiett (after so long and chargeable a contention) by receiving the king's grant, which I doe humblie beseech you [will?] with what speed convenient procure it to him. Hee hath severall licences and certificates heretofore granted by the bishops of Bath and Wells and others which I presume, after ten years possession, and so many verdicts at common law, may bee inducements for procuring the gracious favour from his Majesty. I am, sir, with all my heart,

Your most faithfull humble servant,

Aprill 18th: 1668   JOHN SNELL

This is the first letter known to survive from Snell in his post as seal-bearer. It is written to Joseph (later Sir Joseph) Williamson, 1633-1701, whose life is given at some length in *D.N.B.* At this juncture he was secretary to Arlington, the secretary of state. In a later letter (below, p. 205) Williamson endorses a letter 'cousin Snell', but no relationship, even one by marriage, is known. The Mr. Spence, who is left by Snell to wait at Williamson's office, would seem to be a clergyman who has enjoyed a benefice in the diocese of Bath and Wells for some ten years, by a presentation which has been disputed. The alleged patron of the benefice has not been helpful, and Snell's advice has evidently been that which many modern lawyers might give, to avoid more litigation and accept a royal grant which would side-step the question of legal right.

9 May 1668.

John Tombes to Joseph Williamson.

(Public Record Office, State Papers, Domestic [SP 29], 239, item 173; summarised in *Cal. State Papers, Domestic, Charles II, Nov. 1667-Sep. 1668* (1894), 381-2.)

[holograph]

Your very friendly taking notice of me, together with your readiness to assist me in my addresse to my Lord Arlington, and your wordes to me when I went to Whitehall to return my humble thanks to him for his favour to me, in the business which my Lord Keeper moved his Majesty in on my behalfe, that it was desired that you might heare from me, have moved me to expresse, in this letter to your selfe, my most humble thanks to his Majesty for his royal favour and bounty to me, as also to those noble lords, particularly my Lord Keeper of the Greate Seale, my Lord Privy Seale [and ?] my Lord Arlington for their favour and other actings for me with his Majesty or otherwise, together with the Lord Bishop of Hereford his testimony of me: to all whom, and any other who have showed me any respect, I desire to approve myself as gratefull and observant. And concerning my studies, after the bookes already published about the oath of supremacy, *The Oath Book, Saints no Smiters, Theodulia*, I have on the anvil a book intituled *Theocratia*, or a treatise of the kingdome of God, the main scope whereof is to show that no claim of coercive jurisdiction, either superior or coordinate to the king's, is warranted in any rulers ecclesiastical, by any office or power in the kingdom of Christ in its militant estate, and I have herewith sent you the contents of that which is already composed, which I prosecute the slower because of my absence the last yeare, and my intended absence in Worcestershire (?) this summer, by reason of the decease of my only son and child remaining, March 1, 1666, and his widdow's decease, Sept. 18, 1667, whereby 5 yong orphans are, by providence of God, left on my care. And for printing I finde it more difficult and chargeable, by reason of my dwelling so far from any printing presse, though the bishop of Winchester many yeare since put me in hope of a brotherhood at the Savoy, which Dr Lockey holding, I have been disappointed, and see no likelihood, of it, except something else were gotten in lieu of it, or some other of the brethren there, by way of exchange, or some lecture at Gresham Colledge or elsewhere were obtained for me. There was a motion made to my Lord Keeper of a place at Rochester, in a hospital endowed and to be built according to the will of Bishop Warner, which the Lord Keeper was willing to conferre on me, if Mr Dobson, fellow of Magdalen Colledge in Oxford would relinquish his title to it, whereto to persuade him I wrote a letter to Dr Barlow, which I showed to my Lord Keeper, and left with Mr Snell to be sent to him, but I yet heare nothing of it; onely I have assurance of Sir Stephen Fox his paying me this month. If it please you to present my respects to Mr Snell, my Lord Keeper's pursebearer, and my request of his minding me, I shall take it for a further favour, and for your, or his, former or future manifestations of benevolence to me, shall study to approve myself,

Your thankfull and real servant in any meete office,
JOHN TOMBES

From my dwelling
Castle Streete in
Sarisbury,
May 9th 1668

John Tombes (1603?-1676, see *D.N.B.*) was a baptist divine, ordained in the church of England in or about 1624, whose scruples on infant baptism did not prevent him being greatly admired by some of the most devout and learned members of the established church, though preferment therein had to be denied him. This letter is eloquent testimony to his personal difficulties, after he had to resign his place at the Restoration. We do not know the nature of the business with the king referred to here, in which Bridgman has assisted him, nor the extent of the royal 'favour and bounty', but 'Mr Snell' seems to have been helpful, and more is expected, perhaps, of him in future. On Arlington and Williamson, see above, p. 202. The lord privy seal was John Robartes, a well-known supporter of nonconformity; the bishop of Hereford, Herbert Croft. The work called *Theocratia*, which Tombes has 'on the anvil', does not appear in the list of his publications in *D.N.B.*, but the 'contents' enclosed with this letter are preserved in the file, under forty heads. The 'brotherhood' at the Savoy was one of the four chaplaincies of the hospital of the Savoy in London. See Robert Somerville, *The Savoy: Manor, Hospital, Chapel* (1960), where at p. 243 the list of chaplains includes Thomas Lockey, who was Bodley's librarian, but makes it appear that Tombes was never appointed, as he indeed feared might be the case. For information on this we are indebted to Dr. Gordon Huelin, and Professor Gordon Dunstan. Gresham College in London was, of course, the foundation of the celebrated Sir Thomas, with salaries of £50 a year for the lecturers. Bishop John Warner of Rochester (1581-1666, see *D.N.B.*) is well known as the founder of exhibitions for Scotsmen at Balliol College, Oxford, but the reference here is to the establishment by Warner's will, of which Bridgman was the chief executor, of an institution for the maintenance of twenty poor widows of clergy, to be situated as near as possible to Rochester cathedral, with a chaplain whose salary would be £50 a year. See the will in Anthony Wood, *Athenae Oxonienses* (3rd ed. 1813-20), iii. column 732. It is not altogether obvious why Tombes expected Rochester to suit him better than Salisbury did. Thomas Barlow (1607-91, see *D.N.B.*) was a strong supporter of Tombes, but it is not clear why he should be expected to persuade Mr. Dobson to give up his title to the post at Rochester. Sir Stephen Fox (1627-1716, see *D.N.B.*) was M.P. for Salisbury, and could well afford to pay Tombes for this month, since his fortune was legendary (he was paymaster-general, but it is fair to his memory to add that he was also most generous, and contributed part of the fortune gained from the army as a lavish gift to found Chelsea hospital). The unfortunate Mr. Tombes died at Salisbury, without securing any preferment elsewhere. But evidently his baptist views did not automatically exclude him from candidature for brotherhoods, chaplaincies, and the like.

28 January 1669.

John Snell to Joseph Williamson.

(Public Record Office, State Papers, Domestic [SP 29], 254, item 175; summarised in *Cal. State Papers, Domestic, Charles II, Oct. 1668-Dec. 1669* (1894), 172.)

[*holograph*]

January 28th: 1668 [*i.e., 1668/9*]

Sir,

My Lord Keeper, upon the receit of the instrument you sent, caused the Great Seale to bee affixed to it, but there is one word in it, which though good Latin, yett hee scruples at it as not pertinent, that is *oratori*; the words are *apud magnum Ducem Hetruriae oratori*, therefore hee would have you looke out the coppy of that commission by which hee resides there, and see if by that commission hee bee so named, and if so, then the word *oratori* may stand, because though it bee not a good word in that, yett it is not fitt to alter it. If you have not the coppie of that commission, nor know whether certaynlie hee resides there by the name or title of *orator*, then my lord sayes this word had better be changed, and either *legato, ambassiatori*, or some other word better and more fit, ought to bee putt into its place. I am, sir,

Your most faithfull and most humble servant
JOHN SNELL

Endorsed: [in Williamson's hand] 29 Jan. vicesimo (?) R[egni]
Mr Snell
The Commission to Sir John Finch
The word *orator*
[in Snell's hand] To Joseph Williamson, Esq.,
at the Lord Arlington's Lodging,
at
Whitehall

We see here a glimpse of Snell's routine work at the Great Seal office. The secretary of state (Williamson) has sent a commission for Sir John Finch (a privy seal warrant, perhaps), and Bridgman, as Lord Keeper, has doubts on one detail, asking to have examined the copy of the commission which, in 1665, appointed Finch as minister to the Grand Duke of Tuscany. This would presumably mean looking at the enrolment on the Patent Roll. On Finch, see *D.N.B.* He was born in 1626 and died in 1682: a distinguished physician and diplomatist, and a graduate of Cambridge and Padua, and Fellow of the Royal Society.

22 April 1669.

John Snell to Joseph Williamson

(Public Record Office, State Papers, Domestic [SP 29], 259, item 41; summarised in *Cal. State Papers, Domestic, Charles II, Oct. 1668-Dec. 1669* (1894), 289.)

[*holograph*]

[Apri]ll 22: 1669
Sir,
My lord keeper being altogether a stranger to this affaire, and the sad condicioun of the peticioner, and this reference by his Majesty to the Earle of Clarendon having been unsuccessful, upon what grounds does not appeare, my lord will bee [*sic*] no meanes grant her a breife without a new order from the king, or from the councell. If you think fit to doe the poore woman any kindness in it, I will bee sure to give her all the assistance in the power of, sir,

your most obliged servant,
JOHN SNELL

Endorsed: [in Williamson's hand] 'cousin Snell'
[in Snell's hand] 'To Joseph Williamson Esq.,
at
Whitehall

On the expression 'cousin Snell' used here, see above, p. 202.

7 August 1669.

Joan Snell to Robert Francis.

(Public Record Office, State Papers, Domestic [SP 29], 264, item 1; summarised in
Cal. State Papers, Domestic, Charles II, Oct. 1668-Dec. 1669 (1894), 442.)

[*holograph*]

Sir,

I beseech you doe me the favour to send this enclosed letter to Mr Snell. Sir, I should not have put this trouble upon you, but the gentleman to home [*sic*] Mr Snell gave me derection to send my letters I here is gone in to the contrey for some time; soe that I feare I shall trouble you with a letter or two more before he returns, be pleased to present my humble service to Mr Aldridge and his lady, I peg [*sic*] your pardon for this trouble. I am,

your freind and servant,

August the 7,   JONE SNELL
1669

Sir if any letter come to you for me, I shall be at Mr Pleadal's house at Hallyrood Amney, neer Sisester, in Gloster shire.

This letter, and the following one, also by Joan Snell, John's wife, are written in an unpractised hand. Both letters are in the State Papers only because they enclosed private letters by Joan to her husband, sent to his London office for forwarding to him on his visit to Scotland in 1669. Robert Francis was clerk to Joseph Williamson; Snell calls him 'cosen Francis' below, p. 207, but no relationship between the two men is known. Who the gentleman was who has gone into the country we do not know, but he may have been Joseph Williamson. When Snell wrote to Francis from Edinburgh, on 1 September 1669, he had already received some letters from Joan. Mr. Aldridge is unknown, but may be the same person as Francis's brother-in-law, mentioned in Joan's letter above. Holyrood Ampney is now commonly called Ampney Crucis, Gloucestershire. A tablet in the south transept of the church commemorates Joan's host, Robert Pleydell, and describes him as hospitable (φιλόξενος). He died in 1675. The house, now called Ampney Park, still has the original section where Joan stayed. For information here we are grateful to Dr. A. J. Taylor. Snell probably came to know the Pleydells through Bridgman, who was staying in their house in December 1665 (Hist. MSS. Commission 58, *Bath* [1968], 255). Dr. D. M. Barratt has pointed out to us that from 1673 Snell was involved in some very complex legal proceedings, in which the Pleydells were the principals; see Bodleian library, MS. ch. Oxon. 3293, and the index to Oxfordshire deeds by W. O. Hassall (Oxfordshire Record Society, xliv [1966]), 188-9.

14 August 1669.

Joan Snell to Robert Francis.

(Public Record Office, State Papers, Domestic [SP 29], 264, item 47; summarised in *Cal. State Papers, Domestic, Charles II, Oct. 1668-Dec. 1669* (1894), 449.)

[*holograph*]

Sir,

be pleased to send the in closed for mee to Mr Snell. I have not as yet had any letter from him; pray sir if any come to your hand, be pleased to send them to mee. I am now at Mr Pleadall's house at Hallyrood Amnoy [*sic*], in gloster sheere, neere sisester. I peg your pardon for this trouble. I am,

your freind and servant,

JONE SNELL

Augu ye 14 1669

Endorsed: For Mr Robert Frances, at My Lord Arlington's Lodgings in Whitehall, London

1 September 1669.

John Snell to Robert Francis.

(Public Record Office, State Papers, Domestic [SP 29], 264, item 184; summarised in *Cal. State Papers, Domestic, Charles II, Oct. 1668-Dec. 1669* (1894), 469.)

[*holograph*]

Edenburgh
September 1st: 1669

Good Cosen Francis,

I have received your very kinde letters, for the which I doe heartily thank you, particularly for your kinde conveyance of my wives letters to mee. I am but just now come to this place, and so received all your letters in a crowd together, or else you should have been sure to have heard from me sooner. Wee have litle or no newes here, but that in the west of Scotland, where I have beene, there is a certaine weed, or grayne that growes amongst there oates and barley, which by no arte or industry can be seperated from the corne, of that mischievous effect that one gill of ale or bere, wherein such grayn hath beene, will fudle a man more than a galon of other drink nay the very bread made of it foxes the people, so that in the midle of their labor they fall a sleepe, and many of them [are?] sick a day or two after. It is so generall in some parishes, that it is looked upon as a great judgement from God upon the countrey. Some here call it *roseger*, those that are learned say it is that wee call in Latin *lolium*, but bee what it will, it is a mischievous grayn, as I myself found by experience. Sir I beseech you to convey the enclosed letters with care, and if this come to your hands by the 7th instant, I desire to receive one more from you before I goe hence, which I will doe about the 12th instant. I am, sir,

With very much affection,
Your faithfull cosen and servant
JOHN SNELL

Sir, I pray present my most humble service to all at your brother in lawe's house, and if you know where my wife is, whether at Holyrood Amney in Gloucestershire [*Ampney Crucis*], or at Mr Coopers in Oxford; but if you know it not, I doe pray you give it to Mr Tempest.

Endorsed: To Mr Robert Francis, at the Right Honourable my Lord Arlington, Principall Secretary of State his office at Whitehall.

Snell has been in the west of Scotland and is now in Edinburgh. Writing from there, on 1 September, he confidently expects to have a reply from London before he leaves about 12 September, a fact of some interest in the study of communications. What his official business in the north was we do not know, but presumably he had visited Colmonell. In Edinburgh he would no doubt wish to see his former teacher Lord Stair, now a judge in the Court of Session.

The intoxicating cereal referred to in this letter is the darnel (described in modern science as *lolium temulentum*, the adjective being connected with *temulentia*, drunkenness). The vernacular name 'roseger' is well recorded in Scots texts. There is reason to believe that the ill-effects are not due to darnel seeds *per se*, but to a fungus, analogous to the well known ergot in rye. We are grateful to three experts for advice on this matter: Dr. Brian Flannigan of the Heriot-Watt University, and Professor J. S. Hall and Dr. David Martin of the West of Scotland Agricultural College, Auchincruive. Their quotations from authorities show that darnel is an annual grass, which formerly grew commonly in corn fields, and that we owe it to modern farmers, millers and scientists, that this noxious weed is now absent from our diet. The bread of which Snell speaks (since he refers only to oats and barley) must have consisted of oat-bannocks or barley-cakes. Evidently there had been a recent epidemic of darnel-sickness in the west of Scotland when Snell wrote, and he writes as if he had been a victim.

The post-script must have an accidental omission, for Snell does not say what Francis is to do if he does know where Joan Snell is. Presumably he is to forward a letter to an address, if known, and if not, to give it to Mr. Tempest (see above, p. 201). Mr. Cooper is Snell's Oxford brother-in-law, the registrar of the University, who lived in Holywell street (above, p. 160).

The 12th of September, when Snell intended to leave Edinburgh, happens also to be the date of the tragic death of Janet, Lord Stair's daughter, the event romantically treated in *The Bride of Lammermoor*, but it is unlikely that the news reached him while he was still in Scotland. Such a catastrophe in the family of his beloved master, occurring only some 30 miles from Colmonell, must have been notified to him on his return, by his relatives in Scotland, and have deeply affected him.

26 March 1670.

John Snell to William Blair, regent in the University of Glasgow.

(Original not now known to be extant; text here from *Munimenta Alme Universitatis Glasguensis*, iii. 435. The original is described as 'recently recovered' in *Deeds Instituting Bursaries . . . in the College and University of Glasgow* (1850), 297. Unfortunately the whole letter was not printed in *Munimenta*, and the omitted portion includes the address; we depend for that on the caption by Cosmo Innes in *Munimenta*, given in square brackets below. The entry on p. 297 of *Deeds* says that the letter refers to a visit by Snell to Glasgow 'a short time previously', but it is not clear if this is the visit in the autumn of 1669 (above, p. 167), or a still more recent one.)

[Letter of Mr John Snell of Uffeton to Mr William Blair
Regent in the College.]

26 March, 1670.

.   .   .   .

There is a new book of Criticks coming out upon the Bible, much more methodicall and succinct than that voluminous one of Mr Bee's. It is undertaken by one Matthew Poole. It will consist of two or three volumes. I have the first already. So soone as they are all finished, I will have them bound up and transmitted to your Bibliotheck, for I heartily wish that pyetie learning and ingenuity may flourish and bee encouraged amongst you; which that it may bee is the daylie prayer, and shall bee always the endeavour of,

Sir,
Your and your Universitie's
Most affectionate humble servant,
John Snell.

Poole's work is now in Glasgow University Library (above, p. 183), but it consists of five, not 'two or three' volumes, and was not completed until 1676. The 'voluminous' book of Mr. Bee was the *Critici Sacri* (9 vols., folio, 1660), published by Cornelius Bee, whose curious relationship with Poole is described in *D.N.B.*, *s.n.* 'Poole, Matthew'. Poole was a Presbyterian, who was encouraged by William Lloyd, bishop of Worcester (1627-1717), to undertake this vast synopsis of the work of biblical commentators. It was published by subscription. It is noteworthy that Snell so well appreciated the special merit of the book, which lay in its giving 'the substance of much laboured comment' in 'brief, crisp notes' in Latin. We cite here the praise of the *D.N.B.*

26 May 1670.

Gilbert Burnet, then professor of Divinity at Glasgow, to Thomas Aikman's uncle.
(Aikman papers, The Ross, Hamilton, Lanarkshire, Box II, red-bound autograph book).

[*holograph*]

Glasgow 26 May 1670

Sir,
        Our Mr Snell in England, a great benefactor of our College, hath written to us to send up 3 young men, of good behaviour and expectation, and he will provide and setle them well there. He bids us send one from our selves, one from Ed[inburgh], and on[e] from St. Andrews. Now I find the University here very willing to doe Mr Thomas Aicman all the kindnes they can, and therfor when our Principall writtes to Mr Wm. Collvill, he will desire that they may pitch upon Mr Aicman. It will be nixt week before this letter be written, therfor I have given you this advertisment before hand, that you may send for your nephew, and see how you like of this. Ther is no doubt but he shall be well provided and setled, in one of the Universities. If you and he relish the thing, let application be made to Mr Wm. Colvill before the nixt week, that he may be forstalled, for no doubt he will no sooner gett the letter but manny will give in (?) for it. If Mr Thomas desire me to writte in particular to Mr Collvill I shall, but he may show this to him and that will doe as well. The University here are very glad to have ane occasyon to testify ther respects to your nephew, to whom they are ready to doe all the service they can. No more till meeting.

I am,
Sir,
Your most humble servant,
GILB. BURNETT

(*a later hand adds*: 'who was then a regent in the College of Glasgow, and afterwards Bishop of Salisbury')

The importance of this, and the following, letter for the understanding of Snell's promotion of the careers of young Scotsmen during his lifetime is explained above at p. 168. Mr. Colville is the Principal of the University of Edinburgh. 'Forestall' is used in the sense of forewarned. Evidently Burnet is on familiar terms with the young man's uncle, and expects to meet him shortly, but we know nothing more of their relationship. Thomas Aikman did not in fact, or so it seems, become one of

Snell's protégés. Mr. J. Donnelly, to whom we owe our knowledge of this and the following letter, kindly tells me that in 1671 he appears as a cadet in the Scottish regiment in France, and later as a lawyer. The part of Gilbert Burnet in this matter deserves consideration. He was not, as the later hand says, a regent, but professor of Divinity, working very closely with archbishop Leighton in church affairs, and spending his vacations at Hamilton palace, working on the papers there. He would thus naturally come to know Aikman's uncle, who lived nearby, at the Ross. It may be that Snell sent his offer in 1670 to Burnet, in the first instance, rather than to the Principal, because in 1664 Burnet had spent some time in London in court circles, where he is quite likely to have come to know Snell. On the possibility that discussions with Burnet in London after 1675, when Burnet was chaplain at the Rolls, may have influenced Snell's will, see above, p. 175. Note the expession 'one of the Universities'. It shows that Snell at this time did not regard Oxford as the only possible home for one of his protégés.

28 May 1670.

Edward Wright, Principal of Glasgow College, to William Colville, Principal of Edinburgh College.

(Aikman papers, The Ross, Hamilton, Box II, file 19.)

[*holograph*]

Glasgow 28 May 1670

Reverend and Worthie brother,
                               Their is one Mr John Snell who was bred in this colledg, and now lives in Ingland with my lord keeper, who is a great favourer of his countrie and promover of learning. He hath bein verie beneficiall to this colledg in bestowing many books upon it. We recommended lately a young man to him, whom he hath setled at Oxfuird upon our desire. He hath wreaten to us that three young men more, of good and pregnant abilities, might be sent up to him, and willed us to write to some (?) other universities, and particularly to you, that ye might recommend some one young able man to him. He desires he may have a letter recommendatory from the archbishop, or at least from the principall and masters, under the colledg seal. Wheirfor we would desire you that with all expedition ye would recommend one, and send him up to him, who will not faile to see him placed at Oxfuird. Their is a young man bred at your colledg, called Mr Thomas Aikman, who gave in heir a tryall for a regent's place, who carried himself verie modestly in all his deportment, and gave no small proof of the pregnancie of his spirit, whom we think would be a fitt man to recommend for this tyme. He did so satisfie the masters that they would willingly promove his advancement in what they are able, and if ye will be pleased to recommend him, all the masters will accept it as a speciall favour conferred, and particularly upon,

Your loving brother and servant,
ED. WRIGHT

[*Robert Leighton notes his approval below, in his own hand*]
Though I have not much particular knowledg of the person herein named, yet if it may signify any thing, I dare very confidently, upon the good testimonie of

diverse worthy persons that know him, add my recommendation of him to the favour aforesaid (?).

R. LEIGHTON

Endorsed :   Reverend Mr William Colvill, Principall of the Colledge, Edinburgh, these.

For the general importance of this letter, see the note to the previous letter. Edward Wright was principal of Glasgow from 1662-84; William Colville (d. 1675) of Edinburgh from 1652-3 and again from 1662 until his death: see *D.N.B.* We do not know the name of the young man lately settled by Snell at Oxford, though it may be hoped that one day it will be ascertained, nor do we know anything of the present case, except the suggestion of appointing Aikman. Robert Leighton, of course, was a celebrated archbishop of Glasgow from 1669 to 1674. It is not clear why this original letter should now be at the Ross, rather than in the archives of the University of Edinburgh.

June to August 1670.

Bridgman accounts of disbursements, including sums paid to Snell.

(Staffordshire Record Office, Bradford papers, *ex* D 1287/3/5.)

This is a reckoning of sums totalling £325 16s. 7d., paid out to various persons between 10 June and 20 August 1670, from moneys received as rents on Lady Day of the same year. Only two payments are made to Snell, but we extract a few others, as illustrations of the types of transaction among which his payments appear. The very first is made to him

June 10	Returned upp to London by Mr Smith to Mr Snell	£100	00	00
11	Paid to Mr Thomas Chattock towards his marriage	130	00	00
July 2	Delivered to the butler uppon account	01	00	00
9	Paid to Mr Sadler which he payd to Mr Jenner anon (?) for tent wine for my mistress' use	01	06	10
23	Paid to Mr Sadler for two little silver spones	00	17	00
August 13	Layd out and spent goeing our journey to Olmney	11	00	00
20	Returned upp to London by Mr Smith to Mr Snell	60	00	00

Presumably the large sums sent to London to Snell are not for his own use, but to meet Bridgman's household expenses. 'My mistress' is Lady Bridgman, and 'tent wine' is defined in the Oxford Dictionary as a Spanish wine of dark-red colour and low alcoholic content.

24 January 1671.

John Snell to Sir Thomas Lynch, governor-elect of Jamaica.

(Public Record Office, State Papers, Domestic [SP 29] 287, item 111; summarised in *Cal. State Papers, Domestic, Charles II, Jan.-Nov. 1671* (1895), 43.)

[holograph]

January 24th: 1670/1

Sir,

I have made search at the Petty bagg, the severall offices of the six clerkes in Chancery, and at the crowne office, and cannot in all those places finde the least footstep of any commission to Sir Thomas Moddyford, no not so much as a docquet, which makes me conjecture that it came from the secretaries signed by his Majesty, and by warrant immediately passed under the great seale, and in such case there is nothing remayning with any officer in Chancery, save only the warrant which remaynes with the seale bearer, who was at that tyme one of Mr Kipps, and is not now in London; and the reason of my conjecture is because the revocation of his commission, which came to mee the last weeke, did thus pass, and I have the warrant by me now, and I am sure 3 or 4 years hence, if I should not be sealbearer, there might be as much uncertainty where to finde this as the other. Sir, I did conceive it my duty to signify thus much to you, that you may consider what is fitt to bee done. I am, sir,

Your most faithfull servant,
JOHN SNELL

Endorsed: To Sir Thomas Lynch, at his lodgings in St Alban's street, nere St Alban's tavern:–These

The reason why this letter is now among the State Papers is not clear, unless Lynch for some reason put it in the hands of an official clerk. Sir Thomas Modyford (see *D.N.B.*) governor of Jamaica, was sent home under arrest in 1670, and replaced by Sir Thomas Lynch (see *D.N.B.*). Why the need arose to consult the terms of Modyford's commission we do not know. The letter well shows how familiar Snell was with the complex secretariats of the government in his day. The Mr. Kipps mentioned as one of Snell's predecessors as seal-bearer, figures in Pepys's struggles to secure his patent as clerk of the Acts; Pepys's importunities took him, like Snell, to the Six Clerks office in Chancery Lane, and late at night to Mr. Kipps's lodgings (*Diary*, 12 July 1660). On the petty bag, the six clerks, and the office of the clerk to the crown, see the *Guide to the Contents of the Public Record Office* (London, H.M.S.O., 2 vols., 1963), i. 8-10.

20 May and 24 June 1675.

Snell's evidence in the dispute over a codicil to the will of the late dowager Duchess of Somerset.

(Longleat House, Seymour Papers, Box xi, ff. 399-405; summarised in Hist. MSS. Commission 58, *Bath* iv [1968], 366-7).

(*Snell is the eighth of sixteen deponents in a long enquiry into the soundness of mind of Frances Devereux, dowager Duchess of Somerset (who died on 25 April 1674) when she was alleged to have approved a codicil to her will on 21 April. The present file fills 554 folios*).

20 May 1675. Johannes Snell, beatae Mariae Savoy in le Strand in com' Midd', ar[miger], ortus infra regnum Scotiae, aetatis 47 annorum, aut eo circiter, testis, etc.

Ad decimum-septimum, decimum-octavum, et decimum-nonum [f. 399ᵛ] *articulos dictae allegationis, deponit et dicit*: that this deponent was servant unto the Right Honorable Sir Orlando Bridgman, knight and baronett, late Lord Keeper of the great seale of England deceased, for the space of twenty yeares or thereabouts, and for fifteene yeares of that tyme this deponent well knoweth that the Right Honorable Dame Frances, late duchesse of Somersett dowager, haveing an estate of her owne, when a *feme covert'*, to dispose of, and afterwards [f. 400] when shee became a widow did from tyme to tyme advise and consult with the said Lord Bridgeman, as well before as after hee became Lord Keeper, in and about the managing and ordering of her estate, and [he] beleeveth that for fifteene yeares together her Grace did never signe or seale any document of consequence without his Lordshipp first being consulted therein, and this deponent well knoweth that for fifteene yeares together the Lord Bridgman aforesaid was consulted with all and [f. 400ᵛ] advised with in the making of her will, and this deponent wrote many and severall wills for her Grace within that tyme, drawne upp by the said Lord Bridgeman, and this deponent was a witnesse to may wills by her Grace made within that tyme, and when at any tyme shee altered her said will, this deponent did new ingrosse another by the said Lorde Bridgeman's direction, and was a witnesse to the cancelling of the former and publishing of the latter will, and [f. 401] after the said Lord Bridgman had left the great seale, and this deponent [was] recomended to the now Earle of Shaftesbury, her Grace being unwilling to trust any person, besides the said Lord Bridgman, with the knowledge of the contents of her will, the said Lord Bridgman wrote the will exhibited in this cause, bearing date the seventh day of June 1673, with his owne hand, as his Lordshipp informed this deponent, and by the said writing thereof now showed to this deponent [f. 401ᵛ] is to be seene, and this deponent further deposeth that some few dayes after her Grace death, this deponent was with the said Lord Bridgeman, whoe then, amongst other things, told this deponent that hee was informed that the duchesse had made a codicill to her will, and made some deeds without his being consulted with at all, and that he much wondered thereat that Mr Thyne would doe those things, for hee was confident that her Grace, if shee had beene herselfe, [f. 402] would never have altred any thing of moment or consequence about her will, or disposing of any of her estate, without his advise, and after her death, his Lordshipp being an executor named in her Grace's will refused, as he hath told this deponent, to execute the same, because there was more done thereabout than hee thought was juste, or hee used words to that effect. *Et aliter nescit deponere.*

Super reliquis articulis dictae allegationis non examinatur ex directione, et [f. 402ᵛ] *super interrogatoriis vicesimo quarto Junii 1675 ministratis ex parte Thomae Thyn, ar[migeri], ad tercium interrogatorium respondet*, that this respondent was not present at the time of the signing, sealing, and publication of the same will and codicill alledged in this cause.

Ad quartum et quintum interrogatoria respondet, that hee did transcribe sevrall wills of the late duchesse of Somersett which were drawne or directed by the Lord Bridgman deceased, and [f. 403] afterwards signed, sealed, and published by the said duchesse, and some of such willes this respondent hath read unto her Grace in the presence of the Lord Bridgman. But such persons who were called to be witnesses to such will[s], except his Lordshipp and this respondent, heard not the will read, nor were privy to the contents thereof, as hee beleeveth. *Et aliter nescit responderе*, saving that his Lordshipp at the transcribing of such will[s] wished this respondent to be secret therein [f. 403ᵛ].

Ad sextum interrogatorium respondet that this respondent was not present to his remembrance at any time when his Lordshipp the Lord Bridgman did take any instructions from her Grace, for the making or altering of her will, at any time. *Et aliter nescit respondere.*

Ad septimum interrogatorium respondet that hee doth not know that her Grace did at any time give instructions to the Lord Bridgeman for drawing of her will at any time in the [f. 404] presence of any other person. *Et aliter nescit respondere.*

Ad octavum interrogatorium respondet that hee knoweth that the duchesse of Somerset was a very reserved woman, and carefull and cautious that the contents of her will and codicills might not bee publiquely known untill after her death *Et aliter nescit respondere.*

Ad nonum interrogatorium respondet that at, or in the tyme of, the sicknes whereof the said duchesse dyed, and upon the one and twentieth [f. 404ᵛ] day of Aprill 1674, and for some daies before and after the said one and twentieth day of Aprill 1674, and until and at the death of the said duchesse, the said Lord Bridgman was, as usually, troubled with the goute, and by reason thereof kept his chamber, but knoweth that his Lordshipp was as perfect in his memory and understanding, all the said tymes, as in any tyme of his perfect health, and in particular on the Tuesday, [f. 405] the eight and twentieth of Aprill 1674, his Lordshipp, amongst other things in discourse with this respondent, told him that hee heard her Grace had made such alterations in her will by some codicill that hee wondered at, and that hee thought Mr Thyn, meaning Mr Thomas Thyn, party in this cause, was much to blame therein, and beleeved that her Grace would have done nothing thereabout, if shee had well understood herselfe, [f. 405ᵛ] without his advice, or to that effect. *Et aliter nescit respondere.*

Ad decimum interrogatorium respondet that Thomas Thyn Esq. interrogator, did marry the said duchesse's grandchild, and lived with her Grace in her house *Et aliter nescit respondere.*

Our interest in this recently discovered document is due to the amount of personal information given about Snell. In details it may contribute little that is new (e.g., we knew already that he lived in the parish of 'St Mary-le-Savoy', and the statement that he was aged about forty-seven is superfluous because it does not enable us to calculate the calendar year of his birth); but we can see perhaps more clearly than from any other text how his service with Bridgman introduced him to confidential positions in circles of the highest rank. We learn, at the start, that in 1675 Snell recalled that he had been with Bridgman 'for twenty years or thereabouts'. Since Bridgman died in 1674, we have here our only express date (though one to be used with due regard both to the 'thereabouts' and to fallibility of memory) for Snell's entry to Bridgman's service, that is about 1654. We learn also that Snell had engrossed many wills for the duchess, and witnessed them, and that Bridgman had expressed doubts to him about her latest codicil. We have confirmation also of Anthony Wood's statement that when Bridgman suffered badly from gout, Snell was always in attendance on him (below, p. 218). Those who wish for more details of the dispute about the duchess's will may find them in the volume cited above published by the Historical Manuscripts Commission. The Thomas Thynne (1640-1714) referred to as having married the duchess's grandchild, who is under suspicion here, became Viscount Weymouth, and also came into possession of Longleat, in 1682, whence the presence of this record among the Longleat archives. Note Snell's remark here that 'after Bridgman had left the great seale, and this deponent was *recommended* to the now earle of Shaftesbury' (editorial italics). The same word is used at this juncture in Snell's career by the preface to Bridgman's *Conveyances* (below, p. 219), where the recommender is Bridgman himself.

27 January 1679.

The Duke of Monmouth, to an unnamed 'your grace', perhaps the Archbishop of Canterbury.

(Public Record Office, State Papers, Domestic, Entry Book [SP 44], p. 224; summary in *Cal. State Papers, Domestic, Charles II, 1 Jan. 1679-31 Aug. 1680* (1915), 55.)

[*Register Copy*]

Whitehall, 27 Jan:

Mr Lord,

I sent Mr Snell to acquaint you[r] Grace with my designe to recommend to the University of Cambridge my secretary, Mr Vernon, to bee chosen one of their burgesses att this next election, and to desire your Grace's approbation, and, if you thought fitt, concurrence in it, and if I had mett your Grace att Whitehall I should have made you the same request. Hee is a person that hath already given the University some testimony of his faithfullness to their interests and concerns, which I hope may render him not unfitt to serve them in another station, and if your Grace shall thinke fitt to owne him in a letter from your selfe to any att Cambridge, it would much further his pretentions, and lay an obligation upon,

Your Grace's faithfull humble servant,

MONMOUTH

There is no clue to the identity of the person addressed in this letter except the titles 'my lord' and 'your grace', and no better guess can be hazarded than that of the editor of the State Paper Calendar, that the recipient was the archbishop of Canterbury, William Sancroft, a Cambridge man, and the nephew of a former master of Emmanuel. This was the first general election since that of 1661 and, in view of the recent crises over the popish plot and the exclusion bill, was one of great importance. Professor Roskell has drawn our attention to a letter written by Monmouth, as chancellor of the University of Cambridge, to the vice-chancellor, two days before the above letter, and another, written on 31 January, urging him, in very strong terms, to use his influence in favour of Vernon (*Cal. State Papers, Domestic, ut supra*, p. 53; C. H. Cooper, *Annals of Cambridge*, 5 vols., 1842-1908, iii. 577). Snell became an M.A. of Cambridge, by royal letters, in 1674, probably at Monmouth's instance (above, p. 170). James Vernon was duly elected on 22 Feb. 1679 (*Return of the Name of Every Member of the Lower House* [etc.], *1213-1874* (3 vols., 1878), i. 534). Thanks are due to Mr. Peter Hasler, and to Professor Basil Henning, for help in these matters.

The three versions of Anthony Wood's testimony concerning John Snell.

(These texts are of paramount importance, but their hitherto piecemeal publication has had unfortunate results. The first version (A) was printed in Wood's *Athenae Oxonienses*, vol. ii (1692), before Wood's death in 1695, and again in the edition of 1721. We reproduce it here from the 1692 edition, which is virtually identical with that of 1721. It omits many facts given in B and C, but it was the only version in print until late in the nineteenth century. The second to be printed, (B), appeared in *The Life and Times of Anthony Wood*, ed. by the Rev. Andrew Clark (Oxford Historical Society), ii (1892), 458-9. Even this version, it will be noticed, omitted the important episode of Snell's reception at Hoghton by Lady Margaret. Finally there appeared (C), in *Wood's City of Oxford*, ed. Andrew Clark (Oxford Historical Society), iii (1899), 187-8.

The differences between the texts are not easy to bring out in a parallel arrangement, and we therefore print them here *seriatim*, in order of publication, reproducing the capitals and punctuation of the printed originals, but not their italics. We are indebted to Dr. D. M. Barratt for the help with the details of the 1692 text.)

(A)

Athenae Oxonienses, ii (1692), column 883.
An[no] Dom[ini] 1679, 31 Car. 2.

John Snell born at Comonell in Carrick in the Sheriffdome of Ayre in Scotland, bred in the University of Glascow under Jam[es] Darumpley, Prof. of Philosophy,[119] of which he was afterwards diplomated Mast[er] of Arts, died in the house of Mr Benj[amin] Cooper in Halywell in the suburb[120] of Oxon on the sixth day of Aug[ust] this Year, aged 50 Years (after he had spent some time there) and was buried at the upper end of the Chancel (under the north wall) of the Chap[el] or Church of St. Cross of Halywell. This I mention because that in his last Will and Testament he bequeathed the Mannour of Uffeton, alias Olufeton, alias Ulveton, in the County of Warwick, worth about £450 per an[num] to be employed (after certain years spent, and moneys rais'd and paid thence) for the maintenance of certain Scotch scholars in such Coll[ege] or Hall in Oxon that the Vicechancellour of the Univ[ersity] of Oxon, Provost of Qu[een's] Coll[ege], Master of Ball[iol] Coll[ege] and President of S. Johns Coll[ege] for the time being shall think fit. Their number is not to be above twelve, or under five, to be chosen from Glascow Coll[ege] from the number of such that had spent 3 years, or two at the least, there, or one or two in some other Coll. in Scotland, etc. They are to enjoy the said exhibitions about ten or eleven years, and then they are to return into their own Country to get preferment there, etc.

This estate Mr Snell got by being first a clerk under Sir Orlando Bridgman while he had Chamber-practice in the time of Usurpation. Secondly by being Cryer of the Court of Exchecquer while the said Sir Orl[ando] was L[ord] Chief Baron thereof, and of the Common-Pleas when Sir Orl[ando] was Ch[ief] Justice of that Court, and lastly by being Seal-bearer when he was Lord Keeper. Afterwards, being much esteemed for his great diligence and understanding, he was employed sometimes into Scotland for James, Duke of Monmouth, and bore

[119] To be precise, Dalrymple was a regent at Glasgow, not a professor. In general, see above, p. 153.
[120] Holywell was a 'suburb' only in the sense of being just outside the medieval walls of Oxford.

the seal again when Anth[ony] E[arl] of Shaftesbury was Lord Chancellour of England, etc.

(B)

Life and Times of Wood.

(from Bodleian Library, Wood MS. F. 4, p. 141.)

John Snell, born at Comonnell in Carrick in the sherifdome of Ayre in Scotland, bred in the Universitie of Glasgow under the care of Mr James Darumpley, professor of philosophie, and became Master of Arts there (as his testimonie which I have seen — written some years after his creation — sub sigillo Universitatis Glasgow, dat. 1662 — testifieth),[121] afterwards (in the time of Oliver Cromwell) he came into England verie meane, and being recommended by the Lady Calverley to Sir Orlando Bridgman, who had then much chamber-practice, did write severall conveyances for him. At the king's restauration when Sir Orlando was made Lord Cheif Baron of the Exchequer, the said Snell was made the cryer of that court; in which office he continued after Sir Orlando was made Cheif Justice of the Common Pleas, and when he was made Lord Keeper, he was (at the instance of the Duke of Lauderdale) employed to be the seal-bearer. Being thus esteemed, he was employed sometimes into Scotland for the duke of Monmouth, and bore the great seale while the earl of Shaftsbury was chancellour. He died in the house of Mr Benjamin Cooper situat in Halywell in the suburbs of Oxon on W.,[122] the sixt day of August 1679, aged 50 or thereabouts, and was buried in Halywell chancell by his wive's mother. Arms: 'gules a cross patonce or; impaling, blue a fess ermine between 3 half moons or'.[123] He married Joane, daughter of Vincent Coventry, rector of Begbroke near Woodstock in com. Oxon (sister to the wife of the said Mr Cooper, registrarie of the Universitie) by whome he left issue one onely daughter called Dorothie.

This John Snell bequeathed his mannour of Uffeton, alias Olufeton, alias Ulveton in com. Warwic. (worth about £450 per annum) to be employed (after certain yeares spent, and moneys paid thence) for the maintenance of certaine Scotch scholars in such College or Hall that the vice-chancellor of Oxford, provost of Queen's College, master of Balliol College, and the president of St John's for the time being, shall think fit. Their number not to be above 12 or under 5, to be chosen from Glascow college from the number of such that had spent 3 yeares or two at least there, or one or two in some other college in Scotland, etc. They are to enjoy the said exhibitions about 10 or 11 yeares, and then they are to returne into their owne country to get preferment there, etc.

---

[121] Wood adds a note here 'I have been enformed since I wrot this that the University of Glascow sent him his degree of M. of A. by a diploma dated 1662, and that he was not Master before that time'.

[122] 6 August 1679, was, indeed, a Wednesday; a small tribute to Wood's accuracy.

[123] The addition of an impalement here is an inexplicable error. Though the arms on Snell's tomb have been destroyed with the slab itself, we have a perfect example of his seal as evidence (see above, p. 200). Wood does not make this mistake in his third version below, p. 218.

(C)

Wood's City of Oxford.
(from Bodleian Library, Wood MS. F. 29 A, f. 355ᵛ.)

Holywell, or St. Cross
IN THE CHANCELL

On a black marble, lying at the upper end, neare the north wall:

> *Depositum Johannis Snell, Scoto-Britanni, armigeri, qui obiit vi die*
> *Augusti anno aetatis 50 salutis 1679.*

Arms are 'quarterly or and gules, a cross patonce counterchanged'

This John Snell, the son of Andrew Snell and Margaret his wife (daughter of John Carnahan) was borne in the parish of Comonnell in Carrick in the sherivedome of Aire in Scotland; bred in the Universitie of Glasgow under the care of Mr James Darumpley, professor of philosophie; came into England in the time of Oliver Cromwell in a verie meane condition, and, in his journey through Lancashire, calling at the house of the lady Houghton at Walton neare Houghton tower (one of the daughters of Sir Roger Aston, a Scotchman, who was first king James his barber and afterwards master of the robes) told the person that came to the dore to give him an answer, that 'he was a poore Scotchman and a scholar, and hearing that a gude[124] lady, his countrywoman, lived there, he took the boldness to make himself knowne to her, and to crave some employment in her service'. etc. Whereupon, after the lady had discoursed with him, shee appointed him to keep the accompts, wait upon her, and to say prayers in the family. After he had continued there about an yeare, he upon the recommendations of the lady Calverly (daughter to the said lady Houghton), was taken into the service of Sir Orlando Bridgman, who having much chamber-practice, [Snell][125] did write severall conveyances for him, and was so diligent a servant to him, and to his lady,[126] that when ever the said knight was afflicted with the gout, he was the onlie person who was trusted to attend him.

At the king's restauration when Sir Orlando was made Lord Cheif Baron of the Exchecquer, Snell was made the crier of that court; in which office he continued after Sir Orlando was made Lord Cheif Justice of the Common Pleas; and when he was made Lord Keeper, he was (at the instance of John, duke of Lauderdale) employed to be the seal-bearer. Being thus in esteem he was employed somtimes into Scotland for the duke of Monmouth, and bore the great seal while the earl of Shaftesbury was Chancellour. He married a servant maid in the family of Sir Orlando, named Joane, daughter of Vincent Coventrie, rector of Begbrooke neare Woodstock in Oxfordshire (sister to the wife of Benjamin Cooper, registrarie of the Universitie, in whose house, in Holywell, Snell died), by whome he left issue one only daughter, named Dorothie. At the time of his death he bequeathed his mannour of Uffeton, alias Olufeton alias Ulveton in

---

[124] The spelling 'gude' for 'good' (if not a mere error) may reproduce the Scottish pronunciation used by Snell in talking to Wood.
[125] The word 'Snell' is an editorial addition.
[126] This is the second lady Bridgman, Judith Kynaston, married to Orlando in 1648 (not 1670, as in *D.N.B.*), and described in *D.N.B.* as 'a most violent intriguess in business'.

Warwickshire, worth about £450 per annum, to be employed (after certaine yeares spent, and moneys paid thence for the use of his wife and daughter) for the maintenance of certaine Scotch scholars in such College or hall that the Vice-chancellour of Oxon, Provost of Queen's College, Master of Balliol College, and the President of St John's, for the time being, shall think fit. Their number not to be above 12, or under 5; to be chosen from Glasgow college (from which universitie he received a diploma to be Master of Arts, anno 1662) from the number of such that had spent 3 yeares (or 2 at the least) there, or one or two in some other college in Scotland, etc. They are to enjoy the said exhibition about 10 or 11 yeares, and they they are to returne into their owne native country, to get preferment there.

It will be noticed that nowhere in Wood's testimony is Snell's great benefaction assigned to Balliol College, though the master of Balliol is one of the trustees who are to assign the Scottish scholars to a college when the funds allow the will to take effect in this matter. The reason is that Wood died in 1695, and the first Snell exhibitioners did not go into residence at Balliol until 1699, as a delayed result of the decree of Lord Keeper Somers, made in June 1693.

Extracts from the prefatory materials to
Sir Orlando Bridgman's 'Conveyances', vol. ii.

(For general comments on this text, whose bibliographical history is very complicated, see above, pp. 179-80. In what follows we reproduce the original spelling and capitals, but not the italics, of a copy dated 1699.)

'After all, I think none can reasonably distrust the Genuineness of the present Volume, when they know the whole was Copied by Mr Snell (a Person always near to the Honourable Author, while he lived) who intending this Collection for his private use only, could have no design to impose a Spurious one upon the Publick.

This Mr John Snell was of Scotch extraction, and Educated at the University of Glasgow; but the War breaking out between the king and Parliament, he forsook his Studies to follow the fortunes of the Royal Party, and was present in several Engagements till the Defeat at Worcester: From whence narrowly escaping he sheltered himself in the Family of a Person of Quality in Cheshire, where he had the opportunity of being known to Sir Orlando Bridgman, who was a Native of that Country, and Son to Dr John Bridgman, Lord Bishop of Chester.

Sir Orlando had been Sollicitor to King Charles while he was Prince; and upon the Restoration, His Majesty, in consideration of his Signal Merit and Sufferings, advanced him first to be Lord Chief Baron of the Exchequer, the first of June 1660; and the Twenty second of October following, Lord Chief Justice of the Court of Common Pleas; in both which Places Mr Snell held a considerable post under him: And afterwards on the Thirtieth of August 1667, upon his Promotion to the Dignity of Lord-Keeper, he made Mr Snell his Purse-bearer, an Office of great Trust and Profit. At length, when it was His Majesty's Pleasure he should resign the Seal, he recommended Mr Snell to his Successor, the Earl of Shaftesbury, as a Person of known Fidelity and Diligence. The Earl was soon removed, who took care to help him into the Service of the Duke of Monmouth; whose Secretary he was, and Commissioner for the Management of his Grace's Estate in Scotland. In this Post he died about the year 1678, and leaving no Male Issue behind him, the Oxford Antiquary informs us, he gave his Estate and Mannor of Uffeton in Warwickshire, valued at Four hundred and fifty Pounds per annum, to Baliol College in Oxford, for the Maintenance of poor scholars. By which means his Books, etc., coming to be sold, this Manuscript (among others) fell into my hands; and being perswaded it would be an acceptable Present to the Publick, I was prevailed upon to undergo the Trouble of fitting it for the Press.'

[there follows the text of a congratulatory letter, in Latin, from the University of Cambridge to Bridgman, on his appointment as Lord Keeper of the Great Seal, given 'as I find it Transcribed by Mr Snell, among his Papers'].

The reference to 'the Oxford Antiquary' is shown by a marginal note to mean Wood's *Athenae Oxonienses*; but Wood, of course, says nothing about Snell giving his estate to Balliol, and the author of this preface is presumably using his knowledge that the Snell exhibitions were in process of assignment to Balliol at the time when he was writing (above, pp. 174-5). This misrepresentation should not cause us to distrust the writer in matters where he is the only authority, such as Snell's military adventures in his youth, for, as we show above (pp. 179-80), he may have drawn on family traditions of which we know nothing. Nothing is otherwise known of Snell's books and papers, said here to have been sold before 1699.

The Society acknowledges with thanks contributions from Balliol College, Oxford, and the University of Glasgow towards the publication of this paper.

THE MEMORIALS IN HAGGART AND H. M. ADVOCATE *v.* HOGG AND SOUTAR, 1738*

Edited, with Introduction and Commentary,
by BERNARD S. JACKSON, LL.B., D.PHIL.,†
Professor of Law, Liverpool Polytechnic

Introduction

The case of *Haggart and H. M. Advocate* v. *Hogg and Soutar* represents a crucial bridge between the mediaeval scholarship on *testes singulares* and the modern Scottish 'Moorov doctrine' (which in turn has influenced the recent English development of corroboration by similar fact evidence). A short account of it, against the background of its canonist and English antecedents, was provided in 'Susanna and the Singular History of Singular Witnesses' [1977] *Acta Juridica* 37-54. Here, the memorials are published in full, with the kind permission and approval of the Keeper of the Records of Scotland, from the MS. Book of Adjournal for Feb. 27 1738-June 11 1739. They cast light also on the style of argument and the range of authorities cited at an important transitional stage in the development of the Scottish legal system. Both sides were represented by counsel of great distinction. Apart from the Lord Advocate, Charles Erskine, who had been the first Regius Professor of Law at the University of Edinburgh and was later to become Lord Justice-Clerk, counsel for the pursuer named in the Criminal Letters include a future Professor of Scots Law and curator of the Advocates' Library (Kenneth Mackenzie, Professor of Scots Law, Edinburgh, 1745), two future Deans of the Faculty of Advocates, one of whom was also solicitor-general, Lord Advocate and Lord President (Robert Dundas, solicitor-general 1742, Dean of Faculty 1746, Lord Advocate 1754, Lord President 1760-87; Alexander Lockhart, Dean of Faculty 1764), as well as the celebrated Henry

---

* High Court of Justiciary, 1738
† I am deeply grateful to Mr. C. Gane, of the University of Lancaster, for checking and supplementing the transcript, and for supplying material for the annotations, as signified by [CG]. I take responsibility for the final formulation of these notes. B. S. J.

Home, Lord Kames. Counsel (or prolocutors) for the defence were James Graham, senior, Dean of Faculty 1737-46, and Robert Craigie (Lord Advocate 1742, Lord President 1754-60). There is a short report of the case in Maclaurin's *Arguments and Decisions in Remarkable Cases* (Edinburgh, 1774), no. 95.

There had evidently been a long feud in the parish of Caputh between the laird, David Haggart of Cairnmuir, and the minister, James Hogg, in the course of which Hogg's accounts had come under suspicion, his manse had been burned down, and Hogg had allegedly accused Haggart of incest. A succession of actions was raised: Haggart sued Hogg for defamation regarding the incest charge (368); Haggart sought to prove scandal against Hogg in the Commissary Court (396); and proceedings were taken against Haggart, charging him with responsibility for the burning of the manse. Haggart was detained pending trial, but the prosecution was abandoned before trial when witnesses against Haggart claimed to have been suborned by Hogg. But Haggart was not content. He brought a complaint against the Lord Advocate for conducting a prosecution oppressively — see *Maclaurin*, no. 94 — and he secured a bill of criminal letters against Hogg for subornation. A procession of witnesses testified to approaches made to them by Hogg and his accomplice, Soutar, but no individual approach was evidenced other than by the testimony of the witness whose testimony had allegedly been negotiated, as the jury indicated in its verdict.

The sufficiency of the evidence hung not only upon a determination of the applicable rule of law, but also on two procedural issues. First, the form of the jury's verdict left room for debate as to its proper classification. On the one hand, it used the term 'Proven' with reference to the 'crime . . . as lybelled' (apparently indicating a general verdict against the pannels); on the other, the jury's disquiet regarding the sufficiency of the evidence was indicated by its qualification of the 'Proven' by 'in Sundry Facts, each Fact only by one single Witness' (apparently indicating a special verdict, the effect of which was for the Court to determine). Haggart, of course, pleaded in the alternative: the verdict was conclusive against the pannels (370-4), but even if not conclusive it disclosed a finding of evidence sufficient in law to convict. Hogg was bound to contest both alternatives.

Second, the effect of the indictment fell to be determined. For even if single witnesses could legally be 'conjoined', they could only be so combined for the purposes of proving one and the same charge. (It is significant that there is no hint, on either side, of the modern conception of *mutual* corroboration by single witnesses of a *series* of charges, each attested only by the one witness.) Thus, Haggart sought to interpret the indictment as charging an offence sufficiently general to admit as relevant the evidence of more than one of the witnesses. But it is interesting (in the light of wider conceptions of *nexus* developed in modern law) to observe the circumspection with which Haggart seeks to construct his 'general charge' (375). Sensitive to the argument for the defence (415-17) that such a general charge could be framed no more widely than 'an attempt to suborn witnesses to prove a particular crime' and that the single witnesses must be combined so as to prove subornation to prove that one particular crime, Haggart argued that the jury's verdict must be taken to relate to the suborning of witnesses specifically in relation to the charge of burning Hogg's manse (390). The alleged subornation in relation to the defamation was to be disregarded in the light of the jury's verdict, and that in relation to the scandal proceedings (noted on behalf of

Hogg: 396, 416) is passed over in silence in the argument for Haggart. It seems, therefore, that not even Haggart was prepared to argue that a general charge of subornation could be proved by combining one witness to an approach for evidence against X on a charge of crime A with another witness claiming an approach for evidence against X on another matter.

Haggart was wise to argue for the most narrowly defined 'general charge' which the evidence could be taken to support. For in terms of both logic and history he was arguing for a significant extension of a doctrine which had originated amongst the Canonists and whose ambit had proved highly controversial. The considerable citation and debate in the memorials over foreign authority reflect this background, as indeed does the seventeenth-century English treason law, upon which reliance is also placed. Although Haggart's argument could claim some modest measure of support from foreign authority, Hogg appears to have had the stronger case.

The canonist doctrine of *testes singulares* may be traced back to the Bolognese decretist Rufinus, who recorded in his *Summa Decretorum* (1157-9) the view that *diversitas temporis* and *diversitas locorum* do not universally negate the testimony of the witnesses whose evidence thus diverges. Two classes of case were held to be exceptions: the first where the acts were liable to be repeated (*iterari habent*), the second where they represented a continuing whole (*longa temporis continuatione produci*). The example given of the first was an accusation of adultery where one witness testified to the commission of adultery on one day, while a second witness testified to its occurrence on a different day; that given of a continuing act was the making of plans on different days directed towards the same treasonable plot to kill the king (c. III qu. IX). The initial reaction to this view was favourable with regard to continuing acts but hostile with regard to repeatable acts (see *Glossed Decretum* c. III, qu. IX, no. 16; further Jackson [1977] *Acta Juridica* 41f.).

Some significant elements are added in the treatment by Magister Damasus in his *Summa de ordine iudiciario* (t. LXV, in Wahrmund, ed., *Quellen* IV/4 p. 47). Here we find for the first time the formulation *factum iterabile*, which was to become technical and standard. Here too the example of adultery as a *factum iterabile* is put in terms making it clear that acts of adultery involving the same man and woman are in contemplation. Finally, the text provides what on its face appears to be the earliest example of a distinction which figured prominently in the memorials in *Hogg and Soutar*; rather than rejecting proof of *factum iterabile* by single witnesses outright, the text reads: *et licet discordent in probatione huius criminis unius, id est adulterii in specie, probant tamen, Titium adulterum esse* ('And although they disagree as to the proof of this one crime, that is this particular offence of adultery, yet they still prove that Titius is an adulterer'). The distinction interrupts the logical flow of the passage, and contradicts the later (unqualified) view that *Decretum* 3.9.16 applies so as to exclude such evidence even in cases of *factum iterabile*. Moreover, the distinction does not appear to be paralleled elsewhere in thirteenth-century sources. It is best regarded as an addition by a later hand. This is the distinction later expressed in terms of proof *in genere* or *in specie*, which provided the basis for Haggart's claim that the witnesses against Hogg could be combined so as to prove a 'general charge'. And it is this distinction which was appended by Johannes Andreae in his *Additiones*

(1346) to the influential *Speculum Judiciale* (1276) of Durandus (*ad Spec.* I. iv. 6 no. 16).

By the sixteenth century, a vast body of canonist doctrine on the matter had developed. In 1592 Prosper Farinatius completed an analysis *de testium singularitate* which exceeded 300 numbered paragraphs (*De testibus*, lib. III tit. VII qu. 64). The subject, noted Cravetta (*Tractatus de antiquitatibus temporum*, 1572), *versatur in summo et vasto pelago* (4.1, proem). The treatment by Julius Clarus (1525-75) proved particularly influential. These three writers are all cited in the memorials. But there were numerous others who made notable contributions, including Covarruvias, Mascardi, Bartholemaeus Bertazzolius and Simanca.

Adultery remained the *locus classicus* of *factum iterabile*. There was general agreement that witnesses testifying to different acts of adultery may be adduced to prove that the accused 'is an adulterer' for civil purposes, but the dominant view appears to have rejected such evidence for proof of adultery as a crime. Usury and heresy are frequently discussed in this connection. Treason continued to provide the most fertile context for the admissibility of *testes singulares*, with more general agreement than elsewhere that the effect of such evidence was proof *in specie*, resulting in criminal conviction. The policy argument, that otherwise it would be impossible to secure convictions since the conspirators would ensure that no act was done in the presence of more than one witness (echoed in the memorial for Haggart at 388), is voiced by Mascardi. So too is the argument that sometimes the proof of a general proposition may be provided by evidence (of *singulares*) of different examples of it: *genus enim constat, et perficitur ex pluribus speciebus et particularibus ... quia per singula generis probatur genus* (Cravetta, *Tractatus* 4.4.11). But treason apart, this argument was not taken to support general charges in criminal cases. The analysis by Julius Clarus quoted in the memorial for Hogg (410-12), in which the author identified proof *in specie* with proof for the purposes of criminal conviction and proof *in genere* with proof for other purposes (such as depriving an adulterer of a dowry or disqualifying a witness), was highly regarded, as is evident from the remarks of Bertazzolius (*Decisivarus Consultationum* 20:19) and Farinatius (*De testibus* 3.7.64.229).

This tradition of the learned law is reflected also in the English and earlier Scottish sources cited in the memorials. Significantly, they involve treason (England) and adultery (Scotland): for a brief account, see *Acta Juridica* [1977] 42-6. Since 1708, English treason law had been applicable in Scotland, and both the English judges and Parliament had found it necessary to deal, in the preceding century, with the sufficiency of *singulares* to fulfil the (statutory) corroboration requirement for proof of treason. Of course, Haggart's argument logically involved an analogy (between treason and subornation), but the analogy might be thought a close one. Just as different overt acts might be combined in treason provided that they were committed in furtherance of the same treasonable plot to kill the king (as in Resolution 9 in the case of Regicides (1660) Kelyng 9), so it might be suggested different approaches to witnesses might be combined to prove subornation provided that they were committed with a view to conviction on the same charge. Haggart's concern to specify the general charge as 'subornation to convict Haggart of fire-raising' (rather than 'subornation in actions involving Haggart' — whether fire-raising or defamation or in the scandal proceedings) echoes the limitations of the use of *singulares* in treason. For the English cases show no inclination even to admit within the doctrine different plots to kill (the same or different) king, and the use of *singulares* attesting to acts falling under different heads of treason was specifically excluded by 7 & 8 Will. III c. 3, s. 2.

The English treason sources revealed a further analogy. In Love's case (1651) Sir Thomas Witherington, second counsel for the Commonwealth, recalled a bribery case in Star Chamber:

> I well remember, my Lord, a case in the Star Chamber, against B. of Leicestershire; I think there was an information against him for bribery and extorting of fees. The matter came to the conclusion, that one man proved a bribe of 40*l.* and another a bribe of 40*l.*; but there were several witnesses to several bribes. The question now was, whether he took bribes or no? And these tending to the same general charge, it was the opinion of all the judges, that he did extort and take bribes. The one witness spake to one bribe, and another to another; and in that case, as two witnesses make good a charge against an offender, yet in that case it was taken, that where witnesses, though they speak not in every particular, yet, all tending to the same general charge of bribery, these were taken for plural witnesses, and that was a good conviction. That was the opinion of the judges then. (5 St. Tr. 43, 178-9.)

B. of Leicestershire accepted bribes on different occasions, and these were held admissible in proof of a general charge of taking bribes. Hogg was charged with offering bribes on different occasions, with a view to a general charge of subornation. But though the terminology of general charge is common and the offence is similar, as involving the use of bribes, the analogy is in fact weaker than that with treason, given the background of the canonist conceptions of *nexus*. The only link between the different incidents in the case of B. of Leicestershire was his disposition to take bribes for personal gain (as far as we know); whereas in treason — and in Hogg's case, on Haggart's analysis — the acts showed far more than a disposition to offer bribes, or even to suborn, but rather a continuing course of conduct directed towards one, highly specific end. A closer analogue to the case of B. of Leicestershire may be found in the offence of simony, where the canonists did relax the normal rules of evidence but where the use of *singulares* proved controversial (see Farinatius *De testibus* 3.7.64.274, who accepted it).

Both memorials refer to Mackenzie's treatment of a Court of Session divorce case in which single witnesses to different acts of adultery ('with the same woman', as the quotation for Hogg notes) were admitted (384f., 401f.). The reference is to the *Milntoun* divorce case, appealed to the Court of Session from the Edinburgh Commissary Court in 1667 by the assignee of a liferent-right which would be forfeit if the decreet stood. An account is provided in [1977] *Acta Juridica* 43-6. The argument for Haggart here is self-consciously weak: Mackenzie had observed that 'the Depositions were conjoyned . . . for sustaining a Decreet of Divorce' and had added, as Haggart conceded, 'yet it were hard that these different Probations could have been conjoyned, if the case had been criminally pursued' (*Laws and Customs of Scotland in Matters Criminal* 1678, 1679, II. 26.14, citing Farinatius). But the term 'crime' appears to have had a somewhat loose usage, such as to include our later notion of a 'matrimonial

offence' in the context of divorce — influenced perhaps by the canonist view that
where dissolution of marriage was possible, the criminal standard of evidence
was required. At any rate, Mackenzie himself introduces the *Milntoun* case as one
of 'a Crime which is reiterable' and this no doubt encouraged counsel for
Haggart to argue that 'the Lords found, in proof of the Crime of Adultery, two
witnesses to two different Acts were conjoined to make full Proof of the Crime'
(385). When we turn to the arguments in *Milntoun*, as published in Stair's
Decisions 1683 (i. 453), we find explicit reliance on the canonist doctrine (with
citations of Clarus, Farinatius and Covaruvias), and a formulation which may
further have encouraged the development of the notion of a 'general charge'. For
adultery is there described, even in the context of divorce, as a *crimen genericum*:
'... as in Adultery it is *crimen genericum*, by reiterable Acts, and therefore being
pursued *civiliter* to separat the Marriage, or restore the Joynture, it might be
proven by two witnesses, though not concurring in the same individual time and
place, and therefore singular, albeit not single witnesses'. Scottish advocacy thus
transformed the canonist proof *in genere* into a *crimen genericum*, just as the Star
Chamber constructed a 'general charge' of bribery against B. of Leicestershire.

In sum, there was no direct authority to support the combining of the
testimony in Hogg's case. Apart from treason, there was no clear principle
amongst the canonists supporting the use of *testes singulares* for criminal
conviction: individual crimes were each considered on their individual merits,
and views favouring the device, as in simony, were controversial. The nearest
approach to the use of *singulares* in Scotland had been in *Milntoun*, for proof of
adultery to found a divorce. English law had given statutory authority to the
institution in the context of treason, but no general principle had been developed
or was needed (with the possible exception of practice in the Star Chamber).
Hogg's case therefore represented an extension, though one which could be
justified in terms of the underlying rationale of the treason exception — the
context where the use of *singulares* was most firmly established, in both Canon
and English law. But this justification was based upon a very specific conception
of *nexus*: the witnesses each testified to acts designed to procure the conviction of
the same man on the same charge.

The development from *Hogg and Soutar* to the modern 'Moorov doctrine'
required both the loosening of the required *nexus* between the acts and the
movement from proof of a general charge by evidence of separate instances to
that of the mutual corroboration of instances charged as separate substantive
offences. The history is characterised by the interaction of institutional writings
and case law. While the decided cases and even the examples used by the
institutional writers remained largely within the categories where the canonist
tradition accepted the use of *testes singulares*, the institutional writers constantly
sought statements of general principle such as would both synthesise the
traditional examples and manifest their rationale. This was to lead, eventually, to
the significant extensions of the conception of *nexus* that have been seen in the
present century.

Hume comments on *Hogg and Soutar* thus:

> In this instance, the several acts, though all of one sort, were truly distinct
> crimes, being attempts on the conscience of several persons, though relative

chiefly to one and the same charge, that of fire-raising, and thus far connected one with another. That judgment affords therefore an inference *a fortiori*, with respect to those cases where the accusation is truly of the same crime, such as adultery or incest, committed with the same person on sundry occasions, or during a certain period of time. ... Certainly, however, no inference is to be made from such a case as that of Hog, to one where the several acts, though of the same crime, have no sort of relation to or connection with each other; as, for instance, in the case of successive acts of uttering forged notes to different persons, and at different times and places. (*Commentaries*, 1800, ii, 236-7.)

It is noticeable that Hume relates the different acts, both in the example of adultery and in his description of Hogg's case, not to any general charge but rather to each other. Thus the different acts of subornation are conceived by him as 'truly distinct crimes', and since each involved different parties, the nexus appeared weaker than the example of adultery, at least 'where committed with the same person on sundry occasions'. That is the reasoning behind Hume's *a fortiori* argument. The canonists would surely have disagreed with this assessment of the relative strengths of the two cases. For them, the presence of the same two parties on different occasions of adultery was a requirement relevant to the more controversial case of *testes singulares*, that of *factum iterabile*; it was not required in the case of *factum continuum* (paradigmatically, treason) because the acts there combined were regarded as a unity, as being directed towards one, highly specific end. It was this latter model on which the argument for Haggart had been constructed, and which provided the rationale for the 'general charge'. Hume seems not to have been aware of this background. His lawyer's instincts against vague criminal indictments no doubt made him reluctant to give any support to the use of a 'general charge'. But in the process, he laid the foundations for a doctrine which, in effect, convicts the accused of having a particular propensity. By omitting the general charge, he reduced the significance of the highly specific end which it embodied; and by describing the different acts of subornation as 'truly distinct crimes' he opened the way towards *mutual* corroboration of separate offences charged. (Cf. his remarks at i, 369-71, discussing the specification of time and place in the libel, and comparing treason with incest or adultery 'which have their completion in a single, but withal a reiterable act'.) At the same time, he lent his authority to the proposition — never previously applied in Scotland — that single witnesses to different sexual acts (between the same parties) would suffice for *criminal* conviction (here without Mackenzie's reserve), and his formulation of the *nexus* required in negative terms ('no inference is to be made ... where the several acts ... have no sort of relation to or connection with each other') opened the way to the formulation of *nexus* requirements very much less stringent than in the traditional lore.

Eleven years later, Burnett took a far more traditional view. Whereas Hume had understood *Hogg* in terms of separate repeated acts (in effect assimilating the canonist *factum continuum* to the *factum iterabile*) Burnett approached the matter from the opposite direction: he understood the case of reiterated sexual offences ('with the same person') as the charging of 'one specific crime, consisting of reiterated acts' (in effect assimilating the *factum iterabile* to the *factum continuum*). Burnett was concerned that Hogg's case should not be understood as a broad precedent for the construction of a single offence out of different acts involving different persons: 'This was a peculiar case in various respects; and in this chiefly, that the attempts to suborn applied principally to one and the same fact, the burning of a particular house . . .' (*Treatise*, 1811, 511-14).

The nineteenth-century cases in which the doctrine was applied open with *Landles* v. *Gray* (1816) 1 Murray 79, where slander was held proved on the evidence of single witnesses to the repetition of the slanderous words to different people, in line with the canonist proof of *diffamatio in genere* (also for civil purposes). The court appears to have considered only one slander to have been proved thereby. However, in *Dougall* v. *Dougall* (1833) 11 S. 1020, the Lord President suggested that 'had the issue embraced two occasions of uttering the same slander, and one witness had spoken to each, that might have been legal proof *of both*' (emphasis supplied). In 1834 the issue of single witnesses to acts of adultery arose again in a divorce case: *Sim* v. *Sim* (1834) 12 S. 633. Here the acts of adultery were with different lovers, but on the same night (in the course of, or after, a ball). The witnesses were not, in fact, believed, but the Lord President opined that 'if we could believe these witnesses the case would be very clear'. Half a century later such evidence was accepted, at least by the Lord Ordinary, in *Whyte* v. *Whyte* (1884) 11 R. 710.

Dickson's *Treatise on Evidence* (1855) marks a step towards the modern rationale, while still preserving the traditional distinctions by way of example. Single witnesses are admissible to prove treason or 'a charge of several acts of incest with the same person, or a charge of suborning several persons as witnesses in the same trial'; however, the rationale is now seen in terms of an underlying psychological unity: 'In such cases the different acts are repetitions of the same offence, springing from the same impulses or motives . . .' (§§2039-41; see also Vandore, 1974 J.R. 36-8). Presumably, treason and suborning are cases where the different acts spring from the same motives, whereas incest is a case where the different acts spring from the same impulse. Like the earlier institutional writers, Dickson is anxious to formulate a principle encompassing both streams of canonist tradition, even if the unity of principle is essentially formal. 'Impulses or motives' does reflect the perception of a distinction between the two streams, and Dickson rejects the idea that the principle may be used to admit 'independent instances of the same kind of crime or offence, as, for example, several charges of theft or robbery, or uttering forged notes to several persons at different times and places'.

The courts continued to resist extensions of the traditional conceptions of *nexus* (even where the similar offences were each sufficiently evidenced). In *H.* v. *P.* (1905) 8 F. 232 the Lord President observed of *Whyte* v. *Whyte* that 'the principle laid down there is limited to matrimonial cases, and for this reason, that, it being the duty of the Court to protect the matrimonial bond against grievous injury, the very strict rule has been in such cases somewhat relaxed'. In *A.* v. *B.* (1895) 22 R. 402 a pursuer suing for damages for rape was not allowed to adduce evidence of attempts to ravish other women. Lord M'Laren argued: 'If we were to hold that the statements as to indecent assaults on other women were relevant topics of proof, it would necessarily follow that in an action of fraud it would be legitimate to allow the pursuer to prove that the defender had defrauded other persons under equivalent circumstances' (at 404). In *Inglis* v. *The National Bank of Scotland* 1909 S.C. 1038, Lord M'Laren was able to confirm his *reductio ad absurdum* in a case of fraud (despite an additional element of *nexus*), and to cite *A.* v. *B.* as 'a good authority for the proposition that it is not evidence against a party of having committed a delict to show that he committed delicts of the like description against other persons on other occasions' (at 1040). Yet it was Lord M'Laren who, in the very same year, provided a further impetus on the route to *Moorov* by his dicta in *Gallagher* v. *Paton* 1909 J.C. 50. On a charge of obtaining money by false representations, evidence was admitted of similar representations made by the accused to other persons on the same day. The several incidents here were established by more than a single witness; the issue was proof of the accused's criminal intention. Lord M'Laren observed: 'A false statement made to one person may be explained away, but when a system of false statements is proved, the probability is very great that the statements were designedly made . . . (but) the evidence of like representations must be confined to those that were made about the same time'. In the judgments of the court, temporal continuity thus became a matter of degree; common system was accepted as a form of *nexus*; and appeal was explicitly made to the standards on which people would act in the ordinary course of life. The principle, as applicable to fraudulent statements, was not however applied in *Oswald* v. *Fairs* 1911 S.C. 257.

Dicta in *Kinnear* v. *Brandon* 1914 J.C. 141 and *McVicar* v. *Barbour* 1916 S.C. 567 further set the scene for the emergence of the 'Moorov doctrine'. The first involved proof of charges against an employer of failure to contribute insurance stamps for two employees, the evidence on each of the two separate charges resolving ultimately to the testimony of each employee that he had not received an insurance card. At first instance, the accused was convicted. On appeal the Court divided on the issue of *testes singulares*. Lord Dundas, with whom the Lord Justice-Clerk concurred, doubted that the evidence of each witness could be taken to corroborate that of the other, and found in the stated case no trace of extraneous corroboration of either. Lord Salvesen and Lord Anderson were differently inclined, although finding for the appellant on other grounds. Citing Hume for the proposition that 'the evidence of single witnesses has been held sufficient to establish separate acts of the same kind', Lord Anderson resorted to the strategy of *Hogg and Soutar* (which Hume had avoided in his account of the case): he resurrected the notion of a general charge — even if it was not explicitly laid but had to be reconstructed from the specific charges of the indictment:

> . . . It seems to me that although the complaint apparently contains two distinct charges, it may fairly be regarded as setting forth a general charge of failure to pay the insurance contributions due in respect of the two servants. The two branches of the complaint libel the same *species facti* — in locus, time, and modus. I should therefore have been prepared to hold, in this case, that the two servants might have been taken as corroboration of one another, and, if they said enough, that the case would have been proved on their evidence alone.

If the two distinct charges were, however, to be regarded as 'setting forth a general charge of failure to pay the insurance contributions due in respect of the two servants', it might be concluded that acceptance of the servants' evidence would result in conviction on that one general charge alone. Yet despite this, Lord Anderson spoke in terms of mutual corroboration. The language may be regarded as loose, but still we have a straw in the wind of (real) mutual corroboration (without the intercession of any general charge).

McVicar v. *Barbour* was a case of slander, the statement having been repeated to different persons, but being spoken to by only one witness on each of two occasions. Lord Mackenzie adopted the same strategy as Lord Anderson in *Kinnear* v. *Brandon*, and at the same time suggested what the form of a comparable criminal indictment would be:

> The case must in my opinion be taken as if there was one general issue that, on two separate occasions, the defender used words which did mean that the pursuer had immoral relations with the person named in the issue. If the words used conveyed the same meaning on each occasion, it is sufficient if one witness speak to each occasion. It is analogous to the case of a criminal indictment which sets out that in pursuance of a scheme to obtain money under false pretences, you did first pretend to A and second pretend to B. In a case of that kind it would be competent to prove a general scheme by the evidence of one witness to each occasion.

The analogy is the very case which Lord M'Laren had used, some twenty-one years earlier, as the basis of a *reductio ad absurdum* (in *A*. v. *B., supra*). Fourteen years later, it was to be an indictment in a similar form that brought Samuel Moorov to trial: 'Having formed a scheme for procuring women into his employment, and gaining a domination over them through his relationship with them as their employer for the purpose of compelling them to submit themselves to acts of sexual intercourse with him . . . he did, in furtherance of this scheme, . . . commit certain crimes of assault, indecent assault and attempt to ravish against these women'. In effect, this preamble constituted a 'general charge' (and was so described by Lord Anderson: 1930 J.C. 30, 92). In Moorov's trial, Lord Pitman directed the jury that the Crown had failed to prove the scheme prefaced to the specific counts, and on appeal the Lord Advocate did not seek to contest this. Moreover, the form of the indictment was criticised by some members of the appellate court, and the Lord Justice-Clerk noted with approval an assurance that the preamble would not be regarded as a precedent by the Crown Office (at 78). The general charge was thus put to rest. But mutual corroboration emerged from its ashes.

The Criminal Letters, 3rd July 1738

(JC 3/22, fo. 136) Intran.
Mr James Hogg Minister of the Gospell in Caputh, in the Shire of Perth, and Thomas Soutar late Tenant in Russlo, in the said Parrish of Caputh; — Pannels, Indicted and Accused at the Instance of David Haggart of Cairnmuir, with the Concourse of Charles Areskine Esq. his Majesty's Advocate, for his highness Interest, For the Crime of Suborning of Witnesses; as is more fully mentioned in the Criminal Lybell raised against them there anent, Makeing Mention, That where, By the Law of God, the Common Law, and the Laws of this and of all

other well governed Realms, The Bribeing, Corrupting, Suborning, and Concussing of Witnesses, to bear false Evidence, or to Swear falsely, against any of his Majesty's Leiges, Especially in Matters Capitall or Defamatory, or to Conceall and Deny Truths consisting with their knowledge, when they should be Called up to give Evidence in Matters of Fact, to the Transacting of which they were present; And all Attempts or Endeavours to the above Purposes; The fraudulent Inticeing, Importuning, Soliciting, or Menaceing of any Person or persons, to bear false Evidence, or to Swear falsely, against any Third Person, or to Conceal and Deny Truths consisting with their knowledge, when Called as Witnesses in any Process intented, or to be Intented; by Money actually given, Promises of Rewards and good Deeds; By Importunitys, Threats, Menaces, and Violence, or by other such Corrupt and abominable Means, or any other Sinister Attempts or Methods, to Suppress or withdraw Persons, who might be cited as Evidences in Process Intented or to be Intented by any of his Majesty's Leidges; and all Attempts by fraudulent Means, to Induce others to Defame any of his Majesty's Leidges as Guilty of hainous Crimes, and thereby bringing them under Imprisonment and Trial for the same, and of Consequence under Terrour of Punishment, and even of their Lives and also Subjecting them to great Charges and Expenses; Were Crimes of their own Nature most attrocious, Subversive of all Society and good order; and therefore most severely punishable; Especially where such abominable Practices were the Result of a previous Ill-will and deadly prejudice frequently repeated for the Space of Several Months or years, with a wicked and felonious Intention, to Murder an Innocent Person falsely Slandered, Accused, aspersed or Indicted as Guilty of Capital Crimes; And when Committed by a Minister of the Gospell, to the Scandall of his Profession; And where the Persons so Corrupted, Suborned, or Inticed, or Endeavoured so to be Corrupted and Seduced, were of the Number of those, over whom he was constituted and Ordained Minister, and thereby greatly under his Influence; *NEVERTHELESS*, It was of Verity, That the said Mr James Hogg, and the said Thomas Soutar, shakeing off all Fear of God, and Regard to his Majesty's Laws, had presumed to Committ, and were each of them Guilty Actors Art and Part of all, or one or other, of the Crimes before mentioned, aggravated by all, or one or other of the aforesaid Circumstances; In so far as, The said Mr James Hogg, having for some considerable time, Conceived a most groundless and deadly Ill-will and prejudice against David Haggart of Cairnmuir, venting it on all occasions, even in the Pulpit; and that on account of his having been Instrumentall, in Convicting or Detecting him the said Mr James Hogg, in the year One Thousand and seven hundred and Thirty, before certain of the Ministers of the Presbytery of Dunkeld, and a considerable Number of the Heritors of the Parish of Caputh, of his the said Mr James Hogg's keeping and using a false Balk or Ballance, in Receiving his Stipend Meall; and which Balk or Ballance having been then produced and Examined, by the said Committee of Presbyterys and Heritors, was found to be false, and by their Orders, destroyed; The said Mr James Hogg had since formed a most Malicious Purpose, to bereave the said David Haggart of his Fame, Life, and Reputation; And the said Thomas Soutar, having Conceived the like groundless Ill-will and prejudice against the said David Haggart, for his haveing Removed the said Thomas Soutar from the possession of some Grounds belonging in Property to the said Complainer, Did frequently within the Space of those Twelve or fourteen Months last bypast, with horrid Oaths and Imprecations, Threaten to Murder Cairnmuir, and to Burn him, his House, and whole Family, or to Destroy him by some other Means equally Effectuall; Towards the Accomplishing of which their wicked and Malicious Purposes, as well some short space before, as after the first of March last, when the said Complainer was Committed Prisioner, in order to Triall before the last Circuit at Perth, upon a false and groundless Suspicion, (by virtue of a Warrant of the Sherrif Depute of Perth, dated the said ffirst of March last, of which Warrant an Extract lay in the hand of the Clerk of Justiciary,) Invented and propagated by them the said Mr James Hogg and Thomas Soutar, or one or other of them, of his being Guilty of wilfully Fire-raising, and Burning the Manse of Caputh, when in Reality the same had been accidentally ffired, or by the Negligence of the Ministers' own Servants, or some other such Fatality to which the said David Haggart was an utter Stranger; They said Mr James Hogg and Thomas Soutar, both and each of them, did Endeavour, as far as in them lay, by giveing of Money, Promises of good Deeds and other Rewards, by Sollicitation, Importunitys, and Intreaties, by Threats, Menaces and fforce, To Corrupt, Suborne, Intice, or Concuss a great many different persons, mostly Inhabitants of the Parish of Caputh, under the said Mr Hogg's Charge, falsely to accuse, Declare, and Swear against the said David Haggart, as Guilty of Incest, and of wilfull Fire raiseing by himself or others of his hounding out and Commanding, or at least of Threatenings to Burn the said Mr James Hogg his House or Manse, or of Acknowledgeing to the said Persons, that he had done so, In any Criminal Process, which then was or should be Intented against the said David Haggart, for either of these Crimes; And by the same unjustifiable Means, the said Mr James Hogg, and Thomas Soutar, and each of them did Sollicite, and Endeavour to Induce or Concuss the said Persons when Called as Witnesses in any such Process intented or to be Intented, against the said David Haggart; or when Called as Witnesses in any Process intented or to be Intented, against the said Mr James Hogg himself, as guilty of having Defamed and Slandered the Complainer in these particulars, to Conceall or Deny upon Oath certain matters of ffacts, to which they had been Witnesses, and the truth of which consisted with their knowledge; Particularly during the Dependance of a Process of Scandall, which the said David Haggart had intented against the said Mr James Hogg, for having falsely and Maliciously Slandered and Defamed the said David Haggart, as guilty of Incest with Margaret Halket his own Daughter in law; and which Slander he the said Mr James Hogg had industriously published to several persons, and amongst others to Thomas Thomson Portioner of Caputh; The said Mr James Hogg did, upon the Seventeenth day of November, One thousand Seven hundred and Thirty five, or one or other of the Days of October, one thousand seven hundred and Thirty five, Come to the House of James Stirtoun in Inchstuthill, in the Parish of Caputh, in the Shire of Perth, Father in Law to the above named Thomas Thomson; and after takeing the said James Stirtoun aside, and representing the great Apprehension he had, that the said David Haggart would prevaill against him the said Mr James Hogg, in the forementioned Process of Scandall, unless he the said James Stirton would stand his Friend; He Sollicited, Inticed, and Importuned the said James Stirton, to prevail with Thomas Thomson his son in law, to Say in presence of two Witnesses, that he would stand by the said David Haggart right or wrong, in the Matter of his Evidence with Relation to the before mentioned Scandal, or words to that purpose, which would be sufficient to Cast him as a Witness in that Process; and so there would be no Proof against him, there being but one other Material Witness who heard him utter that Scandall. Likeas upon the Twenty Second day of the said Month of November, one thousand Seven hundred and Thirty Five, or one or other of the days of October, November, or December, one Thousand Seven hundred and Thirty five The said Mr James Hogg Returned again, to the said James Stirton's house in Inchstuthill, and demanded of him, What answer he had got from the said Thomas Thomson? To which James Stirton Answering, that his son in law was offended at the Proposall, and refuses to Comply; Mr Hogg, with redoubled Earnestness and Anxiety again pressed and Importuned him, to Sollicit and Induce his Son in Law, the said Thomas Thomson, when called as a Witness before the Commissar to Deny that he had heard him utter these Scandalous Expressions against the said Complainer. As also, upon the Fourteenth of April, one Thousand seven hundred and Thirty six, being but a few days after the Burning of the Manse of Caputh, (which happened on or about the Ninth of April, one thousand Seven hundred and thirty six) or some one or other of the days of the said Month of April or May, One thousand Seven hundred and Thirty six, the said Mr James Hogg came to the House of James Haggart, (then Tacksman of the Mains of Fordie) in the parish of Caputh, and the Shire of Perth, upon an affected Pretence of Business, when being in private with the said James Haggart he begun to Reflect upon the said David Haggart of Cairnmuir, as the person who had Certainly burnt his Manse of Caputh, and Insisted over and over again, that this must certainly Consist with James Haggart's knowledge; ffor that he could not but know, that none but his Enemy, Cairnmuir could have Set fire to the Manse; which if the said James Haggart would Say, the said Mr James Hogg promised, that he would give him the said James Haggart a large Reward; But which the said James Haggart honestly Rejected, bidding him keep his Rewards to himself, for that he would not be Corrupted to Lie against any Man; And at the same time Cautioned Mr Hogg, to be more careful of what he said of Cairnmuir, for that he had already run a Risque before the Commisary of Dunkeld, for his falsely Scandalizing Cairnmuir of Committing Incest. And likeways, upon the Seventeenth day of May, one thousand four hundred and Thirty Six, or one or other of the days of April or May one thousand seven hundred and Thirty Six, at the Boat of Caputh, in the Parish of Caputh and Sherrifdom of Perth, the said Mr James Hogg did use the like Sollicitations with Alexander Scott late Servant to John Bissett Tenant at the Boat of Caputh, thereby endeavouring to Induce and persuade him the said Alexander Scott, to Join in accuseing Cairnmuir of Burning the Manse of Caputh, or of having acknowledged in presence of the said Alexander Scott that he actually did burn the same, by himself or others of his hounding out and commanding; And in like manner, upon the Thirteenth day of January, one thousand Seven hundred and thirty seven or one or other of the days of the Months of January, February or March, one thousand Seven hundred and Thirty Seven, which was about Nine or Ten Months after the Burning of the Manse of Caputh, the said Mr James Hogg having occasion to pass over the Water of Tay, at a Place called the Garth, near the Manse of Caputh, where John

Neill in Hillhead, sometime Servant to Cairnmuir, was fferrying the said Mr James Hogg over the Water, the said Mr James Hogg, with many Intreaties and Promises of his Kindness, did Intice and Sollicite the said John Neill to Declare and Swear, when called upon as a Witness, That Cairnmuir had Burnt the Manse of Caputh; which John Neill refusing, Mr Hogg, knowing him be very poor, thought to prevail by an offer, which he then made, to give him instantly one Guinea, and was seemingly about to take the same out of his Pockett when the said John Neill Declared his abhorrence of the Proposall, and refused to take the Money; Likeas upon the Twelfth day of October last, or one or other of the days of September, October, or November last, when Christian Grimmon Spouse to James Miller, late Tenent in Cairnmuir, now at the Boat of Coupar, was attending, in the Commisariot Court in the Town of Dunkeld, a Process which the said David Haggart had then depending against her husband for Arrears of Rent; and meeting that day with some Disappointments in relation to the Process, which Ruffled her Temper, and upon which she left the Court in Passion, the said Mr James Hogg, who was always ready upon the Catch, observing the Disposition of Mind in which the said Christian Grimmon was at the time, and thinking this a proper Opportunity for him to Insinuate himself, and to make a Tooll of her to Serve his wicked purposes, he immediately made up to her, upon her comeing out of the Court, and began to Sooth her Passion, by Regrateing that they could never fall upon any means to humble that proud man Cairnmuir; But if she would Say, That it was Cairnmuir who burnt the Manse of Caputh, or that she had heard him acknowledge the same, or words to that purpose, Both he and She would then be sure to get their full Revenge upon him. As also, upon the Sixteenth day of October last, or one or other of the days of the said Month of October, or November last, the said Mr James Hogg having met with James Anderson Boatman at the Boat of Windyedge, in the Wood of Haughend, a little by East the Town of Dunkeld, he the said Mr James Hogg begun, according to his usual Manner, to Insinuate, that the said James Anderson certainly knew, That none but Cairnmuir would have Burnt his Manse; And though James Anderson declared, he knew nothing of the Matter, the said Mr James Hogg pressed and sollicited him in the strongest Manner, by Promises of good Deeds, and Kindness, to accuse Cairnmuir, either of having Burnt the Manse of Caputh, or of haveing acknowledged that he did burn the same; Likeas, upon the Nineteenth day of January, one thousand Seven hundred and Thirty Eight, or one or other of the days of the Said Month of January, or of the month of February immediately following, the said Mr James Hogg came to the House of Cardnoys, belonging to the Laird of Cardnoys, in the Shire of Perth, where finding John Syme Wright in Over Cardnoys at work, he begun a Conversation with him about the Burning of the Manse of Caputh, and after sometime discoursing upon the Matter, did Sollicite and Intice, and in sofar as in him lay did Endevour to Corrupt the said John Syme, to Declare upon Oath, when called on as a Witness, That he had heard Cairnmuir frequently threaten to Burn the said Manse, and after it was burnt had as frequently heard him Acknowledge, that he, in Conjunction with Thomas Soutar, had actually Burnt the same; To which John Syme making no Answer, as being Struck with Horrour at the Proposal, the said Mr James Hogg endeavoured to Enforce what he had proposed, by this Expression, or Words to the same purpose: That, Thomas

Souttar honest man, had already told, that he saw Cairnmuir Burn the Manse of Caputh, and as you John are a poor Man, and I am Resolved to wage Money in this affair; If you will Say or Swear so, I will be ffive pound in your way; By which you will do good Service to God, your Minister, and all good People. And upon John Syme's Enquiring, What he meant by being ffive pounds in his way? The said Mr James Hogg Replied, He would lay that much Money in his Lapp. And as he intended shortly, through the Assistance of God and good People, to Prosecute Cairnmuir, he would then let him the said John Syme know, to whom he was to Declare the same; But the said John Syme having honestly Resisted all these Sollicitations and Promises the said Mr James Hogg earnestly Beseached him to make no mention of what had past in that Conversation. And in like manner, upon the Second day of March, one thousand Seven hundred and Thirty Eight, being the very next day, or soon after that Cairnmuir was Committed Prisoner, in order to Trial, for Burning of the Manse of Caputh, on one or other of the Days of the said Month of March, the said Mr James Hogg Meeting Isabell Tyrie Spouse to John Neill in Hillhead, a little without the North Post of Perth, returning from seeing the said John Neill her husband, who had in like manner been falsely Accused by Thomas Soutar, as Accessory to the Burning of the said Manse, and thereupon also Incarcerated: the said Mr James Hogg Endeavoured at first to Alarm her, with an Apprehension of the Danger her Husband was in; and after having Turned her, as he thought, to his purpose, he Expressed himself of her in these or such like Words, If you will Return and desire your Husband to Concurr with Thomas Soutar, in Saying but two Words against Cairnmuir, you shall get your husband safe home immediately. By which the said Isobell being greatly provocked, Replied with some warmth, You came, Sir, to the Parish of Caputh under pretence of Saving Souls, and would now persuade them to Damn themselves by Swearing the greatest of Falsehoods, since my Husband lay with me all that Night the Manse was Burnt, and knew nothing of it 'till next Morning; And thereupon immediately left his Company. As also, upon the Seventh day of March, one thousand Seven hundred and Thirty Eight, or one or other of the Days of the said Month, or of the Month of April immediately following, after that the said David Haggart was Incarcerated, in order to Trial, for this the said alledged Burning of the Manse of Caputh, the said Mr James Hogg having cast himself so as to meet with Donald Syme, then servant to Cairnmuir, in the Fields betwixt Stentoun and Kirkhill, where it was known he was that day to pass, he the said Mr James Hogg Addressed him with a great deall of Insinuating Language; and having at last told him the said Donald Syme, That Thomas Soutar either then was, or had lately been at Perth, accusing Cairnmuir of Burning the Manse of Caputh he the said Mr James Hogg conduced in these words, or words to the same purpose, That if you Donald will come in there likeways, and Declare or Swear, That you have heard Cairnmuir acknowledge, Drunk or fresh, that he had Burnt the Manse of Caputh, there is a Crown to you, which is all the Money I have at present, but how soon you come in and Swear, I will make it Gold; And if you will say, That Margaret Halket acknowledged to you, that she was with Childe to the said David Haggart Complainer, I will give you Ten Guineas; And the said Donald Syme Refusing to take the Crown, the said Mr James Hogg pressed it upon him, forced it into his hand, and immediately went off, telling him, there was no harm in his takeing it.

Likeas, upon the Seventh day of April last, or one or other of the days of the said Month of April, the said Mr James Hogg went to the House of Bailly Charles Hay in Coupar of Angus, of Designe to pump from the said Baillie Hay, what Conversation had past betwixt him and Cairnmuir, one Night in the End of Harvest preceeding, when he was Informed the Baillie and Cairnmuir had been in Company together; And was so very Inquisitive, as to ask the Bailly, whether he had not that Night heard Cairnmuir Express himself Maliciously or Revengefully against him the said Mr James Hogg? At which Impertinent Questions, Bailly Hay being justly offended, the said Mr James Hogg found it Convenient to go off in quest of other Game; And meeting that same day with Robert Young in Whiteleys, in the Parish of Cargill, and Shire of Perth, as he was just going out of the West end of the Town of Coupar, he the said Mr James Hogg began to Calummiate Cairnmuir, as having been hard upon the said Thomas Soutar, an old acquaintance of the said Robert Young's of Design thereby to animate him against the said David Haggart of Cairnmuir; And Concluded by pressing and Solliciting the said Robert Young, as the best Service he could do to the said Thomas Soutar, To Join with the said Thomas Soutar in Accusing the said David Haggart of Cairnmuir of Burning the Manse of Caputh; Which the said Robert Young observing, it would be Impossible for him to do, though he were willing, Because he was not upon that place when the Manse was burnt; Mr Hogg Replied, You may at least then say, that you heard Cairnmuir give orders to Soutar to Burn it, or acknowledge that he had Burnt it himself; And as ane Encouragement to Robert Young to Comply, the said Mr James Hogg assured him, that Soutar would stand firm while there was Life in him, and that he wanted but one to Concurr; And again, upon the Thirtieth day of April last, or one or other of the Days of the said Month, the said Mr James Hogg, being in Company with William Thomson in Wester Caputh, upon the Road betwixt Dunkeld and Wester Caputh, a little to the East of the House in the Wood of Haughend, in the forsaid Shire of Perth; when the Burning of the Manse of Caputh, was still the Subject of Conversation; Mr Hogg began to Question the said William Thomson, what he thought would become of Cairnmuir? And William Thomson making Answer, That he the said Mr Hogg certainly knew more of that than he did, Mr Hogg frankly Confessed, That he could not Say, What the Event would be, for that they could as yet make nothing of John Neill, though they had taken him up to Logaret Prison, in Sight of the Gallows; So that he still wanted the Assistance of some honest Man, such as him the said William Thomson, who in Concurrence with Soutar would make the affair quite Easy; And therefore Sollicited and earnestly pressed the said William Thomson to Say, That Cairnmuir had desired him to Burn the Manse; upon doing of which, the said Mr James Hogg promised to give him a considerable Reward; But which the said William Thomson refused, and would not be Concerned. And further, upon the ffirst day of February, or one or other of the days of December, January, February, or March last, the said Mr James Hogg did, at the House of Clunie within the Shire of Perth, Sollicite John Pennycook in Clunie, against whom he knew the said David Haggart had shortly before Carried a Process, where he Expected would leave a Resentment in his the said John Pennycook's Breast To Swear and Declare upon Oath, That the said David Haggart had Burnt the forsaid Manse of Caputh, or threatened to do so; and promised him Rewards in

Money and other good Deeds, in Case he would Comply, and second the said Mr James Hogg his wicked purpose against the said David Haggart's life. Likeas, the said Thomas Soutar, being in Company over a Bottle with the said Robert Young in Whiteleys, and John Bisset Elder portioner of Fardle at the said John Bisset's house in Fardle, in the Parish of Caputh and Shire of Perth, upon the Twenty Sixth day of October, or November last, the said Thomas Soutar did, under the promise of secrecy, Acknowledge to those his Comrades, That he himself had Burnt the Manse of Caputh; but pretended that he had done so at Cairnmuir's Desire; Whereupon they having Exhorted him, to be Cautious of what he said, for that an Accusation such as that, would go hard with him, if he could not prove it; Thomas Soutar made Answer, Be not afraid of that, for a Crown piece and a Ribs full of Drink, will make my old Servant John Neill Swear whatever I have a Mind; And as I have got Money from Mr Hogg to make good that Affair, it should not be Starved; Or Words to that purpose and Meaning; And Accordingly the said Thomas Soutar having, in a few days thereafter, that is, upon the thirtieth day of October last, or one or other of the days of the said Month of October, or November last, Mett with John Neill in Hillhead of Caputh, in the house of John Bisset at the Board of Caputh, he did at first Endeavour by fair Means and Sollicitations, to prevail with the said John Neill, to Concurr in Accusing Cairnmuir, of having desired him the said Thomas Soutar, to Burn the Manse of Caputh; which the said John Neill refusing to do, as being intirely Ignorant of the Matter, the said Thomas Soutar put his hands in his pocket, as of Designe to pull out Money, telling the said John Neill, That he had got Three Guineas from the said Mr James Hogg Minister of Caputh, and was to get more, and offered to give the said John Neill the three Guineas, if he would Swear as he desired him; And further, on the ffirst of February, one thousand seven hundred and Thirty Eight, or one or other of the days of that Month, or of the Months of December or January preceeding, the said Thomas Soutar meeting the said Donald Syme, betwixt the Town of Russlo and Caputh, Did Intice, Sollicite, and Importune the said Donald Syme to Swear, That he had heard the said David Haggart Threaten to Burn the said Manse of Caputh or acknowledge that he had done so; and profered if he would Comply, That both he and the said Mr James Hogg would give him a good Reward; At least at that time, threatened under Secrecy to the said Donald Syme, to make an End of the said David Haggart, by Accuseing him of the said wilfull Fire raising; or words to the forsaid purpose; From all which it was plain, That the said Mr James Hogg and Thomas Soutar were each of them Guilty Actors art and part of all or one or other, of the Crimes Particularly before mentioned, aggravated as before set furth, All which, or that the said Mr James Hogg and Thomas Soutar were Guilty Actors art and part of all, or one or other of the aforesaid Crimes, aggravated as before, Being found proven by the Verdict of the Assize, before his Majesty's Lord Justice General, Justice Clerk, and Lords Commissioners of Justiciary, the said Mr James Hogg and Thomas Soutar ought to be most Severely punished, in a most severe and Examplary Manner, in their Persons and Goods, to the Terrour of others to Committ the like in time comeing And ought further to be Decerned in payment to the said David Haggart of Cairnmuir, the Private Party injured and Complaining, of the Sum of Five hundred pounds Sterling, in Name of Damnages, Assythment, and Expenses of Process.

Pursuers
Charles Areskine Esqr
   his Majestie's Advocate,
Mr. James Graham Junr.,
Mr. Alex^r. Lockhart,
Mr. Charles Maitland,
Mr. Robert Dundass,
Mr. Henry Home, and
Mr. Kenneth McKenzie,
   Advocates

Proloq^{rs}in Defence
Mr. James Graham Senr.,
   and
Mr. Robert Craigie,
   Advocates

The Verdict

(JC 3/22, fo. 358)
The Persons who past upon the Assize of the said Pannells Returned their Verdict
in presence of the said Lords; Whereof the Tenour follows:

Edinburgh 17th July 1738,

   The above Assize haveing Inclosed, did Choise William Alexander Merchant
in Edinburgh to be their Chancelour, and John Haliburton Senior Merchant
there to be their Clerk, and having Considered the Criminal Lybell pursued at the
Instance of David Haggart of Cairnmuir, with Concourse of his Majesty's
Advocat, for his highness Interest, against Mr James Hogg and Thomas Soutar
Pannels, with the Lords Commissioners of Justiciary their Interlocutor
thereupon, and Depositions of the Witnesses adducing for proveing thereof,
They (by plurality of voices) Found, That the Crime of Subornation, or
Endeavouring to Suborne People to be Witnesses, as Lybelled against the
Pannell Mr James Hogg, Proven in Sundry Facts, Each Fact only by one Single
Witness; As to Thomas Soutar the other Pannell, They Found him Art and Part
in the said Subornation. In Witness whereof, their said Chancellour and Clerk
have Subscribed these presents in their Names, place, day, Month and Year of
God before written. (Signed)

William Alexander Chancellor
J. Haliburton Clerk

After Reading the above Verdict, Mr Hugh Murray procurator for the Pannells
moved to be heard as to the Import of the said Verdict. The said Lords, In
Respect of the above Motion, Superseded pronouncing of Sentence on the said
Verdict, till Friday next at three o'Clock afternoon, In order that the Procurators
of the Pursuers and Pannels by heard thereon; And ordained Parties then to
attend, and Thomas Soutar Pannel to be Carried back to Prison.

Memorials in Haggart and H. M. Advocate v. Hogg and Soutar

364 Intran.

Mr James Hogg, &
Thomas Soutar,
} Pannels

Indicted and Accused as in the former Sederunts.

Upon a Motion by Mr Alexander Lockhart Procurator for David Haggart, Pursuer, That there was some Variation in Ingrossing the Verdict of the Assize in the Record from the principall Verdict; and Craved that the Seals thereof might be opened.[1]

365 The saids Lords ordained the said principall Verdict to be opened, and Compared with the Record; which being accordingly done in open Court; and the said Verdict being Verbatim Ingrossed without any Variation, the saids Lords Ordained the same to be again Sealled up. (Signed) And^r. Fletcher I.P.D.

The saids Lords Continued advising the Verdict of Assize returned against Mr James Hogg and Thomas Soutar, till the Morrow Eight days being the ffirst day of August next; and Ordained the Proloquitors for David Haggart Pursuer, and the Proloquitors for the Pannels, to give in Memorials to the Clerk of Court, on Friday next, on the Import of the said Verdict.

366   Memorialls for

David Haggart of Cairnmuir, with
Concourse of his Majesty's Advocat,
Pursuer,

Against

Mr James Hogg, Minister of the
Gospell at Caputh, and Thomas
Soutar, Pannels.

The said David Haggart, having been Imprisoned upon Suspicion of Burning the Manse of Caputh, then in the possession of the said Mr James Hogg, suffered a very Severe and tedious Confinement, and was also put to Extraordinary Charges, in Endeavouring, when brought to Trial, to Defend himself against such false Accusation; But so it fell out that the said David Haggart was never put upon Triall, but the Dyet was simply Deserted[2] against him, and he set at Liberty.

367 Mr Haggart who was a Landed Man of Substance, and of Character hitherto unquestioned, having made a Discovery, that these Hardships were brought upon him by the Malice and Wickedness of Persons that bore him no good Will, and particularly of the Pannels, Did, with Concourse of his Majestie's Advocat, raise Criminal Letters against the Pannels, and Charged them with the Crimes of Endeavouring to Bribe, Corrupt, and Suborne Persons, to bear false Evidence against him as the Burner of the Manse of Caputh, and of Solliciting and Enticing them, by Promises of Rewards and Sums of Money, to say and swear that he was in prison upon Suspicion of the said Crime.

And for making out this generall Charge of Suborning, the Lybell
368 particularly Condescends upon Circumstances thereof, upon time and place when and where the pannels, and particularly the Said Mr. James Hogg, did so Sollicite and Endeavour to Corrupt a variety of Persons falsely to accuse him as guilty of the Crime of Burning the Said Manse; And the whole Circumstances of

[1] See Act of 1672, c. 40, Rule 9; Hume, *Commentaries*, ii, 411; Willock, *Jury*, 212f. [CG]
[2] See *MacLaurin*, no. 94 for the details; on the law, see Hume, *Commentaries*, ii, 267. [CG]

Suborning relate to the Burning of the Manse, Except one Single Article of the
Lybell, which Charges Mr. Hogg with haveing Sollicited one person to Conceall
the Truth, when he should be called as a Witness, in a Process raised at Mr.
Haggart's Instance against the Pannell Mr. Hogg, for having falsely defamed him
as guilty of Incest.

   For this Charge of Subornation, the Pannells haveing been Remitted to the
Knowledge of an Assize, in whose presence a proof was led by the Depositions of
369 a great many Witnesses, a Detaill of which it was needless to enter into, because it
was printed at large, and hereto subjoined.

   After adduceing of the Witnesses and hearing of the Proof, the Jury as usual
having been Inclosed, did thereafter Returne to the Court the following Verdict,
viz., "They by plurality of voices[3], Find the Crime of Subornation, or
Endeavouring to Suborn people to be Witnesses, as Lybelled against the Pannell
Mr Hogg, Proven in sundry Facts, each Fact only by one Single Witness; As to
Thomas Soutar the other pannell, wee Find him art and part[4] in the said
Subornation."

   Their Lordships having been pleased, to allow both the Pursuer and pannels
to be heard by their Councill upon the Import of this Verdict, were thereafter
pleased to allow each Party to give in a Memorial to the Court;[5] for a
consequence of which, this was offered upon the part of the Pursuer.
370   The Points then arising from this Verdict, as the Pursuer humbly
apprehended and was advised, Resolved into these two, *Primo*, whether this is a
Generall Verdict upon the Lybell, leaving no Latitude to the Court, other than to
pronounce such sentence, and Inflict such Punishment upon the Pannels, as the
Law directs against Suborners of Witnesses; or *Secundo*, Whether this is a Special
Matter, leaving it to the Court to Determine what arises in Law from the Special
Matter so found by the Jury.

   For other than two such Verdicts, viz., Either General or Special, the Pursuer
humbly apprehended, there were none known in the Law of this or any other
Country.[6]

   And, with Submission, the Pursuer humbly apprehended the Verdict before
371 Recited to be of the First kind, to wit, a Generall Verdict dicisive of the Lybell.
For, as a Jury are the Sole and ultimate Judges of Evidence, and by the Law of
this Country Subject to no Controul, It was noways Materiall whatsoever the
Means were that Induced the Jury so to find, Neither are they bound to Express
them; and though they should, it can make no Alteration, even though perhaps
those Means of Proof might not have given Satisfaction to others, the Jury as said
is being the Sole Judges of Evidence, accountable to none but to God and their
own Consciences.

   And therefore, as they have found the Subornation as Lybelled, proven in

[3] See Willock, *Jury*, pp. 226ff. [CG]
[4] See Balfour, *Practicks*, 2 ed., c. XIX; Hope, *Major Practicks*, VIII, 4, 9; Hume, *Commentaries*, ii,
   218ff.; Macdonald, *Criminal Law* (5th ed., 1948), p. 4. [CG]
[5] This seems to imply oral argument preceding submission of written memorials; in places, the style
   of the latter appears to be influenced by oral rhetoric. That impression is supported by the form of
   the report in MacLaurin, no. 95. [BSJ]. Cf. Willock, *Jury*, p. 219 on oral and written debate
   concerning 'informations'. [CG]
[6] On the classification of verdicts as general or special, see Hume, *Commentaries*, ii, 421f.; Willock,
   Jury, ch. X. [CG]

Sundry Facts, it was noways Material that they have Expressed in their Verdict, as the Cause of their so finding, that each Fact was only proven by one Witness.

372   Because, whether a Lybell be proven by one Witness, or by no Witness, by many Witnesses, or by Facts, Circumstances, and Presumptions, or by Consciousness and private Knowledge; If the Jury think fit to proceed upon such Evidence, and find a Lybell referred to their Inquest proven; Such, with Submission is a General Verdict, and makes an End of the Matter.

There was another Circumstance that seemed highly material, to Denote this to be a General Verdict and not a Special one; For that the Jury, in their above recited Verdict, Find Thomas Soutar the other Pannell art and part in the said Subornation.

And as the Lybell Charges none other Guilty of this Subornation, but Mr. Hogg and Thomas Soutar, and as the Jury have found Soutar not a Principall but an Accessory; Therefore it must follow, that Mr. Hogg is found the Principal Suborner; and Thomas Soutar being an Accessory or art and part in the said Subornation, must mean, that Soutar was art and part in the Subornation found

373 proven against Mr. Hogg: So that the Words in the Verdict, "the said Subornation", must mean, that Subornation wherein Mr. Hogg was principal; Fore where there are no Principals, there can be no Accessories.[7]

And upon these Considerations, the Pursuer humbly submitted to the Court Whether the above recited Verdicts is not Generall, and Decisive of the Lybell referred to the Inquest of the Jury?

For indeed, had the Jury meant a Special Verdict, they could not find the Subornation as Lybelled proven in Sundry Facts, but must have found the Special Facts laid in the Lybell, leaving it to the Courts to Judge, How far those Facts, Returned by them as proven, did amount to the Crimes charged in the

374 Lybell against the Pannels; Because such ffinding, and such only, is of the Nature of a Speciall Verdict.

The next point, with Submission, under their Lordships Consideration might be, Whether, if in Case it should not be found, That the above Verdict is a General Verdict decisive of the Lybell; the Jury's finding Sundry Facts of the Subornation lybelled, each of them proven by one Single Witness only, is such a Verdict as whereon their Lordships ought to pronounce Sentence against the Pannels, and Inflict such Punishment upon them as the Law directs against Suborners of Witnesses?

And the Consideration of this Matter would resolve into this point of Law, Whether in a Lybell, charging a Crime capable of and arising from Reiterated Acts, all tending to the Same End,[8] as of the Same specifick kind, the Proof of one

---

[7] See Balfour, *Practicks*, 549; Hume, *Commentaries*, 279; Gordon, *Criminal Law* (2nd ed., 1978), 137. Cf. Hope, *Major Practicks*, II, 10, 5 & 7; *Regiam Majestatem* IV, 26 (Stair Society, 1947), p. 370f. [CG]

[8] Cf. Cravetta, *Tractatus* 4.4.11: *ideo licet testes deponant de diversis actibus, tamen quia tales actus tendunt ad eundem finem, et ad probationem unius generis, non repelluntur testes, tanquam singulares* ... Although the phrase 'tendunt ad eundem finem' could be used (as in the example of treason) of the specific purpose which gave the course of conduct its unity, it could also be used more generally, of evidence that points in the same probative direction (e.g. Mascardi, *De Prob.* I. concl. 379 nu. 14; Farinatius *De testibus* 3.7.64.6, of a witness and a confession to the same fact; Cravetta, *Consiliorum* 73:34, of witnesses who vary on matters not regarded as *de substantia*, but nevertheless

Act by one Witness, and of another Act by another Witness; or indeed, as in this
375 case, the Proof of a great many Acts by a great many Witnesses, be Legal Proof
Sufficient for Conviction of a Pannell?

And how far such was the Case, the Prosecutor humbly Submitted to their
Lordships, upon the following Considerations.

That where a Crime is Charged of a General Nature, Capable of Reiterated
Acts, every Act laid as tending to the same End, is Qualification and
Circumstance of the General Charge; And, therefore, the particular Circum-
stances may well be conjoined to make out the general Charge, as well as in the
Case of other Circumstantiate Evidence.[9]

And it was hardly hitherto ever been made a Doubt, but that in
Circumstantiate Evidence, one Witness to one Circumstance, and one to
another, may be Conjoined to make good Legal Proof; Whereof Instances
376 occurred every day; Nor has it ever been maintained with any Solid Reason, That
the Law requires two Witnesses to the Proof of each Circumstance.

A very strong Instance of this occurrs from the Law of England, and which
now[10] was the Law of this Country, in the Case of Treason, which being a Crime
of the highest Consequence, and Inferring the Severest Penaltys; Forfaulture of
Life, Lands, and Goods, may be Supposed to require the Strongest Proof.

And in the Case of that Crime, which is generally charged against the
Offenders as Compassing and Imagining the Death of the King;[11] This being a
Crime of a Generall Nature, every ouvert Act tending that way is Charged as a
Circumstance of Guilt, and yet one Circumstance proven by one Witness, and
other Circumstances by another, is held to be good Legal Proof.

---

in agreement *ad eundem finem*). The more technical meaning of *ad eundem finem* would be
appropriate in the present context, even though it was not normally combined with (the alternative
model of) reiterable acts.

[9] Haggart's argument places considerable emphasis on the analysis of the evidence as falling within
the legitimate bounds of circumstantial evidence. There is really one charge — the general one of
which suborning witnesses to convict Haggart of fire-raising — and the several incidents involving
the different witnesses are merely circumstances of it. But the parallel is purely formal. In cases of
'other circumstantiate evidence' the circumstances are all evidence of one temporally-specific fact,
not parts of a continuing course of conduct (any part of which, if sufficiently evidenced, could have
been charged). This difference was well recognised by the canonists, and figured prominently in
Stair's account of the *Milntoun* divorce case, where it was conceded for Whitefoord that witnesses
to distinct circumstances of the same offence could be combined but denied that witnesses to
separate acts of adultery could be similarly treated: see Stair's *Decisions* (1683), i, 453; reproduced
almost verbatim in (1667) Mor. 12101; further [1977] *Acta Juridica* 44. After *Milntoun*, Mackenzie
still insisted on the conceptual distinction, to the embarrassment of the present memorial (*infra*,
385 at n.35). For Hogg's rebuttal, see 425-7 *infra*.

[10] Treason Act 1708, 7 Anne c. 21. Hume, *Commentaries*, i, 369f. notes that a general charge could
sometimes be used in the law of treason: 'The crime of treason also may serve as a farther
illustration: I mean those species of it that consist in rising in arms, or other acts of open and
continued hostility, which are going on publicly in different places, from day to day; and from all of
which proceedings, taken in conjunction, the general charge of levying war, or compassing the
King's death, is inferred, and illustrates this by reference to the last treason trial 'according to the
forms of the law of Scotland'. But the evidence in relation to each of the acts here joined is not
discussed. [BSJ]

For the Old Scots law of treason, see *Regiam Majestatem* (Stair Society, 1947), IV, 1, based on
Glanvill 14, followed by Balfour, *Practicks* 505f.; see also Hope, *Major Practicks*, VIII, 14. [CG]

[11] On the history of which see Jackson, *Essays in Jewish and Comparative Legal History* (1975), pp.
219-22.

377   As may appear from the State Trials, in the Case of Sir William Parkins[12] tryed, anno 1695, for the Assassination Plot; where he Complained to Lord Chief Justice Holt, that he could not be Convicted of the Crime, because that of two ouvert Acts, each was but proven by one Single Witness.

And yet that learned and distinguished Judge, of all others known to be the greatest Maintainer of the Rights and Libertys of the Subject,[13] and the most free from Court Influence, which sometimes is known to take place where political Crimes are charged, told Sir William upon his Triall, That he was greatly mistaken, for that one Witness to one Circumstance and one to another, was good Legal Proof of the Crime; and when Sir William made the Same Objection
378 in Arrest of Judgement, neither the Lord Chief Justice, or any other of the Judges would so much as Listen to him.

And with Submission, it was no Answer at all, that was offered to this by the Councill for the Pannels, viz. That by the Law of England, one Witness was good Proof; for though by the way it was believed that Position was not generally true,[14] Yet however it was, it could not touch the present Instance, for by the Several Statutes[15] antecedent to that Triall, viz. of Edward 6th and Ch: 2^d It is declared, That no Person shall be Convicted of Treason, but upon Evidence of two Witnesses; and it was upon those Statutes that Sir William Parkins made the Objection, and the Answer made to him by the Court was, That one Witness to one ouvert Act; and one to another, was good Proof within the Description of
379 those statutes; and upon Such Proof Sir William was Condemned of Treason.

And by the Seventh of William, Chap. 3^d, Anno 1696, It is now Statuted, That in the Same Species of Treason, one Witness to one ouvert Act, and one to another Shall be good Legal Proof; and such last recited Statute is only held to be Declaratory of what was the Law before.[16]

[12] 13 State Trials [St. Tr.], 63, 131. Other English treason trials in which the issue arose are: *Lilbourne* (1649) 4 St. Tr. 1269, 1401; *Love* (1651) 5 St. Tr. 43, 138-44; *Regicides* (1660) 5 St. Tr. 947, 977, Kelyng 9 (84 E.R. 1057); *Stafford* (1680) 7 St. Tr. 1293, 1527; *Colledge* (1681) 8 St. Tr. 549, 620; *Vaughan* (1696) 13 St. Tr. 486, 535.

[13] Sir John Holt (1642-1710). His libertarian reputation may derive from his resignation in 1687 as Recorder of London in order to avoid passing the death sentence on a prisoner convicted at the Old Bailey of desertion, together with cases like *Ashby* v. *White* (1702) 1 Salk 19, *Somersett's Case* 20 St. Tr. 23, *Smith* v. *Brown & Cooper* 2 Salk 666, *Smith* v. *Gould* 2 Salk 666, *Chamberlain* v. *Harvey* 1 Ld. Raym. 146. [CG]

[14] The reference here be to medieval sources, influenced by the romano-canonical tradition, e.g. *Glanvill* 2.21; *Bracton* f.354b, 410; *Fleta*, ed. Richardson and Sayles (Selden Society, 1955) 2.63. Despite Wigmore's strong denial, the view that early English law accepted the principle *unus testis nullus testis* (see J. W. Salmond, *Essays in Jurisprudence and Legal History*, 1891, p. 28) has survived. See L. M. Hill, 'The Two-Witness Rule in English Treason Trials', *American Journal of Legal History* 12 (1968), 95ff.

[15] 1 *Edw. VI* c.12, s.22. 5-6 *Edw. VI* c.11, s.12. There long remained doubt as to whether the two witness requirement had been repealed by 1 & 2 *P. and M*. c.10, s.7. See Lord Keble in *Lilbourne*'s case (*supra*, n.17); L. C. J. Bridgeman in *Tong, Philips and Stubbs* (1662) Kelyng 18, 84 E.R. 1062. But by *Love*'s case, Lord Keble accepted the need for two witnesses. And this was the view that prevailed. See e.g. Dr. Oldish in *Vaughan*'s case 13 St. Tr. 485, 534; Foster's Discourse of High Treason, ch.3 s.8, at *Reports of Crown Cases* (1792, 3 ed.), pp. 233ff.

[16] 7 & 8 *Will. III* c.3, s.2. For the limitation against the use of witnesses to 'two or more distinct Treasons of divers Heads or Kinds', see s.4. The formulation of s.2, allowing the witnesses to be 'either both of them to the same overt act, or one of them to one, and the other of them to another overt act of the same Treason', in fact echoes that of L. C. J. North in *Stafford*'s case (1680) 7 St. Tr. 1293, 1527. See also L. C. B. Montague and Mr. J. Windham in the same case, and L. C. J. North in *Colledge*'s case (1681) 8 St. Tr. 549, 620, for similar formulations.

Another Instance of what the pursuer here maintained, may be found in the Codex Fabrianus,[17] where the Author was first President of the Senate of Savoy, and Collects the Determinations of that Synod, and Lib. 6 Tit. 2 De Furtis, Defin. 5. treating how Theft may be proven in general, he has these words, "Etsi Furtum, tunc ut Ille, a Sempronio factum esse, probare non potest per Testes 380 Singulares; Si tamen ex plurium Testationibus appareat de diversis Furtis ab eo admissis, non eo minus probatum erit Furtum in genere, ut Concludi possit Sempronium Furem esse; Cujus rei Effectus ille erit, ut Sempronius tanquam Fur Condemnari debeat ad Poenam, non tamen, quod mirum est, ad Rerum quae furto subtractas dicentur Restitutionem.[18] And marks, that the Synod did so Decide. And a little lower down, in his Annotations, he has these words, Nihil enim vetit probare Furtum in genere, quamvis in Specie probare non possis, nimirum cum Testes Singulares tendunt ad eundem finem, et locuntur de Actu Rei reiterabili.[19]

And though in the Case above Collected by him, the Learned President seems to wonder why there was no decree for Restitution, the Reason seemed to the 381 That though the Theft in Generall was proven, yet as no particular Act of Abstraction was proven, So the Party could have no Restitution.

Another Instance where Proof if Conjoined, may be found in Gaill, Observ. pract:[20] Lib. 2. Observ. 66 in these Words: Et regulariter Testes singulares plenam fidem faciunt, quando aliquod in genere probandum est; puta Titium esse Insanium aut furiosum; Due licet singulares sint respectu Actuum, tamen si ratione finis conveniant, integre probant; Secus, Si Super Speciali Actu recepti sint; quia tunc Disparitas Singularitatem inducit, et per Consequens Testes tanquam singulares non probant.[21]

There is a good and Solid Distinction mentioned by the Doctors, viz. That Singular Testimonies may be Conjoined, when Time and place is not of the 382 Substance of the Crime; whereof Carpsovius,[22] Proces. Iuris, Tit. 13. Art. 3 N. 85

[17] A private compilation by Antonius Faber (1557-1624), 1610. See further *Novissimo Digesto Italiano III*, 'Codex Fabrianus'.

[18] 'Even if it is not possible to prove by singular witnesses that a particular theft was committed by Sempronius, if nevertheless it should appear from the evidence of several people that different thefts were committed by him, theft *in genere* will still thereby be proved, so as to lead to the inference that Sempronius is a thief. The effect of this will be that Sempronius ought to be condemned to punishment as a thief, but not remarkably to restitution of the property said to have been stolen by him.' The logic is that we know Sempronius to 'be' a thief (and thus punishable) but there is no evidence in relation to any one act of theft sufficient to prove that particular act against him, and thus to require restitution of property — as the memorial goes on to argue.

[19] 'For nothing prevents the proof of theft *in genere*, even though you cannot prove it *in specie*, especially when the singular witnesses point in the same direction (lit: 'tend to the same end') and speak to the commission of a repeatable act. Here an earlier authority has been found for Haggart's formulation in terms of 'Reiterated Acts, all tending to the Same End' (374; and see n.8 *supra*).

[20] Andreas von Gaill, 1526-87, Germany. The *Observationes Practicae* were published in 2 vols. in 1663 in Amsterdam. The passage here quoted, lib.2, obs.66, nus.11-12, comes from a discussion of proof of a hunting servitude!

[21] 'And singular witnesses commonly inspire full confidence, when something is to proved *in genere*, for example that Titius is insane or raging. In such cases although the witnesses are singular with respect to (particular) acts, nevertheless if they agree as to the end (conclusion), they fully prove it. The matter is different if the witnesses are admitted to prove some particular act. For then their disagreement involves *singularitas*, and as singular witnesses they consquently fail to prove.'

[22] Benedictus Carpzovius, c. 1595-1666, Germany, author of *Definitiones forenses seu Iurisprudentia forensis Romano Saxonica ad constitutiones Saxonicas* (Frankfurt, 1638) and other works. See further Coing, *Handbuch der Quellen und Literatur der neueren Europäischen Privatrechtsgeschichte* (München: C. H. Beck, 1977), vol. II/1, pp. 563, 577.

Etsi Testes Singulares, de diversis Locis ac Temporibus deponentes, non quidem semiplene probent, quando Locus et Tempus est de Substantia Negotii ac rei in Judicio propositis; aliter tamen res se habet in Probatione rei, ubi nec Locus nec Tempus est de Substantia, ut dicimus Supra,[23] &c. And then goes on to give some Instances.[24]

And indeed a Multitude of Instances of this kind might be given from the Doctors; and particularly from Aginon Craveta,[25] in his Treatise De Antiquitatibus Temporum, Part. 4, in that Chapter which treats of Singular, Obstative, Cumulative, and Diversiculative Proof,[26] and the Effects of it; his words are too long to be Inserted; but the whole Chapter is an Elegant Treatise 83 upon that Subject: And in the present Case, it could not be said, That Time or place is of the Essence of the Crime; for it was the same thing; and made no Alteration, at what Time or place the Pannels might have Suborned the Witnesses; The Crime was the Same, and so according to the opinions before given, the Singular Testimonies upon the different Acts at different times and places may be Conjoined.[27]

And here the Learned Council for the Pannells make a great Outcry, and Say, that one Witness upon the Single Acts cannot be received or Conjoined; Because being Single, he may venture to Depone Things, which he would not have done had another Witness been Conjoined with him upon the particular Act; for fear of being Redargued.

But here they seemed to have forgot, That the Same Objection would strick 84 against Singular Adminiculative Witnesses in Circumstantiate Proof, where one Single Witness is received to prove one Circumstance, and another Single one to prove another; And yet no Man ever denied, but that such Single Testimonies might be Conjoined to make out a Proof.[28]

The truth is, the Law must not reject Testimony because there is a possibility of its being otherways; or else no proof could ever be Sustained, the highest Degree of Evidence being no more than Moral Probability; for such is the fallible Nature of Human Affairs, that they do not admitt of Demonstrative Certaintys.

---

[23] 'Although singular witnesses testifying to different places and times do not even provide half proof when time and place are central to the business and matter before the court, nevertheless the matter is different as regards proof of something where neither place nor time are central, as we say above.'

[24] In fact, the examples given are proof of *possessio, iurisdictio* and *aditio haereditatis* — all involving continuing states of affairs, and none of them relevant to proof of crime. Small wonder that the memorial omitted to specify them.

[25] D. Aymo Cravetta, 1504-69, Italy, author of *Consiliorum sive Responsorum* (Frankfurt, 1572); *Tractatus de antiquitatibus temporum* (Frankfurt, 1572). See further *Novissimo Digesto Italiano IV*, 1078.

[26] Such a threefold classification was not confined to Cravetta. See also Farinatius, *De Testibus* 3.7.64.3-4, who tells is that this (as opposed to a rival twofold classification) was the more generally held view. This, of course, was the source of Mackenzie's classification: *Matters Criminal*, II.26.14. At II.24, Mackenzie observes: 'Probation is so fully treated of by the Civilians, and the Cannonists, and we do differ so little from them, that I shall only treat of it here in relation to our own Law.'

[27] Such a view would not have appealed to Farinatius, according to whom time and place are presumed to be *de substantia*, failing special circumstances; thus *diversitas loci vel temporis* was regarded as the prime cause of *singularitas*: *De testibus* 3.7.64. 72, 317-19.

[28] 'Adminiculative' also derives from the canonist classification (*supra* n.26), the unobjectionable form of *singularitas* being termed *adminiculativa* (sometimes, *cumulativa*). But the canonists used this more commonly to refer to evidence resulting from different kinds of proof, e.g. *unus ex visu, unus ex auditu*: Farinatius, *De testibus* 3.7.64. 6, 113.

Neither is this Matter, of Singular Testimonies being Conjoined as to Reiterable Acts tending to the Same End, without Foundation from our own Law; as is plain from Sir George Mackenzie, Title Probation by Witnesses, where 385 he Cites Cases where the Lords found, in the Proof of the Crime of Adultery, two Witnesses to two different Acts were Conjoined to make full Proof of the Crime.[29]

He does indeed subjoine his own Opinion, That such Doctrine would be hard in Criminal Cases; But then, with Reverence, his Opinion did not seem to quadrate right, with what he had writt just a Paragraph or two before, upon the Proof of Crimes by Circumstances, where he admitts, That each Circumstance may be proved by a Single Witness.[30]

The Council for the Pannels upon this head entered upon Declamations, and in common place argued Scripture, where it is Said, Out of the Mouth of two or three Witnesses every Man must be Condemned.[31]

But this was no more but a Rant, and is not the only Instance in this Case, 386 where things Sacred have been Misapplied; For though the Scripture Says what is above Recited, yet it is nowhere Said, That each Circumstance of the Guilt must be proved by two Witnesses; and Indeed, it was humbly thought, That the Resorting to Scripture in this Case was without Foundation; For it was believed, that those Sacred Writings made no Alteration in the Nature of Moral Evidence, but left it just as it found it, namely, to the Consciences and Convictions of Mankind.[32] Some Instances also may be given from the Books of Adjournall, where upon a Verdict returned finding Facts proven but by one Single Witness, without any other to Conjoine with him, or without any Cumulative Circumstance, their Lordships have Condemned even to very Severe Punishment.

Such was the Case of Bisset, who being, in June 1705, arraigned for poisoning 387 his wife, upon a Verdict returned finding the Lybell proven against him by one Witness, Their Lordships Condemned him to be Scourged, Pillory'd and Banished to the East or West Indies; And as the Verdict found, so indeed there was not one Title of Proof against him, but one Single Witness, and who appears not to have been very Clear that the Dose was by him given, knowing it to be poison; And as to the Cumulative Probation found in the Verdicts, It related not to him, but to the other Pannel Joan Currier.[33]

---

[29] See Introduction regarding the use here of Mackenzie's treatment of *Milntoun*; see also n.50 *infra*. The memorial notes that Mackenzie cites 'Cases'. But the second case which he cites was easily distinguished from *Milntoun*; 'For the Lord's thought, that if one witness should peep through a hole, and see Adultery committed, and thereafter another witness should peep in, and see the Adultery likewise committed, yet they were *contestes*, and did prove sufficiently, *etiam ad poenam mortis infligendam*, as was found in the probation of Adultery, led against *George Swintoun*: but in my opinion this case differs from the former, for in *George Swintouns* case, both the witnesses concurred in one Act, but they did not so in the case of *George Maxwel . . .*' — *Matters Criminal*, II.26.14. But at I.17.7 Mackenzie gives the following account of the evidence in Swintoun's case: 'Nothing was proved, but that the Parties were alone, and that the witnesses heard them in Bed together, and the Bed shake.'

[30] On the weakness of this argument, see n.9 *supra*.

[31] *Deuteronomy* 17:6, 19:15.

[32] The argument is in line with Stair's conception of the relationship between biblical 'judicial' law and the 'moral law': *Institutions* I.1.3, I.1.9. See further Jackson [1977] J.R. 142-3.

[33] See Book of Adjournal for Nov. 13 1699 — July 1 1706, pp. 821, 856. The verdict records that the charge was 'proven by one Witness . . . and with a cumulative probation'. The opposing memorial replies to this at 404-6, *infra*.

Another Instance is of Gabriel Clark, arraigned that same Month of June 1705, for Falsifying the Coin, and uttering thereof, where upon a Verdict returned, finding the Uttering of the false Coin proven against him by one Witness, their Lordships Scourged, pillory'd, and Banished him to the Indies; And in this Case the Jury found no other Proof against him but this Single Witness; for as to that part of the Verdict that finds, That the Purse contained false Coin, proved by two Witnesses, it is quite out of the Case, and could not affect the Pannell, because it was not found that Such Purse was his.[34]

But besides the Instances and Authoritys given, the Nature of the present Case speaks Stronger than any of them; That where there is an occult Crime of this Nature, Capable of Reiterated Acts, If one Witness to each Act is not Sufficient, the Crime shall never be proved; for if indeed two Witnesses could have been had to each Act of Suborning, the Pursuer would be of opinion that Mr. Hogg should be Assoilzied, though not for want of Proof, but for Fatuity, or as being non Compos.

Could it be Supposed That in the Crime of Defamation where those Matters are generally transacted by Whispers, If the Defamer shall go through a hundred different People, one only at a time, and propagate things defamatory of his Neighbour, and all those Witnesses, deponing upon the Singular and reiterated Acts, could not be Conjoined to make full Proof of Defamation?[35] And the same may be said of Blasphemy, where a Person should be found to have Blasphem'd the Name of God before a hundred Different People, but before one only at a time.[36]

The Denying that such Proofs could be Conjoined seems so absurd in itself, and Contradictory to Good Reason, that it was humbly thought, it sufficiently refutes itself.

The Pannels were pleased to Object, That the Verdict, finding the Lybell proven in Sundry Facts, was uncertaine; Because, as the Lybell charges different Crimes, It could not be known wherein those facts consisted.

But this seemed to be but a Slight Objection, because in the Lybell there is but one Single Fact Charged touching the Incest, and even that not proven; And therefore, the Sundry Facts in the Verdict cannot relate to it, because Sundry will not apply to a Single Fact: Though in truth it was not very Materiall, Whether the Subornation found proven in the Verdict, related to the Incest or the Fire-raising; In either Case it was a Crime, and so deserved Punishment.

But indeed the Verdict must relate to the Suborning of Witnesses, to accuse the pursuer falsely of the Burning of the Manse, both for the Reason already assigned, and because Soutar is only Charged with the Subornation as to the Fire-raising; and he being found Art and part of the Said Subornation, must

---

[34] Book of Adjournal for Nov. 13 1699 — July 1 1706, pp. 808, 828-9. The opposing memorial replies at 403-4. It may be noted that the offences of both Bisset and Clark were capital, but in fact they were sentenced to transportation — an 'arbitrary' punishment, as the memorial for Hogg suggests. See further *infra*, n.53.

[35] *Diffamatio* was one of the cases commonly accepted as admitting *testes singulares*. See Farinatius, *De testibus* 3.7.64. 223, 279.

[36] Farinatius, *op. cit.*, 287-9, accepts proof by *testes singulares* of *consuetudo blasphemandi*, but denies that the effect of this is the infliction of punishment. See also the passage from Julius Clarus quoted in Hogg's memorial, *infra* at 410-11.

391 show, that the Subornation meant in the Verdict was as to the Fire-raising only.[37]

The Council for the Pannels made a great Rant in this Case, of the Danger of Conjoining Single Testimonys, Because in the present Case there was no Corpus Deliciti[38] proven. But pray, What was that to the purpose? How many Cases are there, where the Nature of the thing does not admitt of a Corpus delicti? Such is the Case of every Crime, where the Nature of it Consists in a Malevolent Intention, expressed by ouvert Acts which have not attained their Execution; and such is the present Case, and which must be evidently highly Criminal, though the learned Council for the Pannels did, contrary to all Reason, maintain that it was not, only because the Witnesses, endeavoured to be practised upon, had the

392 Virtue to Resist, and to prevent the Wickedness being carried to Execution.

And the Pursuer putt it to the Pannels, to Instance where the Corpus delicti is in Blasphemy, Defamation, and a hundred Instances that may be figured; More especially in the present Case, where the Essence of the Crime consists in an Attempt, and in all Cases, as Lawiers say, quorum nulla solent remanere vestigia: Or where is the Corpus Delicti in Treason, as in the Case before recited, and where the Conspirators do not attain to their End? Or if they do attain to their End of Dethroning the King, 'tis generally said, they cease to be Traitors, and turn the Cannon of the Law the other way. The learned Councill for the pannels were pleased Charitably to Say, That the Charge given by the pursuers Councill to the Jury, might have been the Cause that misled them in the Method of their Verdict.

393 But this they apprehended was extremely Injurious: For though, as was their Duty, they Charged the Jury to find the Matter Special in case of Dubiety, yet they did noways Charge them, to find the Subornation as lyoelled proven, and then to Subjoin to their Verdict the Grounds of Evidence upon which they proceeded, That would have been utterly absurd and useless.[39]

The Pursuer in this Case was extremely sorry, that he has had occasion to arraigne so closely a Minister of the Gospell, a Sacred Character for which he had Great Regard; But if persons will be so abandoned as to prostitute that Sacred Character they bear, or if Wolves shall appear in Sheep or Sheepherds Cloathing, it is high time, to look out that the Flock be not devoured.

394 The Pursuer might make some Observations upon the aggravating Nature of this Case; But as he is an Enemy to Invective, as well as Stranger to Rhetorical Declamation, which ought never to be used in Cases of this kind, where a Person stands arraigned of a Crime; because at such time, in not at any, it is unfair to Speak or write to Passions, but only to the Understanding, that things may be Cooly and wisely weighed, and not precipitated and Inflamed with heat and Passion; And therefore the Pursuer should humbly Submit the Case to their Lordships; but with this single Observation,

[37] On the importance of this argument, see the Introduction.
[38] The term appears to refer not to property which is the subject of an offence but to proof of specific acts which constitute the offence in question. Cf. its use in the opposing memorial, *infra* at 403, 406. The wide usage was taken from the learned law.
[39] See the Introduction. The memorial here seeks to avoid the charge that it was the pursuer's own counsel who had induced the jury to render a verdict which combined the formal features of a special verdict (appropriate in cases of doubt, merely stating their view of the evidence) and a general verdict (appropriate to state a conclusion, but without appending its grounds).

That as he had Suffered great hardships and severe Imprisonment, being put to great Charges, heavier than he was able to bear, had been brought upon the Brink of Ruin, and under the nearest approach of Loseing his Life innocently; So there may be now some appearance from whence in a great measure these Hardships have proceeded; and if others may have now fallen into that Pitt which they have digged for him, though not so deep as he must have fallen, they have the Malice of their own Hearts only to blame.

And now it remained only to be Noticed, that this Memorial has drawn out to a greater length than was Intended; And for which the Pursuer humbly askt the fforgiveness of the Court.[40]

Memorial for Mr. James Hogg,
Minister at Caputh,

Against

David Haggart of Cairnmuir,
and his Majesty's Advocat.

A Criminal Lybell was brought at the Instance of Cairnmuir, against Mr. James Hogg, which in the Major Proposition sets forth a Variety of Crimes, and in the Minor[41] Subsumes, "That Mr. Hogg was Guilty Art and part of every one of the Crimes Lybelled in the Major Proposition"; And Qualifies the Same, first in General, tnat Mr. Hogg did Endeavour to Corrupt Witnesses, to accuse Cairnmuir of burning Mr. Hogg's Manse, or of the Crime of Incest, or to Deny the Truth when called as Witnesses in a Proof of Scandall at Cairnmuir's Instance against Mr. Hogg.[42] And the Subsumption further Contains the particular Acts charged against Mr. Hogg, of his having Endeavoured, at the times and places lybelled, to Suborn particular persons or Say or Swear the particulars Lybelled.

That this Lybell was found Relevant, and Mr. Hogg remitted to the knowledge of an Inquest; and the Proof having been adduced, the Jury Returned the following Verdict, viz. By Plurality of Voices ffinds "That the Crime of Subornation, or Endeavouring to Suborn people to be Witnesses, as Lybelled against the Pannel Mr. James Hogg, Proven in Sundry Facts, each ffact only by one Single Witness."

And the Procurators for the Pannell and for the Prosecutor haveing been heard before the Court, upon this Question, Whether a Sentence Condemnatory against Mr. Hogg could pass upon this Verdict? Memorials were directed to be given in; And in the ffirst place, It was observed for Mr. Hogg, That as the Verdict

---

[40] The last four paragraphs read very much like *oral* rhetoric. Perhaps it was based on a speech earlier in the proceedings. But this is unlikely to have been at the oral argument which seems to have followed (immediately) on the jury's rendering its verdict (see 369, *supra*).

[41] On major and minor propositions, see Macdonald, *Criminal Law* (5th ed., 1948), 287ff.; Hume, *Commentaries*, ii, 155; J. Irvine Smith in *Introduction to Scottish Legal History* (Stair Society, 1958), 438. [CG]

[42] On such proceedings, before the Commissary in the Consistory court, see Balfour, *Practicks*, 655ff.; Hume, *Lectures*, III, 153 and V, 282; Erskine, *Institutes*, I.v.30, IV.iv.80-1; G. J. Bell, *Principles of the Law of Scotland* (10th ed. 1899), §2043; G. Donaldson in *Introduction to Scottish Legal History* (Stair Society, 1958), 363ff.; D. M. Walker, *Delict* (2nd ed., 1981), 729. [CG]

was Entered upon Record, So that the Jury could not be again Inclosed to Explain their Verdict, the Verdict alone could be the Rule of the Judgement to be pronounced by the Courts; If Mr. Hogg was Convicted by the Verdict, he behoved to Submitte; But on the other hand, if he was not thereby Convicted, he
398 behoved to be acquitted, there was no Access to Enquire into the Proof, the Verdict was the only Rule.[43]

And taking the Matter in this view, the Import of the Verdict appeared to be this, That the Majority of the Jury found Sundry of the ffacts of Subornation, or Endeavouring to Suborn Witnesses, lybelled against Mr. Hogg, proven by Single Witnesses to each Fact, but there were no Concurring Witnesses to any one of the Facts lybelled.

And when the Verdict is taken in this view, it was argued for Mr. Hogg First, That it was the Rule of the Law of Scotland,[44] founded on the Divine Law and the Common Law,[45] That a ffact proved only by one Single Witness, was not at all proved; Particularly, by the Text in Deuteronomy Cap. XIX. v. 15. The Words are, "One witness shall not rise up against a Man for any Iniquity, or for any Sin,
399 in any Sin that he Sinneth; at the Mouth of two Witnesses, or at the Mouth of three Witnesses, Shall the Matter be Established." And there are a Variety of other Texts in the Old Testament to the same purpose; And the same thing is repeated in the New Testament, which Demonstrates this to be a Moral Precept, binding under the Gospell as well as under the Law, particularly Matthew XVII. v. 16. John VIII. v. 17. 2 Cor. XIII v. 1 and in a Variety of other Texts.[46]

And that this is the Rule of the Common Law, is expressly laid down in L. 20. §1. De Quaestion. and L. 9. §1 Cod. de Test. The words are, Simili modo Sanximus, ut unius Testimonium nemo Judicum in quaecunque Causa facile pateatur admitti; Et nunc manifeste sancimus, ut unius omnino Testis Responsio non audiatur, etiamsi praeclarae Curiae honore profulgeat.[47]

---

[43] In effect, it is here argued that the verdict was tantamount to a general verdict of acquittal, and that the court could not look behind the jury's verdict at the evidence on which it was supposedly based. The arguments in the memorials are consistent with this principle, in that they debate the legal verdict in relation to it. An apparent exception is the argument for Haggart that the verdict must be taken as referable only to the alleged acts of subornation on the fire-raising charge, but in fact this is based not on the evidence but on the form of the lybel (389-91); similarly with Hogg's response (416).

[44] See Bisset, *Rolment of Courtis* ed. P. J. Hamilton-Grierson (Scottish Texts Society, 1920), I, 200; Balfour, *Practicks*, 373; Stair, *Institutions*, IV.43.1, 2 quoted by D. M. Walker in *Introduction to Scottish Legal History* (Stair Society, 1958), 309. Stair further argues that there must be some special significance in the curious biblical formulation 'two or three' IV.43.3. In fact, that expression results from peculiarities of Biblical Hebrew. See further Jackson, 'Two or Three Witnesses', *Essays in Jewish and Comparative Legal History* (1975), ch.VI.

[45] Here in the sense of *ius commune*, as may be seen from the Justinianic passage quoted *infra*, at n.47.

[46] The adoption of the rule in the New Testament (and contemporary sources) has been the subject of a monograph by H. van Vliet, *No Single Testimony* (Utrecht: Drukkerij Kemink en Zoon, 1958). Its use in *2 Cor.* 13:1 is closer to the present problem than the authors of the memorial realised: see Jackson, '*Testes Singulares* in Early Jewish Law and the New Testament', *Essays in Jewish and Comparative Legal History* (1975), ch.VII.

[47] *Codex Justinianus* 4.20.9, of Constantine, A.D. 334: cf. C.Th.11.39.3: 'Similarly we ordained that no judge should readily allow the evidence of a single person to be admitted; and now we make the clearest possible ordinance that the testimony of a single witness should never be heard, even if the witness is distinguished by senatorial office.' The first Roman law reference is to *Dig*.48.18.20 (Paul), but there is doubt as to whether this is good evidence of a general rule in classical times: see Pugliese, *Recueils de la Société Jean Bodin* 16 (1965), 320. Interestingly, there is a more explicit

400   And this Text is express, So the Doctors, on the Common Law don't differ in this point. Wee shall mention but one of great Authority, 'tis Mattheus in his Criminal Treatise, Title de Probationibus, Cap. 3.[48] Where, after haveing laid down the Rule of the Common Law, that one Witness is not Sufficient, he adds, Et sano cum habeat locum in Causis Civilibus, in quibus de re duntaxat pecuniaria agitur; vel maximo in Criminalibus locum habere debet, in quibus de Fama, Fortunis, vita res cernitur, nec more Civilis ea Definitio est, Sed et aequitate Naturali constat, et Autoritate Sacrarum Legum munitur: unde Sequitur, ne Principis quidem Constitutione, qui Legibus duntaxat Civilibus non Divinis Solutus est, offici posse ut uni fides habeatur. Tantum abest ut Statuto id fieri possit, videnturque operam inscribendo abusi qui contra hiscere ausi sunt.[49]

401   And with respect to the Law of Scotland, as 'tis peculiar to our Law, to give less Credit to a Proof by Witnesses than is given by the Laws of other Countrys; In Civil Matters they don't prove above the value of £100 Scots in most Cases, whatever Number Concurr, or of whatever quality they be; Therefore, it would be very extraordinary, if a Single Witness should be Sustained to Convict a Man of a Criminal Fact, without the Concurrence of any Circumstance whatsoever, but the Witness's Single Assertion, and this upon the Simple Emission of Words. Mr. Hogg was advised, that the Rule of our Law was the same with that of the Law of God, That no Iniquity can be proved by less than two Witnesses, that hitherto it never was doubted; and Sir George Mackenzie, in his Title Probation by Witnesses, lays down this as our law, "That where two Witnesses Swear to

402 different Facts, which are Species of the Same Crime, viz. to two different Acts of Adultery, though with the same Woman, they are not probative in a Criminal Prosecution." And though he mentions a Decision of the Court of Session, where two Testimonys upon two different Acts of Adultery were Conjoined, in order to inferr a Divorce;[50] yet Mr. Hogg was advised that this was not held to be Law at this day. In a Late Triall of a Divorce, in the Case of Elderline, two Witnesses has sworn to two different acts of Criminal Conversation he had had, one with Mr. Loan, and another with Moodie; But these two Acts were found to be no Proof, ffirst by the Commissarys, and then by the Court of Session. Mr. Loan and Moodie were allowed to be Examined, in order to Compleat the Proof. It was

---

Digest text, 22.5.12 (*Ubi numerus testium non adicitur, etiam duo sufficient: pluralis enim elocutio duorum numero contenta est*). Perhaps it was realised from the form of the rule (as has more recently been confirmed from the Palingenesia) that this was a rule of statutory interpretation (the original context being the interpretation of *testibus praesentibus* in *furtum conceptum*: see Bruns, *Commentationes Philologicae in honorem Theodori Mommseni* (1877), 495 — a view widely accepted).

[48] Antonius Matthaeus II, 1601-54, Netherlands, author of *De criminibus* (Amsterdam, 1644); see further *Novissimo Digesto Italiano* X, 470.

[49] 'And certainly since (this rule) applies in civil cases, in which only money is being claimed, then most certainly it should apply in criminal cases, in which reputation, property and life are at stake. Nor does the rule derive merely from civil law; it is also in agreement with natural equity, and is secured by the authority of the Sacred Laws. It therefore follows that no ruler (who stands above only the civil and not the divine laws) has the right to enact that a single witness be believed. So far from having authority to enact this, those who have dared to offend against this appear to have wasted their efforts in writing such laws.' This viewpoint contrasts markedly with that adopted by Stair as regards the status of the 'judicial' laws (*supra*, n.32).

[50] Mackenzie opines that *Milntoun* should be restricted to civil cases also at I.17.7, as well as in the passage quoted in the Introduction (II.26.14).

then held, that Single Witnesses Deponing on different Facts could not be
403 Conjoined, even so as to inferr a Divorce.[51]

And if one shall look into the Books of Adjournal, as manifold Instances
occurr where Criminal Lybells have been found not proven where different Acts
of the same Crime have been proved by Single Witnesses; So no Instance is to be
found, so far as could be discovered, where a Verdict has been Returned finding a
Lybell proven, where Single Facts were proven but by Single Witnesses.

Two Instances were mentioned for the Pursuer,[52] the first in the Case of
Gabriel Clark, the 26th June 1705; and the Second in the Case of William Bisset,
the 3rd July the same year; But when the Cases are looked into, they are directly
against him: In the Case of Clark, It was proved by one Witness that he
knowingly uttered false Ducatoons, such as were produced in Court, and by a
404 Variety of Witnesses, that when he was apprehended he was possest of a Purse
with false Ducatoons; By the Verdict, the Coining and venting of false
Ducatoons is found proven by one Witness; and as to the Purse with the false
Ducatoons, it is found proven by two concurring Witnesses. Upon this Verdict,
the Court did not find a Proof by one Witness, a Proof; nor the Returne of such a
Verdict equal to finding the Lybell proven; Nor did they Inflict the pain of Death,
the pain of false Coining; But in respect of the Second part of the Verdict, they
Inflicted an Arbitrary punishment.[53]

And in the Case of Bissett, who was accused of poisoning his wife, It was
proved by one Witness, That by his Direction a Powder was given to his Wife,
that immediately after the powder was given she was Seized with Vomitings and
405 purgings, and Died in a few hours; that the Servant who had given the Powder
Innocently, immediately thereafter gave some of the same powder to a young
Lad, that he might Enquire what it was; That the Husband called for this Powder
from him and Destroyed it; it was found proven, by the opinion of the Physicians
that opened the wife, that Arsenick was found in her stomack, and which was the
Occasion of her Death. The Jury returned their Verdict, finding the Lybell proven
against William Bisset by one Witness; and with a Cumulative Probation, that
the Powder found in the Defunct's Stomack was the occasion of her Death. The
Court did not find this Verdict, finding the Lybell proven by one Single Witness,
was a Conviction of Bisset; for even with the addition of the Circumstances
406 proven, they did not proceed to the Capital Punishment, but to an Arbitrary
Punishment.[54]

And indeed the Pursuer was forced to admitt, That a Single Witness in
ordinary Cases was no Proof, and that Ten different Facts proven each by one
Single Witness, were no more proven than if one fact had been proven in that

[51] However, the principle of *Milntoun* was accepted in *Dun* v. *Bryce* (1746); see *Lord Hermand's Consistorial Decisions 1684-1777*, ed. F. P. Walton (Stair Society, 1940), pp. 130f.
[52] *Supra*, 386-8.
[53] On arbitrary punishments in Scots law, see Mackenzie, *Matters Criminal*, II.30.4. This too derived from the learned law. See John H. Langbein, *Torture and the Law of Proof. Europe and England in the Ancien Regime* (1977), and Jackson's review, 14/4 J.S.P.T.L. 304-5.
[54] This was, perhaps, a dangerous strategy on behalf of Hogg, since it impliedly invited the court to inflict an arbitrary punishment on the pannels, if the evidence was not regarded as sufficient for the legal penalty. Indeed, it seems from Hogg's own memorial (at 417) that this had been suggested by Haggart.

manner. But they Resorted to a Distinction betwixt Generick and Specifick Crimes; That a Specifick Crime behoved to be proved by two Witnesses to the same Fact; but in a Generick Crime, Single Witnesses to Single Facts of the same kind were sufficient to make out the Crime; and they Insisted, That Subornation in general was Lybelled in the present Case, and that the particular Facts lybelled were but the Qualifications of the Generick Crime Lybelled.

It was Answered, first, That the Subornation of Witnesses is in no other Sense
407 a Generick Crime, than Murder, Adultery, or Theft; Suborning of one Witness was equally different from the Subornation of another, as Committing Adultery with one woman was different from committing Adultery with another;[55] or as the Theft of one Cow from one Man was different from the Theft of another Cow from another; And no Solid Reason could be assigned, why one might not be Indicted in General as a Theif, and the Indictment proved by the Oath of one Witness, Swearing that the Pannel one day Stole a Cow from him; and another Witness Swearing that on another day the Pannell Stole a Cow from him; as well as one should be Indicted for Suborning Witnesses in General, and the Lybell Supported, by the Testimony of two Single Witnesses, each Swearing Severally, That the Pannell endeavoured to suborn him at different times and places.[56]

408   But Secundo, Mr. Hogg was advised, That a Criminall Prosecution could not be Carried on for a Crime in Generall, that a Special Fact must be Lybelled and proved, and unless each Fact is proved by two Concurring Witnesses, it is not proved at all; That a Proof of one Crime can be no Proof of another distinct Criminal Fact of the same kind: For Instance, should one be Convicted by two Witnesses today, of Suborning Titius; if the same man should be tried tomorrow for Suborning Maevius, and a Single Witness only adduced for proving Lybell; 'twas believed no Man would adventure to Say, that the former Conviction with a Single Witness should be a sufficient Proof; And if so, could it be pleaded, That the testimony of a Single Witness as to the Suborning Titius should have a Stronger Effect than a Conviction proceeding upon the Testimony of two
409 Witnesses?[57] But more particularly Mr. Hogg was advised, That such a

---

[55] Stress is here being laid upon identity of parties as the *nexus*. It is impliedly conceded (in line with tradition) that different acts of adultery with the same woman might be combined. The alternative canonist model, where the *nexus* is teleological (as in treason) is ignored. Hume too evidently regarded the *nexus* by identity of parties as the more striking; see the Introduction.

[56] The *reductio*, of course, does not work: if the successive acts of subornation are directed towards the conviction of a particular individual on one particular charge, the acts have a teleological *nexus* which is missing from the example of the cattle rustler. Modern law has dispensed with both identity of parties and teleological unity as necessary conditions of the *nexus*, and has substituted notions such as 'striking similarity' (particularly with regard to method). In effect, modern law accepts the present argument, but regards both cases as in principle acceptable.

[57] The argument omits to say whether Titius and Maevius were suborned in relation to the same proceedings (let alone the same charge). The argument is weak also in neglecting the aspect of dual punishment. If the conviction in relation to Titius is admitted also in respect of Maevius, then the accused (who presumably has already been sentenced in relation to Titius) is effectively being punished again in respect of Titius, insofar as that conviction is a necessary condition of his conviction in respect of Maevius. The modern doctrine of mutual corroboration runs into similar difficulties. The general charge strategy, on the other hand, avoids it: the accused is convicted only on the one (general) charge, this being regarded as a *totum* of which the specific offences each provide a *pars* of the proof. Such an argument reflects notions of partial proof which modern law, at least at the formal level, has rejected. The modern all-or-nothing view is reflected in the memorial for Hogg at 418 (rejecting arbitrary punishment).

Prosection for a Generick Crime was contrary to the Natural Rights of Mankind, and without any Foundation in Law, or the practice of Scotland. How is it possible for any Man to defend himself against an Accusation of a Crime laid in the Generall? If a particular Fact is Condescended on with time and place, he can call to mind where he was, and who were present, so as to prepare himself for an Exculpation if he is falsely Accused. But 'tis Impossible to have any Defence against a false Accuser in the Generall especially if Single Witnesses to different facts are admitted; 'Tis Impossible that they can Contradict one another, or be
410 Redargued, or that the Pannel can Escape if they have but Conscience enough to Swear a Crime against him; Innocense itself can be no Protection against such an Accusation.

And in this Mr. Hogg was supported by the General Opinion of the Doctors, who though they Speak and treat of proving a Crime in General, and a Crime in Special, with great Indistinctness; Yet when they are rightly understood, they don't differ, but agree with what wee now plead; particularly Julius Clarus,[58] in his Receptis Sententiis, Lib. 5. §. fin. Quaestio. 53 No. 18. et Seq. where, after having observed, that Single Witnesses don't prove, he adds: Et Haec conclusio de plano procedit, quando agitur de probando aliquo Delicto in Specie, nam eo Casu debent Testes esse contestes ut sufficiant ad Condemnationem; Sed quid Si agatur de probando Delicto in Genere, puta aliquem esse
411 Hereticum, Adulterum, Usurarium, Blasphematorem, vel huius modi, numquid Testes Singulares, qui Deponunt unusquisque eorum de diversis Actibus, Sufficient ad concludentem probationem.[59] And after having observed a Number of the Doctors who were for the affirmative, and others for the Negative, he adds, Ego aliquando cogitabam, quis esset Sensus Doctorum ita loquentium de probando Delicto in Specie, vel de probando Delicto in Genere, et credo quod Secundum eos tunc dicatur agi de probando Delicto in Specie, quando tractatur de puniendo aliquid Criminaliter; Et hoc Casu verior est Secundo Opinio quod Scilicet Testes Singulares non probant aliquem esse Adulterum, vel Hereticum, vel Usurarium, et ita Semper vidi Servari;[60] And after quoting Authoritys, he adds, Tunc vero agi dicunt de probando Delicto in Genere, quando agitur non de poena instigenda, sed ad alium finem, puta excipiendo de Adulterio ad

[58] Julius Clarus, 1525-75, Italy. The *Receptarum Sententiarum Opus* is printed in his *Opera Omnia* (1613). See further *Novissimo Digesto Italiano* III, 344; E. Moeller, *Julius Clarus als Criminalist* (Breslau, 1911); Coing, *Handbuch* (*supra* n.22) III/1, p. 440. Clarus was already being cited with some regularity in Scotland a century earlier: see *Craufurd et al. and King's Advocate* v. *Crombie et al.*, 22nd June 1625; *H. M. Advocate* v. *Mgt. Woode*. 23rd Feb. 1631; *H. M. Advocate* v. *James, Lord Ochitree*, 30th June 1631; *H. M. Advocate* v. *John, Lord Balmerino*, December 1634; *Russell et al. and H. M. Advocate* v. *Bryce and Liddell*, 22nd March 1639 — all in *Justiciary Cases 1624-50*, vol. 1 (Stair Society, 1953). [CG]
[59] 'And this conclusion clearly applies when the proceedings concern proof of some delict *in specie*, for in that case the witnesses ought to be *contestes* (joint witnesses) so that they should be sufficient for the purposes of punishment. But what if the proceedings concern proof of a delict *in genere*, for example that someone is a heretic, an adulterer, a usurer, a blasphemer, or something of the kind? Are singular witnesses, each of them testifying to different acts, to be sufficient to afford a full proof?'
[60] 'I sometimes used to wonder what was the meaning of the doctors who speak in this way of proof of a delict *in specie* or proof of a delict *in genere*, and I believe that when they speak of proof of a delict *in specie* they mean to refer to when one is dealing with the punishment of someone criminally. And in such a case the second opinion is more correct, namely that singular witnesses do not prove anyone to be an adulterer, or a heretic, or a usurer, and thus I have always seen it observed.'

412 privationem Dotis, vel de alio Crimine ad Diminuendum fidem Testis.[61] Here 'tis apparent, that this learned Author had no Notion of a Criminal Accusation for a Crime in General, or of proving a Crime by Single Witnesses to different Acts.

And the same Opinion is delivered by Farinacius,[62] in his Criminal Treatise, De Oppositione Contra dicta Testium, Quaest. 64. No. 200, 217, 218, 228 and 232. That Single Witnesses, Deponing to different Acts of Usury, Adultery, Heresy, and the like, are not a Sufficient Proof so as to Inferr any Punishment; that they may inferr a suspicion so as to be the foundation for Torture, Penance, Abjuration, or the like.[63]

And as to the Law of Scotland, the Pannel had not been able to Discover any one Criminal Lybell, where a Crime in general has been Lybelled, much less where such a Lybell Criminal was Sustained, and the Pannell Remitted to the 413 Knowledge of an Inquest thereon; So that this Notion of an Accusation of a Crime in General, appeared to be a Novelty in the Law of Scotland.[64]

'Tis true, an Experiment was once made in the 1735; a Criminal Lybel was brought against Barrisdale, for an attempt to Suborne Witnesses and the Prosecutor in that Case, in order to obviat the Objection of the Singularity of the Witnesses, set forth in the Minor Proposition of the Lybell,[65] "That the Pannell and others in Combination with him, Intending to accuse and prosecute the Pursuer, as Guilty of certain Thefts, did at several different Times and places betwixt the first of April 1734 and the first of December 1735, endeavour by Rewards, Threatenings, and other undue Methods, to Induce several Persons to give Evidence against the Complainers as Guilty of Stealing or Outhounding 414 Theives"; And then the Lybell proceeds to particular Attempts upon particular Persons, at particular times and places. The Court found the Lybell Relevant as to the particular Facts Lybelled with time and place; But dismissed the Generall Article of the Lybell; and accordingly a Proof came out by Single Witnesses, of the Single Facts particularly Lybelled; and the Jury found the Lybell not proven.[66] This the Defender was advised, is a Decision in point as to the present Question, Whether Subornation in general is a Relevant Lybell? And though in the present Case the Lybel was found Relevant, yet Mr. Hogg apprehended he

---

[61] 'But then they speak of proceedings concerning proof of delict *in genere* when the proceedings do not concern the infliction of punishment but some other objective, such as catching someone in adultery with a view to depriving him of a dowry, or to destroy the credibility of a witness in relation to other criminal proceedings.'

[62] Prosper Farinatius, 1554-1618, Italy; see further *Novissimo Digesto Italiano* VII, 87; Coing, *Handbuch* (*supra* n.22) II/1, p. 446; and Introduction, *supra*, on the *quaestio* of Farinatius, and the repute of this analysis of Clarus. There is a particularly interesting discussion of proof *in genere* by Simanca, *De catholica institutione*, tit.64 (see F. Zillettus, *Tractatus Universi Iuris* (Venice, 1584), vol.XI(2), 202) where the author criticises the idea of proof *in genere* on philosophical grounds. See esp. nu.72: *Genus est, ut Porphyrius caeterique definiunt, quod praedicatur de pluribus differentibus specie: est sane genus, universale, generale, & commune, ... nec visu nec tactu, neque ullo senso comprehenditur, ut civis meus Seneca inquit, sed cogitabile est. Homo generalis sub oculos non venit, sed specialis venit, ut Cicero & Cato. Animal in genere non videtur, sed cogitatur, videtur autem species eius, equus, & canis.*

[63] On suspicion, etc., see further 433 and n.82 *infra*.

[64] See *Justiciary Cases* 1624-50, vol. 2 (Stair Society, 1972), xxii.

[65] See n.41, *supra*.

[66] Book of Adjournal for Feb. 5 1734 — Feb. 9 1736, pp. 898ff. For the argument in support of the general charge, see 927-30; for the argument against, 927-73; for the interlocutor of relevancy rejecting the general article, 999-1001.

had the Opinion of the Court, That no more was Intended by the Interlocutor, but to find the particular facts lybelled Relevant;[67] For when the Pursuer endeavoured to adduce a Witness, not upon any of the particular Facts Lybelled, but upon the general Article of Subornation, and upon a fact not Lybelled, The Court would not allow the Witnes to be Examined; So that the present Trial proceeded not upon the General Crime of Subornation, but upon the particular Facts Lybelled;[68] and as none of those Facts were proven, otherways than by one Single Witness, and as the Verdict finds them only so proven, therefore they are found not proven, and the Pannel ought to be assoilzied.

But in the next place, giving but not granting, That a Lybell of Subornation in General, an Attempt to Suborn Witnesses to prove a particular Crime against a Pursuer, would be Relevant Lybell; and that two or three Single Witnesses, Deponing to different Acts of the same Subornation, might be Conjoined and Sustained as a Sufficient Proof; which however could by no means be admitted; yet even upon that Supposition, no Condemnation could be founded upon the present Verdict.[69]

To Explain this Matter, had Mr. Hogg been Accused only of Suborning Witnesses to prove the fire-raising against Cairnmuir; and the Jury had found several acts proven by single Witnesses, It might upon the present Supposition be pretended, that they Concurred in the same Generick Crime, in proving an Endeavour to Load Cairnmuir with the Fire-raising; But as three different Subornations are lybelled, one to prove the Fire-raising, a Second to prove Incest, a third to Swear falsely in a Process of Scandal before the Commissary;[70] And the Verdict without distinguishing Finds the Subornation in several Instances proven by one Single Witness; It could not possibly from thence appear but that the Instances so found proven, were one of each kind, and which with Submission could not possibly be Conjoined;[71] And as it is a Rule in Criminals, that the Proof must be Clear as Sun Light,[72] this applies to the Verdict of a Jury, that if 'tis uncertain what is found proven, no Sentence condemnatory can go

---

[67] The memorial attempts a difficult argument. In *Barrisdale* the interlocutor of relevancy had specifically ruled 'such of the Articles of the Lybels, where Time and Place were not particularly condescended upon, not relevant'. But in Hogg's case the whole Lybel had been ruled relevant. Nevertheless, Hogg sought to restrict the meaning of the interlocutor in his own case to the particular facts, in the light of the interlocutor in *Barrisdale*.

[68] Non sequitur. The court may simply have been ruling that the only evidence that would be admitted in proof of the general charge was evidence of which notice had been given in the form of one of the specific charges in the lybel itself.

[69] Hogg here pleads in the alternative. Even if a general charge was relevant, it had not been proved according to the verdict actually rendered by the jury. This argument assumes that any such general charge is no wider than 'an attempt to suborn witnesses to prove a particular crime against a Pursuer'; had it been 'an attempt to suborn witnesses against Haggart', the jury's verdict might have been regarded — even on Hogg's argument — as sufficient.

[70] See the Introduction. This charge is not mentioned by Haggart. Apparently it figured only in the specific charges of the indictment, and not in the general article.

[71] A somewhat dubious argument, in the light of the fact that the verdict spoke of 'the crime of subornation . . . as lybelled . . . proven in Sundry facts'. The verdict could hardly have been more ambiguous. What is clear is Hogg's rejection of a *nexus* between suborning on the fire-raising and suborning on any other matter.

[72] A famous maxim of the learned law, its image going back to Cicero, *de finibus* 1.21.71, and reflected also in the seventeenth century English treason trial where *testes singulares* re-emerged: *Love*'s case, 5 St. Tr. 43, 143. It is here applied, by analogy, to the jury's verdict.

upon such an uncertain Verdict: The Rule is, Conclusio Sequitur debiliorem partem, That in the Case of any Uncertainty, that must be taken to be the Meaning of the Verdict that is most favourable for the Pannel; Better two guilty Persons escape than one Innocent Person be Condemned.

And whereas it was Suggested, That though the Crime was not fully proved, this might Excuse from the ordinary punishment, but the Pannel might be still 418 Lyable to a lesser Punishment. But this Distinction, with Submission, is founded in no Law, and appears Contrary to Reason; If the Crime is proved, Why not the Ordinary Punishment? If it is not proved, no Man is to be punished upon Suspicions.[73]

The Pursuer was pleased to lay abundance of Stress upon the Law of England, in the Case of Treason, and to say, that it would look odd, there should several facts of the same kind, proven by Single Witnesses, be found to be no Proof.

But with Submission, as the Law of England, with respect to a Proof by Witnesses led before a Jury, is peculiar to that Country, no Argument can be drawn from the Law of that Country, for proving what is the Law of Scotland. 'Twas well known, that in that Country, the Forms of Trial were in every Respect different from the Laws of other Countrys; No Man could be tried for a Crime 419 untill an Indictment is found against him by Twelve Men of the Country concurring that the Indictment is true; After this he is brought to a Trial, and at common Law, though one Witness is Legal Evidence, but then the whole Jury of Twelve Must Concurr in believing the Evidence; one Dissenter will acquitt the Pannel; So that in the present Case Mr. Hogg behoved to have been acquitted, the Verdict was carried but by a Plurality.[74]

And therefore, it was no Wonder, that when by the Statute of Edward 6th. it was Enacted, That in Indictments of high Treason two Witnesses should be necessary;[75] That it was held, that if both the Witnesses concurred to prove the same Treason, though the ouvert Acts they swore to were different, it was held that they came up to the Rule laid down by the Statute.[76] Witnesses by the Law of 420 England don't mean Concurring Witnesses; But as this remained a Doubt, it was Explained by the Statute or King William the 3d. It was thereby Enacted, that from and after the 25th of March 1696, no Man shall be attainted of high Treason but by the Oaths of two Witnesses, either both of them to the same ouvert Act, or one of them to one, and the other of them to another overt Act of the same Treason; And by another Clause of the same Statute, 'tis Enacted, That if two distinct Treasons be alledged in one Indictment, one Witness adduced to prove

---

[73] See nn.54, 57 *supra.*

[74] The argument in this paragraph should appeal to comparative lawyers. It rejects comparison of isolated rules, in favour of overall comparison of the effect of the rules taken as a whole. One might almost call it structural-functional. In England, it is claimed, the safeguards for the accused reside in the requirements of the grand jury and the unanimous verdict; in the light of this, the evidentiary requirements might reasonably be less stringent. Scotland, lacking the grand jury and admitting majority verdicts, required a strict approach to corroboration in order to safeguard the accused. Even though English law did require corroboration (exceptionally) in treason, an application of English law (including its acceptance of *testes singulares* in this context) would still have resulted in Hogg's acquittal, since the jury had been divided.

[75] *Supra* n.15.

[76] See n.12 *supra.*

one of the said Treasons, and another Witness adduced to prove another, shall not be deemed to be two Witnesses in the Meaning of the Act.[77]

This being the Case, to argue from the Common Law of England, or from the Statutory Law in the Case of Treason, to the Law of Scotland with respect to a
421 Proof by Witnesses is to argue from things that are absolutely different, and the Argument will never Conclude: And with Submission, Mr. Hogg might with the same Justice argue from the Cannon Law,[78] that he, as a Presbyter, could not be Convicted but by the Testimony of fourty four Witnesses; Such Arguments may mislead a Jury, but will never be Listened to by their Lordships.

The Pursuer also founded upon certain Decisions quoted by Huber,[79] in his Title De Testibus, No. 18. and it must be admitted, that the Decisions as they are quoted by him seem to come up to the point, that Single Witnesses to different Facts have been found to prove a Crime in the Courts of Freisland:[80] But whether this ought to be followed as a Precedent in the Law of Scotland, when he himself acknowledges that 'tis Contrary to the general Rules of Law,[81] was humbly
422 Submitted; Especially when, as had been observed already, this has hitherto never been thought of in the Law of Scotland, nor no such General Lybell has ever been Sustained.

The Pursuer also brought a Quotation from Hippolitus Riminaldus, where it was found, that Single Witnesses to different Heretical Expressions, were Sustained as a full Proof of Heresy; So as to Inferr Abjuration.[82] The Answer has

---

[77] *Supra* n.16. It was against the admissibility of *testes singulares* (even as thus restricted) that the draftsmen of the U.S. Constitution reacted: 'No person shall be convicted of treason unless on the testimony of two witnesses concurring to the same overt act, or on confession in open court' — Art.III §3.

[78] 'Cannon Law' here presumably refers to the Law of the Church of Scotland. The memorial here attempts a further *reductio ad absurdum*: if the pursuer seeks to rely on one non-applicable law of foreign origin (treason, now incorporated into Scots law but not applicable in the present case), why should the defender not invoke another non-applicable law of foreign origin — and one which was designed to appear manifestly counter-intuitive. Such a rhetorical technique (again, one might think, more apt to persuade in oral form) seeks to suggest that any law of foreign origin is likely to be equally unreasonable.

[79] But Huber is not cited in the pursuer's written memorial. Presumably, it was adduced by the pursuer at the oral argument. But can one imagine that counsel had Huber at his finger tips at an oral argument immediately following the announcement of the verdict? This may be indirect evidence that counsel were given some opportunity to prepare for that oral argument, and that the written memorials take account, in various ways, of what there took place. See also n.40, *supra*.

[80] *Praelectionum juris Romani*, ad Dig.22.5 tit. *De testibus* nu.18, for the cases of Antonius de By (1645) and Christianus Siamburg (1681). Cf. Huber's *Heedensdaegse Rechtsgeleertheyt* Bk. 5 ch.27 s.42, translated P. Gane *The Jurisprudence of My Time* (Durban, 1939), ii, 295-6.

[81] That is, it belonged to the *ius positivum* of Freisland but not to the *ius gentium*. Such a distinction was perfectly intelligible in Scottish legal circles, where the natural law ideas of Grotius, Pufendorf and Stair were still common.

[82] Again the quotation does not appear in the written memorial for Haggart: see further nn.79 *supra*, 83 *infra*. Proof of heresy by *testes singulares* perhaps originated with the Inquisition (and is so associated in Hogg's memorial) and attracted a voluminous canonist literature. See, e.g., Julius Clarus, *Sententiae* Lib.V haeresis nu.20 (*Opera Omnia*, 1591, p. 181); Farinatius, *De testibus* 3.7.64.201-19 (and see esp. 218 for the proposition in the memorial); Mascardi, *De Probatione* lib.II concl. 857, esp. nus.25-6; Ionnaus Royas, *De haereticis* p. II assert.6, nus.120-49 (in *Tractatus Universi Iuris*, ed. Zillettus, vol.XI(2) p. 225); C. Carena, *Tractatus de officio sanctissimae Inquisitionis* (Bonn, 1668), f.104, 259; D. Guidonis Fulcodii Cardinalis, *Quaestiones Quindecim*, qu.14 esp. nu.10 (on abjuration as one of the possible purposes for which *singulares* could be admitted in heresy; the others mentioned are canonical purgations, torture and extraordinary punishment).On Hippolytus Riminaldus, (1520-89) Italian, see Coing, *Handbuch* II/1, p. 458.

been made already, That such a Proof Inferrs Suspicion and therefore is Sufficient to oblige the Party to a Recantation; But indeed, when the Pursuer argued from the Rules Observed in the Popish Inquisitions, to the Rules of the Law of Scotland, he show'd how much he was Straitned; And as even those won't Serve his turn, 'twas plain that what he plead was not agreeable to the Law of Scotland.[83]

423   It was also said, That if such a Proof were not admitted, Subornation would go unpunished; No Man goes about such a Work in presence of Witnesses; But the Answer was obvious, This is not the only occult Crime, and no Man takes two Witnesses when he is about to committ a Crime; And so farr the Law goes in occult Crimes, that it admitts such Witnesses as were present, though otherways Exceptionable; But if there were no Witnesses, or but one, Non deficit Ius sed Probatio; and this must hold in the Strongest manner in a Case such as the present, where it depends Solely on the Credit of the Single Witnesses, not only Whether the Pannel was Guilty of the Crime, but whether any Crime at all was committed; The Corpus Delicti[84] was proved by a Single Evidence, as well as fixt

424 upon the Pannell.

A good deal of Stress was laid upon a Criminal Prosecution brought against the Pursuer, before the Circuits at Perth, at the Instance of His Majesty's Advocat, for Fire-raising; It was pretended, that it was in order to Support this Prosecution that Mr. Hogg had endeavoured to Suborne the Witnesses:

But, in the ffirst place, Mr. Hogg was no Prosecutor of that Criminal Action, nor was he at all Concerned in the Prosecution; It was directed by people that were far removed beyond the Suspicion of wishing to disquiet or Convict an Innocent Man. And Secondly, of the whole Witnesses upon, upon whom an Attempt was said to have been made by Mr. Hogg, only two were given out in the Criminal Prosecution; and if their Testimonys are at all to be Credited, that they

425 rejected the Proposal with disdain, It cannot be Supposed that it was owing to Mr. Hogg that they were given out in the List of Witnesses; So that the Connection betwixt the Criminall Prosecution at the Circuit, and the pretended Subornation, was meer Imagination.

In the next place, it was said,[85] That in Circumstantial Evidence, it was constantly held, that where all the particular Circumstances were proved by Single Witnesses, the Proof was Sufficient: For Instance, if one saw a Theif go into a Stable without a Horse, and another saw him come out with a Horse, this would be a Proof of the Theft.

But we deny that this is Law; 'Tis true, that in a Circumstantial Evidence 'tis possible, that a Fact proven by a Single Witness may Conjoin as a Circumstance

426 with other Facts that are proven by concurring Testimonys; For Instance, If a Theft were proven by Two Witnesses, that is, that the Pursuer was possest of a Horse, with such Marks, at Night, that the Stable was broken open, and the

---

[83] Hogg argues that not even in Canon law is the heresy fully proved for the purposes of punishment. When the memorial states that 'the Answer has been made already', this may refer to the preceding oral argument. Counsel for Hogg may even have known that the argument was not being repeated in Haggart's memorial; he still includes the rebuttal for the prejudicial effect of associating the pursuer with the 'Popish Inquisitions'.

[84] See n.38 *supra*.

[85] *Supra*, 375-6, 385; and see n.9 *supra*.

Horse amissing in the Morning, and a Single Witness should Swear, that the Pannel was in possession of that Horse at three Miles Distance, early in the Morning, and another that he was in possession of the same Horse at Mid-day, at Twelve Miles distance, the Proof would be Sufficient, Because the Corpus delicti is once proved,[86] and two Witnesses Concurr in pointing out the Theif, by the Possession of the Stoln Horse, which is a permanent Act. But wee deny, that 427 where the Corpus delicti, as well as the Cirumstances pointing out the Criminall, are proved but by Single Witnesses, that this is sufficient Proof of a Crime: And further the Proof before Stated has not the least Resemblance to the present Case, where each Act is quite distinct from the other, and where there is not one Circumstance that is otherways proved than by a Single Witness, that is, not proved at all.

In Respect whereof, etc.

Doom and Sentence, 1st August 1738
(JC 3/22, fo. 489)

The Lord Justice Clerk and Lords Commissioners of Justiciary, having considered the Verdict of Assize Returned, of the Date the Seventeenth day of July last, against Mr James Hogg and Thomas Soutar Pannels, with the Memorials given in thereanent hinc inde, They in respect thereof, by the mouth of Archibald Murdoch, Macer of Court, Decerned and Adjudged both the saids pannels to be Infamous in all time coming; And Decerned them conjunctly and severally, to pay to David Haggart Pursuer, in name of Damnadges and Expences, the Sum of Two Hundred and Fifty pounds Sterling; And Ordained them to be carried to prison in the Tolbooth of Edinburgh and to be Detained there untill they make payment of the said Sum; and further Banished both the said Pannels furth of that part of Great Brittain called Scotland, never to Return thereto; With Certification That if after Six weeks from and after their being set at Liberty out of Prison, they or either of them should be found in Scotland, the person so found should be Set upon the Pillory at Edinburgh, and thereafter Banished to one or other of his Majesty's Plantations in America, and Should be Committed to Prison untill an Opportunity offered of Transporting him or them; ... Which was pronounced for Doom.

(Signed) And[r] Fletcher
Ja Mackenzie. Alex[r] ffraser.
Da Erskine & P. Grant

[86] See n.38 *supra.*

THE ELECTORAL SYSTEM IN THE SCOTTISH COUNTIES
BEFORE 1832

By WILLIAM FERGUSON, M.A., B.A., PH.D.,
Department of Scottish History, University of Edinburgh

The electoral system in the Scottish counties before 1832 should prove of some interest to present day members of the legal profession in Scotland, for the system was a highly legal one founded not only on election statutes but also, and more fundamentally, on the 'feudal law' of Scotland. From first to last, the county franchise was thirled to land tenure, and even as late as the opening months of 1832 the conferring or withholding of the franchise might well turn on an increasingly strained interpretation of feudal law. It is not surprising, therefore, that over the greater part of the period from 1707 to 1832 'the election politicks' formed a very lucrative branch of legal practice. As one acute late-eighteenth century observer noted, 'lawyers are never paid so handsomely as in election causes';[1] and that contention is fully borne out by the costs estimated in numerous volumes of *Old Session Papers* in the Signet Library. Naturally, too, such brisk business gave rise to a considerable literature designed to guide the profession.

Of the older legal works on the subject there are three outstanding treatises that were widely used as working manuals. In assessing them, however, their purpose must be kept in mind: they were not primarily historical works but legal text-books. Thus, while admirable for elucidating the complexities of election law, they rarely give adequate historical accounts of the political manoeuvrings that underlay the leading cases.

The pioneer work in this genre was Alexander Wight's *Treatise on the laws concerning the Election of the different Representatives sent from Scotland to the Parliament of Great Britain*, which was published in 1773. It was soon superseded by an expanded version in two volumes in 1784, Alexander Wight's *An Inquiry into the Rise and Progress of Parliament, chiefly in Scotland, and a Complete System of the Law concerning the Elections of the Representatives from Scotland to the Parliament of Great Britain*, a new edition of which appeared in 1806. This was a work of great learning, and, considering the purpose it was meant to serve, admirable in every way.

Others followed Wight's example. Robert Bell's *Treatise on the Election Laws, as they relate to the Representation of Scotland* was published in 1812, and, as is customary with legal works, it drew heavily on Wight and lesser predecessors, though in some respects giving a fuller and more penetrating

---

[1] John Ramsay of Ochtertyre, ed., A. Allardyce, *Scotland and Scotsmen in the Eighteenth Century* (1888), II, 483.

exposition. Then in 1827 came the last of the three classical studies, Arthur Connell's *Treatise on the Election Law of Scotland*. This was a slighter account than either of its predecessors, to which again it obviously owed much, but, in spite of its inferior quality, Connell's work was in some ways the most useful of the three. Published a bare five years before the demise of the old system, Connell's *Treatise* is the most comprehensive and parts of it are enriched by valuable MS material from the Advocates' Library, some items of which can no longer be traced.

These authors were all Scots lawyers and wrote as practical experts. Wight was one of the leading pleaders in election causes in his day, while Bell was an authority on conveyancing, a subject of exceptional importance to the old system of elections in the Scottish counties. In addition to their strong practical and forensic bents, however, all three authors were scholarly. Their works thus remain authoritative, and they are still indispensable for the study of the eighteenth-century Scottish electoral system. In the following pages, even where no specific references are made to them, the present writer is throughout deeply indebted to the authors of these three classical treatises on pre-1832 Scottish election law.

That subject should also be of interest to historians of modern Scotland, but, for various reasons, it has not so proved. First of all, eighteenth-century historians themselves saw little that was amiss with their world, and, indeed, saw it for the most part as the acme of human progress painfully attained after centuries of medieval stagnation. They did not, therefore, limn their own times 'warts and all'. Warts and other disfigurements were seen as belonging to 'the dark feudal ages' or 'the times of superstition'. To the typical eighteenth-century *savant* élitism came naturally; so a restricted franchise and electoral manipulation were just two of the necessary prices that had to be paid in order to maintain civilisation and ward off democratic anarchy. The radical reformers of the late eighteenth century took the opposite view and tended to attribute all of society's ills to the Rule of Old Corruption.[2] But a condemnatory interest in the old system of elections failed to survive the Reform Act of 1832, which, it was fondly imagined, had curbed the hydra-headed monster of corruption.[3] Disgust at, and distaste for, the old system became the keynote in Victorian times. Victorian historians found eighteenth-century political *mores* hard to swallow and did their best to avoid them. Thus, Cosmo Innes, in editing a volume of family papers, openly admitted that the subject of eighteenth-century political influence raised painful issues and that, for the honour of the house, he had omitted such material.[4]

Later historians as diverse as Peter Hume Brown and Sir Robert Rait agreed in general denunciation of the eighteenth-century political system in Scotland.[5] Hume Brown tended to see history as a branch of moral philosophy, and he

[2] See William Ferguson, *Scotland: 1689 to the Present* (*Edinburgh History of Scotland*, vol. IV, edn., 1978), chs. 8 and 9.
[3] For a discussion of the Reform Act and its meaning, see William Ferguson, 'The Reform Act (Scotland) of 1832: intention and effect', *Scottish Historical Review*, XLV (1966), 105-14.
[4] Cosmo Innes, ed., *The Family of Rose of Kilravock* (Spalding Club, 1848), 440.
[5] P. Hume Brown, *History of Scotland* (Cabinet edn., 1911), III, 281-4, 300; R. S. Rait, *The Parliaments of Scotland* (1924), 123-5.

found the eighteenth-century political system sadly lacking in morals. Rait, dazzled by the Stubbsian vision, saw the Scottish parliament and the election law that served it as 'feudal' and retrograde. More recently Professor T. C. Smout has been rather dismissive about the whole subject, opining that post-union representation at Westminster was for a lengthy (and undefined) period 'scarcely relevant any longer to a general history of Scottish society'.[6] Such facile blanket condemnations fail to convince, the more so as so much depends on how one defines Scottish society. A multiplicity of views is possible here; but it is certainly wrong to overemphasise social and economic developments *in vacuo*, heedless of law and custom or anything else that does not lend itself to quantification or to sociological theorising.

Electoral law, too, has its dry and forbidding technical aspects, and the mechanics of the system were intricate and complex. Most historians find it an uninviting subject; and it is certainly not one likely to inspire deathless prose. Nonetheless, electoral law and procedure in the Scottish counties before 1832 can tell us much about the then state of Scottish society, and in particular it can offer piercing insights into the country's dominant political class — that of the lairds.

It might seem that the logical starting point of the enquiry should be the representation granted to Scotland in the parliament of Great Britain under the terms of the Treaty of Union of 1707. This is not quite the case, however, for the treaty said nothing about franchises or election procedure. The Act of Union determined Scotland's representation at Westminster, allowing forty five seats in the House of Commons and sixteen elected peers in the House of Lords; but the franchises and the machinery of election were accepted as they had already been defined by the law and custom of Scotland, though there was, of course, considerable change in drawing up the new constituencies.[7] What, then, did the law of Scotland before 1707 have to say about the representation of the shires in parliament?

The basic statue is that of 1587 which effectively introduced the system of representation for the shires.[8] It was the essence of the problem that originally all tenants-in-chief, degree unspecified, were required to render suit to the King's Council from which at some indeterminate point in the thirteenth century parliament had emerged.[9] Of its precise early composition little is known; but inability to enforce the attendance of the lesser tenants-in-chief, or small barons, soon came to be a vexed problem. In an attempt to solve this problem James I in 1426 passed an act to ensure the attendance of all 'prelates, earls, barons and freeholders'; but the act's provisions were ignored.[10] The act of 1426 was soon a dead letter. James I then in 1428 passed an act which exempted the

[6] T. C. Smout, *A History of the Scottish People 1560-1830* (1969), 218.

[7] For a summary of the electoral changes after 1707 see Ferguson, *Scotland: 1689 to the Present*, 133-5.

[8] *Acts of the Parliaments of Scotland [APS]*, III, 509-10. For a brief earlier intimation of this legislation, see *APS*, III, 40 (1567); and for general background Gordon Donaldson, *Scotland: James V–James VII* (*Edinburgh History of Scotland*, vol. III, 1965), 278-80.

[9] R. S. Rait, *The Parliaments of Scotland*, Introduction; also A. A. M. Duncan, *Scotland: The Making of the Kingdom* (*Edinburgh History of Scotland*, vol. I, 1975), 609-10; G. W. S. Barrow, *Kingship and Unity: Scotland 1000-1306* (*New History of Scotland*, vol. 2, 1981), 126-9; and Ranald Nicholson, *Scotland: The Later Middle Ages* (*Edinburgh History of Scotland*, vol. II, 1974), 19-21.

[10] Nicholson, *op. cit.*, 302; *APS*, II, 9.

small barons from personal attendance in parliament provided they elected members to represent them.[11] This was the substance of the scheme adopted in 1587, as the act of that year acknowledged. The act of 1587 was, in short, the last of many which had grappled with the problem of the lesser barons. That problem had been forced to a head by the perverse enthusiasm that had brought many small tenants-in-chief flocking to the so-called 'Reformation Parliament' of 1560. They would not come when wanted or stay away when unwanted, and if the composition of parliament were not to be in a state of unmanageable flux this was a matter that had to be resolved. The act of 1587 obliged the small tenants-in-chief to meet annually at the Michaelmas Head Court in each sheriffdom and stewartry, and there to choose 'two wise men, being the kingis freeholders' to represent them in parliament.[12]

The act of 1587 does not use the term 'tenants-in-chief', but like the previous acts, among other terms, speaks of 'freeholders'. This has given rise to some needless confusion. What precisely was meant by a 'freeholder'? As statutes will, the act of 1587 presumed knowledge of its time and did not closely define its terms. Thus today its provisions are by no means self-evident. Grappling with this problem, Lord Cooper showed that 'freehold' could then be accepted Scottish usage for liferent.[13] But his suggestion that the act specifically enfranchised liferenters was rejected by W. C. Dickinson.[14] Liferenters on lands of the requisite valuation held *in capite* were first enfranchised by an act of 1661; and to equate 'freeholder' with 'liferenter' robs the statute of 1587 of all meaning.

What, then, did the word 'freeholder' in the act of 1587 mean? The answer can only be the traditional one: the freeholder mentioned in the act of 1587, and in later representation acts, was simply, whatever the term may have implied in other contexts, a small tenant-in-chief — that is, one who held lands direct of the king but whose lands were of slight extent and had not been erected into a barony. Indeed, the earliest references are usually to barons and freeholders, which is consonant, as Professor Dickinson showed, with the process of differentiation in the estate of the barons that was so well-marked a feature of the fifteenth century.[15] The earliest writers on the county franchise all took a similar view. In 1710 William Forbes defined the position crudely but accurately enough — 'All such as hold their Lands immediately of the Sovereign, are called here Freeholders: whereof some are called Great, and some Small Barons. The Nobility are the Great Barons'.[16] Wight and the other treatise writers held to the same interpretation.[17] Lord Cooper's liferenter is, therefore, in the context of the act of 1587, a red herring.

Closer examination of the act of 1587 drives home the point. It was for its time quite well drafted, and its provisions, so far as the scanty records of the sheriff courts of the late sixteenth and early seventeenth centuries will permit of judgement, were scrupulously observed. Only tenants-in-chief could render suit

[11] Nicholson, *op. cit.*, 303; *APS*, II, 15.
[12] *APS*, III, 509.
[13] Lord Cooper, 'Freehold in Scots Law', *Juridical Review*, LVII, (1945), 1-5.
[14] *Juridical Review*, LVII, (1945), 135-51.
[15] Dickinson, *op. cit.*, 140-1.
[16] William Forbes, *A Letter from William Forbes Advocate to his Friend in England . . . concerning the Law of Election of Members of Parliament etc.* (1710), 4.
[17] Wight, *op. cit.*, I, 50; Bell, *op. cit.*, 26; and Connell, *op. cit.*, 38.

to the Head Courts where the elections were to be held, and furthermore the
freeholders were restricted to those holding by the old feudal tenures of ward and
blench. The king's feuars did not attend the Sheriff Courts, nor were their lands
assessed on the Old Extent. But the 40/- freehold that the act defined, somewhat
hazily, as the qualification for the franchise could only be of Old Extent although
not specifically designated as such.[18] Taking all those points into consideration, it
is evident that the freeholder of the act of 1587 was simply a small tenant-in-chief
infeft in an estate that was held *in capite* either by ward or blench tenure and
valued at least at 40/- of Old Extent. If, therefore, for 'freeholder' we read
'liferenter' the act of 1587 becomes nonsensical. In fact, insistence on the classical
feudal tenures and on Old Extent excluded from the terms of the act of 1587
certain categories of proprietors that were steadily increasing in numbers, wealth
and importance. Notable among those were the king's feuars, and also those who
enjoyed liferent interests in lands held directly of the crown by any tenure.

There is no space to consider at length those provisions of the act of 1587 that
sought to regulate election procedure. They are fully discussed by Rait and need
not be detailed here.[19] It must, however, be said that as to the early procedure that
was actually followed contemporary evidence is scanty and not very revealing. A
few items of information from Aberdeenshire have survived, but they throw little
light on the subject. They do, however, show that only those who owed suit to the
sheriff court might elect. The earliest election recorded, that of 1596, did not take
place at the Michaelmas Head Court but was still described as being made by 'the
haill barrowniss within the Schirefdome of Abirdein'.[20] Nor does it appear that
elections were made annually. They were instead made as need arose, but this was
not outside the terms of the act of 1587, which stipulated annual elections at the
Michaelmas Head Courts but also allowed elections to be made at such other
times as were convenient to the freeholders or to the king. That is the substance of
the act, and there is no need to recite in detail the entire procedure of summons
and returns.

The only other point of interest is that commissions had to bear the signatures
of at least six barons or freeholders, a requirement that was not always easy to
meet since in some of the small shires, like Cromarty or Kinross, the total of
freeholders might well fall short of this number.[21] Finally, as in 1428, the barons
were to defray the expenses of their commissioners; but, since the commissioners
could not bring diligence against defaulting freeholders, this provision seems to
have been generally evaded. Thus, after 1587 the representation of the shires in
parliament was far from complete. Taking the condition of the country and its
poor communications into account the act was possibly over-ambitious, and for
upwards of fifty years after its passing no great enthusiasm was evinced by the

---

[18] Rait, *Parliaments*, 205-10. For a full discussion of Old Extent and the numerous problems
associated with it, see J. D. Mackie's comprehensive Introduction to his edition of *Thomas
Thomson's Memorial on Old Extent* (Stair Society, 1946).

[19] Rait, *op. cit.*, 219.

[20] David Littlejohn, ed., *Records of the Sheriff Court of Aberdeenshire* (New Spalding Club, 1904), I,
372-3.

[21] Because of its udal tenures Shetland had no freeholders and was not represented in parliament until
1832 — Rait, *op. cit.*, 230 n.10. In the late seventeenth century Kinrossshire only narrowly escaped
Shetland's fate — Rait, 216-17.

freeholders in most shires. The Head Courts were busy enough institutions, and the whole question of representation was probably still viewed as a time-consuming and expensive chore.

It was not, indeed, until after the Restoration that a parliament, that of 1681, contained commissioners from every sheriffdom and stewartry. By that time the attitude of the freeholders had changed, for reasons that are well known except to those who resolutely close their eyes to the evidence. The Scottish civil war in the reign of Charles I was not entirely a religious struggle. New social classes, and most notably the lairds, were pushing to the fore and the constitutional element that was so evident in 'the Puritan Revolution' in England was by no means lacking in the Scottish upheavals. Scotland had its corpus of legislation freeing parliament from dependence on the crown and, indeed, making parliament the main engine of government.[22] While it is true that the so-called Act Rescissory of 1661 nullified these measures it required more than a statute, however sweeping, to extinguish the political ideas and aspirations that had been fostered by the brief and stormy life of a parliament untrammelled by the king or a committee of the articles rigged in his favour. All the royal commissioners from the Restoration to the Union found the truth of this; and indeed the ultra-royalist members of the Cavalier Parliament itself could be refractory on occasion.[23] It is, therefore, from the Restoration that parliament began to play a more vigorous part in Scottish life, and, as both cause and effect of this, the barons and freeholders coveted the commissions that entitled them to take part in its deliberations. Double returns became common, and to arbitrate on them a committee anent controverted elections was set up at the beginning of each parliament or convention of estates from 1669 onwards.[24] The work of this important committee furnishes a plethora of evidence of heightened political awareness and activity.

True, the committee anent controverted elections was sometimes used as an instrument of management by a hard-pressed executive bent on securing a tractable house by excluding known supporters of opposition. Such an effort was made by the duke of Lauderdale in 1678, and so successfully according to Bishop Burnet that the duke was master of 'four parts in five of that assembly'.[25] Evidently Lord Danby was not the only Restoration statesman experimenting with solutions for the problems of what was later to be known as 'management'.[26]

[22] C. S. Terry, *The Scottish Parliament 1603-1707* (1905) first gave these developments the prominence they deserve. They are admirably summarised with selections from the main documents in W. C. Dickinson and G. Donaldson, edd., *Source Book of Scottish History* (2nd edn., 1961), III, ch. V. H. R. Trevor-Roper's sophistical attempt to argue a contrary case is demolished by David Stevenson in his article, 'Professor Trevor-Roper and the Scottish Revolution', in *History Today*, vol. 30, February 1980, 34-40. For a detailed account of the constitutional and political history of the period, see David Stevenson, *The Scottish Revolution 1637-44* (1973), *passim*, and the same author's *Revolution and Counter-Revolution in Scotland 1644-1651* (1977).

[23] For some revealing instances, see Sir George Mackenzie of Rosehaugh, *Memoirs of the Affairs of Scotland from the Restoration of King Charles II* (1821), 173, 257. See, too, Earl of Balcarres, *Memoirs touching the Revolution in Scotland 1688-1690* (Bannatyne Club, 1841), 2-3.

[24] *APS*, VII, 552, 19 October 1669, for the introduction of the committee; E. B. Thomson, *Parliament of Scotland 1690-1702* (1929), ch. vi, 55-65, is a useful digest of evidence taken from the committee's deliberations.

[25] Gilbert Burnet, ed. O. Airy, *History of His Own Times* (1900), II, 148-9.

[26] Andrew Browning, 'Parties and Party Organization in the Reign of Charles II', *Trans. Roy. Hist. Soc.* (1948), 21-36.

The committee on controverted elections was also later used by the dominant party at the Revolution to exclude Jacobites. At times of bitter political strife such ploys were inevitable; but abuse of the committee's powers was intermittent and not always successful, and more than anything its activities provide a revealing commentary on the heightened interest in elections after 1669. Indeed, this interest had reached such a pitch that the executive could no longer rely upon rigging elections in the constituencies, the stratagem that had worked well enough in the later years of James VI. In sum, the committee anent controverted elections was by no means a trusty tool in the hands of the executive. Electoral malpractice was steadily increasing as interest in parliament grew, and malpractice had to be curbed. The parliamentary record demonstrates that malpractice was effectively restrained mainly through the activities of the committee anent controverted elections, and those activities were not necessarily or invariably sinister.

Two important post-Reformation statutes illustrate, and also help to account for, this new interest in parliament. Their preambles speak of the growth of electoral abuses and the need to curtail them by more precise and just definitions. An act of 1661 aimed specifically at enfranchising the king's feuars, whilst at the same time the vote was confirmed to the 40/- freeholders, although again not *eo nomine* of Old Extent.[27] For the feuars an alternative qualification was devised, since the great bulk of their lands had not been valued on the Old Extent. It was therefore laid down that those who held lands of the king in feu-ferme should have the right to elect or to be elected for parliament provided their land was of L1,000 Scots valued rent, all feu-duties being deducted. It was on this new qualification based on actual current valuation that in 1661 liferenters and proper wadsetters were also first enfranchised. The introduction of current valuation can readily be explained. In 1587 the payment of feu-duties had been the main charge on the feuars, and the crown felt that those fixed sums, which were rapidly being eroded by inflation, furnished inadequate returns. Then, too, by 1661 the feuars were contributing to the land tax on their actual rent. One of the prime objects of the act of 1661, then, was to enfranchise the feuars in order to secure fuller representation of taxable lands. In addition, the act of 1661 went a long way towards defeating old prejudices against attending parliament by ordaining afresh that the commissioners should be paid L5 Scots for their daily upkeep and also a scaled payment for travelling expenses. This time diligence could be brought against defaulters, and from 1661 until the Union the commissioners from the shires were paid. To encourage attendance from the more remote areas such payment was well-nigh indispensable, and in sharp contrast to English practice where M.P.'s received no payment.

The second Restoration act referred to, that of 1681,[28] was the most important of all, for with few substantial alterations it remained the basis of the system of elections in the Scottish counties until 1832. It was evidently passed to widen the electorate, to define the franchise more strictly, and also to improve election procedure and prevent malpractice. First, the traditional elector, the 40/-

[27] *APS.*, VII, 235-6.
[28] *APS.*, VIII, 353-4.

freeholder, was confirmed in his rights. The franchise was also conferred on those who held lands direct of the crown in feu where the lands were valued at at least 40/- of Old Extent, a fact later accepted by Thomas Thomson, pleading in *Cranstoun* v. *Gibson* in 1812, but with far too many caveats. In particular, Thomson argued that the old kirklands, and feu-lands in general, had never been assessed on what he called 'true Old Extent'. But this, of course, plainly begs the question — what was 'true Old Extent?'

Thomson made a brilliant effort to close with the problem of Old Extent, but, in spite of his immense learning, he cannot be said to have solved it, though the solution was within his grasp. He contended that the so-called Old Extent on which some feu-lands were retoured was 'nominal and factitious'.[29] Had it not been for the requirements of advocacy, the learned and acute Thomson might have seen that 'factitious and artificial Old Extent' was probably the sole reality and that 'true Old Extent' was something of a legal fiction. The matter is complicated by the fact that Sir James Dalrymple of Stair, who drew up the statute of 1681, was very hazy on Old Extent and probably historically wrong in his approach to the problem; but, on the other hand, great lawyer that he was, Stair could not ignore certain anomalous statutory developments. Law, after all, is not such a pure science that it can afford to brush aside 'eccentric' legislation.

In 1594 an act of parliament had ordained that all temporal lands annexed to the crown should remain therewith and that they should be retoured. It was further enacted that all feu-lands whatsoever should be retoured and valued to merk or pound lands, 'That his maiestie may know the owner thairof And being retourit that quhen it sall happin any impost or taxatioun to be raisit that the saidis fewaris sall be chargit according to that retoure'.[30] Obviously, this was an attempt to ensure that feuars would contribute their fair share of taxation. The act, however, is usually regarded as having been abortive, though matters are complicated by the fact that some feu-lands, including some old kirklands, were so assessed. In 1681 Dalrymple seems to have recognised the anomalous situation thus created and that provision ought to be made for those in this vexed category. The act of 1681, therefore, states that all 40/- freeholders of Old Extent were to have the vote, but that in reckoning Old Extent in feu-lands the feu-duties must be kept distinct. Professor Mackie seems at one point to suggest an error in drafting, only to withdraw the suggestion later and so leave the matter a total mystery.[31] It is more likely that Stair, aware of the difficulties and anomalies, took stock of the actual situation and allowed for the small number of cases where feu-lands had been properly retoured on Old Extent.

Such difficulties were compounded by the failure of the act to define the manner in which Old Extent should be proved. In practice it came to be accepted that the best mode of proof lay in the production of a retour on a brieve of inquest which would describe the lands and their Extent. The trouble is that Old Extent rapidly became an antiquarian concept. In the eighteenth century relatively few votes were created on Old Extent, and it is to be feared that the main consequence of Thomas Thomson's brilliant pleas has been to give an exaggerated and

---

[29] Mackie, ed., *Thomas Thomson's Memorial on Old Extent*, 272-3.
[30] *APS*, IV, 75.
[31] Mackie, *op. cit.*, 87.

unwarranted importance to the role of such votes. The fact is that as an actual basis of taxation Old Extent was given up in 1667 and after that year the land tax was raised on current valuations that were worked out by the commissions of supply in each shire. By 1681 it was already becoming difficult in many cases to prove Old Extent. Accordingly an alternative qualification was defined based on a modification of the device used in 1661 to enfranchise the feuars. The real value of L1,000 Scots was given up as being too high, and the qualification was fixed on lands held of the king whose valued rents were not less than L400 Scots. Whatever the origin of the lands, whether old kirklands or not, and whatever the tenure, those, in the words of the statute, 'publickie infeft in property or superiority' of lands of this value held of the king or of the prince of Scotland should have the right to elect or be elected.[32]

But, as it happened, the wording 'in property or superiority' later produced severe problems by seeming to justify the eighteenth-century practice of creating votes on bare superiorities, the vast majority of which votes were based on current valuation. Rait rather attributes this unhappy development to Stair, who in his *Institutions* insisted on the rights of superiority.[33] Stair, however, *pace* Rait, had no choice in the matter. He was forced to take cognisance of the rights of superiority, which were in 1681, and had long been, integral parts of the law of Scotland. One need look no further back than Craig for clear evidence of the concept of superiority as it was understood in the early seventeenth century.[34] Nor can Craig be said to have invented the concept of superiority, which was, in fact, as old as the feudal law of Scotland itself. Indeed, it was *the* fundamental concept in Scottish feudal law and practice, and as such it could not be ignored. Insistence on superiority, too, was consonant with the history of representation in Scotland, where vassals, except in the anomalous case of Sutherland, could not vote.[35] Stair, then, was not pushing the claims of superiority, as Rait seems to suggest, but was merely taking stock of existing realities.

And yet, undoubtedly, the phrase 'in property or superiority' is a puzzle. Faultless phraseology would have been 'infeft in property and superiority'. But it is hard to see how, if this were a slip of the pen, it could have survived to the stage where it was touched by the sceptre, making it law. In short, Stair most likely wrote 'or' instead of 'and' of set purpose. It may be that he was trying to broaden the electorate by bringing in those who enjoyed *dominium utile* as well as those

---

[32] *APS*, VIII, 353.

[33] Rait, *Parliaments*, 213.

[34] Craig's *Jus Feudale*, tr. Clyde (1934), I, 583ff., and numerous other passages.

[35] As already stated the composition of parliament in the Middle Ages is hazy and fluid, as the king could largely determine who should be present. Cf. the act of 1504, *APS*, II, 244, which ordains that 'no baron, freeholder, nor vassal' whose lands were valued at less than 100 merks should be compelled to attend unless the king expressly commanded their presence. But it came to be generally accepted that vassals were not eligible either to attend parliament or to vote for a shire commissioner. Sutherland became the exception here. The sheriffdom was not set up until 1633 when the earl of Sutherland gave up his rights of regality only to lease them again from the crown — *APS*, V, 62-3. Since the earl held most of Sutherland *in capite* and was debarred as a nobleman from electing or being elected for the estate of the barons, his immediate vassals were granted the vote. The act was vague and speaks of the electors as being 'the free barons and other inhabitants', and no franchise qualification was fixed until the act 16 George II (1743) set it at L200 Scots, i.e. half the normal freeholder qualification on valued rent. For this whole matter, see Rait, *op. cit.*, 216 and n.10.

who enjoyed *dominium directum*. The point cannot be proved, but other provisions of the act of 1681 could be held to support this view. Those provisions enfranchised adjudgers and proper wadsetters (but only on the expiry of the legal reversion), apparent heirs, liferenters and fiars, and husbands through the courtesy right. These all represented variations on the theme that the vote lay in land of the requisite valuation held of the crown and that in all possible circumstances the land ought to be represented in parliament.

The act of 1681 also further defined the machinery of the electoral system. Again terminology was none too precise. The word 'freeholders' was now used in a generic way to denote all those electors (barons, feuars, liferenters, wadsetters etc.) whose names, designations and valuations were to be entered in a Roll of Freeholders that was to be compiled in each sheriffdom and stewartry. The freeholders thus defined were to meet annually at the Michaelmas Head Court to correct and adjust this roll. The Michaelmas or Freeholders' Head Court derived from one of the three annual *curiae capitales* of the sheriff court,[36] but under the act of 1681 the Michaelmas Head Court came to have a new life virtually independent of the sheriff, sometimes to the annoyance of that pertinacious maid-of-all-work. The sheriff was restricted to formally convening the meeting but had no part to play in the actual proceedings, though evidently at times this statutory requirement was not observed. In 1700 double returns from Wigtownshire were quashed largely on the grounds that the sheriff had participated in the election and had even had the temerity to claim to act as preses *ex officio*.[37] The Head Courts were also found to be useful meetings where the opportunity was taken to consider a wide range of matters of local concern with none of which the freeholders as such were under statutory compulsion to deal. It was from the Head Courts, indeed, that there evolved the county meetings so often referred to in the late eighteenth and early nineteenth centuries. The Reform Act of 1832 recognised that in this way valuable contributions were made to local government and while abolishing the Head Courts took care to transfer their administrative role to the commissioners of supply.

In the powers of the Head Court and the existence of the roll of electors are to be found the main *differentia* between the county electoral systems in Scotland and England. In England county elections were conducted in haphazard fashion; there the polls dragged over several days, and the unfortunate sheriff, who was expected to scrutinise titles on the spot, could rarely make an adequate check on every self-styled 'freeholder'. Thus copyholders frequently passed themselves off as freeholders; and in general all was not as well with English county elections as Lord Chatham in 1770 fondly imagined.[38] Not until 1832 was an official register

---

[36] W. C. Dickinson, *Sheriff Court Book of Fife* (*SHS*, 1928), XIV-XV.

[37] *APS*, X, 202-3, 223, 224-5. Cf. Dickinson, *op. cit.*, XXI, which shows that the sheriff-principal's right to preside over the Michaelmas Head Court was eroded in practice. And certainly the act of 1681, which constituted the Freeholders' Head Courts, made no provision for the sheriff participating in the deliberations of the freeholders.

[38] E. & A. Porritt, *The Unreformed House of Commons* (1909), I, ch. II, gives a general outline of English practice; Eric G. Forrester, *Northamptonshire County Elections and Electioneering, 1695-1832* (1941), and R. J. Robson, *The Oxfordshire Election of 1754* (1949), give specific insights. For Chatham's eulogy, see D. B. Horn and Mary Ransome, edd., *English Historical Documents*, X (1957), 208.

of electors mandatory in England and Wales, whereas in Scotland the roll of the freeholders played an increasingly important part in county elections from 1681. In Scotland the crucial point was to get on the roll. Before 1707 that could only be done in one of two ways — either by satisfying the freeholders at Head Court or election meeting that the claimant was infeft in lands of sufficient valuation held *in capite* as required by the act of 1681; or, failing that, by successfully appealing the case to parliament, and, if parliament were not sitting, to the Court of Session.

There are, unfortunately, gaps in our knowledge of the operation of the system from 1681 to 1707, mainly owing to the scarcity of freeholders' records.[39] The scraps that have survived are insufficient to give a firm impression of general practice. Indeed, there may well have been no such thing as general practice, for local individualism was still strong and each 'country' tended to follow its own bent. Nonetheless, the system of elections seems to have worked, and not just in the Lowlands but in the Highlands as well.[40] On this whole subject Rait misleads by thrusting back into the seventeenth century the abuses that undoubtedly afflicted the electoral system in the counties in the eighteenth century. He was encouraged to do this by his failure to appreciate adequately a profound change of circumstances that was adversely to affect the system. But, in spite of what Rait has to say, close examination of the evidence that relates to the late seventeenth century proves that, on the whole, the system operated reasonably well until 1707.[41] For example, fictitious votes of the kind that wrought such havoc in the eighteenth century were then unknown. The emergence of votes on naked superiorities looks, on the surface, like a sinister development; but they were, in fact, totally different from eighteenth-century faggot votes and perfectly legal.[42] The only real evidence of vote-making stemmed from trust conveyances, one of the earliest recorded examples of which was a case from Ayrshire in 1701. Here it was alleged that John Campbell could not take his place in parliament as commissioner because he was not a *bona fide* freeholder but enrolled in virtue of lands disponed to him in trust by his brother, the earl of Loudoun. Campbell purged himself of the charge by oath, and he was allowed to take his seat.[43] Before 1707 such trust conveyances were known, but they were not numerous enough to undermine the principle of free election.

In sum, the bare-faced roguery and quasi-legal trickery that enabled eighteenth-century politicians to rig constituencies did not operate before 1707. Legal and parliamentary control over elections was too complete and too rigorously enforced to allow such abuses to prevail. The executive, indeed, occasionally had cause to lament this scrupulosity. As the duke of Queensberry explained to Queen Anne in 1703, it was not possible for even a powerful executive to manipulate elections so as to secure even reasonably predictable

---

[39] The sheriff court records were notoriously ill kept, and only a few shires have freeholders' minutes dating back to the late seventeenth century — e.g. Banffshire (1664), Lanarkshire (1673), Ayrshire (1702) and Haddingtonshire (1702). These, too, are all scrappy.

[40] See, e.g., W. McGill, *Old Ross-shire and Scotland*, II (1909), 98-100.

[41] This statement is based on analysis of the cases considered by the Committee anent Contraverted Elections as given in *APS*, vols. VI-XI.

[42] See, e.g., the case of *John Mitchell of Daldilling, APS*, X (1701), 238. Such cases were few and far between.

[43] *APS*, X, 237.

returns.[44] And, indeed, this very problem had already driven King William's ministers frantic, especially in the preparations for the session of parliament of 1700.[45]

These contentions introduce a major problem: if, as claimed, the Scottish pre-union electoral system was not hopelessly corrupt, whence came those extraordinary practices of which there is so much evidence in the eighteenth and early nineteenth centuries, and which, in the judgement of a recent historian, made Scotland 'resemble one vast rotten borough'?[46] The exaggeration in this view is as obvious as its core of truth, but though the whole matter is easily unriddled the answer is unacceptable to many. The real begetter of those unfortunate defects was undoubtedly the Act of Union of 1707. But the Union of 1707 is commonly regarded as being above criticism; so the traditional reasoning in this matter has to conclude that the fault must lie in the law of Scotland, which is usually flayed for being 'feudal' and backward. Review of the evidence shows how evasive and unsatisfactory this case is. Indeed, the simulacrum of such a case can only be maintained by blandly ignoring the evidence. There is no need to labour the point: the following chief heads of argument must suffice.

Not only did the Union of 1707 drastically reduce the number of shire constituencies in Scotland, thereby increasing competition for returns to a more lucrative source of profit than Parliament House had ever been, but also, and far more serious in the long run, Article XXII of the Treaty and Act of Union failed to provide any effective means of checking the activities of the freeholders. The chief mistake made was to deprive the Court of Session of its review jurisdiction over the acts of the freeholders, and this was done not by statutory enactment but by implication and assumption.

In a late eighteenth century franchise case the judges gave some interesting comments on the position of the Court of Session between 1707 and 1743. From the union until 1743 (when jurisdiction was restored), Lord Eskgrove stated that there was no instance of a man coming before the Court of Session as a freeholder. The Lord President's contribution to the discussion was even more illuminating. According to Ilay Campbell, 'On the abolition of the Scottish Parliament, it would have been a nice question, whether political questions like this could have come here in the recess of Parliament. His Lordship looked for cases in the interval betwixt the Union and 16 George II but he could find none. It was never understood that the Court had a jurisdiction, or at least it was never attempted to be made use of'. The Lord President concluded 'that the hands of the Court were tied up by the terms of the Act 16 George II, the only authority under which they hold their jurisdiction'.[47]

[44] P. Hume Brown, *The Legislative Union of England and Scotland* (1914), 46.
[45] J. McCormick, ed., *Carstares State Papers* (1774), 492-3, 583-6, 598-600.
[46] Norman Gash, *Politics in the Age of Peel* (1953), 36.
[47] Bell, *op. cit.*, 384-6, opinions of judges in *Macleod* v. *Goodsman*, 1791. Cp. Patrick Grant, Lord Elchies, *Decisions*, ed. W. M. Morison (Edinburgh, 1813), II, s.v. 'Member of Parliament' where eighteen such applications to the Court of Session are recorded from 1738 onwards. But the Court of Session was obviously unhappy about these franchise cases and spent much of its time debating its competence to hear them. Some of Elchies's cases also turn upon points of feudal law, which was always, of course, within the competence of the court, and which in these particular instances had a secondary bearing upon elections.

This lapse of jurisdiction after the Union was serious. It was also compounded by the inhibiting effect upon Scottish jurists of the imposition — again unenacted — of the supreme appellate jurisdiction of the House of Lords. This proved to be a most unhappy development in the political no less than the legal sphere and led, as we shall see, to some absurd results. As regards disputed election returns, the House of Commons after 1707 undoubtedly had the right to determine these; but it was soon evident that disputed returns were dealt with on purely partisan lines, and further evident that the great majority of M.P.s had neither the inclination nor the knowledge needed to arbitrate in franchise cases or election disputes from Scotland, the very language of which was foreign to them.[48]

A cardinal fact, then, in the conduct of county elections in eighteenth century Scotland must be that for 36 years after the Union of 1707 there was no real check on the operation of the electoral machinery. As a result some bizarre developments took place which were not sanctioned by the representation acts, though these were often wildly glossed to suit the needs of aspiring parliamentarians. It does not seem unreasonable to suppose that if the Court of Session had been allowed to retain jurisdiction after 1707 corrupt procedures could have been restrained. Historians, however, have mostly failed to recognise this unhealthy result of the Union, and their failure here has seriously distorted historical perspective.[49] This kind of fudging too often palms off as history a mere myth agreed upon.

Naturally, the politicians in Scotland after 1707 were not slow to exploit such a lax and inviting situation. Trust conveyances, known but not widely used before the Union, increased in numbers.[50] By 'trust conveyance' was meant the complete disposition, in both property and superiority, of an estate that qualified for the vote on the understanding, inserted usually in a back-bond, that it would be returned to the original owner on request. The second duke of Queensberry, the first post-Union political manager, was accused of manipulating the general election of 1708 by means of such conveyances.[51] Malpractice was made easier, too, because the Head Courts fell under the sway of cliques whose object was to monopolise the rolls of the freeholders, ruthlessly expunging opponents, sometimes on the flimsiest of pretexts, and enrolling supporters, often on the most dubious of titles, Then, too, the political power of the Scots nobles (supposedly reduced by their meagre representation in the House of Lords) was actually enhanced once techniques had been worked out for the mass manufacture of nominal votes on bare superiorities. In all those respects, and

[48] Bell, *op. cit.*, 30.
[49] E.g., Porritts, *op. cit.*, II, ch. XXXIX; and Holden Furber, *Henry Dundas, First Viscount Melville* (1931), 175-88. Only John Hill Burton seems to have caught a glimpse of the truth. He was an advocate and had better insight into legal and constitutional matters than most general historians. In his *History of Scotland* (New Edn., 1897), VIII, 187, appears a brief but penetrating sentence on the franchise before the Union. It was, he believed, narrow but genuine, and the fictitious vote he regarded as an unintended product of the Union. Unfortunately, he took the topic no further and did not elaborate his argument. Porritt, perhaps following Hill Burton, also sensed something amiss but could assign no real reason for the proliferation of fictitious votes after 1707.
[50] Bell, *op. cit.*, 275ff.
[51] *Somers, Tracts*, XII, 627-8.

many others, abuses multiplied, and the restraints on the freeholders were soon discovered to be inadequate.

As early as 1714 an act was passed in an attempt to prevent electoral malpractice. It sought, in particular, to suppress trust conveyances by obliging claimants for enrolment to take an Oath of Trust and Possession; but this proved of no effect. True, trust conveyances rapidly went out of fashion, but only because they were clumsy and inefficient. In the 1720s and '30s they were completely superseded by more subtle conveyancing forms which took nothing from their authors but empty superiorities and conferred upon the assignees nothing of real value except a claim for enrolment as a freeholder.

The act 12 Anne also sought to prevent registration abuses by requiring that the sasines of claimants for enrolment should be registered for one year before the writ of election was issued. The act, however, was a complete failure. All sorts of malpractices grew, and naturally enough since effective means of restraining them did not exist. Votes on Old Extent were made by splitting retours into as many 40/- lots as possible, though most fictitious votes were manufactured on the alternative qualification of L400 Scots current valuation. The hair-splitting ingenuity of the feudalists had a field day, and it is hard not to be impressed by the professional virtuosity of the conveyancers. But matters became too gross, and the need for some authoritative agency to define and apply the election statutes became clamant. To this problem the Court of Session was the obvious solution, and finally by the act 16 George II (1743) the Court of Session was granted jurisdiction over franchise cases.

This is an important statute but too long to be considered here in the detail it deserves. It sought to do three things. First, it sought to restrain sheriffs and other officials from acting partially at elections. This it achieved by laying down heavy penalties for each transgression, and these penalties of £500 sterling for each transgression on the sheriff's part and £300 on the sheriff clerk's were recoverable by any party having interest to sue by summary complaint to the Court of Session. Secondly, parties dissatisfied with the acts of the freeholders, either regarding enrolments or expungings, might petition the Lords of Session. Thirdly, in order to prevent arbitrary treatment of claims for enrolment, claimants had to go through a statutory procedure; and so, too, in their deliberations should the freeholders.

The act 16 George II was commendable, but paradoxically, while solving some problems (notably malpractice by the sheriffs and sheriff clerks), its shortcomings rather added to the existing confusion. The act's chief defect was that it did not confer a wide enough jurisdiction upon the Court of Session, and the judges at first restricted themselves too narrowly to the express terms of the statute. Nor did the statute adequately define election law and procedure, and as a consequence the questionable practices of the unregulated years between 1707 and 1743 were too often accepted as standard. The freeholders, in particular, were not tightly bound to a prescribed procedure and continued far too much a law unto themselves.

Thus, the problem of Old Extent, whilst seemingly regulated by the act 16 George II, entered into a new and even more tortuous phase. The act scored by requiring that no claim on Old Extent could be considered valid unless based on the production of a retour dated before 16 September 1681, and furthermore that a retour was not divisible. However many multiples of 40/- were represented by the valuation given, a retour could only validate one vote. The number of votes on Old Extent dropped significantly after 1743, but litigation on the subject became extraordinarily complex and confusing. This was partly because in the eighteenth century there was no general agreement as to what Old Extent was.[52] One extreme view held that 'There is but one old extent, whereof we hardly have the date, which remains unalterably the same, being about 50,000 marks for all Scotland'.[53] This crude antiquarianism was accepted as a statement of legal fact by most judges and lawyers because it enabled them to represent as Old Extent any sum so recorded. But the idea that Old Extent was, and always had been, a constant was palpably false, and the result was a grand confusion. The retours, in short, were not the best form of evidence, but the judges were stuck with them.

Furthermore, the Extent had to be entered in the Valent Clause of the retour and not just given in the Descriptive Clause. The reason for this stipulation was that the Descriptive Clause was general and based on consensus, but the Valent Clause had to be sworn to by the jurors under oath.[54] If the Valent Clause were in *cumulo* (i.e. with the valuations on an estate given as a lump sum and not apportioned to individual lands), and if it agreed in every respect with the Descriptive Clause, the retour was found to be sufficient evidence.[55] If for example, the Descriptive Clause of a retour described four separate parcels, of land each valued at 40s of Old Extent, and if the Valent Clause gave the *cumulo* as L8 of Old Extent, then those infeft in the separate valuations as entered in the Descriptive Clause would be entitled to vote. The whole matter, however, became more and more complicated. The precise identification of lands described in old retours or extracts from chancery was by no means easy. The records were not always well preserved; and sometimes names changed, or were transposed to other lands. Sometimes even the sheriffdoms changed, and here the lengthy and sporadic process known as 'the shiring of the north' (the splitting up of the vast medieval sheriffdom of Inverness) created many pitfalls. In all those ways, and others too fine in detail and too numerous to mention, the difficulties associated with the vote on Old Extent steadily grew. This was clearly illustrated in a case from Wigtownshire which involved old kirklands formerly held by the bishop of Galloway: the objections to those claimants on Old Extent were repelled even though it was observed on the bench 'That this was the strongest instance that had ever occurred of a title purely nominal, and which conveyed no real interest in land; but it had been decided in other cases, that no regard was to be had to the *value* of the estate, provided the claimant was really and truly vested in the right such as it was'.[56] The case of the Galloway voters turned entirely on the difficulty of proving Old Extent, and the final decision showed that uncertain legal ground was rapidly developing into a quagmire.

---

[52] Mackie, ed., *Thomson's Memorial*, 89-96.
[53] *Elchies*, II, 274, s.v. Member of Parliament.
[54] David Falconer, *Decisions [D.Falc.]* (Edinburgh, 1746, 1753), I, 83-4, *Sir Michael Stewart* v. *Archibald Campbell of Elderslie*, 19 December 1744.
[55] *Elchies*, II, 263, s.v. Member of Parliament No. 22, *Case of Freeholders of Renfrewshire*, 18 January 1745.
[56] *Faculty Collection of Decisions*, (21 Vols.) 1752-1825 [*F.C.*], 28 July 1761, *Walter Stewart, Advocate and others*, v. *David Dalrymple, Advocate*.

As a result of the difficulty of proving Old Extent most enrolments after 1743 were on the alternative qualification of L400 Scots actual valuation. Statistics cannot be cited to clinch this point, but it is the unmistakeable impression conveyed by the freeholders' records. It is suggestive, too, that of a total number of about 220 franchise cases counted between 1743 and 1832, only twenty eight dealt with Old Extent.[57] That is, in fact, rather a high incidence considering that votes on current valuation were so much more numerous, and it looks as if owing to the difficulty of proving Old Extent a higher proportion of such claims were challenged before the Court of Session. And indeed of the twenty eight cases all, like Thomas Thomson's famous classic, *Cranstoun* v. *Gibson*, are concerned with one crucial point — namely, the difficulty of proving Old Extent.

Numerous objections could also be urged against the claim on L400 Scots of current valuation. Often the commissioners of supply, part of whose duty it was to furnish certificates of valuation, acted in the most arbitrary and sometimes partisan manner. The earliest case on this subject, that of *Abercrombie* v. *Leslie*, was the archetype. At Michaelmas 1752 Colonel Abercrombie complained against the enrolment of William Leslie as a freeholder of the county of Banff on the grounds that no legal evidence of valuation had been produced to instruct the claim. To yield Leslie a franchise qualification a division of *cumulo* had been necessary, but, averred Abercrombie, this had not been carried out by a legal meeting of the commissioners of supply. Instead, four of the commissioners who were friendly with Leslie had convened privately, without legal summons, and had divided the *cumulo*. Although nothing could be said against the accuracy of the decreets of division, the Court of Session found the meeting illegal, and Leslie was accordingly ordered to be expunged from the Roll of the Freeholders.[58] The case of *Cunningham* v. *Stirling*, decided eleven months later, reinforced this decision, although in this case from Stirlingshire the illegal division of *cumulo* had taken place in 1739.[59] Even where honest errors had been made in valuating and the claimants had been enrolled thereon, an offer by the commissioners of supply to furnish a new and accurate certificate could not prevent the freeholder concerned from being expunged.[60] On the other hand, in the case of *Forester of Denovan* v. *Sir George Preston of Valleyfield*, also from Stirlingshire, it was held that the freeholders were bound to accept a certificate of valuation if *ex facie* good.[61] The truth is that it was slowly dawning on the judges that much more was at stake than a few paltry votes, and increasingly, as we shall see, the Court of Session was perturbed by the side-effects of vote-making.

As to the actual valuation of estates the subjects valued were extensive, and, indeed, included anything 'whereby yearly profit and commodity ariseth'.[62] The

---

[57] The number of cases has been estimated as follows: from the *Faculty Collection of Decisions 1752-1825*, then *Decisions 1825-1832*, 196; and from Elchies's *Decisions* (1733-1754), 24. The estimate is rough because some cases went unreported, and on others that were fully reported the fate of a number of claimants or freeholders would depend.

[58] *Colonel Abercrombie* v. *William Leslie of Melross*, 21 February 1753, *F.C.*

[59] *Captain Robert Cunningham* v. *George Stirling*, 9 January 1754, *F.C.*

[60] *John Callendar of Craigforth, Advocate,* v. *Robert Bruce of Kennet, Advocate*, 17 January 1755, *F.C.* This case also came from Stirlingshire.

[61] *Thomas Forester of Denovan* v. *Sir George Preston of Valleyfield*, 18 February 1755, *F.C.*

[62] *APS*, VI, pt. I, 26-36, Act of Convention of Estates, 15 August 1643. Bell, *Treatise*, 46-71, gives an excellent account of valuation as it affected the freeholder's qualification.

income from grain was assessed at the agreed fiars' prices per boll, and the sale of bestial, with yields of teinds, feu-duties, tenements, mills, fishings and boats were all included. In theory the valuation of the county and the apportionment of cess upon the individual proprietors was supposed to be checked and brought up to date on 30 April each year at the statutory meeting of the commissioners of supply; but in practice, once the valuation of the county was established to the general satisfaction, the commissioners rarely bothered to meet regularly. In some counties, too, the freeholders formed the substantial body of the commissioners of supply, and the mixing of freeholder and supply business had obvious enough dangers that were not always avoided.

The importance of the county valuations cannot be overstressed, either from the fiscal or the political point of view. On their basis the land-tax or supply was raised, and this was one of the most important sources of government revenue. The valuations also help to account for the relative number of freeholders in the different shires. No absolute calculus operates here, however, because, of course, in individual shires great estates held by noblemen would account for much of the valuation, although these would contribute a variable quota of freeholders of the nominal type. Thus, Fife, assessed at L363,192 Scots had 206 freeholders on its roll in 1811 (187 in 1788); Perthshire, valued at L339,892 Scots had 177 freeholders (161 in 1788); and Ross-shire, valued at L75,043 Scots had 68 (74 in 1788).[63] The equation between valuation and the number of electors is far from perfect largely because of the nominal votes. Ayrshire in 1811 had 151 freeholders (214 in 1788), although only assessed at L191,605 Scots. Ayrshire, therefore, must almost have reached saturation point as regards nominals, as had Dunbartonshire with 41 freeholders (66 in 1788) for a mere L33,327 Scots of valuation. And, indeed, we know that the shires of Ayr and Dunbarton were racked by savage election contests in the 1770s which threw up large numbers of fictitious votes.[64]

The complex conveyancing needed to create such votes is best described by Bell.[65] What follows is a simplified summary of one of the schemes described. Suppose A to be infeft in property and superiority in an estate valued *in cumulo* at L1,200 Scots. This is divided into three lots valued at L400 Scots each. Assuming A to be a commoner, one such lot will be retained to preserve his own vote. To a friend B he grants a separate feu-charter of each of the other lots, thus separating the superiority (which A retains) from the property. A then resigns the estate, with the exception of the first lot, valued at L400 Scots on which his own vote is to be maintained, and receives a Charter of Resignation. Next, A dispones the lands of lot No. 2 to C, and similarly those of lot No. 3 to D. But in the clause of warrandice of each conveyance he excepts the feu-rights already granted to B. The latter now reconveys the feu-rights to A who thus takes a base infeftment on the property under C and D as his superiors. Finally, the transaction is completed

[63] Information from Anon., *View of the Political State of Scotland at Michaelmas, 1811*, and Adam., ed., *Political State of Scotland in 1788*.

[64] For Ayrshire, see James Fergusson, *SHR* (1947), 'Making Interest in Scots County Elections'; for Dunbartonshire, *Commons' Journals*, vol. 38, p. 14, 7 November 1781, and Joseph Irving, *The Book of Dunbartonshire* (1879), I, 334-7.

[65] Bell, *Treatise*, 74ff.; and Bell, *A Treatise on the Conveyance of Land to a Purchaser* (1815), ch. II, sect. III, i, 'Of Constituting a Vote'.

by having the commissioners of supply split the *cumulo* valuation into three separate parcels valued at L400 Scots each. In other words, he has transferred the superiorities of lots two and three to C and D whose vassal he now becomes. He has sacrificed nothing of real value, but he has placed C and D in a position to claim the vote. Nor did the dispositions to C and D need to be outright alienations. It was more usual for them to take the form of wadset rights redeemable for a slight sum within a term of years, 5 or 7 was common, or else to be conveyed as liferent interests with A as fiar.

For long the proper wadset on a naked superiority was one of the commonest means of creating votes. It was undoubtedly an abuse of the act of 1681, and could not even shelter behind the fig leaf that covered the complete conveyance of a superiority, as in Bell's hypothetical case. The proper wadset sanctioned in 1681 was a definite business transaction; but, clearly, to advance money on a naked superiority of lands valued at L400 Scots, the casualties of superiority being elusory and the wadset redeemable at a fixed date for a ridiculously small sum, was not a normal business proposition. Yet when they first appeared the Court of Session failed to take a decided stand against such wadsets, and they long continued to flourish by no better warrant than some very dubious decisions. One of the earliest of these, *Freeholders of Ross* v. *Munro*, set the tone for many subsequent developments. It was objected that Munro's claim was not founded on a proper wadset, since there was no power given to the disponee to require the money to which he was allegedly entitled. The judges overruled the objection and Munro was among the first of a considerable number of claimants on wadset qualifications to be upheld by the Court of Session.[66]

The main trouble with wadsets of superiority, that they evidently only involved elusory sums, could be obviated in the case of liferent votes. These could be just as nominal, but nominality was not as patent and consequently harder to prove. They were also easily constructed and conferred certain advantages. The proprietor remained as fiar, and thus on the death of the liferenter all rights over the lands concerned would revert to the original owner or to his heir. Frantic conveyancing for electioneering purposes often created impenetrable tenurial tangles but with liferent and fee in time the problems would be resolved. Again, from the purely political viewpoint the vote in liferent and fee had the added advantage that both the liferenter and the fiar could be enrolled, although the fiar could only vote in the absence of the liferenter. This was an increasingly valuable concession, for many freeholders were often unable to attend election meetings, either through ill health, business vocations or military service abroad. If the fiar were, so to speak, a more or less permanent fixture in the shire (and care was usually taken that he should be), then the vote on liferent and fee was seldom wasted. For these reasons such votes were much favoured, particularly by the nobles, who, by using a modified form of this device in which the fiar was seemingly a commoner, could build up sizeable interests.

Such were the main forms of nominal and fictitious votes, but within this general framework variety was considerable. To some extent this morass developed after 1743 because the Court of Session stood in dread of the result of an appeal to the House of Lords.[67] The Court of Session, therefore, tried to play

---

[66] *Elchies*, II, 267, s.v. Member of Parliament, *Freeholders of Ross* v. *Munro*, 18 July, 1745.
[67] Ramsay, *Scotland and Scotsmen*, I, 340-2.

safe and protect the law of Scotland from the wild judgments of the court of last appeal by anticipating verdicts likely to be reached by the Lords. Historically, a fierce election contest in Stirlingshire in 1755 was the background to a leading case which gave the Court of Session's sanction to the creation of nominal and fictitious votes. Nominality was easily proved since the casualties of superiority had been waived; and yet the Court of Session found the titles good.[68] The next major landmark was the case of *Campbell of Shawfield* in 1760, which, among its other interesting features, shows how the making of nominal and fictitious votes enabled noblemen to influence county elections in Scotland. In 1759 the freeholders of Renfrewshire rejected claims for enrolment put forward by Daniel Campbell of Shawfield and William Graham of Gartmore on qualifications bestowed on them by the earl of Glencairn. The lands concerned were proved to belong to entailed estates and therefore incapable of being disponed; but the judges found that the titles in dispute were *ex facie* good, and Campbell and Graham were ordered to be added to the roll of the freeholders.[69] Fortified by such decisions the creation of nominal votes proceeded apace, virtually unchecked and, as precedent piled upon precedent, apparently uncheckable.

Thus, for almost half a century after 1743, the Court of Session was shackled by the very act of parliament that gave it a review jurisdiction in franchise cases. Despite bitter protests from some judges, notably Kames, who would willingly have given the law a stretch to clean up election affairs,[70] it was not until 1790 that the Court won a major victory against corrupt practices in county elections. Indeed, as the purveyor of a 'law' twisted into increasingly capricious shapes, the Court of Session became, most unwillingly, one of the main instruments in perverting county elections in Scotland. From 1743 onwards franchise cases were numerous, and it could easily happen that elections might be determined by judicial decisions either of the Court of Session or of the House of Lords.[71]

As already stated, from about 1743 until 1832, 220 franchise cases have been recorded, a fair number considering the smallness of the county electorate.[72] These cases, as already indicated, are an important source of information, but it is unsound to attempt to construct on them a rigid theory of electoral law and procedure in the eighteenth and early nineteenth centuries. From the view-point of the contemporary practising lawyer this was done in the three classical treatises on election law already referred to, each of which gave the more or less accepted legal position at its time of publication. One can readily see why Wight, Bell and Connell adopted this approach; but one can also readily enough see why for the student of history the approach is wrong.

The truth is that the situation at law was very fluid, and decisions varied

---

[68] *Thomas Forrester of Dunnovan and other freeholders of Stirlingshire* v. *Andrew Fletcher, younger of Saltoun, Lieutenant James Campbell, and David Gourlay of Kepdarroch*, 9 January 1755, F.C.

[69] *Daniel Campbell of Shawfield and William Graham of Gartmore* v. *William Muir of Caldwall*, 5 February 1760, F.C. The interlocutor was sustained on appeal to the House of Lords, 1 December 1706 — *ibid.*, 504, 'Cases Appealed'.

[70] Ramsay, *Scotland and Scotsmen*, I, 341.

[71] As happened, e.g. in the general election of 1768 in Cromartyshire. See *Old Session Papers*, Signet Library, vols. 133, 139, 140, 682 and 684 — especially vol. 684, items 28 and 29.

[72] In 1788 Bute, with 12, had the smallest county electorate, and Ayrshire the largest with 214. The total number of county electors in Scotland was 2,662. See Adam, ed., *Political State of Scotland in 1788*.

greatly from time to time. In the 1740s and '50s the Court of Session was content to restrict itself narrowly to the statutory powers conferred upon it by the act 16 George II; but this restrictive approach bred as many ills as it cured, and in the late 1760s the Court of Session was forced to widen its attitude, particularly as regards nominal and fictitious votes, which were by then assuming dangerous proportions. The ramifications, too, of freehold cases could touch on vital matters of public administration, and when this happened the judges had to take a harder line with freeholders. The conveyancing and registering of lands, their valuations, and the cess levied for the shires were all far too important to be perverted at the whim of freeholders or would-be freeholders. The clash between public policy and private interest came to a head in numerous cases that arose out of preparations for the general election of 1768. Those cases monopolised much of the Court of Session's valuable time between 1765 and 1768, and this, too, was a fact of some weight. The cases from the shires of Forfar and Cromarty were largely instrumental in convincing the judges that new and stricter measures to control the Head Courts were needed, not only to safeguard public administration but also to prevent the time of the Court of Session from being wasted by pettifogging election cases.

In Forfarshire as early as 1765 the earl of Panmure, an Irish peer and the sitting member, became aware that an opposition against him was forming, and so he had recourse to the increasingly popular device of making votes. In 1765, therefore, he created six liferent superiorities on his estate, which were followed by eighteen more early in 1766 and another nineteen in the Martinmas term of that year. He thus created forty three votes in all, a respectable number for a Scottish county. By way of response, the earl of Strathmore, brother of Thomas Lyon, the rival candidate, also began to make votes. Each side, schoolboy fashion, later accused the other of initiating those bad practices, but it is clear from the evidence produced in the relevant Session Papers that, if indeed Panmure was the original offender, it was only a case of getting his blow in first.[73] Strathmore did not long lag behind; but, unfortunately for his brother, the earl found that the valuation available on his estate was insufficient to wipe out the headstart Panmure had won. Another landowner in the county, Hunter of Burnside, was accordingly induced to create votes for the use of Thomas Lyon. This brought about parity. Each interest could count upon as many genuine and as many prospective fictitious votes as its rival. In such a situation adroit control of the commission of supply for the county might well secure victory. The commissioners of supply could so delay or falsify divisions of *cumulo* valuations as to press the advantage of the particular interest that controlled the 'supply meetings'. So each side brought its influence to bear on the commissioners, and, though the precise inducements offered are not known, the upshot is clear enough. The commissioners split into two parties, each claiming to be the legal commission of supply for Forfarshire, and each stigmatising the other as a 'mere junto'. Involved and long-drawn-out legal battles then ensued in the Court of Session to decide which decreets of the commissioners were valid and which

[73] The whole of *Old Session Papers*, vol. 665 is devoted to 'Forfarshire Elections, 1765-9', and is a mine of information on the subject. Only a very brief summary can be given here. I am indebted to the Society of Writers to the Signet for access to their invaluable collections, and to their librarian, Mr. Ballantyne, and library staff for much helpful advice.

invalid. Panmure was finally elected, but only after what was then known in political jargon as 'a vast struggle in the legal field'.

At the same time similar circumstances arose in Cromartyshire where William Johnstone (later better known as Sir William Pulteney) was striving to oust Sir John Gordon of Invergordon. The background to 'the Cromartie politicks' was extremely complicated, as shown by the immense volume of evidence laid before the Court of Session. Harrowing in its detail and difficult to interpret though it is, that evidence is of the greatest value in illustrating the system of elections in the Scottish counties before 1832. The same tricks and stratagems were in general use, and, as in the shires of Cromarty and Forfar between 1765 and 1768, tangles of litigation could easily arise if two more or less evenly balanced interests were determined to carry on an election contest to the very limit of endurance. Cromarty, too, had some unique features that added to the complications.

The ancient shire of Cromarty was one of the smallest in Scotland, and as such was one of the six shires with small electorates that were 'paired' in 1707 — i.e. it took turns with its pair, Nairnshire, to return a Member of Parliament. A further complication lay in the fact that since 1690 the county had been augmented by the addition of enclaves in Ross-shire belonging to the new proprietors of Cromarty, the Mackenzies of Tarbat.[74] For half a century thereafter the Mackenzies of Tarbat, or Cromartie, dominated the politics of Cromartyshire and virtually monopolised its representation. But in 1739 Sir William Gordon of Invergordon gained control of the Head Court, and the fall of the Mackenzies was confirmed by the third earl of Cromartie's forfeiture for his ill-judged participation in the Jacobite rebellion of 1745. The Gordon interest, in the person of Sir William's son and heir, Sir John Gordon, continued to monopolise the representation of the county even though Sir John's position was shaky. His father, at one time a successful London financier, had died bankrupt, and a judicial sale of the estates in 1751 had left Sir John and his nominals on the roll of freeholders but on titles rendered invalid by the sale. By tyrannising over the county and bending the laws to suit his needs, Sir John Gordon nevertheless continued to control the leading political interest in Cromartyshire. Litigious, sharp and brazen, he frustrated an attempt to force on a Head Court in 1753, and even managed to secure his victory by a most curious decision in the Court of Session — namely, that annual Head Courts were permissive and not mandatory. Here a claimant for enrolment petitioned the Court of Session complaining that the freeholders of Cromarty had refused to meet in Head Court to consider his claim for enrolment, which had been properly lodged. It was argued for the freeholders that they were under no statutory compulsion to meet annually, and that the terms of the acts of 1681 and 1743 in this matter were merely permissive. And so the Lords of Session found.[75] Indeed, from 1742, apart

---

[74] *APS*, IX, 194. Sir George Mackenzie of Tarbat, head of this family, became successively viscount of Tarbat in 1685 and first earl of Cromartie in 1703.

[75] *Elchies*, II, 281-2, s.v. Member of Parliament, No. 60, *Case of M'Kenzie etc.* v. *Sir John Gordon*, 20 December 1753. For a fuller account see *Old Session Papers* (Signet Library), vol. 14: 22, *Mackenzie* v. *Gordon*. For some caustic comments on the decision in this important case, see Kames, *Historical Law Tracts* (ed., 1792), Tract VII, 228-9. Elchies says 'we all agreed that it was a great abuse' but that the complaint was incompetent.

from an election meeting in 1754, when naturally Sir John Gordon was returned, the freeholders of Cromartyshire did not meet until Michaelmas 1765.

The Head Court of that year was produced by circumstances beyond the control of Sir John Gordon, who found himself unable to continue his role of masterly inactivity. The intervention of William Johnstone saw to that. Johnstone, a nephew of Patrick, Lord Elibank, was looking for a seat in parliament and thought that Cromartyshire presented the easiest means of gaining one. Sir John Gordon was impoverished, out of favour with government, and highly unpopular locally. It was well known, too, that he and his nominals had no good titles to be on the roll. So, it looked as if all that Johnstone needed to secure the seat was admission to the roll of the freeholders, and the purchase of an estate in the county seemed to furnish him with the necessary means. Sir John, however, took the alarm and got the commissioners of supply to refuse valuations for Johnstone's vote-making schemes. Johnstone riposted by claiming that the true commission of supply was on his side, and that Gordon's commission was, in the current advocates' slang, 'a mere junto'. The Court of Session was soon bogged down in intricate cases brought by both sides in an endeavour to justify their own creations and to nullify those of their rivals as either nominal and fictitious or improperly instructed. The ramifications were wide, and the prospects for the advocates good, for they were paid so much per page of written pleadings and, thus inspired, their splendid eighteenth-century prose tended to gallop repetitively on.

Johnstone saw his easy victory, as it must have appeared when the estate in Cromartyshire was purchased on his behoof in 1763, growing more and more difficult — and more and more expensive. He sought to make use of the usual expedient in such circumstances. He tried to buy off Sir John by offering to purchase his estate, but purely as a temporary vote-making measure. The offer, made in September 1765, was indignantly rejected. The result was three years of desperate politicking and prolonged, and very expensive, litigation. Between June 1765 and February 1767 some forty processes dealing with the politics of this insignificant little northern shire dragged their slow lengths along before weary and bemused judges. Long pleadings — duplies, triplies, reclaiming petitions, eked out by every expedient known to skilled advocacy — were gone through in the Court of Session, and followed by appeals to the House of Lords. Every move, every minute incident in the involved operations of each party was seized upon. The advocates employed all their wiles, and while their paymasters lasted refused to let the causes die. The interlocking processes became one vast labyrinthine tangle, and towards the end the Cromarty cases became grotesquely unreal even to the judges. Their sheer bulk probably exceeded that of the celebrated Douglas Cause; and, indeed, for a time those two gargantuan causes occupied the same sessions. Pelted by the Douglas litigants, with a galaxy of legal talent in full cry, the poor judges were apt to find that the next task awaiting them was yet another of the Cromarty pleas.[76] From 30 April 1765 onwards the course of events becomes obscure and hard to reconstruct, largely because, as their lordships found, the facts of the situation were bandied about in so many

---

[76] For details of the struggle in Cromartyshire, see *Old Session Papers*, vols. 133, 139, 140, 682 and 684.

Petitions and Answers. It became a matter of asseveration and counter-asseveration. Well might the harassed Lord Monboddo exclaim in December 1767, 'There have been extraordinary doings in this country [i.e. county], owing to the madness of elections; votes have been created, commissioners of supply have been created'.[77] And out of the swirling mists of advocacy worse revelations were to come, revelations that proved that, in his desperation, Sir John Gordon had caused the Register of Sasines to be tampered with. He bribed the deputy-keeper of the local register at Inverness to insert sasines under a false date so as to steal a march on the rival interest. The fraud, however, was detected and furnished Pulteney with a powerful weapon in the Head Court of 1766.

The political outcome was touch-and-go all the way. Significantly, too, every swing in the fortunes of the two contending parties was attributable to legal decisions either in the Court of Session or in the House of Lords. Pulteney, who enjoyed ministerial favour and had the greater resources of money and influence, seemed the likelier to win. Thus, it was no surprise when the Gordon interest was decimated in the Head Court of 1766. Most candidates would have given up at this point, but the indomitable Sir John Gordon continued to battle on in the legal field. He won several important cases and reduced the number of Pulteney's votes. Indeed, by the time of the election meeting Pulteney could muster seven votes and Gordon six. Everything turned on the fate of a vote held by one of Pulteney's nominals, Captain Fraser of Culduthill. On 19 February 1768 the judges had come to a strange conclusion in this extremely involved case: they found that Fraser's claim was defective in one vital respect, but they decided that he should not be expunged from the roll! This situation led to a violent election meeting. Sir John Gordon was determined to expunge Fraser, so reducing each side to six votes, in which event Sir John as last elected Member of Parliament would become preses and thus secure his own election by his casting vote. Pulteney finally lost patience and, after a scuffle, seized the minutes of election. The two parties then separated, each making a return, and the double return gave rise to fresh litigation. In the end the election was decided by the House of Commons which, on deliberating on the double return, found in favour of Pulteney.

The great point to emerge from this Homeric contest was how little, relatively speaking, that wealth and influence counted for in a bitter Scottish election contest where the two sides were evenly balanced. The side with the most experience of election law and procedure might well be better off than the one that relied mainly upon ministerial favour. In the Cromartyshire cases the legal honours were about even, and it was this more than anything else that led to such a prolonged struggle and pushed up the costs. The total bill probably came to about £20,000, a crippling sum for an eighteenth century Scottish county election. These cases had also given the judges much to think about, and the first result of their thinking was the introduction of special interrogatories.

For, in far more than their political aspect, these cases from the shires of Forfar and Cromarty were alarming. Quite clearly, if something were not done to keep rival politicians in order, then the whole shaky structure of local

---

[77] Connell, *Treatise*, 120, on *Pulteney* v. *Gordon*, 24 December 1767. Connell derived this information from Session Notes kept by Lord Hailes which cannot now be traced.

government and administration might collapse. The danger was by no means imaginary; and matters were made worse by the fact that the freeholders, the commissioners of supply and local magistrates were often the same persons. The Court of Session therefore determined that, be the consequences what they might, the politicians should no longer tamper with public administration or meddle with supply or with the registration of sasines. In the cases from the shires of Cromarty and Forfar, therefore, the Court of Session made a commendable effort to weed out fictitious votes by putting special interrogatories to claimants, although there was no statutory warrant for such interrogatories. Leading questions were sanctioned, on such lines as: 'who is your author? what returns do you receive from the lands concerned? what was the purchase price? who paid for the completion and registration of titles?' The Court of Session also intended the Head Courts to be empowered to use such interrogatories; and, undoubtedly, those searching questions, answered under oath, would have tended to restrain the creation of nominal votes, for lurking in the background there lay the possibility of a criminal prosecution for perjury.[78] But in 1770 the House of Lords ruined any such prospect by condemning the special interrogatories as *ultra vires*,[79] thus leaving the way open for the mass creation of votes. The one feeble check that remained was the Trust Oath of 1714. But this was a mere formality involving no judicial investigations of any kind. The Trust Oath, which had been nullified for over half a century by perjury unlimited, proved unable to keep the politicians in order.

Public opinion, however, was beginning to be a factor to be reckoned with. It is really from the scandals attending the general election of 1768 that the first demands for reform arose. A writer in the *Scots Magazine* in that year, signing himself 'A Real not a Fictitious Freeholder', led the way. In elections, 'Does not', he asked, 'the highest corruption, prostitution, and venality everywhere appear?'[80] His proposed cure for these ills, to disallow all votes on bare superiorities, was feasible; but no ministry was really eager to sponsor a bill that would outlaw nominal votes and thus increase the difficulty of managing Scottish county elections. A bill on these lines actually introduced in 1775 and seconded, reluctantly, by the Solicitor General Henry Dundas predictably came to nothing.[81] Criticism of the electoral system, however, continued. It increased as a result of the British government's feeble conduct of the American War of Independence. Corruption and mismanagement were blamed for the debacle in America, and many reformers held that reform of representation was necessary to ensure honest and efficient government in the future. In Scotland, too, many freeholders were themselves eager to clean up the system, which was degrading to all but the most brass-necked politicians. Many *bona fide* freeholders resented the tyranny of corrupt cliques, and accordingly a few of the Head Courts passed resolutions calling for the worst abuses of the system to be remedied. There was

[78] Nonetheless, the Court was eager to ensure that the forms of law were rigorously observed by the freeholders, as was made clear in the discussions of the judges in *George Skene etc.* v. *David Wallace and others*, 17 February 1768, in David Dalrymple, Lord Hailes' *Decisions*, ed. M. P. Brown (Edinburgh, 1826), I, 214-16.
[79] Wight, *op. cit.*, I, 266.
[80] *Scots Magazine*, XXX, 176.
[81] *Scots Magazine*, XXXVII, 289-91 and 566-71; also *House of Commons' Journals*, XXXV, 347, 351.

nothing radical about such demands in the 1780s, the main target of which would have been the fictitious vote. This type of conservative reform, however, only enjoyed a brief vogue, due mainly to the panic induced in the propertied classes by the rise of democratic reform movements that were influenced by the French Revolution.[82] In the 1780s, though, a reform act on conservative lines would have been beneficial, without prejudice to further reform and amendment as required, and certainly the want of remedial legislation was severely felt by the Court of Session, which continued to be plagued by franchise cases in which the litigants grew bolder and bolder, frequently flaunting in the Court's very face the law's impotence in these matters.

Clearly, the state of Scottish county elections was bound to become more and more corrupt until such time as the House of Lords, acting as an appeal court, was driven into adopting an attitude more consonant with common sense never mind sound law. So bad did matters become that the freeholders of some counties were at this time obliged to take some extraordinary measures to prevent politics from degenerating into one long, and horribly expensive, nightmare of litigation. For instance, in September 1780 the freeholders of Ayrshire published a notice in the Edinburgh newspapers, from which it appeared that certain lawyers who were also freeholders had been making a ramp of the whole business by taking trumped-up complaints into the Court of Session in the hope of either winning costs or else reaching profitable settlements out of court. In 1780, the two candidates, Sir Adam Fergusson of Kilkerran and Major Montgomerie, agreed that if any of the supporters of either were attacked in this way, for each one so assailed a voter of impeccable standing in the opposite interest would stand down, thus making vexatious litigation pointless.[83] In the event election fever prevailed and the agreement broke down.[84] Nonetheless, the abortive compact perfectly illustrates the awkward predicament of the freeholders: many wished to deal honestly, but, when the law seemed actually to encourage roguery, what were the honest freeholders to do in a crisis? In the last resort, only trickery could counter trickery.

That Scottish county elections were getting out of hand even the House of Lords was at last forced to admit. The House of Lords' belated recognition of longstanding evils resulted from a series of cases that had troubled the Court of Session before and after the bitterly contested general election of 1784. The particular cases that finally forced the House of Lords to reconsider its position came from Aberdeenshire. In 1784 the duke of Gordon and the earl of Fife had fought each other fiercely, and despite the subsequent efforts of Henry Dundas to promote a peaceful compromise the struggle could not be abated.[85] At the by-election of 1786 Fife triumphed, whereupon the duke's interest began to create nominal and fictitious votes on a grand scale. Thus at Michaelmas 1788 twenty six claimants on titles derived from the duke presented themselves for enrolment. The duke of Gordon's interest was in the majority at the Head Court, and, in

[82] H. W. Meikle, *Scotland and the French Revolution* (1912), chs. III-VIII.
[83] *Scots Magazine*, XLII, 555.
[84] *House of Commons' Journals*, XXXVIII, 18ff., *Petition of Sir Adam Fergusson*; *Scots Magazine*, XLIII, 185.
[85] Furber, *op. cit.*, 206-15.

spite of efforts by the opposite faction to apply the special interrogatories formerly sanctioned by the Court of Session but subsequently condemned by the House of Lords, all the Gordon claimants were enrolled.[86] The duke of Gordon could then muster forty four votes in Aberdeenshire, the majority of them more or less nominal, and the earl of Fife could count upon thirty one of the like description. The total number on the Freeholders' Roll was 187, but no other single interest could challenge those of the Gordons or the Duffs.[87] Fife's supporters accordingly appealed to the Court of Session against the duke of Gordon's twenty six new creations. The court, however, was bound to recognise that the special interrogatories it had used in 1767-8 were not competent, and so, in the absence of positive evidence as to nominality, the enrolments were sustained.[88] Fife's interest then appealed to the House of Lords, where the cases were probably decided on political rather than legal grounds, Dundas at that point being keen to humble the duke of Gordon and thus make him more responsive to ministerial commands. And so Lord Chancellor Thurlow, with a spurious air of profound legal learning, and a Pecksniffian sneer at the bewildered 'learned Judges of Scotland', decided that the enrolment of one of the Gordon liferenters, the nabob, Sir John Macpherson (the same corrupt individual who had succeeded Warren Hastings as Governor-general of Bengal in 1785)[89] was wrong, on the score of the nominality of Sir John's title.[90] After this juridical triumph the freeholders in their Head Courts and the Court of Session were at last allowed to use the special interogatories that have already been described.

This decision of the House of Lords on 9 April 1790 really did for a time lead to a diminution in the number of fictitious votes not only in Aberdeenshire but in other counties as well. A comparison of the list of freeholders for the shire of Aberdeen in 1788 with that compiled by an anonymous writer in Michaelmas 1790 reveals striking changes in the roll. The number of freeholders was reduced from 178 to 158, and certainly many of the duke's nominals of 1788 had disappeared by 1790.[91] Other counties also made vigorous efforts to purge their rolls of freeholders. A bold bid was made in Invernessshire, for example, where in recent years nominals had spawned freely. The duke of Gordon, Lord Macdonald, the duke of Argyll, and a comparative newcomer to the great game, Norman Macleod of Macleod, had all created votes. Macleod, another nabob, was bent with the help of Dundas on securing the county for himself, the more so as early in 1790 he had at last succeeded in being returned as its M.P.[92] He now used the outcry against nominals to make a clean sweep of the roll, including those manufactured votes that he himself had created. To different persons Macleod gave differing accounts of his activities. To the duke of Gordon and the

[86] *Scots Magazine*, L, 517.
[87] Sir C. E. Adam, ed., *Political State of Scotland in 1788*, s.v. Aberdeenshire.
[88] The deciding case was *Sir William Forbes* v. *Sir John Macpherson*, 6 March 1789, *F.C.*
[89] Edward Thornton, *History of the British Empire in India* (1859), 186-7; P. E. Roberts, *History of British India* (1947), 221.
[90] Bell, *Treatise*, 285-7, 294-99. The Court of Session had tentatively and hopefully re-opened its attack on nominal votes in some cases from Renfrewshire in 1787, notably *McDowall* v. *Buchanan*, 20 February 1787.
[91] Adam, *op. cit.*, 17; Anon., *A View of the Political State of Scotland, 1790*, 48.
[92] Joseph Foster, *Members of Parliament, Scotland* (1882), 236.

duke of Argyll, for example, he represented himself as forced to expunge nominals by the wrath of the independent freeholders who were led by Forbes of Culloden.[93] But to a personal friend, William Macleod Bannatyne of Kames, he gave another, and very likely more accurate, version of the affair. Wrote Macleod, 'I came down here just in time for the head court; and I proposed a bold measure and carried it; to strike off the roll every nominal and fictitious voter. Our roll is now clear and has just twenty names, being shortened near one hundred'.[94] Evidently objections were made to this arbitrary sweep, but Macleod thought that, on reflection, the protesters would be reasonable. After all, he was magnanimous and willing to restore them to the roll if they insisted, but warned that he would then initiate proceedings against them in the Court of Session. Macleod's coup was not undone: in 1788, before his bold stroke, 103 stood on the rolls for Invernessshire, but in 1811, when next figures are available, there were only 52.[95] Whether Macleod was simply safeguarding his position, or whether his zeal for reform, which later got him into ill odour with Dundas, was genuine is a moot point. The Great Harry, in fact, may have made cunning use of the virtuous decision of the House of Lords to confirm his hold on certain counties. Doubtless, too, the freeholders in the different counties acted on motives based upon local conditions, and these varied widely. In Stirlingshire, for example, only three nominals were expunged, but the freeholders of that county had always carefully regulated their roll and the number of notoriously nominal votes on it was not large.[96]

But the special interrogatories did not invariably prove a lasting check upon nominal and fictitious votes. The freeholders were still allowed too much latitude in their practice; and, indeed, the special interrogatories tended to become useful weapons for dominant parties desirous of maintaining their positions. The Court of Session, in spite of its enlarged powers, was still inadequately equipped properly to control franchise abuses, and the conveyancers, ingenious as ever, soon came up with some tricky solutions that were difficult to counter. Their main answer was to eschew elusory sums and to make it appear that a definite source of income was vested in the claimant. Wadset and liferent interests based upon one penny Scots *si petatur tantum* went very quickly out of fashion. After 1790 they were self-defeating; but the difficulty confronting the freeholders and the Court of Session became that if, on the surface, conveyances were made of real estates which conferred definite profits of, say £10 or £20 per annum, it was, in the absence of incriminating documents that proved nominality, virtually impossible to distinguish the genuine from the false claimant.

Occasionally such evidence was produced and gave rise to revealing cases like those from Renfrewshire in 1817.[97] Each of the cases concerned rose from the

[93] *HMC, Laing Mss.* (1925), II, 536-9, Norman Macleod to duke of Gordon, 6 October 1790, and same to duke of Argyll, 10 October 1790.

[94] *HMC, Laing Mss*, II, 539-40, Norman Macleod of Macleod to William Macleod Bannatyne of Kames, 13 October 1790.

[95] Adam, *op. cit.*, 181; Anon., *View of the Political State of Scotland, 1790*, 111; Anon., *View of the Political State of Scotland, 1811*, 85.

[96] *SRO, Reg. House*, S.C./67/59, 5, Court Book of the Freeholders of the shire of Stirling, 5 October 1790, pp. 1-10.

[97] *Hugh Crawford* v. *John Shaw Stewart*, 12 November 1817, *F.C.*; *William McKnight Crawford* v. *John Shaw Stewart and Robert Stewart*, 7 March 1818, *F.C.*

same general circumstances but ran different courses. Hugh Crawford claimed to be enrolled at the Michaelmas Head Court held at Renfrew in 1816 on lands disponed to him by the earl of Eglinton, but to this John Shaw Stewart objected, alleging that Crawford's superiority was nominal and fictitious. Despite Crawford's offer to take the Trust Oath and to answer all competent interrogatories, his claim was rejected by the freeholders. He then appealed to the Court of Session, whereupon the respondents applied for diligence to recover certain letters. This was granted, and as a consequence several letters between the earl of Eglinton and Hugh Crawford were produced as evidence in court.

The opening letter from the earl to Crawford ran — 'I hope in a short time now to have my dormant freeholds in your country [i.e. county] brought forward, and will be happy that you should have one of them. I believe you understand the footing on which they are to be sold, — for the life of the purchaser; and as to the sum to be paid, five pounds or fifty will make the freehold equally good. Will you have the goodness to write to me on the subject, and hope you will have the goodness to purchase one of them. Few men will be more agreeable to me, being grateful for the friendly support I have received from you.
I remain etc.

Eglinton'.

Crawford replied on that same day 25 January 1815, —

'My Lord,
                    I have had the honour of receiving your Lordship's polite letter of the 25th. I feel very much honoured and obliged by your Lordship's polite information, respecting the division of your Lordship's freeholds in this country; and I shall be most happy to become a purchaser of one of these liferents, so soon as your Lordship shall have made the arrangements and fixed a price'.

Other letters, giving further details of the transaction and proving nominality up to the hilt, were produced. The liferenter was to receive a feu-duty of £5 sterling yearly, and Eglinton stated confidently that 'These freeholds will be as free and independent votes, as any upon the roll of the county and unchallengeable'. On 9 February 1815 Crawford wrote to the earl closing the deal. At the same time he mentioned that his friend MacKnight Crawford of Cartsburn needed L180 Scots of valuation to qualify for the L400 Scots superiority and could the earl oblige him? If not, Cartsburn would buy one of the earl's freeholds should one still be available. On 20 February Eglinton wrote to the various purchasers that he had been advised by his lawyer that, in order to overcome 'the popular prejudice', the price should be increased and not confined to the precise value of the liferent interest in the feu-duty.

On these documents the respondent rested his case. The complainer replied that he had paid a fair price for the estate, and that there was nothing in the correspondence produced to infer, let alone prove, nominality. Crawford again offered to take the Trust Oath and to answer any interrogatories the Court might care to put. In discussing the case the judges made some very interesting comments.

Lord Hermand, an eccentric but able judge, had some particularly interesting and revealing views. He held that liferent qualifications, where properly made, were as valid as any votes could be. Indeed, where legally constituted, he approved of them; for, he said, 'I should like to see the number of independent freeholders legally increased in this country [i.e. Scotland]; but I am afraid that we should not do much to increase the number of independent freeholders by sanctioning the proceedings which are divulged in the proceedings now before us'. Hermand felt that 'the conclusion cannot be resisted that Lord Eglinton was conferring gratuitous rights of voting', and, went on the judge, 'the cases of the Honourable William Elphinston and Sir John Macpherson have never been abandoned, and must be our rule in these cases'.[98] Lord Balmuto was equally clear on the merits of the case. When, said this judge, Lord Eglinton wrote 'I shall be happy to have two such respectable purchasers', he ought to have said, 'I shall be happy to have two such good voters'. Lord Balgray concurred. He went to the heart of the matter: 'It is perfectly possible', he held, 'to make good and effectual liferent freehold qualifications, but these votes have been ill-managed — too many letters have been written — the parties have let us into a knowledge of the views with which they entered into the transaction, and, in doing so, I apprehend that they have made it our duty to refuse their admission on the roll of freeholders'. Lord President Hope agreed; and Lord Succoth also found the votes to be nominal and fictitious. The bench, in fact, was unanimous, rather a rare event in franchise cases which tended to bristle with contentious points. The freeholders were accordingly sustained in their refusal to enrol.[99]

Other claimants on similar liferents derived from Lord Eglinton suffered Crawford's fate, but in the end McKnight Crawford fared differently. The respondents brought against him evidence of the like kind adduced in Crawford's case. Cartsburn, however, was not as directly implicated with Lord Eglinton as Hugh Crawford had been, and Cartsburn also scored heavily by stressing the fact that he was a *bone fide* proprietor in Renfrewshire who had long desired to be an elector but who lacked the requisite valuation. Eglinton could not oblige with a superiority on lands valued at L180 Scots but wrote that he would be gratified if McKnight Crawford would purchase one of his new liferents. Eventually Cartsburn purchased a freehold on the earl's estate of Eastwood. The circumstances, then, were not exactly the same as in Crawford's case. But at first the Court of Session treated the two cases as identical and sustained the freeholders in their refusal to enrol. After hearing a reclaiming petition and answers thereto, however, some of the judges changed their minds, though Balmuto remained convinced that the vote was bad. Lord President Hope pretty well summed up the conclusions of the majority. He had, he said, felt that the interlocutor against Cartsburn was right when made, but at the same time he had been uneasily aware that McKnight Crawford stood in a different position from Hugh Crawford and the other complainers. The Lord President gave as his reason that 'In those other cases, the people had no idea of becoming freeholders in Renfrewshire for any other purpose than to support the interest of Lord

---

[98] Elphinston appealed to the House of Lords against an interlocutor which sustained an objection to his enrolment for the shire of Renfrew, and on 30 April 1787 Lord Thurlow anticipated his verdict in the more famous case of *Forbes* v. *Macpherson*, 19 April 1790. For Elphinston's case, see *F.C.*, IX, No. CCCXV, 489-90, *John Campbell and Archibald Tod* v. *Hon. Wm. Elphinston*, 20 February 1787; also Bell, *Treatise*, 284, and for Thurlow's speech, 288-93.
[99] *Hugh Crawford* v. *John Shaw Stewart*.

Eglinton. This gentleman had not such a view. He had already in his own person a great part of a qualification, and it was natural that he should wish to complete it'. Still the Lord President had a lingering doubt; the vote was, he felt, confidential, and this must destroy it; but, since some of the judges felt differently, he proposed that the Court should put the special interrogatories to the complainer. This was done to the Court's satisfaction, and the interlocutor against McKnight Crawford was reversed. McKnight Crawford was then enrolled as a freeholder of Renfrewshire by decreet of the Court of Session and survived an appeal to the House of Lords.[100]

Those cases from Renfrewshire illustrate the main lines of development in the treatment of nominal and fictitious votes after 1790. Thurlow had concentrated upon *intention*, arguing that it was the *confidential* vote that was bad. But this was not Thurlow's brain-child, as he liked to make out, for the Court of Session had always stressed this idea. Indeed, the entire aim of the special interrogatories devised by the Court of Session in the late 1760s had been to determine this very point. It is not surprising, therefore, that after 1790 *intention* became the touchstone of nominality. This, however, was difficult ground, for it rested largely upon fortuitous evidence. If hard incriminating evidence, such as the correspondence in Crawford's case, could not be produced, then intention became a matter of opinion and averment. And why should one opinion carry more weight than another? Lord Balgray had foreseen this dilemma for, as he acutely observed in Hugh Crawford's case, vote-makers would not always 'let us into a knowledge of the views with which they entered into the transaction'. If vote-makers acted circumspectly, then nominality might be easy to suspect but very difficult to prove in a court of law. Anyway, there was an awkward precedent which left an opening for vote-makers of which the politicians were not slow to avail themselves. In the case of *Freeholders of Kincardineshire* v. *Burnet* in 1745 it was decided that a father might, purely as a mark of parental esteem, confer a nominal estate upon a son with the express intention of enabling him to vote.[101] The principle of natural affection thus accepted was reinforced by other decisions and let to a considerable traffic in nominal and fictitious votes. In a case from Banffshire in 1807 the principle was again upheld. An objection to the enrolment of John Gordon younger of Cluny on allegedly nominal titles bestowed by his father was defeated, although nominality was admitted by the judges, on the plea that 'it is just that the presumptive heir of a large estate should, when he attains majority, be entitled to discharge the political duties of a citizen; and nothing can be more natural than for a father to place him in this respectable point of view'.[102]

Thus if vote-makers took care to cater for natural affections in their operations, or, failing that, saw to it that incriminating evidence as to illegal intention did not reach the courts, their activities were still difficult to foil.

---

[100] *William McKnight Crawford* v. *John Shaw Stewart and Robert Stewart*, 7 March 1818, *F.C.*, at pp. 494-503. Connell, *op. cit.*, 204, shows that the lands concerned were under entail but that this insuperable objection was barely noticed by the Court of Session.

[101] Alexander Fraser Tytler, Lord Woodhouselee, *Decisions* (Edinburgh, 1797), I, s.v. Member of Parliament, at p. 417, *Freeholders of Kincardine* v. *Burnet*, 30 July 1745; D. Falc., I, 146, records that the vote was defeated on other grounds on 19 June 1746. But that the principle of natural affection stood, see Connell, *Treatise*, 184-5.

[102] *Duff* v. *Gordon*, 27 June 1807, *F.C.*

And so in a way that was only slightly modified by the increased powers and vigilance of the Court of Session the old electoral system in the Scottish counties continued until the end came in 1832. The political agitations that gave rise to the Reform Act are well enough known and call for no notice here, except to say that the triumphant Scottish Whigs carefully selected their material to bolster up their contentions. Their moving spirits, after all, were highly skilled practising advocates. Their view of politics was extremely forensic and at times led them to indulge in special pleading. Introducing the second reading of the Reform Bill, Francis Jeffrey relied largely on anecdote. His favourite story told how 'At an election at Bute, not beyond the memory of man, only one person attended the Meeting, except the Sheriff and the Returning Officer. He, of course, took the Chair, constituted the Meeting, called over the roll of the freeholders, answered to his own name, took the vote as the Preses, and elected himself. He then moved and seconded his own nomination, put the question to the vote, and was unanimously returned'.[103] But this engaging tale, even if *ben trovato*, was symptomatic only of the counties with very small electorates — such as Bute or Cromartyshire. And how wildly unlike Jeffrey's story elections in Cromartyshire could be we have seen! The Whigs, however, with their appetites sharpened by half a century in the wilderness (with only brief and partial intermissions in 1806 and 1827) were not in the mood to let logical or historical niceties stand in the way of argument. They dilated on the iniquities of 'closed' counties such as Bute but did not dwell on the electoral history of shires like Stirling, Ayr and Renfrew, which had, in adverse circumstances and with some measure of success, striven to preserve free elections. Such selective evidence enabled Cockburn to reflect complacently that the Reform Bill 'is giving us a political constitution for the first time'.[104] This, of course, was mere political ranting, but it served its turn. By 1830-2 Whig and Radical propaganda of this kind was being mass manufactured, and it would be unwise to swallow it all uncritically.

All the same, it would be a labour of Sisyphus to defend the old system of county elections in Scotland in its last days. In 1823 its defects were tellingly exposed by a Scottish Whig, Lord Archibald Hamilton, who had been M.P. for Lanarkshire since 1802. Lord Archibald proved that the county electors of Scotland numbered no more than 2,889 and thus were a mere handful of the total population, which in 1821 stood at 2,091,521. He further demonstrated that elections almost invariably involved malpractice and legal trickery. As proof of his contentions, he openly admitted that he had held his seat at the last general election because he had created or purchased more nominal votes than his rival. To all this the Tories could only feebly answer that the county franchise and the representation had been settled for all time in 1707 and could not therafter be changed without endangering the Treaty and Act of Union. The House was not convinced by this far-fetched argument, and, in spite of the large overall majority enjoyed by the Tories, Lord Archibald's motion for reform was defeated by a mere thirty five votes.[105] He had, indeed, touched upon a crucial point that

[103] *Hansard's Parliamentary Debates, Third Series*, VII, 529, 23 September, 1831.
[104] *Journal of Henry Cockburn* (1874), I, 13.
[105] W. Law Mathieson, *Church and Reform in Scotland, A History from 1797 to 1843* (1916), 189-90; Foster, *op. cit.*, 169.

transcended party. The truth is that the social and economic conditions that had once given the Scottish representative system some life and vitality were rapidly passing away.[106]

The franchise, and indeed the electoral system as a whole, were, as noted earlier, feudal in origin. Thus the great landed aristocracy and the lairds virtually monopolised political activity and controlled electoral interests. In the early eighteenth century this obvious political fact of life was not wildly at odds with social and economic realities, land still being the basic source of wealth and prestige. But by the early nineteenth century new interests were emerging which differed markedly from the old. In the eighteenth century interests were simply group formations of the politically dominant laird class, but by the early nineteenth century the term 'interests' was increasingly being used to denote economic groupings — such as 'the landed or agricultural interest', 'the manufacturing interest', and 'the commercial interest', whether of East or West Indies.

The older concepts and traditions, however, did not accommodatingly disappear because of the rise of new social and economic realities. The older values were, indeed, deeprooted and tenacious, for not only were the traditional values strongly attached to the idea of prescriptive right but they were also heavily entrenched in the law of Scotland. How to re-define and extend the parliamentary franchise without inflicting damage on the feudal law or introducing democracy became for the Whigs a very thorny question. Scheme after scheme of reform was discussed by the Whigs only to be found wanting. Thus in 1820 Henry Cockburn wrote to his friend Kennedy, 'As to the representation of Scotland, it cannot possibly be worse, and therefore the sooner it is changed the better: but your 40s scheme I fear will never go down. I rather suspect that even the English feel it to be fully low enough; but certainly all Scotland would rise up against it. I should think £20 sufficiently low, or at least £10'.[107] Unable to solve the problem posed by democratic claims and the need to resist them, the Whigs then dropped their projected representation bill and turned with relief to a bill for reform of the criminal jury in Scotland.

The Whigs, in fact, were nonplussed by the problem of electoral reform. They were for it in principle, but only with severe limitations. In practice they found it extremely difficult to decide what precisely electoral reform should entail. Their attitude to this burning question of the day was, in fact, ambivalent. While bitterly denouncing the existing system, which they affected to regard as the corrupt creation of reactionary Toryism, the Scottish Whigs, like Lord Archibald Hamilton, took full advantage of its abuses and wherever possible created nominal and fictitious votes. They felt doubly justified in doing so: such practices supported the Whig parliamentary interest and at the same time extended the franchise. In this way members of what was increasingly coming to be lauded as 'the intelligent and responsible middle class' could be enfranchised

---

[106] The best account of social and economic change in late eighteenth and early nineteenth-century Scotland is R. H. Campbell's *Scotland since 1707: the Rise of an Industrial Society* (1965), Pt. II, 77-224.

[107] *Letters chiefly connected with the Affairs of Scotland from Henry Cockburn ... to Thomas Francis Kennedy 1818-52* (1874), 9. This work is hereafter cited as *Letters on the Affairs of Scotland*.

without danger of the vote being granted to the hare-brained lower orders. Some Tories took a similar view, and believed that nominal votes provided a useful and safe means of broadening 'the political nation'. Rather significantly, the judges in Hugh Crawford's case in 1817, who were Tories to a man, clearly were not hostile to nominal votes as such but only objected to their creators openly flouting the law.

By 1830 there was a wide measure of agreement that the existing system in Scotland needed to be changed. Unfortunately, the consensus did not extend to the precise measures of reform that were needed. Politically, the Whigs used, and duped, the democratic masses. The Whigs relied on popular support, but when Lord Grey formed a Whig administration in November 1830 the new government refused to consider, let alone implement, manhood suffrage or the secret ballot. Consequently, they ran into great difficulties when they sought to introduce a new franchise based, ultimately, on a £10 property qualification, which should sweep away all the old abuses and yet be itself free from abuse. Their best efforts resulted in a hopeless muddle.[108] The measures contained in the Reform Act for Scotland were extremely confused, and, indeed, by making possible the mass manufacture of property qualifications, they helped to produce new and widespread electoral malpractices. Those new abuses were encouraged by the Court of Session's loss of jurisdiction in election causes and the setting up of Registration Courts presided over by the sheriffs. These tended to produce very diverse judgments and to sanction a variety of curious practices.[109]

The principal blame for the unfortunate developments after 1832 must lie with Francis Jeffrey and Henry Cockburn, who, as Lord Advocate and Solicitor-General respectively, were the chief authors of the Scottish Reform Act. In fact, as Cockburn's correspondence proves, he was mainly responsible for framing the bill, Jeffrey apparently making little impact in parliament. Of Jeffrey, Cockburn wrote at the time, 'It is nothing to the disparagement of any man that at his age he has not succeeded in Parliament or in public official life'.[110] Jeffrey's health, too, was not good, and so most of the burden of drafting fell on Cockburn, who, in his zeal for political reform, seems to have forgotten his Scots Law. He was also keen to model the Scottish bill on that for England and Wales, and this, coupled with howlers in enunciating Scots Law, led to his making a hash of the property qualifications. Jeffrey possibly contributed to this poor result. He evidently feared that the bill would fail in parliament, and, as he told Lord Minto, in his eagerness to ensure its passage he felt that it should be as free of contentious measures as possible.[111] This probably led him, among other things, deliberately to ignore the problem of fictitious votes. Many years later, in a letter to the same Lord Minto, Cockburn admitted that in 1832 the Whigs had failed to find a solution for this problem: 'I have often thought', wrote Cockburn, 'of the faggot vote manufactory, but have never been able to devise a practicable way of checking them'.[112] But for his vanity, which was considerable, if benign,

---

[108] W. Ferguson, 'Reform Act (Scotland) of 1832: Intention and Effect', in *SHR*, XLV (1966), 105-14.
[109] These are fully discussed in John Cay, *An Analysis of the Scottish Reform Act with the Decisions of the Court of Appeal* (1850).
[110] *Letters on the Affairs of Scotland*, 334, Cockburn to Kennedy, 23 July 1831.
[111] Minto Papers, *NLS*, MS. 12137, f.1 Jeffrey to earl of Minto, 1 January 1832.
[112] Minto Papers, *NLS*, MS. 12140, f.89, Cockburn to Lord Minto, 25 August 1851.

Cockburn might also have confessed that he lacked the knowledge of feudal law necessary to keep him out of some quite obvious pitfalls into every one of which he tumbled in drafting the Reform Bill for Scotland in 1831-2. Significantly, too, he had no practical knowledge of electioneering, nor of parliament of which he was never a member.

The defects of the resulting act of parliament, which were present *ab initio*, and the ill consequences of these defects, were soon so glaring that a defining act had to be passed in 1835. But the act 5 and 6 William IV c78 merely tinkered with the problems, and electoral abuses continued and actually increased.[113] The aged T. F. Kennedy of Dunure lived to denounce the electoral abuses still rampant in South Ayrshire after the passing of the second Reform Act in 1868, and was particularly incensed by a novel and brazen instance of 'tombstone' voting at Girvan.[114] Not until the passing of the third Reform Act in 1884 were the problems created in 1832 effectively overcome, as the long and as yet incomplete transition from the organic conception of the state to Benthamite democracy gathered momentum.[115]

---

[113] See J. I. Brash, ed., *Papers on Scottish Electoral Politics 1832-1854* (*SHS*, 1974), Introduction.

[114] *Letters on the Affairs of Scotland*, Appendix, pp. XI-XIII, Mr. Kennedy to the Lord Advocate, 17 March 1869.

[115] Elie Halévy, *The Growth of Philosophic Radicalism*, tr. Mary Morris (1928), *passim* and especially 412-17 for the constitutional theories of Jeremy Bentham (1748-1832).

'A MAN OF NO COMMON STAMP':
SIR WILLIAM GIBSON CRAIG OF RICCARTON,
LORD CLERK REGISTER OF SCOTLAND, 1862-1878

By MARGARET D. YOUNG, M.A.,
Assistant Keeper, Scottish Record Office

The above quotation is contained in the obituary of Sir William Gibson Craig which appeared in *The Scotsman* of 13 March 1878. While due allowance must be made for the fulsome elegies produced by newspapers of the period on the death of well-known public figures, Sir William had as good a claim as any to be considered out of the ordinary, not only because of his diverse activities in national and local affairs but also because of his vigorous tenure of an office long considered as a sinecure and even by some as having no justification for its existence at all. Yet the fall in general esteem of the office of Lord Clerk Register is at first sight somewhat surprising for it was of great antiquity, going back to the clerk of the king's rolls of the thirteenth century and the clerk of the rolls and registers of the fourteenth.[1] In the sixteenth and seventeenth centuries his increasing influence is reflected in his title of 'Lord Clerk Register' or 'Lord Register' and he was responsible for the records of chancery, exchequer and parliament and was the custodian of all state papers. In the same period he held an important position in the legal hierarchy, from the emergence of the privy council as a judicial body at the beginning of the sixteenth century, when he was always one of the judges, as he was likewise after the final establishment of the Court of Session as a college of justice in 1532, as well as being responsible for the appointment of the clerks of the court. He was given control over the register of sasines on its establishment in 1617 and later in the century over the registers of apprisings and entails. At the Union of 1707 he is described as 'clerk of the registers and rolls of the council, session and exchequer and of all commissions, parliaments and conventions of estates'[2] but this was more shadow than substance for the Restoration of 1660 had seen a change in the nature of the office. In 1678 the office had been granted during pleasure only and not for life, as hitherto, and it became more important politically because of its connection with parliamentary duties and of the patronage exercised through the gift of clerkships. Legal qualifications were no longer necessary and the holder of the office was no longer a judge of session.

At the Union of 1707 the Scottish parliament and privy council were

---

[1] See A. L. Murray 'The Lord Clerk Register', *S[cottish] H[istorical] R[eview]* (1974). Lists of Lord Clerks Register, with biographical details, and of other record officials, are given in *The Annual Report of the Keeper of the Records of Scotland*, 1974, app. 7.

[2] *Acts Parl. Scot.* [*APS*], xi, 209.

abolished and the exchequer, though retained, was remodelled on English lines and thus outwith the clerk register's control. Both fees and patronage were affected, patronage of the keeperships of the registers and of the various clerkships going to the crown in 1728, and compensation for these losses was belatedly made in 1756 when an increased salary of £1600 was granted, to which was added, by the beginning of the nineteenth century, fees for registration of court business bringing in over £1000 annually.[3] By this time, also, almost the sole responsibility of the Lord Clerk Register was the actual custody of the records, which came to be delegated to his deputies, the deputy clerk register and the deputy keepers. In 1777 the office was again granted for life and in 1817 united with that of the keeper of the signet at an annual salary of £1200 by The Public Offices (Scotland) Act. The Lord Clerk Register also had the function of presiding at the election of Scottish representative peers chosen in terms of the act of union to sit in the House of Lords. Yet if he was a much less prominent figure than his pre-Union predecessors, a holder of the office was still in a position to influence events. Two of Gibson Craig's predecessors, James, 14th earl of Morton, clerk register between 1760 and 1768, and Lord Frederick Campbell, in office from 1768 to 1816, were responsible for obtaining funds for the building of the Register House and for the employment of Robert Adam as architect. Lord Frederick was also responsible for the creation of the office of deputy clerk register in 1806, who became the clerk register's deputy and active head of the department in the nineteenth century.[4]

It has been said that under Lord Frederick Campbell's successors the office of Lord Clerk Register 'moved steadily towards a dignified lack of responsibility'[5] and the appointment of James, 4th earl and later 1st marquess of Dalhousie, to the office on 12 December 1845, raised further questions as to its retention. At the time of his appointment Dalhousie was president of the Board of Trade and in January 1846 he wrote to Sir James Graham, home secretary of state, questioning whether the holding of political office in England might not be injurious to the Scottish office and lead to 'the abolition of one of her State Offices as a sinecure'.[6] He goes on to say that before the death of William Dundas, his predecessor as Lord Clerk Register, the Whig lawyers in Scotland had urged the writer's friends to advise him to apply for the post. On 10 August 1847 Dalhousie was gazetted governor-general of India and Lord Russell, the prime minister, wrote to him enquiring whether he intended to retain the appointment as 'suggestions and applications' made to him in the House of Commons would have to be answered.[7] Dalhousie replied that he had no intention of giving up the office which had been conferred upon him by the Queen in consideration 'of the services I have performed'. He went on to point out that the holding of the governor-generalship with another office was provided for by act of parliament, that the office of Lord Clerk Register was honorary and the business of the Register House would not be affected because 'my predecessor . . . for many years resided permanently in England' and that there were deputies to perform all the

[3] A. L. Murray, op. cit.
[4] See M. D. Young 'The Age of the Deputy Clerk Register', SHR (1974).
[5] A. L. Murray, op. cit.
[6] GD45/14/597 (SRO).
[7] GD45/14/598/14.

necessary duties.[8] Dalhousie's eagerness to retain an office whose utility was in question can only have been from reasons of prestige, for it must be remembered that, however much the powers of the office had diminished, the holder still ranked as a high officer of state in Scotland, taking precedence after the Lord Justice General and before the Lord Advocate. This is exemplified by a letter of congratulation from George Robertson, the deputy keeper, on the appointment '. . . as a Scotchman I cannot help feeling . . . the delight it gives me that the dignity of the office has been kept up by being bestowed upon a Nobleman of Ancient Descent'.[9]

While Dalhousie was in India between 1847 and 1856 he carried on a correspondence with William Pitt Dundas, the deputy clerk register, about all aspects of business in the Register House. Besides Pitt Dundas there were, up to 1853, two deputy keepers and thereafter only one, George Brown Robertson. Between them they carried all the responsibilities for the work of the office and in addition the deputy clerk register became registrar general in 1855, following on the Registration of Births, Deaths and Marriages (Scotland) Act 1854, and was responsible for inbringing the old parish registers from the localities and for overseeing the provision of additional accommodation which led to the building of New Register House between 1859 and 1863. While many of the topics in the letters which passed between the clerk register and his deputy were only of general interest there were certain matters which were particularly brought to his notice. In 1848 the question of certain individuals being allowed to have keys and access to records unsupervised by the deputy keepers should have been referred to the clerk register but, in the event, the deputy keepers were recommended to use their own discretion.[10] Likewise the question of disjoining the register of sasines for Renfrew from that for Glasgow brought the comment from the deputy clerk register that 'I express no opinion without reference to Lord Dalhousie himself'.[11] In 1852, when George Robertson, deputy keeper for forty-three years and in poor health, was proposing to retire and requested a pension, a letter from the treasury remarked that 'it is strongly recommended by Lord Dalhousie'.[12] When it was essential for the deputy clerk register to have a ruling, he consulted either the Lord Advocate or the treasury as in the case of the problem of the sorting of, and accommodation for, the unextracted processes.[13] This practice was also followed after Dalhousie returned home but was not available, as in 1857, when the deputy clerk register wrote to the Lord Advocate concerning a vacancy in the office of the principal keeper of the register of sasines[14] or in the next year when there was to be an election of a representative peer requiring a commission from the clerk register to authorise the clerks of session to act for him, the deputy clerk register remarking 'While he was in India however Lord D. issued a General Commission to all or any two of the Clerks but doubts may be raised how far this is now available'.[15] The commission was, however, obtained and the election proceeded in due form.[16]

[8] GD45/14/597.
[9] ibid.
[10] SRO8/58/1, 119.
[11] ibid., 120.
[12] AD56/293 (SRO).
[13] SRO8/58/1, 204, 207.
[14] ibid., 302.
[15] ibid., 308.
[16] PE.10/140 (SRO).

Yet attempts continued to be made to do away with the office during this period, as in 1849, when Dalhousie wrote from India to the deputy clerk register about rumours of the abolition of the office or at least the salary which Dalhousie did not draw while abroad. He states here that 'They may abolish the salary — but I would rather lay down the GG than the Cl. Reg'.[17] A treasury minute and letter of 27 March 1855,[18] on the occasion of the submission of departmental estimates to parliament, suggested the abolition of the offices of the Lord Lyon, the keeper of the signet and the keeper of the register of hornings, remarking that Lyon had a salary of £555 and the Lord Clerk Register and keeper of the signet of £1200 but that '. . . no functions of public importance attached to these offices . . . no inconvenience to the public can arise from abolition of them'. The Lyon Office might be retained without salary on account of its 'ancient dignity' but many of the ancient offices in Scotland were subject to little supervision and the treasury recommended that any vacancies occuring should be looked at.

The death of the marquess of Dalhousie on 19 December 1860 opened up once again the possibility of abolishing the office of Lord Clerk Register in terms of the treasury minute of 1855, and the treasury was reminded of this in a letter from the Queen's and Lord Treasurer's Remembrancer shortly after the marquess's death.[19] In April 1861, Sir George Lewis, home secretary, wrote to the Lord Advocate asking whether it would be necessary to pass legislation for the abolition of the office, asking 'will the constitution of the office and its legal powers be complete if the principal office is left vacant?'[20] In August of the same year a further step was taken when an Act to repeal the Provisions in certain Statutes relative to the Salary of the Lord Clerk Register of Scotland (24 & 25 Vict, c. 81) abolished the salary of £1200 and, even after Gibson Craig's appointment, the death of the Lord Lyon, the 11th earl of Kinnoull, in February 1866 brought forward suggestions that the offices of Lyon and Lord Clerk Register be combined and 'given to Craig'.[21] Nothing came of this and the Lyon Office was regulated by the Lyon King of Arms (Scotland) Act 1867. In 1862 the office of Lord Clerk Register was revived under the influence of the prime minister, Lord Palmerston. In May of that year the Lord Advocate wrote to the earl of Dalhousie 'I believe Palmerston has written to the Queen proposing Craig as Lord Clerk Register',[22] and his commission was issued on 1 July.[23] On 15 December 1863 Gibson Craig was made a privy councillor, Palmerston having written to him on 21 November saying that 'the high office which you hold in Scotland has usually been filled by a privy councillor'.[24] No evidence has been found as to why Palmerston chose to revive the office and to select Gibson Craig as the holder but it is possible to speculate on the influences governing his decision. The Register House under an active head may have been seen as the instrument for carying out certain necessary reforms coming within its sphere

[17] SR08/66/34.
[18] E.801/23/44 (SRO).
[19] E.801/25/466 (SRO).
[20] AD56/291.
[21] AD56/104.
[22] GD45/14/685.
[23] C. 3/45, no. 74.
[24] SRO 8/203/1.

such as the system of land registration. Moreover, if the office was not to be discontinued and if the conditions caused by the absence of the marquess of Dalhousie in India and the vacancy following his death, whereby the current work of the office went on but there was no incentive for change, were not to continue, then the appointment of a strong and experienced man of affairs with parliamentary and administrative knowledge was essential and such Palmerston knew Gibson Craig to be.

The man who became Lord Clerk Register in 1862 had an ancestry in which law and public service both figured prominently. Among his forebears was Sir Alexander Gibson of Durie, Lord President under Charles I, whose wife was a daughter of Sir Thomas Craig of Riccarton, the great feudal lawyer, and whose son became Lord Clerk Register in 1641. Gibson Craig's father, Sir James, succeeded to the estate by entail in 1823 and took the additional surname of Craig. In 1831 a baronetcy was conferred upon him for public services, for he was a prominent Whig politician of the day, particularly in connection with the passing of the Reform Bill of 1832, and he was also a writer to the signet. Besides law and politics, learning also ran in the family as Sir William's brother James was a bibliophile and one of the original members of the Bannatyne Club, as well as being a partner in the law firm of J. T. Gibson Craig, Dalziel and Brodies, W.S. Sir William Gibson Craig was born in 1797 called to the bar in 1820 and became Liberal M.P. for Midlothian in 1837, which seat he exchanged for the city of Edinburgh in 1841. He succeeded his father in 1850 and his parliamentary career ended in 1852 but he was thereafter greatly involved in local affairs, being a member of the General Assembly of the Church of Scotland and of various boards including that of trustees for manufactures in Scotland and thus involved with the establishment of the National Gallery of Scotland.

More importantly, as regards the Register House, he was the lord of the treasury responsible for the Scottish affairs between 1846 and 1852. This office had evolved as a result of the position which the Lord Advocate occupied as the link between parliament and the execution of government policy in Scotland. To help him he had one of the lords of the treasury, specifically charged with the conduct of Scottish financial matters, who could also in his absence take the Lord Advocate's place in parliament. The tenure of this office gave Gibson Craig an insight into the working of government departments which he put to good use during his period as clerk register, as shown in a letter to the deputy clerk register of 1865 in which he writes 'The present mode of conducting business at the Treasury is quite incomprehensible to me ... This is just the sort of tangle which, when I was at the Treasury, I kept them out of by *insisting* that the whole Scotch business should pass through my hands'.[25] There is a considerable correspondence between the deputy clerk register, the Lord Advocate and Gibson Craig, while at the treasury, touching on almost every aspect of Register House business. In 1847 topics discussed included the abridgements of the register of sasines, the erection of the statue of the Duke of Wellington in front of the Register House and consequent re-siting of the front stairs — causing Gibson Craig to comment 'I will take care that the Town Council do not easily meddle

[25] SRO 8/93/35.

with the Register House' — the sorting and accommodation of the unextracted processes and proposals to publish public law registers in the *Scottish Law Journal*.[26] Between 1851 and 1862 the deputy clerk register is writing to Gibson Craig about alterations to the cupola of the dome of the Register House, peers' elections and the problem of accommodation for the old parish registers following the establishment of the registrar-general's department in 1855.[27]

There is thus no doubt that Gibson Craig was as well qualified as anyone in Scotland to undertake the office of Lord Clerk Register and yet he was unwilling to do so. In practical terms, since he had no intention of treating the office as a sinecure, he realised the work involved and the financial loss he would suffer, as no salary had attached to the office since 1861, and indeed eventual pressure of work forced him to resign his post as referee on private bills to the House of Commons to the value of £1000 a year.[28] Moreover, his experience in parliament and at the treasury led him to believe that he would have difficulties in obtaining what was necessary for the preservation of the records and the staffing and running of the Register House, given the current attitude of both bodies to Scottish interests and needs. There was growing dissatisfaction at this time with Scotland's position *vis à vis* central government. The country was still only represented by fifty-three M.P.s and Scottish business was much neglected, particularly in the large amount of time devoted to Irish affairs, a continuing complaint of the Scottish members. *The Times* of 10 March 1868 stated in its parliamentary report that the Commons had looked forward to the Irish debate ever since reassembling and 'It was almost by a stroke of good luck that such a measure as the Scotch Reform Bill[29] was the order of the day. Nothing could be better fitted to fill up a gap . . A House at once languid and restless assented to the second reading without a division'. These tendencies are illustrated in Gibson Craig's career by the difficult passage of the Land Registers (Scotland) Act 1868 through parliament and the battle with the treasury over obtaining an adequate publications grant, a contributory factor being the time and money devoted to Irish record institutions and publications. Public attitudes might also have to change, since, whatever his intentions may have been, the announcement of his appointment in *The Scotsman* of 1 July 1862 followed the opinion generally held that '. . . the office of Lord Clerk Register in Scotland . . . remains an honorary office'. Nevertheless, as he himself said, he could not refuse the offer as made by Palmerston.[30]

Two aspects of Gibson Craig's activities in the Register House are worthy of notice in detail,[31] namely legislation affecting the land registers of Scotland and the publication of historical material held in the Register House but hitherto unknown. The first created the Sasine Office, the second a series of publications of immense value to scholars which is still continuing at the present day. The Land Registers (Scotland) Act was passed on 31 July 1868 and established the

[26] SRO 8/63-4, 66, 68, 74-5 *passim.*
[27] SRO 8/58/1, *passim.*
[28] *Hansard,* cxcii, 1525.
[29] Representation of the People (Scotland) Act, 1868.
[30] SRO/8/211/1.
[31] Gibson Craig's career as Lord Clerk Register is treated in general terms in M. D. Young, *op. cit.*

present system of land registers by abolishing the particular register of sasines held in the localities and putting the general register of sasines, to be held at Edinburgh, into county divisions. The agitation for reform and the long and laborious measures necessary to achieve it illustrate the increasing tendency towards centralisation by the government, the resistance to it by the localities influenced by vested interests, the ineptitude and apathy of most Scottish M.P.s with regard to such measures and the determination of Gibson Craig to see the measure pass, although he did not approve of all its provisions. From the middle of the eighteenth century commerce in land had been increasing with the growth of industry and the coming of the railways[32] and during the period between 1845 and 1878 in which Lord Dalhousie and Gibson Craig were successively Lord Clerks Register, a great deal of legislation was passed to simplify succession to hereditary rights and the transmission thereof, for the cumbersome feudal procedures involved therein caused quite unjustifiable delays and expense. In 1845 the Infeftment Act changed the form of the instrument of sasine in that the ceremony of giving earth and stone on the ground was abolished and a simpler form of infeftment instituted. In the same year the Heritable Securities (Scotland) Act facilitated the transmission of heritable securities and was further extended by the Heritable Securities (Scotland) Act 1847. Also in 1847 the Service of Heirs (Scotland) Act did away with the necessity of obtaining brieves from chancery while the Crown Charters (Scotland) Act abolished the signature and precept from chancery which had hitherto been required as part of the process of infeftment. The Entail Amendment Acts of 1848 and 1853 relaxed many of the restrictions on the transfer of real property and in 1858 the Titles to Land (Scotland) Act abolished the instrument of sasine completely and simplified the forms and diminished the expense of completing titles. Much of this legislation was brought together in 1868 by the Titles to Land Consolidation (Scotland) Act.

The procedures laid down in the act of the Scottish parliament which set up the register of sasines, reversions and other heritable rights on 28 June 1617,[33] by establishing a general register for the whole country based on Edinburgh and particular registers for the counties and certain specified districts had not been modified to any great extent in subsequent centuries. Thus, while the procedures for the infeftment in, and transmission of, heritable property were being simplified, access to information in the registers themselves and the cost involved was causing difficulties both for members of the legal profession and for the general public, particularly in searches for incumbrances essential before a completion of title. The increase in transactions in heritable property was overburdening a system, adequate when set up over two hundred years previously but now unable to answer current needs. The registers had always been open to inspection in the Register House by the public or their agents, the main work of searching being carried out in the first decades of the nineteenth century by the two deputy keepers who made a handsome living from private searching due to their intimate knowledge of the records for which finding aids

---

[32] The council of the Solicitors before the Supreme Courts noted in a *Report* of 1858 that 'the means of communication which now exist by Railways ... have also had an important effect upon the value of land and the demand for it as an article of sale and subject of investment'.
[33] The Registration Act 1617; *APS*, iv, 545.

were conspicuous by their absence. In 1853 one deputy keeper, who was to do no private work, was appointed instead of two and a searching department was established with a staff of four official and one antiquarian searcher and three clerks.[34] By an Act of Sederunt of 1811 regulating the formation of the sasine registers it was laid down that the minute books should be the basis for indexes of persons and places, to be drawn up by the keepers of the particular and general registers of sasines under the direction of the Lord Clerk Register or the deputy clerk register.[35] In 1819 the first deputy clerk register, Thomas Thomson, proposed a scheme whereby a chronological abridgement of the general and particular registers would be prepared by the keepers which would then be broken down into a county arrangement, to which would be added alphabetical indexes of persons and places. Initially the work was funded by the record commissioners, later, from 1842, by the treasury. The prescriptive period being at this time forty years and the series being produced in 1821, the starting date was taken as 1781.

By the middle of the nineteenth century the inconveniences of the system of land registration and the expense, inaccuracies and length of time involved in searches led to agitation for reform by various bodies connected with the legal profession. A report to the deputy keeper by the dean of the Faculty of Procurators of Glasgow, following on the establishment of the searching department in 1853 and the prohibition of private searching by Register House staff, led to the setting up of a committee of writers to the signet in 1857 to report on searches. The report[36] states that, prior to 1853, searchers were appointed by the deputy clerk register or the deputy keeper who knew them to be suitably qualified people but now these appointments formed part of the patronage of ministers of the crown and consequently serious errors occurred through inexperience or ignorance. An example is given of a search where eight entries had been omitted, one being the proprietor's infeftment in the lands and another securities on the lands to the amount of over £22,000. The minute books of the register of sasines, which an act of parliament of 1693 had regulated so as to serve as both minute and presentment books,[37] were now not suitable for present-day searches as not all the lands were named, many being referred to simply as 'and others'. Searching the minute books was so laborious that the keepers of the registers had taken to making unauthorised markings in the volumes, showing the counties in which the lands lay in the general register of sasines and the parishes in the particular register, and the committee was led to remark that '. . . if the Scottish Parliament had remained, the improvement of the Registers would have kept pace with the national progress'. With regard to the abridgements, the committee pointed out that the index to places was found to be of so little use that it had been discontinued in 1830 and the index of persons they 'found to be equally cumbrous and perplexing'. Where searches were directed with special reference to each individual by whom the lands could have been burdened, the instigator of the search was required to furnish a list of names of such individuals

---

[34] SRO 2/10/1.
[35] *Fourth Annual Report of the Deputy Clerk Register of Scotland*, app. 11-12.
[36] *Report of the Committee of Writers to the Signet upon Searches* (Edinburgh, 1857).
[37] The Register of Sasines Act 1693; *APS*, ix, 271.

and thus anyone who had neither an inventory nor a forty-year progress of titles could not institute a search for incumbrances. The next year the council of the SSC put out a report on registers relative to land rights in Scotland[38] which repeated the complaints made by the WS society committtee the previous year and gave further illustrations of deficiencies in the system. The indexes to places in the abridgements were not detailed enough, a typical entry being 'Gorbals, tenements in', and the abridgements themselves were normally five years in arrears as the volumes of the particular register in the localities had to be completed before being transmitted to the Lord Clerk Register, the minute books being transmitted every six months. As a result, the official searchers made up their own private indexes to persons but general searchers were dependent on the minute books.

This general disquiet led to the setting up of a parliamentary committee to inquire into the state of the land registers in the counties and burghs of Scotland, which made its report in 1863.[39] The commissioners were Charles Morton, WS, of Edinburgh and Andrew Bannatyne, dean of the Faculty of the Procurators of Glasgow. The main recommendations were that there should be one general register of sasines at Edinburgh, to be kept in county divisions with relevant minute and presentment books, the particular registers to be abolished; printed copies of abridgements and indexes and of presentment books to be made up and transmitted periodically to sheriff clerks and town clerks of the royal burghs and to be open to public inspection; a minute of every sasine to be entered on a search sheet and each county to have a book with sheets applicable to every property in the county; probative extracts, either with or without warrants for execution, of deeds previously recorded in the register of sasines should be issued without the deed being again engrossed in the register of deeds; the Court of Session should be empowered, on application by the Lord Clerk Register and the Lord Advocate, to make provision by Act of Sederunt for any further sanctions required, preferably after appropriate professional bodies had been consulted. Gibson Craig, having been appointed Lord Clerk Register during the committee's deliberations, at his request and with permission of the Lord Advocate, had proofs of the report supplied to him, the deputy clerk register, the deputy keeper and the keeper of the sasine registers, John C. Brodie, who were subsequently interviewed by the committee. In his evidence, Gibson Craig was questioned as to the office of Lord Clerk Register and stated that he had been most unwilling to accept it because 'it would give me a great deal of trouble and entail upon me very considerable expense'. In general, he was in favour of the report although against the printing of the abridgements as 'a useless expense'. The two other Register House officials were also generally favourable although they foresaw practical difficulties in operating the search sheets. Brodie, also, was in general agreement and gave evidence which has historical interest in that it lays out the minutiae of the process of registration. The recommendations of the committee brought forth comment and debate from the professional legal bodies

---

[38] *Report by the Council of the Society of Solicitors before the Supreme Courts upon the Registers relative to Land Rights in Scotland* (Edinburgh, 1858).

[39] *Report of the Commissioners appointed to inquire as to the State of the Registers of Land Rights in the Counties and Burghs of Scotland,* (Edinburgh, HMSO, 1863).

and individuals with related interests,[40] the consensus of opinion being in favour
of a single register of sasines to be kept at Edinburgh, and regarding the
amalgamation of the general and particular registers the deputy clerk register
summed up the general feeling with the comment 'No proposed change of such
importance ... ever ... commended ... so unanimous an expression of opinion in
its favour'.[41]

The need revealed by these reports for reforms in the system of land
registration and searching led to attempts to introduce legislation to that end. In
April 1864 the Lord Advocate, Sir George Gray, the home secretary, and Sir
William Dunbar, M.P. for Wigtown burghs, brought forward the Writs
Registration (Scotland) Bill 'to alter and amend the system of Registration of
Writs relative to land in Scotland', based upon the proposals of the Morton and
Bannatyne committee of 1863. The terms of the Bill were favourably received by
the central bodies but met opposition from local officials. On 20 May 1864 the
deputy clerk register wrote to the Lord Advocate giving the reasons why the bill
should go through, especially the amalgamation of the particular and general
registers of sasines for 'it is impossible to estimate too highly the good results
which will follow'.[42] He goes on to point out that postal railway facilities have led
to a preponderance of writs being sent for registration in the general register in
Edinburgh by country practitioners. The opposition by the localities was largely
local feeling against a policy of centralisation, since the keepers of the particular
registers were to be compensated for the loss of their fees. One of the
commissioners of 1863, Andrew Bannatyne, wrote to the Lord Advocate from
Glasgow on 18 May 1864 'A majority of my professional brethern have ...
objected to the transfer of our Glasgow Registers to Edinburgh — It is a narrow
minded, illiberal, selfish policy', pointing out that the opposition had
concentrated on this aspect rather than the benefits.[43] Gibson Craig made every
effort to have the bill passed and in correspondence with the deputy clerk register
he remarked that he had seen as many Scottish M.P.s as possible.[44] One of the
reasons he gives for the bill's failure to pass was that, being Ascot Cup day, there
was a very thin house and he went on to remark 'The debate was not a creditable
one to the Scotch members either as to their intelligence or independence ... their
jealousy of Edinburgh and abuse of Edinburgh lawyers was quite
contemptible'.[45]

The bill was again brought forward in April 1865 by the same sponsors and
not only met with opposition but was faced with a counter-scheme contained in a
bill introduced by Alexander Dunlop, M.P. for Greenock, Sir James Fergusson,
M.P. for Ayrshire, and Walter Buchanan, M.P. for Glasgow. This bill's principal
provision was that the general register of sasines should be discontinued and the
particular registers made the only register, writs relative to lands in more than

[40] See *Report by the Committee of the Faculty of Procurators in Glasgow on the Report of the Commissioners as to the Registers of Land Rights* ... (Glasgow, 1864); *Report of the Committee on Bills of the Society of Writers to the Signet* ... (Edinburgh, 1864).
[41] *Seventeenth Annual Report of the Deputy Clerk Register of Scotland*, 40.
[42] SRO 8/58/1, 414.
[43] AD.56/291.
[44] SRO 8/89/29.
[45] SRO 8/89/30.

one county to be registered in all the relevant counties, and the volumes and minute books to be transmitted to the Lord Clerk Register on completion. Understandably, great differences of opinion were caused by these proposals, and both bills were withdrawn. Another bill, introduced by the Lord Advocate, the solicitor general for Scotland and Sir George Gray, in March 1866, was again withdrawn but led to the setting up of a select committee in April and Gibson Craig, frustrated in all his attempts to get the measure passed, commented 'I know nothing of what the Advocate is doing about the Committee on the Writs Bill, and therefore suppose he is doing nothing'.[46] The report was published in July 1866 and contained a suggestion that an adequate salary should be provided for the Lord Clerk Register since the committee, having heard evidence from Gibson Craig, considered 'that large powers are vested in the lord clerk register and that a considerable amount of labour has already been performed by the present occupant of the post'.[47] Another bill was introduced in July but failed to get through and in a letter written the same month from Gibson Craig to the deputy keeper he comments on the Scottish M.P.s' attitude 'There has always been a shabby spiteful feeling among them which induces them to obstruct anything that is proposed to be done for Scotland (Edinburgh especially) or any Scotchman and therefore I have never troubled myself about the salary of the Lord Clerk Register believing there would be such a yelping raised against it, it would never be obtained'.[48] Some of the 'yelping' had been done by local registrars in Scotland who, earlier in the year, had sent a pamphlet to their local M.P.s alleging that the office of Lord Clerk Register was a sinecure and the Writs Bill only a scheme to get its holder a salary.[49]

Nothing was achieved in the parliamentary session of 1867 but in 1868 the Lord Advocate introduced another bill which received the royal assent on 31 July. The Land Registers (Scotland) Act contained the main provisions already put forward including that for a salary for the Lord Clerk Register. The report of the select committee of 1866, which had unanimously recommended a salary, was the basis on which Sir William Stirling-Maxwell, M.P. for Perthshire, and others brought forward the case for the insertion of a clause to this effect in the bill,[50] and during the debates about the bill in June George Waldegrave-Leslie, M.P. for Hastings, quoted the findings of the same committee and expressed the view that such extensive powers as those enjoyed by the Lord Clerk Register should not be vested in an unpaid officer, that the Land Registers Act would increase that officer's duties and that Gibson Craig's loss of the annual £1000 as referee to the House of Commons should be recompensed.[51] The opposition brought up the usual arguments, the main one being that the work was done by deputies. James Moncrieff, who had been Lord Advocate when the salary was abolished in 1861,[52] gave his opinion that 'The office ought never to have been a sinecure' and since Lord Dalhousie had given up the salary while governor-

[46] SRO 7/66/2.
[47] *Report from the Select Committee on Writs Registration (Scotland) Bill, 1866.*
[48] SRO 14/28/17.
[49] SRO 8/96/63.
[50] AD 56/291.
[51] *Hansard*, cxcii, 1525.
[52] Above, p. 298.

general of India, it had had to be abolished thereafter but should now be restored.[53] In its parliamentary report of 13 June 1868 *The Times* made special mention of the salary clause noting that the select committee of 1866 had felt 'astounded at the work performed by the present Lord Clerk Register'. The salary clause was finally passed by a majority of fifty-three votes, seventy-two for and nineteen against. In March 1869 the treasury wrote to Gibson Craig telling him that the chancellor of the exchequer had approved the salary of £1200 on condition that, should the office of Lord Clerk Register become a sinecure again 'as it was in the time of your predecessor', the salary would be withdrawn.[54]

While the main provisions of the Land Registers Act, namely the centralisation of the sasine registers and the provision of adequate finding aids for searching, were long overdue, new problems were created thereby. The support given by Gibson Craig to the bill and encouraged by him in others might not have been so wholehearted had he foreseen the consequences with regard to the balance of power in the Register House. In 1868 the sasine office already occupied nine rooms as offices, five rooms for the abridgers and one for the searchers' clerks while the volumes of the register took up much of the space in the legal search room and in adjoining storage rooms.[55] By 1872, after the particular registers of sasines had been brought in, nine more rooms had been taken over and in 1877 the large front room on the first floor, the Lord Clerk Register's room, was also being used, so that in the last two decades of the nineteenth century working conditions and record storage were alike unsatisfactory. The sasine office finally got its own building, to the rear of the Register House, in 1904 and since 1976 it has occupied even larger premises at Meadowbank House, where the recent introduction of registration of title marks yet another change in the transmission of heritable rights in Scotland. As regards the abridgements and their indexes, these had been régulated by sections 9-11 of the act but, excellent though the regulations were in theory, in practice the execution was not only far from easy but also brought to the surface latent differences between Gibson Craig and John C. Brodie. At the beginning of the 1870s the Lord Clerk Register was being harried by parliamentary questions and articles and corresondence in newspapers. In 1871 and 1872 questions were asked in the Commons as to why the abrdigements and indexes were so slow in being sent to the localities,[56] and it was reported that in 1872, 1204 volumes remained to be done. A further question concerned a proposal to copy out the indexes of persons to the abridgements for the use of the localities but the Register House officials showed that this was impossible, as the indexes consisted of 278 volumes and the cost of copying would be enormous apart from shortage of staff to do the work.[57] Complaints having been made to Gibson Craig by certain legal practitioners about the failure to implement the act, the Court of Session set up, at his instigation, a committee composed of Lord Curriehill and Lord Gifford 'to inquire into the mode of Indexing the Register of Sasines and the mode of making

[53] *Hansard, op. cit.*
[54] SRO/8/211/7.
[55] SRO 2/3, 250.
[56] SRO 2/5/9.
[57] SRO 2/5/11.

searches in the said Register ...' which reported in 1875.[58] The committee is important, not only because it put forward various suggestions, including the use of search sheets, which Brodie supported and Gibson Craig opposed, but also because disagreement took place between Gibson Craig and the Court of Session about the extent of the latter's authority *vis-à-vis* the office of Lord Clerk Register. The court was doubtful about prescribing the form indexes should take and about laying down regulations under which searches should be made for they considered these matters to be the responsibility of the Lord Clerk Register under the 1868 Land Registers Act and the committee therefore would not recommend the court to pass an Act of Sederunt or interfere in any way with the Lord Clerk Register's discretionary powers. Nevertheless Gibson Craig insisted that the enquiry be held so that any new arrangements made under the Act would at least have the approbation of the court' who have always exercised an ultimate and supereminent control over all public registers in Scotland',[59] and because he considered it was the judges' duty as part of the *nobile officium* of the court.

The setting up of the Curriehill committee was undoubtedly an attempt on Gibson Craig's part to avert the day when alterations to methods of indexing and the introduction of search sheets, changes supported by Brodie and by members of the legal profession,[60] would come about so that he would at least have the authority of the Court of Session behind him. In December 1875 Brodie said as much in a letter to Gibson Craig, expressing his anger at the latter's refusal to forward an application by Brodie to the treasury for an increase in staff for the sasine office until the findings of the Curriehill committee were made known. Brodie repeated the assertion of the committee that the Land Registers Act laid the duty of carrying out its provisions on the Lord Clerk Register and 'by declining to interfere or take any responsibility unless "under the direction of the Court" you neither in fact abstain from interference nor free yourself from responsibility ... you have ever since been vainly endeavouring to induce the Court to accept the responsibility of performing for you your statutory duty'.[61] The clash between Gibson Craig and Brodie was partly one of temperament, partly a genuine belief on Gibson Craig's part that some of the reforms would affect the accuracy of searches and partly a justifiable fear that the Register House would suffer at the expense of the Sasine Office. The treasury, never the most understanding of masters and certainly uncaringly ignorant of Scottish insititutions, was unwillingly involved in the dispute. In March 1877 Gibson Craig wrote to them commenting on the long and fruitless correspondence between them and his difficulty in making them understand the legal business of the Register House. Moreover, he maintained that the ordinary business and administration of the office did not come within the treasury's competence and 'if I received any directions which I considered would be injurious to or derange what is in fact legal procedure so long established I might feel compelled by my public duty to refuse to obey them unless under the sanction and approval of the

[58] AD 56/293; SRO 2/6/5.
[59] *ibid.*
[60] See SRO 2/5/23, 'Report of Writers to the Signet as to the General Register of Sasines', 1872.
[61] SRO 6/121/14.

Court of Session'.[62] Finally a conference was held in 1878 between the Lord Advocate, John C. Brodie, the Queen's and Lord Treasurer's Remembrancer and the crown agent as to the best arrangements for the abridgements and indexes and a report submitted to the treasury led to the transference of their management to the sasine office.[63] By section 25 of the Land Registers Act the treasury was given power to amend the table of fees for registration inasmuch as 'the Fees to be drawn from the said Department shall not be greater than may reasonably be held sufficient for defraying the expenses of the said Department or the Improvement of the System of Registration'. A parliamentary question as to why fees had not been reduced led Gibson Craig to write to the treasury in July 1872 saying that of those having authority to amend the fees in the terms of the act namely himself, the Lord President, the Lord Advocate and the Lord Justice Clerk, he had consulted the Lord President and the Lord Justice Clerk but no decision had been reached.[64] Another parliamentary question put at the same time was whether all expenses of the Register House should not be defrayed by the treasury but Gibson Craig replied that 'the principle on which the Scotch system of Legal Registration was originally established was that it should be self-supporting ... and any reduction in fees should take this into account'.[65] The next year the treasury again wrote about the reduction of fees on the sasine registers, warning Gibson Craig that the Register House estimates would not be presented to parliament until the Commons had been told that fees would be reduced.[66] In reply he suggested that reductions should be made particularly on extracts from the registers, where charges were prohibitive, and produced a table of fees[67] which, as amended by the treasury, was approved in February 1873.[68] Throughout Gibson Craig's period of office he put forward at every opportunity the idea that the surplus produced in the Register House each year should be used for increased salaries for the staff and better preservation of the records, as in 1874, when the new system of fees had been running for a year and there was a larger surplus than estimated for.[69] Naturally this tendency of the Lord Clerk Register's to regard the Register House as a separate entity based on self-help did not find favour with the treasury and the annual surplus continued to go to the exchequer.

If the Land Registers Act of 1868 marks the piece of legislation with the most far-reaching effects on the Register House during Gibson Craig's term of office, then his achievements in the field of publications brought historical records hitherto unknown to public notice and provided a lasting service to scholars. He expressed his general aim quite clearly in a letter of 1866 saying that 'The Register House has never been in its proper position in Public estimation as the co-equal in status with the Public Record Offices of London and Dublin, but I hope to accomplish this before I have done ...'[70] During the period when Thomas

---

[62] SRO 2/6/92.
[63] SRO 2/6/151.
[64] SRO 2/5/9.
[65] ibid.
[66] SRO 2/5/177.
[67] SRO 2/5/181.
[68] SRO 2/5/224.
[69] SRO 2/5/577.
[70] SRO 2/13/80.

Thomson had been deputy clerk register and also a sub-commissioner for the Record Commission, this body had been responsible for funding the publication of the national records and from this period come some of the basic printed sources.[71] A precedent had also been set for looking furth of Scotland for material to supplement native sources which produced the *Rotuli Scotiae*, comprising Scottish rolls in the tower of London and chapter house at Westminster, 1290-1509, published between 1814 and 1819, and *Documents illustrative of Scottish History* using material in the English exchequer, published in 1837. The record commissioners ceased to function in the 1830s and, as far as Scotland was concerned, the production of printed historical material was left to the publishing clubs such as the Bannatyne and the Maitland. In England, record publication had been undertaken by the record commissioners and the state paper commissioners from the early nineteenth century. Their function was taken over by the Master of the Rolls who, in terms of the Public Record Office Act 1838, was empowered to print calendars and other forms of publications from records in his charge. Calendars first appeared as separate publications in 1856 continuing the work of the state paper commission, just as the rolls series, begun at the same time, carried on the work of the record commission.

The Register House had, since its inception, always been thought of primarily as a repository for the legal records and registers and was still so regarded throughout the nineteenth century but with the completion of the building in the 1820s, the large room at the back, now the historical search room, was considered as a suitable place in which to house the historical records. An increasing interest in these led in 1847 to such records being made available to those interested in historical or literary research free of charge, as is still the case. At the same time, a superintendent of historical searches was appointed under the direction of the deputy keepers and at the Lord Clerk Register's pleasure. In 1854, Joseph Robertson, who had been 'antiquarian assistant' since 1853, was appointed to the post and was later designated 'curator of historical records'. He was a man of great learning and industry and it was to him that Gibson Craig turned, shortly after his appointment as Lord Clerk Register in 1862, for advice on the initiation of a programme of record publications. Robertson produced a memorandum in 1864 listing suitable material and he also noted that a series of calendars had been in course of publication for some years under the direction of the master of the rolls which included material outside the Public Record Office 'But the series must obviously be imperfect, unless it include the State Papers and Documents preserved in Her Majesty's General Register House at Edinburgh'.[72] He goes on to mention the two facsimile volumes of Domesday Book recently reproduced by the process of photozincography, an early form of photo-lithography, as used in the productions of the Ordnance Survey Office at Southampton and suggests that Scottish historical documents of importance and interest should be similarly reproduced, not only for general information but also because, in spite of the utmost care, 'some of the more ancient and important are preceptibly wasting away'.

Gibson Craig put Robertson's memorandum up to Gladstone, chancellor of

---

[71] For details of record publications see *British National Archives*, sectional list 24 (HMSO).
[72] *Seventeenth Report of the Deputy Clerk Register of Scotland*, app. VI.

the exchequer, who sent it to Lord Romilly, Master of the Rolls. The outcome
was a letter from the treasury to Gibson Craig of 12 July 1864 allowing the
employment of 'one fit person' to produce a calendar of state papers in
consultation with the Master of the Rolls.[73] No other documents were to be
calendared but the proposal to publish the national manuscripts by photozincography was agreed to. Gibson Craig arranged for notices to be put in *The
Times* and *The Scotsman* announcing the new publications in a general way,
explaining to Robertson that '... it is very important that we should at once
assume the *position* and get it established in the Public mind that we are really
undertaking a great National work'.[74] The Lord Clerk Register probably knew
that he would meet opposition to the programme from various quarters for he
continues 'This will facilitate immensely our arrangements with the Treasury'. In
Robertson's reply he tells him that the announcement has been much talked
about but he is afraid it may be misunderstood in some quarters for '... the great
mass of the public — I might say the great mass of the legal profession too — are
ignorant of the great value and extent of our Records ... They seldom think of
the Register House as anything more than a repository of Sasine Registers, Court
of Session processes and Letters of Horning'[75] and he fears that such people may
see the historical publications as interfering with improvements in the legal
department of the Register House. The announcement of the forthcoming
Scottish publications was perhaps premature, since both the treasury and officials
of the Public Record Office objected to various aspects of the proposals.
Publications suggested for the first year included the acts of the Scottish
parliaments between 1639 and 1650, missing at the time of Thomas Thomson's
publication of *APS* but since recovered from the State Paper Office, state papers
of Queen Mary's reign, 1542-67, and the accounts of the treasurer, the estimated
cost being £2412. The treasury were unwilling to fund *APS*, as they did not want
to finance unfinished works of the record commission. They also proposed that
there should be one grant for Scotland and England under the Master of the
Rolls but Gibson Craig immediately saw the danger that the two series would be
in perpetual competition. The Lord Clerk Register enrolled the aid of Sir William
Dunbar, M.P. for Wigtown burghs and auditor general of the exchequer, in
trying to obtain a grant of £2000 and writing to him on 14 February 1865 he
pointed out that England received an annual grant of £5000 for publications.[76] In
March Gibson Craig wrote to tell the treasury that the Master of the Rolls had
refused to make any part of his grant available to Scotland and therefore '... the
publication of our MSS is to be doled out to us at the pleasure of the Record
Office'.[77] By a treasury minute of 17 April 1865[78] a grant of £1000 annually for
five years was given, the work to be under the direction and supervision of the
Lord Clerk Register, exclusive of printing costs, an additional £200 a year to be
added to Joseph Robertson's salary in recognition of the extra work involved and

[73] SRO 2/13/5.
[74] SRO 8/90/33.
[75] SRO 8/90/34.
[76] SRO 2/13/25.
[77] SRO 2/13/26.
[78] SRO 2/13/29.

his exceptional qualifications. On 9 October 1864 Gibson Craig proposed that an assistant to Robertson should be appointed[79] and this was agreed by the treasury and in June parliament voted the grant.

During the remainder of his term of office the Lord Clerk Register continued to agitate for an increase in the grant. In March 1866 he wrote to the treasury urging its inadequacy and pointing out that the importance of the project was appreciated because 'many of the most distinguished literary men in Scotland are willing to give their assistance as Editors'.[80] Correspondence with the treasury was printed as a return moved in the Commons by Sir William Stirling Maxwell, M.P. for Perthshire, and in the Lords by earl Stanhope[81] and Gibson Craig commented in June 1866 '... having made the Scotch M.P.s aware of the importance of the work, I shall throw the responsibility on them of getting me enabled to carry it out efficiently. As old Barbour says

"Full little knowest thai that hast not tried
What hell there is in suing long to bide"

and I am sick of that part of the work'.[82] When the treasury wrote proposing to stop the grant in 1872, Gibson Craig went to see Law, private secretary to the chancellor of the exchequer, who had signed the letter but knew nothing about it so 'I made him send for the Papers when it appeared it was Mr Baxter alone (a Scotchman!!) who announced the stoppage of the grant on his own authority',[83] and the grant was restored. In spite of all difficulties, by 1873 a number of the proposed publications had appeared, including volumes one and two of the *National Manuscripts of Scotland* and volumes five and six of *APS*. During this period Joseph Robertson died, in 1866, leaving an irreplaceable gap since his assistant had had to retire because of ill health. Gibson Craig thus was faced with not only running the historical department but dealing with publications currently in preparation. In 1867 he is arranging with the treasury for the distribution of the first volumes and with the stationery office for binding them in the same style as the English series but 'I intend that the Scottish series shall be blue which is the proper Scotch colour'.[84] There was trouble with the stationery office about who should print the work but Gibson Craig put a stop to this by interviewing the official concerned, saying 'I let him see it would be no use fighting with me ... if I had not been able to beard him and known how to deal with those English heads of departments it is quite clear he would have rode roughshod over us'.[85] In 1876 further publications were arranged so that, at Gibson Craig's death in 1878, there were completed the index to *APS*, the first volume of the *Accounts of the Lord High Treasurer of Scotland* and the first and second volumes of the *Register of the Privy Council of Scotland* and the *Exchequer Rolls*.

If Gibson Craig had to look to Joseph Robertson for advice on suitable historical material for publication then both had to look to the Public Record Office in London for information about the editing and financing of the Scottish

[79] SRO 8/90/40.
[80] SRO 2/13/60.
[81] SRO 2/13/90.
[82] SRO 2/13/83.
[83] SRO 8/119/2, 7, 9.
[84] SRO 8/100/8, 26.
[85] SRO 2/13/70.

publications. In October 1864 Joseph Robertson went to London to consult J. Duffus Hardy, the deputy keeper there, and other officials, who were helpful with advice although possibly only because they thus hoped to keep some control over the Scottish publications and they undoubtedly influenced the treasury in the matter of the Scottish grant. In March 1865 Gibson Craig wrote to Robertson about a meeting at the treasury with the Master of the Rolls when he found the latter 'much irritated and actuated by the most bitter jealousy'; an acrimonious discussion took place which had one good effect in that the treasury official realised that Scotland should be independent of England in publication matters because 'it would not be proper that the Lord Clerk Register should be subjected to have constantly such sort of discussions'.[86] In April of the same year Robertson wrote to the Lord Clerk Register impressing upon him the need to get the Scottish publications started for 'Until we set our Scottish series of Chronicles and Memorials fairly afloat, the Master of the Rolls and Duffus Hardy will still be working against us at the Treasury in the hope of getting that branch of our Record Publications transferred to the Master of the Rolls' series'.[87] Robertson reports an interesting conversation which Cosmo Innes, the record editor responsible for the index to APS, had with Duffus Hardy in April 1865 in which Innes tried to avoid the subject of publications but found that Duffus Hardy could not keep off it and 'avowed that he is the prompter of Peel [a treasury official] — "Peel sent for me" — "I said to Peel" etc. etc. He took credit for having overcome difficulties in increasing *your* income',[88] presumably a reference to the addition of £200 to Robertson's salary. Just as the time given to Scottish matters in parliament suffered because of the bias towards Irish affairs, so Gibson Craig found that attention was being diverted from Scottish record publications to Irish records. In 1864 Duffus Hardy produced a report on the Irish record establishment which was in very bad case and it was shown in confidence to Robertson. A treasury minute of 20 April 1866 setting forth publications to be undertaken in the United Kingdom showed clearly that the greater part of the funds available were to go to England and Ireland.[89] Gibson Craig commented 'I am surprised to see how much has been done for Ireland. It is very meagre in regard to Scotland ... The contrast between the illiberality shown to Scotland compared with the other kingdoms may be made good use of ...'[90] so that, when the treasury threatened to withdraw his grant in 1873, he wrote to them 'I must now beg to know why Scotland is to be dealt with so differently and illiberally as compared with England and Ireland ... I must protest in the strongest manner against the injustice with which Scotland is treated'.[91]

Sir William Gibson Craig died on 12 March 1878 and the subsequent history of the office of Lord Clerk Register leads one to wonder whether his active participation in affairs was a factor in it being stripped of its powers. Although criticisms could certainly be raised against particular aspects of his admini-

[86] SRO 8/94/18.
[87] SRO 8/207/13-16.
[88] SRO 8/207/8-9.
[89] SRO 10/109.
[90] SRO 2/13/71.
[91] SRO 8/121/3.

stration of Register House affairs, especially a conservative turn of mind which tended to regard innovations as naturally to be avoided, on occasion he was right to be cautious. In 1869, when the treasury suggested the use of photozincography for registration, the record officials objected that, among other reasons, the results would not be sufficiently legible and in fact the quality of reproduction in the *National Manuscripts of Scotland* was far below requisite standards, although a remarkable achievement for the time. He was prepared to take on the most senior officials, as in the case of finding a successor to Joseph Robertson in 1866. The Lord Advocate gave him a final date in January by which an appointment had to be made, to which Gibson Craig replied 'this is not the manner in which the Lord Clerk Register should be treated by any Lord Advocate nor is it the manner in which the public business ought to be done' and, on the principle that the best form of defence is attack, he continued 'I am not aware that you were ever in the Historical Department and you certainly know nothing of what it contains'.[92] George Skene was finally appointed in June 1867 and there is an interesting postscript to these events in 1895 when Stair Agnew, the deputy clerk register, wrote to the Scottish Office concerning the appointment of a curator of historical records stating that, following Joseph Robertson's death in 1866, 'the post was informally offered to, and accepted by, the late Professor Skene and Dr Dickson, by the lord advocate and the lord clerk register of the day respectively, through inadvertence, each being under the impression that it lay with him to recommend for the appointment which was then in the patronage of the Treasury'.[93] On the question of patronage Gibson Craig was firmly against it in the Register House, believing in promotion by merit and qualifications, remarking 'I always wished the holders of any of my offices to be immortal'.[94] When it was proposed in July 1866 to put all Register House appointments under the treasury Gibson Craig objected that this would make the appointment a political one, commenting 'I shall resist it to the uttermost. If there are any malcontents in the office ... they had better not let me discover who they are, because if I do their chances of promotion will be small.'[95] His attitude to officials could not have endeared him to them, one of whom he described as 'a pig-headed meddling animal',[96] but he could resort to kinder methods on occasion, as in 1865, when he told the deputy clerk register that he had come to a satisfactory understanding with a treasury official because 'There is no better lubricator to business than a little good claret which I took care he had had'.[97] If, on the whole, Gibson Craig was swimming against the tide as, for example, in his attitude to a burgeoning Sasine Office which eventually far outgrew the Register House, his career shows than an active and interested Lord Clerk Register could still make a valuable contribution to record-keeping in Scotland. A touch of the determination he showed over publications appeared in 1873, when he reminded the commissioners of supply in Renfrewshire of their duty to make better provision

[92] SRO 9/67/1.
[93] SRO 22/6/8.
[94] SRO 9/70/5.
[95] SRO 14/28/17.
[96] SRO 8/93/34.
[97] SRO 8/93/58.

for the records of the county.[98] With hindsight it is possible to speculate on whether the survival of the Lord Clerk Register with all the prestige effeiring to his ancient office but also possessing powers approximating to those of the Master of the Rolls might not have prevented the neglect both of the national records and of local records in the half century which followed the death of Gibson Craig.

The office of Lord Clerk Register remained vacant until the appointment of George, 6th earl of Glasgow, on 21 February 1879. During the vacancy two bills were introduced by the government in May 1878, one to make provision for the conduct in parliament of business relating to Scotland and for that purpose to appoint another secretary of state. The scope of the second bill was to deprive the office of Lord Clerk Register of the salary and of the principal duties now attached to it, the salary to be used to pay for the new secretary of state. The idea of a Scottish secretary of state was not new. In 1709 a third secretary, with a special oversight of Scottish affairs, was added to the two secretaries of state already in existence but the appointment made little impact and the office was allowed to lapse. Demands for its revival in the nineteenth century[99] stemmed from the contention that the office of Lord Advocate entailed far more work than it could carry and Scottish affairs suffered thereby. As a result of this agitation a committee of the treasury was set up in 1869 to enquire into certain civil service departments in Scotland and from evidence submitted by Sir William Gibson Craig his opinion on the question of the Lord Advocate and a secretary for Scotland is known.[100] He saw insuperable difficulties in finding a suitable person as secretary and in defining his duties and he wanted the office of Lord Advocate retained but considered that the powers of the Scottish lord of the treasury, a position which he himself had once held, should be increased.

Nothing further was done until the introduction of the two bills in 1878 and after their second reading a committee was set up, who reported that the appointment of an under-secretary for Scotland would diminish the office of Lord Advocate 'a high office of state of great antiquity', so they came out against the proposal.[101] With regard to the office of Lord Clerk Register, the committee wanted it retained, quoting Lord Palmerston's opinion when the question of a Scottish secretary was raised in 1858, 'I cannot agree that, if it is desirable to create a new office, we should go foraging among the different departments of the State in order to find some retrenchment . . .', and such must have been the impact of Gibson Craig's term of office that the committee even proposed that, if an office had to be sacrificied, it should be the lesser one of deputy clerk register. Of particular interest is a letter written by Patrick Fraser, dean of the Faculty of Advocates, and published in the *Edinburgh Courant* of 21 June 1878. He had recently gone to London to explain the Faculty's views 'as to the impolicy and injustice of the scheme set forth in these two bills'. The salary freed by the death

---

[98] SRO 2/5/241-50.
[99] See *Hansard*, cxxxix, 19; clxxv, 1167.
[100] *Report of the Commissioners to inquire into certain Civil Service Departments in Scotland* (1870 C-64), 33-9.
[101] SRO 14/43/4.

of Gibson Craig had given Cross,[102] the home secretary, the idea of diverting it to create an under-secretary of state. After giving the history of the office of Lord Clerk Register, Fraser goes on to say that the bill proposed to leave a Lord Clerk Register in name only, with two functions, keeper of the signet and the office of presiding at the election of representative peers which 'are of the most trifling description ... The mechanical operation of affixing the Signet makes little demand upon the intellect.' He points out that the law regarding the appropriation of fees in the Register House was clearly laid down in the Land Registers Act of 1868 and their use for payment of the salary of an under-secretary would be a violation of the law. The whole scheme should be denounced as 'an attempt to perpetrate a gross and scandalous injustice' and he remarks that, if it had happened in Ireland, the Irish members of parliament would have spoken against it with one voice but 'a number of our Scottish members ... have been somewhat perverted in this case by mean and petty ambitions. The office of Under-Secretary would suit a number of them very well — in their own estimation.' Lord Curriehill, one of the commissioners reporting in 1875,[103] hoped that 'the dignified office [of Lord Clerk Register] might be conferred upon some Nobleman of position and influence possessing antiquarian tastes ...' with an experienced and well-paid deputy appointed by the crown. This is indeed what happened, for on 11 August 1879 the Lord Clerk Register (Scotland) Act was passed whereby the Lord Clerk Register was to continue as one of the officers of state, with precedence after the Lord Justice General, to be keeper of the signet and to preside at peers' elections but all his rights and privileges were to be vested in the deputy clerk register. The bill put forward by the home secretary came to nothing but the office of a Scottish secretary was finally established in 1885 with the passage of the Secretary for Scotland Act.

[102] Richard Assheton Cross, cr. Viscount Cross of Broughton-in-Furness, co. Lancaster, 19 August 1866.
[103] Above, p. 307.

INDICES

LIST OF CASES

INDEX

THE STAIR SOCIETY

Instituted in 1934 *to encourage the study and advance the knowledge of the History of Scots Law*

OFFICE-BEARERS 1984

President: THE RIGHT HON. LORD AVONSIDE.

Vice-President: PROFESSOR GORDON DONALDSON, M.A., PH.D., D.LITT., HON.D.LITT., F.B.A.

Chairman of Council: SHERIFF J. IRVINE SMITH.

Vice-Chairman: SHERIFF PETER G. B. McNEILL.

Council: W. D. H. SELLAR; J. M. PINKERTON; J. J. ROBERTSON; JOHN BLACKIE; A. FORTE; DR. ATHOL MURRAY; T. DAVID FERGUS; HECTOR MacQUEEN; PROFESSOR WILLIAM GORDON.

Literary Director: W. D. H. SELLAR, B.A., LL.B.

Secretary and Treasurer: I. R. GUILD, W.S., 16 Charlotte Square, Edinburgh EH2 4YS.

Auditor: RICHARD B. ANDERSON, C.A.

Secretary for the U.S.A.: PROFESSOR W. A. J. WATSON, M.A., LL.B., D.PHIL., The Law School, University of Pennsylvania.

333

CONSTITUTION

1. The Society shall be called 'The Stair Society'.

2. The object of the Society shall be to encourage the study and advance the knowledge of the history of Scots Law especially by the publication of original documents, and by the reprinting and editing of works of sufficient rarity or importance.

3. Membership of the Society shall be constituted by payment of the annual subscription, and shall cease if this be in arrear for one year.

4. The amount of the annual subscriptions shall be fixed by the Council from time to time, and shall be payable in advance on 1st January in each year.

5. The management of the affairs and funds of the Society shall be vested in a Council consisting of the President, Vice-President, a Chairman, a Vice-Chairman and not more than ten ordinary elected members.

6. The President, Vice-President, Chairman and Vice-Chairman shall be elected annually at the Annual General Meeting, to hold office for the following calendar year, and shall be eligible for re-election. Those elected at the Inaugural Meeting shall hold office until 31st December, 1935.

7. The ordinary members of Council elected at the Inaugural Meeting shall hold office from that date. At every Annual General Meeting thereafter the Society shall elect members to fill any vacancies on the Council that may have occurred, or that may be due to occur at the end of the year, members so elected to hold office from the ensuing 1st of January. The original members of Council shall hold office until 31st December, 1939, and, at the Annual General Meeting to be held in November, 1939, all of these members, except two (selected by agreement or by lot), shall be eligible for re-election. The two so selected shall retire as at 31st December following, and shall not be eligible for re-election for one year. Thereafter at each Annual General Meeting two of the ordinary members of Council shall retire as at 31st December following, and shall not be eligible for re-election for one year. The two members to retire annually shall be those who have the longest continuous period of service, and, as among those of equal service, shall be selected by agreement or by lot.

8. In addition to the elected members, the Council shall have power to co-opt as additional members of Council any member of the Society who, in their opinion, may be fitted to render special service in promoting the work of the Society. Such co-opted members shall hold office for such period, not exceeding five years, as the Council may in each case determine. At no time shall the co-opted members of Council exceed three in number.

9. The Society at the Inaugural Meeting, and thereafter at the Annual General Meeting, shall appoint a Literary Director or Directors, a Secretary and a Treasurer, and such other officers as may from time to time be deemed necessary, who shall be subject to the direction of the Council in the performance of their duties, and who shall receive such remuneration as the Council may determine. Those so appointed shall not be members of Council, but may be invited to attend any meeting of Council.

10. Any casual vacancies in the offices of President, Vice-President, Chairman,

Vice-Chairman or elected members of the Council, or among the officers of the Society, may be filled up by the Council, appointments so made to be for the period till the 31st of December following the next Annual General Meeting.

11. In any year in which a volume is published each member who has paid his subscription for that year shall be entitled to receive one copy.

12. The Annual General Meeting shall be held between 1st November and 31st March at such time and place as may be fixed by the Council. If the Meeting is not held until after 31st December in any year, office-bearers and members of Council then due to retire shall remain in office until the Meeting is held. The Council may also at any time call a Special General Meeting of the Society, and shall do so on a requisition from not less than ten members, which shall specify the object for which the Meeting is to be called. Seven days' notice shall be given of all General Meetings.

13. The Constitution of the Society as contained in these Rules may be amended at any General Meeting on twenty-one days' notice of the proposed amendments being given to the Secretary and included in the Agenda circulated for the Meeting.

PUBLICATIONS OF
THE STAIR SOCIETY

1. AN INTRODUCTORY SURVEY OF THE SOURCES AND LITERATURE OF SCOTS LAW. By various authors. With an introduction by The Rt. Hon. Lord Macmillan, P.C., LL.D., Lord of Appeal in Ordinary. 1936.

1a. AN INDEX TO VOLUME NO. 1, compiled by James Cowie Brown, M.A., LL.B., Ph.D., was issued in 1939.

2. ACTA CURIAE ADMIRALLATUS SCOTIAE, 6th September 1557—11th March 1561-2. Edited by Thomas Callander Wade, M.A., LL.B., Solicitor, Falkirk. 1937.

3. HOPE'S MAJOR PRACTICKS, 1608-1633. Edited by The Rt. Hon. James Avon Clyde, LL.D., formerly Lord Justice-General of Scotland and Lord President of the Court of Session. Vol. I. With portrait. 1937.

4. HOPE'S MAJOR PRACTICKS, 1608-1633. Edited by The Rt. Hon. James Avon Clyde, LL.D., formerly Lord Justice-General of Scotland and Lord President of the Court of Session. Vol. II. 1938.

5. BARON DAVID HUME'S LECTURES, 1786-1822. Edited and annotated by G. Campbell H. Paton, M.A., LL.B., Solicitor, and Assistant to Professor of Law in the University of Glasgow. Vol. I. With portrait. 1939.

6. LORD HERMAND'S CONSISTORIAL DECISIONS, 1684-1777. Edited by F. P. Walton, K.C.(Quebec), LL.D., Hon. Fellow, Lincoln College, Oxford, formerly Director, Royal School of Law, Cairo. With Biographical Sketch of Lord Hermand by James Fergusson. With portrait. 1940.

7. ST. ANDREWS FORMULARE, 1514-1546. Text transcribed and edited by Gordon Donaldson, M.A., Ph.D., and C. Macrae, M.A., D.Phil. Vol. I. 1942.

8. ACTA DOMINORUM CONCILII, 26th March 1501—27th January 1502-3. Transcribed by J. A. Crawford, M.A., LL.B., Advocate. Edited with an Introduction by The Rt. Hon. James Avon Clyde, LL.D., formerly Lord Justice-General of Scotland and Lord President of the Court of Session. 1943.

9. ST. ANDREWS FORMULARE, 1514-1546. Edited by Gordon Donaldson, M.A., Ph.D., with Prefatory Note by David Baird Smith, C.B.E., LL.D. Vol. II. 1944.

10. THE REGISTER OF BRIEVES, 1286-1386, as contained in the Ayr MS., the Bute MS., and Quoniam Attachiamenta. Edited by The Rt. Hon. Lord Cooper, LL.D., Lord Justice-Clerk. THOMAS THOMSON'S MEMORIAL ON OLD EXTENT. Edited by J. D. Mackie, C.B.E., M.C., M.A., Professor of Scottish History and Literature in the University of Glasgow. 1946.

11. REGIAM MAJESTATEM AND QUONIAM ATTACHIAMENTA, based on the text of Sir John Skene. Edited and translated with Introduction and Notes by The Rt. Hon. Lord Cooper, LL.D. 1947.

12. THE JUSTICIARY RECORDS OF ARGYLL AND THE ISLES, 1664-1705. Transcribed and edited, with an Introduction, by John Cameron, M.A., LL.B., Ph.D. Vol. I. 1949.
13. BARON DAVID HUME'S LECTURES, 1786-1822. Edited and annotated by G. Campbell H. Paton, M.A., LL.B., Solicitor. Vol. II. 1949.
14. ACTA DOMINORUM CONCILII ET SESSIONIS, 1532-1533. Edited by Ian H. Shearer, M.A., LL.B., Advocate. 1951.
15. BARON DAVID HUME'S LECTURES, 1786-1822. Edited and annotated by G. Campbell H. Paton, M.A., LL.B., Advocate and Lecturer in the History of Scots Law in the University of Glasgow. Vol. III. 1952.
16. SELECTED JUSTICIARY CASES, 1624-1650. Edited and annotated by Stair A. Gillon, B.A., LL.B., Advocate. Vol. I. 1953.
17. BARON DAVID HUME'S LECTURES, 1786-1822. Edited and annotated by G. Campbell H. Paton, M.A., LL.B., Advocate and Lecturer in the History of Scots Law in the University of Glasgow. Vol. IV. 1955.
18. BARON DAVID HUME'S LECTURES, 1786-1822. Edited and annotated by G. Campbell H. Paton, M.A., LL.B., Advocate and Lecturer in the History of Scots Law in the University of Glasgow. Vol. V. 1957.
19. BARON DAVID HUME'S LECTURES, 1786-1822. Edited and annotated by G. Campbell H. Paton, M.A., LL.B., Advocate and Lecturer in the History of Scots Law in the University of Glasgow. Vol. VI. 1958.
20. AN INTRODUCTION TO SCOTTISH LEGAL HISTORY. By various authors. With an Introduction by The Rt. Hon. Lord Normand, P.C., LL.D., Lord of Appeal in Ordinary, 1947-1953. 1958.
21. THE PRACTICKS OF SIR JAMES BALFOUR OF PITTENDREICH. Edited by Peter G. B. McNeill, M.A., LL.B., Ph.D., Advocate. Vol. I. 1962.
22. THE PRACTICKS OF SIR JAMES BALFOUR OF PITTENDREICH. Edited by Peter G. B. McNeill, M.A., LL.B., Ph.D., Advocate. Vol. II. 1963.
23. THE ORIGINS AND DEVELOPMENT OF THE JURY IN SCOTLAND. By Ian D. Willock, M.A., LL.B., Advocate and Professor of Jurisprudence in the University of St. Andrews. 1966.
24. WILLIAM HAY'S LECTURES ON MARRIAGE. Transcribed, translated and edited by The Right Rev. Monsignor John C. Barry, M.A.(Cantab.), D.C.L.(Rome), Rector of St. Andrew's College, Drygrange, Melrose; Consultor to the Pontifical Commission for the Revision of the Code of Canon Law. 1967.
25. THE JUSTICIARY RECORDS OF ARGYLL AND THE ISLES. 1664-1742. Edited by John Imrie. Vol. II. 1969.
26. MISCELLANY I. By various authors. With a Preface by The Rt. Hon. Lord Clyde, LL.D., Lord Justice-General and Lord President of the Court of Session. 1971.
27. SELECTED JUSTICIARY CASES, 1624-1650. Edited with an Introduction by J. Irvine Smith, M.A., LL.B., Advocate, Sheriff of Lanarkshire at Glasgow. Vol. II. 1972.
28. SELECTED JUSTICIARY CASES, 1624-1650. Edited with an Introduction by J. Irvine Smith, M.A., LL.B., Advocate, Sheriff of Lanarkshire at Glasgow. Vol. III. 1974.

29. THE MINUTE BOOK OF THE FACULTY OF ADVOCATES, 1661-1712. Edited by John M. Pinkerton, Clerk of Faculty. Vol. I. 1976.
30. THE SYNOD RECORDS OF LOTHIAN AND TWEEDDALE, 1589-96, 1640-49. Edited with an Introduction by Dr. James Kirk of the Department of Scottish History, Glasgow University. 1977.
31. PERPETUITIES IN SCOTS LAW. By Robert Burgess, LL.B., Ph.D., Senior Lecturer in Law in the University of East Anglia. 1979.
32. THE MINUTE BOOK OF THE FACULTY OF ADVOCATES, 1713-1750. Edited by John M. Pinkerton, late Clerk of Faculty. Vol. II. 1980.
33. STAIR TERCENTENARY STUDIES. By various scholars. Edited by David M. Walker, Q.C., M.A., LL.D., F.B.A., Regius Professor of Law at the University of Glasgow. 1981.
34. THE COURT OF THE OFFICIAL IN PRE-REFORMATION SCOTLAND. By Simon Ollivant, M.A., Ph.D. 1982.